A Companion to the British and Irish Novel 1945–2000

Blackwell Companions to Literature and Culture

This series offers comprehensive, newly written surveys of key periods and movements and certain major authors, in English literary culture and history. Extensive volumes provide new perspectives and positions on contexts and on canonical and post-canonical texts, orientating the beginning student in new fields of study and providing the experienced undergraduate and new graduate with current and new directions, as pioneered and developed by leading scholars in the field.

Published

A COMPANION TO

THE BRITISH AND IRISH NOVEL

1945 – 2000

EDITED BY **BRIAN W. SHAFFER**

Blackwell
Publishing

BLACKWELL PUBLISHING
350 Main Street, Malden, MA 02148-5020, USA
108 Cowley Road, Oxford OX4 1JF, UK
550 Swanston Street, Carlton, Victoria 3053, Australia

First published 2005 by Blackwell Publishing Ltd

Library of Congress Cataloging-in-Publication Data

A companion to the British and Irish novel 1945–2000 / edited by Brian W. Shaffer.
   p. cm.—(Blackwell companions to literature and culture)
   Includes bibliographical references and index.
   ISBN 1-4051-1375-8 (hardcover : alk. paper)
   1. English fiction—20th century—History and criticism—Handbooks, manuals, etc. 2. English
fiction—Irish authors—History and criticism—Handbooks, manuals, etc. 3.Ireland—Intellectual life—
20th century—Handbooks, manuals, etc. 4.Ireland—In literature—Handbooks, manuals, etc. I. Shaffer,
Brian W., 1960– II. Series.

PR881.C655 2005
823'.91409—dc22
2004007691

A catalogue record for this title is available from the British Library.

Set in 11/13 pt Garamond 3
by Kolam Information Services Pvt. Ltd, Pondicherry, India
Printed and bound in the United Kingdom
by TJ International Ltd, Padstow, Cornwall

The publisher's policy is to use permanent paper from mills that operate a sustainable forestry policy, and
which has been manufactured from pulp processed using acid-free and elementary chlorine-free practices.
Furthermore, the publisher ensures that the text paper and cover board used have met acceptable
environmental accreditation standards.

For further information on
Blackwell Publishing, visit our website:
www.blackwellpublishing.com

Contents

Notes on Contributors

Chris Ackerley is Associate Professor and Head of English at the University of Otago, in Dunedin, New Zealand. The author of numerous articles on the work of Samuel Beckett, Malcolm Lowry, J. G. Farrell, James Joyce, and Vladimir Nabokov, he is also the co-author, with Lawrence J. Clipper, of *A Companion to* Under the Volcano (1984) and, with Stanley E. Gontarski, of *The Grove Press Companion to Samuel Beckett* (2004).

James Acheson is Senior Lecturer in English at the University of Canterbury, in Christchurch, New Zealand. He is author of *John Fowles* (1998), *Samuel Beckett's Artistic Theory and Practice* (1997), and either editor or co-editor of *Contemporary British Poetry* (1996), *British and Irish Drama Since 1960* (1993), and *The British and Irish Novel Since 1960* (1991). He is currently working on a book on contemporary British historical fiction.

M. Keith Booker is Professor of English at the University of Arkansas in Fayetteville. He is the author of numerous books on literature and literary theory, including *The Post-Utopian Imagination: American Culture in the Long 1950s* (2002), *Ulysses, Capitalism and Colonialism: Reading Joyce after the Cold War* (2000), *The Dystopian Impulse in Modern Literature* (1994), *Dystopian Literature* (1994), and *Literature and Domination: Sex, Knowledge, and Power in Modern Fiction* (1993).

Gerard Carruthers is Lecturer in the Department of Scottish Literature at the University of Glasgow. He is co-editor of *English Romanticism and the Celtic World* (2003) and *Beyond Scotland: New Contexts for Twentieth-Century Scottish Literature* (2003), and has published widely on eighteenth- and twentieth-century literature.

Bryan Cheyette is Chair in Twentieth-Century Literature at Southampton University. He is the editor of five books and the author of *Muriel Spark* (2000) and *Constructions of "the Jew" in English Literature and Society* (1993). He is currently completing *Diasporas of the Mind* for Yale University Press.

Peter Childs is Professor of Modern English Literature at the University of Gloucestershire. As well as writing articles on a wide range of subjects in twentieth-century and postcolonial literature, he has published ten books to date, including *Modernism* (2000), *Post-Colonial Theory and English Literature* (ed., 1999), and *The Twentieth Century in Poetry* (1998). He is also the author of a forthcoming book, *British Fiction 1970–2003*.

Reed Way Dasenbrock taught at New Mexico State University for twenty years before becoming Dean of the College of Arts and Sciences at the University of New Mexico in 2001.His publications include *Truth and Consequences: Intentions, Conventions, and the New Thematics* (2001), *Imitating the Italians; Wyatt, Spenser, Synge, Pound, Joyce* (1991), and *The Literary Vorticism of Ezra Pound and Wyndham Lewis* (1985).

Damon Marcel DeCoste is Associate Professor of English at the University of Regina, Saskatchewan, where he teaches and studies British and American literature of the twentieth century. He is the author of essays on Richard Wright, Malcolm Lowry, Graham Greene, Graham Swift, and Evelyn Waugh, and is completing a book-length study of British novels of World War II and their indebtedness to the historical outlook of high modernism.

James F. English is Associate Professor of English at the University of Pennsylvania. He is the author of *Comic Transactions: Literature, Humor, and the Politics of Community in Twentieth-Century Britain* (1994) and of a forthcoming book entitled *The Economy of Prestige: Prizes, Awards, and the Circulation of Cultural Value*. He is editor of the journal *Postmodern Culture* and of the forthcoming *Concise Companion to Contemporary British Fiction,* and is currently at work on a study of cultural trade between the US and the UK entitled *Translated from the English*.

Judith Kegan Gardiner is Professor of English and of Gender and Women's Studies and Interim Director of the Center for Research on Women and Gender at the University of Illinois at Chicago. She is the author of *Craftsmanship in Context: The Development of Ben Jonson's Poetry* and *Rhys, Stead, Lessing, and the Politics of Empathy* (1989); and editor of *Provoking Agents: Gender and Agency in Theory and Practice* (1995) and *Masculinity Studies and Feminist Theory* (2001). She is also co-editor of the *Routledge Encyclopedia of Men and Masculinities*.

David Goldie is Senior Lecturer in the English Department at the University of Strathclyde, in Glasgow. He is the author of *A Critical Difference: John Middleton Murry and T. S. Eliot in English Literary Criticism 1919–1928* (1998) and is the editor, with Gerard Carruthers and Alastair Renfrew, of the forthcoming *Beyond Scotland: Scottish Literature in the Twentieth Century*.

S. E. Gontarski is Sarah Herndon Professor of English at Florida State University where he edits the *Journal of Beckett Studies*. His books include *The Grove Press Reader, 1951–2001* (2001), *Modernism, Censorship, and the Politics of Publishing: The Grove Press Legacy* (2000), *The Theatrical Notebooks of Samuel Beckett, Volume IV: The Shorter Plays*

(1999), *Samuel Beckett: The Complete Short Prose, 1928–1989* (1996), and (with C. J. Ackerley) *The Grove Press Companion to Samuel Beckett* (2004).

Erika Gottlieb teaches at Ryerson Polytechnic University in Toronto. She is the author of *The Orwell Conundrum: A Cry of Despair or Faith in the Spirit of Man* (1992), *Dystopian Fiction East and West: Universe of Terror and Trial* (2001), and *Lost Angels of a Ruined Paradise: Themes of Cosmic Strife in Romantic Tragedy* (1982).

Nico Israel is Associate Professor of English at Hunter College, City University of New York. He is the author of a book, *Outlandish: Writing between Exile and Diaspora* (2000), and of essays on Conrad, Adorno, and Stevens, among others. He is also a frequent contributor to *Artforum* International magazine and has published more than fifty catalogue essays, previews, and reviews for contemporary art exhibitions. His next book project, tentatively titled *Globalization and Trauma*, will explore intersections among literature, contemporary art, and critical theory in the post-1945 period.

Feroza Jussawalla is Professor of English at the University of New Mexico. She is the author of a poetry collection, *Chiffon Saris* (2003), and of *Family Quarrels: Towards a Criticism of Indian Writing in English* (1984), the editor of *Conversations with V. S. Naipaul* (1998), and the co-editor (with Reed Way Dasenbrock) of *Interviews with Writers of the Post-Colonial World* (1992).

Donald P. Kaczvinsky is Professor of English and Director of the Honors Program at Louisiana Tech University, where he holds the Mildred Saunders Adams Endowed Professorship. He is the author of *Lawrence Durrell's Major Novels* (1997) and of essays on the work of James Joyce, Margaret Atwood, Graham Swift, and Alasdair Gray. He is currently the Vice President of the International Lawrence Durrell Society and is at work on a book entitled *Storied Lives: Narrative and the Self in Postmodern British Fiction*.

Cheryl Alexander Malcolm is Associate Professor of English at the University of Gdańsk, Poland. Her books include *Understanding Anita Brookner* (2002), *Jean Rhys: A Study of the Short Fiction* (with David Malcolm) (1996), and two collections of poetry under the pseudonym of Georgia Scott, *The Penny Bride* (2003) and *The Good Wife* (2001).

Kevin McCarron is Reader in English Literature in the School of English and Modern Languages at the University of Surrey, Roehampton. He has published numerous articles in scholarly journals and has contributed chapters to over thirty books on a wide variety of subjects including tattooing, cyberpunk, popular music, horror fiction, dystopian literature, drug addiction and alcoholism, and blasphemy. He is the author of *The Coincidence of Opposites: William Golding's Later Fiction* (1996) and *William Golding* (1995), and the co-author of *Frightening Fictions* (2001), a study of adolescent horror narratives.

Patrick A. McCarthy, Professor of English at the University of Miami, has written or edited ten books, including *Malcolm Lowry's "La Mordida": A Scholarly Edition* (1996) and *Forests of Symbols: World, Text, and Self in Malcolm Lowry's Fiction* (1994), and, with Paul Tiessen, *Joyce/Lowry: Critical Perspectives* (1997). Recently he edited and annotated *Star Maker* by Olaf Stapledon (2004). His current project is a study of bodies in Samuel Beckett's fiction and drama.

Brian McFarlane is Honorary Associate Professor at Monash University, in Melbourne, Australia. He is the author of numerous articles on British cinema and adaptation, and his more recent books include: *Lance Comfort* (1999), *An Autobiography of British Cinema* (1997), and *Novel to Film: An Introduction to the Theory of Adaptation* (1996). He was a compiler, editor, and chief author of *The Encyclopedia of British Film* (2003) and co-edited *The Oxford Companion to Australian Film* (1999). He is currently co-authoring a book on the British 'B' movie.

Merritt Moseley is Professor of Literature and Director of the Honors Program at the University of North Carolina at Asheville. He is the author of *Understanding Julian Barnes* (1997), *Understanding Kingsley Amis* (1993), and *David Lodge* (1991), and the editor of four volumes of the *Dictionary of Literary Biography, British Novelists Since 1960*. Current projects include a book about Michael Frayn and a collection on Booker Prizewinners.

Nicola Pitchford is Associate Professor of English and Comparative Literature at Fordham University, New York, where she specializes in contemporary British literature and culture. She is the author of *Tactical Readings: Feminist Postmodernism in the Novels of Kathy Acker and Angela Carter* (2002) and of articles on James Kelman and the Booker Prize, Gertrude Stein, and feminism's pornography debates.

Donna Potts is Associate Professor of English at Kansas State University. The author of a book, *Howard Nemerov and Objective Idealism* (1994), she also has published articles on Seamus Heaney, Patrick McCabe, Frank McCourt, Margaret Atwood, Katharine Tynan, and Nuala Ni Dhomhnaill.

Julius Rowan Raper is Professor Emeritus of English at the University of North Carolina, Chapel Hill. He is the author of *Narcissus from Rubble: Competing Models of Character in Contemporary British and American Fiction* (1992), three books on the southern American novelist Ellen Glasgow, and is the editor of *Lawrence Durrell: Comprehending the Whole* (1995).

Margaret Moan Rowe is Professor of English and Vice Provost for Academic Affairs at Purdue University. She is the author of *Doris Lessing* (1994) and of essays on a wide range of nineteenth- and twentieth-century British writers, including Charlotte Brontë, George Eliot, W. H. Auden, and Muriel Spark.

Roberta Rubenstein is Professor of Literature at American University in Washington, DC, where she teaches courses in fiction by women, feminist theory, and modernism. She is the author of *Home Matters: Longing and Belonging, Nostalgia and Mourning in Women's Fiction* (2001), *Boundaries of the Self: Gender, Culture, Fiction*

(1987), and *The Novelistic Vision of Doris Lessing: Breaking the Forms of Consciousness* (1979). She has published over thirty articles on modern and contemporary women writers, including Woolf, Lessing, Atwood, Drabble, and Morrison.

Dale Salwak is Professor of English at Southern California's Citrus College. His publications include *A Passion for Books* (1999), *The Literary Biography: Problems and Solutions* (1996), *The Wonders of Solitude* (1995), and the forthcoming *Living with a Writer*. He also has authored studies of Kingsley Amis, John Braine, Philip Larkin, Barbara Pym, and John Wain.

Margaret Scanlan specializes in comparative literature and has, since 1976, taught at Indiana University South Bend, where she is currently Professor and Chair of English. She is the author of *Plotting Terror: Novelists and Terrorists in Contemporary Fiction* (2001) and *Traces of Another Time: History and Politics in Postwar British Fiction* (1990). She is currently at work on a book about contemporary Irish culture.

Peter J. Schakel is the Peter C. and Emajean Cook Professor of English at Hope College, in Michigan. He is the author of three books on C. S. Lewis: *Imagination and the Arts in C. S. Lewis: Journeying to Narnia and Other Worlds* (2002), *Reason and Imagination in C. S. Lewis: A Study of Till We Have Faces* (1984), and *Reading with the Heart: The Way into Narnia* (1979), and is the editor of *The Longing for a Form: Essays on the Fiction of C. S. Lewis* (1977) and (with Charles A. Huttar) of *Word and Story in C. S. Lewis* (1991).

Bernard Schweizer is Assistant Professor of English at Long Island University, Brooklyn. He has written two monographs, *Rebecca West: Heroism, Rebellion, and the Female Epic* (2002) and *Radicals on the Road: The Politics of English Travel Writing in the 1930s* (2001). He has edited Rebecca West's previously unpublished work *Survivors in Mexico* (2003), and is currently editing an essay collection on Rebecca West, as well as an anthology of essays on the female epic.

Brian W. Shaffer (Editor) is Professor of English and Associate Dean of Academic Affairs at Rhodes College, in Memphis. He is the author of two books, *Understanding Kazuo Ishiguro* (1998) and *The Blinding Torch: Modern British Fiction and the Discourse of Civilization* (1993), and of numerous essays in such journals as *PMLA, ELH, Journal of Modern Literature,* and *James Joyce Quarterly.* He is co-editor (with Hunt Hawkins) of *Approaches to Teaching Conrad's "Heart of Darkness" and "The Secret Sharer"* (2002) and is currently at work on a monograph, *Reading the Novel in English: 1945–2000.*

John Skinner is Professor of English Literature at the University of Turku, Finland. His book-length studies include *Raising the Novel: An Introduction to Eighteenth-Century Fiction* (2001), *The Stepmother Tongue: An Introduction to New Anglophone Fiction* (1998), *Constructions of Smollett: A Study of Genre and Gender* (1996), *The Fictions of Anita Brookner: Illusions of Romance* (1992), and *Tell-Tale Theories: Essays in Narrative Poetics* (1989). His current interest is Indian writing in English.

Claire Squires is a Senior Lecturer in Publishing at Oxford Brookes University. Her publications include *Philip Pullman's* His Dark Materials *Trilogy: A Reader's Guide* (2003), *Zadie Smith's* White Teeth: *A Reader's Guide* (2002), and "Toby Litt" for the *Dictionary of Literary Biography: Twenty-First Century British and Irish Novelists* (2002). She previously worked at Hodder and Stoughton, publishers.

John J. Su is Assistant Professor of English at Marquette University, Milwaukee. His recent articles have appeared in *Modern Fiction Studies, Twentieth-Century Literature*, and *Critique,* and he is currently completing a book manuscript entitled *Narratives of Return: Nostalgia and Contemporary Anglophone Literature.*

Rebecca L. Walkowitz is Assistant Professor of English at the University of Wisconsin, Madison. She is the author of several articles in the fields of British fiction, modernism, and cultural theory, including "Ishiguro's Floating Worlds," "Shakespeare in Harlem," and "Conrad's Adaptation." An editor of five books in the field of literary and cultural studies, she is completing a book on the aesthetics of cosmopolitanism in twentieth-century British fiction and cultural theory.

Cedric Watts is Research Professor of English at the University of Sussex. His many books include: *A Preface to Greene* (1997), *A Preface to Conrad* (2nd edn., 1993), *Joseph Conrad: A Literary Life* (1989), *The Deceptive Text* (1984), *R. B. Cunninghame Graham* (1983), and (with John Sutherland) *Henry V, War Criminal? And Other Shakespeare Puzzles* (2000).

Patricia Waugh is Professor of English Literature at the University of Durham. Her publications include *Revolutions of the Word: Contexts for the Study of Modern Literature* (1997), *Harvest of the Sixties: English Literature and its Backgrounds, 1960–1990* (1995), *Practising Postmodernism/Reading Modernism* (1992), *Feminine Fictions: Revisiting the Postmodern* (1989), *Metafiction: The Theory and Practice of Self-Conscious Fiction* (1984), and (with David Fuller) *The Arts and Sciences of Criticism* (1999). She is currently editing *The Oxford Guide to the Theory and Practice of Literary Criticism* and is completing a book entitled *Literature, Science, and the Good Society.*

Timothy Weiss is Professor of English at the Chinese University of Hong Kong, where he teaches postcolonial, Caribbean, and African literature. He is the author of two books, *Translating Orients: Between Ideology and Utopia* (2004) and *On the Margins: The Art and Exile of V. S. Naipaul* (1992), and of essays on Naipaul, Rushdie, and other contemporary writers.

Lynn Wells is Associate Professor of English at the University of Regina, Saskatchewan. Her areas of specialization are contemporary British fiction, postmodernism, and urban representations in fiction. Her publications include *Allegories of Telling: Self-Referential Narrative in Contemporary British Fiction* (2003) as well as articles on A. S. Byatt's *Possession,* virtual textuality, and Mary Shelley's *The Last Man.*

Anne Whitehead is Lecturer in Contemporary Literature and Theory at the University of Newcastle upon Tyne. She has published numerous articles on trauma theory and modern fiction and has two forthcoming books: *Trauma Fiction* and *W. G. Sebald: A Critical Companion* (co-edited with J. J. Long).

Kenneth Womack is Associate Professor of English and Head of the Division of Arts and Humanities at Pennsylvania State University, Altoona. He has published widely on twentieth-century literature and popular culture and serves as editor of *Interdisciplinary Literary Studies: A Journal of Criticism and Theory,* and as co-editor of Oxford University Press's *Year's Work in English Studies*. He is author of *Postwar Academic Fiction: Satire, Ethics, Community* (2001) and co-author (with Ruth Robbins and Julian Wolfreys) of *Key Concepts in Literary Theory* (2002).

Cynthia F. Wong is Associate Professor of English at the University of Colorado, Denver, where she teaches modern and contemporary world fiction and ethnic American literature. She is the author of *Kazuo Ishiguro* (2000) and is presently at work on a book concerning early twentieth-century British narratives of Antarctic exploration.

Preface

In this sea are situated two very large islands, the so-called British Isles, Albion and Ierna, which are greater than any which we have yet mentioned ...

(pseudo-Aristotle, *De mundo* c.iv)

{P}rose art presumes a deliberate feeling for the historical and social concreteness of living discourse ... a feeling for its participation in historical becoming and in social struggle; it deals with discourse that is still warm from that struggle and hostility ...

(Bakhtin, *The Dialogic Imagination*)

The subject of this work, the British and Irish novel between the close of World War II and the turn of the millennium, is as vast as it is rich and heterogeneous. This volume concerns novelists of that half-century who are indigenous to Britain or Ireland or who have emigrated to one of these "two very large islands" (usually but not invariably settling in greater London) and who have written novels of acclaim that have significantly engaged with and influenced the indigenous literary culture.

Collectively, the essays that follow implicitly (and at points also explicitly) test and explore the meaning of the term "novel" and gauge the pressures on the form brought about by extraliterary developments in the publishing industry, in critical and cultural theory, in film and video, and in literary credentialing (e.g. the rise of the literary prize phenomenon). Whatever we might mean by "novel," the ideas of "expansiveness" and "newness" (engagement with the present) seem to be central to it. In *Aspects of the Novel* (1927), for example, E. M. Forster addresses the first point by calling "expansion" an "idea the novelist must cling to." "Not completion," Forster adds; "Not rounding off but opening out" (quoted in Danow 1991: 43). And M. M. Bakhtin, a leading twentieth-century theorist of the novel, addresses the second point by claiming that the novel – because it is oriented toward the here and now and is characterized by its "evolutionary nature, its spontaneity, incompleteness and inconclusiveness, by its ability and commitment to rethink and reevaluate" – is "the quintessential register of society's attitudes toward itself and the world" (Danow 1991: 50, 43). In contrast to the epic, which presents itself as "completed, conclusive and immutable," the novel "is a genre that is ever questing, ever examining itself and subjecting its established forms to review"; it is the genre with the most "contact with the present (with contemporary reality) in all its openendedness" (Bakhtin 1981: 17, 39, 11). One might conceive of Bakhtin's perhaps overly neat "epic/novel" distinction in terms of a series of dichotomies – "centrifugal" versus "centripetal," "becoming" versus "being," and "dialogic" versus "monologic" – that collectively make the case for the potentially liberating energies of prose fiction. Akin to Bakhtin's distinction between "epic" and "novel" is Frank Kermode's distinction between "myth" and "fiction." In *The Sense of an Ending* (1967) Kermode argues that while "myths" presuppose definitive answers and "total and adequate explanations of things" as they are and were, "fictions" exist for the purpose of "finding things out":

> they change as the needs of sense-making change. Myths are the agents of stability, fictions the agents of change. Myths call for absolute, fictions for conditional assent. Myths make sense in terms of a lost order of time . . . ; fictions, if successful, make sense of the here and now. (1967: 39)

In the spirit of Forster, Bakhtin, and Kermode, then, the present volume approaches the novel of the period as an open-ended, engaged, exploratory genre, one that challenges and stretches the conventions of perception, subjectivity, and literary representation in its attempts to probe and depict an evolving contemporary reality.

In this spirit too one might view the British and Irish novel of the period as a battleground on which competing artistic, philosophical, social, and political agendas wage war (for Bakhtin, a novel's discourse is "still warm from that struggle and hostility" (1981: 331)). Although it is all but impossible to draw a neat circle around the immensely varied novels treated in this volume and summarize what makes them distinctive as a group in time or place, a few generalizations, all pertaining to the relationship of fiction and history, do present themselves. First, however different these various novels are to each other, they collectively suggest that it is no longer possible to affirm, with James Joyce's Gabriel Conroy, that "literature" is "above politics" (Joyce 1993: 171) – that it inhabits a separate ontological status. Although Joyce may have been ironic in giving this thought to his protagonist in "The dead," Gabriel's wish attests to the currency of this notion in early twentieth-century fiction as an ideal worth upholding. The idea that art can function as an escape from worldly power struggles (and the violence and strife these entail) finds expression, in different ways, in many modern novels, from Forster's *A Room with a View* (1908), to Joyce's *A Portrait of the Artist as a Young Man* (1914), to Virginia Woolf's *Mrs Dalloway* (1925). By contrast, the novels of the second half of the twentieth century, almost without exception, attest to the inescapability of the sociopolitical fray – and to the inescapability of history. To quote a Joycean protagonist once again, this time Stephen Dedalus in *Ulysses* (1922), the idea that "History" is "a nightmare" from which one might hope "to awake" (Joyce 1986: 28) – the idea that one can shake off one's national and cultural history – is all but ruled out in novels of this later period. As different as Lowry's *Under the Volcano*, Orwell's *Nineteen Eighty-Four*, Golding's *Lord of the Flies*, Tolkien's *The Lord of the Rings*, Spark's *The Prime of Miss Jean Brody*, Lessing's *Golden Notebook*, Rhys's *Wide Sargasso Sea*, Rushdie's *Midnight's Children*, Ishiguro's *The Remains of the Day*, Swift's *Waterland,* Byatt's *Possession,* and McCabe's *The Butcher Boy* are from each other, each of these works attests to the inescapability of the past and to the inter-animation, indeed to the blurring, of "fiction" and "history." Moreover, the novels of this period may be said to obsess over history, whether in the sense of being preoccupied with historical events or in the sense of thematizing history itself and of musing on historiography. It is difficult to overlook the explicit meditations on history – the inescapably fictive nature of history and the inescapably historical nature of fiction – in so many of the novels discussed in this volume.

I intend this Companion to function both as a reference guide and as an extended introduction to the field, for scholars, teachers, and students alike. This volume makes no pretensions to being a definitive literary history of the period. Rather, these inter-linked essays that concern texts, topics, and controversies of the last five decades of the twentieth century seek to stimulate the study of the contemporary British and Irish novel and to demonstrate the vitality and diversity of the critical and contextual lenses by which this recent fiction is being viewed and understood.

I have divided the volume into two sections, in the hope of making it more easily navigable for a variety of different readers with a variety of different scholarly needs and agendas. The essays in Part I, "Contexts for the British and Irish Novel, 1945–2000," focus on overarching sociocultural and literary movements and trends, and on the impact that such sociocultural developments have had on the novelistic production of the period. These chapters situate the British and Irish novel of the half-century within a number of contexts to which it responded, among these: the elitist orientation of literary modernism; the rise and fall of European fascisms and, later, of the Cold War; the decline and demise of the British empire; the post-1968 explosion in critical theory and the rise of postmodernism; the literary prize phenomenon and developments in the publishing industry and in film and video; the effect on "British" and "English" literature by Irish and Scottish national identities; and the challenge posed to male-dominated and ethnically British literary traditions by feminist and black-British authors, among others.

These and other informing frames of reference are also used to illuminate the specific novels (and novelists) discussed at greater length, and in more focused treatments, in the second part of the volume. The essays in Part II, "Reading Individual Texts and Authors," probe key texts, figures, and sub-genres of the period. Included here are discussions of "canonical" works by authors long familiar to readers (Samuel Beckett, Evelyn Waugh, George Orwell, Graham Greene, William Golding, Iris Murdoch, and Jean Rhys); more recent works by authors currently on the scene (Margaret Drabble, V. S. Naipaul, Salman Rushdie, Julian Barnes, Kazuo Ishiguro,

Ian McEwan, Graham Swift, A. S. Byatt, and Pat Barker); and works by authors with popular or even "cult" followings that continue to animate our literary culture in significant ways (Malcolm Lowry, C. S. Lewis, J. R. R. Tolkien, and Kingsley and Martin Amis). Separate chapters on the campus satire subgenre, the Scottish "new wave," and the Irish novel after Joyce attend to topics of interest that embrace numerous authors. The primary objective of this section is to "read" individual works and authorial careers that continue to inform and energize literary culture today, on both sides of the Atlantic and beyond.

REFERENCES AND FURTHER READING

Aristotle (1931) *Works of Aristotle, translated into English under the editorship of W. D. Ross, vol. III.* Oxford: Clarendon Press.

Bakhtin, M. M. (1981) *The Dialogic Imagination*, trans. C. Emerson and M. Holquist. Austin: University of Texas Press.

Danow, D. K. (1991) *The Thought of Mikhail Bakhtin: From Word to Culture.* New York: St Martin's Press.

Forster, E. M. (1927) *Aspects of the Novel.* New York: Harcourt, Brace, and World.

Joyce, J. (1986) *Ulysses.* New York: Vintage.

——(1993) *Dubliners.* New York: Vintage.

Kermode, F. (1967) *The Sense of an Ending.* Oxford: Oxford University Press.

Acknowledgments

I am grateful for the resources that Rhodes College made available to me as holder of the Charles R. Glover Chair of English Studies during the period in which this volume was being prepared. I would also like to thank my colleagues at Rhodes – in particular Jennifer Brady, Michael Leslie, Cynthia Marshall, Steven McKenzie, and Lynn Zastoupil – for their ongoing support and encouragement of my work; the Dean of the College, Robert R. Llewellyn, for his support of this project and faculty development at Rhodes; and Mimi Atkinson and Judith Rutschman, of the Rhodes English and computer departments, respectively, for their gracious help in preparing the typescript. Thanks also are due to Andrew McNeillie, Jennifer Hunt, Emma Bennett, Karen Wilson, and Mary Dortch at Blackwell Publishing for their expert advice and tireless efforts on behalf of this volume. As always, I am deeply grateful to my wife Rachel, daughters Hannah and Ruth, and mother Dorothy for making everything possible and worthwhile.

PART I
Contexts for the British and Irish Novel, 1945–2000

1

The Literary Response to the Second World War

Damon Marcel DeCoste

> *My subject is War, and the Pity of War.*
> *The Poetry is in the pity.*
> (Wilfred Owen)

> *It wasn't only evil men who did these things. Courage smashes a cathedral,*
> *endurance lets a city starve, pity kills...*
> (Graham Greene, *The Ministry of Fear*)

If one war most influenced British literature in the last century, that war was certainly Wilfred Owen's, the Great War, 1914–18. From Rupert Brooke's sonnets of 1914 to Pat Barker's *Regeneration* trilogy of the 1990s, the First World War has inspired British writers like no other. Indeed, Paul Fussell argues that this war defines subsequent British culture more generally, engendering a uniquely "modern understanding [that is] essentially ironic" (2000: 35). As part of this privileged place in the nation's cultural memory, the Great War has, through the writing of Owen and others, become *the* war of twentieth-century British literature, that which defines for popular memory what war is and what war writing should be. In Samuel Hynes's words, this war's "image of total annihilation is our tragic myth of modern war" (1998: 53), one that shapes how we approach both later conflicts and the literature about them. Indeed, the Great War's grip on literary representations of war is such that the Second World War poet Vernon Scannell confesses, in his "The Great War," that he remembers "Not the war I fought in / But the one called Great / Which ended in a sepia November / Four years before my birth" (Stephen 1993: 312). By so functioning as the definitive war writing of the last century, the canon of Great War literature has furnished later generations not only with the images and emotions taken to be the truth of modern warfare, but also with a model of the war writer himself, who emerges as a fairly homogeneous figure having undergone a specific set of experiences and drawn particular lessons from them. If the First War assumes a mythic stature in twentieth-century culture, then, for Scannell, "the War Poet [is] at once a propagator of the myth and one of its creatures" (1976: 14). This figure of the War Poet, modeled on such writers as Owen himself, is, above all, a combatant, one "who [has] endured battle" and recorded, with unflinching fidelity, "what it was like to be a fighting man in the first Great War of the twentieth century" (1976: 7).

From such frontline testimony emerges a literature marked by two salient traits, which, because of the unique place held by the Great War in modern memory, come to be held as definitive of modern war writing generally. First, this war writing is a literature of disillusion, of young soldiers educated in ideals of manly and patriotic conduct that are blown apart by industrial warfare. It is thus a literature recording the death of what Owen dubs "the old Lie" of martial glory (1965: 55), a literature of brutally disappointed expectations, or in Fussell's terms, of that irony that typifies modernity: "the Great War was more ironic than any before or since" (2000: 8). Second, if, as Hynes suggests, the Great War is memorialized as tragedy, then this writing foregrounds one of the two emotions Aristotle deemed essential to that genre, namely pity (Aristotle 1988: 48). As my first epigraph indicates, pity is at the heart of much of the best remembered of Great War literature, pity for the "doomed youth" sent by ignorant civilians to "die as cattle" (Owen 1965: 44). While excoriating those who, safe on the home front, support the war, such writing nonetheless aims to elicit our sympathy for combatants cast as helpless innocents, even, as in Owen's "Parable of the old man and the young" (p. 42), as sacrificial victims, and to lead us to understand the meaning of war primarily in terms of their suffering.

Another significant body of British war literature from the last century does not, however, fit this mold. British fiction of the Second World War is not primarily the testimony of frontline witnesses; it is not, for the most part, a literature of combatants at all. Of the authors to be dealt with here, only two – Anthony Powell and Evelyn Waugh – served with the armed forces during the war. One of the consequences of this "deviation" from the model of the War Poet is that fiction of the Second War is not a literature of the battlefront. Indeed, battles play an astonishingly small part in this body of writing, making brief appearances in Waugh's *Sword of Honour* trilogy (1952–61), say, or Olivia Manning's *Levant Trilogy* (1977–80), but otherwise being most conspicuous by their absence. Rather than the testimony of infantrymen disillusioned by combat, British fiction of the Second World War offers us the war away from the front, and especially on the home front. Its war is the war of black-outs, evacuees, rationing, aerial bombardment and industrial mobilization. It is a home-front fiction for what was, for long stretches of time, really a home-front war. As Angus Calder notes, during the German Blitz from the air of 1940–1, over 43,000 Britons were killed on this "front," and it was not until three years of war had passed that armed forces fatalities exceeded those of civilians (1969: 226). As Margot Norris observes, the home front became "the arena of combat" (2000: 32), and this fiction tends to fix its gaze not on distant trenches, but on the lives of Britons at home, producing an apt wartime literature nonetheless at odds with the Great War model.

Nor does this wartime fiction rehearse that narrative of disillusion so central to the literature of the First War. While there are exceptions – Waugh's *Sword of Honour*, for example, charts Guy Crouchback's slow surrender of his belief in honorable warfare – for the most part this fiction has no investment in Owen's "old Lie," and so little in its dismantling; that work had already been done by an earlier war and its well-known literature. As Scannell observes, "[t]he serviceman of 1939–45 could not be disillusioned because he held no illusions to start with" (1976: 17). Indeed, Waugh himself, despite Crouchback's illusions, entered service, as a 1940 letter reveals, understanding war to entail the undermining of one's ideals and so, to an extent, already having undergone a process of disillusionment: "I know that one goes into a war for reasons of honour & soon finds oneself called on to do very dishonourable things" (1980: 141). The war is thus, as Hynes argues, reflected in the literature less in terms of ideals and their betrayal, than in terms of grim necessity (1998: 111). The grimness of this fate is almost always stressed in wartime fiction, even in novels that predate the war itself, so that there remains little room for narratives of lost illusions, though still enough for treatments of this Second War as "a great tragedy" (Manning 2001: 571). But if the literature of the Second World War, like that of the First, can write its war as tragedy, it does so by eliciting, not pity for the innocents, but rather Aristotelian terror in the face of a global conflagration that would claim some 60 million lives.

British fiction's Second World War is not a war of pathos. As a war that involves the home front, which makes everyone a participant, this total war targets everyone both for suffering and for potential culpability. If, for Hynes, the Second World War "was everybody's war" (1998: 113), then British fiction tends to treat such universal participation as a universal responsibility that makes the identification of "innocents" for whom we may feel Owen's pity a difficult, even morally suspect, enterprise. For Graham Greene, this second global war served as a moral judgment on European culture, a fitting end for a corrupt world undeserving of our pity: "Violence comes to us more easily because it was so long expected – not only by the political sense but by the moral sense. The world we lived in could not have ended any other way" (1969: 447). Greene's *The Ministry of Fear* (1943) and *The Heart of the Matter* (1948) go further, identifying pity itself as allied to the corrosive pride that enables murderous acts. Thus of *The Heart of the Matter*'s Scobie we are told, "Pity smouldered like decay at his heart" (1968: 170). While Greene's war on pity is peculiarly his own, wartime fiction is remarkably lacking in pity for the war-torn lives it traces, tending instead to pass austere judgment on those who suffer the war's ravages as themselves part of the problems that have unleashed this war. The tragedy staged by these novels, then, is one in which weariness and moral horror seem, more than pity or identification, to be the governing responses.

The Invisible War

While I have sketched some features of British fiction of the Second World War, what has commonly been taken to be such literature's most salient trait is its absence. For most of the second half of the twentieth century, the Second World War was the invisible war, so far as literary studies were concerned. Unlike the Great War, the Second War has tended not to be treated as a discrete moment in British literary history, nor has it been seen to offer a clear canon of worthwhile texts and authors to be studied as wartime literature. This process of defining Second War literature as the literature that wasn't is as old as the war itself. As early as December 1939, reviewers in the *Times Literary Supplement* were bemoaning the apparent lack of writers willing to render the present conflict (Abrams 2000: 2525). This sense of a literary void persists well beyond the war's conclusion, with, for example, Robert Hewison treating the war as an era of endings: of Auden and Isherwood's emigration to America (1977: 8), of the cessation of such periodicals as *The Criterion* and *New Verse* (p. 11), and of a fall in numbers of books published (p. 22). Thus, for Hewison, "the number of writers able to carry on their trade was small; their facilities were restricted" (p. 56). Fussell, too, reads the onset of the war in terms of a depressed silence on the part of major writers (1989: 133) and warns that "[d]isappointment threatens anyone searching in published wartime writing for a use of language that could be called literary" (p. 251). Indeed, this sense of the war as not being written, or as having produced but literary ephemera, is one that plagued wartime writers themselves. George Orwell, for one, in a 1941 letter to *The Partisan Review*, decried what he saw as a dearth of good novels; new writing, in his opinion, comprises nothing but hasty pulp fiction "of a trashiness that passes belief" (1968: 54).

The duration of such sentiments was such that Alan Munton could justly begin his pioneering study, *English Fiction of the Second World War* (1989), by claiming that his "is a virtually untouched subject, as far as criticism is concerned" (p. ix). The years since the late 1980s have seen the partial redressing of this critical gap, with the appearance of several books aimed at tackling this subject and at establishing wartime fiction as both worthy of scholarly comment and as benefiting from being treated specifically as wartime writing. Munton's groundbreaking work was soon followed by Sebastian Knowles's study of seven British writers of the Second World War in *The Purgatorial Flame* (1990). Gill Plain's 1996 examination of women's writing of this period has been supplemented by Karen Schneider's 1997 study of "the war/gender matrix" in this fiction (p. 8) and Jenny Hartley's comprehensive survey of women's wartime novels in *Millions Like Us* (1997). More recently, Mark Rawlinson has undertaken a similarly extensive overview, in *British Writing of the Second World War* (2000), identifying such germane features of this writing as its presentation of a conflict "in which seemingly everyone was both a target and a belligerent producer" (p. 23). Such scholarship has begun the long-deferred task of recognizing the merits of much neglected wartime fiction, and of defining the Second World War as a meaningful period in British literary history, one of signal importance to several major novelists of the last century: Evelyn Waugh, Graham Greene, and George Orwell, to name but three who have chapters devoted to them in this volume.

Yet that such critical work was so long in coming is itself worthy of remark. What creates this impression of a literary void during the Second World War? The reasons for the "invisibility" of this war are many. While several works by major writers are, in fact, being published in the midst, much less in the immediate wake, of the war, both production and publication of new novels did, as Hewison observes, decline in wartime. The rationing of paper shortened publishers' book lists, and the Blitz likewise took its toll on new literary work. On December 29, 1940, German bombers hit the center of the London book trade, destroying over 5 million unissued volumes in warehouses there; over the course of the Blitz, 20 million new volumes would be lost (Hewison 1977: 32). The literary scene also suffered from the fact that most writers of note were active in the war effort. Powell and Waugh spent much of the war in uniform. Orwell was occupied, from 1941 to 1943, with work for the BBC's Eastern Service. Henry Green served with the National Fire Service, while Graham Greene moved from a post as a London air raid warden to serving British Intelligence in Sierra Leone. Countless other writers found themselves drawn into war work and away from their writerly routines, thus contributing to that drop in literary output so often noted by critics. Moreover, certain writers felt themselves "blocked" by the momentous and intrusively present history through which they were living. Orwell, for instance, remarked during the Blitz that "[o]nly the mentally dead are capable of . . . writing novels while this nightmare is going on" (1968: 54), and such writers as Elizabeth Bowen, whose *Heat of the Day* (1948) was five years in the making, and Evelyn Waugh would similarly complain of the difficulties of executing major work amidst war's upheavals.

Despite all this, wartime fiction, and certainly postwar novels that chronicle Britain's Second World War, are scarcely negligible in either quantity or quality. In fact, the long-standing "invisibility" of Second World War fiction seems to have less to do with any actual paucity of works dealing with this conflict than it has with such works' "failure" to be the kind of war literature the critics want. That is, the Second War has long been elided in literary histories of the twentieth century primarily because novelistic responses to that war do not fit the model for war writing bequeathed to literary scholars by the Great War. Instructive, in this regard, is the abbreviated "Voices from World War II" section of the latest edition of *The Norton Anthology of English Literature*. Comprising but five such "voices," and no fiction, this sampling is guided by that notion of the War Poet treated above. Four of the five writers are servicemen, three of these poets, one of them the RAF memoirist Richard Hillary. That this section is considerably shorter than the anthology's "Voices from World War I" is no surprise, for in attempting to represent World War II writing primarily through the figure of the soldier-poet, the anthology limits its field and misrepresents the literature, and most certainly the fiction, of this war. As noted above, literary responses to the Second World War diverge in both spirit and focus from Great War verse, and searching for writing that will replicate that verse leads only to a "discovery" of lack. If the Second War has, then, been characterized as a literary hiatus, this has resulted more from scholars' looking for what isn't there than from their critical examination of what is.

The All-too-visible War

If, however, the Second War has not been treated as its own literary epoch, this may in part be due to the fact that the war, as a literary event, so predates the actual outbreak of hostilities. Certainly, one of the reasons this war's fiction avoids a narrative of shock and disillusionment is that this sequel war was so long anticipated by British novelists. Variously dubbed by literary historians "[t]he Literature of Anticipation" (Knowles 1990: 2), the literature of the "prelude" (Plain 1996: 35), or the "Literature of Preparation" (Hynes 1979: 341), this literary imagining of an all-too-visible future war is something peculiar to the Second War and central to its depiction as one in which Owenesque pity is inappropriate. While Bernard Bergonzi locates the emergence of this prophetic literature only in the year leading up to the war (1978: 87), the development of such an anticipatory fiction reaches much further back. As early as 1930, Evelyn Waugh's *Vile Bodies* introduced readers to a world of frenzied, joyless revels, overshadowed by the certainty of a second war; as Waugh's Father Rothschild tells us, "Wars don't start nowadays because people want them . . . and soon we shall all be walking into the jaws of destruction again, protesting our pacific intentions" (1965: 133). And indeed Waugh's characters take this walk, as their creator sets their ironically titled "Happy Ending" on "the biggest battlefield in the history of the world" (p. 220).

While *Vile Bodies* may be, as Hynes contends, the earliest work of anticipation (1979: 60), it was soon enough followed by others. The year 1936 produced both Graham Greene's *A Gun for Sale* – with its headlines of "Europe mobilising" (1961: 7) and its grotesque gas-masked crowds preparing for aerial assault (pp. 181–2) – as well as Orwell's study of rancorous would-be poet, Gordon Comstock, tantalized by visions of "[t]he whole western world going up in a roar of high explosives" (1986: 26), in *Keep the Aspidistra Flying*. As the decade drew to its close, such prophecy became only bleaker and more urgent. Stevie Smith's *Over the Frontier* (1938) presents the often surreal first-person narrative of Pompey Casmilus, who noting that "our times have been upon the rack of war. And are, and are" (1989: 94), metamorphizes from amanuensis into secret soldier in a war that seems already ongoing and that takes her, on clandestine missions, into Germany. Published mere weeks before Britain's declaration of war, Orwell's *Coming Up for Air* (1939) chronicles George Bowling's search for the romanticized world of his childhood as an escape from a present in which he is convinced that "[w]ar is coming" (1990: 238). Indeed, this "prelude" fiction extends into wartime, with Virginia Woolf's posthumous *Between the Acts* (1941), begun in 1938 and eventually set in the summer of 1939, treating a rural pageant of British history played to an audience acutely aware of "[t]he doom of sudden death hanging over [it]" (1990: 71).

To a degree, such fiction merely registers the mood of the 1930s. Certainly the history of the years preceding the war offered grounds for such expectation. From

Hitler's rise to power in 1933, a series of harbingers of European war punctuated the decade and could only help fuel anxiety, even certainty, concerning a second Great War. The steady rearmament of Germany from 1934 forward, the German reoccupation of the Rhineland in 1936, the Axis alliance forged that same year, the absorption of Austria in 1938, the annexation of the Sudetenland under the terms of 1938's Munich agreement – such proofs of Nazism's expansionist aims were made only more worrisome by the victory of fascism in the Spanish Civil War (1936–9) and Japan's 1937 invasion of China. War had, in fact, become a reality well before the Allied powers made it official in September 1939. Such developments made the 1930s themselves a decade of anticipation in which, says Hynes, "it was clear not only that a war would come, but who the Enemy would be" (1979: 140). In part, then, this preparatory fiction only records a common expectation of its day, a sense of protracted lead-up to the inevitable, nicely rendered by Anthony Powell in *The Kindly Ones* (1962):

> war was now materialising in slow motion. Like one of the Stonehurst 'ghosts', war towered by the bed when you awoke in the morning; unlike those more transient, more accommodating spectres, its tall form ... remained ... a looming, menacing shape of ever greater height, ever thickening density. (1976b: 87)

But this fiction is significantly more than reportage. While often it ties its predictions to contemporary events – certainly Bowling mentions war in Spain and China, and the singularly menacing figure of Adolf Hitler (Orwell 1990: 9, 165) – it helps establish the outlook of later war fiction by treating the inevitability of the coming war as deriving from a deeper cultural malaise in which Britons themselves, and not just foreign regimes, are implicated. Like much subsequent war fiction, this "prelude" literature is focused almost exclusively on the home front, and it sees there a world like that described by Graham Greene above, that is, a *Britain* that is so corrupt that war is its only fitting future. The war being anticipated in the 1930s, then, is not one brought to Britain by foreign enemies alone. Rather than casting their English characters as simply the victims of other nations' sins, as, that is, fitting objects for readerly sympathy, these novels disclose enemies within the British state, and within the British soul, and so make the prewar home front in part responsible for its own, apparently fated, suffering. Thus the war that threatens Greene's England in *A Gun for Sale* is one plotted by the arms manufacturer, Sir Marcus, on English soil. Likewise, Gordon Comstock, seeing only "[d]esolation, emptiness, prophecies of doom" in modern English culture (Orwell 1986: 21), discerns there, too, "the reverberations of future wars," for which he himself longs (pp. 22, 26). For Smith's Pompey, the enemy is best denominated by the first-person plural, as the lesson she draws from having passed over into "enemy" territory is that *we*, Britons at home, are all fascists and warmongers in embryo, and always have been: "Power and cruelty are the strength of our life" (Smith 1989: 272). Such a diagnosis of an innate bloodlust at home, as well as abroad, is echoed by Orwell and Woolf. Bowling gets his first taste of the war as bombs are dropped on his childhood home not by German, but by British planes (Orwell 1990: 234), a fitting conclusion for a novel that reveals the sources of war to be as much rooted in our own hatred as in continental turmoil: "The same thing over and over again. Hate, hate, hate. Let's all get together and have a good hate" (p. 156). Similarly, Woolf's war-haunted parody of British history in *Between the Acts* locates the roots of wars, past and present, in an erotics of violence that her characters cannot escape. While Isa Oliver agonizes over how "[l]ove and hate [tear] her asunder" and longs for "a new plot" by which to live (1990: 134), the novel ends with the insistence that the old plots – of love and hate, eros and violence – must be rehearsed by her and her husband, Giles: "Before they slept, they must fight; after they had fought, they would embrace. . . . But first they must fight, as the dog fox fights with the vixen" (p. 136).

By thus locating the urge to war in the heart of Britain, the literature of anticipation inaugurates a sense, sustained in later war fiction, that this is a conflict in which our heroes are also villains, the victims also culprits, a depiction of the war that discourages readerly readiness to pity or to cheer Britain's hardships or valor. So far, too, as it identifies aggression as a ubiquitous element of the human constitution, this fiction also presents the war as part of a history inevitably, repetitively, marked by war, even simply defined as war's repetition. Certainly such a sense of repetition plagues Isa, and informs the pageant's staging of British history in terms of the same old plots of love and hate. According to Fussell, it was also deeply felt by those who would fight this *Second* World War: "Among those fighting there was an unromantic and demoralizing sense that it had all been gone through before" (1989: 132). This demoralizing view of history, fostered by the war's status as sequel, remains a central one in fictional responses to the war, at least up to Penelope Lively's *Moon Tiger* (1987). In this novel, Claudia Hampton, in the process of writing her deathbed "history of the world" (p. 1), declares, "All history, of course, is the history of wars" and so of ostensibly unstoppable repetitions (p. 66). Lively reinforces this point with her title itself, which refers to a brand of mosquito repellent, "a green coil that slowly burns all night" (p. 75), making its fiery circles much as Claudia's history of the world seems to do. The impact, then, of this prewar literature is far-reaching, and it creates a starting point for wartime fiction that helps account both for its common pessimism and for its often highly critical presentation of the home front.

From "Phoney War" to Blitz

Its focus on the home front is one of the clearest legacies of this prelude literature to the war fiction that follows. While certain war novels are set far from England, this fascination with the war away from the battlefield remains a prominent feature of virtually all British fiction of the Second War. Although Olivia Manning sets her two trilogies, *The Balkan Trilogy* (1960–5) and *The Levant Trilogy*, in continental Europe and the Middle East, her tale of Guy and Harriet Pringle's travels nonetheless approaches the war through the lens of domesticity and, but for a few scenes involving the young officer, Simon Boulderstone, avoids the frontlines. Manning's world is still a noncombatants' world, her story that of colonies of academics, journalists, diplomats, and expatriates awaiting news of a war that is happening elsewhere, and not, for the most part, of soldiers in the heat of battle. Indeed, even works such as Powell's *The Valley of Bones* (1964) and *The Soldier's Art* (1966), which focus on the serviceman's experience, tend to eschew depictions of combat and to situate themselves firmly in a British milieu. Powell's Nick Jenkins thus spends two novels and two years of the war being shuttled, in England and Northern Ireland, from one non-combat role to another, and experiencing the war most powerfully in the Blitz's claiming of the lives of friends and relatives. Even this soldier's war, then, is primarily the war at home.

In part, this concern with life behind the lines merely reflects the kind of war that finally arrived in 1939. As Plain notes, "expectations of absolute war were confronted by the actuality of absent war" (1996: 119), as between the fall of Poland and the German *blitzkrieg* in the spring of 1940, the war so long awaited seemed, from a British perspective, still in abeyance. Britain's war begins with what has been variously termed the "phoney war," the "funny war," or the "Bore War" (Calder 1969: 57), a period of about seven months in which virtually no military actions were engaged by British forces. This was, instead, a period of mobilization on the home front, of civilians evacuating urban centers, dealing with new wartime strictures, and seeking places to contribute to the war effort. After the evacuation of British forces from Dunkirk, the war shifted to an even more emphatically home-front conflict, with the Battle of Britain developing into the sustained German bombing program – the Blitz – which lasted from September 1940 to May 1941. With the military largely expelled from Europe, Britain's war became one of nightly raids on major cities, and so one largely "fought," or at least suffered, by civilians. The exigencies of this home-front war, the fact that it was borne by civilians and dictated sacrifices across class lines, helped generate a wartime rhetoric of this being a war for the social transformation of Britain herself, a "People's War" of "stoical resistance and social solidarity" in which old hierarchies were swept away (Donnelly 1999: 37). In fact, for Munton and Hartley, this notion of social reform by means of a "People's War" is a galvanizing premise for much wartime fiction.

Yet while one can find literary celebrations of the war in these terms – for example, J. B. Priestley's *Daylight on Saturday* (1943), with its paean to the collective efforts of munitions workers, without whom "we could not survive in wartime" (1967: 9) – the literature of the phoney war and of the Blitz tends instead to mock such portraits of social solidarity, seeing on the home front, rather, an egotism and fractiousness that reflect, and help account for, the war that home front has to suffer. As regards the vaunting of the "common people," the tartness of Muriel Spark's *The Girls of Slender Means* (1963) – which opens by observing that, "[l]ong ago in 1945 all nice people in England were poor, allowing for exceptions" (p. 1) – is itself at least as common as Priestley's hero-worship. Certainly such cynicism is rife in the works of the England's prime chronicler of the phoney war, Evelyn Waugh. The wartime "Prologue" to *Brideshead Revisited* (1945), with its unflattering portrait of the "common man," Hooper, and its description of wartime social change in terms of civilization being *"over-run by a race of the lowest type"* (1962: 13), testifies to Waugh's impatience with the ideal of a People's War. Likewise, in *Put Out More Flags* (1942) and *Men at Arms* (1952), Waugh depicts a home front typified less by noble sacrifice and collective effort than by petty strife and treacherous self-seeking. Thus the central character of the earlier novel, Basil Seal, is a man whose wartime conduct "ran parallel to Nazi diplomacy" (1943: 49). Motivated by the desire to "[do] well out of the war" (p. 46), Basil exploits the evacuation of urban children, by threatening billets with the destructive Connollys unless they pay him off, before betraying his friend Ambrose Silk by reporting him as a fascist sympathizer. Such egotism is the rule for this novel's cast of characters and works both to deface the "People's War" portrait of the home front and to highlight that home front's emulation of the amoral conduct of the "enemy." Indeed, in *Men at Arms*, the enemy Waugh's officers are keenest to engage is one another, as the prime struggle of this novel is no heroic engagement with either social injustice or the Nazi foe, but rather the absurd war waged between Apthorpe and Brigadier Ritchie-Hook over control of the former's "thunder box," a chemical toilet. Childish squabbling, not selfless labor, is the essence of Waugh's phoney war, which reveals the home front as a kind of farcical reflection of the enemy.

Comparable petty strife in the Auxiliary Fire Services animates much of Henry Green's phoney war novel, *Caught* (1943). Protagonist Richard Roe's story is defined largely by the insults and intrigues of his fellow firemen, and the most traumatic event of his war, until the book's conclusion with the onset of the Blitz, is the attempted abduction of his son, Christopher, not by some foreign enemy, but by the sister of his Fire Services instructor, Pye. While Roe's closing account of the AFS's efforts on the first night of the London Blitz seeks to memorialize them in terms of heroic solidarity, this tale is disturbingly punctuated by his son's own eagerness to play "German policeman" beating Poles (1965: 188), suggesting once more that the will to power at the roots of this war is present even in English "innocence." Such uneasy diagnoses of native British virtue are common to other Blitz fictions. These novels, to be sure, typically stress how bombardment transforms the landscape of home, making it alien, even surreal. For example, Powell's *Casanova's Chinese Restaurant* (1960) describes a bombed-out pub as a vision out of fairy tales: "a triumphal arch erected laboriously by dwarfs, or the gateway to some unknown, forbidden domain, the lair of sorcerors" (1976a: 1). Such an insistence on the supernatural also marks Bowen's "phantasmagoric" London, a haunted landscape in which "the wall between the living and the dead thinned" (1976: 91, 92). But along with this sense of the familiar being defamiliarized, one finds in Blitz fiction the assertion that war is simply uncovering what was always there, revealing how the values of "private" life mirror, and enable, the war of "public" history. As Harrison, in *The Heat of the Day*, says, "War...hasn't started anything that wasn't there already" (p. 33).

Here the Blitz is as much exposé as transfiguration. Indeed, for Greene, such exposure is the essence of bombardment, which "land[s] you naked in the street or expos[es] you in your bed or on your lavatory seat to the neighbours' gaze" (1978: 28). What is thus exposed, for Blitz fiction, is how the war has been bred on the home front, indeed, even in domestic space itself. This latter is the argument advanced by Bowen, who presents the Second World War as a conflict engendered and waged in private homes: "The grind and scream of battles, mechanized advances excoriating flesh and country... were indoor-plotted; this was a war of dry cerebration inside windowless walls" (1976: 142). This is borne out by the love affair of Stella Rodney and Robert Kelway, fostered by war and ultimately doomed by Robert's status as a home-grown exemplar of the psychology that mandates this war. Raised at Holme Dene, a quintessentially English country home, Robert has been reared on a diet of surveillance, emotional repression, and obliquely but savagely expressed will to power. Fittingly, this home is described in terms borrowed from across the Channel, with its "swastika-arms of passage leading to nothing" (p. 258). What, in fact, it has led to is Robert and his nihilistic worship of might, a stance that makes of this scion of Englishness a traitor in the service of Nazism. Similar affinities are uncovered by Greene's *Ministry of Fear*, whose protagonist, Arthur Rowe, welcomes the destruction of London, willing to buy his longed-for escape from his own past at the cost of others' loss: "After a raid he used to sally out and note with a kind of hope that this restaurant or that shop existed no longer – it was like loosening the bars of a prison cell one by one" (1978: 22). Indeed, the past for whose obliteration he yearns is one that allies him with the novel's Nazis. Rowe is haunted by his having murdered his ill wife out of pity for her sufferings. It was an act whose rationale the text presents as dangerously presumptuous and in accordance with the very credo of such Nazi agents as Dr Forester, who, a champion of euthanasia, "was quite unmoved by the story of the Nazi elimination of old people and incurables" (p. 182).

In both novels, the world uncovered by the Blitz is one not of heroic, if stoic, resistance, but of kinship with the very evil the war is being fought to vanquish. Their home front is one riddled with the same sickness that threatens from abroad. Indeed, it is noteworthy that both these Blitz texts are also spy novels, tales of intrigue, but even more, of treachery. Robert Kelway has betrayed his country in time of war. Arthur Rowe's story centers upon his entanglement with a spy circle, including native Britons, operating on English soil. These novels thus literalize that sense of the enemy within which animates not only such other wartime fiction as Green's, but both the literature of anticipation and postwar renderings of the period, as well. For, guided by this intuition of corruption on the home front, later novels make treachery a mainstay of British fiction's Second World War. Thus, in Waugh's *Officers and Gentlemen* (1955), the gravest threats come from figures such as Ivor Claire, who betrays Britain in Crete by deserting his command in the face of the enemy, or Ludovic, who murders Major Hound to save himself. Likewise, in Manning's *Balkan Trilogy*, the Pringles are most endangered by the malfeasance of their fellow Britons, falsely reported to the Germans as saboteurs by their beneficiary Yakimov, and almost abandoned to the advancing

Germans in Athens by the decamping Major Cookson. Far from celebrating British valor, or sympathizing with "innocent" civilians targeted by this home-front war, British war novels dismiss any pretensions to heroism or innocence and, by revealing the causes and dangers of this war to lie as much within as without, obscure from view any obvious candidates for our pity.

The Gendered War

Were this an earlier war, or a different war literature, innocence might indeed be located on the home front, and more especially, seen to repose in the figure of Woman. The traditional gendering of war, according to which male soldiers fight, in part, to preserve the purity of women on the home front, in fact persists in twentieth-century war writing, making an appearance, for example, in Jimmy Cross's idealization of Martha in Tim O'Brien's collection of Vietnam War stories, *The Things They Carried* (1990). But just as the Second World War transformed the home front into the frontline, so too did it turn British women from wards of fighting men into active participants in the war. Britain's war marked an unprecedented movement of women out of the domestic sphere and into both the work force and auxiliary arms of the military. Indeed, 1941 saw the conscription of young British women, something Calder calls a first in "civilized" nations (1969: 267). Women took up war-related posts in munitions factories, in adjuncts to the armed forces, in government ministries, even at anti-aircraft batteries (p. 268). The war thus entailed a liberation, for women, from homebound roles of wife, mother, and housekeeper, a liberation that involved the novelty of considerable sexual freedom, a development revealed by the tripling of illegitimate birthrates over the course of the war (p. 312).

This broader scope of opportunities for women is reflected in British war fiction, in which female characters take an active part in the war and fill a host of untraditional roles in public life. Thus Greene's *Ministry of Fear* offers us the portrait of Mrs Wilcox, an air raid warden who dies heroically in the line of duty (1978: 83). Bowen's Stella Rodney is, likewise, a contributing member of British Intelligence, "employed, in an organization better called Y.X.D., in secret, exacting, not unimportant work" (1976: 26). The fiercely independent Claudia Hampton of Lively's *Moon Tiger* insists both that "[h]istory [is] in the public domain" (1987: 50) and that she be part of it, by traveling to Egypt to act as war correspondent. British fiction, then, offers no shortage of strong female characters, eager to take full advantage of the war's opportunity for a less cloistered role in the life of their nation. What it does not offer, however, is any simple celebration of this new personal and professional liberty. While British fiction of the war duly records the changes in women's lives brought about by the conflict, it does not always do so favorably. Indeed, the response to these changes in gender roles is typically ambivalent in fiction by men and women both.

Perhaps predictably, male writers often view these developments with suspicion, if not outright hostility. Their criticism tends to focus on either the "unnatural" character of women's wartime work or on the dangers posed by a newly liberated female sexuality. Greene's Mrs Wilcox, for example, hero though she be, is derided by the narrator, castigated as a "masterful wife" and mocked for her "hockey-playing" heartiness (1978: 81, 80); her valor is thus undercut by the insistence that there is something farcical in her playing at hero at all. Green's *Caught* fixes an even more baleful gaze on female promiscuity in wartime. While Green's Roe pines for his dead wife, he views the amorous habits of the novel's women as tawdry and contemptible:

> As they were driven to create memories to compare, and thus to compensate for the loss each had suffered, he saw them hungrily seeking another man, oh they were sorry for men and they pitied themselves, for yet another man with whom they could spend last hours, to whom they could murmur darling, darling, darling it will be you always. (1965: 63)

Neither Roe nor his creator spare any pity for these women and their loss, however, and virtually the last words of the novel are Roe's angry declaration that "you get on my bloody nerves, all you bloody women with all your talk" (p. 196). Female sexual licence, the decided lack of feminine "innocence" at home, becomes an even deadlier matter for Powell. Indeed, the first fatality recorded in Nick Jenkins's war chronicle is the suicide of Sergeant Pendry, an act to which he is driven by his wife's infidelity (1976c: 99–102). Likewise, in *The Military Philosophers* (1968), the beautiful Pamela Flitton, with her passion for "[g]iving men hell" (1976e: 74), is cast as a veritable succubus, pursuing an ambitious campaign of affairs for the sole apparent purpose of inflicting suffering.

Not all male renderings of women's conduct in wartime veer in such misogynistic directions. Indeed, Green's own *Back* (1946) tells the tale of returned war amputee Charles Grant and his surrender of delusions that he is being persecuted by his former lover, Rose, and her family. In coming to accept that Nancy Whitmore is not his dead lover refusing to acknowledge him, but her half-sister, Charles discovers both a new love and a secret that centers not on womanly perversity, but on the infidelity of Rose's father. More recently, Sebastian Faulks makes a sexually active woman committed to a meaningful role in the war effort the eponymous hero of his *Charlotte Gray* (1998), which tells the tale of her secret missions to assist resistance efforts in Vichy France. But if male authors can prove themselves amenable to the more active and public woman of wartime, female writers are often critical and uneasy in dealing with this same figure. Spark relates the story of her "girls of slender means," with their ever-shifting retinue of lovers, in tones scarcely less caustic than Green's in *Caught*; thus, for example, does she describe literary London in 1945 in terms of "young male poets in corduroy trousers and young female poets with waist-length hair, or at least females who typed the poetry and slept with the poets, it was nearly the same thing" (1963: 75). Yet even women authors who eschew such mockery betray a certain allegiance to, or nostalgia for, more traditional feminine roles. In fact, the stories of their seemingly independent female protagonists typically suggest that fulfillment for these characters lies in an adherence to at least modified forms of conventional feminine roles of mother, wife, or faithful lover, and in the private domain of the courtship narrative.

Thus what hope is discernible at the end of Bowen's *Heat of the Day* seems borne by the single mother, Louie Lewis, and her newborn son, Tom, who, between them, offer the promise of life's persistence. While Louie has been unfaithful to her now-dead husband and has stepped outside the nuclear family, it is nonetheless in the role of mother that she discovers "her now complete life" (1976: 329). Similarly, Manning's Harriet Pringle identifies herself, in the end, with her marriage to Guy, despite her brief flight to Syria and Palestine. Though frustrated through two trilogies by Guy's taking her for granted, by his preference for a public, over a private, existence, Harriet feels bound to him and returns less out of resignation than of hope: "Guy and Harriet smiled at each other, aware that they were joined by [their] shared memories and the memories would never be lost" (2001: 567). Even Lively's Claudia Hampton, with her insistence on living and recording the "public" affairs of world history, ultimately writes a more private, and more traditionally feminine, love story. While she has never married and has been far from a conventional mother to her daughter, Lisa, the heart of her history is the war in Africa, and more specifically, her love there for tank officer Tom Southern, which remains, to her dying day, the most vivid of her experiences, just as his death in war creates the greatest lack in her life. Likewise, Faulks's Charlotte, for all of her "masculine" efforts in the world of espionage, is prompted to them by her own romantic plot, her love for the pilot, Peter Gregory. It is in hopes of finding him that she undertakes her mission to France, and she herself treats her tale as a conventional romance: "I'm just a romantic girl who's come to find her lost lover" (2001: 341). Thus while British war fiction may not present its women as retiring paragons of traditional feminine virtues, writers both male and female seem to express a longing for a womanly "innocence" effaced by war's transformation of gender roles, and for a home front that might be imagined as distinct from, and untainted by, the violence and treachery of war.

War without End

If Britain's literary war is remarkable for having its outbreak so amply forecast, it is likewise notable for having its conclusion all but overlooked. While history's Second World War culminates in Allied victory, the war recorded by British fiction fails often to end at all, and when it does, does so with little sense of triumph. Thus Bowen, while constructing *The Heat of the Day* around such events as the evacuation of Dunkirk, the Blitz, and Montgomery's success at El Alamein, takes her reader to the Allied invasion of Normandy and no further. Final victory is left tantalizingly out of reach, though hinted at in the middle name of Louie's newborn son: Victor. Waugh's *Sword of Honour* trilogy elides the war's end, its final volume, *Unconditional*

Surrender (1961), leapfrogging from the defeat of German forces in Yugoslavia to a postwar reunion dinner for the officers of Guy Crouchback's Halberdiers. Similarly, Powell's *Military Philosophers* shifts abruptly from the autumn of 1944 to the summer of 1945, omitting thereby any record of Allied victory in the Europe. While this novel concludes with a Victory Service at St Paul's Cathedral, the description of this ceremony is markedly devoid of celebration or even relief. The mood, instead, is somber and spent: "The country, there could be no doubt, was absolutely worn out.... One felt it in St. Paul's" (1976e: 217–18). Even Manning, having devoted six novels to the Pringles' wartime experiences, brings their narrative to a halt a full two years before the war's end, with only a cursory "Coda" gesturing towards a future of "precarious peace" (2001: 571). For the writers compelled to treat this conflict, then, the Second World War is not best grasped in terms of victory or defeat, winners and losers, so that even when some attempt is made to represent the war's conclusion, British novelists insist on deflating any urge to triumphalism.

Hynes argues that this difficulty with rendering the war in terms of unambiguous victory has to do with the very nature of this war's finale. For him, "its progress toward inevitable victory was interrupted and altered by two events," namely, the liberation of the Nazi death camps and the dropping of the atomic bombs on Hiroshima and Nagasaki (1998: 175). Such a claim is, to an extent, borne out by Faulks's *Charlotte Gray*, which instead of ending with British triumph, concludes with a wartime wedding, the description of which eerily echoes an earlier scene of two Jewish French boys' arrival at Auschwitz (2001: 370, 399); Faulks ends his war not with victory, but with the haunting reverberations of the Holocaust. Yet Hynes's account seems off the mark, for, in fact, the Nazi Holocaust leaves astonishingly little imprint on most war novels. While the persecution, even execution, of Jews in wartime is dealt with in *Unconditional Surrender* and Manning's *Balkan Trilogy*, these texts are more the exception than the rule. And indeed, these texts both deal with the homegrown anti-Semitic violence of Yugoslavia and Romania, respectively, and not with Hitler's genocidal "final solution." Waugh's Kanyis are tried and killed by a "Peoples' Court" [*sic*] in Tito's Yugoslavia (1975: 236), and Manning's Sasha and his family are dispossessed by a Romania itself no stranger to historical pogroms. But these texts, and British war writing more generally, skirt the horrific specters of the death camps and of the programmatic murder of some 6 million Jews, an aversion which, it may be noted, helps this fiction present the war as no fit occasion for readerly pity. It is fair to say, however, that Faulks's tale of the doomed André and Jacob Duguay is designed to elicit this emotion.

Rather than stemming from the specific shocks of genocide or atomic warfare, then, British fiction's reluctance to admit a meaningful victory in this war has its roots in that very sense of Britain's own corruption that pre-scripts the war in the literature of anticipation. If, after all, the war is to be understood as something dictated as much by the culture and psychology of the homeland as by those of hostile nation-states, then simple victory over foreign enemies resolves very little indeed. If, as this literature typically maintains, this war is preordained by a drive to dominance and an erotics of power that defines the "us" as much as the "them," then "their" unconditional surrender means only that this installment of what Lively's Claudia deems history's endless war narrative has come to a close, not the bloody story itself, nor the pathology that authors it. Thus, even when British writers do, as in Spark's *The Girls of Slender Means*, present us with scenes of victory celebrations, their rendering of such festivity is bleak and works to undercut any sense of triumph by foregrounding the terrifying potential for inhumanity on the home front itself. Spark's novel concludes with London crowds marking victory over Japan, but this moment of national jubilation is presented as something sinister; the cheering crowd is cast as a fearsome agent of senseless violence, as Spark's Nicholas witnesses a woman being stabbed amidst the riotous throngs (1963: 181). Screams of other victims are heard as well. This, for Spark, is what our "glorious victory" amounts to (p. 183), the age-old war returned, for a time, to within our borders.

This sense of defeat in victory accounts for British fiction's reticence concerning the war's "successful" conclusion and finds its clearest expression in novels that foresee not peace, but ceaseless war. As noted above, Lively's novel treats war and history as coterminous, thus understanding this second total war to have brought nothing to an end. Manning, too, can only reach towards a peace she nonetheless characterizes as "precarious," unlikely to last. Other novels use the war as the occasion for a more explicit treatment of perpetual war fueled by the power and cruelty which, as Smith maintained, are "the strength of our life." Set in a London – with its bombed-out buildings, its ubiquitous government ministries, its rationing, and ceaseless news from the front – that mirrors the city that weathered the Second World War, Orwell's *Nineteen Eighty-Four* (1949) might be seen as the quintessential expression of the British novel's treatment of that war. Orwell's Airstrip One, Britain's incarnation as part of Big Brother's Oceania, is the most extreme version of that common diagnosis of the home front's own embodiment of the evils ostensibly resisted in the Second World War. Here, totalitarianism reigns in a manner not even Hitler could quite effect, and far from having been imposed from without, it has arisen from within, born of a lust for power, defined as "inflicting pain and humiliation" (1976: 214), that typifies "victorious" London as much as her fallen foes. Moreover, this "postwar" Britain has become not only the very thing it fought in that war, but also an engine of never-ending warfare, of continuous wars with Eurasia and Eastasia, in part because such conflict is the necessary issue of homegrown dreams of the future as "a boot stamping on a human face – for ever" (p. 215). Having long forecast a war they deemed inevitable, in part at least because of the will to power definitive of a native psychology, British novelists posit no sudden cure for this malaise at war's end, and so can see no reason for this war not to be endlessly rehearsed. Thus they write the ending of the war in terms of its potentially infinite extension. In so doing, it may be argued, they leave to later writers an apt, if dark, lens through which to view the second half of the twentieth century.

REFERENCES AND FURTHER READING

Abrams, M. H., et al. (eds.) (2000) *The Norton Anthology of English Literature*, 7th edn., vol. II. New York: W. W. Norton.

Aristotle (1988) *On the Art of Poetry*, in *Classical Literary Criticism*, trans. T. S. Dorsch (pp. 29–75). Harmondsworth: Penguin.

Bergonzi, Bernard (1978) *Reading the Thirties: Texts and Contexts*. London: Macmillan.

Bowen, Elizabeth (1976) [1948] *The Heat of the Day*. Harmondsworth: Penguin.

Calder, Angus (1969) *The People's War: Britain, 1939–1945*. New York: Random House.

Donnelly, Mark (1999) *Britain in the Second World War*. London: Routledge.

Faulks, Sebastian (2001) [1998] *Charlotte Gray*. London: Vintage.

Fussell, Paul (1989) *Wartime: Understanding and Behavior in the Second World War*. New York: Oxford University Press.

——(2000) [1975] *The Great War and Modern Memory*. Oxford: Oxford University Press.

Green, Henry (1965) [1943] *Caught*. London: Hogarth Press.

——(1946) *Back*. London: Hogarth Press.

Greene, Graham (1961) [1936] *A Gun For Sale*. London: Heinemann.

——(1978) [1943] *The Ministry of Fear*. Harmondsworth: Penguin.

——(1968) [1948] *The Heart of the Matter*. Harmondsworth: Penguin.

——(1969) *Collected Essays*. London: Bodley Head.

Hartley, Jenny (1997) *Millions Like Us: British Women's Fiction of the Second World War*. London: Virago.

Hewison, Robert (1977) *Under Siege: Literary Life in London, 1939–1945*. London: Weidenfeld and Nicolson.

Hynes, Samuel (1979) *The Auden Generation: Literature and Politics in England in the 1930s*. London: Faber and Faber.

——(1998) *The Soldier's Tale: Bearing Witness to Modern War*. New York: Penguin.

Knowles, Sebastian (1990) *A Purgatorial Flame: Seven British Writers in the Second World War*. Philadelphia: University of Pennsylvania Press.

Lively, Penelope (1987) *Moon Tiger*. London: André Deutsch.

Manning, Olivia (1998) [1987] *The Balkan Trilogy*. London: Arrow Books. (First published 1960–5, in separate volumes).

——(2001) [1982] *The Levant Trilogy*. Harmondsworth: Penguin. (First published 1977–80, in separate volumes).

Munton, Alan (1989) *English Fiction of the Second World War*. London: Faber and Faber.

Norris, Margot (2000) *Writing War in the Twentieth Century*. Charlottesville: University Press of Virginia.

Orwell, George (1968) *The Collected Essays, Journalism and Letters of George Orwell*, vol. II: *My Country Right or Left, 1940–1943*, ed. Sonia Orwell and Ian Angus. New York: Harcourt, Brace and World.

——(1976) [1949] *Nineteen Eighty-Four*. Harmondsworth: Penguin.

——(1986) [1936] *Keep the Aspidistra Flying*. Harmondsworth: Penguin.

——(1990) [1939] *Coming Up for Air*. Harmondsworth: Penguin.

Owen, Wilfred (1965) *The Collected Poems of Wilfred Owen*, ed. and with introduction by C. Day Lewis. New York: New Directions.

Plain, Gill (1996) *Women's Fiction of the Second World War: Gender, Power and Resistance*. New York: St Martin's Press.

Powell, Anthony (1976a) [1960] *Casanova's Chinese Restaurant* (A Dance to the Music of Time, 2: Summer). New York: Popular Library.

——(1976b) [1962] *The Kindly Ones* (A Dance to the Music of Time, 2: Summer). New York: Popular Library.

——(1976c) [1964] *The Valley of Bones* (A Dance to the Music of Time, 3: Autumn). New York: Popular Library.

——(1976d) [1966] *The Soldier's Art* (A Dance to the Music of Time, 3: Autumn). New York: Popular Library.

——(1976e) [1968] *The Military Philosophers* (A Dance to the Music of Time, 3: Autumn). New York: Popular Library.

Priestley, J. B. (1967) [1943] *Daylight on Saturday*. London: Pan.

Rawlinson, Mark (2000) *British Writing of the Second World War*. Oxford: Oxford University Press.

Scannell, Vernon (1976) *Not Without Glory: Poets of the Second World War*. London: Woburn Press.

Schneider, Karen (1997) *Loving Arms: British Women Writing the Second World War*. Lexington: University Press of Kentucky.

Smith, Stevie (1989) [1938] *Over the Frontier*. London: Virago.

Spark, Muriel (1963) *The Girls of Slender Means*. London: Macmillan.

Stephen, Martin (ed.) (1993) *Poems of the First World War: "Never Such Innocence."* London: J. M. Dent.

Waugh, Evelyn (1943) [1942] *Put Out More Flags*. Harmondsworth: Penguin.

——(1962) [1945] *Brideshead Revisited: The Sacred and Profane Memories of Captain Charles Ryder*. Harmondsworth: Penguin.

——(1965) [1930] *Vile Bodies*. Harmondsworth: Penguin.

——(1970) [1952] *Men at Arms*. Harmondsworth: Penguin.

——(1975) [1961] *Unconditional Surrender*. Harmondsworth: Penguin.

——(1980) *The Letters of Evelyn Waugh*, ed. Mark Amory. London: Weidenfeld and Nicolson.

——(1985) [1955] *Officers and Gentlemen*. Harmondsworth: Penguin.

Woolf, Virginia (1990) [1941] *Between the Acts*. London: Hogarth Press.

2

The "Angry" Decade and After

Dale Salwak

The impact that a promising generation of irreverent and iconoclastic novelists made on the English reading public in the 1950s marked the emergence of a new literary movement, as a name and as a myth. Fifty years later, the myth is still with us. It is the "Angry Young Man."

To understand the origins of the label, we must go back at least to 1945. Aldous Huxley, Graham Greene, Evelyn Waugh, C. P. Snow, and Anthony Powell, among others, had made their reputations before the war and continued to be the major literary voices at that time. Most of them had come from upper- or upper-middle-class homes and been educated in private schools, then at Oxford or Cambridge, so their novels were likely to revolve around fashionable London or some country estate. Often they confined their satire to the intellectual life and the cultural as well as social predicaments of the upper middle class. The occupations of the characters, even their temperaments, varied little from book to book.

But as Britain struggled to redefine itself in the aftermath of World War II and the consequent political upheaval, writers, too, struggled to find a voice appropriate to the changed circumstances of an emergent postwar society. As Malcolm Bradbury noted, the war had "created not only a new political, social and ideological environment but inevitably a new intellectual and artistic environment as well" (1972: 319). With the exception of the playwright Christopher Fry and the novelist Angus Wilson, however, few signs pointed towards the development of any new writers. Thus, in the final editorial for his magazine, *Horizon*, at the end of 1949, Cyril Connolly wrote: "it is closing time in the gardens of the West and from now on an artist will be judged only by the resonance of his solitude or the quality of his despair"; and T. C. Worsley noted in the *New Statesman*: "Five years after the war there is still no sign of any kind of literary revival; no movements are discernible; no trends" (Jacobs 1995: 165). Some critics got into the habit of remarking that the novel, as a literary form, was probably dead.

John Wain's assignment in 1953 to succeed John Lehmann as editor of the BBC's *Third Programme* ("New Soundings") was to fill the vacuum. He described his policy as "consolidation," a reaction against modernism, a return to traditional forms as he introduced promising young writers to the public (Wain 1963: 205). But from Wain's "new Elizabethan era," to Anthony Hartley's "New University Wits" and the "Metaphysicals," to Donald Davie's the "new Augustans," nothing caught on. What was needed – and what stubbornly failed to materialize – was a tangible literary movement.

It is generally agreed that something new in Britain's intellectual and imaginative life finally surfaced, however, with the appearance of three astonishingly assured, inventive, and funny first novels: John Wain's *Hurry on Down* (1953), and Iris Murdoch's *Under the Net* and Kingsley Amis's *Lucky Jim* (both 1954). These works, and others soon to come, had developed an interest in that aspect of English literary tradition that resisted the technical innovations in fiction and poetry especially predominating between the wars and finding full flower in the work of Joyce, Woolf, and the writers of the *nouveau roman*. Critics have distinguished between the "modern," experimental novel and what is sometimes called the "contemporary," realistic (or "common-sense") mode of writing (Lodge 1966; Rabinovitz 1967). The new generation fell into the latter camp by virtue of its firm rejection of such experimentation. In 1958 Kingsley Amis wrote:

> The idea about experiment being the life-blood of the English novel is one that dies hard. 'Experiment', in this context, boils down pretty regularly to 'obtruded oddity', whether in construction – multiple viewpoints and such – or in style; it is not felt that adventurousness in subject matter or attitude or tone really counts. Shift from one scene to the next in mid-sentence, cut down on verbs or definite articles, and you are putting yourself right up in the forefront, at any rate in the eyes of those who were reared on Joyce and Virginia Woolf...(Amis quoted in Rabinovitz 1967: 40–1)

Unlike their modernist predecessors, Amis and his contemporaries saw themselves as serious writers who had grown increasingly impatient with technical innovations for their own sake. Their interest was not in testing the limits of expression but in having their books read and understood – an approach that they developed early in their careers and followed assiduously. Melvyn Bragg described them as "resolute" in their "dedication to the idea of a novel as something which can be picked up and read with pleasure by all and sundry" (Salwak 1992: 34). Wallace Robson pointed to their "businesslike intention to communicate with the reader" (Robson 1970: 154); and Norman Macleod found in their writing "a communication shared between listening reader and informally talking author" (Macleod 1990: 107). The likelihood of readers shutting books or even throwing them aside in boredom and frustration was an ever-present dread underlying many of their critical observations. They were, indeed, *conscious* artists wedded to the principles of good narrative rather than the lure of verbal pyrotechnics. Kingsley Amis spoke for his generation when he said:

What I think I am doing is writing novels within the main English-language tradition. That is, trying to tell interesting, believable stories about understandable characters in a reasonably straightforward style: no tricks, no experimental foolery. As the tradition indicates, my subject is the relations between people, and I aim at the traditional wide range of effects: humor, pathos, irony, suspense, description, action, introspection. (Gindin 1982: 28)

Rarely ambiguous and with a usually straightforward and unbroken narrative line, their novels resolved mystery and contained, as James Gindin wrote of Amis's novels,

nothing of the thematic corollaries of the open-ended, of introspection, self-doubt, emotional turbulence, indecision, or romanticism. In his knowable world, characters learn to adjust, earn the rewards of prize jobs and prize women by not deluding themselves and sensibly squelching their own deviations from the reigning axioms of the society. (1971: 360)

Because their fiction reflected a determination to speak to a wider range of readers than did their modernist predecessors, it reflected, too, their faith in the common reader's ability to recognize and respond to traditional philosophical concerns. Avowed realists, these writers would aim for both physical and psychological reality, and they would adapt the techniques of Dickens, Smollett, and Fielding, whose ability to bring immense variety and plenitude to their work without reverting to obscurity or stylistic excess appealed to them. With their entertaining, episodic plots, realism, and clear, unadorned style, their novels reminded readers of the conventional picaresque tale – a convention as old as the novel itself.

Along with their style, what was unmistakable was their new voice. A few socially minded critics saw in these writers an attempt to articulate, realistically and comprehensively, several highly relevant concerns: the social frustrations and aspirations of many people of that time, including a concern for the condition of the working and lower middle classes after the war; a discontent that the Welfare State had not reached far enough in eliminating remaining class privileges and inequalities; an implicit criticism of the British class structure; a distaste for the profit motive; a mockery of the old bases of morality and of any kind of gracious living; and a loathing of all forms of pretentiousness. Feeling uprooted in a no-man's-land between one class and another, these writers challenged with relish Prime Minister Harold Macmillan's famous pronouncement: "You've never had it so good."

Thus, their politically disillusioned heroes – or antiheroes, as it became fashionable to call them – were seen as apt spokesmen for the post-Romantic, post-Freudian age, which, having witnessed an economic depression and several wars, had rediscovered the fact of man's limitations. Malcolm Bradbury described this new tone as "a serious progressive severity, a new critical instinct [which seemed] determined to dispense with the experimentalism of the 1920s and 1930s, with the romanticism and apocalypticism of the 1940s [and with] the Beckettian despairs emanating from Paris, though there is an underlying existentialist influence" (1988: 76–7).

At the mercy of life, sometimes capable of aspiration and thought, their fumbling antiheroes are not strong enough to overcome an entrenched social order and carve out their destiny in the way that they wish. Frequently they are dreamers, tossed about by life, and also pushed about, or at least overshadowed, by the threats in their lives. Wain's Charles Lumley (*Hurry on Down*) and Edgar Banks (*Living in the Present,* 1955), Amis's Jim Dixon (*Lucky Jim*), Murdoch's Jake Donaghue (*Under the Net*), Braine's Joe Lampton (*Room at the Top,* 1957), and Sillitoe's Arthur Seaton (*Saturday Night and Sunday Morning,* 1958) all bear the marks of a character type that had been anticipated earlier in William Cooper's *Scenes from Provincial Life* (1951) and echoed in Philip Larkin's novel, *Jill* (1946). In their search for social readjustment, there is discernible in all of these characters a vague discontent, sometimes anger, and a yearning for some person or set of circumstances beyond their reach. On occasion the sense of disenchantment with life as it is becomes so great that the individual expresses a desire not to live at all.

Most attractive of all was that these novels also offered good entertainment, providing comic relief for a reading public weary of self-absorbed, tormented, alienated artists and tired of despairing about the future of a world seemingly bent on self-destruction. Implied in the satire was a criticism of some of the cultural values that had been passed on to the postwar society – most comically expressed by Jim Dixon's loathing of the snobbish, Bloomsbury style culture of his academic superior, Professor Welch, and this superior's pseudo-artist son, Bertrand. As a young lecturer in medieval history at a provincial university, and as an opponent of pretentiousness and dilettantism of all kinds, Jim Dixon must depend upon his wits, his adaptability, and his good luck to escape from the trap of the wrong woman, the wrong town, and the wrong job – indeed, the snare of an entire moral and aesthetic system that he finds tiresome and unreasonable. Because he is not morally committed to any of them, he is able to discard them all for the promise of better opportunities. His triumph emerges naturally and deservedly as a fitting conclusion to all the comic misfortune that had befallen him beforehand.

Like Jim Dixon, the hero of *Hurry on Down* is also a creation of the postwar Welfare State. As a discontented youth on his own for the first time, he feels that neither his upbringing nor his university education has prepared him for making a satisfactory living. Because he has a driving obsession to avoid the phoney in life, he detests the world he sees and rebels against whatever is bourgeois and commonplace. Ironically, each of his jobs carries with it some sort of class identification: window cleaner, delivery truck driver, hospital orderly, night club bouncer, radio show comedy writer, even car thief. By the end of novel he realizes that the individual and his own values are more important than any badges of class. He settles for marriage to the girl he has always wanted (but could not get) and a modest "pot of gold" through the help of the wealthy Mr Roderick.

At first reading Jake Donaghue, the happy-go-lucky bohemian hero of *Under the Net*, resembles Jim Dixon and Charles Lumley in that he, too, is earthy and unsettled.

But he is Irish and not a product of the Welfare State; in personality and philosophy he bears a resemblance to Sartre; and he lives in an unsettled world of writers, artists, theater people, and left-wingers while he scrapes together a living as a translator of French novels. His adventures begin after he is thrown out of his flat and is forced to take stock of his life. Several factors conspire to make this happen, including an inability or refusal to see people as they really are. A variety of comical situations leads him finally to decide to give up translating and become a serious creative writer.

No doubt another reason that Amis, Wain, and Murdoch were thrown together in the minds of many journalists is that through their characters there ran a consistent moral judgment that advocated the virtues of hard work, responsibility, decency, and love – an enduring if beleagured value system that defends the English language, traditions, customs, and freedoms against all of their assorted enemies. "Almost all of the fiction is comic," observed Gindin, "satirizing man's pretenses ... using sharp, contemporary, and very funny images to reduce human posture to the mundane. The comic iconoclasm is social as well as individual, mocking various forms of govern-mental, religious, or institutional truth" (1971: 357). These writers, Bradbury said,

> looked across a landscape that was deeply changed by the world of the welfare state, was divided by war from the past generation, and was probably more comfortable than the depression age of the 1930s, even though it was pressed by nuclear anxiety. Mores, manners and social accents were changing, in life and fiction, and the writing was amenable, open, speaking plainly, from recognized social positions, in clear rhetorical tones; it had few oblique angles, few signs of avant-garde displacement, and it offered to return the literary arts to the accessible ways that prevailed before the coming of modernism; an artistic spirit, Philip Larkin suggested, that could only interest Ameri-cans and had as its two main concerns mystification and outrage. (1988: 207)

Because Amis, Wain, and Murdoch seemed to express similar concerns about social and cultural values, had attended Oxford, and taught for a time at provincial universities, critics soon identified them as a trio of rebellious young writers; indeed, here was the "movement" that had been missing from literature for several years.

Ironically, the phrase "Angry Young Man" was first used by the Christian apologist Leslie Paul as the title of his autobiography (1951), a book that had nothing to do with the phenomenon that appeared five years later, except that it is an account of disillusionment with the "isms" of the 1920s and 1930s. For the purposes of this study the most immediate sources of the phrase are John Osborne's play *Look Back in Anger* (launched May 8, 1956 at the Royal Court Theatre) and Colin Wilson's quasi-philosophical *The Outsider* (published May 26, 1956). On the surface, Wilson's *Outsider* is in tune with the theme of the alienated intellectual that underlies much mid-1950s writing. His book emphasized the decay of conventionally held cultural values and stirred the emotions of those who felt divided from their society. Above all, the title of his book and the treatment of his theme in terms of a personality added a new and easily identifiable character to "the chorus of disenchanted fictional personalities who were voicing their dissatisfactions with the way society had developed" (Hewison 1981: 132). In *Look Back in Anger*, on the other hand, the protesting individual is not a character in a book but a walking, and endlessly talking, figure on stage. Jimmy Porter is the archetypal dissatisfied, unpleasant, but articulate young man. Although university-educated he is nevertheless enraged by the middle-class values he would have to adopt to get a "good" job. Instead, he maintains a market stall in a provincial town, from which he vents his anger against the bomb, the government, Sunday newspapers, education, love, marriage, T. S. Eliot, the Church, his mother-in-law, even his wife. Typical of Osborne's invective is Jimmy's oft-quoted tirade which begins: "There aren't any good, brave causes left" (Maschler 1958: 51).

The "Angry" myth gathered momentum when the theater's press officer, George Fearon, told a journalist that Osborne was a "very angry young man" (Jacobs 1995: 167). The press ran with the label, and Dan Farson in the *Evening Standard* and *Daily Mail* suggested that anger unified several contemporary poets, novelists, and play-wrights. J. B. Priestley discussed both the book and the play in an article for the *New Statesman*, one of the first places where the phrase "Angry Young Men" was applied to these writers. The *Daily Mirror* picked up the phrase in its comments on "an angry play by an angry young author," and the London *Times* called Jimmy "a thoroughly crass young man." Kenneth Tynan, himself a rebel, treated Jimmy in a rave review for *The Observer* as though he were a real person: "The Porters of our time deplore the tyranny of 'good taste' and refuse to accept 'emotional' as a term of abuse; they are classless, and they are also leaderless. Mr Osborne is their first spokesman in the London theatre" (Salwak 1992: 78).

A certain "loose similarity" is bound to exist between artists of the same gener-ation, John Wain noted (1963: 121); and so, when Osborne's play was launched, critics did not have to look far for other writers whose work had covered some of the same ground: "Amis and Wain prepared the stage for the angry young man," said Robert Hewison. "Colin Wilson gave him an identity as an outsider, John Osborne gave him a voice" (1981: 135). All that remained was for later novelists to turn out more examples of the genre.

It has been suggested that the early novels of Keith Waterhouse (*Billy Liar*, 1960), Stan Barstow (*A Kind of Loving*, 1960), David Storey (*This Sporting Life*, 1960) and, most prominently, John Braine and Alan Sillitoe, appealed to a set of expectations that had been introduced, but not fully satisfied, by their predecessors. Both Braine's *Room at the Top* and Sillitoe's *Saturday Night and Sunday Morning* project the same ethos of dissatisfaction that Jimmy Porter expressed so violently on the stage by focusing on the consciousness of one central character, a rebellious young man from a proletarian background.

Arthur Seaton (in *Saturday Night and Sunday Morning*) is an angry Midlands bicycle-factory hand who escapes from his physically dirty job on weekends by taking women to bed and by going on drunken sprees – all because he lacks a meaningful place in society. As a West Riding working-class hero, Joe Lampton (in *Room at the Top*) also has the characteristic social background; but unlike the other heroes, he knows that he wants to reach the top of society. The novel dramatizes the difficulties and hazards of the slow rise, for in the process Lampton destroys the integrity of both himself and his personal relationships. With their emphasis on youth and energy, their predisposition for social satire, and their cynical attitude towards establishment assumptions and class structures, these writers too became known as angry young men.

Eventually, the sheer quantity of media coverage of these writers – in what Hewison calls a combination of "historical truths and popular distortion" (1981: 127) – generated high sales in both Britain and America; but the nature of the coverage obscured the novels and their authors under a layer of categorization from which their reputations would not escape for many years. Once the myth had emerged, it took on a life of its own; it could not be reshaped by facts. Photographs of angry young men appeared in *Saturday Review*, *Life*, and *Mademoiselle*. The *Western Political Quarterly* solemnly analysed their politics; and commentators eagerly began to sub-classify this new collection of writers into mystics, provincials, radicals, nonconformists, humanists, neutralists, emotionalists, and lawgivers. Robert Coughland labeled them "the chroniclers of Britain's shrinking-pains" (Salwak 1992: 79). *Pravda* accused them of selling out. A Polish critic wrote: "we in Poland value *Lucky Jim* greatly – it mirrors the struggle of our young men against Stalinism" (McDermott 1989: 20). Others related this phenomenon to the equally nebulous Beat Generation – a connection that Amis firmly rejected. Kenneth Allsop viewed these writers and their heroes as "a new rootless, faithless, classless class" and went on in his book *The Angry Decade* to say that "the phrase Angry Young Men carries multiple overtones which might be listed as irreverence, stridency, impatience with tradition, vigour, vulgarity, sulky resentment against the cultivated" (1958: 51).

Not all critics received these new authors with pleasure, however. Philip Toynbee and Cyril Connolly, for example, regarded them as drab and uninspiring; and W. Somerset Maugham (whose literary award Amis had, ironically, just won for *Lucky Jim*) called their heroes "mean, malicious and envious.... Charity, kindliness, generosity, are qualities which they hold in contempt. They are scum" (Salwak 1992: 79). Never mind that Amis's hero wins out in the end because he is fundamentally decent while those around him are not; Maugham, who was firmly rooted in the old order of English novelists and thus saw the Angry Young Men as antithetical to all he stood for, said he counted himself fortunate that he would not live to see what they would make of his country. In an earlier period – say in 1900 – these heroes would never have attained a university education, and their energies would have been channeled into working-class occupations. But the establishment of new universities and grants allowed them to become educated. They were excluded from working-class lives but remained unacceptable, generally, to the Establishment.

By 1958 practically everybody was referring to any kind of misfit as an outsider – or an angry young man. Some reviewers even confused the characters with the authors themselves. Amis's Jim Dixon was contemptuous of the tedium and falseness of academic life; therefore, he was interpreted as a symbol of anti-intellectualism. Jim taught at a provincial university; therefore, he became a symbol of contempt for Cambridge and Oxford. Amis himself taught at a provincial university; therefore, he and Jim became one and the same in the minds of many readers. Even intelligent readers, it seems, could not help confusing author and protagonist.

While admirers praised *Lucky Jim* as the funniest book they had ever read, funnier even (though not wittier) than Evelyn Waugh's *Decline and Fall*, some detractors were shocked by its seeming attack on civilized cultural values. Nancy Mitford wrote that the book saddened her, "as do all evidences of declining civilization." Wyndham Ketton-Cremer, while amused, was "unable to forgive some of Jim Dixon's reflections on the arts." In reaction to the controversy, C. S. Lewis came to Amis's defence, telling him that he was "a very ill-used man; you wrote a farce and everyone thought it a damning indictment of Redbrick. I've always had great sympathy for you. They will not understand that a joke is a joke. Everything must be serious" (Salwak 1992: 79).

At the Edinburgh Festival in 1957, where the film version of *Lucky Jim* was screened, Amis recalled that he encountered one fan who asked him if he was satisfied with the results:

> "Yes, indeed. You see, I intended it to be a funny book and so – ."
> "But surely, Mr Amis, the sociological implications of your satire
> have been altogether lost, haven't they?"
> "I'm afraid I don't bother with any of that because the chief
> thing to me is that it's supposed to be a funny – ."
> "But surely, Mr Amis, you wrote a comedy of manners in the
> Welfare State." (Salwak 1992: 79)

And so it continued. On another occasion Amis met a Yugoslavian professor who said that students at home identified very closely with Jim. "He represents their own struggle against Stalinism," he whispered. Another critic called *Lucky Jim* "a fever chart of society"; and when he went into a bookshop he was told that they had sold a hundred copies that morning. "What caused that?" Amis asked. "The Irish have just put it on the banned list," was the reply (Salwak 1992: 80). For the next couple of years Amis was widely represented by the press as one of the "group's" leading and most controversial figures. It was the kind of attention from which a lesser novelist might never have recovered.

Although the writers were aware of the publicity value that talk of a "movement" or "school" made possible, they have always rejected the label and refused to be linked closely with any of their supposed philosophical compatriots. In 1957 Osborne declared, "I have only met Mr Amis once, and I have never met Mr Wain, nor any of the rest of these poor successful freaks" (Maschler 1958: 52). When asked by the editor, Tom Maschler, to contribute to *Declaration* (1950) – a collection of essays in which Wain, Osborne, Wilson, Doris Lessing, Lindsay Anderson, Stuart Holroyd, Kenneth Tynan, and Bill Hopkins defined their positions in society – Amis refused and wrote back: "I hate all this pharisaical twittering about the 'state of civilization', and I suspect anyone who wants to buttonhole me about my 'rôle in society'. This book is likely to prove a valuable addition to the cult of the Solemn Young Man; I predict a great success for it" (Maschler 1958: 8–9).

Other writers also resented being so labeled. Lindsay Anderson disliked any association of Osborne with Amis and Wain, the latter two of whose views – "anti-idealist, anti-emotional, and tepid or evasive in their social commitments" – were, he thought, fashionable precisely because their views were the direct opposite of Osborne's (Maschler 1958: 147). Wain's publicist tried in vain to prevent such labeling: "when I was in danger of getting sucked into the 'Angry Young Man' circus, my publishers . . . put out a display card bearing a picture of me and the legend 'John Wain is *not* an Angry Young Man'. . . . The display card wasn't very effective; I did my term as an 'Angry Young Man' in the press. . . . I, meanwhile, sit in my book-lined cave, getting on with my work" (Wain 1963: 196–7). He called the term "irksome" because:

(1) it is the creation of journalists who know nothing, and care less than nothing, for the art to which my life is dedicated; (2) it is a hindrance to anyone who holds serious opinions and is able to be genuinely serious about them; and (3) because I refuse to be institutionalized, whatever may be the immediate advantages in terms of hard cash. (1963: 225)

John Braine explained:

Well, of course journalists talk about the Angry Young Men. You can't blame them; they have to put something together in two hours. So naturally they make generalizations like that. If they had time to think, say, six hours, you'd never have heard about the Angry Young Man. (Salwak 1984: 51–2)

Alan Sillitoe called the label "just a journalistic catch-phrase. Nobody should have taken it seriously, but then people jump onto catch-phrases because it helps them to classify certain people and render them harmless" (Salwak 1992: 81).

Amis had mixed feelings about the label:

It is difficult to sound sincere in repudiating free publicity, so I was lucky in never having to. In my case, the simplifications and distortions inevitable in gossipy booksy journalism fell short of tempting me irresistibly to break the writer's first rule and start explaining what I 'really meant' by my books. And if it was boring at times to be asked by a new acquaintance what I was so angry about, I was amply repaid on other occasions by seeing people wondering whether I was going to set about breaking up their furniture straight away or would wait till I was drunk. (Salwak 1992: 81)

Since the 1950s, the angry young men have moved so far from one another that few critical generalizations truly apply to them. The most we can say is that they harnessed their undeniable novelistic skills to promote clarity, honesty, and reason in their fiction, and that they distrusted excessive emotion and technical experimentalism for its own sake. Wilson suggested that there might have been more sense in calling the new hero an "outsider," or even an "alienated young man" (Maschler 1958: 3, 41). This alienation certainly was what these heroes all had in common – from Murdoch's and Doris Lessing's to Amis's and Sillitoe's, from J. P. Donleavy's Ginger Man to the characters of Harold Pinter, Joe Orton, and Tom Stoppard. But to treat writers of such formidably varied backgrounds, education, and experience as even a loosely organized group is to chart a perilous course. While in retrospect we can identify and admit to certain similarities between and among these authors, their personalities, like their writings, elude facile characterizations or labels.

A final question now presents itself: how does the myth of the "Angry Young Man" look if we base our study on each writer's later publications rather than on the first? In the years to follow, each of these authors achieved a vigorous reputation in contemporary English letters, and, as is so often the case today, the measure of their respective qualities does not depend upon any single creation. It is rather the totality of their work that we should consider. Amis and Murdoch, for example, proved themselves to be restless and ambitious writers who seldom repeated themselves and who used their powers of observation and mimicry both to illuminate changes in English society following World War II and to suggest alternatives of behavior. Wain grew into a genuine man of letters as he continued to produce work of high standard while staying on the fringes of the academic world, as a Professor of Poetry at Oxford in 1973 and by writing criticism and biography. With each succeeding work by Braine, Sillitoe, and the others, we see an ever more marked contrast between their efforts and those of their predecessors.

None of this is meant to underestimate the commercial or historical importance of the label. "The Angry Young Man is a myth," said Robert Hewison; "yet myths are imaginative versions of the truth, and advertisers know that the best way to present a product is to exaggerate its novel – and truthful – qualities. . . . Accurate or not, Angry Young Man was a compelling slogan" (1981:130). I cannot improve upon that judgment.

References and Further Reading

Allsop, Kenneth (1958) *The Angry Decade*. London: Peter Owen.

Bradbury, Malcolm (1972) "The novel," in C. B. Cox and A. E. Dyson (eds.) *The Twentieth Century Mind: History, Ideas and Literature in Brief*. Oxford: Oxford University Press.

——(1987) *No, Not Bloomsbury*. London: André Deutsch; New York: Columbia University Press.

Gindin, James (1962) *Postwar British Fiction: New Accents and Attitudes*. Berkeley: University of California Press.

——(1971) "Well beyond laughter: directions from fifties' comic fiction." *Studies in the Novel*, 3: 357–64.

——(1982) "Kingsley Amis," in James Vinson (ed.) *Contemporary Novelists*.. New York: St Martin's Press.

Hewison, Robert (1981) *In Anger: British Culture in the Cold War 1945–60*. London: Weidenfeld and Nicolson; New York: Oxford University Press.

Jacobs, Eric (1995) *Kingsley Amis: A Biography*. London: Hodder and Stoughton.

Karl, Frederick (1972) *A Reader's Guide to the Contemporary English Novel*. London: Thames and Hudson.

Lodge, David (1966) *The Language of Fiction*. London: Routledge and Kegan Paul.

McDermott, John (1989) *Kingsley Amis: An English Moralist*. London: Macmillan; New York: St Martin's Press.

Macleod, Norman (1990) "The language of Kingsley Amis," in Dale Salwak (ed.) *Kingsley Amis: In Life and Letters*. London: Macmillan; New York: St Martin's Press.

Maschler, Tom (1958) *Declaration*. London: MacGibbon and Kee; New York: E. P. Dutton.

Morrison, Blake (1980) *The Movement: English Poetry and Fiction of the 1950s*. Oxford and New York: Oxford University Press.

Rabinovitz, Rubin (1967) *Reaction against Experimentalism in the English Novel: 1950–60*. New York: Columbia University Press.

Ritchie, Harry (1988) *Success Stories: Literature and the Media in England, 1950–1959*. London and Boston: Faber and Faber.

Robson, Wallace (1970) *Modern English Literature*. Oxford: Oxford University Press.

Salwak, Dale (1984) *Interviews with Britain's Angry Young Men*. San Bernardino, CA: Borgo Press.

——(1992) *Kingsley Amis: Modern Novelist*. Hemel Hempstead: Harvester Wheatsheaf; New York: Barnes and Noble.

Sillitoe, Alan (1973) *Men, Women and Children*. London: W. H. Allen.

Smith, Bruce M. (1981) "Looking back at anger: the novels of Kingsley Amis, John Wain, John Braine, David Storey, and Alan Sillitoe." PhD dissertation, Indiana University at Bloomington, IN.

Stevenson, Randall (1986) *The British Novel Since the Thirties: An Introduction*. London: Batsford; Athens: University of Georgia Press.

Swinden, Patrick (1984) *The English Novel of History and Society, 1940–80*. London: Macmillan; New York: St Martin's Press.

Van O'Connor, William (1963) *The New University Wits and the End of Modernism*. London: Feffer and Simons; Carbondale: Southern Illinois University Press.

Wain, John (1963) *Sprightly Running: Part of an Autobiography*. London: Macmillan; New York: St Martin's Press.

3

English Dystopian Satire in Context

M. Keith Booker

Dystopian literature might be defined as imaginative literature that constructs flawed fictional societies the shortcomings of which satirize ideal utopian societies, or specific real-world societies, or both. Dystopian fiction became a major mode in the twentieth century, though it has roots that go back still further. This is especially the case with English literature, which was at the forefront of the turn from utopian to dystopian visions of the future at the end of the nineteenth century, especially in the early works of H. G. Wells. In any case, Aldous Huxley's *Brave New World* (1932) can be considered the first truly important twentieth-century dystopian novel in English, while it joins Evgeny Zamyatin's *We* (1924) and George Orwell's *Nineteen Eighty-Four* (1949) to constitute the three central works of modern dystopian narrative. Orwell's novel is probably the most important and influential of the three. Indeed, one could make a viable case that *Nineteen Eighty-Four* is not only the central work of English dystopian fiction but also one of the pivotal works in all of twentieth-century global culture. All subsequent English dystopian fiction has been influenced to some extent by Orwell's vision, though it is also important to recognize that Orwell's work itself had numerous important predecessors, especially in the numerous antifascist dystopian satires produced by British leftist writers during the 1930s.

Dystopian fiction is typically an individualist genre, opposing the special desires and inclinations of its protagonists to the demands of an oppressive regime that makes true individualism impossible. In this sense, one might be tempted to see dystopian fiction and utopian fiction as polar opposites, given that fictional constructions of utopia have typically emphasized the community rather than the individual, envisioning a world in which individual eccentricities take a back seat, to the greater good of the greater number. Indeed, one of the central premises of most dystopian fiction is that one person's dream might be another person's nightmare, so that even an achieved utopia from the point of view of some might be a dystopia from the point of view of others. Of course, this very premise suggests that the opposition between dystopia and utopia is neither absolute nor simple. Among other things, while both dystopian and utopian fiction tend to be set in worlds that are distant in space or time from that of the author, both modes are often intended as satirical critiques of specific trends in the author's own world, the displacement in setting merely providing exaggeration and emphasis of the kind that is central to all satire.

For example, *Brave New World* can be taken as a satirical rejection of modern capitalism, including the turn toward consumerism that marked capitalism in the 1920s. Huxley creates a nightmare future world so devoted to capitalist ideals that its central hero is Henry Ford, who is worshiped almost as a god. Here, Fordist production has helped to create a high level of affluence, so much so that most individuals spend most of their time in the pursuit of instant happiness through sex, drugs, and mind-numbing multisensory entertainments like the popular "feelies," which are continually broadcast to keep the minds and senses of the citizenry occupied at all times. However, the emphasis on pleasure in Huxley's future society masks a deep-seated lack of individual liberty. Indeed, the sex, drugs, and popular culture are intended primarily to divert attention from social problems and to prevent individuals from developing any sort of strong feelings that might lead them to challenge official authority.

In addition, citizens do not share equally in the affluence of this future society, which retains rigid class distinctions. Using advanced techniques of genetic engineering, Fordist manufacturing methods are extended even to the assembly-line production of human infants, who are designed according to the strict specifications of the class to which they will belong. The "Alphas" – members of the highest class who will occupy positions that require advanced intelligence – are endowed with high IQs, while low-class citizens, the "Deltas" and "Epsilons," are mass-produced with low intelligence but high physical strength and endurance, so that they can perform menial tasks. This genetic engineering is supplemented by a massive program of indoctrination designed to make them content with the roles that have been designated for them.

Of course, it is important to understand the thoroughness of Huxley's critique of modern consumer capitalism within the context of the Depression-ridden time in which it was written. Indeed, the 1930s saw the emergence of a number of dystopian fictions aimed at capitalism, many of which also react directly to the threat of fascism, while collectively providing a crucial literary background to the later, better-known dystopian novels of Orwell.

In *To Tell the Truth . . .* (1933), Amabel Williams-Ellis presents a satirical reversal of the anti-Soviet travelogue by detailing the visit of a young Russian, Pavel Pedersson, to Britain, where he hopes to learn about the workings of capitalism. Set in the early 1940s, the book imagines a Britain in which the worst tendencies of the early 1930s have continued to develop, producing a grim, authoritarian, and impoverished (though in many ways technologically advanced) society. Meanwhile, in a motif that echoes *Brave New World*, Pedersson discovers that the cultural apparatus in Britain has been almost entirely successful in suppressing any sense that concerted working-class action might bring about a change in the grim conditions he has observed.

   If Williams-Ellis projects, in a dystopian mode, the gradual development of the capitalist status quo, works such as Storm Jameson's *In the Second Year* (1936), Ruthven Todd's *Over the Mountain* (1939), and Katharine Burdekin's *Swastika Night* (1937) react directly to the threat of fascism, imagining a grim future Britain in the aftermath of a fascist takeover. Identified by Andy Croft as "the most original of all the many anti-fascist dystopias of the late 1930s," Burdekin's book is probably the most important of these (Croft 1990: 238). It is set in the far future, more than seven hundred years after the initial Nazi victory, when the entire world is split between two vast empires, one ruled by Germany, the other by Japan. Burdekin's book focuses on the German empire (which includes all of Europe and Africa), but implies that the two empires are rather similar in their ideologies, though competition over resources has frequently led to warfare between the two regimes. The dissemination of information in this future world is strictly controlled. Books, in fact, have been entirely banned (except for one sacred "Hitler book"), and virtually all citizens are illiterate. History has been almost entirely forgotten, the only records of the past being highly mythologized versions in which Hitler has been promoted to the status of a god and all memories of any civilizations before German Nazism forgotten.

   Within the confines of its minimal plot, Burdekin is able to carry out a satirical assault on fascism, militarism, and, especially, patriarchy as crucial to the ideology of fascism. However, Burdekin's book, while aimed very directly at German fascism of the 1930s, is careful to suggest that fascism has its roots in patriarchal attitudes that go well beyond that specific phenomenon. Among other things, the book suggests that the ideology that drives the British empire is not as different from the ideology of Burdekin's fictional German empire as some might like to believe. The book's clear support for pacifism seems, in retrospect, problematic, while some of the book's portrayal of gender verges on essentialism. Nevertheless, *Swastika Night* calls attention to a number of crucial issues of the 1930s that remain important for us today.

   Swastika Night anticipates Orwell's *Nineteen Eighty-Four* in some fairly obvious ways. Indeed, one of the least appreciated aspects of Orwell's dystopian writings of the 1940s is the extent to which they are rooted in the numerous antifascist satires produced by British writers of the Left during the 1930s. Given Orwell's own extensive (though problematic) participation in the cultural Left during the 1930s, this connection comes as no surprise. However, the connection does shed important new light on Orwell's work, which was so often appropriated during the Cold War as an anti-Soviet and even antisocialist statement.

   Granted, Orwell's first postwar novel, *Animal Farm* (1946), is aimed rather transparently at the Soviet Union, and in particular at Stalin. An allegorical commentary on the tendency of revolutions to lead not to utopian reform, but to dystopian oppression, *Animal Farm* resembles a number of dystopian works, particularly Zamyatin's *We*. While the parallels between Orwell's plot and the history of the Soviet Union are obvious, Orwell's displacement of the Bolshevik Revolution and its

Stalinist aftermath into the framework of an animal fable provides a satirical commentary on those events that is far from trivial. Indeed, *Animal Farm* is one of the best-known (and probably one of the most effective) political satires of the twentieth century. Its depiction of Stalin as a drunken pig who betrays Lenin's revolution, scapegoats Trotsky to cover his own perfidy, fraternizes with the enemies of Communism, and becomes himself a reincarnation of the tsars is striking, to say the least.

But *Animal Farm* has a relevance that goes well beyond its primary satirical target. The allegory form generalizes events in the Soviet Union to suggest that all revolutions are in danger of similar betrayal. Ultimately, however, the book is not a sweeping rejection of revolutionary change so much as a cautionary tale suggesting that those involved in such change must remain ever-vigilant lest their revolutions similarly decay. After all, Orwell's satire is aimed not at the Revolution itself but at the betrayal of that Revolution. In this sense, *Animal Farm* again echoes *We*, which suggests that revolution must be an ongoing process lest it lead to tyranny. The fairy-tale-like atmosphere of *Animal Farm* also makes it an especially interesting companion text for Orwell's *Nineteen Eighty-Four*, which deals with very much the same subject matter, but in a mode of stark realism.

Nineteen Eighty-Four also differs from *Animal Farm* in that the dystopian state of Oceania depicted in the book is ruled by a ruthless Party that makes no pretensions to utopian benevolence, but rules with an iron hand, overtly seeking only to perpetuate its own power. In short, the Party is consciously seeking to create the ultimate dystopia, a world that "is the exact opposite of the stupid hedonistic Utopias that the old reformers imagined" (1961: 220). The Party employs every resource at its disposal to maintain its power, but the two most striking motifs in *Nineteen Eighty-Four* are the revisionist manipulation of history in order to provide support for the programs of the ruling Party, and the attempt to institute a new language that will allow expression only of ideas that are consistent with the Party's policies.

Indeed, the most potentially powerful force for government control of the population of Oceania is probably language itself. Orwell's Party diligently works not only to produce mechanical cultural products but to make language itself mechanical through the development of "Newspeak," an official language the authoritarian intentions of which are made clear in the book. The basic goal of Newspeak is simple: to deprive the populace of a vocabulary in which to express dissident ideas, and therefore literally to make those ideas unthinkable. Not surprisingly, the Newspeak project extends to works of literature as well, since the classics of past literature are informed by precisely the kinds of polyphonic energies and human passions that the Party seeks to suppress. Therefore, the works of writers such as Chaucer, Shakespeare, Milton, and Byron are in the process of being translated into Newspeak and thereby rendered ideologically orthodox.

The party's textualization of history – in which history is altered by altering the historical record, a record constantly being revised to suit the political needs of the moment – threatens to strip the experiences of the real people who live through history of all significance. With no tangible evidence to the contrary, Party members tend to accept official accounts of the past even when those accounts contradict their own memories. The dictatorship of the Party in Oceania is relatively new, and citizens can commonly still remember the days before the Party's rule. Yet the revisionary history of the Party has been so effective that even direct memory is becoming less and less effective as a counter to official fictionalizations of the past.

In both its manipulation of language and its continual revisions of history, Orwell's Party can again be taken as a satirical commentary on the Stalinist regime in the Soviet Union. On the other hand, a closer look shows that *Nineteen Eighty-Four* is aimed just as much at ominous trends Orwell believed he detected in the democratic societies of the West. Indeed, the book seems almost prescient in its anticipation of the textualization of history – and reality – that observers such as Fredric Jameson have seen as crucial to the ideology of "late capitalist" societies in the era of postmodernism.

For example, one of the main ways the Party manipulates the feelings of its members is through direct control of Oceania's culture industry. All culture in Oceania is produced directly by the Ministry of Truth, which works to supply Party members with "newspapers, films, textbooks, telescreen programs, plays, novels – with every conceivable kind of information, instruction, or entertainment" (p. 39). The most striking example of this cultural production resides in the ever-present telescreens that convey a constant stream of officially endorsed programming, even as they also serve as part of an extensive surveillance network. Orwell thus anticipates the crucial power of television in western societies in the decades after World War II, even before television had become a powerful cultural force. In Oceania, members of the Party are kept under particularly strict surveillance and control, while the masses of "proles" are largely judged to be too politically impotent to require such close scrutiny. But even the proles are not exempt from more subtle controls via the content of the popular culture they consume; one of the reasons they need not undergo constant surveillance is that they are effectively kept in line by the Ministry's departments of proletarian culture, which produce a variety of products (mostly sentimental or pornographic) aimed at the Party's perception of proletarian taste.

Whatever Orwell's intentions, his book was typically read during the peak Cold War decade of the 1950s as a denunciation of Soviet Communism. It could be effectively appropriated in this way partly because its thoroughgoing rejection of utopianism was so much in tune with a prevailing western Cold War ideology that equated utopianism with the presumably failed Soviet project, completely dismissing both the Soviet Union and utopianism in general. This ideological climate made it rather easy to read *Nineteen Eighty-Four* as a satirical critique of the Soviet Union, while ignoring the obvious ways in which it commented on western capitalist societies as well. On the other hand, this climate made it difficult for Orwell's book to function effectively as a satirical critique of western democracies. Indeed, if the anti-utopian suspicions of the Cold War virtually wiped out utopian literature in the West during the 1950s, it was also the case that the entire decade of the 1950s was a particularly slack period for western dystopian satire.

With the advent of the 1960s, important English satirical works in the dystopian mode once again began to appear. For example, L. P. Hartley's *Facial Justice* appeared in 1960, satirizing the conformist inclinations of the 1950s with its vision of a dystopian "New State," in which enforced conformity extends to the state operation of plastic surgery centers where women go to have their faces altered to match the declared norm. On the other hand, *Facial Justice* is a complex text, and Hartley seems to endorse some policies of the New State, and especially of its rather jovial leader, the "Darling Dictator." That the dictator dies and is replaced by a rebel leader in the course of the narrative – with the general public being none the wiser – can be taken as a satire of British politics in the 1950s, with its shifts from Labour to Conservative governments making little difference to much of the population.

More harrowing dystopian visions were on the way. In *The Wanting Seed* (1962), Anthony Burgess depicts conditions in a future England in which overpopulation has led to a serious decline in the quality of life. All inhabitants live in extremely crowded conditions and must deal with ever-present shortages, a situation that leads to considerable unrest and to repressive responses to that unrest by the government. Meanwhile, those who contribute to the population problem by having too many children are subject to considerable social and economic persecution, finally culminating in the institution of strong government measures to limit additional population growth by creating a corps of "Population Police" whose job it is to enforce these measures.

In a global situation that obviously comments on and extrapolates the oppositional nature of global politics during the Cold War, most of Burgess's future world is under the domination of one of the two great superpowers, the "Enspun," or English-speaking union, and the "Ruspun," or Russian-speaking union. Meanwhile, in the course of his depiction of this future society, Burgess launches a number of satirical assaults on his own 1960s England, many of which are quite humorous, even if grimly so. For example, in a comment on the growing power of popular culture, religion has been banned, and the authoritative figure of God has been replaced by "Mr. Livedog," a comic cartoon character.

Such humor aside, the problem of world overpopulation on which Burgess's book focuses is obviously a serious one. Indeed, the directness with which *The Wanting Seed* responds to a specific real-world issue potentially makes the book especially effective as a cautionary tale. However, Burgess's ultimate pessimism about the possibility of a solution to the problem of overpopulation seems seriously to undermine the effectiveness of his book as a warning. As Robert O. Evans puts it, the novel seems to be not so much a warning against a preventable catastrophe as "an expression of vast loathing over what the author, a realist of no mean talent, makes us believe may almost be inevitable" (1987: 262).

The grimness of Burgess's vision in *The Wanting Seed* shows, among other things, a strong Orwellian influence. Indeed, Burgess acknowledges this influence in his own book-length "response" to Orwell, entitled *1985* (1978), in which Burgess presents a long discussion of *Nineteen Eighty-Four* (which he finds to be largely a satire of postwar

England, rather than the Soviet Union), then presents his own novelized account of the near future, which can be read as a parody of Orwell's novel, but one that still shows the powerful effect of Orwell's vision. And, if this rather comic approach to dystopia seems odd, one need only remember that Burgess had already established his own reputation largely on the strength of the darkly comic *A Clockwork Orange* (1962), one of the most compelling dystopian satires since *Nineteen Eighty-Four*.

A Clockwork Orange is a dystopian fiction set in a nightmarish near-future England that centrally focuses on the "nadsat" dialect spoken by Alex, its narrator and central character. Alex is a teenage gang member, and this dialect provides a private language in which he and his fellow delinquents ("nadsats") can communicate. Dr Branom, one of the psychologists who participate in the later forced conditioning of Alex to remove his violent antisocial inclinations, explains the composition of nadsat language: "Odd bits of old rhyming slang. A bit of gipsy talk, too. But most of the roots are Slav. Propaganda. Subliminal penetration" (1963: 113). Indeed, most of the roots of nadsat words (including "nadsat," the suffix of Russian numbers from eleven to nineteen) do appear to be Russian, though the nadsats have anglicized some of them in colorful ways, as when *khorosho* ("good" or "well") becomes "horrorshow."

There is, of course, a not-very-subtle irony in Branom's suggestion that the Russians have brainwashed the rebellious youth of Burgess's British dystopia, especially since brainwashing is precisely the job of Branom himself. One potential message of Burgess's book (echoing *Nineteen Eighty-Four* as it does in other ways as well) is thus that there is no point in turning Britain into a totalitarian state from within in order to resist the threat of totalitarianism from without. Indeed, this Russian invasion of the language of the teenagers of Britain would seem to function largely as a parody of western paranoia over the potential influence of Communist infiltration on the hearts and minds of capitalist youths, though it is a sort of unstable parody that leaves open the possibility of an entirely straightforward interpretation: perhaps the nadsats really *have* been brainwashed by the Russians, a reading that suggests that Alex's conflict with British authority is not a confrontation between free choice and conditioning so much as a clash between two different conditioning programs. Indeed, though Alex himself at one point rejects the suggestion that his social environment may have contributed to his delinquency, it is rather naive to view Alex as entirely free before undergoing treatment by the Ludovico Technique that makes him incapable of violence. Even if Alex and his fellow gang members have not been subtly influenced by Russian propaganda they, like everyone, have been exposed to a number of other influences throughout their lives. In the book's final chapter (significantly omitted from American editions of the book prior to 1987) Alex himself seems to recognize this point, comparing his early self to a wind-up toy. On the other hand, in *1985* Burgess seems to suggest that before his conditioning Alex does evil by his own free choice. Burgess further makes clear his support for the right to such a choice, arguing that "if I cannot choose to do evil neither can I choose to do good. It is better to have our streets infested with murderous young hoodlums than to deny individual freedom of choice" (1978: 96).

The nadsat language spoken by Alex and his mates at first appears to be a form of linguistic rebellion, a way of rejecting the official ideology of the society around them by rejecting the language of that society and replacing it with one strongly informed by the language of a feared enemy. For one thing, the plural sources of this language invest it with a heteroglossia that powerfully opposes any attempt at the imposition of monological ideas. For another, this private language furthers a sense of solidarity among the nadsats that contributes to their resistance to the rule of official authority – just as the distinctive slangs employed by youth cultures were beginning to gain power in Burgess's own England.

Nevertheless, despite the fact that Burgess's delinquents seem to rape and pillage almost at will (at least after dark) in his dystopian London, superior power in *A Clockwork Orange* still rests with traditional authority, as it generally does in dystopian fiction. Indeed, the only thing more frightening than the youth gangs of the book is the official response to those gangs, and it is owing to this dual horror that *A Clockwork Orange* has had an impact on the popular consciousness not achieved by dystopian fiction since *Nineteen Eighty-Four*. Spurred by Stanley Kubrick's 1971 film adaptation, Burgess's book still contains some of the most widely recognizable images of the future in all of western culture.

British science fiction as a whole, overshadowed by American science fiction for decades, rose to a new prominence in the 1960s and 1970s, owing partly to the participation of "respected" authors such as Burgess and partly to the central role played by author/editors such as Michael Moorcock in science fiction's so-called new wave. Ultimately, however, the most important British science fiction writer of those decades was surely John Brunner, largely on the strength of a sequence of impressive dystopian satires that included *Stand on Zanzibar* (1968), *The Jagged Orbit* (1969), *The Sheep Look Up* (1972), and *The Shockwave Rider* (1975). Each of these four volumes is strongly rooted in the political concerns of the late 1960s and early 1970s, constructing future societies in which trends of Brunner's own day have continued to horrifying extremes. The Hugo Award-winning *Stand on Zanzibar*, for example, follows Burgess's *The Wanting Seed* in its central emphasis on the effects of overpopulation, though it is a massive and highly ambitious novel that employs a number of complex literary strategies to explore several issues in its fictional world of the early twenty-first century. *The Jagged Orbit*, meanwhile, focuses on racism and the criminalistic tendencies of the military-industrial complex; *The Sheep Look Up* explores ecological concerns in its projection of future environmental degradation; and *The Shockwave Rider* focuses on the impact of a worldwide communications explosion, in many ways anticipating the later (largely American) phenomenon of cyberpunk science fiction, a movement that has itself shown considerable dystopian leanings.

The title of *Stand on Zanzibar* refers to its central emphasis on overpopulation, in particular to the fact that the world population has reached the level where, for the first time, it would no longer be theoretically possible for all of the world's people to stand shoulder-to-shoulder on the island of Zanzibar. In the book, international strife is a fact of life, with the United States and China engaged in an interminable war of attrition that bears obvious similarities to the war in Vietnam, ongoing when the book was written.

Stand on Zanzibar, like much of Brunner's work, focuses on the United States, depicted as the world's richest – but also most violent – nation, replete with commodities, but also with economic inequities that keep most urban areas on the verge of riots. Gender relations in an overpopulated America ruled by strict eugenic legislation are also rather strained, though Brunner does relatively little to explore the implications of the fact that so many young women, unable to have children under the current circumstances, are reduced to the status of roving sexual objects, or "shiggies," drifting from one man to another, providing sexual favors in return for food and lodging. The American social fabric is further disrupted by the terrorist activities of pro-Chinese partisans and by the ever-present threat of "muckers" – individuals who snap under the pressure of modern life and run amuck, killing and maiming anyone in their path. Most of the populace cope with these pressures via an array of strategies that include drugs, casual sex, and popular culture. Indeed, the latter is a particularly powerful force as new technologies allow the media to extend their reach worldwide. This phenomenon is symbolized by the fact that the chief figures in global advertising are the allegorical Mr and Mrs Everywhere, who can be made to resemble (via special high-tech televisions) whoever happens to be watching at the time.

Brunner presents this vision of the future via a complex literary form that is clearly reminiscent of John Dos Passos's *U.S.A.* trilogy, though Dos Passos's later *Midcentury* may have been an even more direct inspiration. Relatively brief narrative segments that advance the major plot sequences are interspersed with other sections that contribute primarily to the elaboration of the texture of life in this future world, through either additional narratives relating the experiences of an array of minor characters or through non-narrative segments involving collages of discourse from advertising, popular culture, and other sources. Many of the latter include quotations from the works of the anti-authoritarian pop sociologist Chad Mulligan, who also becomes an important character in the second half of the book.

Stand on Zanzibar is far less directly plot-driven than most science fiction, concentrating instead on creating a complete fictional world. There are, however, two major plot sequences, respectively centering on the experiences of Norman House and Donald Hogan, who begin the text as roommates in New York but then go their separate ways. The African-American House, an executive with the gigantic General Technics Corporation (GT), becomes involved in a massive project to develop the "backward" African nation of Beninia (in the process creating new markets for GT products). Hogan, meanwhile, after ten years of employment in "research" for the US government, is pressed into active service as an espionage agent and sent to the Asian island nation of Yatakang; he is to investigate reports that a world-famous Yatakangi scientist, Dr Sugaiguntung, has developed new genetic techniques that will allow the Yatakangis to produce genetically superior human beings. Hogan, having been "eptified" into an efficient killing machine, eventually goes insane after he kills a number of people in the course of his mission, finally including Sugaiguntung himself. House, meanwhile, becomes the effective head of the Beninia project, employing Mulligan as a principal adviser.

Much of the suspense of the plot involves the attempts of House and other westerners to unravel the mystery of the fact that life in Beninia, which is economically impoverished to the point of squalor, seems unaccountably richer and more humane than life in the "advanced" countries of the West. The entire country of Beninia operates like one large family, under the benign leadership of its patriarch, President Zadkiel Obomi, whose impending death has triggered the GT project. Beninia is a land essentially free of violent crime, with a language that makes it almost impossible even to describe anger, except as a form of temporary insanity. As such, the book explores contrasts between the individualism of modern capitalist society and the communalism of traditional African society in potentially productive ways. Unfortunately, Brunner's depiction of the Beninians has a tendency to succumb to colonialist stereotyping; for example, ancient Beninia is described as a timeless land without history, inhabited only by the peaceful Shinka tribe until slave trading brought an influx of foreigners into the region. Most important, the mystery of Beninian tranquility and cooperation is ultimately attributed not to social but to biological differences. Mulligan discovers that the Shinkas bear a mutant gene causing them to secrete a substance that suppresses the normal human (masculine) tendency toward aggression; it thus makes not only them, but those they encounter, behave in peaceful and cooperative ways.

This appeal to biological difference comes dangerously close to stereotyping in terms of both race and gender. Indeed, the highly patriarchal nature of this ideal Beninia is extremely problematic. In the end, Mulligan assumes, somewhat to his own horror, that capitalism will appropriate the Shinka mutation, developing a way to synthesize and market the secreted substance, then distributing it to prevent the human race from destroying itself. But this seemingly optimistic turn in the text does not address the fundamental incompatibility between capitalism, built on competition and aggression, and the Shinka mutation, which may spell the doom not only of the GT project to develop Beninia along capitalist lines but also, if widely distributed, of capitalism itself.

Ultimately, then, Brunner misses a number of opportunities to make important political points, perhaps because of his own apparent assumption that human social problems arise primarily from the biological predilections of the human race and are therefore not amenable to solution by social and political means. Indeed, while the book's critique of capitalism is sometimes trenchant, it does not offer socialism (or anything else) as an effective alternative. The book is, in fact, sometimes quite critical of the Communist regime in its future China, though it does suggest that western complaints about the lack of individual freedom in China reflect a lack of understanding of the Chinese situation, which has been substantially improved under Communism (2000: 586). Though John J. Pierce describes *Stand on Zanzibar* as a Wellsian satire "committed to utopian socialism and a world state," the book ultimately has no clearly articulated political agenda (Pierce 1987: 189). It is also, as science fiction goes, not particularly imaginative in its projection of the impact of technology on future human societies. For example, the computer technologies that are central to much of the book are rather clunky in comparison with what has actually occurred in the past thirty years – or with what Brunner himself would later envision in *The Shockwave Rider*, with its anticipatory versions of the internet and computer viruses. But Brunner's book is clearly more a satirical commentary on his present world of 1968 than a literal attempt to envision the future. Moreover, *Stand on Zanzibar* is extremely insightful in its projection of a media-dominated world system that again reflects the spread of what Jameson has called late capitalism. It also dramatizes, in a vivid and effective fashion, the inability of relative material comfort to compensate for the dehumanizing consequences of this system.

If anything, Brunner's dystopian vision becomes bleaker as his dystopian series proceeds. *The Sheep Look Up* is particularly powerful in its depiction of a future America in which capitalist greed has destroyed the environment and threatens to make the country, and perhaps even the world, uninhabitable. Americans are plagued by a variety of diseases, many directly caused by a lack of clean air and water, though overuse of antibiotics has also helped to produce resistant strains of bacteria that contribute to the health crisis. In the meantime, overuse of pesticides has contributed not only to the contamination of the environment but to the rise of new insect mutations that attack crops and contribute to a general decline in the food supply. The government of the United States, led by an anti-environmentalist President (popularly known as "Prexy") who seems to be all bluster and little action, has done very little to improve the situation, which also includes deteriorating social conditions and rising crime rates. Meanwhile, the global operations of the American government and American corporations have helped to further anti-American feeling around the world. US troops are involved in a variety of local wars, especially in Central America, where Tupamaro guerrillas are waging an increasingly successful war of liberation against American domination, sometimes even taking the war to US soil through terrorist attacks.

The Sheep Look Up is a complex novel with numerous characters and multiple plot strands, constructed somewhat in the manner of *Stand on Zanzibar*, with the main narrative segments interspersed with documents, news accounts, and so on. One of the most important plot strands involves the ultra-rich Bamberley family, one of whose charitable organizations distributes contaminated food in Africa and Central America, which causes outbreaks of homicidal madness among those who consume the food. Given the generally predatory nature of the Bamberley corporate operations, many suspect that the contamination was an intentional plot in the interests of American imperialism. It turns out, however, that the contamination was caused by experimental chemical weapons developed by the US army, which have leaked into the ground water around Denver, Colorado, where the food is being produced. Eventually, this contamination causes general outbreaks of madness in the Denver area as well, leading to near-apocalyptic chaos in the area and across the nation.

Perhaps the most important single figure in the text is one Austin Train, a formerly prominent environmental activist who has, at the time of the book, gone underground, partly for his own safety and partly to live among the common people so that he can better understand their lives. Meanwhile, "Trainite" groups have sprung up around the country to protest against environmental degradation and are beginning to employ increasingly violent methods, of which Train does not necessarily approve. Eventually, in a move sanctioned by the President himself, Train is brought up on charges of kidnapping a member of the Bamberley family. His easy demonstration of his innocence in a nationally televised trial increases his popularity even further, leading to a resurgence in Trainite activity and bringing the country to the brink of revolution. Train himself is killed as a Trainite bomb explodes in the courthouse, and many of the other characters are also killed in the violence and destruction that reigns in the country. The book ends as Thomas Grey, former chief actuary for a major insurance company and now a Bamberley employee, announces on national television that his computer modeling has indicated that the global environment can be saved only if "we exterminate the two hundred million most extravagant and wasteful of our species" – a number, of course, that roughly matches the population of the United States.

Brunner's warnings in *The Sheep Look Up* (and, for that matter, all of his dystopian fictions) are all the more striking for the extent to which they seem in so many ways to have anticipated developments in the decades after its publication. Most important, of course, is the worsening environmental crisis, but more specific projections of the book have also proved accurate, including the increasing mediatization of American society, the increase in global American military interventions, and the uncanny resemblance between Prexy and US President George W. Bush. Nevertheless, it is true of Brunner's dystopian fictions, as with those of predecessors such as Huxley, Burdekin, Orwell, and Burgess, that the works function primarily not as predictions of the future but as satires of the present.

The same continues to be the case for more recent works, such as those of Ian McDonald. For example, *Out on Blue Six* (1989) depicts a failed utopia in a way that clearly responds, as did much British science fiction of the period, to some of the concerns of the Thatcher years. Science fiction works of the 1990s, such as Ken MacLeod's *The Star Fraction* (1995), envision a dystopian future that directly engages with contemporary British politics as well. In addition, by the 1990s, writers with reputations in genres other than science fiction were producing dystopian visions of the future. A notable case is the respected Scottish writer Iain Banks, who has written (as Iain M. Banks) a number of science fiction novels focusing on a rather utopian interstellar "Culture" that is sometimes contrasted with dystopian enemies.

One of the most interesting English dystopian satires of the 1990s was written by the noted mystery writer P. D. James. In *The Children of Men* (1992), all of the world's sperm (including supplies frozen in sperm banks) are suddenly and inexplicably rendered inert in 1995, leaving humanity with no prospects of continuing the species beyond the generation born that year. Left without such hope for the future, humanity sinks into despair. British society, on which the book focuses, becomes decidedly dysfunctional, until a dictatorial "Warden" manages to re-establish order at the expense of dystopian repression. By the year 2021, in which the book is set, the general population, having grimly acknowledged that humanity is doomed anyway, accepts this repression without complaint. However, the book ends on a seemingly hopeful note: not only is the Warden killed, but a baby is born, generating new hope that others will be born as well. On the other hand, in an ominous development, the book's protagonist, an Oxford historian who has been appalled by the policies of the Warden's regime, prepares to assume the mantle of the Warden (his cousin) with hints that he may follow directly in his predecessor's footsteps. All in all, James's elegantly written novel nicely dramatizes the importance of hope in human life, a key point made in the work of such modern utopian theorists as Ernst Bloch. At the same time, James's book suggests an expansion of dystopian satiric fiction in ways that indicate a rich and hopeful future for the genre.

References and Further Reading

Booker, M. Keith (1994a) *Dystopian Literature: A Theory and Research Guide*. Westport, CT: Greenwood.
——(1994b) *The Dystopian Impulse in Modern Literature: Fiction as Social Criticism*. Westport, CT: Greenwood.
Brunner, John (1969) [1968] *Stand on Zanzibar*. New York: Ballantine.
——(1976) [1975] *The Shockwave Rider*. New York: Ballantine.
——(2000) [1969] *The Jagged Orbit*. London: Gollancz.
——(2003) [1972] *The Sheep Look Up*. Dallas, TX: BenBella Books.
Burdekin, Katharine (1985) [1937] *Swastika Night*, Old Westbury, NY: Feminist Press.
Burgess, Anthony (1963) [1962] *A Clockwork Orange*. New York: W. W. Norton.
——(1976) [1962] *The Wanting Seed*. New York: W. W. Norton.
——(1978) *1985*. Boston: Little, Brown.
Croft, Andy (1990) *Red Letter Days: British Fiction in the 1930s*. London: Lawrence and Wishart.
Evans, Robert O. (1987) "The *nouveau roman*, Russian dystopias, and Anthony Burgess," in Jack I. Biles (ed.) *British Novelists Since 1900*. New York: AMS Press.
Hartley, L. P. (1966) [1960] *Facial Justice*. Harmondsworth: Penguin.

Huxley, Aldous (1998) [1932] *Brave New World*. New York: Perennial Classics.
James, P. D. (1992) *The Children of Men*. New York: Alfred A. Knopf.
Jameson, Fredric (1991) *Postmodernism, or, The Cultural Logic of Late Capitalism*. Durham, NC: Duke University Press.
Kumar, Krishan (1987) *Utopia and Anti-Utopia in Modern Times*. Oxford: Blackwell.
MacLeod, Ken (1995) *The Star Fraction*. London: Legend.
McDonald, Ian (1989) *Out on Blue Six*. New York: Bantam.
Moylan, Tom (2000) *Scraps of Untainted Sky: Science Fiction, Utopia, Dystopia*. Boulder, CO: Westview.
Orwell, George (1946) *Animal Farm*. New York: New American Library.
——(1961) [1949] *Nineteen Eighty-Four*. New York: New American Library.
Pierce, John J. (1987) *Foundations of Science Fiction: A Study in Imagination and Evolution*. Westport, CT: Greenwood.
Wegner, Phillip E. (2002) *Imaginary Communities: Utopia, the Nation, and the Spatial Histories of Modernity*. Berkeley: University of California Press.

4

The Feminist Novel in the Wake of Virginia Woolf

Roberta Rubenstein

The title of this chapter is problematic in at least two senses. First, just as there is no simple definition of "feminism," there is no single definition of "feminist novel." Second, while Virginia Woolf has been a vital inspiration for female writers, few novels written by women during the second half of the twentieth century demonstrate the direct influence of her masterpieces of formal experimentation and unique poetic language. Rather, for the purposes of this discussion, Woolf's "wake" was formed principally by her groundbreaking feminist essays, most notably *A Room of One's Own*. The essay, which began as a series of lectures at Cambridge, was published in 1929 and subsequently went out of print for several decades – a period not particularly hospitable to Woolf's important argument that a woman needed £500 and a room of her own in order to write. During the 1960s and 1970s – formative years of the women's movement – the essay was rediscovered and enthusiastically embraced by writers and feminist scholars. In succeeding decades, it has remained required reading for anyone interested in women and writing, and, of course, in Virginia Woolf herself. Among the essay's many unforgettable images and observations are the author's plea for the rebirth of the imaginary Judith Shakespeare – the spirit of women's writing – and her contention that "we think back through our mothers if we are women" (Woolf 1989: 76). The latter phrase remains an essential touchstone for regarding the literary history of women's writing.

During the half-century encompassed by this volume, the discourses and meanings of feminism, shaped by the multiple contributions of feminist activism, theory, scholarship, and literature, have continued to evolve. To further complicate this discussion, even the term "British" is somewhat problematic; some postcolonial literary critics use the term to include all writers of the former British Commonwealth. To narrow the otherwise impossibly large scope of this discussion, I include only writers who were born in Britain or Ireland and writers of other national origins who immigrated before or during the early years of their literary careers and are permanent citizens of those countries.

Quite apart from matters of nationality, even for writers who identify themselves as feminist, not all of their fiction can (or should) be described by that term; most have published novels with strong feminist themes among other works of fiction with entirely different emphases. Furthermore, an author's own judgment is not the sole determinant of the feminism of her fiction. For example, Doris Lessing was disappointed with the initial responses to her groundbreaking novel, *The Golden Notebook* (1962). In her own estimation, the novel was a failure because readers embraced it as "a kind of banner" of feminism, at the expense of what its author regarded as its "carefully constructed" and innovative narrative form (Howe 1966: 9). By contrast, when asked how the women's movement influenced her as a writer, Fay Weldon responded, "I like to think I influenced *it*! I started writing in England at the same time as the women's movement there got going, so we were more or less contemporary phenomena. The writer and the movement [began] to feed into each other" (Kumar 1995: 16).

What, then, is a feminist novel? To answer this question, I define the project of this chapter in two ways. First, I identify as feminist novels those narratives that take as their central subject the lives and experiences of women while implicitly acknowledging, if not explicitly critiquing, patriarchal social structures. Second, I use historical chronology to highlight by decades key themes and ideas. These approaches are necessarily suggestive rather than definitive; writers, novels, and ideas do not fit neatly into these admittedly arbitrary intervals. Moreover, space constraints necessitate exclusion of many worthy novels that focus on female experience as well as full commentary on the thematic and formal elements that distinguish the narratives included for consideration. Nor can this discussion encompass the history of feminism or the influential body of feminist theory and scholarship that has shaped interpretations of women's writing. Rather, this chapter focuses on novels by British and Irish women writers who, in my estimation, have significantly contributed to the evolving feminist discourse. Incidentally, their fiction also intersects with the evolution of narrative forms and new theoretical approaches that have emerged during the second half of the twentieth century.

1950s–1960s: Growing up Female, the Quest for Selfhood and Identity, Marriage, Motherhood, Confinement

Although the historical time frame of this volume begins with the postwar period, it was not until nearly a decade later, when the situation of women in patriarchy had begun to generate its own discourse, that the first "feminist" novels appeared. In *The Second Sex,* published in English in 1952, French philosopher Simone de Beauvoir argued that the overlapping effects of biology, culture, economics, and history had shaped human sexual arrangements, reinforcing female subordination over time. Her critical insight was that women's secondary status throughout history and across cultures was not innate but culturally produced – and reproduced – by the social structure known as patriarchy. As she so memorably phrased it, "One is not born, but

rather becomes, a woman" (Beauvoir 1952: 267). Her detailed critique was foundational for what was to develop into the Women's Liberation Movement. Betty
Friedan's *The Feminine Mystique* (1963) also contributed influentially to the emerging
awareness of women's situation in patriarchy. Friedan articulated "the problem that
has no name" (Friedan 1964: 11), identifying as particularly destructive to women
the unequal gender relations that structured heterosexual relationships and marriage.

Not surprisingly, then, among the defining themes of the early feminist novels of
the 1950s and 1960s is the quest for female selfhood and identity – including what it
means to "become a woman" in patriarchy – along with attention to the experiences of
marriage and motherhood and representations of literal or figurative confinement.
Despite Doris Lessing's own dismay noted above, her novels are an important starting
point for the literary representation of these ideas. A member of the first generation of
novelists considered here, Lessing (b. 1919) introduced the major themes of feminist
fiction published during the 1950s and 1960s, and thus stands as both an essential
voice and a significant shaper of the feminist novel. As one of several writers
considered here who spent her formative years in a British colony (Fay Weldon
spent her childhood in New Zealand, and Buchi Emecheta immigrated to England
from Nigeria as a young adult), Lessing drew on her own experience growing up in
Southern Rhodesia (now Zimbabwe) to chronicle from childhood through young
adulthood to middle age the life of Martha Quest, the protagonist of the five-volume
Bildungsroman, *Children of Violence* (1952–69).

In *Martha Quest* (1952) and *A Proper Marriage* (1954), Martha emerges as a curious,
intelligent, and introspective girl who, despite her idealized visions of a different life,
finds herself propelled to follow the traditional path toward womanhood. Driven by
social and biological forces so overbearing that she feels powerless to resist them, she
chooses marriage at 19 to an utterly conventional young man, followed soon afterward
by motherhood. Through the detailed rendering of Martha Quest's emotional and
psychological growth, Lessing charts the power of biological and cultural conditioning for girls and women, reinforced by her protagonist's own deep ambivalence:
Martha wants simultaneously to be like her peers and to resist the traditional patterns
that determine their lives.

Eventually, breaking radically with prescriptive social expectations, Martha is
radicalized by leftist politics (*A Proper Marriage*, 1954; *A Ripple from the Storm*,
1958; *Landlocked*, 1965) and takes the unprecedented step – as did the author herself
– of leaving her husband and young child to pursue a more authentic life. Though
later tormented by guilt, at the time Martha earnestly believes that her departure will
set her daughter free from the "tyranny of the family" (Lessing 1964a: 343). Still later,
disillusioned by Communism, a second unsatisfactory marriage based on political
rather than emotional compatibility, and a passionate love affair with a married man,
she leaves Zambesia (Southern Rhodesia) for England.

Martha Quest's moral and spiritual quest takes her on a complex path through the
London of the 1950s and 1960s, including residence with the Coldridge family; over
time, the Coldridge house, shared by occupants of several generations and diverse

backgrounds, evolves into a collective center for emotional and spiritual growth. Martha is profoundly affected by her friendship with the visionary Linda Coldridge, a woman who is able to "see" in ways that ordinary people cannot but who is unable to function in their world. Through relationships (mostly unsatisfactory) with men, Martha explores her sexual and emotional capacities and experiments with altered states of consciousness and extrasensory perception; through these and other experiences, Lessing richly documents the countercultural strands of the 1960s. With the final volume of *Children of Violence, The Four-Gated City* (1969), the themes and ideas of the series expand in multiple directions, culminating in a post-apocalyptic Appendix. Martha Quest's achievement of full self-realization must be understood as only one of many dimensions of her emotional, intellectual, and spiritual transformation from girlhood in southern Africa to mature womanhood in England.

Lessing interrupted the writing of *Children of Violence* to write what many regard as her masterpiece, *The Golden Notebook.* Although this novel merits a more detailed discussion, it must be at least briefly noted here because of its significance to the subject of this chapter. Lessing's protagonist, Anna Wulf (note the echo with Virginia Woolf), a writer who feels artistically blocked, nonetheless writes voluminously in four different notebooks that embody her inner self-division, including her experiences as a writer, a Communist, a sexual being, and a mother; intervening segments of a conventional novel called "Free Women" offer a more objective – and ironic – parallel narrative that highlights, among other things, female friendship. As minutely recorded through her multiple notebooks, Anna is driven to mental breakdown by the dissonances among her disparate identities and by her emotionally destructive relationships with men. Her effort to reconcile her self-division through *writing* is reflected in the novel's innovative metafictional structure, in which both process and form are its subject. Though Anna's tormented struggle to overcome psychological fragmentation may be resolved by the novel's end, the absence of a true conclusion suggests that what it meant to be a "free woman" in the 1950s and 1960s remained more question than answer.

Unlike Doris Lessing, Penelope Mortimer (1918–99) focuses on women who are so entirely defined by traditional female roles that they have virtually no sense of an "I" apart from marriage and motherhood; she rarely imagines possible strategies for her characters' liberation from their emotional prisons. If at least two of her novels nonetheless qualify as feminist, it is because they stand as early literary representations, and implicit critiques, of women's socially-determined compliance with their subordinate positions as "housewives." Mortimer's *Cave of Ice* (1959) pivots on a teenage girl's unwanted pregnancy that, ironically, duplicates her mother's pregnancy out of wedlock years before; Angela Whiting's conception resulted in her parents' obligatory and sterile marriage, for which Ruth Whiting has never quite forgiven her daughter. In addition to tracing the difficulty of obtaining an illegal abortion in the 1950s, the narrative also explores a relationship important to the feminist novel: the mother–daughter bond. In this instance, the termination of pregnancy, rather than drawing the two women closer, drives them apart. While Angela releases herself from the grip of her mother's guilt and unconscious rejection by leaving home, Ruth remains trapped in the emotionally deadened "cave of ice" that her life has become.

During the 1960s, the "problem that has no name" was represented in a number of feminist novels by British (and North American) writers in the form of stories about "mad housewives" – "mad" meaning either crazy or angry, or both. Concurrently, early feminist novels repeatedly examined the ambivalence of the maternal role; motherhood represented the juncture – and, frequently, the point of conflict – between biology and ideology, between obligation or responsibility and personal freedom, between erotic and maternal love. One of the first narratives to explore these tensions is Penelope Mortimer's most significant novel, *The Pumpkin Eater* (1962), published the same year as Lessing's *The Golden Notebook*.

Mortimer's narrative unfolds as a monologue "spoken" to an unsympathetic psychiatrist-like doctor by Mrs Armitage, who, tellingly, never reveals her first name; she exists only as the auxiliary of her fourth husband, Jake. Mother of a brood of children, Mrs Armitage finds in compulsive procreation both a substitute for sexual intimacy and her only means of self-confirmation. However, Jake emphatically opposes her next pregnancy and compels her to have not only an abortion but surgical sterilization. Though she feels sexually and emotionally liberated by the surgery, she later realizes that, in passively submitting to the procedures, she has continued to abdicate responsibility for her own life. Only late in the narrative does she acknowledge the forces that perpetuate her self-destructive behavior. Although Mrs Armitage never entirely escapes the "pumpkin shell" that circumscribes her life, the reader sees the thickness of its walls and comes to appreciate the difficulty of escape.

The protagonists of Margaret Drabble's early novels are also preoccupied with the tensions between confinement and liberation. Typically, as educated young women on the verge of adult life, they discover to their chagrin that the choices available to them are quite different from those promised by their educations and expectations. Although at the time Drabble (b. 1939) was "not conscious of [herself] as a woman writer" (Kenyon 1989: 45), she later described the circumstances of her own life that impelled her to write about the difficulty of being a "free woman" in the restrictive social climate of the 1960s:

> When we left college we had babies, fed the family, did a day's work, served Cordon Bleu meals by candlelight and were free to have intellectual conversation all evening. But the freedom was a mockery because we were all overloaded, exhausted. And out of that feeling arose the women's novel of the sixties … Edna O'Brien, Doris Lessing, Penelope Mortimer … Fay Weldon, beginning to express these feelings of rage. We were not actually blaming men but we felt caught in a trap and did not know how to get out. (Kenyon 1989: 27–8)

Later in the same interview, Drabble added, "My protests were mild, but I felt I had to express them. This was the first time women novelists dealt frankly with subjects not considered 'polite', such as breastfeeding, hysterectomy, wanting too much" (p. 45).

In Drabble's *A Summer Bird-Cage* (1963), a novel of manners in the tradition of Jane Austen, Sarah Bennett has no idea of a career or vocation, despite her first-class honors degree from Oxford. As the title suggests, the conflict between emotional confinement and independence is central to the narrative. After focusing almost obsessively on the wedding of her older sister Louise, Sarah admits that she has been "delaying the problem of marriage" (Drabble 1981a: 74) for herself. The novel also pivots on the siblings' powerful rivalry. Ultimately, Louise's marriage is exposed as a sham and Sarah ponders, with renewed anxiety, the pressures that compel her female peers to marry unsatisfactory men rather than to pursue the alternatives that their elite educations should encourage.

Emma Evans of *The Garrick Year* (1964) is already married, but not happily so. The mother of a toddler and an infant, she is submerged to the point of drowning in the routines of child-rearing and eagerly anticipates a promised job as a television news announcer. However, because her actor husband has been cast in a role that will require the family to relocate, she cannot accept the position. As she resentfully comments,

> After three years of childbearing and modeling maternity clothes, I felt in serious need of a good, steady, lucrative job. I could hardly believe that marriage was going to deprive me of this too. It had already deprived me of so many things which I had childishly overvalued: my independence, my income, my twenty-two inch waist, my sleep, most of my friends who had deserted on account of David's insults, a whole string of finite things. . . . (Drabble 1981b: 10)

Emma's dissatisfaction with the constraints of domesticity lead to complications in her life that recall those of her adulterous French namesake, Emma Bovary. Though the novel concludes with Emma's reconciliation with her contrite husband, the core of the narrative is her struggle to keep her head above the waterline of domestic chaos rather than drown in it.

A number of feminist novels published before reliable contraception and legal abortion were available focus on female characters who, like Penelope Mortimer's women, face unchosen pregnancies. Drabble's *The Millstone* (1965) develops that uniquely female complication of experience along an unconventional trajectory. The novel's first-person narrator, Rosamund Stacey, is an intelligent young woman in pursuit of a doctorate in English; she is also an inhibited virgin who fears emotional intimacy. Ironically, her sole experience of sexual intercourse leads to pregnancy. She fatalistically decides she will have the child but never informs its unsuspecting father. As an unmarried woman seeking prenatal care in public health clinics, she is exposed for the first time in her privileged life to working-class and immigrant women whose circumstances challenge the unexamined liberal values she has acquired through her family and education.

The Millstone is a love story that focuses not on heterosexual but on maternal love. Indeed, for a number of Drabble's protagonists, the two are virtually incompatible.

The author has commented that "the mother–child relationship is a great salvation and is an image of unselfish love, which is very hard to get in an adult relationship ... if not impossible" (interview quoted in Creighton 1985: 24). In *The Millstone,* Rosamund Stacey's deepest feelings of attachment and relationship are born along with her daughter, Octavia. Near the end of the narrative, Rosamund accidentally encounters the child's father and, as if compelled to maintain the exclusivity of her devotion to her daughter, she does not reveal his relationship to the child. Although the author's moral position is complicated – some critics accused Drabble of endorsing illegitimate pregnancy while others praised her depiction of female autonomy through her protagonist's choice of single motherhood – Rosamund's position is unambiguous: while she continues to sidestep sexual intimacy, during the course of her story she grows from intellectual self-centeredness to emotional connection: from living in her head to living with her heart.

Like several of Drabble's other protagonists, Jane Gray of *The Waterfall* (1969) – one of the author's most technically accomplished and morally complex novels – is an educated young woman who is married to a man she no longer loves. The mother of one child, she gives birth to another early in the narrative, an event that precipitates a passionate affair with her cousin's husband. Both the timing of the birth and its vocabulary are crucial: the novel pivots on the multiple meanings of "delivery," a term associated not only with maternity but with spiritual pilgrimage. Through adulterous passion, Jane discovers herself. Ultimately, she also pays a price for that discovery through a car accident that seriously injures her lover. Her inner division is expressed through the narrative structure, which alternates between first- and third-person perspectives. As both author and subject of her narrative, Jane Gray is an unreliable narrator who offers conflicting accounts of the same events, both to rationalize her actions and to make sense of them; it is through *telling* her story of illicit passion and its resulting sexual and spiritual awakening that she plumbs its meaning.

The early novels of Fay Weldon (b. 1931) also focus on domestic and maternal confinement. Esther Wells, the protagonist of Weldon's first novel, *The Fat Woman's Joke* (1967), feels trapped: in her body, her house, and her marriage. Leaving the "crushing weight" (1986: 10) of her partnership of two decades – a flight precipitated by a mutual diet whose strains drive the couple apart – she proceeds to eat compulsively. The symbolic meanings of hunger and appetite figure centrally in the narrative's exploration of female subordination and marital dissatisfaction; overeating is Esther's protest against the reality that "men ... control the world" (p. 137).

Irish writer Edna O'Brien's trilogy – *The Country Girls* (1960), *The Lonely Girl* (1962), and *Girls in their Married Bliss* (1964) – traces a strong female friendship and offers an unusually frank portrayal of growing up female at a time when fiction was far more discreet about female sexuality. Beginning with the youth and adolescence of the romantic Caithleen (Kate) and the rebellious Baubra (Baba), O'Brien (b. 1932) traces the girls' lives through convent school in Ireland, to young adulthood and employment at menial jobs in Dublin, to loss of sexual innocence and subsequent relationships with men. Though Kate's attraction to older married men leads to repeated disappointments in love, by the final volume of the trilogy both she and Baba arrive at the altar pregnant. Kate finally marries the divorced man with whom she has been in love for years; ironically, the marriage marks the death of love, for it was the lure of the unattainable that had sustained their relationship over time. When Kate's husband secretly leaves Ireland with their young son, she never recovers from the emotional devastation and loss. In an epilogue to the trilogy published twenty years later, the reader learns that, soon after being abandoned by her husband, Kate drowned herself, imitating her mother's death years before.

In one of the few explicitly feminist statements in the *Country Girls* trilogy, the unmarried Baba visits a doctor to confirm her pregnancy. When the doctor advises her to relax during the pelvic examination, she thinks,

> Relax! I was thinking of women and all they have to put up with, not just washing nappies or not being able to be high-court judges, but all this . . . poking and probing and hurt. And not only when they go to doctors but when they go to bed as brides with the men that love them. Oh, God, who does not exist, you hate women, otherwise you'd have made them different. And Jesus, who snubbed your mother, you hate them more. (O'Brien 1986d: 473)

O'Brien's trilogy, with its irreverent jabs at Catholicism and religious faith and its candid portrayals of female sexuality outside of marriage, attempted self-induced abortions, and divorce, was not well-received in Ireland.

It is worth noting here that O'Brien published a play based on the life of Virginia Woolf (O'Brien 1981).

1970s: Sexuality and the Body, Gender Identity, the Domestic Maternal, Mid-life; Postmodern and Postcolonial Intersections

The 1970s brought major critical discourses such as postmodernism, deconstruction, psychoanalysis, and New Historicism into the arenas of the academy and imaginative writing. Concurrently, British women had begun to approach, if not achieve, greater social, legal, and economic parity with men. Feminist novels of the 1970s included – along with continuing attention to sexuality, female confinement, and the domestic maternal – narrative experimentation and representations of new aspects of female experience.

Fay Weldon's novels of the 1970s are by turns acerbic and comic critiques of the condition of women before feminism. *Down among the Women* (1971), chronicled by a narrator who sits on a park bench and cries "for all the women in the world" (1973: 118), articulates a collective complaint; the title phrase recurs as a kind of refrain. The narrative's three generations of women are economically and emotionally dependent on indifferent or even abusive men. There are few supportive relationships between women, even mothers and daughters, because all are driven by competition for a scarce resource: men. If sexual relationships only occasionally include love, some unions endure despite the absence of both love and sex. Even motherhood brings more difficulties than satisfactions, while age further reduces the choices available to women. As the narrator phrases it, "There is nothing more glorious than to be a young girl and there is nothing worse than to have been one" (p. 6).

In the era before reliable contraception or legalized abortion – opportunities for which feminists successfully struggled in the 1960s – women were at the mercy of their bodies; those, like 20-year-old Scarlet, who becomes pregnant out of wedlock, face limited opportunities to achieve self-sufficiency. Like Weldon herself (who was for a time a young unmarried mother), Scarlet is driven by economic desperation, along with the wish for her young son to have a proper father, to marry a significantly older, asexual man whom she does not love. Weldon obliges her readers to see women as not only economically and sexually oppressed but domestically oppressed by what has traditionally been regarded as women's work:

> We are the cleaners. We empty the ashtrays which tomorrow will be filled again. We sweep the floors which tomorrow will be dusty. We cook the food and clean the lavatory pans. We pick up the dirty clothes and wash and iron them. We make the world go round. Someone's got to do it. When she dies it will be said of her, she was a wonderful wife and mother. She cooked a hundred thousand meals, swept a million floors, washed a billion dishes, went through the cupboards and searched for missing buttons. (Weldon 1973: 83)

Elaborating on the preoccupations of *Down Among the Women*, Weldon's *Female Friends* (1974) is a virtual anatomy of – if not diatribe against – male subjugation of women and women's complicity in it. Chloe, Marjorie, and Grace meet as girls during the war, when they are evacuated from London for protection from German bombing raids. In later life they are united by their difficult childhoods – their "inner homelessness" (1988: 33) as offspring of mothers from whom they remain estranged. When they enter young adulthood, they find no alternative to remaining with men who use them. Children, even when desired, are the source of their mothers' suffering. As the narrator acerbically phrases it, "childbirth may be a miracle for the child but it is not for the mother" (p. 182). Chloe, who has more miscarriages than successful pregnancies, becomes the substitute mother for her friends' children, who are rather casually passed around as divorces and sexual liaisons scramble traditional family bonds.

Whether intentionally or not, Chloe's name invokes Virginia Woolf's wish that friendships between women might become the subject of fiction: "Chloe liked Olivia. . . . Sometimes women do like women" (Woolf 1989: 82). In *Female Friends,* Chloe *dislikes* Oliver, her duplicitous husband, but draws sustenance from her friends. Ultimately, with their support, she leaves her suffocating marriage. As the narrator observes, "What progress can there be, from generation to generation, if daughters do as mothers do?" (1988: 233)

Praxis (1978), one of Weldon's finest novels, was short-listed for the 1979 Booker Prize and judged by A. S. Byatt to be "(apart from *The Golden Notebook*) the single best modern novel about the condition of women" (Byatt 1979: 10). The first-person narrator, Praxis Duveen – whose first name, according to Weldon, alludes to the "moment when theory takes actual practical form" (quoted in Kenyon 1988: 114) – tells her story in two time frames: recently, she has been discharged after two years of incarceration for a crime not revealed until the novel's end; through the intercut retrospective narrative that functions as a confession, she reconstructs the story of her life in order to explain and justify it. At the end, the two narratives converge as Praxis' crime – the mercy killing at birth of her surrogate daughter's Down's Syndrome infant – is disclosed.

Praxis chronicles her miserable childhood as an illegitimate and rejected child whose mentally ill mother was institutionalized by the time Praxis was 15. As her story unfolds, she comes to resemble a modern-day Moll Flanders/ Everywoman, a picaresque figure who embodies more experiences than would be likely for any individual woman, from the conventional (sexual initiation, marriage, motherhood) to the unconventional or unlawful (prostitution, incest, infanticide). Looking back, Praxis acknowledges the socially approved masochism of her role as helpmate: in support of her husband's education and career, she had subordinated her own talents. The pattern of self-erasure persists in Praxis' later life when, in her job as a researcher for the BBC, she finds her name always missing from the credits. Taking stock of the economic and sexual pressures she shares with other women, Praxis polemically observes the "betrayal on all sides" that defines women's lot:

> Our bodies betray us, leading us to love where our interests do not lie. Our instincts betray us, inducing us to nest-build and procreate – but to follow instinct is not to achieve fulfilment, for we are more than animals.... Our brains betray us ... keeping [us] one step, for the sake of convenience, to avoid hurt, behind the male. We betray each other. We manipulate, through sex: we fight each other for possession of the male .... We prefer the company of men to women. (Weldon 1990: 205–6)

As with Margaret Drabble's Jane Gray, *telling* her story is a way for Praxis to examine the choices she made, including her crucial act on behalf of all of her "sisters," to smother "nature's error" (1990: 242). For the first time claiming her symbolic name, Praxis insists on accepting full responsibility for her deed, resulting in her punishment by law. As the two strands of the narrative – confession and current commentary – converge at the end, she feels redeemed.

Several of Weldon's other novels published during the 1970s and 1980s qualify as feminist novels because of their renderings, in both realistic and fantastic narratives, of aspects of women's lives in patriarchy, from marriage and maternity to the revenge of wronged wives: *Remember Me* (1976), *Words of Advice* (1977), *Puffball* (1980), and *The Life and Loves of a She-Devil* (1983).

Among the first British women writers to situate feminist preoccupations within a postcolonial context, Buchi Emecheta (b. 1945) documents her own life in her autobiographical second novel, *Second-Class Citizen* (1974). Emecheta, who immigrated to England from Nigeria in 1962, traces the determined Adah Ofili from her Ibo (Igbo) girlhood in a culture in which female children are devalued, to early marriage to an Ibo man who expects her to support him financially while he pursues an accountancy degree in England, to years of continuous maternity: five children born during the six years before her twenty-third birthday. Adah's job as a librarian is the burgeoning family's sole source of income. Francis is a lazy, abusive husband who beats Adah for a variety of reasons, including her reasonable decision, after the complicated delivery of their third child, to use birth control; he is incapable of seeing his wife apart from the satisfaction of his own needs. Though Adah endures numerous abuses, when her husband maliciously burns the manuscript of her first novel, *The Bride Price* (a novel eventually published by Emecheta in 1976), she finally claims her anger and leaves Francis. In the court proceedings that formalize their separation, Francis crassly argues that they were never legally married and refuses to pay child support for their four children and the fifth on the way. Emecheta's novel documents the difficult struggle of an intelligent woman who confronts both the sexism of her own culture and the racial prejudice and economic hardship she experiences once she leaves it.

Several women writers of the 1970s, moving beyond portrayals of intelligent but confused young women confined by marriage and maternity, introduced somewhat older female protagonists who face issues more pertinent to women at mid-life, when the maternal role ceases to be so all-consuming. Kate Brown of Doris Lessing's *The Summer before the Dark* (1973) is the wife of a successful neurologist and the mother of four children in various stages of adolescence. Her identity has been so shaped by the conventional cultural scripts for women – supportive wife and nurturing mother – that she has no idea who she "is" apart from those roles. One summer, when her husband and children are all engaged away from home, Kate is catapulted into a radical break with her conventional life. Taking a temporary job as a simultaneous translator at an international conference, she discovers that her real skill, developed during years of mothering, is not as a translator but as a "tribal mother" (1973: 51) who intuitively responds to others' unstated, and usually unconscious, needs.

The key task of Kate Brown's subsequent travels, including an interior journey that parallels a geographical one, is to discover an identity apart from her role as nurturer. Crucially, a series of dreams involving an injured seal disclose aspects of Kate's denied self, enabling her to recognize that years in the service of others' needs have left her deepest self emotionally starved. Ultimately, transformed by her summer of outward adventure and inner exploration, she returns to her family, having found a core of identity separate from her relationships with them. Tellingly, she has discovered that "the light that is the desire to please had gone out" (p. 269). The novel is also a chronicle of female accommodation with aging. Kate Brown, having discovered her authentic self, permits her once-dyed hair to return to its natural gray.

Margaret Drabble's *The Realms of Gold* (1975) is also an affirmative exploration of female mid-life. Frances Wingate, divorced and the mother of grown children, is a distinguished archeologist who discovers not only an important trade site in Saharan Africa but, figuratively, unexpected archeological layers and sites in her own personal life. One of the novel's several strands concerns Frances's conflict over whether to return to her married lover or to retain her personal independence. Drabble places her protagonist's successful life within a larger context of disturbing and tragic events: a family history of depression briefly darkens her life and, for a troubled nephew, culminates shockingly in suicide and infanticide. Indeed, for Drabble, as for the early Lessing, Mortimer, and Weldon, the interventions of chance and fate form a background of determinism against which their female characters struggle. The happy ending for which Frances Wingate is destined by an occasionally intrusive narrator may seem almost too "golden." Nonetheless, *The Realms of Gold* is noteworthy for its portrayal of a woman who, having overcome an entrapping family and a destructive marriage, feels herself a free agent in her emotional choices and intellectual endeavors; her success in the world, while aided by a degree of good fortune, is convincingly predicated on her own capabilities. Drabble's ruminations on time, death, and loss add depth to her female protagonist's excavations of her material and psychological past.

Drabble's *The Middle Ground* (1980) is of particular interest in the context of Virginia Woolf's wake, for a number of motifs and events in the narrative allude to *Mrs Dalloway* (Woolf 1925). In both novels, a middle-aged woman residing in London reminisces about the past and re-evaluates former relationships, including one with a person once quite close to her named Peter; several other characters figuratively "complete" her; at times she finds herself teetering on the edge of sanity; she is released from emotional stagnation through (among other things) an accident that happens to someone else; in preparation for a party she will host later on a particular day, she goes to a florist shop to buy flowers. (Of note, earlier in her career, Drabble published an essay acknowledging her debt to Virginia Woolf. See Drabble 1973). However, unlike Clarissa Dalloway, Kate Armstrong is an independent professional woman, a journalist who writes on women's issues, living in London a half century later.

A year before the narrative present, told in a flashback, the divorced Kate finds herself unexpectedly pregnant after her lover has left her. Approaching 40, with three nearly grown children, she agonizes over whether to allow the pregnancy to proceed, only to discover through amniocentesis that the fetus is severely deformed. The abortion and sterilization that she voluntarily but reluctantly undergoes haunt her. Though rationally she knows she made the right decision, emotionally she feels that "Maternity had been her passion, her primary passion in life, and she had been forced to deny it. . . . *Doing the right thing has destroyed me*" (1980: 211, emphasis in original). Although she recovers from that despairing view, she is compelled to acknowledge the end of her reproductive years, the end of her relationship with her lover, and the intrusion of chance and tragedy that she and her friends face as they reach "the middle years, caught between children and parents, free of neither" (p. 165).

While most of the novels considered thus far can be termed realistic, Angela Carter (1940–92) took the feminist novel in refreshing and innovative directions through her introduction of fantasy and postmodern narrative strategies. Looking back at the early years of feminism in her own life, she acknowledged the importance of her discovery that "femininity" was a "social fiction" and her desire to imagine "a 'new kind of being', unburdened with a past" (1983: 70, 74). Whether intentionally or not, Carter's *The Passion of New Eve* (1977) also imaginatively renders ideas articulated by two French feminists in 1975. Catherine Clément and Hélène Cixous challenged traditional ideas of the feminine, proposing the idea of *la jeune née* – the "newly born woman" – and arguing for the innate bisexuality of women. Although their collaborative views (published in English in 1986) were subsequently challenged as biologically reductive, their influential writings directed attention to the male bias of psychoanalysis and the instability of socially constructed ideas of gender.

The Passion of New Eve also follows explicitly in Virginia Woolf 's wake: like Woolf's Orlando (1928), Carter's Evelyn (a name of ambiguous gender) undergoes a radical gender metamorphosis. As he travels through a post-apocalyptic United States, he also journeys backwards through time into history and myth. In place of realistic characters, Carter populates her phantasmagoric narrative with exaggerated or parodied figures from classical and contemporary western mythology, ranging from Eve and the Great Mother Goddess to Hollywood screen goddesses. Ultimately Evelyn reaches Beulah – an imagined time and place in human history during which matriarchy flourished – and endures a violent "apprenticeship in womanhood" (1977: 107). Following an inverted rape by the Great Mother herself, he involuntarily undergoes "exemplary amputation" (p. 69) along with psychological "re-programming." Through Evelyn's painful metamorphosis into Eve, Carter satirizes the idea that "One is not born, but rather becomes, a woman" (Beauvoir 1952: 267). In an "anti-mythic" novel that she calls a "feminist tract about the social creation of femininity" (1983: 71), Carter imaginatively exposes the fault lines between biological sex identity and culturally constructed gender identity.

1980s: Deconstructions (Love, Marriage, Sexuality, Desire), Female Friendship, the History of Women, Postmodern Transformations (Fantastic and Grotesque)

In addition to her play with narrative reality through fantastic or magical realism, Angela Carter introduced to the feminist novel a Rabelaisian blend of the comic, the vulgar, and the grotesque. *Nights at the Circus* (1985), set at the turn of the twentieth century, features the larger-than-life Sophie Fevvers, a trapeze artist – and perhaps also a con artist – with wings. Or, rather, she *may* have wings; the narrative pivots on the impossibility of verification. Describing, and perhaps inventing, the key events of her biography to the enthralled American journalist, Jack Walser, Fevvers is another "new Eve," a woman who virtually constructs herself. After "hatching" from an egg like the mythical Helen, she spent her childhood in a brothel, sprouted wings at puberty, learned to fly, played the role of the Angel of Death in a chamber of horrors, and, repeatedly, narrowly escaped men who sought to possess a woman with wings.

While the unique Fevvers obviously commands power as both trapeze artist and Scheherazade-like storyteller, a number of secondary characters in *Nights at the Circus*, from the passive Mignon to other subordinated circus performers, exemplify female victimization in patriarchy. However, the often topsy-turvy world of the carnival is an arena in which all roles, including gender roles, become fluid. Even Jack Walser undergoes a comic shamanic initiation. Tracking multiple complications in Fevvers's and Walser's separate picaresque journeys, the narrative becomes even more exaggerated as it moves from London to St Petersburg. In the concluding comic reunion, Fevvers exults that she has "fooled" the once-skeptical Walser into believing that she is the "only fully feathered intacta in the history of the world" (Carter 1985: 294). Carter, winking at the reader as she deconstructs ideas of the feminine, the New Woman, and fictionality itself through her "Mae West with wings" (Haffendon 1985: 88), leaves unknowable what has fooled Walser: the authenticity of Fevvers's wings or of her virginity. For another example of the author's use of fantasy to explore feminist ideas, see *The Bloody Chamber* (1979), a collection of provocative revisions of traditional fairy tales. In her non-fictional work, *The Sadeian Woman and the Ideology of Pornography* (1978), Carter critiques the power men wield over women through exploitative sex.

Like Angela Carter, Jeanette Winterson (b. 1959) uses fantasy and postmodern narrative strategies to expose and subvert conventional assumptions about gender. In her first novel, *Oranges Are Not the Only Fruit* (1985), Winterson weaves biblical stories, myths, quest legends, fairy-tale narratives, and dream fantasies into her autobiographical account of her childhood and adolescence as the adopted daughter of working-class parents in the industrial Midlands. Through her mother's zealous Pentecostal evangelism, the character Jeanette discovers her spiritual calling. However, defying her mother's equation of sex with sin, Jeanette also discovers her sexuality through her passionate attraction to another girl, Melanie. Indeed, "sometimes women do like women" (Woolf 1989: 82).

Though Jeanette's lesbianism marks her, according to her mother and her Church, as one possessed by demons, an exorcism and other punitive efforts fail either to expunge the "demons" or to discourage her passionate attraction to others of her own sex. Demons and sorcerers both guide and mock Jeanette in her attempts to understand the "Great Struggle between good and evil" (Winterson 1985: 16) that seems to be expressed not only in the world but in her own body. In one fantastic dream sequence, she finds herself in the city of Lost Chances where, "if you've already made the Fundamental Mistake," you end up in the "Room of the Final Disappointment" (p. 111). In addition to alternate sexualities, Winterson explores alternate times and histories, expressing her character's theory that "every time you make an important choice, the part of you left behind continues the other life you could have had. . . . There's a chance that I'm not here at all, that all the parts of me, running along all the choices I did and didn't make, for a moment brush against each other" (p. 169). Moreover, the protagonist's name, duplicating the author's, complicates the boundaries between fiction and autobiography.

While Carter and Winterson stretch the possibilities of the novel form through their experiments with fantasy and magical realism, Pat Barker's *Union Street* (1982) and *Blow Your House Down* (1984) represent the other extreme, grim realism. However, like Winterson's first novel, Barker's first two novels focus on women whose experiences are typically absent from feminist novels: working-class women. *Union Street,* set in the industrial north of England, is a series of vignettes of the lives of seven women of different ages and circumstances, loosely linked through their residence in an economically depressed factory town. Like Fay Weldon in *Down among the Women*, Barker (b. 1943) chronicles women's difficult lot: a young girl's rape; women's unhappy marriages and unwanted pregnancies; menial employment; and degradations that stem from economic hardship.

In the moving final portrait in *Union Street,* the incapacitated 76-year-old Alice Bell struggles to maintain her independence and personal dignity, even as her son arranges for her admission to a nursing home. Reminiscing about her life, Alice finds her memories overwhelming. "These fragments. Were they the debris of her own or other lives? She had been so many women in her time" (Barker 1999b: 239). The girl who comes to greet her at the moment of death is one of those women: her own younger self. Her death is a lyrical epiphany that, like a number of other passages in Barker's narrative, illuminates and elevates an otherwise bleak life, "[s]o that in the end there were only the birds, soaring, swooping, gliding, moving in a never-ending spiral about the withered and unwithering tree" (1999b: 241). Barker's *Blow Your House Down* is a dark account of a community of working-class women with no education and few economic skills. As wives of abusive men or as single mothers, they find themselves driven to extreme choices, including prostitution, and are terrified by a serial rapist/murderer.

Several of Margaret Drabble's novels of the 1980s also focus centrally on affirmative bonds between women; coincidentally, two feature a serial killer. What distinguishes the trilogy – *The Radiant Way* (1987), *A Natural Curiosity* (1989), and *The Gates of Ivory* (1991) – is not the domestic and maternal preoccupations that characterize Drabble's earlier novels but its focus on successful professional women in mid-life. The richly textured narratives follow three women, whose friendships began during their years at Cambridge, through a cross-section of experiences that reflect life in late twentieth-century Britain and elsewhere. The divorced psychiatrist Liz Headleand discovers previously-unknown family members and travels in war-torn Cambodia in search of a missing friend. The happily married and socially committed teacher Alix Bowen is strangely fascinated with the grisly murder, and then with the psychotic murderer himself, of one of her troubled female students. The unmarried Esther Breuer pursues her aesthetic passion, Renaissance painting. Although the women's different interests lead them to dissimilar destinations, each novel concludes with a symbolic reunion: the women gather together to celebrate their sustaining friendship at (respectively) a birthday party in London, a picnic lunch in Italy, and a London memorial service for their friend who died in Cambodia. Drabble's trilogy ultimately affirms both the power of enduring friendships between women and the gratifications of mid-life.

Eva Figes's *The Seven Ages* (1986) stresses the bonds between women not only in contemporary life but throughout history. The voice of the central narrator, a contemporary midwife who reflects on her life in the healing profession upon her retirement in rural England, mingles with those of midwives whose experiences extend back nearly a millennium, to Britain's "dark ages." From their perspective, multiple pregnancies, often the result of rape, are women's inevitable destiny; the only form of childbirth is "natural" and many women are permanently injured or die during the birth process. The midwives rely on herbal balms, spells and charms, leeches, and – the core of Figes's imaginative history of women's culture – old wives' (midwives') tales: the stories and lore passed down from mother to daughter to soothe a woman during labor and distract her from pain. Closer to the present era, during the early years of struggle for women's suffrage, an enterprising woman invents the first birth-control device, the pessary (sponge). When one woman comments that "most of the women we knew had more use for a rubber pessary than having a vote," another responds, "why not have both?" (Figes 1986: 178).

Figes (b. 1932), who was born in Germany, is also the author of a highly-regarded history of the women's movement, *Patriarchal Attitudes* (1970). Several of her novels reveal her debt to Virginia Woolf's poetic language and narrative experimentation: *Days* (1974), *Waking* (1981), and *Light* (1983) express transient moments of consciousness and the flux of experience.

1990s: The Body and Desire (reprised), Sisterhood, the Coming of Age

In an influential and controversial essay, "The laugh of the Medusa" (1976), French feminist Hélène Cixous argues that women writers, rather than acceding to cultural assumptions about female sexuality rooted in patriarchal psychoanalytic theory, must exuberantly define their sexuality in their own terms; they must "write through their bodies" (Cixous 1981: 256). Jeanette Winterson's *Written on the Body* (1993) would seem to be a direct application of Cixous's exhortation. The narrator, whose gender identity is never revealed, repeatedly falls in love with married women. One woman in particular, Louise, inspires the deepest of passions. For several months, the two fulfill their erotic desires for each other, until Louise is diagnosed with leukemia; only her doctor husband's interventions can assure her appropriate treatment. The excluded lover, prompted by objective descriptions from an anatomy textbook, literally "writes through the body," offering a series of lyrical and erotic elegies to "the cells, tissues, systems and cavities" (Winterson 1993: 113) of the now-unattainable Louise. Meditating on her body, the narrator comments, "I dropped into the mass of you and cannot find the way out. . . . Myself in your skin, myself lodged in your bones, myself floating in the cavities that decorate every surgeon's wall. That is how I know you" (p. 120). Only through such intimate knowledge of the corporeal can the narrator reach the loved one's soul.

By the 1990s, it was possible to examine the evolution of both the theories and the practices of feminism. Fay Weldon's *Big Girls Don't Cry* (1997; published in Britain as *Big Women*) is a sardonic history of "sisterhood" and of the feminist movement in Britain from the 1970s through the 1990s, spiced with Weldon's characteristic satire. A core of five female characters represent different ideological branches of feminism, including the radical ideologue, Layla; the intellectual and theorist, Alice; the pragmatist, Steph; and the workhorse, Nancy: "four women who changed the world" (1997: 346). The fifth woman is the oppressed Zoe, who, despite her secret efforts to write what is clearly an autobiographical book on "the fate of the woman graduate: *Lost Women*" (p. 117), can only extricate herself from her unhappy marriage through suicide. The novel revisits early feminist consciousness-raising meetings, era-defining slogans such as "the personal is the political" (p. 41), and women's struggle during the early years of feminism to put theory into "praxis" (p. 28). As in many of Weldon's novels, what disrupts women's loyalties to one another is men. Early in the narrative, while most of the women are preoccupied with establishing a female publishing collective, suggestively named Medusa, one of them is upstairs in bed with another's husband. On the other hand, as Layla wryly observes, "If you can't have sex with a man and be a feminist, it's going to be a pretty small movement" (p. 164).

Two decades later, as the women of the collective celebrate the success of their enterprise and the profound influence of feminism on women's lives, the narrator offers the mellow conclusion that

> They had got things wrong, personally and politically, but who ever got everything right? . . . If the separatists had won over the socialists and the radicals, if young women everywhere assumed men were an optional extra . . . that too in time would shift and change, and become more merciful. Men are people too. Gender, like the state in Marxist aspiration, might in the end wither away, and be relevant only in bed and the approach to it, and the aftermath. There is no harm living in hope. (Weldon 1997: 338)

Finally, as writers of the first generation of the second wave of feminism have grown older, "the coming of age" (Beauvoir 1972) has moved to the narrative foreground. Among the novels that reflect, both positively and negatively, on female aging are Doris Lessing's *The Diary of a Good Neighbor* (1983), *If the Old Could . . .* (1984), and *Love, Again* (1996). The protagonist of the last novel, Sarah Durham, is an unattached professional scriptwriter in her mid-sixties. Though she has not been in a man's arms since her husband's death twenty years earlier, during her involvement in the production of a new opera, she finds herself sexually attracted to men young enough to be her sons. As Sarah laments the discrepancies between her youthful inner image and her reflection in the mirror, Lessing registers the powerful social conditioning that dictates the trajectory of female aging, including cultural assumptions about older women as asexual, emotionally desiccated beings.

In an uncharacteristically optimistic view of the same subject, Fay Weldon makes the protagonist of *Rhode Island Blues* (2000) an octogenarian. As revealed through narrative flashbacks, 83-year-old Felicity Moore, the widowed or divorced veteran of three unhappy marriages, has lived an unintentionally adventurous life; currently, she feels that her future holds few appealing options. Following conventional expectations for women of her age and circumstance, she sells her house and moves to a retirement/ nursing home. However, unlike most of its residents, Felicity is far from "elderly" in either behavior or attitude. Finding herself attracted to a man eleven years her junior, she worries about her suitor's motives, even as – in the habit of a younger woman – she purchases cosmetics and lingerie to make herself appear more attractive. The most delicately realized dimension of Weldon's elder-fairy tale is her treatment of sexuality, which she renders with both sensitivity and genial humor. Felicity concedes that "as you got older desire presented itself in a different form . . . as a restless sense of dissatisfaction, which out of sheer habit you had the feeling only physical sex would cure. It was generated in the head, not the loins, the latter these days admittedly a little dried up, and liable to chafing rather than the general luscious overflowing which had characterized their prime" (Weldon 2000: 108).

Felicity Moore is a rare character in the feminist novel: a woman who, despite her advanced age, not only asserts that "she did miss being in love" (p. 108) but who emphatically resists cultural assumptions about older women's (and men's) physical and emotional diminution. As Felicity's surprised granddaughter observes, "One tends to write off women in their mid-eighties as simply hanging around until death carries them away. One is wrong" (p. 140). By the novel's end, Felicity is on the verge of a secret escape from the retirement home and elopement with her younger suitor.

Conclusion

Since the mid-twentieth century, feminist novels have expressed two divergent though often overlapping perspectives: critiques of the confining circumstances of women's lives in patriarchy before feminism; and celebrations of the increasing potentialities for the growth, self-discovery, and full humanity that feminism has made possible. However, these novels are not simply sociological treatises but richly imagined, and often formally innovative, renderings of female experience. Their artistry – nuances of style, characterization, point of view, dialogue, humor, satire, and narrative design – merits considerably more analysis and commentary than space permits here.

In 1929 Virginia Woolf, anticipating the endeavors of future women writers, speculated in *A Room of One's Own* that "if we have the habit of freedom and the courage to write exactly what we think . . . the dead poet who was Shakespeare's sister will put on the body which she has so often laid down. Drawing her life from the lives of the unknown who were her forerunners ... she will be born" (1989: 114). As is demonstrated by the many fine novels that have been published in Woolf's wake, Judith Shakespeare is most certainly alive – and flourishing.

References and Further Reading

Barker, Pat (1999a) [1984] *Blow Your House Down*. New York: Picador.

——(1999b) [1982] *Union Street*. New York: Picador.

Beauvoir, Simone de (1952) *The Second Sex*, trans. H. M. Parshley. New York: Alfred A. Knopf. (First published in French as *Le Deuxième Sexe* in 1949).

——(1972) *The Coming of Age*, trans. Patrick O'Brien. New York: Putnam. (First published in French as *La Vieillesse* in 1970).

Byatt, A. S. (1979) "A. S. Byatt on the Booker shortlist," *The Literary Review* (Edinburgh) November: 10–11.

Carter, Angela (1978) *The Sadeian Woman and the Ideology of Pornography*. New York: Pantheon Books.

——(1979) *The Bloody Chamber*. New York: Harper and Row.

——(1982) *The Passion of New Eve*. London: Virago.

——(1983) "Notes from the front line," in Michelene Wandor (ed.) *On Women and Writing*. London: Pandora.

——(1985) *Nights at the Circus*. New York: Viking.

Cixous, Hélène (1981) "The laugh of the Medusa," trans. Keith Cohen and Paula Cohen, in Elaine Marks and Isabelle de Courtivron (eds.) *New French Feminisms*. New York: Schocken. (First published in French as *Le Rire de la méduse* in 1975).

Clément, Catherine and Cixous, Hélène (1986) *The Newly Born Woman*, trans. Betsy Wing. Minneapolis: University of Minnesota Press. (First published in French as *La Jeune Née* in 1975).

Creighton, Joanne V. (1985) *Margaret Drabble*. London: Methuen.

Drabble, Margaret (1967) *Jerusalem the Golden*. New York: William Morrow.

——(1969) *The Waterfall*. London: Weidenfeld and Nicolson.

——(1973) *Virginia Woolf: A Personal Debt*. New York: Aloe Editions. (Originally "How not to be afraid of Virginia Woolf," *Ms.* magazine, 1 (November 1972): 68–70, 71, 121).

——(1975) *The Realms of Gold*. New York: Alfred A. Knopf.

——(1980) *The Middle Ground*. New York: Alfred A. Knopf.

——(1981a) [1963] *A Summer Bird-Cage*. Harmondsworth: Penguin.

——(1981b) [1964] *The Garrick Year*. Harmondsworth: Penguin.

——(1981c) [1965] *The Millstone*. Harmondsworth: Penguin.

——(1987) *The Radiant Way*. New York: Alfred A. Knopf.

——(1989) *A Natural Curiosity*. New York: Viking.

——(1992) [1991] *The Gates of Ivory*. New York: Viking.

Emecheta, Buchi (1994) [1974] *Second-Class Citizen*. Oxford: Heinemann.

Figes, Eva (1970) *Patriarchal Attitudes*. New York: Stein and Day.

——(1974) *Days*. London: Faber and Faber.

——(1981) *Waking*. New York: Pantheon.

——(1983) *Light*. New York: Pantheon.

——(1986) *The Seven Ages*. New York: Pantheon.

Friedan, Betty (1964) [1963] *The Feminine Mystique*. New York: Dell.

Haffendon, John (1985) "Angela Carter," in *Novelists in Interview*. London and New York: Methuen.

Howe, Florence (1974) [1966] "A conversation with Doris Lessing," in Annis Pratt and L. S. Dembo (eds.) *Doris Lessing: Critical Studies*. Madison: University of Wisconsin Press.

Kenyon, Olga (1988) *Women Novelists Today*. New York: St Martin's Press.

——(1990) [1989] *Women Writers Talk: Interviews with 10 Women Writers*. New York: Carroll and Graf.

Kumar, Mina (1995) Interview with Fay Weldon, *Belles Lettres*, 10/2 (Spring): 16–18.

Lessing, Doris (1962) *The Golden Notebook*. New York: Simon and Schuster.

——(1964a) [1954] *A Proper Marriage*. New York: Simon and Schuster.

——(1964b) [1952] *Martha Quest*. New York: Simon and Schuster.

——(1966a) [1958] *A Ripple from the Storm*. New York: Simon and Schuster.

——(1966b) [1965] *Landlocked*. New York: Simon and Schuster.

——(1969) *The Four-Gated City*. New York: Alfred A. Knopf.

——(1973) *The Summer before the Dark*. New York: Alfred A. Knopf.

——(as Jane Somers) (1983) *The Diary of a Good Neighbor*. New York: Alfred A. Knopf.

——(as Jane Somers) (1984) *If the Old Could...* New York: Alfred A. Knopf.

——(1996). *Love, Again*. New York: Harper Collins.

Mortimer, Penelope (1959) *Cave of Ice*. New York: Harcourt Brace.

——(1962) *The Pumpkin Eater*. New York: McGraw Hill.

O'Brien, Edna (1981) *Virginia: A Play*. New York: Harcourt Brace Jovanovich.

——(1986a) [1960] *The Country Girls*. London: Weidenfeld and Nicolson.

——(1986b) [1962] *The Lonely Girl*. London: Weidenfeld and Nicolson.

——(1986c) [1964] *Girls in their Married Bliss*. New York: Random House.

——(1986d) *The Country Girls Trilogy and Epilogue*. New York: Farrar Straus Giroux.

Weldon, Fay (1973) [1971] *Down Among the Women*. Harmondsworth: Penguin.

——(1976) *Remember Me*. New York: Random House.

——(1977) *Words of Advice*. New York: Random House.

——(1980) *Puffball*. New York: Summit Books.

——(1983) *The Life and Loves of a She-Devil*. New York: Pantheon.

——(1986) [1967] *The Fat Woman's Joke*. Chicago: Academy Chicago Publishers.

——(1988) [1974] *Female Friends*. Chicago: Academy Chicago Publishers.

——(1990) [1978] *Praxis*. Harmondsworth: Penguin.

——(1997. *Big Girls Don't Cry*. New York: Atlantic Monthly Press. (Published in UK as *Big Women*. London: Flamingo).

——(2000) *Rhode Island Blues*. New York: Atlantic Monthly Press.

Winterson, Jeanette (1985) *Oranges Are Not the Only Fruit*. New York: Atlantic Monthly Press.

——(1993) *Written on the Body*. New York: Alfred A. Knopf.

Woolf, Virginia (1953) [1925] *Mrs Dalloway*. New York: Harcourt.

——(1956) [1928] *Orlando*. New York: Harcourt.

——(1989) [1929] *A Room of One's Own*. New York: Harcourt.

5

Postmodern Fiction and the Rise of Critical Theory

Patricia Waugh

Jean-François Lyotard's elegy on modernity, *The Postmodern Condition,* appeared in English in 1984. The book effectively declared the end of that idea of nature (as a rationally intelligible structure whose truths might provide the grounds for all those grand and utopian narratives of historical emancipation and the discovery of a perfect order of natural justice) that had come to be associated with Enlightenment thought. For Lyotard, "postmodernity is not a new age, but the rewriting of some of the features claimed by modernity, and first of all modernity's claim to ground its legitimacy on the project of liberating humanity as a whole through science and technology." The goal of theory for Lyotard must be that of exposing the inability of realist science to legitimate itself within the terms of positivist reductionism; it would be achieved by revealing how that legitimation is always finally dependent upon a narrative imagination, a *mythos*, which is also now defunct in its grand form of a narrative of the Laws of Nature. In a post-industrial world, which has seen the erosion of customary knowledge as an overarching mythic framework, the grand narrative has lost its credibility and there are only contestatory and agonistic little narratives left to play with; we have even, he says, lost the nostalgia for the lost narrative, the grand teleological picture of Nature that might sanction and orient our purposes and values. Even before the publication of Lyotard's era-defining work, however, it was evident that the shift from the ideal of a common culture to a more fractured, pluralistic, and multicultural society had already deeply eroded the postwar cultural consensus and had produced an increasingly relativized account of cultural values. The philosophical, cultural, and political instability of the contemporary world, and the difficulty of knowing it, would become intense theoretical preoccupations from the seventies onwards.

Certainly a postmodern kind of "mood" began to gather in all advanced Western European cultures from the sixties on, when two sets of changes coincided: cultural changes (the emergence of post-industrialization; increased technologization; expanding consumerism; widening democracy, and the proliferation of subcultures;

globalization and the boom in information technologies; new bio-technologies and the development of molecular biology and genetics; the retreat from both colonialism and utopianism in politics and the rise of new identity or micro-political movements) with changes in literary and artistic expression and an intensified "linguistic turn" in intellectual thought; this produced significant critiques firstly of the western meta-physical tradition and subsequently of the positivistic credentials of modern science. Modernism had been preoccupied with a perceived tension between the desire for a narrative transcendence, which might arrive at truth, and the suspicion that the inventions of fiction might be the only source of redemption in a world that is ultimately a chaos of sensation. For the postmodern sensibility, however, it seems virtually impossible in any discourse – aesthetic, philosophical, or scientific – to move beyond and outside our linguistic instruments of interrogation in order to make contact with a reality that exists beyond construction or projection. Fiction is all. Even the consciousness of imprisonment in a language game can never arrive at any certainty about its condition, for such a statement would constitute an attempt to confer an illegitimate decidability and to ignore the *aporia* of self-referential paradox.

As Samuel Beckett had anticipated in the last book of his trilogy, the world, indeed, had begun to seem unnameable. Ihab Hassan, an important early commen-tator on postmodernism, saw it as a vast unmaking of the western mind. Closure is not only impossible but is even a mark of the totalitarian: indeterminacy, deferral, and dissensus are the new signifiers of pluralistic and multicultural liberal democracies. Such cultural relativisms were increasingly supplemented from the early seventies by a pervasive and growing epistemological relativism developing within the academy and associated specifically with the rise of "theory" within literature departments. The sustained and skeptically relativist critiques of philosophical foundationalism in the work of theorists such as Jacques Derrida, Michel Foucault, Roland Barthes and, more specifically, of modern realist science and positivism in those of Lyotard, would then feed back dialectically into an increasingly "inward turn" in fiction: a contestation and interrogation of the conventions and claims of representation – that language might bear a truthfully descriptive relation to the world – which had underpinned the mimetic assumptions of realism. Modern literary theory initially took hold in the British academy as a reaction against what it regarded as "expressive realism": a broadly mimetic view that language delivers up truths about life and the human condition, and of reality as a coherent whole standing behind its formulation in words. Fictional realism comes to be seen as a discursive mode in which there is an attempt to impose on the text this kind of illusory consensus about the real by suppressing and disguising the contradictions or *aporias* opened up in all discourses by the metaphoric and differential nature of a language that can finally never command the subject matter it purports to represent. Theorists, however, recognized that their own discourses must inevitably partake of similar blindnesses and that there is a performative contradiction built into the very attempt to demonstrate that all language misrepresents and, in describing the real, must inevitably go astray. Indeed, the very concept of postmodernism is subject to this kind of circularity, for much more so than modernism, it has always been a cultural phenomenon created as much through academic theory as through actual literary and aesthetic practices.

Theorists themselves often seem to want to claim both creative and scientific credentials. Fredric Jameson has argued that "theory" in this sense is itself simply one more manifestation of the postmodern as the cultural logic of late capitalism, but in so doing he is of course implicitly claiming for himself the "scientific" legitimation of a Marxian economic reading. Theory like fiction, therefore, has had to keep avowing its resistance to theory. The word "theory" implies an authoritative metalinguistic relation to the literary text, criticism as a kind of science, but the preoccupation with the impossibility of naming or asserting propositional truth seems to bring theory closer to the epistemological status of fiction. In Jameson's reading, all postmodern discourses are caught in a flight from propositional truth, foundations or origins, affirmative content or closure, and show a pronounced preference for modes of self-reference, indeterminacy, undecidability, and intertextual excess as a repudiation of the autonomy of the individual text or subject or author. As he puts it:

> the crucial feature of what we have called a theoretical aesthetic lies in its organisation around this particular taboo, which excludes the philosophic proposition as such, and thereby statements about being as well as judgements about truth. (Jameson 1991: 392)

The theoretical turn seemed to bring criticism and creative writing into closer proximity. One effect of this has been to elevate the status of the theorized literary critic to that of a creative author. Creativity is then seen to lie in a linguistic and intertextual playfulness designed to disparage and displace traditional or Romantic ideas of authorial expressivity by actually borrowing the rhetorical strategies of the literary author. This occurs just at the moment when metafictional self-consciousness in the novel appeared to be relegating the literary text to an introverted critical commentary on itself. Novelists and theorists alike seem to share a mutual anxiety of influence, and from Muriel Spark to John Fowles, Julian Barnes to Martin Amis, Margaret Drabble to Doris Lessing, there are few novelists from the seventies onward whose work does not reveal, in a variety of ways, a self-conscious anxiety about the authority and ontological status of the authorial voice of the novelist.

For contemporary theory has also demonstrated a concomitant desire to arrogate to itself the authority and legitimation of science as the dominant paradigm of knowledge in the western world. The "theoretical revolution" began with a professionalized assertion of the objectivity of criticism; the various formalisms and structuralisms of the sixties were attempts to establish a scientific poetics in an academy where, increasingly and *pace* C. P. Snow, the paradigms of knowledge and research were led by the hard sciences. Theory implicitly claims to be more than speculation or hypothesis, regards itself as in some way analytic, but certainly not subject to the same degree of verificationist or falsificationist rigor, of testing and inference and formulation of laws, assumed in the development of any scientific theory. Indeed, one aim of "theory" is to draw out the contradictions at play in any supposed analytic proof or scientific demonstration, so that its playfulness and aestheticization is in the service of a greater claim to knowingness that there simply cannot be any secure knowledge. Theory plays back and forth between science and fiction. So Lyotard legitimates his critique of scientific legitimation by hauling in Heisenberg, Gödel, and Neils Bohr as new scientific authorities, to imply that his vision of radical indeterminacy, undecidability and uncertainty is authenticated and underpinned by the very latest sciences. It seems no coincidence that the year Crick and Watson described DNA as a writing, a code that carries the genetic information, Barthes published his *Writing Degree Zero,* which also called for a new materiality of writing. Later he would claim that meaning comes not from the antecedent intentionality of an author but from a play of intertextualities, a writing that writes, a figure that insistently becomes its own ground, so that it is "language that speaks and not the author" (Barthes 1977: 143). A decade later Richard Dawkins would also announce that "what lies at the heart of every living being is not fire, not a warm breath, not a spark of life. It is information, words, instruction" (Dawkins 1986: 12). By the eighties, the scriptoral metaphor played back and forth in Borgesian fashion between novelists, scientists, and literary theorists. Virtual realities, artificial intelligence, digital life, bodies that are written, and cyborg post-humans seem to spring up everywhere in fictional and theoretical discourses alike.

Turning specifically to the novel in the period, it would certainly seem to display all of the preoccupations and motifs of theory: labyrinths, mirrors, architexts, Chinese boxes, *mise-en-abyme* effects; contested worlds and disruptions of ontologies; authors becoming characters in their own fictions and characters trying to break out of their scripts; historical personages wandering into fantastic worlds; space fragmenting or shrinking; and time running in reverse. These are the fictional equivalents of such theoretical and cultural preoccupations. Novelists such as Muriel Spark, Doris Lessing, John Fowles, Angela Carter, Alisdair Gray, Martin Amis, Fay Weldon, and Ian McEwan had for some time before 1984 shown an experimental interest in a range of self-referential aesthetic practices involving playful irony, parody, parataxis, nestings and framings, self-consciousness, and the mixing and meshing of high and popular culture. Yet for the most part, the British and Irish novel has resisted the more exuberant textual playfulness or, indeed, apocalypticism and paranoia, of its American counterpart, as it has similarly disdained (with a few exceptions such as the writing of Christine Brooke-Rose) the rather more austere verbal experimentation of the French nouveau roman. This may account for the academic perception of the British novel of the seventies as stagnant and backward-looking and for the critical tendency to privilege novelists such as Angela Carter and Salman Rushdie, for example, who more explicitly engage with postmodern and poststructuralist ideas.

However, it may be that one unfortunate consequence of the popularization of theory and the dissemination of reductive versions of postmodernism has been the neglect of novelists whose experimentation has operated through an attempt to negotiate theoretical ideas through the framework of a contested empiricism. Such writers demonstrate an ongoing attachment to both the realist tradition in fiction and an indigenous British tradition of philosophically-rooted moral and cultural critique. Postmodern theory, as a view from everywhere, has tended to ignore the specificity and particularity of expressions of the postmodern as they emerge from and are situated in indigenous intellectual and cultural traditions (ironically so, given its insistence on the local and the situated and the particularity of language games). Academic critical commentary on fiction in the seventies and eighties largely ignored the specifically British historical and intellectual contexts of the novel, and drew its inspiration either from accounts of the postmodern in writing by American cultural commentators such as John Barth, Susan Sontag, Ihab Hassan, or Leslie Fiedler, or turned to continental intellectual traditions for philosophical and political orientation.

Continental theory seemed much more excitingly radical and in tune with the apocalypticism of a new generation of intellectuals retreating from Marxism, recovering from utopianism, and confronting the regeneration of neoliberal and monetarist economics, breakdown in political and cultural consensus, the emergence of new political identities, and of a new technologically driven information culture. But British novelists on the whole responded somewhat cautiously to the contemporary theoretical turn by assimilating continental versions of textual self-referentiality and social constructionism into an indigenous fictional tradition. There realism has largely tempered romance, and ethical commitment has often allied itself with a broadly empiricist tradition surviving into the twentieth century and still perceptible in novelists as different as Virginia Woolf (with her Bloomsbury affiliations with Moore and Russell's Cambridge realism) and George Orwell (whose work continuously makes a connection between the "theory" of intellectuals and a misplaced faith in abstract argument, which is ultimately complicit with totalitarianism). This fictional orientation has meshed with a mainstream intellectual tradition broadly liberal in ethos; concerned with moral considerations and the ongoing need for contracts protecting human rights; and requiring the belief that being reasonable requires assertions to be supported by verifiable evidence that is not simply the property of a particular language game or cultural group, but is, as far as possible, universalizable and applicable to all human beings. It is a tradition that has always been skeptical about rationalistic grand narratives. As far back as Orwell's journalistic essays or Wittgenstein's "turn" towards the end of the *Tractatus*, this tradition of writers already preferred to do its social theorizing in a piecemeal and tentative fashion through "ordinary language" or fiction, rather than through grand theory and technical vocabularies, jargon, neologism, and global pronouncement.

In the British context, then, even overtly experimental novelists have usually conducted their textual playfulness in tension with an underlying if conflicted attachment to an attenuated realism. B. S. Johnson, for example, one of the most formally experimental British novelists of the mid-sixties to seventies, seems to have waged a metafictional war against a philosophically textualist anti-realism by producing a series of novels between 1963 and 1973 committed to an almost Platonic insistence that "telling stories is telling lies." His work oscillates between darkly humorous and ultimately nihilistic fictions which advertise their fictionality as a badge of "truth" and a refusal of the consolations of lying, and a bleak autobiographical confessionalism whose abandonment of formal containment self-consciously insists on the random moral indifference of material being. (*The Unfortunates* (1969), for example, was presented loose-leaf in a box decorated with enlarged photographic images of cancer cells.) Realism is engaged in his adherence to an empiricist episte-mology and rebuked in the intensity of his ethical nihilism. The position can be traced back to the post-Humean argument developed in T. H. Huxley's "Evolution and ethics," or to G. E. Moore's repudiation of the naturalistic fallacy in his *Principia Ethica* of 1903, and in the later more emphatic logical positivist separation of facts and values. It is the problem of how to come to terms with a scientific realism that builds a picture of physical Nature entirely unable to legislate for, or sanction, human purposes or ends. The problem haunts British modernism from Hardy through Conrad, Lawrence, and Woolf, and is in many ways resolutely at odds with the rationalisms of the French tradition or the German tradition of Romantic Idealism, or even the pragmatism of American thought, whose legacies would resonate throughout the so-called "theory" revolution from the seventies onward. Indeed, twentieth-century English criticism was itself established as a professionalized aca-demic discipline within the terms of this empiricist tradition with the founding of the Cambridge School of English under the aegis of I. A. Richards. He was a former pupil and protégé of Moore, who developed the first rigorously formalist criticism in Britain. Richards famously proclaimed that in an age of mass culture and scientific rationalization only the arts might be our storehouse of recorded values. Literature could not, like science, make claims to knowledge, consisting only of pseudo-statements which did not refer to or hook up with the world; but as a formally orchestrated discourse offering a unique experience of value in its capacity to release and order psychic and emotional energy, literature for Richards was badly in need of a formally rigorous and scientific criticism.

F. R. Leavis would then develop his own version of the argument that literature was a vital source of cultural value in a utilitarian and technologically-driven age, but with the important difference that, for him, values are an intrinsic aspect of the human relation to *knowledge*. Leavis shaped a view of literature, in contradistinction to that of the prevailing positivist perception, as vital to culture as a source of value precisely because it offers an alternative and more important kind of knowledge than that of science. The struggle with positivism has helped to shape a mainstream intellectual tradition in Britain, which had for long been engaged not so much with the repudiation of metaphysical truth (the focus of logical positivism), nor even with the undermining of scientific truth, but with the desire to reclaim from positivism the possibility that there are different kinds of knowledge and that fiction possesses its own kind of cognitive persuasiveness. This is an ability to imagine and offer the vicarious experience of being subjectively situated in other worlds and other minds and simultaneously to offer a more impersonal reflection upon the world and that experience as a necessary prelude to informed ethical judgment. For Leavis, literary experience preserves and makes possible a collaborative form of knowledge, neither subjective nor objective, neither verifiable nor purely private. Human knowledge arises out of a fundamentally tacit and already value-laden understanding of the world that precedes the explicit knowledge offered by science or philosophy. Such knowledge is most adequately preserved in great works of literature and most adequately defended by the trained and professional literary critic.

Given its empiricist orientation, the ongoing engagement, positive or negative, with the positivist legacy has been more central to British intellectual culture. It is evidenced in the early sixties, for example, in the infamous and ill-tempered "two cultures" debate between F. R. Leavis and C. P. Snow, and has helped to shape important political movements such as the New Left, and to provide a context for the reception of theory which was always oriented to the culturally materialist and towards an ethical and political liberal communitarianism. Writers such as Iris Murdoch, William Golding, Doris Lessing, and John Fowles, for example, both anticipate and reflect the preoccupations of high theory; but if we are to understand their work it needs to be contextualised within this somewhat differently inflected intellectual culture. And the same is true for the later generation of innovative novelists such as Kazuo Ishiguro, Martin Amis, Ian McEwan, Graham Swift, Margaret Drabble, and A. S. Byatt.

One could argue, however, that the assimilation of theory into Britain was very much shaped by the desire to abandon as parochial the prevailing tradition of *Kulturkritik* in its Leavisian mode. The repudiation of this kind of expressive realism became an abiding concern in a way that introduced a marked dissociation between the culture of academics and the broader culture outside the academy: in the seventies, it produced something of a stand-off between novelists and academic critics. Writing in 1980, the literary theorist Catherine Belsey, for example, described the dominant ideology of letters as "empiricist-realist" and characterized it as a view where

> common sense urges that "man" is the origin and source of meaning, of action and of history (humanism). Our concepts and our knowledge are held to be the product of experience (empiricism) and this experience is preceded and interpreted by the mind, reason or thought, the property of a transcendent human nature whose essence is the attribute of each individual (empiricism). (Belsey 1980: 7)

In this view, the grounding assumptions of humanism presuppose that experience is prior to language and language is conceived merely as a tool to express the way that experience is felt and interpreted by the unique individual. Literature is then the expression of gifted individuals who are able to capture elusive but universal truths of human nature through the sensuous crafting of words. Modern literary theory – structuralism, poststructuralism, feminism, New Historicism, deconstruction, post-colonialism, postmodernism – thus embarks upon the task of overcoming and displacing such assumptions. The recovery of the work of the Swiss linguist Ferdinand de Saussure was instrumental in the early theoretical critique of realism, substituting a constructivist and conventionalist account of language which rejects the notion that language simply "names" the world in any correspondent fashion, and insisting that language is a system of difference where any one term only has meaning by virtue of its differential place within the system of language as a whole.

Read alongside the work of Karl Marx, for whom it is the underlying system of economic and social relations that conditions the forms of culture, and incorporating the Freudian account of unconscious desire as a primary process logic which undoes and subverts the possibility of self-knowledge, this reading of Saussure began to unravel assumptions about authorial intention, autonomous subjectivity, the possibility of knowledge, and the idea of pure or non-ideological value. If it is impossible to move beyond and outside of our instruments of interrogation (primarily language); if knowledge is always situated and unstable and if there can be no perfect account of justice or account of the "good" deriving from a secure epistemological foundation, then it would seem that the Enlightenment and humanist discourses of knowledge, emancipation, and universal justice are no longer defensible. We are caught within incommensuarable language games only ever offering a knowledge of the world relative to the scope of their conceptual frameworks, but we delude ourselves by positing transcendental origins which might provide a position outside of and therefore able to ground and encompass our various discourses. For modern literary theorists, there has for too long been a naive and "logocentric" faith in the capacity of language to mirror nature and a deluded belief that the meaning of the word somehow has its origin in the nature of the real and can therefore reflect its structures in the mind as a "metaphysics of presence." Now we can see that truth is a kind of fiction, reality also an appearance, depth only ever another surface, history an endless regress of texts, and reading always a mode of misreading. We inhabit not the real, but always our representations of it.

By the 1970s, the theoretical assault on metalinguistic foundations was developed into the postmodern insistence that objects of knowledge are not so much entities on which language reflects as artifacts actually constructed through and within language. In such a condition, fiction, as a world-creating activity, inevitably takes a turn towards philosophical self-interrogation of its own epistemological and ontological status, and philosophy and criticism as metalinguistic discourses have to confront the demise of any secure claim to objectivity or validity in interpretation or evaluation. For if language no longer refers to a realm that is independent of language, then any attempt to stand outside, and to offer critique, of a particular cultural or philosophical perspective, is no longer simply to offer a different version of the world but actually to construct a wholly alternative one. Each "world" becomes a construction only comprehensible within its own terms for, if there is no independent reality against which to compare the perspectives, each becomes a discrete language game and it is no longer possible to determine the validity of any claim independently of the cultural or linguistic context in which it is made. As Beckett's unnameable had put it, some twenty or so years before the rise of theory: "speak of a world of my own, sometimes referred to as the inner, without choking. Doubt no more. Seek no more" (Beckett 1959: 394).

Accordingly, novelists begin to experiment, for example, with effects of infinite regress: Beckett's narrators endlessly telling themselves stories that are made to correspond, through their own conceptualizations, with the apparent structure of their lives, which itself turns out to be simply the story they are narrating. Or they may transgress ontological levels between story and discourse as in Fowles's *The French Lieutenant's Woman*, which pastiches the style of numerous Victorian novels through the discourse of an author who sometimes appears in the novel as a character, sometimes uses and abuses the omniscience of the implied author of realism, and sometimes personalizes himself as a narrative construction of the post-Barthesian age of authorial death. Sometimes novels play metafictionally on the contradictions of a metaphysics of presence, as in Muriel Spark's first novel, *The Comforters* (1957), where the grossly physical and morally self-righteous but hypocritical Mrs Hogg, described by another character as "not all there," simply vanishes from the text, enforcing an ethical point about those whose private lives do not match their publicly professed moralities, and an ontological point about the status of fictional objects as linguistic constructions. As a minor character in the plot, Mrs Hogg does indeed disappear when the discourse no longer requires her presence. In *The Driver's Seat* (1968) too, Lise sustains the plot momentum in her search for a man who will murder her, describing this as yet unknown man as "not really a presence, the lack of an absence." And in his story "The enigma" in *The Ebony Tower* (1974), Fowles plays on the textual possibilities of the missing person motif of traditional detective fiction, refusing to resolve the mystery, in order to allow his character freedom, for if "he's traced, found, then it all crumbles again. He's back in a story, being written"; Fielding only exists if he is not "traced," but only exists as the effect of a linguistic trace. Fictional statements exist and have their "truths" within a fictional world that is also created by the fictional statement: everything that is described is simultaneously created. And yet such worlds can never be autonomous: they are endlessly caught in a web of intertextualities.

There are plenty of examples of such overtly self-referential play to be found in British fiction, even before the academic dissemination of continental theory in the seventies, and they seem to suggest a compatibility of concern. But the immediate cultural context for the novelistic metafictional turn in British writing of the sixties and seventies also grew out of a pervasive concern with the overextension of the positivist paradigm of knowledge evident in a culture which seemed to have become obsessed with managerialism, cultural planning, and social rationalization. This version of the critique of method, however, was equally concerned to resist the countercultural retreat from reason that appeared in the decade of the sixties. The first generation of experimental writers who reached maturity in the sixties and early seventies, including Murdoch, Spark, Golding, and Fowles, had grown up during the Second World War and, after Nazism, it seemed evident to them that the projection of Promethean desire beyond the controlled realm of art had, as often as not, realized a hell of violence rather than an aestheticized utopia. In a desacrilized society, aesthetic vision may seem liberating but in fact may represent a potentially and powerfully destructive force. The countercultural and situationist slogan of taking one's desires for reality, even more than the technocratic state, could be seen to invest in a potentially destructive aestheticization of experience. There was therefore already an inbuilt indigenous resistance to the later and stronger postmodern aestheticization of the real, which reflects both the prevailing tradition of empiricism in Britain and a differently inflected tradition of *Kulturkritik* and liberal and radical dissidence. Novelists of this period were more preoccupied with self-consciously *differentiating* between the identifiable and intentional fictions of the artistic imagination and those epistemologically distinct orders in the world beyond art, so the metafictional turn usually remained the ethical tool of an epistemological interrogation rather than an indiscriminate ontological pluralization and relativization of worlds.

Novelists remained within the frame of Popperian empiricism and anti-utopianism, with its commitment to piecemeal and empirically grounded social change. Popper's work provided a powerful critique of metaphysical thinking as a dangerous pseudo-science, where an aesthetic design betraying the desire for a perfect order is presented under the mantle of a rationalist metaphysics masquerading as "science." As art is not open to the kind of disconfirmation or proof required in scientific thought, such aesthetic narratives, presented as the laws of history, are projected on to and disseminated through the real with disastrous consequences. The temper of the decade was more inclined toward the careful discrimination of varieties of fictionality. This weaker mode of postmodern engagement shares with the stronger modes the recognition that science does project models on to the world and that there is finally no way of getting outside of the model to check its correspondence: there is always an ironic gap between language and the world. But recognition of the gap need not bring everything to a condition of indiscriminate fictionality. In a pure fiction there is no gap between the world and its representation because the world is entirely textual and representational. Ironic awareness of narrative in the framing of scientific or historical accounts is not the same as saying that scientific or historical knowledge is always just another story and that there is no distinction to be made at all between invention and discovery, fiction and truth.

Novelists of the time (for example, Muriel Spark in *The Prime of Miss Jean Brodie*, *The Abbess of Crewe*, or *Not to Disturb*; Iris Murdoch in *A Fairly Honourable Defeat*, *The Black Prince*, or *The Sea, The Sea*; John Fowles in *The French Lieutenant's Woman*, *The Magus*, and *Daniel Martin*; William Golding in *Free Fall* and *Darkness Visible*) explore the ways in which indiscriminate aestheticization facilitates playing God with the real. Novels such as *The Prime of Miss Jean Brodie* (1961) and Murdoch's *A Severed Head* (1961), ostensibly about trivial love affairs, charismatic schoolmistresses, and the adulterous deceptions of the high bourgeoisie, are also studies of the psychological and myth-making imperatives of power politics and totalitarianism. Jorge Luis Borges' story "Tlön, Uqbar, Orbis, Tertius" in the collection *Labyrinths* (1962) was an influential fictional parable that explicitly addressed such concerns. In the story, the imaginary and ideal world of Tlön, a cosmos brought into existence by the conjunction of an encyclopedia (knowledge) and a mirror (narcissistic desire), is figured metafictionally as an aesthetic world that has seeped outside the covers of the book. Tlön is a fantastic cosmos, an idealist fiction that has infiltrated the historical world, its imaginary orders becoming indistinguishable from empirical fact. Borges explicitly relates his parable to the rise of National Socialism; the desire for the submission of the historical world to the perfect order of Tlön is seen to reflect our dangerous yearning for a metaphysical order read as the scientific laws of nature from which we might infer our human values. The story can be read as a paradigmatic Popperian fable about the necessity for discrimination of knowledges and orders of being and, although Borges is regarded as a key postmodern figure whose work is often read through the stronger versions of textualism and fictionality, his metafictional techniques are ultimately in the service of a desire to hold on to an Enlightenment insistence on reason and discrimination.

For metafictional strategies serve an important ethical function in a world which increasingly, and dangerously, neglects to discriminate between different orders of fictionality. Perhaps the first British critic to recognize the ethical implications of this metafictional turn was Frank Kermode, in his important book of 1967, *The Sense of an Ending*. Kermode drew on the insights of the philosopher H. Vaihinger's *The Philosophy of As If* (which had been translated in 1924 by I. A. Richard's sometime collaborator C. H. Ogden), to argue for the crucial importance of always remembering that fictions are neither myths nor hypotheses and that you can neither arrange the world to their template, nor test them by experiments, as in the gas chambers. Metafictional self-consciousness protects against dangerous tendencies toward myth-making. Kermode's defence of the necessity for discrimination between orders of fictionality would regard as equally dangerous the stronger postmodern insistence that all truths are fictions, or that all knowledge is relative to the perspective of the situated observer. Authentic fiction manages to achieve a balance between a formal consolation provided by the illusion of correspondence between desire and the world, and an ethical refusal of such consolation, which reminds us that in the end fictional form is inevitably a mode of aesthetic seduction. Both Popper and Kermode reflect the problematization of positivism and recognize that there is always an aesthetic dimension to knowledge. But they are also very much part of a long-standing British intellectual and novelistic tradition concerned with the absolute need for ethical and epistemological discrimination. This "weaker" form of postmodernism was the preferred mode of postmodern fiction in Britain.

A glance at the work of Doris Lessing and Iris Murdoch in the earlier years of the period, and Kazuo Ishiguro in the next generation of novelists, suggests ways in which the epistemological focus of self-conscious fiction in Britain has continued to exist within a broader tradition of moral critique. Both Murdoch and Lessing might be regarded as novelists who attempt to sustain collectivist or even transcendent modes of representation whilst trying to reconcile them with a sense of identity as perspectival and radically situated in specific bodies. Both interrogate grand narratives but find them wanting from the woman's point of view. In *The Golden Notebook*, Lessing had expressed her longing to write a book "powered with an intellectual or moral passion strong enough to create order, to create a new way of looking at life" (Lessing 1973: 7). But her problem is whether conventional realism can any longer express the complex fragmentariness of late modernity in terms that neither reduce social experience to particularized flashes of insular personal emotion, nor subsume the particular into the generalized impersonality of the rationalized discourses of political science and sociological theory. Initially, Anna Wulf, the writer, tries to work her way through the problem and overcome her writer's block (also Lessing's, before she wrote the novel), by separating herself into distinct fictionalized voices, one for each of the four notebooks, convinced that if the essence of neurosis is conflict, then scientifically dividing up, separating out the voices in the manner of sociological role play, is the way to stay sane. In the final, golden notebook, however, she begins to break down and to experience a dissolution of the voices into each other, and into those of the other characters in the novel, and to recognize through the abandonment of a compartmentalizing rationalist logic that "the cruelty and the spite and the I I I I of Saul and Anna were part of the logic of war" (p. 568). Lessing introduces a theme she pursues throughout her career: the spiritual and moral bankruptcy of the West in its blind adherence to a narrow and instrumental concept of rationality. In her later novel, *Memoirs of a Survivor* (1974), she would describe this rationalism as an intelligence that could "make a rocket fly to the moon or weave artificial dress materials out of the by-products of petroleum," and that has created weapons of such horrifying destructive potential that "as we sit in the ruins of this particular variety of intelligence it is hard to give it very much value" (Lessing 1976: 74).

Like Lessing's, Murdoch's fiction searches for a model of self-reflexive consciousness as an opening on to the world that proceeds from a radical embededness, in which the body is not simply a text overwritten by culture but a situation through which we experience our very subjectivity. Murdoch also uses her fiction to demonstrate the negative consequences for human flourishing of scientific liberalism's acceptance of the logical positivist separation of fact and value. Much of her philosophical writing is also an extended critique of Moore's naturalistic fallacy and a response to the positivistic revival in the fifties marked by the reissue of A. J. Ayer's *Language, Truth and Logic*, first published in 1936. For Ayer, all scientific assertions were to be grounded in facts open to observation; scientific theorems are axiomatic systems whose connection to experience is to be achieved by the discovery of strict rules of interpretation, and the deductive derivation of facts is to be explained from empirical laws that act as premises of the deductive argument. Meaning pertains only to those propositions that can be empirically verified or falsified; truth is ultimately a function of the productive tautologies of mathematics and formal logic; and metaphysics, art, and ethics therefore belong merely to that irrational if consolatory realm of the fictional, of nonsense, of those infantile parts of ourselves that still need to believe in stories. Murdoch develops her fictional response through her notion of character as ethos. Characters in her novels are embodied but self-reflexive consciousnesses engaging a world that never presents itself simply as neutral "facts." In this world, goodness ever escapes the frantic egomaniacal fantasies and desires of her loquacious male wordsmiths, artist-narrators, and enchanters, and is more often to be found in the muted and tacit responses of female characters, or her "feminized" males who, accepting the contingent, brute materiality of the world, serve (often self-sacrificially) as the means to expose the seductive egotism of masculine desire in its will to absorb the world and the other into self-projected and abstractly crystalline schemes (Murdoch's version of "clear and distinct ideas").

Kazuo Ishiguro's 1989 novel *The Remains of the Day* is similarly a study of the way in which servitude to an impoverished model of reason that separates thought from feeling produces moral and spiritual blindeness. Like the "weaker" Enlightenment critiques of philosophers such as Charles Taylor and Alisdair MacIntyre (both formative influences on the New Left in Britain and both working in the Murdochian tradition), and the critique of method being developed by Hans-Georg Gadamer, Ishiguro uses the aesthetic as a mode of neo-Aristotelian practical wisdom, one that challenges the Kantian exclusion of feeling or compassion from the stern rationalism of his ethical categorical imperative. Stevens, the butler, practices a version of Stoicist extirpation of emotion in his blind obedience both to the profession of butlering and to his Nazi-collaborating master. The Stoic cultivates detachment and rationality in the belief that emotional connection to things or people leaves the self vulnerable to forces beyond instrumental control. Stevens remains in a condition of moral blindness, however, until the belated recognition of his love for Miss Kenton allows him to see his complicity in both the inhumane treatment of his father and in the fascist politics of his master. Again the novel proceeds in broadly realist fashion, but like Borges's Tlön also provides a moral allegory suggesting some of the ways in which the denial of feeling, of compassion and human empathy, and the separation of reason from feeling, have served not only to fuel the contemporary authoritarian politics of self-reliance in the context of a managerial and bureaucratized society, but also the blind obedience and apathy that facilitated the "banality of evil" that was National Socialism. Ishiguro's critique avoids the blanket condemnation of Enlightenment reason in the strong versions of postmodern theory, but he suggests ways in which human ends defy formulation through scientific models of rationality, and require a model of reason that refuses the Cartesian separation of mind and body. *Contra* Kantian rationalism and the positivist separation of facts and values, epistemology and ethics are seen as indissolubly linked.

Indeed, as early as the fifties and sixties, in the work of writers such as Beckett and Murdoch, there is already a proto-postmodernism flourishing in the novel and arising out of a critique of positivist method. Derrida admitted in an interview in 1989 that he had never written on Beckett, because "this is an author to whom I feel very close, or to whom I would like to feel myself very close; but also too close.... How could I avoid the platitude of a supposed academic metalanguage?' (Derrida 1992: 60). Derrida's anxiety is that Beckett has already outperformed deconstruction, already collapsed the boundaries between the creative and the critical text. Beckett's work in the fifties already provides the gloss on Derrida's much misunderstood remark that "Il n'y a pas de hors-texte," suggesting not that reality does not exist except as an illusion constructed through verbal artifice (vulgar postmodernism), but demonstrating that it is impossible categorically to distinguish what is inside and what is outside of the text, that there is no way within language to know what it is that language can finally know about the world (the platitude of an academic metalanguage). Or, as the narrator of *The Unnamable* puts it: "that's what I feel, an outside and an inside and me in the middle, perhaps that's what I am the thing that divides the world in two...I'm neither one side nor the other...I'm the tympanum, on one hand the mind, on the other the world, I don't belong to either" (Beckett 1959: 386). Though published as early as 1952, the third volume of Samuel Beckett's trilogy, *The Unnamable*, anticipates most of the themes and preoccupations of postmodernism. The novel opens with the words:

> Where now? Who now? When now?...I seem to speak, it is not I, about me, it is not about me. These few general remarks to begin with. What am I to do, what shall I do, what should I do, in my situation, how proceed? By aporia pure and simple? Or by affirmations and negations invalidated as uttered, or sooner or later?...The fact would seem to be, if in my situation one may speak of facts, not only that I shall have to speak of things of which I cannot speak, but also which is even more interesting, that I shall have to, I forget, no matter. (1959: 293–4)

Beckett's narrator is caught between a sense of the exhaustion of those discourses of Enlightened modernity – positivistic science (no matter) and the human limitations of Cartesian rationalism (I forget) – whilst recognizing that the attempt to move beyond those *aporias*, those irresolvable hesitations between competing meanings, brings one to the Wittgensteinian insight that whereof one cannot speak one must remain silent. But in a world without guarantors of truth or value, then the desire for consolation propels an endless babble, a filibustering against the void, a necessary and desperate capitulation to negative capability as a late modern substitute for a failed *cogito* and the self-cancelling rigors of method. Beckett speaks – having no voice and nothing to express – through his endless narrators, talking heads, whose inventedness must be flaunted as the only remaining marker of authenticity:

> I invented it all, in the hope it would console me, help me to go on, allow myself to think of myself as somewhere on a road, moving, between a beginning and an end ...but somewhere in the long run making headway. All lies...I have to speak, whatever that means. Having nothing to speak. (1959: 316)

Beckett's texts endlessly expose Cartesian *aporias* through the Wittgensteinian recognition that the subject can know itself only by becoming the object of its own consciousness, but then ceases to be itself:

I have no voice and must speak, that is all I know, it's round that I must revolve, of that I must speak, with this voice that is not mine, but can only be mine, since there is no one but me, or if there are others, to whom it might belong, they have never come near me. (1959: 309)

Beckett's novel prefigures not only the practices of deconstruction, but also specific critical texts such as *Roland Barthes by Roland Barthes*, and later postmodernist fiction such as Julian Barnes's *Flaubert's Parrot* (1984). In this novel, the search for authorial origins and real parrots is playfully exposed as a mode of linguistic parroting behind which the real Flaubert is gradually absented from the text.

For the renunciation of positivism in terms which presage the linguistic and narrative turn of modern literary theory was apparent even in the last sections of Wittgenstein's *Tractatus,* where he began to open up the possibility that even in science, as well as metaphysics, there can be no pure correspondent language, no theoretical foundation, and no certain beginnings. Wittgenstein already saw the problem of linguistic self-reference central to later poststructuralist theory: positivism limited knowledge to true meaningful statements but, logically, must then provide a definition of meaningful statements that could include the statement itself; but as positivism had defined all meaningful statements as those which can be empirically verifiable, any statement of limits inevitably fell outside of its own limits and was therefore not a meaningful claim by its own criteria. Later, in the *Philosophical Investigations*, Wittgenstein would elaborate on the insight in his famous image of language as an ancient but sprawling, ever-evolving, and uncontainable city, "a maze of little streets and squares, of old and new houses, and of houses with additions from various periods: and this surrounded by a multitude of new boroughs with straight regular streets and uniform houses" (Wittgenstein 1978: 8). A recursive metaphoric transfer confers on the city a palimpsestic textuality, and on language the quiddity of the phenomenally real. Wittgenstein had alighted on the problem of self-reference and the paradoxical relations of figure and ground that would become central to later theoretical assaults on both metaphysics and positivistic thought and to metafictional play with the world and the book. However, none of the major theorists associated with the theoretical turn in the seventies engaged either with Wittgenstein's work or, specifically, with logical positivism and the Murdochian tradition of critique of method. It was not until the publication of Lyotard's work in the eighties that the Wittgensteinian critique was revived. But it was already an important context for British novelists from the fifties onward and one of the reasons why the postmodern novel in Britain seemed less of a radical break with past traditions than its counterparts in Europe and America.

By the eighties, however, both the novel and theory in Britain seemed equally preoccupied with the sense that one of the effects of modernity is that knowledge reflexively enters and shapes experience in the world and is then shaped by it in an unprecedentedly self-conscious fashion. Once knowledge is thus reconceived in constructivist or situational terms, however, then rationality may no longer be grounded in a self that is somehow transparent to itself; truth may no longer be discovered by a consciousness operating through a systematic process of doubt, a *cogito* fathoming in solitude its own foundations to arrive at those clear and distinct ideas to deliver the truths of both cosmos and consciousness. Nearly twenty years after the publication of Beckett's text, his performance of unnamability had already been made over into an explicit theorization, which began to surface in a pervasive fashion in both literary fiction and criticism. John Fowles would proclaim in one of the first "historiographic metafictions," *The French Lieutenant's Woman,* that "fictionality is woven into all" and that he finds "this new reality or unreality more interesting" (Fowles 1977: 87).

Both novelists such as Amis, Rushdie, Byatt, Swift, and Peter Ackroyd and the newest variety of historicist literary critics became increasingly preoccupied with the sense that if language did in some sense mediate the real, then that reflection could only ever be a perverse one. The world reflected was already thoroughly fictionalized, "socially constructed," already imbued with stories and narratives and texts, a plurality of islands of discourse or mobile armies of metaphors, which could not finally be detached from the institutionally generated discourses which must therefore construct both object and all attempts at knowledge of or reflection upon that object. Historiographic metafiction prefigures the New Historicist turn in criticism and opened up the novel to a more fantastic turn in the writing of Rushdie, Winterson, and Carter, for example, and to a more explicit engagement both with postmodern theory and with those New Sciences so much favoured in the anti-realist epistemologies of postmodern theorists such as Lyotard and Baudrillard. Even here, though, the assumption that theory and postmodern fiction are somehow interchangeable requires some qualification.

One illustration of this is the preoccupation with the body which surfaces in postmodernized feminist theory of the eighties and nineties. In many ways, the postmodern body has begun to look curiously complicit both with the Cartesian project and the discourses of contemporary techno-biology. For if, to quote Judith Butler, gender is a "free-floating artifice, with the consequence that man and masculinity might just as easily signify a female body as a male one, and women and feminine a male body as easily as a feminine one," then the body, paradoxically, as in the Cartesian *Discourse on Method,* ceases to matter, and as matter, becomes expendable in the very construction of subjectivity (Butler 1990: 6). Butler claims that the sexed body is always ever an imitation that actually produces what it claims to imitate: another version of Flaubert's parrot, in effect. And, also like Barnes's parrots, this performative body too becomes so much a textual construction that it is effectively disembodied. Bodies, monstrous, engineered, fantastic and hybrid, stalk the pages of postmodern fiction: in Spark's *The Hothouse by the East River* (1973), Weldon's *The Life and Loves of a She-Devil* (1983), Lessing's *The Fifth Child* (1988), Carter's *The Passion of New Eve* (1977), and Winterson's *Sexing the Cherry* (1989), to name but a handful. In such postmodern fictions, the monstrous body functions as a means to voice and overcome anxieties concerning the construction of femininity as uncontrollability, but also concerning the contingency of materiality as a threat to the crystalline perfections of rational theory. Carter's Fevvers in *Nights at the Circus* poses the question to Walser, what is natural or unnatural, whilst the text repeatedly and metafictionally raises the issue of whether she is fact or fiction. Walser himself ponders whether Fevvers's freakishness lies in the fact that she is indeed a bodily "freak" (paradigmatic object of the gaze) or whether her true freakishness lies in the power of her performance thus to convince her audience and thereby to turn the gaze to her own advantage. He reflects that if

> she were indeed a *lusus naturae*, a prodigy, then – she was no longer a wonder . . . no more the greatest Aerialiste in the world, but – a freak . . . a marvellous monster, an exemplary being denied the privilege of flesh and blood, always the object of the observer, never the subject of sympathy, an alien creature forever estranged. (Carter 1985: 161)

But Carter's own postmodernist performance keeps us guessing about Fevvers's real bodily condition and she is allowed to demonstrate her physical prowess in overcoming all those who would simply kill her into symbolic life (a warning to read the text as more than a postmodern parable of an all-pervasive textuality). But the theoretical body has long since dissolved into a condition of semiosis and organic and material evacuation that bears an uncanny resemblance to the contemporary discourses of genetic- and bio-engineering. Here again it would seem that the theoretical resistance to theory still prompts writers of fiction into their own novelistic resistance to the theoretical resistance to theory. And who better than Beckett as *the* postmodernist writer of the body to have the last word on theory and the current state of affairs: "if its not white it's very likely black, it must be admitted the method lacks subtlety, in view of the intermediate shades all equally worthy of a chance. The time they waste repeating the same thing . . ." (1959: 377).

REFERENCES AND FURTHER READING

Barthes, Roland (1977) "The death and return of the author," in Stephen Heath (ed.) *Image-Music-Text*. London: Fontana.

Beckett, Samuel (1959) *Molloy/Malone Dies/The Unnamable*. London. John Calder.

Belsey, Catherine (1980) *Critical Practice*. London: Methuen.

Butler, Judith (1990) *Gender Trouble: Feminism and the Subversion of Identity*. London and New York: Routledge.

Carter, Angela (1985) *Nights at the Circus*. London: Picador.

Connor, Steven (1996) *The English Novel in History, 1950–1995*. London: Routledge.

Dawkins, Richard (1986) *The Blind Watchmaker*. Harmondsworth: Penguin.

Derrida, Jacques (1992) *Acts of Literature*, ed. Derek Attridge. London: Routledge.

Fowles, John (1977) *The French Lieutenant's Woman*. St Albans: Panther.

Gasiorek, Andrzej (1995) *Post-War British Fiction: Realism and After*. London: Edward Arnold.

Head, Dominic (2002) *Modern British Fiction, 1950–2000*. Cambridge: Cambridge University Press.

Hutcheon, Linda (1995) *A Poetics of Postmodernism: History, Theory, Fiction*. London: Routledge.

Jameson, Fredric (1991) *Postmodernism, or, the Cultural Logic of Late Capitalism*. London and New York: Verso.

Lee, Alison (1990) *Realism and Power: British Postmodern Fiction*. London: Routledge.

Lessing, Doris (1973) [1962] *The Golden Notebook*. St Albans: Panther.

——(1976) [1974] *The Memoirs of a Survivor*. London: Picador.

McHale, Brian (1991) *Postmodernist Fiction*. London: Routledge.

Sage, Lorna (1992) *Women in the House of Fiction: Post-War Women Novelists*. Basingstoke: Macmillan.

Waugh, Patricia (1995) *Harvest of the Sixties: English Literature and its Background 1960–1990*. Oxford: Oxford University Press.

Wittgenstein, Ludwig (1978) *Philosophical Investigations*. Oxford: Blackwell.

6

The Novel and the End of Empire

Reed Way Dasenbrock

English literature was for centuries the product of a small nation on part of an island off the coast of Europe; now, literature in English is a global enterprise, produced on every inhabited continent by writers with a once unimaginable variety of mother tongues, backgrounds, and cultural commitments. For this transformation to have taken place, two developments were necessary. First, the English and the language they spoke had to insert themselves into the plethora of sites and situations where English is now spoken and used as a medium of creative expression. Second, people other than the English needed to take up, master, and creatively adapt the English language for their own purposes and occasions. These are quite different aspects of the evolution of literature in English over the past half-millennium. It is the first development that is my focus here, more precisely the last chapter of that development; the second development – arguably responsible for the most vital contemporary literature in English – is the focus of another essay in this collection.

All of these aspects of contemporary literature in English must be seen against a long backdrop of social and political history if they are to be understood: there would be no postcolonial literature in English if there had been no colonialism; the novel of the end of empire – my subject here – presupposes by its very nature both the fact of empire and that fact mattering for literature in a number of concrete respects. But why should the fact of empire matter for literature? Some background is needed.

For a fairly long time, it did not matter that much. England was of course a somewhat belated and even reluctant entrant into the European colonization of the world. The Iberian and Catholic nations of Portugal and Spain were off the mark first, and their aims were fully imperial from the first, embracing both conquest and conversion to Catholicism as explicit aims of their voyages of discovery. The English went to sea (or more precisely to non-European waters) in the sixteenth century above all to fight the Spanish: it was the conflicts in Europe that drew them outside Europe. A secondary aim that came to the fore once the threat of a Spanish conquest of England receded after 1588 was trade and commerce. The rapid growth of what has come to be known as the first British empire, from 1607 – the date of the first English settlement in what is now the United States – until the loss of the United States in 1783, was less a function of state policy than a complex mixture of motives in which trade and commerce reigned supreme.

In this period, themes of empire are remarkably absent in English literature. In saying this, I am not ignoring the work of scholars such as Stephen Greenblatt who have done a great deal to explore the engagement of Shakespeare, Spenser, and others with the Renaissance discovery of the New World. But I think it worth noting that it took until our time to read these texts in this way. In contrast, the major work of Portuguese literature of the Renaissance, Camoens's *Os Lusiados,* has as its explicit subject Vasco da Gama's voyage to India in 1497–8. The masterpieces of English literature do not so directly engage the subject of discovery or empire at this early date, and I think this reflects both the somewhat unintended nature of England's empire-building, and perhaps more importantly the fact that the dominant cultural dynamic of the period for the English was the European struggle between the Protestant North and the Catholic South. *The Tempest* is, of course, the play of Shakespeare's in which the exploration of the New World comes most to the fore, yet the play is set in the Mediterranean with Italian dynastic intrigues driving the plot, and this reflects the limited role the New World played in English politics and in the English imagination at this point. Whatever the reason, Renaissance drama and poetry in English does not center on the non-European engagements of English society. The subject is left to one side, treated primarily in the extensive but quite utilitarian narratives of discovery and exploration represented by the work of Hakluyt, Purchas, and others.

Things changed somewhat during and after the great worldwide struggle with the French, which reached its height in the Seven Years War (1756–63), the War of American Independence (1776–83), and, finally, the Revolutionary and Napoleonic Wars (1792–1815). By the end of this period, Great Britain (England and Scotland shared a common monarch from 1603 and were united administratively by the Act of Union in 1707) had lost and regained an empire and had bases and colonies, not just in North American but also in Africa, India, and the West Indies, in addition to island bases throughout the world. By this point, Britain's imperial commitments and ambitions were clear, even to itself, and those commitments found institutional expression in the East India Company, the army, and above all the Royal Navy, as well as in other civil institutions.

The poetry and drama of the eighteenth century were little more attuned to these events than they had been two centuries earlier, but the explosion of the reading public and the expansion of printing helped create the new genre of the novel. The novel became the genre after travel literature most engaged with empire and with Britain's increased interpenetration with the non-European world. The novel is of course not an unequivocal genre, and although generalizations are quite tricky here, I think it fair to say that the strain of English fiction during the period of imperial expansion and empire building (up to, say, 1901) most highly regarded by critics remained English in its orientation. It is true that one can find echoes of the imperial experience even in the more domestic of English novels, and Edward Said's discussion of Jane Austen's *Mansfield Park* and the role of the family's estate in Antigua in the events of the novel is a good example of this. The forms of English society depicted in English fiction rest on an imperial economic base in much the way certain mythologies assert that our world is held up at the base by a giant turtle. But Fielding, Richardson, Austen, Dickens, Eliot, Hardy – Leavis's "Great Tradition" and others added to that canon – do not for the most part go out and take a look at the turtle. By and large, they take the existence of the empire for granted. It makes at most an occasional appearance on the stage, as characters return from the sea or from a colonial possession to the place in English society where they are seen to belong, even if their re-entrance into society is frequently financed by that colonial sojourn.

But this "high," England-centered tradition competes for the very core of the English novel with a tradition of fiction far more focused on travel, adventure, and empire. Neither Stephen Greenblatt nor Edward Said was needed to tease out the imperial subtext of Daniel Defoe's *Robinson Crusoe* or *Moll Flanders* or *Captain Singleton*, since these novels clearly tell stories of overseas travel, commerce, and colonization that are part of the development of the empire. Defoe is only the first of many such writers of fiction in English, who are more oriented towards travel than domesticity, adventure than marriage, war than peace, and this body of fiction best reflects Britain's active role in the world. Nonetheless, during the entire period of imperial expansion from the publication of *Robinson Crusoe* in 1719 to the death of Queen Victoria in 1901, this body of work – best represented by such widely-read writers as Smollett, Scott, Marryat, Disraeli, Collins, Stevenson, and Kipling – was defined as lesser in quality than the great tradition. This should not occasion a great deal of surprise. If one reads extensively in "serious" fiction from the United States since 1945, only in a handful of cases (Mailer, Pynchon, DeLillo) does one find serious engagement with America's dominant role in the rest of the world. It is to the popular fiction designed for consumption on airplanes and beaches that one must turn to find fiction responsive to the age of the American empire.

Less well regarded does not mean less important, of course, and Martin Green has argued for an important social role for the tradition inaugurated by Defoe, in fueling in its readers a desire for adventure that in turn helped man (and man is the right word here, not staff) the British empire. Moreover, it is from this fiction of imperial adventure that many of the genres of popular fiction have sprung. The mystery story, the spy novel, the thriller: these have their seeds in the fiction of adventure inspired by the British empire. (Conan Doyle's reliance on Indian settings and backgrounds for so much of the Sherlock Holmes corpus is one of the points where this can be seen most clearly.) All of these fields of culture lie outside the scope of this essay, though it is perhaps worth noting that a major subfield of such adventure writing today – primarily in Britain – is historical fiction set in the British empire. C. S. Forester, Bernard Cornwall, James Clavell, Wilbur Smith – to mention just a few names – are imitators of Kipling and Buchan and Marryat, and pay these writers the compliment of setting their own contemporary books in these earlier times. That this genre can rise to the level of great literature is shown above all by the work of Patrick O'Brian, whose splendidly inventive twenty-volume series set during the Napoleonic Wars about the adventures of Captain Jack Aubrey and the surgeon and quondam spy Stephen Maturin is among the great achievements of contemporary British literature. O'Brian clearly writes with an awareness that what he writes about has passed away, is history, but he regrets that passing; and it is his refusal to adopt a deprecating stance towards the fact of empire that establishes his deep kinship with the novelists of the imperial age.

O'Brian died in 2001, but if we can assign a single date for the end of the confident imperialism that his work depicts, it would be exactly one century earlier. When Queen Victoria died in 1901 the sun indeed did not set on the British empire. It was the largest empire the world had ever seen, and the extent of British territory around the globe was perhaps less important than its military, industrial, and commercial domination. As is the case with the United States today, there was only one global power, one power with a presence in every part of the world, and this presence was a function of its colonies, its bases, its direct overseas investment, and its role in the culture of its time. (Paul Kennedy (1987) draws this analogy with considerable precision.) London was – as it would be put a few years later by Wyndham Lewis – the great vortex of the world, drawing much of the world to it and then recirculating these people around the globe. One consequence of the spread and dynamism of the British empire is that English became an important world language, spoken and written by many people who were not in any sense English. The first such nomad to acquire stature as a great writer is Joseph Conrad, the Polish exile who became a sea captain and then a novelist in English.

Conrad could be said to be the novelist laureate of the apogee of the British empire, except that his attitudes towards imperialism were sufficiently complex that controversy still roils about them. His work, along with that of E. M. Forster, who though younger ceased publishing fiction before Conrad died, properly initiates the fiction about the end of empire I have been trying to place in perspective. Conrad wrote in many different veins, of course. A good deal of his work is essentially adventure fiction as described above, with perhaps the aptly titled *Romance* (1903), co-authored with Ford Madox Ford, serving as the best example. Although the bulk of his work does not simply or straightforwardly endorse the values of adventure, the plot of adventure nearly always provides the essential narrative framework. *Nostromo* (1904), for instance, like *Romance* set in Latin America, is about a secessionist movement in a Latin American country loosely based on the American-engineered breakaway of Panama from Columbia. The novel ultimately stresses the continuity between the straightforwardly despotic *ancien régime* and the new era of neocolonialism directed by foreign Anglo-American capital, in that the life of the people and their lack of autonomy remains essentially unchanged. But this point is carried by – or perhaps hindered by – a convoluted romance plot involving stolen treasure and a man in an adulterous relationship with his wife's sister that cannot be taken quite as seriously.

A plot structured by action coexists uneasily in *Nostromo*, and much of Conrad, with a complex reflection on the value of action and, more specifically, on the actions central to the novel.

Through this reflection, Conrad nearly always questions the value of the imperial enterprise that he first was part of and then wrote about. Nowhere is this better shown than in the frame for *Heart of Darkness* (1902), in which the story Marlow tells about the Belgian Congo is told on a yacht in the Thames, downriver from London. To the listeners, the two rivers seem diametrically opposed: they sit in the center of the civilized world, hearing a story about the antithesis of that civilization, the "heart of darkness." But *Heart of Darkness* begins with Marlow making a point about the context-specific nature of darkness by talking about how where they are hearing this story would have been viewed 1900 years earlier. The Thames also "has been one of the dark places of the earth" (1999: 5); for the Romans, as Marlow points out, the Thames would have been regarded much as Europeans regard the Congo in Conrad's day. Marlow's Roman analogy can be taken in two different ways, and these correspond to the two principal lines of Conrad criticism. First, one can see this analogy as a critique of imperialism, reminding those currently in a dominant position that there is nothing inherent about their circumstance and that if history tells us anything, their moment on top will be brief indeed. (Of course, a century later, with Britain cast in the role of America's sidekick, this point needs little emphasis.) This is certainly the main line of Conrad criticism, which stresses the author's position as a Pole subject to Russian imperialism, and which sees him as reflecting the growing current of doubt in late Victorian and Edwardian England about the validity of the structures of dominance that sustained the British empire. In this regard, *Heart of Darkness* functions as a literary analogy to J. A. Hobson's 1902 classic, *Imperialism*.

However, the one thing not questioned in Marlow's moment of questioning is the civilization/barbarism antithesis that structures the passage. Those assigned to each category may change across time, but the structure that creates the distinction is not questioned. More specifically, nothing about this passage questions the notion that at present the Thames represents civilization and the Congo savagery. Marlow says in a famous passage that "the conquest of the earth, which mostly means the taking it away from those who have a different complexion or slightly flatter noses than ourselves, is not a pretty thing when you look into it too much. What redeems it is the idea only" (1999: 7–8). But it is an open question – one answered differently by different readers – how deep Conrad's irony runs here: does he leave room here for a conquest that is redeemable?

The action that follows, too well known to need detailed retelling, certainly underscores Marlow's ironic comment about conquest not being "pretty." Little about the "civilized" side of the antithesis seems civilized as we see how the Belgians systematically pillage and depopulate the Congo. Kurtz at the heart of darkness itself clearly represents no civilizing mission, as we see in his final comment, "exterminate the brutes." And *Heart of Darkness* has predominately been represented as a devastating critique of the pretensions of empire to improve. It is the desire to dominate and conquer, not the desire to ameliorate, which is at work here. But African critics have seen this differently: just as Conrad saw little difference between liberal apologies for empire and conservative celebrations of it, these critics have seen little difference between liberal critics of empire such as Conrad and the empire they criticize. Chinua Achebe is the key figure here, and in his "An image of Africa" he presents a blistering critique of Conrad as an apologist for European domination. Although there is much that is uncharitable in Achebe's reading of Conrad, he correctly points out that while the novel does not endorse Kurtz's call to "exterminate the brutes," neither does it lead us to see the Africans as anything other than brutes. Much of this is a function of the novelistic form in which *Heart of Darkness* is cast: it is a narrative of action, and the European adventurer – Marlow going up the river to find Kurtz – is in a position of agency. Neither Marlow in his story nor Conrad in his gives the Africans genuine agency, nor do they represent the African outside of the imperialist assumptions that govern the site Conrad is depicting.

Another way of putting this is that Conrad is a chronicler of empire, caught ineluctably in its structures of representation and its characteristic anxieties, whatever his own attitudes towards empire might be. The complex, perhaps uncomfortable but certainly fascinating space his work explores is a space explored by a number of subsequent writers. Crucial in sustaining this imaginative literature about the empire is a shift in demography. By Conrad's time, families – not just young men looking for fame and fortune – were leaving Britain and migrating to the empire. The many places the British controlled can be roughly divided into categories according to whether the British immigration constituted the majority of the population or whether it was numerically insignificant with respect to the indigenous people, constituting essentially an administrative and governing cadre. In the first category, generally known as the dominions, one finds of course Canada, Australia, and New Zealand, areas that moved by a series of steps towards self-government and finally independence; in the second, the colonies, comes virtually everyone else, with India – with a population of hundreds of millions ruled by several hundred thousand British – as the prime example. Blurring this distinction are those areas with a strong but minority white settler presence: the Caribbean was initially such an area, although the emancipation of the slaves in 1833 led to the demise of the plantation economy and a slow repatriation back to Britain, while much of East and Southern Africa remained in this category until independence, and indeed South Africa does so today.

In all these cases, however, the British and other Europeans came to live in varying numbers, and whatever their fraction of the population, the settlers had jobs and raised families. Some of those children became writers; to name a few: Olive Schreiner, born in 1855 in Cape Colony, South Africa; Katharine Mansfield, born in 1888 in New Zealand; Jean Rhys, born in 1890 in Dominica in the West Indies; George Orwell, born in 1903 in Bengal in British India; Lawrence Durrell, born in 1912 in the Punjab in British India; Doris Lessing, born in 1919 in Persia and raised in Rhodesia. Others not born in the empire nonetheless came to live or spent formative years there: Karen Blixen, a Danish aristocrat, came to Kenya to grow coffee and started writing in English under the pseudonym Isak Dinesen; Paul Scott was stationed in India during World War II; Ruth Prawar Jhabvala was born in Poland but escaped the Nazis, married an Indian in Britain and moved to India with him after the war; Tom Stoppard was born in Czechoslovakia but was raised in Singapore and India before moving to England after the war, after his widowed mother married a British army officer.

These writers pose complex questions for how we categorize literature. For where they were born or lived remain important for their writing in a way that differentiates them from the English writers of their own time, yet they are also clearly distinct – as Achebe's critique of Conrad will serve to illustrate – from the indigenous writers of their places of origin. To call Lawrence Durrell Indian would be absurd given the enormous gap between him and Indians, but to call him English (without any further qualification) ignores a different gap. In practice, we tend to treat writers from the dominions differently: as early Australian or South African writers. But the others – born in a place then under British control which has by now undergone decolonization – fit only with some important angle of difference into the general label of English literature. Their own lives saw or have seen the end of the empire which shaped their lives and work. The empire, which as recently as 1947 was the largest the world had ever known, has now shrunk to a few spots scattered around the globe, which are now either places for off-shore banking and tourism – the Cayman Islands, the British Virgin Islands, Bermuda – or places the British refuse to give to their neighbors – the Falklands, Gibraltar – from a complex mixture of pride, principle, and sheer stubbornness. These writers therefore lived in a culture that ended in their lifetime; or, to put this another way, the "England" they were born into – though a vital and enduring aspect of English history and identity – in an important respect no longer exists.

This is the political, social, and historical context these writers have in common, which makes the disparate nature of what they write about that much more remarkable, and which makes a summary of the kind needed in an essay such as this one all the more difficult to write. It should be pointed out first of all that a colonial upbringing or significant colonial experience does not necessarily shape every aspect of a writer's oeuvre. George Orwell, for instance, was born in Bengal into a family with long Indian and colonial associations, and after his education at Eton he returned to Asia and was a policeman in Burma from 1922 to 1927. But aside from the classic essays, "Shooting an elephant" and "A hanging," this experience led only to his first novel, *Burmese Days* (1934), and it was only through his engagement with the struggle against fascism and Communism after his return to Europe that Orwell found his voice as a writer.

Lawrence Durrell, also born and raised in India in a family that was in India for two generations, never drew on this experience directly in his fiction. But he matured as a writer while working for the British Foreign Office on and off from 1941 to 1953, living in Egypt during the war and then in Rhodes, Argentina, and Yugoslavia. This work led most directly to one spy novel, *White Eagles Over Serbia* (1957), as well as some humorous writing about the Foreign Office in the vein of P. G. Woodhouse. He moved to Cyprus in 1953 intending just to write, and while living on Cyprus from 1953 to 1956 he did write *Justine*, the first novel of the *Alexandria Quartet*. But Cyprus was undergoing a violent anticolonial movement, and Durrell went to work again for the British government on Cyprus, an act that made his position on the island untenable but also led to a nonfiction work about the Cypriot struggle, *Bitter Lemons* (1958). This wartime and postwar experience of the empire and decolonization is a crucial part of the background for his masterpiece, the *Alexandria Quartet* (1957–60), discussed in a separate essay in this volume. It cries out for a colonial/postcolonial reading it has not yet received, given its setting in Egypt under British colonial rule and its subplot concerning resistance to that rule. This is especially prominent in the third novel of the *Quartet, Balthazar*, the most naturalist and least modernist of the novels. Following the *Alexandria Quartet*, Durrell's fiction is set primarily in Europe, reflecting his residence in Southern France after he had to leave Cyprus. Although his later fiction, especially *Tunc* (1968) and *Nunquam* (1970), is fascinating and has not received its due, it is arguable that after 1960 Durrell turned away from the richest vein of his work and that the implicit imperial subtext of his earlier work is that vein.

Those who do explicitly engage the subject of the empire in their work can be arranged on a continuum according to their attitudes towards empire. After the struggle for Indian independence had intensified under Gandhi's leadership, writers recognized that British rule was contested in a way it had not been a half-century earlier. But this did not mean that they, any more than anyone else, reacted in the same way. Karen Blixen (1885–1962), the Danish aristocrat who wrote under the pen name Isak Dinesen, was certainly an unconventional figure among the settlers in Kenya, where she ran a coffee plantation from 1914 to 1931. The most famous of her works about those experiences, *Out of Africa*, was published in 1938, but she continued mining this vein after the war, in *Shadows on the Grass* (1961). (These works are ostensibly memoirs, but it has become clear that they are at least quasi-fictional and therefore merit mention here.) Nonetheless, from our vantage point today, her work is quite vulnerable to a criticism along the lines of Achebe's critique of Conrad. Like Conrad, her narratives are ones in which the actors are European, and in which Africa provides a "setting and backdrop which eliminates the African as human factor" (Achebe 1977: 788). The very land that Dinesen was able to buy for her farm had been taken away from the Kikuyu in a series of alienations and expropriations early in the century. The Kikuyu were then allowed to move back, as "squatters," on to uncultivated parts of land owned by Europeans in return for up to 180 days of labor each year. Both *Out of Africa* and *Shadows on the Grass* reveal Dinesen's deep affection for her African servants, and she was clearly more liberal in her treatment of Africans than the average settler, working hard to provide them with health care and to ensure that they could continue to live together after she had to sell her farm in 1931.

Nonetheless, nothing in either book allows us to see the "Natives" – as they are always referred to – from any other perspective than hers, and her perspective is explicitly one that endorses European colonization: "We ourselves have carried European light to the country quite lately, but we have had the means to spread and establish it quickly" (1961: 9). Another way of putting this is that while Dinesen was not, as Achebe has dubbed Conrad, "a bloody racist," she was in some sense a racist in her belief that the intelligence of an individual reflects the people he or she belongs to. We can see this in the way she differentiates Somalis from Kenyans: "In my day there were a large number of Somalis in Kenya. They were greatly superior to the Native population in intelligence and culture" (p. 9). Admittedly, these are not aspects of her narrative that are foregrounded by Dinesen, and they were pushed back even further in the film version of *Out of Africa,* which starred Robert Redford and Meryl Streep. But a juxtaposition of Dinesen's work with, say, the early novels of Ngugi wa Thiong'o such as *The River Between* and *Weep not, Child,* which cover the same historical terrain, allows one to see the difference. Here, a colonial perspective is confronted with a postcolonial one in a way that calls into question the adequacy of the self-representation of the former.

That there was nothing preordained about this celebration of European settlement in Africa can be shown by the example of Doris Lessing, born in Persia in 1919 of English parents, who in 1924 began to farm in Southern Rhodesia (now Zimbabwe), where she lived until she moved to England in 1949. Lessing is one of the best known and most highly regarded novelists writing in English today, and her work defies easy summary, extending as it does to science fiction and opera libretti. Her acknowledged masterpiece, *The Golden Notebook* (1962), is the subject of a separate essay in this volume. *The Golden Notebook,* though set in London, includes a good deal of African material, as the protagonist, Anna Wulf, usually taken as an autobiographical representation of Lessing herself, is the author of *Frontiers of War,* a novel set in Rhodesia about a group of Communist activists opposed to colonization and to the "colour bar." Much of the novel is made up of excerpts from *Frontiers of War,* so there is an oscillation in the novel between Anna's London present and African past. Most of Lessing's writing before *The Golden Notebook* is set in Africa, and this work includes a nonfiction book, *Going Home* (1957), a body of short fiction re-collected in *African Stories* (1964), her first novel, *The Grass is Singing* (1949), and most substantially a quintet ultimately titled *Children of Violence,* published between 1952 and 1969. This narrates the evolution of Martha Quest from a young woman on an African farm, in a series of deeply autobiographical novels about Lessing's turn first to Communism and then to her own particular form of feminism, a theme that has made her work the focus of a kind of devotion seldom received by contemporary writers.

If Lessing is clearly anticolonial (one measure of this is the incorporation of *The Grass is Singing* in Heinemann's African Writing Series) and therefore has not been subjected to the kind of postcolonial critique aimed at Dinesen, nonetheless her long residence in England, and more importantly the London setting of most of her fiction written after 1960, means that her work is not consistently seen in terms of the colonial frame we are concerned with here. One novelist who is, the one writer discussed in this essay who is frequently presented as a postcolonial – not a colonial –

writer, is Jean Rhys. Rhys was born in Dominica in 1890, moved to London in 1907, and spent the rest of her long life in England. The author of four well-regarded but not widely known novels published between 1924 and 1939, she fell out of sight for many years, only to make a triumphant return with *Wide Sargasso Sea* (1966). *Wide Sargasso Sea* is also the subject of an essay in this volume, so I will simply note here that if a major theme of postcolonial literature and criticism has been to "write back" by taking canonical works and subjecting them to the kind of critique Achebe has made of Conrad, Rhys herself does this in *Wide Sargasso Sea*. *Wide Sargasso Sea*, as is well known, takes as its intertext *Jane Eyre*. It tells the story, from childhood on, of the West Indian wife locked in the attic in Rochester's house as mad. Rhys's novel shares with the work of Lessing and Dinesen a concern for the position of women, represented here as essentially chattel once married, and largely defenseless if not married. But for Rhys, race is at least as crucial a form of oppression as gender, and her sympathy for and identification with the black characters in the novel is what differentiates her most sharply from Dinesen. Key here is the figure of Christophine, Antoniette Cosway's nurse, who is seen as the one figure with genuine agency in the novel, given her reputation as an *obeah* (or voodoo) woman. This agency does not, of course, give her the power to alter the tragic events of the novel any more than it gives her the power to alter the oppressive structures of colonialism in the West Indies, but she is consequently able to resist and that resistance gives her a sense of identity and self-worth that is not shared by anyone else – white or black – in the novel.

Such resistance was ultimately effectual, as between 1947 and 1964, first India, then other British possessions in Asia, Africa, and the West Indies gained their independence. The novels we have discussed so far might be called novels of the beginning of the end of empire, novels in which other political, social, and cultural possibilities are glimpsed and sometimes advocated, but never actually realized. There is, however, one great work that takes a remarkably detailed look at the moment of decolonization itself: Paul Scott's the *Raj Quartet*. The *Raj Quartet*, published between 1966 and 1975, with a related sequel volume, *Staying On*, published in 1976, is in some senses the most complete flowering of the fiction of the end of empire described here, but Paul Scott was not in any sense typical of the writers of such fiction. He was not born in Bengal or anywhere in the empire, but rather in London, in 1920, and his contact with India was relatively brief, essentially the period 1943–6, when he served in the British army (with additional visits in 1964 and 1969).

The *Raj Quartet* is a complex enough work to defy easy summary, but briefly, it takes as its scope the history of India from the Quit India movement launched by Gandhi in 1942 to the communal violence that attended the separation of British India in 1947 into the separate countries of India and Pakistan. The initial point of focus in the first novel, *The Jewel in the Crown*, is the rape of Daphne Manners in the town of Mayapore in British India. Suspicion falls on a British public-school-educated Indian, Hari Kumar, who was innocent but in fact had been having an affair with Daphne. Scott has been criticized for taking many elements of this situation from

E. M. Forster's 1924 novel, *A Passage to India*, which centers on a mistaken and later withdrawn allegation of rape lodged by Adela Quested against the Indian Aziz. The echo is intentional, but *The Jewel in the Crown* is less an imitation of *A Passage to India* than a variation on it, a variation that shows how decisively the situation had been transformed in the intervening years. On the one hand, the Anglicization of India had proceeded to the point that a figure like Hari Kumar is possible, someone of Indian descent whose English accent and education is of much higher class than the policeman Ronald Merrick, who imprisons him unjustly because he is also interested in Daphne. However, the rape in *The Jewel in the Crown* is a real one, even if the wrong person is imprisoned for it; the tension in India has been heightened enormously since *A Passage to India*. The Raj – as British rule over India was characteristically called – had lost all pretense of legitimacy. One claim to legitimacy was the claim to amelioration, to raising India's standard of culture, but the contrast between Merrick and Kumar shows this to be either outdated or false. The other was the claim to arbitration, that the British could somehow unite a divided and complex subcontinent under their rule, and this is also clearly outdated yet now ironically true: the British have brought the Indians together, as they are now united by their desire to get the British to quit India. What is left is Ronald Merrick, a closet homosexual who brutalizes prisoners of greater culture and knowledge than his; all that is left is the naked fist of power, except that this fist is deformed (as Merrick's is, literally) by the awareness that the Japanese are on the India-Burma border and have shown themselves to be as adept at modern war as any white nation.

But the *Raj Quartet* does not stop there, with a celebration of decolonization as a victory over oppression. It is not that easy. The focus on the Manners-Merrick-Kumar plot set in Mayapore gives way to other plot complexities, those concerning the Muslim-ruled princely state of Mirat and a relationship between Ahmed Kasim and Sarah Layton, another idealistic Englishwoman anxious to put the differences between East and West behind her. But by 1947, the date of the events in the last novel in the *Quartet, A Division of the Spoils,* the primary struggle is no longer between the British and the Indians, but rather among the Indians themselves about the future of their subcontinent. Ahmed's father, Mohammed Ali Kasim, although Muslim, refuses to break with the Indian Congress and support the creation of a separate Pakistan. Despite this, Ahmed is killed in the communal rioting that follows Partition.

A Passage to India ends with a famous image of Aziz going out for a ride with Fielding, the one Englishman who has supported him. Aziz takes the occasion to utter a speech in favor of Indian independence, which concludes in this way:

> "Clear out, you fellows, double quick, I say. We may hate one another, but we hate you most. If I don't make you go, Ahmed will, Karim will [Aziz's children], if it's fifty-five-hundred years we shall get rid of you; yes, we shall drive every blasted Englishman into the sea, and then" – he rode against him furiously – "and then," he concluded, half kissing him, "you and I shall be friends." (1945: 282)

Fielding asks, "Why can't we be friends now?" "It's what I want. It's what you want."
If for a moment this seems to indicate a possibility of English–Indian amity, the
horses themselves break the image by riding off in different directions. By the end of
the *Raj Quartet*, we have lived out the prophetic end of *A Passage to India*, and the
British are clearing out. The tensions building throughout *A Passage to India* in terms
of both British–Indian relations and communal relations between Hindus and
Muslims have exploded, leading to Independence, Partition, and the massacre of
millions. The deepest debt of Scott to Forster lies not in the resemblance of their
plots, a resemblance that lasts only for *The Jewel in the Crown*, but rather in terms of
the values advanced by their conclusions. By the end of the *Raj Quartet* all that stands
against this dismal record of violence in which there seem to be no clean hands are a
number of tenuous relationships and friendships. Like Forster, Scott nonetheless
focuses on those relationships and the characters that create them: the *Raj Quartet*,
though it narrates some of the most complex events in the history of the British
empire, is ultimately a novel of characters, not of action. The best of these characters
demonstrate a confidence not found in *A Passage to India* that it is possible to cross the
divides depicted in these novels. Perhaps that is where any hope for the future lies.

   Partition seems like a good place for a discussion of fiction about the end of empire
to end, as Indian independence in 1947 certainly marked the beginning of the end of
empire, with the decolonization of most of Britain's colonies in Asia, Africa, and the
West Indies to follow in the next twenty years. But if the fiction about empire from
Defoe to Scott has been the crucial element in reducing the insularity of English
fiction, what continues this impulse after the end of empire? One way this has been
continued has been through the visual media, as nearly every book mentioned in
this essay has been the subject of transformation into film or television, with the
mini-series of the *Raj Quartet* having perhaps the greatest impact of all. Another,
perhaps more enduring force is the arrival in England of writers from the former
colonies: India and Britain are still connected, less by a British presence in India than
by the vital Asian presence in British life and culture. The lines continue to be
difficult or impossible to draw, and this is all to the good even if it complicates
the task of writers of essays such as this one.

References and Further Reading

Achebe, Chinua (1977) "An image of Africa," *The
   Massachusetts Review*, 18/4 782–94. Originally
   the Chancellor's Lecture at the University of
   Massachusetts, February 1975.
Conrad, Joseph (1999) *Heart of Darkness* and *Selec-
   tions from the Congo Diary*. New York: Modern
   Library.

Dinesen, Isak (1961) *Shadows on the Grass*. New
   York: Random House.
Forster, E. M. (1945) *A Passage to India*. London:
   J. M. Dent.
Green, Martin (1979) *Dreams of Adventure, Deeds of
   Empire*. New York: Basic Books.

Greenblatt, Stephen (1991) *Marvellous Possessions: The Wonder of the New World.* Chicago: University of Chicago Press.

Hobson, J. A. (1965) [1902] *Imperialism: A Study.* Ann Arbor: University of Michigan Press, 1965.

Kennedy, Paul (1987) *The Rise and Fall of the Great Powers: Economic Change and Military Conflict from 1500 to 2000.* New York: Random House.

Lapping, Brian (1985) *End of Empire.* New York: St Martin's Press.

Leavis, F. R. (1963) *The Great Tradition: George Eliot, Henry James, Joseph Conrad.* New York: New York University Press.

Said, Edward W. (1993) *Culture and Imperialism.* New York: Alfred A. Knopf.

7

Postcolonial Novels and Theories

Feroza Jussawalla

The past few decades have seen an explosion of interest in the field of postcolonial literature and theory. Postcolonial literature in English emerged after the dissolution of the British empire on the Indian subcontinent, on the continent of Africa, and on certain of the islands of the Caribbean. At first labeled "Commonwealth literature," as countries gaining independence continued to stay connected to the British government via the "Commonwealth," this literature was then re-labeled "postcolonial literature" by American critics. Fredric Jameson's famous 1986 conference at Duke University on Third World literature, at which he presented his talk, "Third World Literature in an era of multinational capitalism," formally subsumed literatures from the Commonwealth under the aegis of "postcolonial literatures." "postcolonial," then, is a term that emerged from the American academy, building upon Senator Daniel Patrick Moynihan's plea to the US Senate to erase the debt of nations recovering from colonialism.

Nomenclature

The question of a term has plagued this literature, and continues to do so, as theoretical concerns pervade the academy, and questions such as whether James Joyce classes as a postcolonial or a modernist author, continue to be asked. The writers creating this literature in English did not fall easily into the familiar categories of Victorian, modern, or postmodern. If E. M. Forster's writing about India was considered Anglo-Indian, then should Indians writing in English be classified as Indo-Anglian? For a period of time it was. As K. R. Srinivasa Iyengar has humorously noted in the introduction to his book, *Indian Writing in English,* it was even referred to as Indo-Anglican literature. As late as 1991, the Indo-British writer Salman Rushdie (b. 1947) used this same term in his book *Imaginary Homelands*. As growing nationalisms created dissatisfaction with the term "Commonwealth," the notion of "world literatures written in English" came about. Even the term "postcolonial" came under fire in certain quarters for overplaying the connection with the colonizer; writers wished instead to be identified within their own national categories. The consideration of diaspora or immigrant writers is even more complicated. Both Salman Rushdie and V. S. Naipaul (b. 1932) now prefer to be called British writers, regardless of their countries of origin or of the fact that Rushdie is living in New York. Similarly with Bharati Mukherjee (b. 1940), who wrote of her origins in Calcutta in her fictionalized memoir, *The Tiger's Daughter* (1972), but who now sees herself as an American writer.

In his book *In Theory* the Marxist theorist Aijaz Ahmad maintained that the term "postcolonial" has been overused and used altogether too loosely. In a now famous review of one of the major books on postcolonial literature and theory, Bill Ashcroft, Gareth Griffiths, and Helen Tiffin's *The Empire Writes Back*, critics Vijay Mishra and Bob Hodge agree with Ahmad that it is important to use the term "post-colonial" (that is, with a hyphen) to denote an exact moment in time – the chronology of post-coloniality. But they also say that the term "postcolonial" can be used metonymically without the hyphen to indicate what might be called "an attitude" of postcoloniality, one that challenges the dominant hegemony and embodies notions of nationalism and liberation. Thus postcolonialism would neither be restricted to a period in time nor to those geographic regions affected by colonialism, but would include even works of British literature that embodied the attitude characteristic of "postcolonial" literature.

The literatures of Australia, New Zealand, and Canada have posed particular challenges to nomenclature, especially to the term "postcolonial," as critics have questioned whether "white" writing from settler colonies can properly be considered postcolonial. Mishra and Hodge (1994) justify the inclusion of literature by "white writers" from white settler colonies such as Australia, Canada, and South Africa and that of, say, indigenous peoples within the Americas, metonymically, since actual postcoloniality has not yet occurred. Indeed, some of the finest postcolonial writing is emanating from the indigenous writers of Australia and New Zealand, such as Patricia Grace (b. 1937), Keri Hulme (b. 1947), and Witi Ihimaera (b. 1944), the latter now famous for the Academy award nominated film *Whale Rider* (2003), based on his novel and screenplay. Here a young girl finds her origins in the complex, conflicted world of tradition in a struggle with modernity by connecting with her grandfather's tradition and by coming to an awareness of her Maori-ness. This is an example of the "attitude" of postcoloniality.

However, it must be acknowledged that this anti-imperial literature flowed almost directly from the tradition of British literature and was created by those well versed in English literature and skilled in the use of the language. Thus the irony of the term: although postcolonial literature is widely understood to be a literature that writes against empire, it is nevertheless a literature born of empire and one influenced by English literature – by, as Spenser put it in *The Faerie Queene*, "the well of English undefiled."

In introducing his Minute to Parliament in 1832 on English education in the colonies, T. B. Macaulay said:

> We have to educate a people who cannot at present be educated by means of their mother tongue.... The claims of our own language it is hardly necessary to recapitulate... The scepter may pass away from us.... But there are triumphs which are followed by no reverse. There is an empire exempt from all natural causes of decay. Those triumphs are the pacific triumphs of reason over barbarism; that empire is the imperishable empire of *our* arts and *our* morals, *our* literature and *our* laws. (quoted in Jussawalla 1985: 192–3)

Thus was invoked an empire on which the sun would never set. Macaulay did acknowledge, however, that "there are in [London] natives quite competent to discuss... with fluency and precision in the English language." Indeed, Indians were already creating (and continued to create) a literature written in English to express "their" India in contrast to that of British writers from William Makepeace Thackeray to E. M. Forster. Henry Derozio (1809–31), Kashiprasad Ghose (1809–73), Michael Madhusudhan Dutt (1827–73), and Bankim Chandra Chatterjee (1838–94) were some of the early colonials using English for their social and creative purposes. It was Mahatma Gandhi who turned English into an anti-hegemonic tool by using it to unify India's many different language speakers. For this he credits Ruskin's *Unto this Last* and Mr Bell's *English Reader*: "Mr. Bell rang the bell of alarm in my ear" (Iyengar 1973: 250).

Characteristics of the Postcolonial Novel

What most convincingly defines a postcolonial novel, then, is the author's attitude towards his or her country and its culture, an attitude of its distinctness and difference from that of the European colonizer. In the "postcolonial *Bildungsroman*," a favored form for the postcolonial writer, this attitude is reflected in the hero or heroine's developing affirmation of his or her native culture and history. In such novels, the process of the *Bildungsheld*'s personal growth and development almost always reflects his or her growing sense of national and ethnic belonging. This sense of national awareness, as opposed to a simple "coming of age," is a characteristic of the German *Bildungsroman* from Weiland to Hermann Hesse. Martin Swales notes that in Goethe's *Wilhelm Meister's Years of Apprenticeship* the awareness that the hero achieves is an awareness of both national and class identity. These two characteristics make this subgenre particularly relevant to the postcolonial literary tradition, as questions of both nation and class are raised by most of the protagonists in this literature.

A quick survey of postcolonial novels, beginning with R. K. Narayan's *Swami and Friends* (1935), often considered the first "postcolonial" novel written in English (though written more than ten years before Indian independence), to Salman

Rushdie's *Midnight's Children* (1981) and Arundhati Roy's *The God of Small Things* (1997), reveals that virtually all of these works follow the form of a young child coming of age within the context of his or her concerns over national, cultural, and class identity and belonging.

It is interesting to ask why this is so. The answer is that English language and literary education particularly influenced writers in the colonies. In his memoir, *My Days* (1974), Indian novelist R. K. Narayan notes that when he started writing, his uncle asked if he could write like Dickens. He also notes the influence of canonical British literary works: "Keats, Shelley, Byron and Browning. [These poets] spoke of an experience that was real and immediate in my surroundings and stirred in me a deep response" (1974: 58). The importance of English literary education even in postcolonial India is underscored in Vikram Seth's *A Suitable Boy* (1993), in which we are shown an Indian university's English department meeting regarding the possible inclusion of James Joyce in the canon to be taught: "If Joyce goes in, what comes out?" (1993: 52)

Lewis Carroll's *Alice in Wonderland* was one of the classics, widely read and taught, in the colonies. The story of a young girl growing up into a knowledge of herself, as belonging to England, even while wandering through a topsy-turvy world, was no doubt an influence not just on Anglo-Indian writers such as Frances Hodgson Burnett (as in *The Secret Garden*) but on "Indo-Anglian" writers such as R. K. Narayan. Even *Alice* can be read, metaphorically, as a "postcolonial *Bildungsroman.*" Here a little girl falls into the colonies, which interestingly are called "the antipathies," and who discovers in this world turned "mad" a sense of her own Englishness. She may not like the duchess and the Queen, *her* queen, Victoria, but she is English after all and stands up for British justice, fair play, and everything that embodies her culture. Certain dimensions of the *Bildungsroman* were borrowed from other novels that Indian writers read: Mark Twain's *The Adventures of Huckleberry Finn* (1884), Rudyard Kipling's *Kim* (1901), which seems distinctly to have influenced Rabindranath Tagore's *Gora* (1923), and James Joyce's *A Portrait of the Artist as a Young Man* (1917).

A comparison between an Indian novel and a Kenyan novel from the period under consideration demonstrates this influence further. When R. K. Narayan's *Swami and Friends* (1935) first opens, we encounter the 5- or 6-year-old Swami getting ready to go to the Albert Mission School that his father has chosen for him with great care because he wants Swami to get an English education so that he can gain a good government position, like his own, in the Indian Civil Service. One of the first classes he attends is "Scripture," in which "Mr. Ebenezer asks, 'Oh, wretched idiots!... Why do you worship dirty, lifeless, wooden idols and stone images?'" Mr. Ebenezer, a dark-skinned Indian Christian, further provokes the boys' ire by asking, "Did our Jesus practice dark tricks on those around him?" This form of colonial indoctrination and humiliation is also experienced by children in Kenyan writer Ngugi wa Thiongo's *Weep Not, Child* (1964). The headmaster in this novel believes that the best, the really excellent could only come from the white man. He brought up his boys to copy and cherish the white man's civilization as the only hope of mankind and especially of the black races. (1964: 115)

In a conversation with his girlfriend, Mwihaki, the protagonist of the novel, Njoroge, says:

"All this land belongs to the black people."
"Y-e-e-s. I've heard father say so. He says that if people had had education, the white man would not have taken all the land. I wonder why our old folk, the dead old folk had no learning when the white man came?"
"There was nobody to teach them English." (p. 37)

This process of inculcating in colonized people the belief in the supremacy of the European is the shared experience of all formerly colonial cultures. In *Weep Not, Child*, for example, we read that "Njoroge came to place faith in the Bible and with the vision of an educated life in the future was blended a belief in the righteousness of God. Equity and Justice were there in the world" (p. 49). In Ngugi's *The River Between* (1965), the young people come to feel ambivalence towards the initiation ritual of female circumcision and would rather be westernized and Christianized. But they are soon to be disillusioned. Swami's Albert Mission School friend, the westernized Rajam, does not care about Swami when he disappears before the all-important cricket match in which they plan to lick the "local" boys. Njoroge finds that his schoolmasters, whom he greatly respects, turn him over for torture and questioning about the killing of a white man. It is this betrayal at the hands of those they had admired and a consequent sense of disillusionment and anger at the colonial regime that proves to be the essential knowledge gained by these "colonial Adams."

Another important characteristic of postcolonial authors, whether they write in English or in French, is the effort of taking the colonizer's language and making it their own. This is another aspect that is borrowed from Mark Twain and James Joyce. While Twain was really the first postcolonial writer to change and vary English to express his native voice, a call taken up so well by James Joyce, it was Indian writer Raja Rao (b. 1909), in his Preface to *Kanthapura* (1938), who gave voice most eloquently to this decolonizing effort:

One has to convey in a language that is not one's own the spirit that is one's own. One has to convey the various shades and omissions of a certain thought-movement that looks maltreated in an alien language. I use the word "alien," yet English is not really an alien language to us. . . . We cannot write like the English. We should not. We cannot write only as Indians. We have grown to look at the large world as part of us. Our method of expression therefore has to be a dialect which will some day prove to be as distinctive and colorful as the Irish or the American. (1960: vii)

In February 1922, when James Joyce's *Ulysses* was first published, what was to become the postcolonial novel received its greatest gift – the gift of the permission to experiment with the English language. G. V. Desani's *All About H. Hatterr* (1948), a picaresque adventure that plays on *Alice in Wonderland,* won the most western encomia for being "modernist" in its approach to language experimentation. Salman Rushdie was directly influenced by Desani's word-play and temporally disjointed picaresque style. At first Rushdie disavowed any influence, claiming that his influences were "post-Joycean/sub-Joycean," but then in the special issue of the *New Yorker* that he edited for the fiftieth anniversary of India's independence, Rushdie acknowledged Desani's influence. In African literatures, the call to stylistic experimentation was taken up by the Nigerian writer Amos Tutuola (b. 1920) in his work *The Palm Wine Drinkard* (1953), which when he sent it to Faber and Faber was championed by T. S. Eliot, who urged a junior editor, "Surely keep 'drinkard.'" Ayi Kwei Armah's *The Beautyful Ones Are Not Yet Born* (1968) continued this experimental tradition in African literatures.

Within this tradition of linguistically experimental postcolonial fiction, the quint-essential "postcolonial" novel, Salman Rushdie's *Midnight's Children* (1981), takes its place. Told in picaresque style and in Indian English, with much word-play and punning, *Midnight's Children* is the *Bildungsroman* of Saleem Sinai, who is born at the exact moment of India's independence, August 15, 1947. Exchanged at birth with the actual Saleem Sinai, a child of a wealthy family, the hero's plight revolves around this switch and mistaken identity. Saleem goes through the process of rejecting his Catholic school education, playing with the English language and making fun of it – while also making fun of the way in which it is used in India — until such time as Saleem can assert his Indianness, even if both the character and his creator seem to be criticizing the "neocolonialism" of Indira Gandhi in India. Similarly, in *The Satanic Verses* (1989), Rushdie's character Gibreel Farishta, bowler-hatted and English, meta-morphoses from a monstrosity into a human when he discovers his antecedents in the Muslim community located in the Shandaar Café. He discovers that he wants to belong to his Muslim community despite having criticized his religion and his prophet. Indeed, each of Rushdie's three major works, *Midnight's Children, The Satanic Verses*, and *The Moor's Last Sigh*, is a *Bildungsroman* in which the main character comes to identify himself with his indigenous self – whether Muslim or Indian. *The Satanic Verses* and *Midnight's Children* reveal that Rushdie's chosen mode is social satire. Although this mode got him into trouble before (with Mrs Gandhi, who banned *Midnight's Children*), it was *The Satanic Verses,* most famously and decisively, that landed Rushdie in hot water. No other postcolonial novel has provoked such a reaction – either among certain Muslim clerics or in postcolonial theoretical circles. Rushdie had become a victim literally of "the death of the author" and of the condition of postmodernity, whereby authority was wrest from his hands and laid in the hands of warring groups of readers, who determined the "true" meaning of his novel. Prufrock-like, Rushdie said, "this is not what I meant at all": "*The Satanic Verses* was never intended as an insult . . . and [was] not representative of the point of view of the author" (1991: 431).

Female postcolonial novelists seem also to have drawn on the subgenre of the *Bildungsroman.* Bapsi Sidhwa's *Ice-Candy-Man,* originally published in Britain in 1988

and re-published in the US as *Cracking India* in 1991, and made into Deepa Mehta's
film *Earth* (1998), for example, is probably the most famous of these coming-of-age
novels. Lenny, a young Parsi girl, neither Hindu nor Muslim and from a community
with loyalties to the British, grows up in Lahore, in un-partitioned India. She
overhears political discussions – talk of independence, partitions, and Hindu–Muslim
hatred – by hiding under the table. She has polio and understands that such diseases
were brought by the British. But she loves her *ayah* or nursemaid, who is a Hindu.
Although the Muslims capture *ayah* by tricking Lenny, her sense of nationalism leads
her to the awareness that she belongs in Lahore, which thereafter becomes Pakistan.
This same pattern is followed in Sidhwa's *An American Brat* (1993), in which the main
character, Feroza, finds that despite being Americanized she is really a Parsi subcon-
tinental, one who wants to carry out her religious rituals in Idaho. These patterns were
laid out by the earliest and one of the finest of Indian women writers, Kamala
Markandaya, in such novels as *Nectar in a Sieve* (1954) and *Two Virgins* (1973). Her
novel *Some Inner Fury* (1955) most closely resembles the pattern of Narayan's *Swami*,
with the club-going father who at the time of independence tugs on the children's
loyalties. Anita Desai's *Where Shall We Go This Summer?* (1975) is another *Bildungsroman,* while her *Voices in the City* deals with the serious issue of bride burning.
Nigerian writer Buchi Emecheta's *Second-Class Citizen* (1974) and Caribbean writer
Jamaica Kincaid's *Lucy* (1991) are the *Bildungsromane* of immigrant young people
coming to an awareness of themselves as belonging to their communities in the
western world – one in Britain and one in the US. Despite leaving behind their
cultures with disgust, they find that they do not belong in the new world, either. This
is what might be called the *Bildungsroman* of "unbelonging," after the black-British
Caribbean writer Joan Riley's novel of that title, *The Unbelonging* (1985). The
Bildungsroman of belonging and of unbelonging in England is also the favored form
for Parsi novelist and British television producer Farrukh Dhondy's young adult
novels, *Come to Mecca* (1978), *Trip Trap* (1982), and *East End at Your Feet* (1976).
This pattern is continued in the black-British postcolonial novel of the present,
among these Hanif Kureishi's *Buddha of Suburbia* (1990) and Zadie Smith's *White
Teeth* (2000), and in the queer postcolonial novel, among these P. Parviraj's *Shiva and
Arun* (1998) and Shani Mootoo's *Cereus Blooms at Night* (1999).

Post-1945 Indian Writing in English

R. K. Narayan followed up his Swami trilogy with an expression of his disillusionment with India's leaders in *Waiting for the Mahatma* (1955), in which waiting for
Gandhi is rather like *Waiting for Godot*. In *The Painter of Signs* (1976) Narayan
humorously probes the wrongs of the Indira Gandhi government, particularly in
relation to "the family planning" initiative, which is also taken up in Rohinton
Mistry's *A Fine Balance* (1995). Mulk Raj Anand (b. 1905) and Raja Rao both had

careers spanning the century, from pre-independence days to the present, with Raja Rao having published his most recent book, *The Chess Master and his Moves,* in 1988.

In *Imaginary Homelands*, Salman Rushdie names those writers who have kept Indian literature in "excellent shape": Vikram Seth, Allan Sealy, Amitav Ghosh, Rohinton Mistry, Upamanyu Chatterjee, and Shashi Tharoor (1991: 3). Since then, both Amitav Ghosh (resident in New York) and Rohinton Mistry (resident in Canada) have gained great prominence. Ghosh's *The Circle of Reason* (1986), *In an Antique Land* (1992), *The Calcutta Chromosome* (1996), and, most recently, *The Glass Palace* (2000) have contributed greatly to postcolonial and postmodern fiction. Of course, Rushdie could not have predicted the immense popularity of Arundhati Roy's *The God of Small Things*, the *Bildungsroman* of a pair of twins coming to an awareness of themselves as belonging to their home state, Kerala, in south India despite their disillusionment with the Communist-dominated government of that state. Nor was Rushdie to have known of the subsequent great success of "writers of Indian origin" (after the new category created by the Indian government) such as Jhumpa Lahiri, the author of *Interpreter of Maladies* (1999) and *The Namesake* (2003). In the latter work, yet another *Bildungsroman* of identity, we read that "Being a foreigner is sort of a lifelong pregnancy – a perpetual wait, a constant burden, a continuous feeling out of sorts" (2003: 49).

Post-1945 African Literature in English

Postcolonial literature from African countries developed later than that from India. Alan Paton's *Cry, the Beloved Country* (1948) established the resistance novel on the African continent. South African novelists who challenged the racism of the apartheid regime became the first writers of "postcolonial intent" in Africa. Among these early novelists must be numbered Nadine Gordimer, who began writing in 1949 and won the Nobel Prize in 1991, and J. M. Coetzee, whose work comes later but is also part of that foundational generation of "African" writers in English (and who won the Nobel Prize in 2003 as well as being awarded two Booker Prizes). Unfortunately, these very writers have met with a sort of reverse racism in certain circles, stemming from Gayatri Spivak's seminal essay in postcolonial and feminist theory, "Can the subaltern speak?" which asks the question, "who can speak for whom?" that has become central to what has come to be called "subaltern studies." Both Nadine Gordimer's *Burger's Daughter* (1979) – another *Bildungsroman* - -and J. M. Coetzee's *Waiting for the Barbarians* (1981) (as also Athol Fugard's plays) poignantly treat the crimes of apartheid. The crumbling of post-apartheid society and frustrations with neocolonialism are reflected in Coetzee's *Disgrace* (2001). In recent years there has been a surge of African novels in English, including the work of South African novelist Lewis Nkosi and Nigerian novelist Ben Okri, the latter of whom writes in the vein of Achebe's *Things Fall Apart* and is often classified as "black British."

Frustration with "neocolonialism" and a dogmatic nationalism on the part of one's own people is echoed in the works of Kenyan and Nigerian postcolonial writers, the most famous of these being Ngugi wa Thiong'o in Kenya and Chinua Achebe (b. 1930) in Nigeria. Ngugi was expelled from Kenya for criticizing the "neocolonial" regime there in his play *I Shall Marry When I Want* (1982). Under the regime of Arap Moi, Ngugi was a wanted man. There was even a warrant issued for the arrest of his character from the novel of the same name, *Matigari* (1988). Achebe rightly belongs to that first generation of postcolonial/Commonwealth writers that included the earlier Indians, as he is among the first of the "black" African writers to write in English. After the great and enduring success of *Things Fall Apart* (1958), Achebe's *No Longer at Ease* (1960) and *A Man of the People* (1966) expressed disillusionment with the neocolonial government, leading to Achebe's long silence during the period of Nigeria's turbulent years.

In 1957 when Albert (later Chinua) Achebe went to attend the British Broadcasting Corporation's staff school, he became the first of the "colonial" writers to benefit from the BBC. One of the faculty members at that school, Gilbert Phelps, even helped him find a publisher for *Things Fall Apart*. The BBC also broadcast several other such novels for the "cultural" benefit of British overseas officers. This was the beginning of what might be called "the great school of BBC novels and writers." Cyprian Ekwensi and the dramatist Wole Soyinka also found there not only a new outlet for their creativity but also sources of employment. Edward Blishen ran a program called *A Good Read*, which covered writers from Achebe to Tsitsi Dangaremba and featured, among other writers, Okello Oculli (Uganda), Tayeb Salih (Sudan), James Ngugi (Kenya; later Ngugi wa Thiong'o), Mbella Senne Dipoko (Cameroon), and Ama Ata Aidoo (Ghana).

Perhaps the finest African novelist to experiment in a postmodern vein is the Somali writer Nuruddin Farah (b. 1945). *From a Crooked Rib* (1972) and *Variations on the Theme of an African Dictatorship* have female voices and concern female oppression. Farah tends to write in trilogies: *Sweet and Sour Milk* (1979), *Sardines* (1981), and *Close Sesame* (1983); and *Maps* (1986), *Gifts* (1993), and *Secrets* (1998). M. G. Vassanji, whose novel *The In Between World of Vikram Lal* won the Canadian Giller Prize in 2003, is an African writer living in Canada, but one who is proud to identify as an African writer. Born in Kenya, raised in Tanzania, and educated at MIT and at the International Writer's Program at the University of Iowa, Vassanji explores themes of memory, identity, and rootedness, particularly with respect to certain Asian communities in Africa.

Post-1945 Caribbean Writing

Vidiadhar Surajprasad Naipaul (b. 1932), born in Chagunas, Trinidad but who eschews the label of "Caribbean writer," clearly acknowledges the BBC for employing him, for getting him out of the nervous depression he was in at Oxford, and for providing him and C. L. R. James (whose cricket memoir *Beyond a Boundary* has become an important analogical source for that part of postcolonial theory called "border studies") with a room, not only one in which they could write, but also one in which they could share their drafts and thoughts. From what we know of the two and their respective politics now, it is hard to believe that they had this close relationship. Above all, though, V. S. Naipaul was launched as a journalist and author by his interviews with writers and his weekly column in *The Listener*, the BBC's magazine. Naipaul is probably the postcolonial novelist with the most substantial body of writing but the one most difficult to place. He has never wanted to be classified as a Caribbean. And he would particularly balk at being categorized as "black British," as this would run counter to his identity as a Hindu Brahmin (some Brahmins liked to see themselves as a "fairer" caste). From his *A House for Mr Biswas* (1961), another *Bildungsroman*, onwards, through his many novels and travelogues to his essays about writing, *The Writer and the World* (2002), Naipaul has deployed a pungent style to criticize practically all groups: British, Indian, Caribbean, and particularly Muslim communities. Some postcolonial critics have even claimed that his 2001 Nobel Prize was a reaction to the anti-Islamic feeling prompted by the 2001 destruction of the World Trade Center. His autobiographical *Enigma of Arrival* (1987) traces his coming to an awareness of himself as "a person of Indian origin," connecting with the chanting of the Gayatri mantra, "Om Bhur Buh Svaha," after having made his way through Anglicization, Stilton cheese, and all. It is in his "Hinduness" that Naipaul's identity lies. Raja Rao-like, he would say, "My India I carry with me." And this, despite his severe criticisms of Hindus in *A House for Mr Biswas*, *An Area of Darkness*, *India: A Wounded Civilization*, and *India: A Million Mutinies Now*. Notwithstanding notions of the "death of the author" and the post-structuralist sense that a text can be understood without reference to the author and to authorial intention, Naipaul's case, like Salman Rushdie's, demonstrates the importance of archival and interview records that indicate the writer's sense of identity and belonging.

Caribbean novelists who see things very differently than V. S. Naipaul include George Lamming, whose *Castle of My Skin* is a classic postcolonial *Bildungsroman*, Sam Selvon (1923–98), Wilson Harris (b. 1921), Earl Lovelace (b. 1935), and Caryl Phillips (b. 1958). Wilson Harris's *Guyana Quartet* (1960–3), starting with *The Palace of the Peacock* (1960), makes a major contribution to the postmodern-postcolonial novel. Earl Lovelace, whose novels are set in Trinidad and Tobago, is perhaps the Caribbean novelist most rooted in the West Indies. *The Wine of Astonishment* is probably his best-known novel to explore the juxtaposition of western Christianity and his indigenous vernacular culture. Caribbean literature is the model, within postcolonial studies, for a world-wide creolization that is developing. The poet Edward Kamau Braithwaite was the first writer to use the term "creolization" to embrace all of the cultures of the Caribbean that were oppressed by slavery and colonialism. Increasingly, with the importance of "hybridity" as a concept in post-colonial studies, notions of "creolization" and Eduard Glissant's *Poetics of Relation*

(1990) are helping to establish a "creolite" movement, one which dovetails nicely with postmodern notions of the fluidity of identity and consciousness.

The writers of the female *Bildungsroman* in the Caribbean, in the wake of Jean Rhys's *Wide Sargasso Sea*, tend to write novels that challenge colonial depictions of female natives. Novelists Michelle Cliff (b. 1946) in *Abeng* (1984) and *No Telephone to Heaven* (1987), Paule Marshall in *Brown Girl, Brownstones* (1959), and Jamaica Kincaid (b. 1949) in her fiction all explore female coming of awareness within the context of postcolonial ethnic and national identities

Theoretical Challenges

Postcolonial literature, especially of the Anglophone world, is a rich and heterogeneous field. Much of the early criticism focused on classifying and describing this vast new literature. This early work was carried out by such critics as William Walsh, David McCutchion, C. D. Narasimhaiah, Meenakshi Mukherjee, Bruce King, G. D. Killiam, and, most importantly for African literatures, Bernth Lindfors. But in more recent years, with the development of postcolonial theory, questions of language and authenticity, nationalism and identity have been revived in theoretical terms. Some of these theoretical concerns reiterate those that have been touched upon above: (1) the political implications of the novelist's choice of language as a medium of expression, (2) problems of identity and national belonging, (3) hybridity and the place of postcolonial literature in an increasingly globalized world, and (4) the positioning of the critic in relation to the novel and the world.

The most important theoretical question concerning "postcolonial" writing has been that of the chosen language of the author. While engaged by postcolonial theorists it is the novelists themselves who addressed this question first. In India this question was raised over and over again, until the poet R. Parathasarthy finally dismissed it as akin to flogging a dead horse. Some Indian authors, Arundhati Roy among them, affirm that they write in English because in India English is the first language for most writers and readers. *Los Angeles Times* editor Steve Wasserman asked Nadine Gordimer to explain her choice of English as the language of her novels, only to be told that she regretted having lived in South Africa for so long and not having learned an African language. She felt that the most vibrant writing coming from the Third World was in its indigenous languages. In African postcolonial literature this issue has been central ever since Ngugi wa Thiong'o proclaimed years ago that he would no longer write in English but would write instead exclusively in his mother tongue. By contrast, Chinua Achebe wrote his great paean to the English language in *Morning Yet on Creation Day* (1975), in which he argued that the English language should continue to be the language in which postcolonial literature is written. In his essay, "The African writer and the English language," Achebe stressed the importance of English as the language through which all African writers could talk to each other:

If it failed to give them a song it at least gave them a tongue for sighing. There are not many countries in Africa today where you can abolish the language of the erstwhile colonial powers and still retain the facility for mutual communication. Therefore those African writers who have chosen to write in English or French are not unpatriotic smart alecks with an eye on the main chance – outside their own countries. (1976: 77)

This was not, however, Ngugi wa Thiong'o's complaint against the English language. His complaint was that reading and writing in English would, in effect, continue the process of colonizing the mind of the formerly colonized peoples; that it would be a form of continued intellectual imperialism. As the title of his book, *Decolonizing the Mind,* suggests, Ngugi believes that completing decolonization requires a shedding of the oppressor's language altogether.

Early critical and theoretical attempts to grapple with issues of authenticity, indigeneity, and hybridity were to be found in the Negritude movement and the work of Aimé Césaire and Frantz Fanon, who believed in the importance of cultural affirmation and resisted the deracination that coincided with colonialism. In the wake of critic Homi Bhabha's theory of hybridity, which dismisses questions of nationalism and indigeneity as essentialist, "nativist" critics have resurrected not only the question of belonging and identity but that of "who can speak for whom." Fanon's *Black Skin, White Masks* (1952) argues against the deracination that comes with assimilation or what Bhabha has called "colonial mimicry." Half a century ago, Fanon articulated what writers and individuals reaching for hybridity today seem only now to be discovering: that for the dominant majority, those aspiring to the condition of "hybridity" will never be acknowledged as "white." However creolized and globalized the world is becoming, a sense of indigenous identity seems to be reasserted in the novels of many young writers, among them Chitra Divakurani Bannerjee (b. 1956), in which the mixing and merging of cultures seems to fail the characters. In her book, *A Mistress of Spices* (1997), for example, an Indian, Tilo, tries hard to westernize, even to the point of connecting with another indigenous culture, the Native American, but has to retreat back into her Indianness. Fanon would say that this is a classic example of the colonizer not allowing the colonized to become assimilated or "white," which allows the colonizer to continue not to recognize the colonized person as an equal. Fanon urged resistance to the "internalized guilt" of not being white and of trying to be white – particularly in the case of mixed race women who saw themselves as superior because of their "whiteness." In the early resistance to colonialism, therefore, it was important for the writers not to be "Calibans," as Aimé Césaire has said.

Raja Rao, who was educated at the Sorbonne, said in an interview that his early efforts to assert his Indianness in writing style and content stemmed from the intellectual company of colleagues such as Césaire and Amilcar Cabral, who asserted the importance of a "national culture" (Jussawalla and Dasenbrock 1992). But Fanon also notes that it is the "colonialists who became the defenders of the native style." In other words, the colonialists wanted the colonized to remain exoticized but denigrated "others" – different from and never equal to them. This more or less becomes the premise of Edward Said's *Orientalism* (1978), a book that is a cornerstone of postcolonial theory, as it explores how natives are represented by colonials and how that representation takes on a politically diabolical life and character of its own, not just in the colonial encounter but in current politics. Said's example is Henry Kissinger's portrayal of Palestine and, more recently, the American demonization of Islam in general. With the explosion of the Rushdie affair, this latter issue caught Said in a bind. Although Said had always criticized Naipaul for his characterization of Islam, it was Said's friend, Salman Rushdie, whose portrayal of Islam raised many more hackles (during the *Satanic Verses* controversy Said was embarrassingly quiet).

This typifies a dilemma of a number of postcolonial theorists. Gayatri Spivak, for example, argues in her famous 1988 essay, "Can the subaltern speak?" that the indigene female wishing to commit *sati* (the Hindu widow's "suicide" by burning on her husband's funeral pyre) should be allowed to "speak" for herself. She even makes the case for this "subaltern's" authentic Indianness and cultural rootedness, seemingly arguing for the Hindu widow's right to continue this barbaric tradition and for the colonizer not to interfere in the practice. While *Orientalism* questioned the colonial representations of indigenous subjects, Spivak raised the issue of who can adequately represent the colonial and gendered subject. In her most recent book, *A Critique of Postcolonial Reason* (1999), Spivak returns to the *Srimadbhagvatgita* (commonly referred to as the *Bhagvad Gita*) because she is "an Indian and born a Hindu," and feels obligated to "interpellate" her "native informant/postcolonial voice" (1999: 40). While "Can the subaltern speak?" was criticized in some quarters for being "essentialist" in nature, and while Spivak herself has disavowed national identities, in this new tome she indeed seems to have reverted, Naipaul-like, towards her Indian Brahmin, Hindu self. Like a *Bildungsroman,* Spivak's recent book explores her own coming into awareness of herself as Indian.

Of all the changes that have recently come to postcolonial studies, the change that is perhaps least welcome is a sharp and growing disjunction in the field. Those interested in postcolonial literature are increasingly divided into two groups: those who are interested principally in the literature and the writers who produce it and those who are interested principally in the theory of the "post-colonial" situation. This unfortunate division is at least partially a generational one, between older scholars who "discovered" Commonwealth literature and have worked to bring it to public awareness and younger scholars who approach the literature through the perspective of the theorists who have brought the literature to their awareness. Perhaps in the future this gap can be narrowed. Theorists of the field should welcome the opportunity to test the adequacy of their theories against more than a limited set of examples, while scholars of the literature should welcome the insights into the novels provided by fresh theoretical approaches. The study of postcolonial literature and theory should be two sides of the same coin, not two increasingly divergent intellectual discourses, as it has been of late.

Another unfortunate consequence of the rise of postcolonial theory is the unwillingness of some proponents to see anything in postcolonial literature except its challenges to hegemonic forces. Indeed, some novelists have articulated a sense of frustration with continually being tied to the colonial millstone. V. S. Naipaul for example, at a 2002 postcolonial writers' conference in Delhi, abruptly interrupted Nayantara Sahgal to note that to define oneself against colonialism is not to become "post-colonial."

It has been widely argued and even more widely assumed that postcolonial literature is necessarily anti-canonical, part of the current movement away from a fixed canon of "great works" taught in the curriculum. Obviously, a great deal of the controversy over the teaching of this literature has focused on this issue. In my *Interviews with Writers of the Post-Colonial World*, many of the authors attempted to extricate themselves from any associations with an anti-canonical movement and to argue that their works are connected to and logically part of a larger canon of world literature. Moreover, their texts themselves seem to stand in a relation to central texts of western literature, as a number of these titles – *Things Fall Apart*, *A Grain of Wheat*, *Omeros* – suggest. In fact, Edward Said's *Culture and Imperialism* (1993) demonstrates that native identity is not fashioned by rejecting everything colonial but sometimes, for example in the case of Ngugi's *The River Between*, by reviving the western literary tradition. Another example of this is to be found in Derek Walcott's *Omeros*, an epic poem that rewrites Homer (and Dante) in the context of contemporary St Lucia in the Caribbean. In a clear parallel to James Joyce's *Ulysses*, Walcott's work of postcolonial literature is intertextually related to the canon.

Perhaps the most prominent school of postcolonial theory, one that concerns itself with the economics of imperialism, is the "Subaltern Studies group" (which takes its name from the British army's word for a "private," the lower level soldiers who would not bite the bullets greased with pig fat in the Indian mutiny of 1857, a term that comes to us via the work of the Marxist theorist Gramsci). As noted above, this group is largely led and promoted by Gayatri Spivak. In addition to Spivak and Said, the list of major postcolonial theorists includes Homi Bhabha, whose growth as a critic seems to be in direct opposition to this pattern, as he seeks to "de-privilege specific subaltern histories and identities" (1994: 192–3). He has moved over the course of his career from a focus on "colonial stereotypes" and "mimicry" to his notion of "hybridity." Instead of thinking in terms of essential identities and narratives of originary and initial subjectivities, he now maintains that the "social articulation of difference, from the minority perspective, is a complex on-going negotiation that seeks to authorize cultural hybridities that emerge in moments of historical transformation" (p. 2). Bhabha rejects what he calls "nativist" positions that set up "binary oppositions" (p. 35) between the first and third world. His aim is to revise precisely the kind of "nationalist/nativist" binary discourse that is reflected in much postcolonial theory and criticism.

Much postcolonial theory relies on and takes its terms from European Marxism and psychoanalysis, and for this it has been criticized as being Eurocentric and as continuing to colonize as opposed to challenging European hegemonic forces. Homi Bhabha has therefore borrowed from articulations of the postcolonial condition by indigenous thinkers such as Frantz Fanon and Amilcar Cabral. But since these too follow in the traditions of western psychoanalysis and take their terms from western models, there is a growing feeling that the criticism and theory do not do justice to the literature and that new terms need to be articulated. The stark polarities that currently structure postcolonial theory become more complex and therefore less starkly polarized when we turn to the literature to see how they play out.

This study of the Anglophone literature of the countries that were formerly part of the British empire was until recently a marginal part of English studies; "Commonwealth literature" was seldom an integral part of undergraduate or graduate curricula. However, the continuing achievement and remarkable power of writers in English from the Indian subcontinent, Africa, the Caribbean, and other parts of the English-speaking world is now all but impossible to ignore. Many of these writers have attained considerable prominence on the international literary scene, and prizes such as the Booker Prize and even the Nobel Prize (following in the footsteps of Rabindranath Tagore, who was awarded the latter prize in 1913) have increasingly gone to writers from the postcolonial world. What had been a marginal and arguably neglected field can complain of neglect no longer.

REFERENCES AND FURTHER READING

Note: I have discussed the importance of the German *Bildungsroman* for postcolonial coming-of-age novels in "Kim, Huck and Naipaul: using the postcolonial *Bildungsroman* to (re)define postcoloniality," *Links & Letters*, 4 (1997): 25–38 and "(Re)reading *Kim*: defining Kipling's masterpiece as postcolonial," *Journal of Commonwealth and Postcolonial Studies*, 5/2 (Fall 1998): 112–29.

Achebe, Chinua (1976) "The African writer and the English language," in *Morning Yet on Creation Day*. Garden City: Anchor.

Ahmad, Aijaz (1992) *In Theory: Classes, Nations, Literatures*. London: Verso.

Bhabha, Homi K. (1994) *The Location of Culture*. New York: Routledge.

Fanon, Frantz (1967) *Black Skin, White Masks*. New York: Grove Press.

Iyengar, K. R. Srinivasa (1973) *Indian Writing in English*. Bombay: Asia Publishing.

Jussawalla, Feroza (1985) *Family Quarrels: Towards a Criticism of Indian Writing in English*. Berne and New York: Peter Lang.

——(1997) *Conversations with V. S. Naipaul*. Jackson: University Press of Mississippi.

Jussawalla, Feroza and Dasenbrock, Reed Way (1992) *Interviews with Writers of the Post-Colonial World*. Jackson: University Press of Mississippi.

Lahiri, Jhumpa (2003) *The Namesake*. New York: Houghton Mifflin.

Mishra, Vijay and Hodge, Bob (1994) "What is post(-)colonialism?," in Patrick Williams and Laura Chrisman (eds.) *Colonial Discourse and Post-Colonial Theory: A Reader*. New York: Columbia University Press.

Narayan, R. K. (1974) *My Days*. New York: Viking.

——(1980) *Swami and Friends*. Chicago: University of Chicago Press.

Ngugi wa Thiong'o (1964) *Weep Not, Child*. London: Heinemann.

——(1986) *Decolonising the Mind: The Politics of Language in African Literature*. London: James Currey.

Rao, Raja (1960) [1938] *Kanthapura*. New York: New Directions.

Rushdie, Salman (1991) *Imaginary Homelands*. New York: Viking.

Seth, Vikram (1993) *A Suitable Boy*. New York: HarperCollins.

Spivak, Gayatri Chakravorty (1994) [1988] "Can the subaltern speak?," in Patrick Williams and

Laura Chrisman (eds.) *Colonial Discourse and Post-Colonial Theory: A Reader.* New York: Columbia University Press.

——(1999) *A Critique of Postcolonial Reason; Toward a History of the Vanishing Present.* Cambridge, MA: Harvard University Press.

Swales, Martin (1978) *The German Bildungsroman from Wieland to Hesse.* Princeton: Princeton University Press.

Williams, Patrick and Chrisman, Laura (eds.) (1994) *Colonial Discourse and Post-Colonial Theory: A Reader.* New York: Columbia University Press.

8

Fictions of Belonging: National Identity and the Novel in Ireland and Scotland

Gerard Carruthers

I

Yeats Is Dead! (2001) is a cooperative novel written by fifteen Irish writers in aid of Amnesty International. It both utilizes and subverts strongly received ideas about Irish expression. The very device of relay composition, each of its authors taking a chapter in the novel, parodies notions of Irish sociability and loquacity. The novel is gossipy, full of innuendo and knowing insider jokes centered on the pursuit of a lost 600-page manuscript by James Joyce. Throughout, however, moments often hilariously couched but encoding serious concerns puncture supposed common Irishness, the mythology of which was so cemented in the generation of Yeats. For instance, Roddy Doyle presents us with a character who controls "a global empire from the back garden of a corporation house, bang in the middle of the Celtic Tiger's litter tray" (O'Connor 2001: 13). The recent economic pride of Ireland, imaged in such romantic, animate terms masks a story of profound urban rot, acknowledged by Doyle's socially aware subversion of the trope, as well as wider problems of social dislocation with which the old organic national iconographies cannot cope. If the center cannot hold, no one has told Ireland. One of Frank McCourt's characters bitterly complains, "Everyone in Dublin is writing a fucking memoir. Thank God Limerick has been spared" (p. 271), and so points to the metropolitan self-importance of the capital. If Joyce had fled a city of parochial claustrophobia, things are perhaps no better a century later in the navel-gazing that is here diagnosed. As *Yeats Is Dead!* frequently makes clear, the pursuit of literature, so central to the self-imaging of Ireland in the Revival of the early twentieth century and amidst its struggle for independence in 1916, now in the twenty-first century in the search for the missing Joyce text, has become a matter of commodity (given the prospect of an American library buying the manuscript if found) and of the professional reputations of "the jackeen academic gang [in Dublin] – UCD and Trinity, one as bad as the other" (p. 271). In this latter remark we see another skepticism, this time towards the religious divide of Ireland (University College Dublin being Catholic, Trinity being Protestant) as being no longer an important cultural factor in the nation. Ireland's old distinctions of identity, even where these were crucially problematic before, are now witheringly viewed. *Yeats Is Dead!* is full of enjoyable knockabout fun, but it is also a compendium of serious complaint that Ireland remains as unrealistically attainable as ever even though, and perhaps because, the issues that are central to the lives of its inhabitants are more to do with a global culture of human avarice than with a mere national condition.

Skepticism towards the vitality of post-independence Ireland is a phenomenon visible in fiction from around the time that Irish independence was theoretically increasing with the Free State becoming a republic in 1948 and leaving the Commonwealth in 1949. This is at first somewhat oblique, however, in the work of Mervyn Wall (1908–97), whose novel *The Unfortunate Fursey* (1946) burlesques Celtic Christianity; the hapless monk, Fursey, visited in his cell by Satan and unable to expel this visitation, goes on a heroic quest in search of a lady love. We are into a cultural landscape that is puritanical and misogynistic and romantically driven in turn, and Fursey, unsure whether to follow the nomadic, pagan life-style of the heroes associated with the Fionn cycle of tales or the strictures of Christianity, and uncertain, generally, about the action that is most appropriate to create a sense of wholesome order in his life, is a figure who exposes the rather mixed up foundational myths of victim, saint, and warrior in modern Irish identity. At around the same time Ireland's most brilliant contemporaneous writer, Samuel Beckett (1906–89), increased his modernist disaffection with the country of his birth. Already resident in France and feeling increasingly irritated with cultural and philosophical conservatism in both Britain and Ireland, he began to write in the language of that country in the early 1950s. His trilogy of novels, *Molloy* (1951), *Malone Dies* (1953), and *The Unnamable* (1953), represents an important part of an oeuvre whose "language of exhaustion and abjection famously demystified the whole notion of identity and the concept of an indigenous tradition" (Ryan 2002: 147).

It is an interesting phenomenon of the 1950s that second- and third-generation Irish were producing a more expansive fiction of "community" outside Ireland. *Home is the Stranger* (1950), by Edward A. McCourt (b.1907), follows a couple from Ulster to the vast expanses of Canada, where they find their lives making much more sense than before, now that they are removed from the cramped, competitive culture they have left behind. *The Last Hurrah* (1956), by Rhode Island writer Edwin O'Connor (1918–60), deals with the confident, streetwise, though morally complex world of Irish-American city politicians. Both of these books find prominent place in the Cork University Press anthology, *Irish Writing in the Twentieth Century* (2000), pointing to the increasing conception of Irish culture as something not to be constrained by simple geographical boundaries (Pierce 2000: 1321). Such a maneuver makes clear historical sense in keeping with the diasporas of Irish history, but the very wide anthologizing energies of recent Irish Studies so strongly licensed by the post-national and postcolonial moods of western culture perhaps raise a problem nearer to home in Ireland. Edna Longley has most eloquently drawn attention to the sometimes all too facile canonization of Irish literature in the contemporary period (Longley 1994: 22–44). The biggest instance here, arguably, would be the bold profligacy with which the hugely impressive *The Field Day Anthology of Irish Writing* collects together writers from the Irish Republic and from British Ulster. For all that this project is explicit about issues of belonging and proceeds in a finely nuanced, scrupulously scholarly fashion, it carries out a *fait accompli* by subsuming too many writers underneath a blanket Irish identity, and might be judged to be appropriating rather than including. Questions both of how geographically far one might travel across the world and how near to the island of Ireland one can go when defining Irish literature remain problematic. To take one further example that is telling in terms of the novel, what is one to do in the case of Iris Murdoch (1919–99)? Her milieu might well be thought to be that of Oxford and the perplexities of postwar philosophy, but, born in Dublin, she has herself emphasized her Anglo-Irish identity, and two of her best novels, *The Unicorn* (1963) and her *The Red and the Green* (1965), a moving account of events surrounding the Irish rebellion of 1916, are set in Ireland. Why can the *Irish Writing in the Twentieth Century* include extracts from McCourt and O'Connor but nothing from Murdoch?

One writer who emigrated to North America in 1948, Brian Moore (1921–99), has been among the leading novelists documenting social conditions in postwar Northern Ireland. His portrayal of Belfast in particular finds a place of almost unremitting stasis and bleakness. Characteristically writing a highly accomplished prose that fluently manages a welter of realistic detail, Moore has perhaps been most successful in his portraiture of Irish women. *The Lonely Passion of Judith Hearn* (1956) is a novel that sets out the excruciating physical and social claustrophobia of a respectable spinster lady eking out the end of her economically frugal existence in a Catholic boarding house. Obliquely drawing upon a pietistic Catholic vocabulary that is most explicitly registered in the title, the "passion" of Judith Hearn is her mental scourging in a thousand little indignities and a slow trudge to death in a life that is publicly coffined. Bleakly, even when Hearn forms a relationship of sorts, with James Madden, he turns out to be a sadist. The Catholic repression of Ulster turns out to be as puritanical, repressive, and warping as anything Presbyterian Ulster might have to offer. Full of dark, rain-filled skies and a very dismally described Belfast Lough, the novel is in keeping with a Joycean tradition of portrayal of stagnancy and lack of hospitability in the natural as well as the urban Irish setting. *Cold Heaven* (1983) is a novel full of grim inversions and uncomfortably unresolved questions, as the adulterous atheist Marie Davenport (or, nearly a pun, "Mary Divine Port") undergoes a series of Marian visions. Is she the sinner sought out by divine agency, or the woman whose attempts to have personal life experiences are crushed by a deep, psychologically penetrating and insidious culture that can countenance no image of proper womanhood except upon the model of Mariology? The exchanges that follow between the clergy who learn of her visions and Marie are also ambiguous, either suggesting that she is not to be allowed to describe them in her own terms, or that the Church is genuinely attempting to make sense of her experiences.

In an Ireland where the censorship of the literary representation of sexual activities (particularly any involving the act of contraception) was not truly relaxed until the 1980s, the novels of Edna O'Brien (b.1930) shocked mainstream Ireland more than any others in the second half of the twentieth century. *The Country Girls* (1960) was the first book in a trilogy that made an impact by detailing the awakening emotions and physicality of country convent girls (such licentiousness, then, was not merely to be associated with the debauched city, but was available in the rural setting that in many ways has traditionally represented the spiritual heartland of Ireland). The implicit optimism that forms one strand of these books, and a veritable catalogue of strangely irregular liaisons that is found in much of the rest of O'Brien's work in this period, are a curious sign of the female revolution of the 1960s that, arguably, did not actually occur in Irish society. In her later works, O'Brien dissects an increasingly dark feminine experience, including incest in *Down by the River* (1996). In seventy-two short chapters fragments of detail (obvious but not pieced together by those who had the power to do so), the miserable splinters of Mary MacNamara's life, a 14-year-old being raped by her father, are set out. At one point this metaphor becomes all too literal as Mary's father exacts on her a terrible punishment with a broom handle in response to her attempts to run away: "She could not tell how deeply it had plunged, all she felt was the wooden teeth cutting and the splinters snagging" (O'Brien 1997: 121). The writing in the novel is sometimes more graphic even than this and indicates O'Brien's anger over the real-life case of a 14-year-old who five years earlier had been refused permission to leave the republic for an abortion after she had been raped. Sexual repression and, indeed, that which it smothers, healthy sexual expression, have been predominant themes in post-1960s fiction. This fiction now attempts to essay a hidden Ireland, an Ireland that seems to many writers to have been kept inordinately obscure by the apparatus of the state. John McGahern (b. 1934) fell foul of the Censorship of Publications Act (1929) with his novel *The Dark* (1965), and was consequently removed from his state position as a teacher. This story of a boy growing up, piecing together what inklings he can of the power of sexuality, as he lives somewhat awkwardly with his widower father, and *Amongst Women* (1990), another tale of difficult communication between a father and his children, both question Ireland's conceit of itself as a healthy, family-centered society and, particularly, expose the expressive insecurities of Irish masculinity. The work of John Broderick (1927–89) connects with that of O'Brien and McGahern in its gamut of shoddy institutional and personal behavior on the part of middle Ireland in the 1960s and 1970s.

Alongside Broderick and McGahern another male writer has been particularly expert at picking at the hard male institutional contours of Irish society. Bernard Mac Laverty (b. 1942) has the unique distinction of being claimed not only by Irish literature, but also by Scottish literature, owing to his many years resident in Islay and Glasgow. In the latter place he befriended and shared readings with such writers as Tom Leonard and James Kelman, making him a bright presence in the west of Scotland literary firmament (Gifford et al. 2002: 942). His first novels, written while a teacher in Scotland, are very much about his Ulster background. *Lamb* (1980) deals with a tragic lack of love in a borstal run by a religious order and *Cal* (1983) provides a shockingly tender portrait of love between a young Catholic who has been complicit in the murder of a Royal Ulster Constabulary police officer and his unsuspecting widow. These beautifully cadenced but very dramatic stories of victims of the large-scale cultural situations pertaining in Northern Ireland give way to a no less moving but altogether quieter, more mundane scenario in *Grace Notes* (1997). The novel is set in Glasgow, the highlands, and Eastern Europe, as well as Ulster, and Mac Laverty's love of music is to the fore as composer Catherine McKenna, estranged daughter of a devout Catholic Ulster publican, returns from Glasgow to attend her father's funeral in understandably reflective mood. Unsentimentally, she realizes that her alienation from her family, amidst their disapproval of her pregnancy out of wedlock, relationship failure, and near total personal breakdown, gives her a particularly profound desire to renew contact with them. The harrowing events that have led to her estrangement have not made her give up on the idea of the harmony that is so often difficult and absent from the human condition, but have heightened her awareness of its necessity as an aspiration that bolsters the business of living. Mac Laverty spent many years working on *Grace Notes*, and this effort is rewarded in his execution of a complex and lavish but unpretentious musical detail and imagery throughout the novel, which extends to a crosscutting, or contrapuntal, mode of narration between different times. At the heart of the novel is the public performance in a converted church in Glasgow of Catherine's composition incorporating the drums of the Orange Order, which her background ought to make her despise:

> The Lambegs have been stripped of their bigotry and have become pure sound. The black sea withdraws. So too the trappings of the church – they have nothing to do with belief and exist as colour and form. It is infectious. On this accumulating wave the drumming has a fierce joy about it. Exhilaration comes from nowhere. The bell-beat, the slabs of brass, the whooping of the horns, the battering of the drums. Sheer fucking unadulterated joy. Passion and pattern. An orchestra at full tilt – going fortissimo – the bows, up and down, jigging and sawing in parallel – the cellos and basses sideways. The brass shining and shouting at the back. The orchestra has become a machine, a stitching machine. The purpose of training an army is to dehumanise, to make a machine of people yet here all this discipline, all this conformity was to express the individuality and uniqueness of one human being. (Mac Laverty 1997: 276)

Here we see Catherine extracting a sense of harmony not only for herself but also for her community, including her father. In no way an act of defiance, the father's daughter will overcome his visceral hatred of the drums for him and in tribute to him, precisely because she cares for him and laments the circumstances that had embittered him and so many others in Ulster. In the present-tense narration and the exhilarated musical moment, historically thrawn circumstances, such as the

"Troubles" of Ireland and Catherine's awkward personal history, are erased. Music is proof of the strength of the uncorrupted life-urge and the possibility of "unadulterated joy," even if fleetingly evidenced, and is the most effective way of Catherine rendering a heartfelt and loving version of the traditional Irish address to the bereaved, extended to her whole community, "I'm sorry for your trouble."

Like Mac Laverty, William Trevor (b.1928) and John Banville (b.1945) are to be included among Irish writers whose reputations mushroomed abroad during the 1980s. Trevor has an eye for eccentric and grotesque portraiture. This can take particularly dramatic and rebarbative substance as in the characters of child abusers in *The Old Boys* (1964) and *Felicia's Journey* (1994). It is more likely to emerge from the quirks in behavior and circumstances of normal people, as in the case of so many of his fine short stories, perhaps Trevor's true métier, and in a novel, *Mrs Eckdorf in O'Neill's Hotel* (1970); this collides clinical observation and moments of dark humor to suggest that the human condition ought to be seen sardonically with regard to its place within the physical and social worlds that surround it. The peculiar effect of this latter mode found across Trevor's oeuvre is the creation of a particularly ironic sympathy. John Banville has been as equally at home with non-Irish as Irish subjects in his fiction. Partly, perhaps, in deliberate reaction against the expectations of the rootedness that an Irish writer should display, Banville produces a sequence of novels, including *Doctor Copernicus* (1976) and *Kepler* (1981), on the rational lives of scientists, depicting an intensity in these lives which is charged with aesthetic as well as scientific formal predilections. In *The Untouchable* (1997) the real-life British spy affair with Anthony Blount at its center is transmogrified into a situation where an Irish, or at least Anglo-Irish, protagonist is involved. As ever with Banville's fiction we are reminded of how translatable the concerns of individuals are across the boundaries of nationality (just as they are across boundaries such as those supposed between artists and scientists). One has the impression that Banville's many years as the literary editor of that core cultural institution, *The Irish Times*, has confirmed him in his universalism of outlook. Jennifer Johnston (b.1930) is the other Irish novelist most adept at dealing with intense feelings, of love as well as of professional purpose, which transcend boundaries either within Ireland, or with other locations. Her *The Old Jest* (1979) is one of the finest fictions dealing with the Anglo-Irish war of 1919–21, but her entire oeuvre, consistently well written, makes her a writer who ought to be better known in the English-speaking world.

The proliferation of Irish experience, in keeping with postmodernist and post-nationalist sensibilities, is marked in a range of normative, fragmentary life-style fiction. Deirdre Madden (b.1960) in *One by One in the Darkness* (1996) produces a beautifully interwoven novel of past and present which interrogates the relationship of the individual to family identity. The IRA is about to declare the first of its historic ceasefires in 1994 and the Quinn sisters are haunted by the tragic event of the murder of their father, mistaken for another man, during the "Troubles." On the one hand, the family is brought closer together by their loss; on the other, each of the three sisters to some degree derives a heightened awareness of their individuality.

The pattern of history (a sequence of landmark events from the quarter-century of armed conflict in Ulster is impressively rendered) is reviewed against the ordinary lives that this history crushes. The supposed order of history imposed, as ever, retrospectively does not sit easily with the tragic randomness experienced by the Quinns and leads them both to value their familial relations and their rootedness in Ulster, but to realize that these things are not to be taken for granted, nor described by the narratives of others. *One by One in the Darkness* is simultaneously one of the most sensitive and hardheaded novels of the Troubles. Dermot Bolger (b. 1959) had at the beginning of the 1990s "generated high praise as well as considerable rancour" (Ryan 2002: 159) in producing his *The Journey Home* (1990), a portrait of a state strongly resembling the traditional conception of the Republic and, in its swathing in rural, romantic imagery, somewhat at odds with the often vicious control exercised by those in power. This operates obviously enough at the level of withering and despondent national satire; but the sharply drawn, disconnected, and alienated individuals who inhabit this country formulate a clear-sighted symbolism for the vast but practicable emotional recapitulation that the powers that be in modern Ireland must undertake if the nation is to attain any kind of new coherence.

Much modern Irish fiction takes location, or, indeed, dislocation much more for granted in pursuing social experiences that, while circumscribed by Irish circumstances, are cognate with problems of belonging elsewhere. Roddy Doyle (b.1958), finding great popularity with the youth market, has perhaps been more immediately successful in his fiction than any of the Irish writers who preceded him (and whose concerns were far from being dissimilar to those he presents) in drawing attention to the "normal" problems of a patriarchal society in a liberal capitalist western nation. *The Woman Who Walked Into Doors* (1996) is a typical, flippantly couched tale of a battered wife (acknowledging in the clichéd excuse of its title the frequency and ubiquity of this experience). His chronicling of the working-class Dublin Rabbitte family in *The Commitments* (1989) and elsewhere opened up to an audience beyond Ireland the housing-scheme environments of Dublin in a way that genuinely extended the perception of Irish reality. His Booker Prize-winning *Paddy Clarke, Ha Ha Ha* (1993), the story of a pre-adolescent boy observing the collapse of his parents' marriage, confirmed Doyle's ability as a writer of great emotional empathy alongside his well-attested talents as a social satirist.

Emma Donoghue (b.1969) has produced thoughtful, funny "gay" fiction that challenges homophobia with the sheer normalcy of lesbian living, though that normalcy is something that is made puzzlingly difficult for her protagonists by the "straight" world that surrounds it. In one sly, but also touching episode in her *Hood* (1995), a private lesbian wake occurs, and in this novel that as a whole encompasses that supposedly very Irish concern of death, we are made powerfully aware of the centripetal and centrifugal forces that operate in human identity. Gay writing, arguably, has been slower to occupy the mainstream than elsewhere within the British Isles, but striking instances occur. Colm Tóibín (b. 1955), as an additional example, produces in *The Blackwater Lightship* (1999) a harrowing but lyrical account of the dying of an AIDs victim.

The comment by Frank McCourt (b.1930) in *Yeats is Dead!* that Limerick is thankfully untouched by the Irish mania for biographical writing is, of course, an arch reference to the phenomenal success of his own "memoirs" of growing up in that town, *Angela's Ashes* (1996). Huge sales worldwide and an extremely well-crafted film version, a success such as this book has had both in popular and critical terms, has made McCourt the most successful communicator of the impulse of revisionist Irish history in the latter half of the twentieth century. This portrait of a miserable, uncharitable post-independence Ireland is all the more telling in that it comes from the pen of another "exiled" writer who has spent most of his life in New York, a location that has been a bastion of the most sentimental imaging of the "old country." The present-tense narration of the struggle of the family of young Frankie McCourt to survive the Limerick slums during the 1930s and the vividly character-ized dialogue of the protagonists provide deliberate uncertainty over the extent to which this book is fiction. The title itself clearly suggests that it is a novel and is grimly elegiac in alluding to the benign intentions but eternally compromised position of Frankie's mother. All of her loving schemes for her children will perforce turn to dust during her life amidst a society that is economically unjust but morally crushing as it pays loud lip service to Christian ideals of love and the family. McCourt's literary rhetoric starts his book in a grimly bathetic way that leaves the reader in no doubt about the internally cosseted problems of Ireland in the first part of the twentieth century and beyond: "Worse than the ordinary miserable childhood is the miserable Irish childhood and worse yet is the miserable Irish Catholic childhood" (McCourt 1996: 1). This is a historical book that is compellingly modern in implying that belonging to the nation is not easy.

Irish fiction in the second half of the twentieth century implicitly raises the question of who or what it is, precisely, that tells the Irish that they cohere as a group. Nation, history, family, and other traditional tropes of belonging are all found wanting as these constructed conceits are seen, very often, to bring destructive pressures. It is in the strategies of social realism and demythologization that Irish fiction is helping to make the nation a place much easier to locate, though no less problematic than it has ever been.

II

The end of the wartime "home front" in Britain did not immediately lead to a resurgence of separatist feeling in Scotland. Politically, it took until the 1960s for the Scottish National Party to make significant electoral progress; and culturally the postwar period found a Scotland where the anti-metropolitan modernist mythologies that had often powerfully supported the aspiration of independence in the 1920s and 1930s were suddenly much less potent. A new skepticism, carrying deep scars from the recent race-fuelled human conflagration, is seen clearly in the work of Robin Jenkins (b. 1912). Among his first novels, *The Thistle and the Grail* (1954) shows some continuity with a prewar literary agenda in castigating the poor material health of urban, lowland Scotland; it also casts a withering eye on the mob mentality of working-class culture while dealing with the obsession of a depressed industrial town in propelling its football team, Drumsaggart Thistle, towards winning the "holy grail" of a trophy. The sardonically inflated symbolism of the novel's title scathingly points to self-aggrandizing parochialism as a frequent condition in Scotland. Even more critical of received notions of community in Scotland is Jenkins's *The Cone-Gatherers* (1955), one of the most often taught texts in Scotland's schools and universities. Set on a patriarchal Argyllshire estate during World War II, it finds two misfit brothers aiding the war-effort by gathering tree-cones alongside conscientious objectors. However, the malevolent gamekeeper, Duror, harbors murderous intent toward the brothers, most especially the younger Calum, who is deformed in body though possessing a beautiful face and who is mentally challenged, something seen in his all too simple love of nature. For Duror, the coexistence of beauty and ugliness, innocence and folly in Calum is an affront to the ideal purity of categories in the world, and spurs him on to annihilate this aberrant individual. The irony, of course, is that the war against the Nazis rages at large outwith, but here too on the home front primal loathing is to be found, and the conflict between "good" and "evil" is ubiquitous and eternal. *The Cone-Gatherers* opens with the heavily symbolized Edenic quality of the Scottish landscape and becomes increasingly Gothicized as it portrays the descent into hysterical hatred by Duror, a "Green Man" figure stalking Calum through the woods. In a final moment of heavy symbolism, Lady Runcie Campbell, who is left in charge of the estate while her husband serves in the army, sees Calum as a Christ-figure, finding exultant catharsis in his death even though she had feared his pacifist influence while alive upon her seemingly effeminate young son, Roderick. Calum, then, becomes an all too iconic figure of good to add to the other misapprehension of his presence by Duror as overwhelmingly corrupt. Extreme, mythical perceptions are the stock-in-trade of the novel and this extends to the polar depictions of the Scottish forest-scape. The reader also has to be wary of judging the scenario with too ready a preordained vision.

   Calvinism is to the fore in *The Cone-Gatherers* as, on one level, the novel can be read as affirming this religion's traditional mistrust of the world as a fallen, deceitful place. The character of Duror, however, who believes himself to be absolutely damned, also represents a variation on the all too certain "justified sinner" type, a figure who believes that he is allowed to pass judgment on others because of the Calvinist notion of "the elect," those preordained by God for salvation. James Hogg in his *Private Memoirs and Confessions of a Justified Sinner* (1824) was the first to explore in Scottish fiction the ambiguities of the Calvinist worldview and, perceptively, Cairns Craig has remarked on the republication in 1947 of a highly successful edition of Hogg's novel, introduced by André Gide, which makes it "part, almost . . . of twentieth-century rather than nineteenth-century Scottish writing" (Craig 1999: 38). It is certainly the case that Scottish writers in the latter half of the twentieth century have had frequent recourse to the oxymoronic Calvinist character-type, not necessarily to mount an internal, historical critique of the mentality of Calvinism in Scotland, but as a device allowing more universal purchase on a post-1945, postmodern world where truth and conviction are such contested concepts.

Muriel Spark (b. 1918) has minted the most celebrated version of the "justified sinner" in *The Prime of Miss Jean Brodie* (1961), the most famous Scottish novel of the twentieth century. Spark's own fluid identity, of mixed Jewish, Gentile, Scottish, and English blood, has been the foundation, perhaps, for her fiction of heterogeneous reality. As an educator, Jean Brodie is involved in an activity of prodigious historic Scottish pride, but she is "eccentric," attempting to impose her own very partial beliefs about art, literature, and politics upon the girls she teaches. Brodie is an unorthodox entity partly because of her personality and partly because of historical circumstance: she is one of the "war-bereaved spinsterhood" (Spark 1961: 42), an outwardly respectable 1930s "schoolmarm " though minimally qualified, who would not have the position she has in her prestigious school but for the traumatic changes (including a shortage of available manpower) following the Great War. From this basis of being a new and insecure career woman, Brodie is unable openly to enjoy a love-life, since marriage would most likely spell an end to this career; and so alongside other illicit affairs, she attempts to place one of her pupils, whom she wrongly perceives to be possessed of a Lawrentian spirit, as her proxy in the bed of the art teacher, with whom she is herself in love. Brodie is, then, a character whose behavior can repel as she places her own career and the conviction of her superior aesthetic sensibility above the lives of others. She attempts to predestine the lives of her pupils, though this turns out to be largely unsuccessful: only two girls are spectacularly but oppositely influenced by their teacher, with one running off to fight and be killed in the Spanish Civil War by the forces of Franco, whom Brodie has naively sent her off to join, and the other becoming a Catholic nun in rebellion against her apprehension of Brodie's Calvinist mindset. Nonetheless, Brodie is a character often sympathetically and even lyrically drawn, a site of contradiction who embodies the disparate iconic qualities of historic Scotland, being seen at different points as behaving like John Knox or Mary, Queen of Scots. Her enigmatic, heterogeneous character, in turn culpable and innocent, is not finally to be summed up or judged entirely, since this would be to abrogate the role of God.

Much of Spark's fictional oeuvre has to do with the difficulty of fixing identity in the modern world, which can be seen to be too smugly certain in its contemporary, secular values. *The Ballad of Peckham Rye* (1960) intrudes a Scottish demon into urban, working-class London, a figure in part constructed from Spark's reading of ballads and the Scottish supernatural tradition. In this novel she exuberantly teases the "modern" mindset with a Scottish "bogeyman" and ideas of morality and eternity that it feels it has become too sophisticated to countenance. *The Driver's Seat* (1970) is altogether bleaker in tone as a young woman frustrated by her alienated, characterless life in the city sets out to orchestrate her own death, a situation that the reader only gradually works out, having previously believed the woman to be irrationally fussy and awkward. The truth is that this character, Lise (a sad and chilling development of the Jean Brodie character, though in her abject isolation shorn of any precise location of origin), in counterpoint to her prior drabness of existence, is constructing a story-like enigma around her final days, which people will remember. Spark herself has presented to Scotland a somewhat difficult figure, as a female, member of a racial minority, convert to Catholicism, and writer as often about London, Italy, South Africa, and America as about Scotland. Her own trammelled makeup and concerns fly in the face of the vestigial longings that linger in Scottish culture for solidity of identity. Yet it is her salutary, challenging cosmopolitanism that makes her the most exemplary of late twentieth-century Scottish writers.

At least one Scottish writer has explicitly opposed cosmopolitanism to what he takes to be the prevailing parochial mentality of late twentieth-century Scotland. The Italian-Scot, Alexander Trocchi (1925–84), felt particularly alienated from intellectual conditions in Scotland. He claimed that the problem of cultural mentality in Scotland, and, indeed, in Britain, was due to the dominance of an English philosophical tradition of utilitarianism unreceptive to continental thinking. Self-exiled in Paris and New York for much of his life, he produced in *Young Adam* (1954 and 1961, first published in Paris and only later under his own name) a novel that, to its author's delight, shocked Scotland. It is an existential tale of meaningless, unsatisfying sexual exploits, and successfully suppressed guilt, on the part of a young man employed on a barge travelling the Forth and Clyde canal – the old industrial heartland of Scotland that until the 1970s continued to give the nation its modern, "British" *raison d'être*.

Among those writers disillusioned by the collapse of traditional industrial identity in Scotland, the most powerful has been William McIlvanney (b. 1936). In a series of novels from the 1960s to the 1990s McIlvanney has chronicled the decline of working-class structures of community, never with more sensitivity than in *The Kiln* (1996), a novel that alternates between the late 1950s, when Tom Docherty is about to go to university, and the 1990s, by which time he is a moderately successful author with the debris of a failed marriage and post-Thatcherite Britain all around him. Two iconic figures, Alexander Fleming, discoverer of penicillin (and like Tom Docherty hailing from industrial Ayrshire), and Margaret Thatcher frame the novel. Fleming historically is a "lad o' pairts," someone from a relatively humble background but possessed of innate ability and powerfully supported by the Scottish educational system, so that he achieves much and gives much back to the wider community. He is an oblique foil to Margaret Thatcher and, especially, her infamous pronouncement that society does not exist. The story of *The Kiln* begins in 1955, the year of Fleming's death and the birthing year of rock n' roll and a new youth global youth culture, a point at which the world seems to be full of promise for Tom Docherty. The post-industrial landscape of rampant individualism experienced by the middle-aged Tom is a disappointment for him in its dislocations of family and community, but he reflects too on the old patterns and expectations that previously restricted people of his class in their choice of life-style. The kiln of industrial west-of-Scotland community made strong and often admirable individuals, but in its patriarchy and gender stereotyping it was far from completely healthy. It is unfortunate that McIlvanney, a writer who specializes in profound but unpretentious thought-processes in his characters, has had one partial Hollywood success with the adaptation of his novel, *The Big Man* (1985), about an unemployed steel worker drawn into the murky world of illegal prize-fighting in order to support his family. The film tended towards glamorization of the male violence that McIlvanney has consistently critiqued. It thus reinforced the anachronistic figure of the "fighting Jock" that reached its garish height in the 1930s and that the west of Scotland in particular has found so hard to shake off. *The Kiln* contains an excellent riposte to those who have lazily condemned McIlvanney for the machismo evident in a number of his characters, such as "the hardman" in the kiln-factory, where Tom Docherty works briefly before commencing his studies, who falls over and disablingly ruptures his piles as he is about to administer a beating to Tom, whose family and education he despises.

Apart from his series of twentieth-century historical novels charting the fortunes of the Docherty clan, McIlvanney has led the way in adapting a darkly intelligent detective novel to the Scottish setting. *Laidlaw* (1978) and *The Papers of Tony Veitch* (1983) feature the unconventional Inspector Jack Laidlaw, whose philosophical literacy enables him to contemplate the problems, economic and social, of a malfunctioning, modern Scotland and provides the structural context to the individual crimes that he solves. McIlvanney has been followed by a very striking list in the genre of detective fiction that explores decayed criminal minds arising from the condition of Scotland. A number of exemplars here also consciously reprise the particular "Scottish" concern, as so powerfully practiced by Robert Louis Stevenson and pioneered by James Hogg, of exploring the extent to which cultural context rather than individual volition accounts for evil. Frederic Lindsay (b. 1933) in *Brond* (1983), Christopher Brookmyre (b. 1963) in *Quite Ugly One Morning* (1996), and Ian Rankin (b. 1960), with his hugely successful series of novels featuring the religiously haunted John Rebus, all highlight the whodunit as a serious literary mode of choice in modern Scotland.

A marker of this phenomenon is found also in one of Scotland's most experimental writers of fiction, Frank Kuppner (b. 1951), whose blend of documentary research and lyrical *pensée*, *A Very Quiet Street* (1989), reopens the infamous Glasgow murder case during the early years of the twentieth century when, owing largely to institutional anti-Semitism, Oscar Slater was wrongly imprisoned. Kuppner's fictional narrator trawls through the real archives to name a much more credible killer, though one in his day shrouded by the cloak of respectability. This, along with the narrator's self-reflexive analysis of his increasingly troubled mind, makes for a scrupulous scrutiny of the vulnerability of the individual in relation to versions of reality promulgated by powerful cultural institutions. Kuppner's sardonic identification of such institutions is extended in *A Concussed History of Scotland* (1991), where the problems of Scotland are shown to be a subset of wider abuses of power meditated upon by a philosophical but socially misfit narrator from his bedsitter in Glasgow; and in *Something Very Like Murder* (1994), which brings together reflections on the denial of real-life human rights, both Scottish and international, and lyrical but unsentimental episodes from the lives of a Scots-German family (very closely resembling in places Kuppner's own).

Kuppner is sometimes compared to Alasdair Gray (b. 1934), but while the two writers share a vision that is often absurd in its humor even as it is passionately committed, Gray is more acutely interested in the particulars of the national as well as the personal condition in modern Scotland. He is an observer of the unreflective, unimaginative, "historyless condition in which Scottish society has been trapped" (Craig 1996: 53); and we see this interest pursued in Gray's *Lanark: A Life in Four Books* (1981), the novel that has often been seen by Scottish and even English critics as the one undoubtedly great Scottish novel of the second half of the twentieth century – a novel, paradoxically, in which the supposed, long-standing cultural deficit of Scotland is translated into gain of sorts. *Lanark* is a tale of immense physical and mental pain on the part of its central protagonist, Duncan Thaw, a sickly, emotionally constipated and sexually inept art student in 1950s Glasgow. The problems of Thaw are transmogrified in a fantastic landscape of staggering negativity where Thaw's alter-ego, Lanark, is plunged into the threatening, Kafkaesque "Institution," where his social ineptness is to be corrected, and into the dystopian city of Unthank, where people live lonely, disconnected lives and mysteriously disappear in the normal course of events. The novel is a veritable compendium of images of detachment, decay, and dissolution. And yet, while it is to be read as an excruciating allegory of personal depression on the part of Thaw, the novel also speaks to the post-industrial, dysfunctional reality of Glasgow; this is a city depopulated in its traditional engineering and heavy industry activities but possessed of a growing underclass disenfranchised of any real quality of life on its bleak, sprawling housing schemes. For Gray, this state of affairs is the ultimate consequence of Glasgow's and, indeed, Scotland's historic inattention towards imagining itself. "No-one imagines living here" (Gray 1981: 243), says Thaw of Glasgow as he alludes implicitly to the denuded aesthetic experience of Calvinistic Scotland and a nation that has often been functionally servile to the mercantile and imperial priorities of the British superstate. As he interweaves the joyless reality of the life of a Scottish art student (embarked, then, on the archetypal bohemian life-style), and the grimmest of dystopias, Gray taunts Scotland as a place devoid of a positive aesthetic atmosphere. A moment of *reductio ad absurdum*, emblematic of Scotland's historical emptiness of aesthetic facility, is found as Thaw, recently released from hospital, is allowed by a kindly minister to paint a huge mural, à la Michelangelo painting the Sistine chapel, in his Presbyterian church. Ridiculously, Thaw perseveres in this task, almost to the point of mental breakdown, in spite of his knowledge that the church is due soon for demolition.

Gray's diagnosis of Scotland's crass Protestant-British history has led him into nationalist polemic such as the provocatively titled, *Why Scots Should Rule Scotland* (1992), and to surprisingly optimistic and flamboyant exhortation such as is to be found on the ornate cover of the first edition of his *Unlikely Stories Mostly* (1983): WORK AS IF YOU WERE / LIVING IN THE EARLY DAYS / OF A BETTER NATION / SCOTLAND.

Gray's therapeutic manner is continued in the novel, *1982, Janine* (1984), in which once again a neurotic central character is tortured by the personal failures of his life flashing before him over the course of one evening, and finds that a particular blight upon his own behavior, and that of Scotland also, has been the aggressive male mentality. *Poor Things* (1992) caricatures the icon of the practical Scot by satirizing the Dr Frankenstein-like activities of a public health officer in nineteenth-century Scotland, whose papers are purportedly found by the narrator in a manner that echoes a prominent device of Hogg's *Justified Sinner*. Here we see Gray visiting poetic justice upon his country by heaping it with a scurrilously salacious history, in order to counterpoint what he diagnoses as the lobotomized consciousness of the actually harmful historical progress of Scotland.

Alongside Gray, James Kelman (b. 1946) is the Scottish writer who has played best to an international audience since Muriel Spark; and Kelman has been particularly successful in a British context. His *How Late It Was, How Late* (1994) won the Booker Prize, but not without much controversy over the supposed profanity of his work. Joe Samuels, newly blind and amnesiac, perambulates Glasgow as he attempts to piece together the events of recent days lost to heavy drinking, to negotiate the menacing presence of the police, and to extract assistance from the social security system. "Sammy" may or may not have been involved in criminal activity (the police are particularly suspicious of him because of his Irish drinking cronies), but he is stoical in his puzzled predicament, a quality we are intensely aware of in the narration of the novel through his stream of consciousness. We are never allowed to escape his intimate physical pain nor his expletive encoded defiance and so, even as we are plunged, narrative-wise, into a traditional relationship of sympathy towards the character, we are made uncomfortable with his basic unattractiveness (including questionable personal hygiene as part of his alcoholic degradation) and his aggressive manner. Quality and tabloid press alike in Britain made much of the frequency of the word "fuck" in the novel and, in opposition to his strong supporters among the London critics, some commentators have implied that Kelman is a "Jock on the make," peddling visceral paranoia and successfully passing it off as art to a gullible metropolis. The hallmark of Kelman's fiction is marked precisely by this challenge to sympathy, as his marginalized, underclass protagonists often seem to lack hope or purpose; irritably alienated in a blighted, post-industrial urban landscape, they refuse to cooperate with the assumption of others, including sometimes more cheerful characters from their own class, that the world is a place of easily discernible and correct moral order. Kelman's most pointed exploration of this scenario is found in *A Disaffection* (1989), featuring that frequent Scottish fictional protagonist, the schoolteacher. Patrick Doyle plays hookie from his job by drinking and frittering away his time; when in class he indulges in quite astonishing dialogues (which perhaps exist only in his mind) with his pupils over philosophy and classical geometry. In his escapism and his intensity, Doyle is a strange new version of Jean Brodie; both characters are responses to the belief that the much-vaunted Scottish ideal of education is too often about conformist rote-learning and not enough about genuine breadth of mind.

Kelman's unapologetic use of the Scots vernacular by his characters has been an inspiration to numerous writers of fiction who follow him; it is in prose rather than in poetry that this language is most vibrant of the last thirty years of the century, in contrast to the opposed situation that pertained for most of the twentieth century, until the 1970s. The most successful of the writers enabled in part by Kelman is Irvine Welsh (b. 1958), another uncompromising exponent of (Edinburgh) working-class patois. His best work, *Trainspotting* (1993), is a tour de force in stitching together the diverse narrative points of view of a cast of drug-raddled or otherwise marginalized and fearful characters in a manner that makes for a dissonantly vibrant expression of culture. Interestingly, the film version of 1996 accentuated the national dimension, so that among numerous brilliant moments of comic bathos to do with the supposed culture of both nationality and community, the group of substance-abusing friends go on a day-trip to the Scottish mountains and find this experience entirely alien. One of them also expresses the idea that it is "shite being Scottish", the comment is in part due to the humiliating fact that Scotland has been colonized by the English, who are "wankers." Entertainingly, what is punctured here in a self-ironizing mode of aggressive expression is another national shibboleth, the martial prowess of the Scot (or "the fighting Jock"). The film version followed the book in its intelligent discussion of drug and youth cultures, though Ewan MacGregor's starring role brought to the film a glamorous screen presence not entirely consonant with the original scenario of the work, and a middle-class Perthshire accent that fails to replicate the linguistic energy found in the book.

Next to the "urban fiction" of Gray, Kelman, and Welsh, the most notably cognate grouping in the modern Scottish novel is that of "women's fiction," including Janice Galloway (b. 1956) and A. L. Kennedy (b. 1965). Galloway's *The Trick is to Keep Breathing* (1989) provides yet another rendition of the Scottish schoolteacher; this time a woman is ostracized after the accidental death of her lover while they are on holiday together, he having recently left his wife for her. Portraying the relentless laceration of the central character by her community, the novel presents her excruciatingly shredded sensitivities, or a breakdown, amidst a world lacking in sensitivity. Contemporary Scotland is as cruel and lonely a place as any for the female, especially the educated female, in Kennedy's *So I am Glad* (1995), a novel of bitter magic realism in which the central character imports Cyrano de Bergerac to modern Glasgow to be her lover. Similarly to the case of Gray's *Lanark*, then, the Scottish location is energized by a very sharp transfusion of "culture" to counterpoint a previously unimaginative place. Even as Cyrano's presence in the city jars, however, his ability to brawl with street thugs finds him perfectly at home. This is a novel that suggests that the imagination and grounded normality need not be polar opposites, not only in Glasgow but also in a detached, commercialized world, generally, where the mass media promulgates a bloodless language and slickly edited reality that is harmful to the human condition.

Along with fiction dealing with the urban underclass and the situation of women, gay writing has ensured that if Scotland, with its Calvinist-rooted culture, was even more puritanical than other places, this is no longer the case. A hugely sensitive, unapologetic gay fiction is found in Thomas Healy (b. 1944), perhaps the most underrated of all contemporary Scottish novelists, Christopher Whyte (b. 1952), and Ali Smith (b. 1962). Amidst the prominence of this fiction a complaint has arisen in the past decade: that the "middle- class" voice is being marginalized in Scotland. Certainly, we might consider the case of Allan Massie (b. 1938), a man unfashionable in his Tory politics but who has written historical fiction that stands comparison with that of William McIlvanney, although it is much less noticed, dealing as it does with the likes of ancient Rome or Vichy France. Ronald Frame (b. 1953) provides in his fiction a very different, indeed, middle-class, west of Scotland than the more popular literary representations of the region by Kelman and others. His terrain is in the icily sensitive area of human relationships that are as difficult and as psychologically interesting for his bourgeois protagonists as for anyone else. Iain Banks (b. 1958) is a hugely popular writer of science fiction, but also writes about middle-class angst. His *Whit* (1995), about a religious cult operating in rural Stirlingshire, is one of the funniest and one of the best-constructed novels in Scotland in the second half of the twentieth century. Modern, indeed post-Modern Scotland, in that it appears as fragmented and decentered as anywhere else in its cultural expression, finds itself at the center of concerns important anywhere in the West.

Like the contemporary Irish novel, the postwar Scottish novel has expressed skepticism about the national condition. If in Scotland the mythology of the nation that has been interrogated possesses an anti-romantic image (in contrast to the received romantic image of Ireland), the results of the fictional inquiry are similar in locating a place that is much wider and more worldly than might previously have been imagined. In its maturity, Scottish fiction, like Irish fiction, has a stronger sense of place than ever before.

REFERENCES AND FURTHER READING

Craig, Cairns (1996) *Out of History: Narrative Paradigms in Scottish and British Culture.* Edinburgh: Polygon.

——(1999) *The Modern Scottish Novel.* Edinburgh: Edinburgh University Press.

Deane, Seamus (ed.) (1991–2002) *The Field Day Anthology of Irish Writing.* Derry: Field Day Publications.

Gifford, Douglas, Dunnigan, Sarah, and MacGillivray, Alan (eds.) (2002) *Scottish Literature.* Edinburgh: Edinburgh University Press.

Gray, Alasdair (1981) *Lanark: A Life in Four Books.* Edinburgh: Canongate.

Longley, Edna (1994) *The Living Stream: Literature and Revisionism in Ireland.* Newcastle upon Tyne: Bloodaxe Books.

McCourt, Frank (1996) *Angela's Ashes.* London: HarperCollins.

Mac Laverty, Bernard (1997) *Grace Notes.* London: Jonathan Cape.

O'Brien, Edna (1997) [1996] *Down by the River.* London: Phoenix.

O'Connor, Joe (ed.) (2001) *Yeats is Dead!* London: Jonathan Cape.

Pierce, David (2000) *Irish Writing in the Twentieth Century: A Reader.* Cork: Cork University Press.

Ryan, Ray (2002) *Ireland and Scotland: Literature and Culture, State and Nation, 1966–2000.* Oxford: Oxford University Press.

Spark, Muriel (1961) *The Prime of Miss Jean Brodie.* London: Macmillan.

9

Black British Interventions

John Skinner

An obvious problem in attempting a survey of such a wide and variegated subject is that of categories and labels. Indian-born (and later American-resident) Salman Rushdie did not protest about being categorized as a "black British writer," which suggests that the term might be ideological rather than geographical – and, least of all, chromatic. On the other hand, Britain's most famous Caribbean-born writer, V. S. Naipaul, whose ethnic origins are also Indian, declined to be included in Onyekachi Wambu's fine *Empire Windrush* (1998) anthology of Caribbean and black literature. In terms of cultural background, however, the cosmopolitan Naipaul and Rushdie do not fit very comfortably into the categories of Indian or Asian, either.

A representative essay in *Wasafiri*, Britain's leading journal in the field, refers to "African, Asian, Caribbean and Black British" writing; relations between the four fields are ambivalent, although, in the broadest reading, all writers of the first three categories are subsumed within the fourth group. In his critical survey of black British literature, Prabhu Guptara thus suggested: "Being 'black' is a matter of visibility, with social and political consequences. Being a writer is a matter of culture. Being 'British' is a matter, not of culture, but of what passport you carry" (1986: 14). Such sweeping definitions contrast with those of critics who would limit the term "black British" to writers of African or Caribbean (and possibly Asian) descent, born in Britain.

It is not possible to be prescriptive on this issue and one should simply try to understand the assumptions or implications behind each definition: social and political solidarity or multicultural inclusiveness versus a more limited concept somewhat analogous to that of African-American writing. Bharati Mukherjee and Maxine Hong Kingston in the United States are not normally regarded as "black" authors, although a similar desire for solidarity and inclusiveness has produced the concept "women of color." In a broader perspective, finally, it is worth noting that the currently fashionable label, "black British," might have been thought derogatory in the 1970s and, in another few decades, may be found dated: as well insist on Hanif Kureishi being a black British writer as George Eliot a white one.

The present chapter is a guide to novels and novelists, however, rather than an ideological debate; and the compromise solution adopted is that of using the shortest viable rubric, with the chapter itself divided into two sections, featuring novelists of (geographically) Caribbean or African and Asian origins, respectively. Towards the end of each section, the categories Caribbean/African or Asian then inevitably merge into that of black British. Most writers in either group actually born in Britain can be usefully regarded as "black British writers," although the label does not seem quite apt for a Kazuo Ishiguro or a Timothy Mo. Even among Afro-Caribbean writers, moreover, distinctions should be used with care. Caryl Phillips, who might otherwise seem an exemplary case, was born abroad and actually arrived in Britain from his native St Kitts at the age of six weeks. That said, Phillips himself has paid tribute to the legacy of George Lamming and Sam Selvon, who emigrated to Britain as adults and spent much of their creative lives outside the country in establishing a "black British canon."

There is a shorter caveat to be made regarding the apparently innocent term "interventions." (The term here has no specific ideological connotations and certainly no sense of restriction or interference, but simply refers to all significant critical, theoretical, or ficitional contributions to the field.) Some writers from whichever category – say Guyana's Roy Heath or India's Kamala Markandaya – have in a literary sense, notwithstanding a lengthy residence in Britain, never really forsaken their country of origin, rather as Joyce may be said never to have left Dublin. Others – Hanif Kureishi immediately springs to mind – have set their fiction almost exclusively in Britain. But quite naturally, perhaps, the greatest number – such as Trinidadian Sam Selvon or Nigerian Buchi Emecheta, not to mention Rushdie and Naipaul themselves – have crossed these particular geographical and cultural divides in countless ways, whether between novels or within the same fictional work. With regard to the concept of "interventions," then, this chapter proposes two referents for the term: the direct result of thematizing such topics as the (im)migrant experience, ethnic identity, or the new multiculturalism of Britain; and the less easily defined achievements of revising, or in some cases simply rewriting, the country's entire literary map.

Prior to the discussion of individual novels and novelists, it is also worth revisiting two theoretical configurations, the postcolonial and the postmodern. In his extremely helpful *Beginning Postcolonialism*, John McLeod suggests three areas of activity relevant to "postcolonial studies." These include reading texts produced by writers from countries with a history of colonialism; reading texts by those who have migrated from countries with a history of colonialism or are descended from migrant families; and, in the light of colonial discourses, rereading texts produced during colonialism (2000: 33).

The first category, of writers who remained in their country of origin, is marginal in the present context. The second category has an obvious relevance to first-generation immigrants, whether or not these individuals later repatriated or moved on. It is even more fundamental for raising the issue of "diaspora": originally referring to the historical dispersal of the Jews, the term has now become widely used for the mass displacement of Africans by the slave trade or Indians under the system of "indenture," or contract labor, that followed it (the large Asian populations in the Caribbean and East Africa were a direct result of this). And when West Indians, as well as Indians from outside the Indian subcontinent, emigrated to Britain in considerable numbers during the postwar period, one could even speak of a "double diaspora." In any case, diaspora itself is a key concept in a number of critical studies (King 1996; George 1999; Nasta 2002). The third category, that of writers who reread texts produced during colonialism, would be less relevant here were it not for the fact that many of those discussed in this chapter have already done precisely that, producing revisions, adaptations, or parodies of canonic literary works. Key target texts here include Defoe's *Robinson Crusoe*, Conrad's *Heart of Darkness,* and, above all, Shakespeare's *The Tempest* (Childs 1999; Thieme 2001).

On the other hand, postcolonial theory seems of little relevance to the latest novel of black urban life, a context where a postmodern approach – reinforced by the insights of cultural studies – is certainly more helpful. In the 1970s, when financially aided repatriation for immigrants ("sending them back where they came from") was still a serious alternative for the political far right, a celebrated black Bradford-based comedian said he would be happy to take the money and go: he came from Sheffield. The story belongs with a fund of home truths, whether bluntly analytical ("we're here because you were there") or ironically perceptive (Britain as the last colony). It is in any case also an invitation to transcend simple binaries and redefine who or what is British.

Critic and theorist Homi Bhabha, among others, has done just this. In the context of a landmark conference organized by the British Council in 1997 under the rubric "Reinventing Britain: A Forum," Bhabha looked for "redefinitions of the concepts of culture and community that emerge from the hybrid cosmopolitanism of contemporary metropolitan life." Bhabha's specially commissioned manifesto for the conference went on to claim: "The new cosmopolitanism has fundamentally changed our sense of the relationship between national territory, and the attribution of cultural values and social norms."

Bhabha's manifesto privileges identity as personal and performative within a pluralistic and multicultural society. It also echoes the postmodernist rejection of the "grand narratives" (liberalism, the Enlightenment, Christianity, Marxism, etc.) with its own implied dismissal of certain rather less "grand" narratives concerning myths of Britishness or Englishness (see Gikandi 1997). Whereas Bhabha discusses "nation" and "culture" at greater length elsewhere (1990, 1994), this particular manifesto is reprinted in *Wasafiri*, in a special issue entitled *Black Writing in Britain* (Spring 1999). Bhabha's hypothesis also connects neatly with the ideas of two major British cultural critics: with Paul Gilroy, whose rejection of *roots* for *routes* – his seminal essay is called "It ain't where you're from, it's where you're at" (1993:

120–45) – seems to coincide exactly with Bhabha's concepts of the personal and the performative; and with Stuart Hall, whose *Critical Dialogues in Cultural Studies* (1996) insistently links postmodernism with questions of ethnicity and new identities.

Caribbean Writers

The Caribbean is is an excellent starting point for a fictional survey, since the strong West Indian literary presence in Britain coincides precisely with a new migration pattern from the region. This is linked in turn to a particular event at the beginning of the period covered by this Companion. In response to a labor shortage after the Second World War, the British government actively sought immigrants from the Caribbean, and the first contingent of 492 arrived in Britain on the *Empire Windrush* in 1948. In the eyes of white Britain, the early immigrants were generally lumped together as "Jamaicans." It was an inaccurate label not least in literary terms, since early arrivals included George Lamming (b. 1927) from Barbados and Sam Selvon (1923–94) from Trinidad, who travelled on the same boat in 1950. Their rough contemporary, V. S. Naipaul (b. 1932), came to England in the same year, but on an Oxford scholarship rather than as a simple immigrant.

Lamming is, in many ways, the paradigmatic Afro-Caribbean novelist and his best critic, Sandra Pouchet Paquet, offers an exemplary list of his thematic interests, including colonialism and nationalism; emigration and exile; history and myth; tradition and modernity; and cultural hybridity, identity in the context of race (*DLB* 125: 55). While Lamming's first novel, *In the Castle of My Skin* (1953), is the classic Caribbean *Bildungsroman* and his last one, *Natives of My Person* (1972), is a historical reconstruction of a slaving voyage, the second and third, *Of Age and Innocence* (1958) and *Season of Adventure* (1960), are, above all, political dystopias set on the fictional, but highly generic, Caribbean island of San Cristobal. Lamming's other two novels, *The Emigrants* (1954) and *Water with Berries* (1971), could be more literally seen as black British "interventions." The first of these uses the device of the ship sailing to Britain with its cargo of West Indian immigrants, whose subsequent experiences of alienation and loss are then depicted in detail. The second follows a trio of West Indian artists in Britain – Derek, an actor; Roger, a musician; Teeton, a painter – and the racial hostility from the white community that they encounter. In the latter, however, Lamming provides a classic example of "canonical counterdiscourse" or writing back against the canon (John McLeod's third category above) through an appropriation of *The Tempest*. His new versions of Caliban, Prospero, Ferdinand, and Miranda offer a parable of colonization in reverse. In this way, the novel is also closely linked with Lamming's seminal essay collection, *The Pleasures of Exile* (1960), containing a radical rereading of Shakespeare's final play, now rejecting the white magician, Prospero, and identifying with the prototypical colonial subject, Caliban.

The central figure in the context of early West Indian immigration, however, is Sam Selvon, although his early novels, *A Brighter Sun* (1952), and its sequel, *Turn*

Again Tiger (1958), depict the Trinidadian Indo-Caribbean environment in which he grew up. In his third novel and the first set entirely in Britain, *The Lonely Londoners* (1956), Selvon then abandons his Indo-Caribbean alter ego, Tiger, for a pioneering attempt to record the experiences of Caribbean immigrants in a cold and inhospitable postwar Britain. The tragi-comic existence of the apparently Afro-Caribbean Moses Aloetta and his fellow West Indians is also remarkable for being recorded throughout in a fairly mild but consistent representation of creolized English. Although some of the same themes were repeated in *The Housing Lark* (1965), the true sequels to *The Lonely Londoners* are two more vernacular novels of "episodes" or "ballads," as Selvon described them – *Moses Ascending* (1975) and *Moses Migrating* (1983) – together forming what is generally known as either the *Moses* or the *London* trilogy.

The third of the pioneering novelists is V. S. Naipaul, whose fastidious prose may seem, at first glance, remote from that of Selvon. Critical opinion generally sees Naipaul as abandoning the model of Dickens in his early comic novels with their Trinidad setting for the dystopic, cosmopolitan vision of a Conrad. *A House for Mr Biswas* (1961), inspired by the struggles of the novelist's father for material independence and the climax of this first phase, is a classic realist text, although it may be noted that the stories of *Miguel Street* (1959), the first of Naipaul's books to be written, actually use the same kinds of "ballads" and "episodes" in a Port of Spain setting as those Selvon exploited in *The Lonely Londoners*. In both cases, orality, vernacular, and Trinidad's indigenous calypso tradition are formative elements.

Of Naipaul's prolific output, both fictional and nonfictional but almost inevitably autobiographical in either case, the two most significant novels for our purposes are *The Mimic Men* (1967) and *The Enigma of Arrival* (1987). The first, constructed around a failed West Indian politician writing his memoirs in a London boarding-house, thematizes the imitative compulsions of the colonial subject, introducing in its title a classic trope for this experience. The second, far more ambitious in scope and considerably challenging the reader's concept of what a novel might involve, provides an extended meditation on a myriad of topics, including Britain's past glory and present decay, or the constant contradictions between a Britain fantasized in anticipation and one lived in the present – all from the authorial persona of a writer living in a rented house in rural Wiltshire.

On a practical level, the first postwar generation of West Indian writers in Britain received valuable exposure in the celebrated BBC radio program, *Caribbean Voices*, transmitted for half an hour on Sunday afternoons from 1946 to 1958. Besides the three writers already mentioned, contributors over the years included Edgar Mittelholzer (Guyana) and Michael Anthony (Trinidad), as well as the Jamaican, Andrew Salkey, who chronicled the lives of alienated black immigrants in *Escape to an Autumn Pavement* (1960) and *The Adventures of Catullus Kelly* (1969). Salkey was also at the heart of another important initiative for the Caribbean expatriate literary community, CAM or the Caribbean Artists' Movement, which was founded in 1966. It held many private and public meetings as well as two major conferences over the next two decades. The year 1966 also saw the launching in London of the pioneering independent West Indian publishers, *New Beacon Books*, named for a radical Trinidad journal of the 1920s. The remarkable concentration of West Indian writing talent in the London of the 1950s and 1960s also included the Jamaicans John Hearne and Roger Mais. The whole generation is usefully surveyed in the "Brit'n" section of Louis James's *Caribbean Literature in English* (1999).

Although Naipaul, particularly after the award of the Nobel Prize in 2002, is certainly the most prominent English-language novelist with Caribbean antecedents, some critics still regard the less famous Wilson Harris (b. 1921) as the most profoundly original novelist from the region. A Guyanan of mixed ancestry and a trained surveyor, Harris emigrated to Britain in 1959 and has lived there ever since. His fiction draws on his wide knowledge of history, mythology, and anthropology – Guyanan, Amerindian and other – in an extensive series of novella-length narratives, ranging in technique between traditional realism and metafictional experiment. The first of these, *Palace of the Peacock* (1960), the fantastic and largely allegorical account of a river journey into the Guyanese hinterland – and thus inevitably compared to *Heart of Darkness* – is still the most highly regarded. It was later combined with three other short fictions to form Wilson's best-known work the *Guyana* quartet. A few Harris texts, including *Black Marsden* (1972) and *The Angel at the Gate* (1982), are set exclusively or partially in Britain, as much as concrete setting is relevant to this author's dream-like narratives.

Two of Harris's compatriots should also be mentioned here. Even more focused on his native Guyana, but now on the communal "yards" of the capital, Georgetown, is Roy Heath (b. 1926), who moved to England in 1950 and had a long teaching career. Heath's central achievement is the unjustly neglected *Georgetown* trilogy (1981), consisting of *From the Heat of the Day*, *One Generation*, and *Genetha*, chronicling three generations of the Armstrong family and contrasting with the writer's more uncanny fiction such as *A Man Came Home* (1974). Characteristic of the author is a total rejection of his long immigrant experience in Britain as potential fictional material.

This is not the case, however, with Heath's fellow Guyanan, Beryl Gilroy (1924–2001), who follows a common West Indian paradigm by producing fiction set in either Britain or the West Indies, and located in either the past or the present. Arriving in 1951, Gilroy was also a career teacher, becoming London's first black school principal. These experiences inspired her autobiography, *Black Teacher* (1976), and – less directly – the novel *Boy-Sandwich* (1989), a sensitive representation of the immigrant experience and multicultural consciousness. Gilroy also broke new ground for West Indian fiction with her portrayal of a vital and independent old woman in a Caribbean setting in *Frangipani House* (1986), besides writing two short historical novels, *Steadmann and Joanna* (1996) and *Inkle and Yarico* (1996), connected with the legacy of slavery.

Certain of the first-generation Caribbean novelists in Britain are sometimes seen as the founding figures of a "black British canon": Caryl Phillips (b. 1958) and others have recognized the legacy of Selvon and Lamming. Phillips himself, born on the island of St Kitts but taken to England as an infant, is one of a talented second-generation of Caribbean writers, including David Dabydeen (b. 1956) and Fred D'Aguiar (b. 1960), both with Guyanan childhoods behind them, although D'Aguiar was actually born in Britain.

Common to all three novelists is their interest in the African diaspora, explored by narratives designed to fill what Edward Said has poignantly described as "the gaps and silences of history." Phillips, who made his first trip to St Kitts at the age of 22, wrote a traditional novel of immigration with *The Final Passage* (1985) and depicted the alienation and frustration of the Caribbean returnee in *A State of Independence* (1986). But his subsequent fiction characteristically features postmodern collages of juxtaposed narrative voices: an articulate plantation slave and a visiting Englishwoman in *Cambridge* (1991) and – most memorably – a range of historical black voices, framed by the lament of an African father obliged to sell his children, in *Crossing the River* (1993). A later novel such as *The Nature of Blood* (1997), employing the same techniques as it moves between medieval Italy, the Jewish ghetto in Othello's Venice, the Holocaust and the modern state of Israel, suggests both Phillips's impressive range and the restrictive nature of such literary labels as Caribbean or black British writer.

D'Aguiar also created a short slave narrative in *The Longest Memory* (1996) before expanding his historical interests in *Feeding the Ghosts* (1997). The latter novel is motivated by the notorious Turner painting, *Slavers Throwing Overboard the Dead and Dying* (1840), connected in turn with the contemporary scandal of the *Zong*, whose captain had done precisely this, to be able to make insurance claims for lost cargo. Like Phillips, Dabydeen also produced two earlier and more conventional novels. The first of these, *The Intended* (1991), is a kind of black British *Bildungsroman*, plotting the experiences of four Asian schoolboys growing up in England in the 1980s: the title is an oblique reference to the fiancée of Kurtz in *Heart of Darkness*, while the novel itself is a witty reversal of the colonizing process, as Dabydeen's Indo-Guyanan protagonist penetrates the darkness of contemporary London. Its successor, *Disappearance* (1993), is a realistic but richly allegorical account of a Guyanese engineer working on a project to prevent a Sussex cliff-top village from subsiding into the sea. Dabydeen is also a widely respected academic, who – in addition to chronicling a multicultural Britain – is a historian of the black presence in the country, which he dates back to Roman times. His historical studies contributed to two later novels, *The Counting House* (1996), narrating the tragic experiences of an Indian couple in nineteenth-century colonial Guyana, and *A Harlot's Progress* (1990), inventing a story for the black slaveboy painted in 1732 by William Hogarth.

The question of which writers of directly African origin can be fairly linked to Britain is even more problematic than is the case with those of the Caribbean. Whereas the novelist Chinua Achebe has no physical links at all, the historical legacy of British colonialism and the destruction of traditional Nigerian society is at the center of his most famous novel, *Things Fall Apart* (1958), and the so-called *African* trilogy it initiates. Other African writers were resident in Britain for various periods, often in the context of higher education or political exile: Wole Soyinka, not only a dramatist and a poet but also the author of an important novel, *The Interpreters* (1965), is a good example. Conversely, a younger writer such as Nigerian-born Ben Okri might be considered a "black British" writer in the broadest sense, although one can hardly speak of (direct) interventions in an author whose major fiction is set exclusively in a country unnamed, but highly reminiscent of his native Nigeria.

Somewhere between Okri, on the one hand, and the Nigerians, Achebe and Soyinka, on the other is Buchi Emecheta, who significantly won a "Best Black Writer in Britain" award for her most highly acclaimed work *The Joys of Motherhood* (1980). With several novels reflecting the immigrant experience in Britain and complementing the fiction set in her native Nigeria – a contrast not unlike that exemplified by Selvon – Emecheta is good figure to begin with. Her early books, *In the Ditch* (1972) and *Second-Class Citizen* (1974), are essentially fictionalized autobiographies, depicting the author's immigrant experience: the first based on the life of a lone parent with five children in a London housing estate, the second following the same life over an earlier period, including childhood and adolescence in Nigeria, followed by marriage and separation in Britain.

Ben Okri himself (b. 1959) was born in Nigeria, but moved to Britain at the age of 18 and, after studying at the University of Essex, began a long-term residence in London, although his fiction, as already noted, does not reflect this experience. After two early novels, *Flowers and Shadows* (1980) and *Landscapes Within* (1981), representing African variants of the *Bildungsroman* and *Künstlerroman*, respectively, he produced the startlingly original *The Famished Road* (1992), on which his current reputation largely rests. This scathing account of a barely disguised contemporary Nigeria is structured around the adventures of Azaro, a spirit-child or *abiku*, the Yoruba term for the offspring of a woman who has suffered repeated miscarriages or infant deaths, on the assumption that the new infant has finally developed the will to remain in the human world. Azaro thus has both a human and a spiritual dimension, with the result that Okri's novel is a dazzling mixture of European realism and traditional African folklore and oral tradition. *The Famished Road* may be compared with the magic realism of García Márquez or Rushdie, with Azaro's gifts even recalling the special powers of Saleem Sinai in *Midnight's Children*. Students of Nigerian literature in English, however, will also be reminded of the fantastic tales of Amos Tutuola, such as those in *The Palm Wine Drinkard* (1952), which was inspired in turn by the Yoruba-language novelist D. A. Fagunwa. Okri continued in the same fantastic vein with *Songs of Enchantment* (1993) and *Infinite Riches* (1999), the latter explicitly described as "volume three of the Famished Road cycle."

A less ambivalent claim to being a black British writer is held by Diran Adebayo (1968), born in north London of Nigerian parents. His *Some Kind of Black* (1996) also represents one of the more nuanced representations of the contemporary black urban experience. The formative influences on the life of Adebayo's protagonist, the black Oxford law student, Dele, include his harshly autocratic, Seventh Day Adventist Yoruba father, various patronising university contemporaries, and an ethnic rainbow of girlfriends, together with his delinquent but streetwise Brixton friend, Concrete. The novel is notable for its emphasis on intra-community, as much as inter-community, relations. Its title refers to the protagonist's feelings of ambivalence in the black community, as the author's sharp vignettes of London life often move beyond facile ethnic polarization to record "the games that black folk play on one another."

In most recent black British writing, the urban ghetto, with its sub- and counter-cultures, is far more prominent than any native Caribbean echoes. The controversial but successful X-Press, which brought a new dimension to popular publishing with such novels as Victor Headley's *Yardie* (1992) and its sequel *Excess* (1993), may be felt to sensationalize criminality and drug culture. But others would argue that fiction such as *The Scholar* (1997) and *Society Within* (1999) from Courttia Newland (b. 1973), or *Bad Friday* (1982) by Norman Samuda-Smith (b. 1958), the first black British-born novelist to be published, are an accurate representation of urban life.

The writing of several contemporary women novelists of Caribbean origin, including Joan Riley (b. 1958) and Andrea Levy (b. 1956), is sometimes a more nuanced counterpart to modern ghetto fiction: while moving in similar landscapes of urban deprivation, it also highlights the more traditional themes of painful uprooting and traumatic relocation. Riley's poignant first novel, *The Unbecoming* (1985), thus depicts the trauma of an 11-year-old girl transplanted from rural Jamaica to inner-city Britain on the summons of a father she has never known. Its successor, *Waiting in the Twilight* (1987), portrays the immigrant experience of an older woman, while a third novel, *Romance* (1988), is the story of two sisters whose world is turned upside down by the arrival in England of their Jamaican grandparents. British-born Levy, whose Jamaican parents actually came to Britain on the *Empire Windrush*, fictionalizes this journey in *Every Light in the House Burnin'* (1994) and explores council-estate life in *Never Far from Nowhere* (1996). *Fruit of the Lemon* (1999), however, is a more ambitious returnee novel, with action in Panama and Cuba.

Ultimately, however, there are novels which, either through their originality or their comprehensiveness, transcend the ethnic labels sometimes attached to their authors. In the first group, Jackie Kay, a black British writer who grew up in Edinburgh, won the 1998 Guardian Fiction Prize for her remarkable first novel, *Trumpet*, about a Scottish jazz trumpeter who was discovered on his death to have been a woman. In the second, Zadie Smith, an icon of contemporary black British writing, produced the best-selling *White Teeth* (2000): there is still little comment on the novel that is critical or analytical rather than merely promotional, but it is safe to predict that it will win lasting recognition – in the open category – for an epically inclusive depiction of a multicultural contemporary London.

Asian Writing in Britain

To some readers, the use of a subheading for the second part of this chapter might seem redundant. In the introduction to his excellent anthology, *Empire Windrush*

(1998), subtitled *Fifty Years of Writing about Black Britain*, Onyekachi Wambu lists a first generation of writers representing the "post-Empire black imagination," including Lamming, Harris, Selvon, and Salkey, and later generations including, among others, Salman Rushdie, Timothy Mo, and Hanif Kureishi. As already noted, however, some writers of Asian origin would feel uncomfortable in this category, not least V. S. Naipaul, who – it will be remembered – declined to be included in the anthology. Potential terminological controversy can be avoided by returning to the concept, introduced above, of the Indian (or Asian) diaspora. It is worth remembering, however, that the writers now discussed belong to a category variously seen as complementary or tangential to – even sometimes identical with – that of black British writers.

Extensive postwar immigration to Britain from the Indian subcontinent began a little later than that from the Caribbean. The British Nationality Act of 1948 took away allegiance to the Crown as the basis for British citizenship and gave the same rights and privileges as those of British subjects to citizens of all countries joining the Commonwealth. This was particularly relevant to India, which had become an independent republic in 1947. While South Asian immigrants faced the same prejudice and discrimination in postwar Britain as West Indians, the acculturation process was often even more difficult because of such issues as language, religious observance, and traditional gender roles. In 1958 there were widespread racial disturbances in the East Midland city of Nottingham and the Notting Hill district of London.

Public hostility to what was seen as excessive numbers of new immigrants (both Asian and Caribbean) hastened the introduction of the more restrictive Commonwealth Immigration Act of 1961, which actually came into force in the July of the following year, with systems of quotas and employment vouchers. The delay naturally led to a temporarily sharp increase in immigration, as many tried to beat the new deadline. The acceptance of Indians with British passports who were forced to leave Kenya and Uganda in the 1960s caused renewed public alarm. The situation was then exacerbated by the inflammatory rhetoric of Conservative politician Enoch Powell: in a 1968 speech, he infamously prophesied "rivers of blood." A new Commonwealth Immigrants Act of 1968 distinguished between British citizens who were "patrials," i.e. with identifiable ancestors within the British Isles, and those who were not. This clearly discriminatory piece of legislation in favor of white people sat strangely with the Race Relations Act of the same year, outlawing discrimination in employment or housing. However, in spite of such major setbacks as the Brixton riots of 1981 and widespread disturbances in 1985, race relations continued to make slow and painful progress together with the growing multiculturalization of Britain. Such historical detail may be usefully juxtaposed with the early representational fiction of writers such as Dabydeen and Kureishi, or the trenchant social commentary of Rushdie.

Various Indian novelists, such as Mulk Raj Anand (b. 1905), resided for long periods in Britain prior to the Second World War, and thus long before the arrival of any of the so-called *Windrush* generation. Kamala Markandaya (b. 1924) married an Englishman and has been living in Britain since 1948. Her long series of novels, of which *Nectar in a Sieve* (1954) is currently the only one easily available, frequently thematize the clash between Indian/eastern and western/British values, but their settings – whether contemporary or historical – are generally Indian. The exception is *The Nowhere Man* (1972), dealing with the acculturation problems of an Indian family living in London. The cosmopolitan Zulfiqar Ghose (b. 1935), born in the Punjabi city of Sialkot – now India, then Pakistan – spent the years 1952 to 1969 in England, and explored the trauma of exile in his fine second novel *The Murder of Aziz Khan* (1967). He even used a lonely London-born schoolteacher for the (anti)hero protagonist of his third book, *Crump's Terms* (1968), arguably a more successful attempt than V. S. Naipaul's rather feeble *Mr Stone and the Knights Companion* (1963) to use a native English protagonist.

In retrospect, however, the focal point of late twentieth-century fiction in English by writers of Asian origin can only be Salman Rushdie. A highly privileged immigrant from an affluent Kashmiri family that had resettled in Bombay and later moved to the newly independent Pakistan, Rushdie was educated at an exclusive British private school, and then at King's College, Cambridge. Rushdie is presented individually later in this Companion, so it is not necessary to discuss any of his novels in great detail here. It is nevertheless worth considering briefly what the implications of the word "interventions" might be for a novelist of Rushdie's stature.

In the context of literary history, *Midnight's Children* (1981) "intervened" by virtually redrawing the map of English fiction. Rushdie achieved this with large doses of Latin American-style magic realism – even if Gunther Grass is his first acknowledged model – and postmodernist "historiographic metafiction" (Hutcheon 1988), the parodic and playfully subconscious subversion of the historical novel. Rushdie also provided a liberating impulse for many Indian novelists in English, whereas indigenous British fiction arguably has no direct imitator, but only a kindred spirit of the fantastic in Angela Carter.

This is not the place to discuss Rushdie's shifts between the postmodern and the postcolonial, but it is worth stressing both his gift for satire and his compulsion towards allegory, both of which transcend the generic division proposed. *Midnight's Children*, *Shame* (1984), and *The Satanic Verses* (1988) effectively form a trilogy, with each volume concentrating on one of Rushdie's past homes: India, Pakistan, and Britain. For besides everything else, *The Satanic Verses* is a novel of immigration, with its satirical exposure of an inhospitable Thatcherite Britain in the 1970s. Moreover, if the immigrant genre has been wittily characterized as "traveling light" (George 1996: 171ff.), then Rushdie's Gibreel Farishta and Saladin Chamcha, floating gently down on to British soil from exploding Air India flight 420, could hardly be traveling lighter. And, to continue the novel's refreshingly direct allegorical mode, the public-school and university-educated Chamcha makes a career as an impersonator: "a thousand voices and one voice," to recycle a literary association dear to the author, or simply as Rushdie's "mimic man."

Rushdie has also published two collections of miscellaneous essays and criticism, *Imaginary Homelands* (1991) and *Step Across This Line* (2002), where – as literary critic and cultural commentator, respectively – he provides other memorable examples of both kinds of intervention suggested here.

In her important study of the South Asian diaspora in Britain, Susheila Nasta (2002) discusses a number of post-Rushdean novelists working consciously within their double cultural heritage, suggestively dividing them into two contrasting subgroups: those who thematize the immigrant experience in the new multicultural Britain and those who concentrate on evoking the lost homeland. Her examples of the first category include Hanif Kureishi (b. 1954) and Ravinder Randhawa (b. 1952), while the second group contains Romesh Gunesekera (b. 1954) and Sunetra Gupta (b. 1965).

Kureishi, whose celebrated *The Buddha of Suburbia* (1987) depicts a young Asian boy's process of cultural assimilation, spoke honestly about his own situation: whatever people thought, he himself felt quite British and it was rather his father who was "caught between two cultures." Randhawa is probably a better example of an individual genuinely trapped in a hybrid existence, unable to belong fully to either British or Asian culture. And such is the underlying theme of her impressive first novel, *A Wicked Old Woman* (1987), which concerns an elderly Indian protagonist brought to England while still a young girl and which features a whole gallery of displaced Asian women.

The other two novelists are described by Nasta as "birds of passage"; Rushdie himself used the suggestive phrase "tellers of migrant tales." Gunesekera was born in Sri Lanka and moved to Britain in 1972 via the Philippines; Gupta, one of a large number of Asian diasporic writers with Bengali origins, had an even more cosmopolitan upbringing. Whatever the origins, however, novels such as Gunesekera's *Reef* (1994) or Gupta's *The Glassblower's Breath* (1993) are more concerned with the weaving of the fabric of memory than with the immigrant's task of assimilation.

A number of Asian diasporic writers can be linked with one or other of the two poles proposed by Nasta. Leena Dhingra's *Amritvela* (1988) is another novel dramatizing cultural clashes; but it achieves originality through its reverse focus on a British-educated Indian girl returning to her extended family in India. Farrukh Dhondy's *Poona Company* (1900), on the other hand, is a sensitive evocation of the author's Indian childhood; its successor, *Bombay Duck* (1990), is a more ambitious, Rushdiesque celebration of hybridity and cultural diversity, as it ranges with its actor protagonist between Edinburgh, London, and Bombay.

An Indian English novelist who would be more difficult to limit to a single category is Amit Chaudhuri (b. 1962). After evoking the existence of a young Indian student at Oxford in *Afternoon Raag* (1993), Chaudhuri set his second novel, *Freedom Song* (1998), against a backdrop of growing communal tensions in his native Calcutta in the 1990s. *A New World* (2000) depicts a visit to India, although the writer-protagonist, recently divorced, is returning to his elderly parents from America. Chaudhuri also deserves mention for a fine anthology of Indian Literature (2001), notable for its generous coverage (in translation) of fiction in India's indigenous languages. The anthology thus provides a counterweight to an earlier collection, edited by Rushdie and Elizabeth West (1997), containing the notorious claim that contemporary Indian writing in English is a "more important body of work" than that produced in India's other sixteen official languages combined.

The majority of Asian writers in Britain, or in the English language for that matter, are part of an Indian or, more accurately, South Asian diaspora. Among individual writers falling outside this category the most remarkable include Timothy Mo (b. 1950) and Kazuo Ishiguro (b. 1954). Mo, who was born in Hong Kong to an English mother and Cantonese father, was nevertheless educated in England and has lived for long periods in London. He used a contemporary Hong Kong setting in *The Monkey King* (1978) and a historical one in *An Insular Possession* (1986), before expanding his range to guerrillas in a barely disguised East Timor (*The Redundancy of Courage*, 1992) and Chinese-Americans in the Philippines (*Brownout on Breadfruit Boulevard*, 1995). With his cultural hybridity and multicultural perspectives, Mo is another example of those authors characterized by Salman Rushdie as writers of "migrants' tales."

Mo's most interesting novel in the present context is *Sour Sweet* (1982), set in London's Chinese community in the 1960s. It depicts the existence of a humble Chinese waiter, Chen, and his family as they become unwillingly involved with the criminal activities of a Hong Kong triad. In addition to its tragic dimension – Chen is "washed" by the Triad society, who wrongly believe he has been cheating them – the novel provides a fairly comic, even satirical, account of the acculturation process (or lack thereof), with its humor derived as much from the British as seen through Chinese eyes, as from the resistance of Chen and his family to new ways.

Kazuo Ishiguro (b. 1954), finally, is an example of an Asian writer without the remotest colonial connection. He came to Britian in 1960 and received an exclusively British education, including enrolment at the University of East Anglia on one of the few academic creative writing courses to have actually produced distinguished creative writers. Numbering Angus Wilson and Malcolm Bradbury among its past teachers, the program also includes Ian McEwan among its graduates. Although Ishiguro's first two novels, *A Pale View of Hills* (1982) and *An Artist of the Floating World* (1986), with their evocations of devastated postwar landscapes, have explicit Japanese links, his better-known *The Remains of the Day* (1989) – made even more famous by a memorable screen adaptation – has an entirely English setting. Merely as a "novel of manners," minutely depicting the prewar rituals of a fading aristocrat through the perspective of its butler, Stevens, reminiscing from the bleaker 1950s, the book is suggestive; with its invitation to allegorical readings (not admittedly from Ishiguro himself) of the inexorable decline of a whole social class, a whole way of life, or a whole country, it is remarkable.

It is helpful to recall in conclusion what has been excluded by imposing certain divisions and restrictions, or – which often amounts to the same thing – to consider how some of the tendencies in British fiction outlined here might be extrapolated in other directions.

While it is understandable that poetry and drama are excluded from a survey of this kind, a few examples of shorter fictional forms should be briefly mentioned. In an Asian context, this would certainly apply to the two short-story collections of Aamer Hussein (b. 1955), *Mirror to the Sun* (1993) and *This Other Salt* (1999). Born in Karachi, moving between Indian and Pakistan in his early years and finally emigrating to Britain with his family in the 1970s, Hussein is an eloquent chronicler of the experiences of cultural loss and displacement. Another interesting example is Bombay-born Suniti Namjoshi (b. 1941), who moved from the Indian Administrative Service to Canadian academia and, finally, in the mid-eighties, to rural Devon. Her rewritings of traditional stories from East and West in *Feminist Fables* (1981), and her satirical blend of myth, fable, and the fantastic in *The Conversations of Cow* (1985), are highly original contributions to Indian diasporic writing. In the Caribbean context, is Guyanan-born Pauline Melville (b. 1948). Although Melville has written one novel, *The Ventriloquist's Tale* (1997), set in Georgetown at the beginning of the twentieth century, her characteristic fascination with metamorphosis and disguise is still better known from two remarkable collections of short stories, *Shape-shifter* (1990) and *The Migration of Ghosts* (1998).

However one defines and understands "black British" fiction, the tradition should not be limited to the representation of inter-ethnic relations or the acculturation process undergone by the writer's alter ego in the United Kingdom in the second half of the twentieth century. Many novelists have also dealt with the legacy of colonialism *outside* the British Isles, with one of the most fertile approaches here being the rewriting of canonical English texts directly or indirectly related to empire. One key focus of what was defined above as "canonical counterdiscourse" has been *Heart of Darkness*: rewritings of the Conrad text such as Achebe's *Things Fall Apart* or Kenyan novelist Ngugi wa Thiong'o's *A Grain of Wheat* (1966) fall outside the present survey, but Wilson Harris's *Palace of the Peacock*, V. S. Naipaul's *A Bend in the River* (1979), and David Dabydeen's *The Intended* are obviously central to it.

Other target texts include *Robinson Crusoe*, comically inverted in Sam Selvon's *Moses Ascending*, and, above all, *The Tempest*, the intertextual model for George Lamming's *Water with Berries*. The most profoundly original rewriting of Shakespeare's final play, however, is surely Marina Warner's *Indigo* (1992). But in spite of this author's century-old family links with the Caribbean – from the direct ancestor who established the first British settlement on St Kitts in the seventeenth century to a grandfather who was Attorney General of Trinidad – Warner is excluded from the present chapter by ethnicity. The same is true of white Dominican Creole Jean Rhys, whose *Wide Sargasso Sea* (1966) is an even more famous example of canoncal counterdiscourse with its fictional recreation of the life of the first Mrs Rochester from Charlotte Brontë's *Jane Eyre*.

It is also worth noting that a number of black or Asian novelists have focused on such topics as alienation, discrimination, hybridity, or multiculturalism, but in the context of Canada or the United States, reflecting the fact that writers of the black or Asian diaspora may just as well be living in New York or Toronto as in London. Sam

Selvon, in many ways the representative West Indian writer of the *Windrush* generation, actually emigrated to Canada in 1976 and lived the last eighteen years of his
life in Toronto. And to return to an author justifiably prominent in this chapter: even
Rushdie finally abandoned the empire, as one critic has noted, and relocated to New
York. Nevertheless, wherever one draws the boundaries, or however one groups what
remains within them, one claim may be strongly argued: the black British contribution to English fiction in the second half of the twentieth century deserves wider
critical attention than it has hitherto received.

REFERENCES AND FURTHER READING

Note: The entries for Dance and Nelson are structurally similar, basic handbooks for Caribbean and Asian
   Diasporic writers, respectively.
Volumes 112, 125, and 157 of the huge *Dictionary of Literary Biography* (DLB) have longer esssays on
   Caribbean and black African writers, although there are no separate volumes yet on Asian writers in
   English.
Wasafiri is a London-based journal featuring "Caribbean, African, Asian and associated literatures in
   English," with frequent coverage of black British writing. *The Journal of Commonwealth Literature*,
   notwithstanding its rather dated name, is another excellent journal with comprehensive annual
   bibliographies.

Bhabha, Homi (ed.) (1990) *Nation and Narration*.
   London: Routledge.
——(1994) *The Location of Culture*. London: Rou-
   tledge.
Childs, Peter (ed.) (1999) *Post-Colonial Theory and
   English Literature: A Reader*. Edinburgh: Edin-
   burgh University Press.
Chaudhuri, Amit (ed.) (2001) *The Picador Book of
   Modern Indian Literature*. London: Picador.
Dance, Daryl Cumber (ed.) (1986) *Fifty Caribbean
   Writers: A Bio-Bibliographical Critical Sourcebook*.
   New York: Greenwood Press.
George, Rosemary Marangoly (1999) *The Politics of
   Home: Postcolonial Relocations and Twentieth-Cen-
   tury Fiction*. Berkeley: University of California
   Press.
Gikandi, Simon (1997) *Maps of Englishness:
   Writing Identity in a Culture of* Colonialism.
   New York: Columbia University Press.
Gilroy, Paul (1993) *Small Acts: Thoughts on the
   Politics of Black Cultures*. London: Serpent's Tail.
Goonetilleke, D. C. R. A. (1998) *Salman Rushdie*.
   London: Macmillan.
Guptara, Prabhu (1986) *Black British Literature:
   An Annotated Bibliography*. Aarhus, Denmark:
   Dangaroo Press.

Hall, Stuart (1996) *Critical Dialogues in Cultural
   Studies*, ed. David Morley and Kuan-Hsing
   Chen. London: Routledge.
Hutcheon, Linda (1988) *A Poetics of Postmodernism:
   History, Theory, Fiction*. London: Routledge
James, Louis (1999) *Caribbean Literature in English*.
   London: Longman.
King, Bruce (1996) *New National and Post-
   Colonial Literatures: An Introduction*. Oxford:
   Clarendon Press.
——(2003) *V. S. Naipaul*. New York: Palgrave
   Macmillan.
Ledent, Bénédicte (2002) *Caryl Phillips*. Manches-
   ter: Manchester University Press.
McLeod, John (2000) *Beginning Postcolonialism*.
   Manchester: Manchester University Press.
Nasta, Susheila (1988) *Critical Perspectives on Sam
   Selvon*. Washington, DC: Passeggiata Press.
——(2002) *Home Truths: Fictions of the South Asian
   Diaspora in Britain*. London: Palgrave.
Nelson, Emmanuel, S. (ed.) (1993) *Writers of the
   Indian Diaspora: A Bio-Bibliographical Critical
   Sourcebook*. New York: Greenwood Press.
Newland, Courttia (ed.) (2001) *The Penguin Book of
   New Black Writing in Britain*. Harmondsworth:
   Penguin.

Paquet, Sandra Pouchet (1983) *George Lamming.* London: Heinemann.

Phillips, Mike and Phillips, Trevor (eds.) (1999) *Windrush: The Irresistible Rise of Multi-Racial Britain.* London: HarperCollins.

Rushdie, Salman and West, Elizabeth (eds.) (1997) *The Vintage Book of Indian Writing 1947–1997.* London: Vintage.

Thieme, John (2001) *Post-Colonial Contexts: Writing Back to the Canon.* London: Continuum.

Wambu, Onyekachi (ed.) (1998) *Empire Windrush: Fifty Years of Writing about Black Britain.* London: Phoenix.

10

The Recuperation of History in British and Irish Fiction

Margaret Scanlan

The historical novel, Andrew Graham Dixon writes, is "a literary form at war with itself"; the very term implies "a lie with obscure obligations to the truth" (quoted in Lee 2000). Though its pleasures are many, most of historical fiction's theoretical interest lies along this border between documented public history and the literary. Dixon's "lie" is presumably the imaginative, or the invented; we might equally think of the literary in terms of the aesthetic, of figurative or experimental language. For its great nineteenth-century practitioners, for Scott, Hugo, and Tolstoy, the art of the historical novel required concealing the junctures between history and fiction, much as a skilled cabinetmaker smooths the seams between two pieces of wood. Its major characters are representative figures, eyewitnesses to history: Scott's Waverley the Jacobite, Hugo's Marquis de Lantenac the dispossessed noble of 1793. The author makes readers at home in history, encourages them to share the characters' enthusiasm for Bonnie Prince Charlie, provides images that make the battle of Borodino come alive. And since history is organic, developing as people do according to principles the novel can articulate; since nations, like persons, have character traits that determine the patterns of their behavior; since the nation's past explains its present, then nothing in history is entirely alien to us.

One reason the historical novel flourished in the time of Scott and Hugo is that historians and novelists shared many basic premises; in an age of biography and narrative history, one might argue that they wrote in the same genres. While best-selling historical fiction and best-selling history books still share many narrative and stylistic features, changes in historiography and literary theory, and over a century of experiment in narrative form, have combined to complicate the relationship between history and fiction in the historical novel. The major changes in both historiography and literary theory reflect the influence of poststructuralism. One of the most important of these is a diminished belief in originality, or in the possibility of retrieving the pure original version of anything, which is summed up in Derrida's principle that "everything is always already written." Another is the Foucauldian view that great men and ideas do not produce change; instead, change occurs through gradual shifts in attention and in ways of explaining the world. After Foucault, we see an increasing sense of ruptures in history, of the otherness of the past, as well as a reluctance to discern patterns or identify causes of change. Finally, in Lyotard's formulation, we find thinkers distrustful of "grand narratives," of systems such as Marxism or orthodox Christianity that offer comprehensive explanations of history or human behavior. When we add the influence of the *Annales* historians, who argued for studying history in terms of subtle changes occurring across the *longue durée*, rather than as a series of events; the still-powerful Marxist claim that ideology masks economic interests; and the burgeoning interest among historians in the working class, women, gay people, and ethnic minorities, we can see how thoroughly "history," as a subject, has changed. All of these intellectual developments promote innovation in the historical novel.

Nor, of course, should we discount postwar social and political changes in Britain and Ireland, many of which work in tandem with developments in theory. Throughout the 1950s and 1960s, as the British rebuilt their cities and saw the hardships of the immediate postwar period give way to consumer comforts, their nation's international power diminished. The empire was lost, piece by piece, in every decade after the war: from British India in 1947 to Hong Kong in 1997. The 1963 news that the head of SIS's Soviet section, Kim Philby, had been a Soviet agent since 1936 became emblematic of lapsed judgment and an excuse for American domination during the Cold War. On the other hand, the Labour government's postwar guarantee of free access to medicine, education, affordable housing, and a tax system to support them realigned the social classes at home. Millions of Commonwealth immigrants moved to the United Kingdom, provoking a backlash of immigration curbs and racial strife but also creating, in the larger cities, a newly multicultural Britain. Under Margaret Thatcher (1979–90) the United Kingdom reversed many social policies of the previous thirty-three years, privatizing utilities and transportation, reducing public spending, and curbing labor unions. The UN reported that the index of "income poverty" rate increased 60 percent in the United Kingdom between 1979 and 1991, but Thatcher's supporters saw greater stability at home and restored prestige abroad; they heralded the Falklands victory as a return to glory. After eighteen years in opposition, a Labour Party government under Tony Blair was elected in 1997. Domestically, "New" Labour sought a middle course between the socialism of the 1950s and Thatcherite conservatism; when Blair committed troops to Iraq in 2003, many members of his own party resisted what they saw as endorsement of US neo-imperialism.

In Northern Ireland, the most visible events were connected with the Troubles, which began in 1968 with violence against Catholic Civil Rights marchers and officially ended with the Good Friday Peace Agreement in 1998. During this period, over 3,200 people lost their lives; billions of dollars in property was destroyed; and terrorist violence was endemic, particularly in working-class Catholic and Protestant neighborhoods in Belfast and Derry, and in rural South Armagh. Five years after the agreement, paramilitary violence continued on a reduced scale and so did political divisions: in April 2003, the new Assembly was dissolved and Northern Ireland's government was placed under direct British control. The Republic of Ireland, as the Irish Free State was renamed after withdrawing from the Commonwealth in 1948, had a continuous and peaceful parliamentary system. Culturally and economically, however, it has changed dramatically. Once one of the poorest countries in Europe, in 2003 the Republic ranked twelfth in the UN's Human Development index, just ahead of the United Kingdom. Much of this transformation came in 1987–97, when economic growth averaged over 5 percent per year, more than double the figure for the European Union as a whole (O'Connell 1999: 4). At the same time, the Catholic Church's influence declined; one study puts the figure for weekly Mass attendance, which was 91 percent in 1974, at 57 percent in 1999 (Irish Council of Churches 2000). In 2000, an *Irish Times* poll reported that only "four out of 10 people overall and only 14 percent of young people see weekly Mass attendance as 'very important'" (Brennock 2000). The economic, social, and religious changes I have noted are consistent with the movement away from Great Men and Events in academic history; in the novel, too, history has become decentered. Given the traditional exclusion of women from parliaments and armies, it is hardly surprising that history in women's novels, or "domestic fiction," is usually seen from the margins.

Elizabeth Bowen's *The Last September* (1927), *The Heat of the Day* (1948), and *Irish Stories* (1978) are influential examples. Set in London during the Blitz, with an extended excursus to rural Ireland, *The Heat of the Day* is largely seen through the consciousness of Stella, an employee of a secret government agency; Harrison, employed by another, discovers that Stella's lover, Robert, is a Nazi spy. Harrison blackmails Stella into continuing the relationship so that he can keep Robert under surveillance; in the meantime, a family death leaves Stella's son, an army recruit, heir to an Anglo-Irish estate and a recognition that he may not survive to occupy it. Drawing on her own experience of being bombed out, Bowen provides harrowing descriptions of the Blitz, when a civilian at home might face greater danger than an officer in India. The war blurred distinctions between the home and the front, between the experiences of men and women. But Bowen also articulates a deeper continuity: "The grind and scream of battles . . . tearing through nerves and tearing up trees, were indoor-plotted; this was a war of dry cerebration inside windowless walls. No act was not part of some calculation . . . any action was enemy action now" (1962: 142). On this view, an account of the Battle of El-Alamein that disregarded the politics and psychologies of the London bureaucracy would be incomplete, even naive.

Other novels about the Second World War by women, including Muriel Spark's *The Girls of Slender Means* (1963), Olivia Manning's *Balkan* and *Levant* trilogies (1960–80), and Penelope Lively's *Moon Tiger* (1987), also emphasize that what matters most in history is often experienced on its margins. Anita Desai's *Baumgartner's Bombay* (1988) adds a postcolonial perspective. As the war began, British officials rounded up German Jewish refugees to be interned with other Germans as enemy aliens. Most refugees were soon released, but Desai's research showed that some were held in India for six years. Her novel follows Hugo Baumgartner from a comfortable childhood in Berlin to an increasingly difficult adolescence; in the eleventh hour, an old Gentile friend who commandeered the family business after his father's suicide finds him a place with an export firm in Bombay.

Seen through Hugo Baumgartner's troubled eyes, European and Indian history are a tale of mutual incomprehension. Nazi ideologues persecute Jews in the camp; the bullying continues for months because the camp fails to distinguish between Jewish and Gentile holders of German passports; to their Indian guards, the prisoners all look alike. European battles come to Hugo in Nazi broadcasts monitored on hidden radios: Churchill "blows up the whole French fleet, the madman"; not a word about Auschwitz (Desai 1989: 114). When Baumgartner returns to Calcutta after the war, he is astonished to learn that thousands died there in a 1943 famine; when Partition brings the deaths of 20,000 people in three days he is bewildered because, like his Indian guards, he thinks all foreigners are the same.

For the rest of his life, Baumgartner constructs "a wall against history" (p. 118). He prospers in Bombay under the sponsorship of an Indian businessman, but after his death the man's sons cheat him. He lives in squalor, begging scraps to feed an adopted horde of semi-feral cats. His kindness to a passing German drug addict leads the young man to murder him for his only valuable possession, a silver trophy won by a horse he and his Indian partner owned. An Indian perspective allows Desai to show, without relativizing Nazi brutality, that the bigotry, violence, and betrayals of Baumgarner's youth follow him in later life. She portrays a sense of history as the *longue durée*; in addition to the horror of events, of Kristallnacht or Count von Stauffenberg's execution, we follow the sustained miseries of a life irretrievably damaged in childhood, dragging on into decrepit old age. Similarly, the casual violence of a young German tourist against an aging Jewish refugee suggests that the half-life of the Third Reich is incalculable.

Pat Barker's *Regeneration* trilogy (1991–5) moves back to the First World War, as seen through the eyes of characters introduced in an Edinburgh hospital for shell shock victims. In some respects, the trilogy is closer to the nineteenth-century model of historical fiction than is Bowen's, or Desai's, work: virtually all of the characters considered at any length are male; well-known historical figures, psychotherapist W. H. R. Rivers and poets Siegfried Sassoon and Wilfred Owen, mingle with fictional characters; flashbacks to combat appear in the first two volumes, while the third ends with a long section taking the fictional Billy Prior to France to die with Owen at the Sambre-Oise canal. Yet Barker focuses on the war's psychological impact on soldiers, rather than on public issues of politics and military strategy, both of which, whenever briefly noted, appear as out of touch with reality as do the hallucinating patients. The homosexuality or bisexuality of the major characters is treated at length in the second volume, *The Eye in the Door*, which deals with an actual defamation suit against Noel Pemberton Billing, an MP who claimed to have a list of 47, 000 mostly lesbian, gay, and feminist spies corrupted by German agents. In her treatment of the repression of peace activists and the gay community, Barker suggests that the normative community is engaged in a "reaction formation," a pathological wartime hyper-masculinity worthy of one of Dr Rivers's patients. A feminist emphasis similarly emerges in the parallel drawn between the symptoms of prewar hysteria patients, virtually all female, and shell shock victims.

Although traditionally realistic, Barker's trilogy also introduces, as Anne Whitehead argues, a postmodern conception of the Great War. Many of Rivers's patients suffer from memory loss accompanied by hallucinations, paralysis, or mutism. Rivers's associates use hypnosis to help patients retrieve suppressed memories. Once the missing episode is retrieved, the "patient repossesses his own history" and his identity consolidates around it: "The past becomes a possession; the ability to narrate the event acts as proof of its ownership" (Whitehead 1998: 678). If all goes well, a patient with a restored memory will no longer need the symptom that blocked it. However, according to Rivers and Barker, the patient's past is insistently invading the present; the traumatic shock is an event that was "not experienced at the time," a view consistent with postmodernism's emphasis on history's ruptures and discontinuities (p. 678). Further, Rivers resists hypnosis because he fears producing a Jekyll and Hyde split in men already inclined to dissociate. His realization that the war demands this compartmentalization, producing it in pathological form in vulnerable patients, reinforces a sense of a public history as anything but organic and whole. As Whitehead concludes, "Barker's text leaves us finally in an uneasy 'no-man's-land' between past and present; although the past cannot be 'regenerated' . . . its specters compulsively haunt the present and do not readily submit to the processes of narrative transformation" (p. 692).

As Great Britain, once the center of international trade and politics, moved into the shadow of the conflict between the United States and the Soviet Union, fictional accounts of the past became increasingly critical. Victorian self-confidence, the civilizing mission of the empire, and notions of national character featuring pluck, bravery, and emotional restraint became particularly vulnerable. J. G. Farrell's *Empire* trilogy – *Troubles* (1970), *The Siege of Krishnapur* (1973), and *The Singapore Grip* (1978) – offers an ironic look at three events on the periphery: the Irish War for Independence (1919–21), the Sepoy Mutiny (1857), and the fall of British Singapore to the Japanese (1942). *Troubles* is seen through the eyes of Major Brendan Archer, a shell-shocked veteran visiting a fiancée he barely knows in Ireland. Her father, Edward, owns a resort hotel, but, since tourists avoid guerrilla wars, the only guests at the once resplendent Majestic are elderly widows of colonial administrators. His psyche already damaged, the Major can neither find his way around the massive and decaying hotel nor make sense of local politics.

His war experiences have not shaken his patriotism; to him, the British "presence" in Ireland "signified a moral authority" (Farrell 1971: 51). Yet Edward's fanatic anti-Catholicism, his conviction that "you might as well dress up a monkey in a suit" as send an Irish boy to a good school, his refusal to let his starving tenants eat the grain they grow on his fields, and his zeal to protect his zinc statue of Queen Victoria from the Sinn Fein, defy the Major's notions of British fair play (p. 187). Grotesque events in the hotel, however, mirror the political history to which the novel seldom alludes directly. As the old ladies' sedate dogs, with their sweaters and British names, age and weaken, a vicious family of feral cats, led by a ferocious orange female with "bitter green eyes" (p. 234), terrorizes the dogs and their owners. Enraged, Edward and the Major gun down the cats, who shriek "as if it were a massacre of infants" and leave a "dreadful mess: blood on the carpets, there forever, ineradicable, brains on the coverlets" (p. 327). Inevitably, the cat massacre invites an invasion of rats.

The Major's abstract beliefs are defeated, in these scenes and elsewhere, by the dreadful viscosity of fact: by damp sheets, crumbling plaster, a rotting sheep's head in a chamber pot. In the end, he goes mad, urging a last-ditch defense when even Edward presses him to "listen to reason"; it all ends with the old ladies rescuing him from the beach, where the IRA have buried him up to his neck; he will survive to become a POW of the Japanese in the *Singapore Grip*. A similar destruction of imperial idealism, and more generally of ideas and culture, characterizes *The Siege of Krishnapur*, in which the central figure is the Collector, or local administrator, of a remote district. Before the terrible siege that kills half of the British residents, the Collector embodies enlightened imperialism. The many useful inventions displayed at the Great Exhibition of 1851 ("an instrument to teach the blind to write . . . a fire annihilator . . . a domestic telegraph") demonstrate the progress Britain is bringing to India (1974: 51).

But after weeks of starvation, filth, and misery, which Farrell describes with inimitable wit and compassion, the Collector is a changed man. A cannon saves the British remnant; when soldiers run out of ammunition, they load into it all the symbols of British civilization and cultural superiority, from silverware to art. As Judie Newman notes, "Predictably Shakespeare proves particularly deadly" (1995: 2). In London years later the Collector seems almost Marxist, declaring that "Culture is a sham . . . a cosmetic painted on life by rich people to conceal its ugliness." Perhaps, the narrator notes, by the end of his life the Collector came "to believe that a people, a nation, does not create itself according to its own best ideas, but is shaped by other forces, of which it has little knowledge" (Farrell 1974: 343).

Many other postwar historical novels offer ironic readings of events known to generations of schoolchildren as stirring adventures. George Macdonald Fraser's popular Flashman novels take the bully of Thomas Hughes's *Tom Brown's Schooldays*, his character unimproved with age, into all the hot spots of empire. Whether assisting at the Charge of the Light Brigade or the Sepoy Mutiny, Flashman can be counted on for an unheroic performance and a debunking account of once-celebrated events. William Boyd's *An Ice-Cream War* (1984), set during the First World War, features an obscure conflict between Germans and Englishmen in colonial Africa; in *The New Confessions* (1988), the hero experiences the horrors of trench warfare, but his uncle soon rescues him, putting him to work making propaganda films.

In *The Remains of the Day* (1988), Kazuo Ishiguro focuses not Churchill or the Blitz, but on the British aristocracy's infatuation with fascism in the 1930s. In the unreliable eyes of his butler, Stevens, Lord Darlington's meetings with von Ribbentrop and

Oswald Mosley are noble diplomatic initiatives; hardly aware of having emotions, this butler immerses himself in his role and obeys Darlington perfectly. Stevens reflects on his life, framing it as an academic question, "What is a great butler?" But even this question has political overtones: "a great butler is bound, almost by definition, to be an Englishman," because the profession requires the "emotional restraint which only the British are capable of" (Ishiguro 1993: 43). The novel reminds readers of an inglorious chapter in the nation's history with a troubling suggestion that the national character might incline one to edit out painful realities. Yet readers of an earlier Ishuguro novel, *An Artist of the Floating World* (1986), the story of an equally deluded painter who spent the war years designing propaganda posters for the Emperor, will recognize Ishiguro's interest in the capacity of human beings to mistake the prevailing discourse for the self's authentic promptings. In this sense, Ishiguro takes us full circle from the old historical novel in which great men made history to a fully realized world in which the blur and buzz of an unarticulated public history shape human beings.

Novels about the Irish past also grow increasingly critical of national mythology, but with a distinction that stems from literary and political differences. For if it was a moral advantage to the Irish to have been, historically, the oppressed rather than the oppressor, the political enthusiasms of the Irish Renaissance proved a difficult inheritance. W. B. Yeats, J. M. Synge, Lady Augusta Gregory, Douglas Hyde, Patrick Pearse, and George Russell envisioned a Celtic Ireland with a heroic past and a sacrificial revolutionary tradition. That Sean O'Casey, James Joyce, Flann O'Brien, and Samuel Beckett offered an ironic, even debunking version of the national myth did not loosen its grip on the popular imagination, in part because the Free State banned many of their works. One of the first postwar novels to tackle the literary legacy of romantic nationalism was Iris Murdoch's *The Red and the Green* (1965). The Dublin-born author uses her Anglo-Irish heritage as a basis for re-imagining Easter 1916 as a family with alliances on both sides of the hyphen experienced it.

The founding event of the Irish Republic was the capture of the central post office in Dublin by revolutionaries during Easter week, 1916. Although the rebellion was quashed in a week, Britain's subsequent execution of fourteen leading revolutionaries led to public outcry and created the support needed to win independence in 1921. In patriotic retellings, the Easter Rising and the birth of a free Ireland from the martyrs' blood became virtually indistinguishable from Catholic Ireland's sanguinary Christ story. Yeats's "Easter 1916," with its sonorous refrain, "all, all are changed utterly / A terrible beauty is born" expresses reservations about revolutionary violence, but suggests that the executed rebels transformed their colonized homeland into the heroic Ireland they had imagined. In *The Red and the Green*, a text dense with allusions to Yeats and Joyce, Murdoch deconstructs both this patriotic version of the rebellion and the modernist impulse to recover the past as a coherent whole. Key characters, such as the artistic revolutionary Pat Dumay, are constructed of traits that Joyce treats as incompatible. In a walk along the sea, one such character, a spoilt priest with more than a passing resemblance to Leopold Bloom, follows the path Stephen took in

Portrait of the Artist after he renounced his vocation. But Barney sees a different view: "two tall rival spires at Kingstown, Catholic and Protestant, shifting constantly in their relation to each other except when from the Martello tower at Sandycove they could be seen superimposed" (1965: 98).

Murdoch asks readers to consider how irresponsibly literature shapes history. The title comes from a patriotic song, "Sure 'twas for this Lord Edward died and Wolfe Tone sunk serene / Because they could not bear to leave the red above the green." Pat Dumay argues that death has nothing to do with sinking serene and that "bad poetry is lies," but the damage is already done; "I'm going to die young," his younger brother affirms (1965: 104, 108). Yet great literature too, in Murdoch's austere analysis, also shapes a lethally oversimplified patriotism. Pat's cousin Andrew, a British cavalry officer who will die at the rebels' hands, "would have blushed to admit how much his zeal depended on early impressions of the more patriotic passages of Shakespeare and a boyish devotion to Sir Lancelot" (p. 9). While Murdoch sees our tendency to fictionalize history as a perennial danger, her Easter 1916 offers an unglamorous alternative, reflecting the perspectives of a wide range of characters and attentive to details of their daily lives to which no political abstraction seems adequate.

With the outbreak of the Troubles in 1969, people were once more dying for a cause that echoed the rhetoric of 1916, with an equally violent and intransigent Unionism as the declared enemy. In the North, the Field Day movement led by Seamus Deane, Tom Paulin, Seamus Heaney, Thomas Kilroy, Michael Longley, and Brian Friel mobilized writers to imagine an alternative vision of Irish history, a mythical "fifth province" where Protestant and Catholic claims could be reconciled.

While Field Day's poetry and plays remain better known than its fiction, Kilroy's *The Big Chapel* (1971) illustrates the Field Day project of re-imagining the past in order to promote a peaceful future. Set in the early 1870s, *The Big Chapel* focuses on the debate over National Schools. Established by the British, they were usually under secular control, with a standard curriculum that included the Protestant King James Bible and excluded the Irish language. The Catholic Archbishop, Paul Cullen, advocated reforming these schools and creating Catholic secondary schools and universities. Kilroy tells the story of a local priest who opposes the bishop's decision to replace the national school with one run by the Christian Brothers. The headmaster of the National School, a Catholic married to a Protestant, fights to preserve it as the town's only genuinely integrated institution.

The sectarian violence of 1971 guarantees an unhappy ending for *The Big Chapel*; the moderates are pushed to madness and the townspeople are further polarized. Yet the novel's modestly experimental treatment of history proves liberating. Kilroy emphasizes the undecidability of historical questions, facts that have been lost, distortions of memory, and the strong misreadings of the partisan: "It is difficult to decide between truth and lie...each side claimed to have acted in extravagant contradiction to what the others represented as the true account" (1971: 17). These uncertainties do not so much signal the irrelevance of fact as the need to remain open to nuances and alternative explanations. When Northern Ireland seemed gripped in the dead hand of myth, Kilroy suggested that reading fiction might be a model for historical and political interpretation, a movement of consciousness among alternatives. For if even the past is open to changing interpretations, the future need not be rigidly determined by ancient injustices.

John Banville's *Birchwood* (1973) is a more thoroughly postmodern treatment of the Irish past, but the author's 1992 remark that he had only realized retrospectively "how much of the early seventies there was in it. When Northern Ireland was beginning to be really bad" suggests its continuity with *The Big Chapel* (quoted in Hand 2002: 37). It is impossible to specify the time of Banville's novel; at the beginning, when the eponymous Big House is equipped with a telephone and the narrator refers to the new state, we might assume that it is roughly 1923. However, after the narrator joins a circus, a potato famine strikes; later, he alludes to the Molly Maguires, the Irish secret society remembered for its role in the Pennsylvania coal mine strikes of the 1870s. The book's time, then, is an Irish Anytime in the Past Two Centuries, populated by characters based on the stereotypes of the Anglo-Irish Big House novel, from the mad mother to the menacing peasants. For novelist Colm Tóibín, *Birchwood*'s publication was a landmark event that "offered closure, tried to put an end . . . to certain tropes and themes . . . it made fun of rebellion and land wars and famine, Irish myths of origin . . . Full of dark laughter, *Birchwood* was, more than any historian's work, the most radical text in Irish revisionism" (2000: xxxi).

Joseph O'Connor's *Star of the Sea* (2003), a story of a voyage to America in the famine year 1847, continues this revisionism. Framed as a limited-edition reprint of a contemporary travel narrative, the novel observes some mid-nineteenth-century conventions, including chapter headings such as "The Visions at Delphi, In which the wretched Husband of Mary Duane, quite undone by the Evil of Want, records his Last and Terrible thoughts" (2003: 34). The book's frankness about the symptoms of syphilis introduces a note of anachronism, as do stories assuming a knowledge of later events. Thus a famine victim driven to crime in London falls into conversation with a novelist, to whom he confides the story of an imaginary Jew who runs a school for young thieves; Dickens swallows it whole, including the name "Fagan," which belongs to the most anti-Semitic Irish priest Mulvey knows. Like Banville, O'Connor also recreates familiar Big House figures: both Mulvey and the Anglo-Irish landlord David Meredith are in love with the peasant colleen, Mary Deane. Incest and assassination loom; Mary is revealed to be Meredith's half-sister; a secret society has put Mulvey on board to murder him.

O'Connor's realistic descriptions of starvation and life below decks show no irony about the famine. Indeed four quotations that stress British responsibility for the famine and indifference to its victims preface the text, including *Punch*'s infamous characterization of the Irish as the missing link between "the gorilla and the Negro." Similarly, Mulvey's mission to kill Meredith, although fully authorized by romantic mythology, creates agonizing conflict for the intended assassin, whom the revolutionaries are blackmailing. Further acquaintance with Meredith creates sympathy for an imperfect man who once dreamed of becoming a model landlord. Instead, he has himself been bankrupted by the famine; although doubtless many of the tenants whose tickets to Canada he paid for will die on the terrible passage, he did what he could for their future. Contemporary Irish readers who enjoy a comfortable middle-class life do not have the luxury of execrating this traditional enemy; instead the novel challenges them to see in Meredith's relationship to the starving and homeless peasants a reflection of their own relationship to, say, present-day refugees from African famines.

While a critical or ironic tone characterizes many postwar British and Irish historical novels, victory in the Falklands seemed to occasion a return to a more patriotic recuperation of history that Joseph O'Connor complained of as "an odd kind of retro-drama of English culture, as writers retreat into a miserable invented version of a cosy Victorian past which never existed in the first place" (1995: 142). More charitably, Suzanne Keen observes the creation of a new genre she calls the "romance of the archives." In such novels, a researcher tracks down material traces of the past in a literal archive. This exciting quest ends pleasurably, in the discovery of a truth that "not only fascinates, but...yields tangible benefits" (2002: 42). Though the researcher "as action hero" may seem an unlikely figure, Keen traces him, or her, through such popular works as P. D. James's *Original Sin* (1994) and A. S. Byatt's *Possession* (1990). In these romances the past is "approachable...mapped onto recognizable places" (2002: 130); its figures are linked to the researcher by continuities as indisputable as evidence of mitochondrial DNA (p. 207). This healthy dose of sameness, then, enables Barry Unsworth to restore the true history of Liverpool's role in the slave trade in *Sugar and Rum* (1988) and permits an empathic researcher in Stevie Davies's *Impassioned Clay* (1999) to restore a suppressed episode of lesbian history.

As these last two examples suggest, the romance of the archive is not necessarily a work of political reaction, though Keen notes many examples, such as *Possession* and Peter Ackroyd's *Chatterton* (1987) and *English Music* (1992), that "pay homage to the English tradition" (p. 127). She sees the genre's relationship to debates in Britain over the heritage industry and the history curriculum for national schools and to fears that disrespectful postcolonials would appropriate the nation's history. In Keen's view, Byatt, Ackroyd, and Robert Goddard, offered a choice between a history that evokes guilt and one that evokes pride, opt for the feel-good alternative every time. Even writers who excoriate the British past "contribute to nostalgic fantasies about the uses of the past...the endogamous Englishness of the past discovered...can add to a celebratory narrative of homogeneity, continuity, native virtues, and cultural survival." Few use the recovered past to reconsider "the national identity" (p. 215).

Ian McEwan's *Atonement* (2001) offers an interesting variation on Keen's romance of the archives. As the novel begins in 1935, Briony Tallis, a privileged 13-year old, is planning a family production of her romance play, *The Trials of Arabella*, since current issues such as the Abyssinia Question and rearmament are unsuitable for literature. The day ends disastrously, for Briony's cousin is raped and Briony, misinterpreting a note from her older sister Cecilia's boyfriend, Robbie, falsely accuses him of the crime.

Robbie is jailed until released to join the army at the outbreak of World War II; he participates in the British expedition that culminated in the Dunkirk evacuation, now safely enshrined as a heroic moment but at the time a defeat.

Part Two of the novel takes Robbie across France; Part Three returns to Briony, who has joined Cecilia as a nurse in London. "Atonement" is already a theme in Briony's life; she feels as responsible for betraying the lovers as if she had been an adult at the time, rather than a 13-year old who could hardly be expected to fathom the nuances of adult sexuality. The hardships of the Blitz offer one form of atonement; another is Briony's gradual coming to terms with the damage the incident did. She constructs a plausible hypothesis of the rapist's real identity, and approaches Cecilia with a plan to change her testimony. Cecilia swears never to forgive her; Robbie, who walks in on the conversation, scoffs at the idea that "growing up" provides an adequate explanation of her change of heart. Nonetheless, the lovers give her detailed instructions for writing a statement exonerating Robbie before dismissing her to spend an hour alone before returning to duty.

Only at its end does the reader understand that Part Three is a fiction, a "new draft, an atonement," completed in 1999. Briony is an old woman, a celebrated writer; having suffered a series of small strokes, she understands that she will soon lose her memory to vascular dementia. As her family gathers to celebrate her seventy-seventh birthday with the performance of *The Trials of Arabella* canceled sixty-four years ago, Briony reflects on war and writing. Since the rapist and his victim – who have been married to each other for almost sixty years – are still alive and litigious, the true story can only be published after her death. But publishing the truth, which would include Robbie's death at Bray Dunes in June 1940 and Cecilia's in the bombing of London's Balham station in September, no longer seems important. Atonement is impossible, for the writer in her own novel, like God, has the "absolute power of deciding outcomes...No atonement for God, or novelists, even if they are atheists" (2001: 350, 351). Like Keen's romancers of the archive, McEwan respects patriotic history; Robbie and Cecilia are admirably brave and the war is just. Nor is the gap between fiction and history an occasion, as in Murdoch, for deploring the power of fiction to mislead. The impulse to atone, to allow Robbie to survive Dunkirk and join Cecilia in London, to omit their early deaths, affirms an older conception of art as a transformation of life. Yet the knowledge that the lovers died young and the author is doomed to lose her mental powers prevents us from confusing the imagined outcome with the actual one, the fiction with the history.

As we have seen, one might define serious historical fiction by its self-consciousness about the relationship between history and fiction, which postwar writers configure in multiple ways. The genre Linda Hutcheon dubbed historiographic metafiction is even more "intensely self-conscious" about how we narrate the past (1988: 113). In such examples as Anthony Burgess's *The End of the World News* (1982), John Fowles's *A Maggot* (1985), or J. M. Coetzee's *Foe* (1986), history is even more diffuse than in Farrell or Barker; the reader is invited not so much to ponder the inadequacies of a familiar history as to confront the paradoxes of fictive/historical representation, the particular/the general, and the present/the past. And this confrontation is itself contradictory, for it refuses to recuperate or dissolve either side of the dichotomy, yet is . . . willing to confront both. (Hutcheon 1988: 106)

The writer assumes that both history and fiction derive from and produce texts; this assumption, however, is not tantamount to a "loss of belief in a significant external reality." Rather than assert that, since history is a fiction, all variants are equally valid, historiographic metafiction reveals "a loss of faith in our ability to (unproblematically) *know* that reality, and therefore to be able to represent it in language" (p. 119).

The French Lieutenant's Woman (1969) revolves around the fascination of Charles Smithson, a Victorian gentleman, with Sarah Woodruff, a mysterious young woman believed to have been seduced and abandoned by the eponymous lieutenant. Set in Lyme Regis, the novel cuts a broad swathe through Victorian debates about science, religion, and gender roles, barely mentioning political and military events. Deliberate anachronisms – references to the Gestapo, to film, to the atom bomb, to twentieth-century publicists and the *Valley of the Dolls* – continually remind readers that they, and the narrator, belong to a later period. Differences between the way the characters understand themselves and the way we do are underscored: "We could not expect [Charles] to see what we are only just beginning . . . to realize ourselves: that the desire to hold and the desire to enjoy are mutually destructive" (Fowles 1981: 60). Similarly, the narrative highlights the significance of events as seen from our perspective, not the characters': "At Westminster only one week before John Stuart Mill had seized an opportunity . . . to argue that now was the time to give women equal rights at the ballot box." His contemporaries laughed, but "March 30th, 1867, is the point from which we can date the beginning of feminine emancipation" (p. 95).

Fowles's narrator also intrudes, breaking in to set a watch back to give the characters more time, or flipping a coin to determine what will happen next. In extended asides, Fowles reproduces a Victorian convention, but takes a contemporary perspective. For example, when an imagined reader objects that his intrusions undermine belief in his characters, he makes a twentieth-century response: "A character is either 'real' or 'imaginary'? If you think that, *hypocrite lecteur*, I can only smile. You do not even think of your own past as quite real . . . you fictionalize it" (p. 82). Calling attention to the artificiality of literary endings, the narrator proposes to give us at least two.

The first ending tidies up the plot to accord with Victorian convention; Charles marries his fiancée and never sees Sarah again. In the second ending, Charles finds Sarah and makes love to her, surprised to discover that she is a virgin. Swearing she is unworthy of him, she flees; alone in an empty church, he realizes that the Victorian era, with its certainties and repressions, is "the great hidden enemy of all his deepest yearnings" (p. 285). After nearly two years of roaming, he finds her again in London, living with the Rossettis. Although Sarah has given birth to Charles's daughter, she refuses to marry him, making a twentieth-century speech about needing space and "congenial work" (p. 353). Which ending we consider plausible, Fowles suggests, depends not on the logic of the characters, but on our philosophical biases and our assumptions about narrative.

Graham Swift's *Waterland* (1983) is another novel that foregrounds the nature of history. Its second chapter, "About the end of history," literally refers to the plight of Tom Crick, a history teacher in the East Anglian fens forced into early retirement under a new regime that wants to focus on the future. As in Fowles, plot revolves around personal relationships, in this case three deaths in the summer of 1943 for which Crick feels responsible. Not one of these is a casualty of war, yet the world wars are continually evoked; Crick's grandfather turned his mansion into a hospital for shell shock victims, one of whom became his son-in-law; bombers fly overhead, interrupting conversation; much is made of the resemblance between the muddy fens and the infamous Flanders mud. Crick understands that modern, scientific history requires solid facts, not stories, mysteries, the supernatural. Yet as his career and marriage collapse, he begins to tell his class "fairy tales" about his family's history, which is entwined with the history of how the fens were reclaimed and how the family brewery brought them prosperity. Only occasionally does he return to the proper topic for the class, the French Revolution.

Thus the question of what history is, why it matters, and how we can understand or narrate it drives the book at least as much as its rather Gothic plot, which uncovers a case of father–daughter incest, a botched abortion, a murder, and a suicide. The draining of the fens, their elaborate maintenance with a system of locks and perpetual dredging, becomes what cetology is in *Moby Dick*: an arcane lore that demonstrates desire for knowledge and mastery of nature. Land reclamation is also a metaphor for history: "forget ... your revolutions, your turning-points, your grand metamorphoses of history. Consider, instead, the slow and arduous process, the interminable and ambiguous process – the process of human siltation" (Swift 1992: 10). Crick tells the children that we begin to desire history when life slaps us with the Here and Now and we start asking why and when everything went wrong. "History is that impossible thing: the attempt to give an account, with incomplete knowledge, of actions themselves undertaken with incomplete knowledge" (p. 108). Next to this desire to know why, the revolutionary impulse, the desire for change and progress, will always fail. The symbol for this failure is the flood of 1947 that breaks the Atkinson Lock; the sea comes rushing in, restoring its old boundaries, like Napoleon following on the wake of the Terror. Yet Crick's own sad fate, and the recognition that "progress doesn't go anywhere," does not keep him from valuing history:

> It's progress if you stop the world slipping away. My humble model ... is the reclam-
> ation of land ... repeatedly, never-endingly retrieving what is lost. A dogged, vigilant
> business ... But you shouldn't go mistaking the reclamation of land for the building of
> empires. (p. 336)

Like Fowles and Swift, Salman Rushdie has written several historiographic meta-fictions. Like them he injects commentary about narrating fiction; like them he favors digressions and shifting chronology. But Rushdie's historiographic metafictions – *Midnight's Children* (1981), *Shame* (1983), and *The Satanic Verses* (1988) – also engage contemporary political controversy. The origins of the Indian and Pakistani states, the role of religion in public life, political corruption, military adventurism, and the treatment of women are topics that refuse to stay safely in the past. Rushdie adds elements of magical realism: an Anglicized Indian who morphs into Satan, a child born at the hour of Indian independence who can tune in to the thoughts of every other person born in India then, a retarded daughter called "shame" who commits gruesome murders and finally explodes into a fireball, burning down her family's home. The savage indignation of Rushdie's political novels stems most distinctively from this mixture of fantasy and the too-incredible-to-be-true facts of his homeland's history.

Thus the talkative narrator of *Shame* suggests that he is the author's stand-in, telling anecdotes about his family and friends, confessing at one point to the ease with which he himself entertains incompatible ideas and at another to understanding a Pakistani immigrant who murdered his daughter for sleeping with an Englishman. He describes himself as an exile, writing in a foreign language, whose very right to tell the story will be questioned by some Pakistanis. But he also insists that he is only telling a fairy tale, because a realistic novel would require unsavory facts – an aside that permits him to provide such examples as "genocide in Baluchistan" and officially tolerated heroin smuggling (1989: 67). Better to tell a tale about Beauty and the "Beastji," a lovely girl who feels the shame her country's rulers cannot feel and, having felt it, violently acts out "the collective fantasy of a stifled people" (p. 279). The narrator suggests that the distortions of fairy tale are hardly more exaggerated than the distortions of their nation's history its new rulers imposed in 1947, and have been revising ever since. "Pakistan" was invented in England, by Muslim intellectuals, who returned to make a "palimpsest" country, where the Indian centuries were covered up and "the past was rewritten" (p. 86). Thus the text proposes its own mind-boggling stories about a boy with three mothers or a political prisoner who hears Machiavelli speaking to him in an irritating sing-song as no less fictional than the official "justifying myth of the nation" that imposes an alien Islamic fundamentalism (p. 266).

The Ayatollah's *fatwa* of 1989 illustrated dramatically the differences between the postmodernist assumptions of western fiction and the fundamentalist conception of an inerrant Qu'ran. In the offending sections of *The Satanic Verses*, Rushdie re-imagined the origins of a religion called "Submission," a literal translation of "Islam." Mahound, an all-too-human character standing in for the Prophet, arranges with the heathen to give three of their goddesses special status in exchange for a peaceful conversion. Rushdie hoped that providing a playful but critical alternative to a received truth might seem liberating and hopeful; instead his book was burned in Bradford and its author sentenced to death.

Doubtless western writers who rallied to his support were genuinely outraged, but one senses a certain envy of Rushdie, whose audience takes its history, and its fictional transformation, so much to heart. For English-born writers contemplating their nation's history, Julian Barnes's *England, England* (1999) must propose a more likely fate. In that novel, an entrepreneur decides to make English history more accessible to American tourists, who find it inconvenient to travel from, say, the Tower of London to another site, such as Anne Hathaway's Cottage. How much better to take the Isle of Wight, and transform it into a replica of England's history, without all the boring contemporary industrial wasteland in between. When the nation's heritage is reduced to a saleable commodity, an agreed-upon fiction, critical historical fiction hardly seems necessary.

References and Further Reading

Acheson, James (ed.) (1991) *The British and Irish Novel Since 1960.* New York: St Martin's Press.

Barker, Pat (1991) *Regeneration.* New York: Plume.

Bell, Ian A. (1995) *Peripheral Visions: Images of Nationhood in Contemporary British Fiction.* Cardiff: University of Wales Press.

Bowen, Elizabeth (1962) [1948] *The Heat of the Day.* Harmondsworth: Penguin.

Brennock, Mark (2000) "Mass very important to only 40%," poll, *The Irish Times,* December 27. <http://www.ireland.com/newspaper/front/2000/1227/fro2.htm>

Connor, Steven (1996) *The English Novel in History, 1950–1995.* London: Routledge.

Davis, Alistair and Sinfield, Alan (2000) *British Culture of the Postwar: An Introduction to Literature and Society 1945–1999.* London: Routledge.

Desai, Anita (1989) [1988] *Baumgartner's Bombay.* Harmondsworth: Penguin.

Farrell, J. G. (1971) [1970] *Troubles.* New York: Alfred A. Knopf.

—— (1974) *The Siege of Krishnapur.* New York: Harcourt.

Fowles, John (1981) [1969] *The French Lieutenant's Woman.* New York: Signet-NAL.

Hand, Derek (2002) *John Banville: Exploring Fictions.* Dublin: Liffey.

Higdon, David Leon (1985) *Shadows of the Past in Contemporary British Fiction.* Athens: University of Georgia Press.

Holmes, Frederick M. (1997) *The Historical Imagination: Postmodernism and the Treatment of the Past in Contemporary British Fiction,* English Literary Studies 73. Victoria, BC: University of Victoria.

Human Development Report 1997 (1997) United Nations Development Program. New York: United Nations Human Development Report Office. <http://www.undp.org/>

Human Development Report 2003 (2003) United Nations Development Program. New York: United Nations Human Development Report Office. <http://www.undp.org/>

Hutcheon, Linda (1988) *A Poetics of Postmodernism: History, Theory, Fiction.* New York: Routledge.

Irish Council of Churches (2000) "Statistical snapshots on the state of religion in Ireland." <http://www.irishchurches.org/Statistics/body_statistics.html> September 22, 2003.

Ishiguro, Kazuo (1993) *The Remains of the Day.* New York: Vintage.

Keen, Suzanne (2002) *Romances of the Archive in Contemporary British Fiction.* Toronto: University of Toronto Press.

Kennedy-Andrews, Elmer (2003) *(De-)constructing the North: Fiction and the Northern Ireland Troubles since 1969.* Dublin: Four Courts.

Kilroy, Thomas (1971) *The Big Chapel.* London: Faber and Faber.

Lane, Richard J., Mengham, Rod, and Tew, Philip (eds.) (2003) *Contemporary British Fiction.* Cambridge: Polity.

Leader, Zachary (ed.) (2002) *On Modern British Fiction.* Oxford: Oxford University Press.

Lee, Richard (2000) "The problem of truth in history and fiction." <http://www.historicalnovelsociety.com/> September 16, 2003.

McEwan, Ian (2001) *Atonement.* New York: Doubleday.

Murdoch, Iris (1965) *The Red and the Green.* New York: Bard-Avon.

Newman, Judie (1995) *The Ballistic Bard: Postcolonial Fictions.* London: Arnold.

O'Connell, Philip J. (1999) *Astonishing Success: Economic Growth and the Labour Market in Ireland*, Employment and Training Papers 44. Dublin: United Nations International Labor Organization.

O'Connor, Joseph (1995) [1994] *The Secret World of the Irish Male*. London: Minerva.

—— (2003) *The Star of the Sea*. New York: Harcourt.

Rushdie, Salman (1989) [1983] *Shame*. New York: Vintage.

Ryan, Ray (2002) *Ireland and Scotland: Literature and Culture, State and Nation, 1966–2000*. Oxford: Oxford University Press.

Scanlan, Margaret (1990) *Traces of Another Time: History and Politics in Postwar British Fiction*. Princeton: Princeton University Press.

Swift, Graham (1992) [1983] *Waterland*. New York: Vintage.

Tóibín, Colm (2000) *The Penguin Book of Irish Fiction*. New York: Viking.

Whitehead, Anne (1998) "Open to suggestion: hypnosis and history in Pat Barker's *Regeneration*," *Modern Fiction Studies*, 44/3: 674–94.

11

The Literary Prize Phenomenon in Context

James F. English

Let me begin by stating the obvious. Over the last several decades, literary prizes in Britain have become vastly more numerous, more widely publicized, more symbolically potent, more lucrative in themselves, and more capable of increasing book sales than ever before. In terms of scale and impact, the phenomenon is simply unprecedented, and no history of postwar British literature can afford to overlook the role played by prizes in the more general reshaping of literary culture.

The phenomenon has not, however, been a strictly local or a strictly literary one. Since the inaugural Nobel Prizes (awarded in 1901), there has been an increasingly rapid and widespread proliferation of prizes across all the fields of art and culture. In the last quarter of the twentieth century, this process began escalating almost to the point of frenzy and became truly global in scope. Indeed, of the many gripes about the contemporary book-prize scene in Britain, one of the most common is that its vigorous expansion over the last few decades represents an encroachment upon the domestic literary culture by essentially subliterary and, above all, *foreign* (especially American, neo-imperial) influences. Whether this view is expressed in terms of the "Hollywoodization" of literature, the "triumph of television" over literature, or the deformation of literature after the model of "Miss World contests" (all of these jibes taken from recent articles about literary prizes in the British press), the underlying assumption is that book prizes and the hoopla of publicity that surrounds them have been imposed on Britain by outside forces bent on undermining traditional British cultural values and (perhaps for these critics it amounts to the same thing) the values proper to the field of literature itself.

This particular form of hostility to the literary awards industry obviously bespeaks anxieties that go well beyond the literary: anxieties regarding the consolidation of a global cultural and economic order still dominated by English but no longer centered on the British Isles. It is also the case that this view of prizes as an imposition on rather than an expression of the internal logics and energies of the (national) literary field is prevalent everywhere prizes have proliferated, which is to say everywhere, period – even, albeit less stridently, in the USA. Nevertheless, one of the things that has made the British book-prize scene so much more animated than many others, and so much more central to literary life, is precisely the strong national tradition of animosity toward awards. Prize-bashing is good sport wherever there are prizes; but nowhere is the game played with more spirit and pleasure than in Great Britain. The recent flourishing of British literary awards cannot be understood without considering this deep and enduring strain of anti-prize sentiment.

Historical Background: Prizes and the National Disposition

Though my purpose in this essay is to trace the history of book prizes since World War II, and especially since the important turning point of roughly 1968–72 (the point at which they seem to have attained cultural escape velocity), I will begin by recounting briefly an episode from the very early days of the modern literary prize – which for Britain would be the first decades of the nineteenth century. Already, in this period of prizes' first emergence, the essential aspects of the anti-awards position, together with its most potent rhetorical strategies, were manifest. The episode I have in mind is that of George IV's proposal, in 1821, to found a Royal Society of Literature and to award, through that institution, annual Gold Medals in honor of lifetime achievement in letters. Prior to these Society medals (the first of which were presented in 1823), Britain had lacked any sort of national bureaucracy to exercise control over the distribution of literary prestige. By contrast, the French Academy, on which the Royal Society was clearly modeled, had existed for two hundred years. And while the French Academy was never, perhaps, quite the "supreme court for literature" that its founder, Richelieu, had envisioned, it undeniably exercised considerable symbolic power both negatively, through its acts of condemnation and censorship, and positively, though its distribution of honors and its self-declared monopoly on literary *immortalité*.

In Britain, literary awards had, until the early nineteenth century, largely been restricted to the schools and universities – institutions within which it was, after all, normal practice to promote competition among individual writers and to rank their works according to precise hierarchies of value. To some extent, these devices of the educational apparatus anticipated later, extra-curricular forms of the literary prize, with their tendency to become entwined with political and commercial agendas. The tradition of honoring "prize poems" on a set topic at Oxford and Cambridge, for example, was annexed in the eighteenth century to the political project of imagining Britain as a national community and thus in effect "creating" Britons (Simpson, forthcoming); by the turn of the nineteenth century the practice was being exploited by publishers in the form of prize-poem anthologies and advertisements touting a work's award-winning stature, forerunners of the now ubiquitous book-cover stickers and blurbs that say, for example, "Winner of the Orange Prize for Fiction." Major Victorian careers, even as late as Oscar Wilde's, were launched on the publicity generated in connection with Oxford's Newdigate Prize. But on the whole, Britain clearly lagged behind the European nations in systematically producing, administering, and exploiting literary awards. The idea that the entire literary field might be structured along the lines of a school (an Academy), with prizes and ribbons for those at the top of the class and various forms of honorable mention for the also-rans, had a difficult time gaining traction on the English side of the Channel.

In effect, partly owing to Britain's rivalrous relationship to France, but certainly also to other and more complex factors, an amused disdain for cultural prizes in general and literary prizes in particular had become, in the eighteenth and nineteenth centuries, part of the national literary habitus, part of the shared disposition or outlook that defined a British man of letters. The classic statement of this attitude is that of Sir Walter Scott in a letter so thoroughly and mockingly dismissive of the entire Royal Society/Gold Medal scheme that he felt obliged to follow up with a note of apology, urging that only his opinions and not his actual words be shared with the King.

Briefly, Scott's objections were as follows. First, he dismissed any justification of valuable gold medals or cash awards as a modern form of patronage, declaring them "completely useless" in that respect (Grierson 1934: 398). As he saw it, the rise of the private booksellers meant that any major national literary figure of the sort who might properly receive a royal Gold Medal would already command very substantial sums in the marketplace. Far from assisting writers in need, the £100 medals (about £5000 today) would simply add a small supplement to the bank accounts of writers who had succeeded in the new commercial environment. Second, he observed that, since they lacked neither money nor reputation, and in fact stood to lose more than they might gain by accepting the Royal Society's (as yet untested) symbolic currency, Britain's leading writers might be expected to maintain a certain distance between themselves and the Society, declining election to its membership, refusing its proffered medals, and generally "stand[ing] aloof" in postures of contempt or condescension. Third, he predicted that the kinds of writers who *would* be attracted to the Society were precisely those "whose mediocrity of genius and active cupidity of disposition would render them undeserving of the Royal benevolence or render the bounty of the Sovereign ridiculous if bestowed upon them" (p. 399). The Society's inevitable tendency to assemble and promote these errant mediocrities would in turn further alienate writers of "true genius," leading to further embarrassments for the sponsoring King as his awards, lacking the crucial legitimacy of first-rank judges, fell into a hopeless spiral of symbolic erosion (p. 400). Fourth, Scott anticipated that, even if a few writers of real merit could be persuaded to participate in what they would surely regard as the "odious" task of prize judging, the deliberations by their very nature would devolve into "a sequence of ridiculous and contemptible feuds, the more despicable that those engaged in them were perhaps some of them men of genius" (p. 402). Finally, Scott warned that all these unavoidable embarrassments and crises of legitimacy would prove an irresistible attraction for journalists, who would seize on the "quarrels fracasseries lampoons libels and duels" as a way to amuse readers while also undermining the Society's credibility and so, by implication, the Sovereign's claim to exercise monopoly governance over matters of literary value. In short, the whole scheme would be self-defeating, a colossal "jest" on the unwitting King (p. 401).

Scott had it wrong, of course; lucrative, nationwide literary prizes have not imploded but exploded; far from undermining themselves, they have proved to be the kind of cultural phenomenon that self-replicates like a virus. Yet his objections are worth recounting because they remain so surprisingly resonant in Britain even today. How often do we hear that the really valuable book prizes – the only ones anyone pays any attention to, and the only ones you could actually live off of for a while – go to the very authors who are least in need of them? Much was made of the fact that A. S. Byatt spent her Booker Prize winnings on a swimming pool for her house in Provence, for example, or that Ian McEwan's annual earnings, as had been reported at his divorce trial, were some twenty times the value of *his* Booker. The point of such invidious accounting, of course, is that prizes, their investment in "serious" or "literary" fiction notwithstanding, are on the whole sufficiently well aligned with the market for books that a genuinely struggling or impoverished writer scarcely stands a chance. Patronage of such writers is far from a central aim of the contemporary book-prize industry. That task is left to the Arts Council and other distributors of small grants and fellowships, an important but distinct set of institutions.

Scott's second objection, that the true geniuses of the literary world are bound to express more hostility or condescension than appreciation for the prize and its sponsor, brings to mind the many episodes of ingratitude and crankiness on the part of eminent prizewinners: from John Berger, whose novel *G* fairly swept the field of fiction awards in 1972, denouncing Booker plc as an imperialist enterprise and vowing to give his winnings away to militant black nationalists; to J. M. Coetzee, who became in 1998 the first author to win the Booker Prize twice, while declining both times even to attend the award ceremony.

As regards Scott's third criticism, many commentators today would credit his prediction that the judging of these prizes would end up being done not by the nation's greatest writers but by elderly pedants and rank mediocrities. Few aspects of contemporary book prizes have come in for as much abuse as the judging, with particular venom directed at know-nothing "celebrity" or "ordinary-reader" judges on the one hand and hopelessly scholastic "professor types" on the other. The view that book prizes are a celebration of the mediocre by the mediocre, that the most exciting and original and pathbreaking writers – those who will be rewarded by posterity – are largely overlooked (as James, Hardy, Conrad, Kafka, Proust, Joyce, and Woolf all were by the Nobel), is one of the most frequently rehearsed of all awards truisms.

Scott's fourth objection, that the whole process of selecting "winners" on the field of letters must inevitably devolve into squabbles and feuds – that, far from adding luster to the activities of the literary world, the proceedings would deprive that world of even its normal degree of dignity and decorum – again appears difficult to dispute. Quarreling among judges, or between judges and administrators, or between winners and losers, has become so commonplace that such headlines as "Prize Fest Turns into Prizefight" have become a journalistic cliché.

And this brings us to Scott's final argument against the establishment of literary awards: that they would be a magnet for bad publicity, a field day for hostile journalists, a cause of much high-profile embarrassment for their sponsor as well as for many of the participants. This would seem to be Scott's most prescient argument of all, the point at which he most accurately projects the contemporary situation of prizes. For, of all the features of the contemporary prize scene in Britain, none is more striking than its capacity to fill column-inches with catty gossip, embarrassing reports of scandal and outrage, or sheer journalistic invective.

And yet, it is here, at the intersection of literary prizes with journalism, that Scott's analysis falls short. Already in the early nineteenth century, the relationship between literary prestige and journalistic publicity (including the publicity attendant on episodes of cultural "embarrassment" or "scandal") was more symbiotic than Scott seems to have recognized; this was, after all, the age of Byron. With the rise of advertising, radio, cinema, television, and other technologies of wide and rapid cultural dissemination, the distinction on which Scott's analysis depends, between cultural prestige on the one hand and mere visibility or (more or less scandalous) celebrity on the other has become even less supportable (English 2002). As I will discuss below, it is the capacity of prizes to effect rapid conversions of cultural scandal and embarrassment (what we might think of as a form of journalistic capital) not only into financial windfall (economic capital) but into cultural prestige (literary capital), that would ultimately make Great Britain an especially fertile ground for their propagation.

The point here, however, is that Scott's overdetermined but largely negative attitude toward literary prizes – at once amused and horrified, loftily dismissive and intimately concerned (he takes for granted his personal stake in this emergent economy of prestige, not to mention his own claim on a Gold Medal, which in fact he received in 1827) – informs the whole modern history of such prizes in Great Britain, right up until the period of study. The earliest of the nation's established prizes, the Hawthornden and the James Tait Black (founded in 1919 and 1920, respectively), seem to have been subdued, publicity-shy affairs by design. Although their format was essentially that of the Prix Goncourt, the father of all national book-of-the-year awards (first awarded in 1902), and though they were exactly contemporaneous with the US's Pulitzer Prize for Fiction, those prizes were veritable publicity machines, the former orchestrated by France's major publishing houses, the latter by newspaper owners and editors in the US. In contrast with the front-page coverage accorded the Goncourts and Pulitzers, and the frequent scandals of corruption, imbecility, or merely bad behavior that animated such coverage, neither the Hawthornden nor the James Tait Black ever sought or received much attention. They were, as far as possible, "private" awards, pointedly lacking any public face, much less any PR strategy, and eschewing the typically overblown language of greatness, immortality, and literary pantheons to which the French and American prizes freely appealed.

Of the two, the James Tait Black might have been expected to generate more excitement and controversy. While the Hawthornden combined fiction and nonfiction into a single broad category of award, the Black was divided into two separate prizes, thus assuring an annual prize for the best work of fiction (nearly always a novel), which had proved in France and America to be the most volatile category. But the Black was administered in Edinburgh, far from the main hub of publishing, journalism, and literary affairs – and, arguably, at some distance from the dominant literary habitus, as well. It was judged by a single person (who thus had no one with whom to engage in quarrelsome deliberations), and that judge was not chosen or elected as such (through some potentially acrimonious or contestable system) but simply assumed the role as part of his responsibilities as Regius Chair of Rhetoric and Belles Lettres at the University of Edinburgh. In contrast with the Pulitzer fiction prize – with its journalist-controlled Advisory Board, which receives from a Fiction Jury (itself appointed by a separate administrative arm) a ranked list of nominees, which the Board is then free to re-rank or (as it has done on several notorious occasions) to reject entirely – the James Tait Black seems astonishingly simple and non-bureaucratic, resolutely modest in format and intention. It is a prize perfectly in keeping with a literary culture that is not very comfortable with prizes.

Postwar Prizes, and the Breakthrough of the Booker

Given this determinedly low-key starting point, it is not surprising that the first book prizes to emerge in the postwar years did not announce themselves as antagonists or competitors to the Black and the Hawthornden. In France, the Goncourt had quickly inspired a number of hostile literary groups to launch their own anti-Goncourts, beginning with the Prix Femina (a feminist prize administered and judged by women rather than men) and then the Prix Renaudot (a noncommercial or "independent" prize judged by writers and critics not beholden to the major publishing houses). And this process of negative emulation has continued to characterize the French prize scene for more than a century. (A recent success has been the Prix Décembre, which pointedly refuses to coordinate its announcement date with the other prize organizations and with the publishers' fall schedules.) Likewise, in America, after twenty-five years of timid and often dubious Pulitzer selections (the most adventurous juries having typically been overruled by the Advisory Board), the National Book Awards were launched in 1945 as an ostensibly bolder alternative, with no meddling from non-literary overseers. Another twenty-five years after that, the National Book Critics Circle Awards were founded by a group of book-reviewers in New York to counter the commercialism of the publisher-sponsored NBAs, which, from the perspective of professional critics, made these prizes just as philistine a venture as the Pulitzers.

Nothing of this kind occurred in Britain, where the John Llewellyn Rhys and Somerset Maugham prizes, founded in 1942 and 1947 respectively, were given quiet and non-acrimonious launches. The one point of differentiation between these second-wave prizes and the earlier ones was that the former restricted eligibility to younger writers (under 35). This restriction reflected the concern expressed by Scott, that prizes could never be justified as a new form of patronage since their general tendency would be to pad the fortunes of the already successful rather than to assist those in need. But if the new prizes managed to limit their complicity in this winner-take-all environment, their willingness merely to assist the promising rather than to consecrate the great gave them an even more modest cast than the Hawthornden and Black. Whereas the tendency elsewhere was for leading prizes to contend with each other over questions of purity, legitimacy, and predictive power, each new prize claiming to be a more accurate and incorruptible barometer of literary genius than its predecessors, the British prizes coexisted amiably, each with its own idiosyncrasies, exercising a common preference (apparent also in their aesthetic choices) for less over more, for the minor over the major. Indeed, as though in approbation of the John Llewellyn Rhys award, founded in memory of a young writer killed in the war, the 1942 Hawthornden was awarded posthumously to John Llewellyn Rhys himself, an author beyond any criterion of promise or need and plainly destined for minor status at best.

Thus when, in 1964, Tom Maschler of Cape, addressing the Society of Young Publishers, observed that even insiders like themselves were scarcely aware of the British book prizes and had no idea "who the previous award winners have been," no one could disagree (Strachan 1989: ix; Maschler 1998: 15). Britain was not a place where literary awards mattered much, even to literary people. What was unusual was that Maschler found this aspect of the national literary habitus irksome, and set out to correct it. Within a few years, he had secured a sponsor, the farming and food-services company Booker Brothers (later Booker McConnell, then Booker plc), for a new, big-budget prize modeled more closely on the foreign example of the Goncourt than on the homegrown Tait or Hawthornden. That is, it would actively court publicity and would work with publishers unashamedly to maximize its commercial as well as its symbolic impact. The earliest years of the Booker (which was first awarded in 1969) involved quite explicit attempts by its organizing committee to make the prize more Goncourt-like. The eligibility, nomination, and judging deadlines were shifted over to the Goncourt's more publisher-friendly timetable, and a meeting was called at which journalists were asked for their assistance in making the prize "more of an excitement among the reading public, as is the Prix Goncourt in France" (English, forthcoming).

Yet, for all its bold intentions to break with the national pattern, the Booker might well have settled into position as just one more British book-of-the-year award, worth more cash than the rest (initially £5000, or about £20,000 in 2000 currency), but not otherwise easily distinguishable from the first- and second-generation prizes or even from its more immediate contemporaries, such as the W. H. Smith (founded 1959), the Guardian (1965), the Faber (1965), the Silver Pen Award (1968), and the Whitbread Novel Award (founded, along with other Whitbread literary awards, just after the Booker, in 1971). In its first three years, the prize achieved such sparse notice and had such little effect on sales that some publishers became reluctant to pay the small fee required to nominate a book. Judges of real distinction in the literary world proved hard to come by; just as Walter Scott had anticipated, they "stood aloof," regarding their hard-won prestige in British literary circles as more likely to be eroded than augmented by an association with this brash, Francophilic venture. Maschler continued to put his energies into the project, but as the editor for a publishing house whose books would perforce be among the contenders, he made an unsuitable overseer, and his vigorous meddling caused much internal strife and resentment. These problems in turn led to second thoughts among the executives at Booker Brothers. The company had hoped to tone up its image as it diversified outward from its traditional core in colonial agribusiness (it already had a small but profitable literature division that contrived tax-shelter schemes for best-seller writers), but now Booker was threatening to pull the plug when its seven-year contract came up for renewal (Sutherland 1981).

Yet before that date arrived, the prize had turned things around dramatically, establishing a decisive advantage over all previous British book awards and positioning itself as the model (either positive or negative) for all the many prizes that have sprung up since then. It effected this sharp turnaround by inserting itself rapidly and strategically into an emergent space of cultural journalism where the seeming illegitimacy and, in the national context, obnoxiousness of its claim to symbolic power could be leveraged into actual power. Its successful strategy was, to be sure, partly a product of good luck, but also of good luck seized upon and exploited skillfully by Martyn Goff, who was brought in as the new chief administrator when the enterprise appeared to be unraveling in 1971. Goff may have been the first literary prize administrator in Britain to recognize that, given a national context in which prizes serve chiefly as objects of embarrassment (among writers) and derision (among cultural journalists), with a strong tendency to erupt into "quarrels fracasseries lampoons libels and duels," the way to succeed is not to maintain a dignified distance from the apparatus of publicity but to make a virtue of necessity, situating the prize at the very vortex of literary scandal, making it an irresistible magnet for national anxieties over literary value, cultural commerce, and the meanings of Britishness itself.

While most commentators have dated the Booker's rise from the early 1980s – and these were indeed the years of its greatest commercial impact – I want to stress that the decisive break from the traditional pattern comes at this earlier point, around 1972 (when, as reported at the annual meeting of the Booker's Management Committee, "publicity for the prize had gained its own momentum"). Not coincidentally, this is the point at which historians have drawn the period marker between the key phases of western capitalism in the twentieth century, a relatively stable period of Fordist industrialism giving way, under pressure of overproduction, to a series of crises and crashes (Harvey 1990; Arrighi 1994; Hobsbawm 1994). During this latter period, a new capitalist economy emerges, characterized by more intensive and extensive dealings in pure numbers, increasingly frenzied financial and land speculation, an eclipse of industrial goods by "weightless" information products, and increasingly global consumption of increasingly ephemeral fashions and cultural goods. The sudden emergence of prizes from the arcane recesses of British literary life into the spotlight of national fascination must be seen as part of this radical reconfiguring of the economic and cultural fields. In particular, the sped-up and intensified appetite of cultural consumers for "events" or "happenings," as opposed to cultural works as such, exerted a certain pressure on the literary field to produce its own brand of ephemeral spectacle or excitement (Harvey 1990). The rise of television, the great medium of cultural ephemera, to its position of dominance in British cultural life raised the question of how such a supremely untelegenic practice as literature could attract the attention of a mass viewership.

One way for this to occur was through crossover figures who enjoyed both the celebrity of television stars and the status of serious authors or critics. In 1971, his first year of running the prize, Goff installed as chair of judges Malcolm Muggeridge, a conservative literary critic/journalist and Sunday-morning Christian program host for the BBC, widely known as "St Muggs." Muggeridge lasted until mid-summer, at which point he abruptly withdrew from his post, writing in a letter to the Booker secretary that the nominated books "seem to me to be mere pornography in the worst sense of the word, and to lack any literary qualities or distinction which could possibly compensate for the unsavouriness of their contents." Goff promptly issued an enticing press release which made sure to emphasize Muggeridge's charge of "pornography," and the Sunday papers, capitalizing on St Muggs's ubiquity in their readers' living-rooms, obliged with the Booker's first real dose of publicity.

Providing resonance to a question of literary value (concerning the post-sixties prevalence of explicit sex scenes in works of literary fiction) via the mediation of television celebrity, this scandal, though rather muted and today largely forgotten, in fact prepared the ground for the succession of scandals with which the Booker Prize came to be associated in the 1970s and the 1980s. It would be wrong to suggest that these episodes were simply manufactured by Goff and his staff, or that they were a matter of mere play-acting on the part of writers, critics, and journalists. On the contrary, they were events in which genuine divisions of ideology and interest were at stake. But those divisions or struggles were here provided a forum where they might be staged in such a way that a television-dominated culture would attend to them. John Berger, whose notoriously ferocious acceptance speech the following year (1972) ignited perhaps the single most important scandal in the prize's history, was a committed man of the Left, deeply opposed to everything Booker plc stood for. He was also, however, a crossover figure *par excellence*: respected as a novelist, just coming off the successful run of his *Ways of Seeing* series on BBC, and about to spin off from that program a major nonfiction bestseller. His highly principled intervention, by means of which he intended to expose the foundation of racist exploitation that had long supported not only Booker's corporate profits but British literary culture itself, thus also functioned as a natural conduit between that rather insular culture and the wider public of the BBC. The clear implication of Berger's speech was that the Booker Prize represented a kind of cultural laundering of dirty money, an attempt to convert labor value extracted from black plantation workers in Guyana into symbolic capital among London's literary elite. Goff and Michael Caine (Chairman of Booker and chief supporter of the prize within the corporation) both took the speech, quite correctly, as an affront. But it was not lost on these men that, in the days and weeks after the award banquet, the Booker Prize reaped an enormous amount of publicity, at least four times as much coverage as even the Muggeridge affair had generated. Goff may have found Berger's speech painful to sit through, but he did not in the least hesitate to invoke this scandalous episode as a way of heightening journalists' interest during the run-up for the 1973 prize. And it was partly owing to this priming of the journalistic pump that J. G. Farrell's much more gently critical speech that year – which would not normally have attracted much notice – was seized upon as yet another outrageous display of ingratitude, yet another well-deserved embarrassment for an illegitimate institution, yet another scandalous exposure of the sordid reality of literary life.

By this point the prize had developed a capacity to function as a "serial" event, scandal building upon scandal, expectations not so much of triumph but of disgrace aroused and satisfied on an annual basis. The importance of television to achieving Maschler's original vision of Goncourt-like hoopla around a British book prize had begun to be clear. The event would not literally be televised for three more years, and it would take a few more years after that for the BBC to work out a successful format for live broadcast of the award ceremony. Goff, meanwhile, would adjust rules and procedures along the lines of big-time televised awards shows: maximizing the advance speculation, the suspense, and the anguish of the also-rans by widely publicizing the shortlist while delaying the judges' decision until the last possible moment. But already by 1973 the Booker Prize had begun the process not only of articulating the struggle over literary value with the television medium, but of recognizing that the scandalous nature of that articulation underscored a more general paradox of legitimacy: that the only form of success available to a British book prize was *success de scandal*.

In this respect, then, what began to happen to British book prizes at the start of the 1970s was something driven by larger economic and cultural tendencies, but intensified and accelerated by a peculiarly strong and enduring anti-prize tradition. Though Britain was notably late to produce a widely visible and symbolically powerful literary award, it was among the first in the world to offer live, prime-time, nationwide television coverage of an award ceremony (only Austria, with its start-to-finish television coverage of the Bachmann Prize dating from 1977, was earlier). Even today in the US, where there are hundreds of niche cable channels, no book prize has duplicated the feat. (And this is despite the National Book Award's deliberate attempts to "Bookerize" itself in the 1980s (Lehman 1986) and, more recently, to raise its public profile by presenting medals to Oprah Winfrey and Stephen King.) Those who lament the rise of prizes as an encroachment of alien, televisual values on British literary culture need to recognize that this convergence of books and television around the nexus of award scandals is something that has been uniquely perfected in Britain; it is one of the most distinctive facets of literary life in the UK.

If we turn to the substantive content of these early scandal-driven successes, we can see again that what drove the Booker Prize (and thereby the whole concept and institution of the literary award) into the national limelight were debates over value that erupted because of post-sixties global political and economic shifts, but took their particular form and urgency from Britain's special cultural predicament as the most recently fallen empire. Berger's denunciation of Booker, for example, was clearly motivated by the broad trends that we were not yet calling globalization: the effects, on peoples of the periphery, of neo-liberal economic policies, neocolonial business enterprises, neo-imperial cultural practices, and the metropolitan racism that informs them all. But much of what gave his speech its force was specific to the British context. As a prize open to all authors of the Commonwealth and the Irish Republic, the Booker claimed the cultural authority to judge the merits of literature produced by writers who had been born and raised under various forms of British colonial authority – writers from the Caribbean, for example, where Booker Brothers had profited from vast plantation holdings. It was a postcolonial prize by means of which London could – couldn't *not* – reaffirm its domination of the formerly colonized space. And it was paid for by a company eager to put literature in service of rehabilitating an ugly colonial past. As Graham Huggan has argued, an important part of what animated the Booker Prize was its role in managing the basic postcolonial contradiction "between anti-colonial ideologies and neo-colonial market schemes" (Huggan 1997). This is what was behind the veil of cozy celebration, and what Berger's speech in 1972 was pointing toward. By the early years of Thatcherism, with their urban race wars, re-ascendant imperial and militarist ideologies, and emergent forms of "black British" cultural production, the Booker would be in position as a perfect lightning rod for all the many anxieties and antagonisms of the postcolonial metropole – as well as serving, according to Huggan, in the unavoidable commercial exploitation of this situation through its consecration of the "postcolonial exotic" (Huggan 1994).

Prizes that have emerged to compete with the Booker have all had to contend with this problem, not only on the level of literary evaluation and competing "regimes of value" but, preliminary to that, with respect to the basic question of cultural jurisdiction or terrain. Those that have cast their nets of eligibility still wider than the Booker (to include all novels written in English, or even all novels published in English, whatever their language of origin) can appear even more guilty of metropolitan arrogance. Yet those that have narrowed their emphasis to just the UK, or just Great Britain, or even just a particular region of England, have not by any means escaped the political dilemmas of postcoloniality. For there are, after all, domestic literatures of black resistance and of postcolonial exoticism as well as international ones. The Commonwealth Writers Prize, founded in 1987, and the *Irish Times* Aer Lingus International Fiction Prize, founded in 1990, are interesting cases, since both of them roughly duplicate the Booker's criteria of eligibility while shifting the sites of administration and judgment away from London. The *Irish Times* Prize is administered in Dublin, while the Commonwealth Prize, though founded by a London-based foundation (and, since 1999, partly administered by Booktrust), uses regional judging panels to establish finalists for an overall prize that has been judged and awarded in Toronto, Edinburgh, and other Commonwealth cities. Whether the regime of value is much altered by this decentering of the core of symbolic power is debatable; recent winners of the Commonwealth Prize include J. M. Coetzee and Peter Carey, who hold the distinction of being the only double winners of the Booker Prize; one of the first winners of the *Irish Times* prize, A. S. Byatt (who won for *Possession*), was likewise a former Booker winner, and Coetzee has won the *Irish Times* prize, as well. Such duplications have fed into the ongoing debates over the geopolitics of literature in English, serving as evidence either of London's enduring capacity to impose its literary tastes on subordinate centers of literary life, or as a happy consensus of readers and critics across the entire Commonwealth, or of a pernicious political correctness leading to postcolonial bias among the London literati who judge the Booker.

Even the Orange Prize, founded in 1996 and mainly known for its restriction to women authors, has attracted controversy as a result of its handling of the jurisdiction or core/periphery problem. In this case, the point of contention has not been how and where to legitimately assess postcolonial literary value as such, but the related concern of how to foster specifically British (even, perhaps, English) literary values on a field of global English literature no longer dominated by England or Great Britain but, increasingly, by the US. The Orange Prize's extension of eligibility to American writers was denounced in some quarters as a kind of cultural treason. If the proliferation of prizes in Britain was itself a symptom of creeping Americanization, here was a sign of outright capitulation to American cultural hegemony. The debates and quarrels over this eligibility question have ebbed and flowed depending on whether the Orange Prize is indeed awarded to an American in any given year. But they have been extremely helpful to the Orange Prize administrators in drawing scandalized attention to this latecomer on the scene, which has quickly become one of the most important prizes in the UK. The venerable James Tait Black Prize followed the Orange's example, opening to US authors in 2001, and the Booker itself took the opportunity of its change in sponsorship that year to hint that it might similarly reconfigure its rules of eligibility. One strongly suspects that as far as the Booker is concerned this was merely a publicity ploy; at any rate, it attracted what must have been a welcome storm of objections from those who feared that such a change would further erode the British novel's position on the field of English-language literature. Thirty years after Berger's scandalous speech gained it national attention, the Booker Prize was still profiting from after-empire anxieties about the status and function of specifically British literary values in a vast, complex, and rapidly globalizing world of English-language cultures.

Book Prizes in the Boom Years, 1980–2000

Historical accounts of Britain's contemporary fiction prizes – of which Richard Todd's (1996) is the best and most detailed – tend to regard the 1980s as the period of their great emergence. And while I have tried to suggest that the foundations of that emergence were laid down a decade earlier by the Booker Prize, there is no denying the seismic shifts that took place during the Thatcher decade. If the 1970s was the decade when book prizes finally achieved symbolic importance in Britain – not only as formidable badges of prestige for authors but, inseparably from that function, as serial occasions for public excitement and controversy over matters of cultural value and national identity – the 1980s was the decade when they finally achieved real economic importance. The Thatcher years were, like neo-liberal environments generally, conducive to markedly divided fortunes, with tremendous economic gains for some set against deepening immiseration for others. For publishers, booksellers, and literary entrepreneurs, these were unquestionably boom years, bringing overall levels of production back for the first time to pre-World War II levels, and offering suddenly wider opportunities for innovation and profit.

This was, for example, the period of the revolution in book retailing, when small, independent bookshops began rapidly to be replaced by large, attractively modern chain stores offering more titles, faster receipt of special orders, and ultimately (with the collapse of the Net Book Agreement in the mid-1990s) widespread discounts. The Dillons chain was launched by the Pentos Group in 1977, and Waterstone's, which would later merge with W. H. Smith, in 1982. Over the next fifteen years, these two retailers became increasingly powerful players in the world of literary fiction, such that by the 1990s ambitious book prizes like the Orange were focusing much of their promotion and publicity budgets on in-store promotions. Waterstone's even initiated its own prize-like promotional device in 1990, Waterstone's Book of the Month, whose fiction selections were often the very books that contended for the Booker and other major prizes.

Another characteristic innovation of the 1980s was *Granta* magazine's Best of the Young British Novelists, a prize-like device cooked up by the Book Marketing Council in 1983 and then repeated in 1993 and 2003. Here again, one finds many of the same authors who would land on the shortlists or podiums of the major prizes; the first BYBN issue featured Salman Rushdie, Ian McEwan, Rose Tremain, Kazuo Ishiguro, Martin Amis, Julian Barnes, Pat Barker, Graham Swift, William Boyd, and Timothy Mo – all writers who would soon boast prize-studded resumés.

These kinds of overlapping and interrelated devices, to which one might add the increasingly ubiquitous top-ten and top-100 best-novel lists; the discernible shift in book-chat radio toward "Book of the Month" (Radio 3), "Book Choice" (Radio 4), or "Big Read" listener's-poll (BBC) formats; and the dramatic expansion of the literary festival circuit (which has made increasing use of tie-ins both with radio polls and with prize shortlists), all signal not just a period of vigorous literary entrepreneurship but a period in which such entrepreneurship took place within what Todd has called "a general atmosphere of contemporary canon-formation" (1996: 101). And the more closely the apparatuses of marketing and sales became entwined with the apparatuses of contemporary canon-formation, from the early 1980s onward, the more there came to be real money at stake in "serious literary fiction." To be accorded recognition as Britain's most "important" young novelist, or as "Novelist of the year," was no longer just to receive a nice plaque and a slightly better shot at the course syllabi of the future, but to be embraced from several directions as a genuinely hot commercial property.

With its proven and steadily increasing capacity to attract public attention to the struggle for contemporary canonicity – and to do so in many cases by attaching an air of scandal or controversy to the winners of this struggle, thereby augmenting their celebrity appeal – the Booker Prize quickly became the center of this commercially enriched field of literary activity. Booker winners of the early 1980s saw hardcover sales rise immediately through the roof in the days and weeks after the award ceremony, often creating some difficulty for publishers who had not yet caught on to the prize's commercial impact and could not print enough copies to meet demand (Todd 1996: 104–5). But as the Booker consolidated its position of dominance among the British fiction prizes, a host of new prizes – labeled "Baby Bookers" in the press – sprang up in its shadow. Most of these prizes differentiated themselves from the Booker and from each other by establishing somewhat different rules of eligibility or criteria of evaluation. The Betty Trask (1984) was to be oriented toward more "traditional" fiction, including quality romance novels; the *Sunday Express* Prize (1988) claimed a more populist orientation toward the "good read"; the *Irish Times* Aer Lingus (1989) positioned itself as more international in scope, more cosmopolitan in outlook; the David Cohen Prize (1993) proposed to serve as an instrument both of consecration and of patronage by offering both a cash award and supplemental money for the winner to put toward assisting younger writers; the Orange Prize, as mentioned, set out to correct an unmistakably male bias in British fiction prizes dating all the way back to the Hawthornden and notably including the Booker. But, apart from the Orange's feminist slant, these sorts of distinction are not always easy to communicate or even (as in the case of the *Sunday Express*'s populism) to maintain in practice. An easier way for a start-up prize to draw serious notice on this increasingly crowded and commerce-oriented field was simply to step into the ring with a bigger winner's check than any of the others. Each of the prizes just named did exactly that, and those that have survived have continued to play a kind of economic leapfrog with each other right down to the present day. When the Man Group assumed sponsorship of the Booker Prize, the Booker came back in the lead with its £50,000 winner's check, but we can expect that amount to be superseded before long.

These are not negligible sums, and it would be going too far to say that such cash awards as these are essentially symbolic, like the fifty francs presented to the winner of the Prix Goncourt. But taking account of the broader economics of prizes, they are often a surprisingly small piece of both the sponsor's costs and the winner's gain. As regards the latter, while only the Booker exerts a really profound influence on sales (and even that impact pales in comparison with what the Goncourt, or Italy's Premio Strega, can do), the prizes do pay off economically in a variety of important ways. The author's stature as, say, "winner of the Orange prize" virtually guarantees the publication of all her future books, as well as increasing the likelihood of republication of her earlier ones. It might also result in, for example, a well-compensated university post as Writer in Residence a few years later. The prize is in this respect an enduring and transferable credential, a typical feature of what Randall Collins called the "credential society." There can also be opportunities for the literary capital of a prize to produce profits on other, adjacent fields. It is striking that five of the twelve Booker winners from 1982 to 1992 went on to become films, three of them Academy Award winners (*Schindler's List*, *The Remains of the Day*, and *The English Patient*). By comparison, the shortlisted novels from the same period were adapted only one-tenth as often: just five out of fifty-four. Apart from their value to the author in film rights, cinematic adaptations tend to give a second life to the novel, often boosting its sales beyond those of its original prize-driven success. The outstanding example of this is *Schindler's Ark*, which, having sold a remarkable 300,000 paperback copies after its Booker win in 1982, sold another 900,000 (as *Schindler's List*) in the wake of Spielberg's film in 1994 (Todd 1996: 316–17).

As regards the economics of sponsorship, when Orange agreed in 1995 to sponsor "the most lucrative fiction award in Britain," the £30,000 necessary to claim that title was already covered by arrangement with an anonymous donor. But the other costs associated with a major award – which in this case included extensive point-of-sale promotions, book-club tie-ins, and other innovative promotional devices – would amount to at least six or seven times that much: about a quarter million pounds annually, according to Peter Raymond, who orchestrated the deal. Figures for the Booker Prize are even more lopsided. When the Big Food Group, having absorbed Booker plc and thus inherited the Booker Prize, took a look at the expense ledgers in 2001, the company was spending £350,000 per annum to support the £21,000 prize, and decided it was high time to bow out. But the new sponsorship agreement that was secured with the Man Group was even richer, not only raising the prize amount by £29,000, but increasing the overall budget to at least half a million pounds annually (Thorncroft 2002).

Figures like these – ten pounds to the booksellers, publicists, caterers, travel agents, administrators, and others behind the scenes for every pound that is visible to the public – make us realize just how much money there really is in the burgeoning book-prize industry. While the state continues to support writers and artists in a small way (the Arts Council distributes something less than £100,000 per year to writers, with no discernible impact on book sales), the task of arts sponsorship has, since the 1970s, basically shifted over to the private sector. Though the resulting corporate takeover of the cultural economy has meant reduced funding in many quarters, it has clearly led to much larger outlays for prizes and awards. This is partly because even a major prize, highly lucrative by the standards of the field, is a relatively inexpensive proposition in comparison with, for example, sponsorship of an opera company or a symphony orchestra, yet stands a chance of attracting far more publicity. The bottom-line calculation will often suggest the prize as the vehicle of greatest leverage for a given marketing budget. We should note, too, that much of the labor that prizes require goes virtually unpaid. Administrators are rarely well compensated and judges generally perform their duties for free (or rather for the subsidiary honor of having their authority recognized in this way, and for the possible longer-term financial value of that recognition). The judging of a book prize is especially labor-intensive; with as many as two or three hundred titles nominated for some of the prizes, judging involves at minimum something like a thousand hours of fast reading. The sheer impracticality of performing this job thoroughly – reading every book through to the end – has led to the much ridiculed but unavoidable practice of "pre-judging," by means of which anonymous office assistants or local graduate students effectively narrow the field to a manageable 20–30 titles before the "real" judges step in. Even with this quiet assistance, some judges have confessed to skimming or relying on reviews. While this has predictably scandalized commentators, the real scandal is that the prize industry has managed to grow so large and so powerful without compensating monetarily those who do the lion's share of the work and on whom the legitimacy of prizes ultimately depends. The new economics of arts sponsorship has, through its penchant for fiction prizes, created an enormous burden of work for literary people while contriving to pay for this work not with new money from the corporate sponsors but rather through a recirculation of symbolic capital supplied by these literary people themselves.

Just how much of a financial windfall the prize phenomenon has brought to the British literary community as a whole is thus a difficult question to answer. But there is no doubt that prizes have emerged, over a remarkably short span of time, to assume a commanding position in the literary economy more broadly conceived – the economy, that is, where not only money but social, political, and symbolic capital are involved in every exchange. Finding that, in the age of media overload and global English, their traditional lack of credibility in Britain made them more rather than less powerful instruments for conducting transactions in literary value, prizes have quickly installed themselves at the very heart of the literary system. To the extent that their legitimacy remains in doubt, their power and ubiquity will make many of us uncomfortable. But it is difficult at this point even to imagine British literary culture without them.

REFERENCES AND FURTHER READING

Arrighi, G. (1994) *The Long Twentieth Century: Money, Power, and the Origins of Our Times*. New York: Verso.

Behr, S. (ed.) (2000) *The Book Trust Guide to Literary Prizes*. London: Book Trust.

Collins, R. (1979) *The Credential Society: An Historical Sociology of Education and Stratification.* New York: Academic Press.

English, J. (2002) "Winning the culture game: prizes, awards, and the rules of art," *New Literary History*, 33: 109–35.

—— (forthcoming) *The Economy of Prestige: Prizes, Awards, and the Circulation of Cultural Value.* Cambridge, MA: Harvard University Press.

Firth, G. (1984) "Financial facts of fiction: the Booker Prize," *Financial Times*, October 6.

Grierson, H. J. C. (ed.) (1934) *The Letters of Sir Walter Scott 1819—1821,* vol. 6. London: Constable.

Harvey, D. (1990) *The Condition of Postmodernity: An Enquiry into the Conditions of Cultural Change.* Cambridge, MA: Blackwell.

Hobsbawm, E. (1994) *The Age of Extremes: The Short Twentieth Century, 1914–1991.* London: Michael Joseph.

Huggan, G. (1994) "The postcolonial exotic: Rushdie's Booker of Bookers," *Transition*, 64: 22–9.

—— (1997) "Prizing 'otherness': a short history of the Booker," *Studies in the Novel*, 29: 412–33.

—— (2001) *The Postcolonial Exotic: Marketing the Margins.* New York: Routledge.

Lehman, D. (1986) "May the best author win – fat chance," *Newsweek*, 107 (April 21): 82.

Maschler, T. (1998) "How it all began," in Booker plc (eds.) *Booker 30: A Celebration of Thirty Years of the Booker Prize for Fiction, 1969–1998.* London: Booker plc.

Miller, P. (1982) "Booker triumph 'Like avalanche smothering you'," *Sunday Times*, October 24.

Simpson, E. (2004) "Minstrelsy goes to market: prize poems, minstrel contests, and romantic poetry," *English Literary History*, 71 (Fall).

Strachan, A. (1989) *Prizewinning Literature: UK Literary Award Winners.* London: Library Association.

Sutherland, J. (1981) "The bumpy road to the Booker 1981," *Times Higher Education Supplement*, October 30.

Thorncroft, T. (2002) "New sponsor for the Booker Prize," *Financial Times*, April 26.

Todd, R. (1996) *Consuming Fictions: The Booker Prize and Fiction in Britain Today.* London: Bloomsbury.

12
Novelistic Production and the Publishing Industry in Britain and Ireland

Claire Squires

Introduction

The decades following 1945 were a time of great reorganization in the British and Irish publishing industry, and the production of the novel would be affected by great upheaval in terms of ownership, operation, and competition. The ideology and culture of publishing would also be re-evaluated. In his memoir *Kindred Spirits: Adrift in Literary London* (1995), the publisher Jeremy Lewis depicts the upheaval by describing the changing office spaces in which he has worked:

> [T]he last ten years I spent with a small but well-regarded firm, which has since been absorbed into an American conglomerate and transplanted to a modern office block, all open-plan and winking VDUs, but was, when I went there in the late 1970s, the epitome of an old-fashioned literary publisher...
> [T]he floors were covered with blue lino, the telephones were Bakelite and the furniture Utility... and the place was staffed by loyal, long-serving spinsters in cardigans and sandals, and – for much of the firm's history at least – amiable and highly civilised men with large private incomes...(Lewis 1995: 3)

Lewis here hints at some of the major changes in publishing history: the consolidation of small, often family-run companies into global multimedia conglomerates; the resulting new operational paradigms and in particular the ascendancy of marketing; and the cultural transition from an industry populated by "amiable and highly civilised men with large private incomes" to a highly commercialized, market-focused work force. This chapter addresses these changes, alongside key developments including the impact of new technologies, alterations in the retail environment, and the interaction of publishing and society. The final section of this chapter then draws some preliminary conclusions about the impact of these changes on novelistic production.

The title of this chapter contentiously refers to "the publishing industry" in Britain and Ireland, rather than their "publishing industries." However, Irish publishing has largely been, throughout its history, a subaltern industry to the British, or rather the English, or even London-based, industry (Scottish, Welsh, and English regional presses are similarly relegated). From the relatively late arrival of the printing press, to the non-extension of the British Copyright Act of 1709 to Ireland, to the more effective marketing and distribution mechanisms of London throughout the eighteenth, nineteenth, and twentieth centuries, Irish writers have frequently looked abroad for a more efficient, more legally safeguarded, more remunerative and – as the section on censorship later in the chapter details – freer publishing industry (Kinane 2002). There are notable exceptions to this rule: a publishing revival in the later nineteenth and early twentieth centuries, a mini-boom during and shortly after the Second World War, a period of excitement in the 1970s, when British publishers were suffering recession and during which publishers in both Northern Ireland and in the Republic were established, including the Irish Academic Press, Wolfhound, the O'Brien Press, Blackstaff, and Appletree. A special report in *Publishers Weekly* in 1981 optimistically entitled "Ireland: A New Flowering," analysed this difficult history:

> Ireland was for centuries politically and economically dominated by the British and failed to produce publishers to match its poets. Only after 60 years of nationhood has Ireland's book world been able to acquire a measure of independence. (Davis 1981: 63)

The London publishing industry, though, would strengthen once more in the 1980s and 1990s, and would continue the "Dublin raid," where English publishers seek Irish writers for their lists. Neil Jordan, Bernard MacLaverty, and Julia O'Faolain were all poached in this way, following earlier departures of censored writers including John McGahern and Edna O'Brien (Davis 1981: 78–9). This chapter, therefore, largely considers the British and Irish publishing industries as one, following the traditional territorial pattern of their production for "one market" (Brown 1981: 86). Where the chapter departs from this is in its consideration of the specific social conditions of the two nations, above all in their differing attitudes towards censorship.

The Legacy of the War and Postwar Markets

The immediate postwar publishing industry in Britain was a depressed one. The book trade had been hit hard by the war. In *A History of British Publishing* (1991), John Feather enumerates publishing's threefold loss: of staff, who left to fight in the war; of paper, now in short supply; and also – in addition to the similar losses suffered in the

First World War – of stock, offices, and records, which were destroyed by enemy bombing. Much of Britain's paper was imported, and the domestic paper-making industry was heavily reliant on imported raw materials. In 1940, paper rationing was introduced and foreign imports were banned. The trade negotiated the Book Production War Economy Agreement, which specified tightly-spaced print on thin paper. Book production in the war halved, falling from a total of 14,904 new books in 1939 to a wartime low of 6,705 new books in 1943 (Norrie 1982: 91–2, 220).

Paper rations to publishers were based on their paper use in the year preceding the war. Penguin, the paperback company set up by Allen Lane in 1935, was one of the few companies to do well out of this arrangement, as 1938–9 had been an extremely successful year. Moreover, the 'Penguin Specials' – short, topical, and quickly produced books on current world issues – along with the production of books for the Forces Book Club and the POW Book Service, placed Penguin at the heart of Britain's war effort. In *Penguin Portrait: Allen Lane and the Penguin Editors 1935–1970*, Steve Hare observes that "the rationed and restricted war years became not a period of retrenchment and consolidation but a period of intense and spectacular growth" (Hare 1995: 90). This was in contrast to the experience of the majority, and would be a crucial factor in Penguin's emergence in the postwar years as the pre-eminent British publisher. Penguin also had an advantage over many publishers in Lane's choice of location for its warehouse. After early years in central London, the company moved to Harmondsworth, in Middlesex. Other publishers and wholesalers, however, remained in London during the war years, and suffered badly during the Blitz. The gutting of the wholesaler Simpkin Marshall in 1940 was particularly harmful to the trade, taking its total stock, records, and a large part of the distribution arrangements for the nation's book industry (Norrie 1982: 87).

Like many other aspects of life in Britain, then, postwar publishing entered a time of austerity. Paper rationing was in place until 1949. The editor Diana Athill evokes in her memoir of the period "those book-hungry days" of "the post-war book famine" (2000: 34). She recounts how this "famine" encouraged a serious attitude to publications at Allan Wingate, in which books on the list "were of a sober – almost stately – kind," and for which "the reissue of classics was felt as a need" (p. 34). Penguin was engaged in a similarly high-minded project, with E. V. Rieu's translations of the *Odyssey* and the *Iliad*, and the establishment of the Penguin Classics list. In *Penguin Portrait* Hare comments that "Rieu's series [was] inaugurated with the specific aim of making the Classics accessible to the widest possible audience, primarily for their enjoyment" (1995: 189).

The high-minded ideals of these postwar publishers were encouraged by educational reforms. The great reforms of the late nineteenth century had done much to educate the nation as a whole, but the early twentieth-century rise of the educated working classes was cemented by the 1944 Education Act, which established free and compulsory secondary education until the age of 15. Penguin was again central to these developments in its provision of affordable reading materials to new readers. Richard Hoggart, himself the epitome of the working-class scholarship boy, was heartfelt in his appreciation of Penguin in the celebratory volume *Penguins Progress 1935–1960* (1960); and in his key work, *The Uses of Literacy* (1957), he applauded his peers' use of Penguins and Pelicans (Hoggart 1957: 261–2). The expanding markets made available by self-education and the 1944 Education Act are important contexts by which to understand the postwar development of the publishing industry which, once the problems of rationing and distribution were resolved, had an unprecedented opportunity to feed the nation's hunger for books.

Britain was not the only market to which the British publishing industry catered. The traditional British publishing territories of the Commonwealth provided publishers with a substantial proportion of their trade. Immediately after the war, publishers were heavily encouraged by the government to reconstruct their export trade (Feather 1991: 220). In 1949, 29 percent of the value of all book sales made was to export, rising to 38 percent in 1959, and hitting a peak of 47 percent in 1969 (Norrie 1982: 223). Publishers that had already set up branch offices or subsidiaries expanded, while newer enterprises also opened overseas ventures. Heinemann Educational Books, for example, set up subsidiaries in Australia, New Zealand, South-East Asia, East and West Africa, and Canada (Norrie 1982: 105), and would go on to found the influential African Writers Series, in 1962 (Hill 1988).

However, the export market would also face serious challenges in the decades after the Second World War. India gained independence from the British empire in 1947, and subsequent waves of decolonization followed in Africa. The desire of these freshly independent nations for indigenous industries would pose a challenge to traditional British markets. Moreover, and perhaps more harmfully to the British industry, traditional trade arrangements were attacked. US publishers questioned the UK's exclusive rights to publish in the vast majority of the English-speaking world. The booksellers of Australia and New Zealand in particular were frustrated in being bound to trade with the UK, rather than having access to cheaper US editions. The British Commonwealth Market Agreement was successfully challenged in 1976 by the US Department of Justice, which considered it to be illegal under existing anti-trust laws (Feather 1991: 221). Markets were eventually forced open, jeopardizing British profits and forcing down the percentages of sales to export markets. Nonetheless, other forms of legislation protected British publishing, notably the granting of exclusive territorial rights in author–publisher contracts (Clark 2001: 62).

The legacy of the traditional British Commonwealth territorial rights, and of London's long-established position as a metropolitan center of publishing, meant that "British" publishing had a enduring (post)colonial shape beyond the age of empire, particularly in relation to its novelistic production. Thus writers from postcolonial countries continued to seek publication, effective marketing and distribution and, ultimately, validation via London publishing companies. This has been a significant effect of the postcolonial but globalized world created by the end of empire.

Social and Legal Contexts

The publishing industry both reflected and influenced the great social changes of the postwar period, notably in the 1950s and 1960s, through some of the more contentious materials it produced and the censorship battles it underwent. Publishers were prosecuted throughout the 1950s for obscenity, with Hutchinson (for Vivian Connell's *September in Quinze*, 1952), Secker and Warburg (for Stanley Kaufmann's *The Philanderer*, 1953), and Heinemann (for Walter Baxter's *The Image and the Search*, 1953) all brought to the dock. The latter two were acquitted, but the former was found guilty, and both publisher and printer were heavily fined (Norrie 1982: 181). The pulp fiction writer Hank Janson was also successfully prosecuted in the 1950s, pornography was seized from London bookshops, and even stock of Boccaccio's *Decameron* was destroyed (Bloom 2002: 71). The feverish nature of legal activity against publishers, printers, and writers was such that better-defined laws were called for and, in 1959, a new Obscene Publications Act was passed.

The first trial held under the new law was that of Penguin's edition of D. H. Lawrence's *Lady Chatterley's Lover* (1928), in 1960. The book had originally been privately published, and already existed in an expurgated UK edition as well as in full-text imported copies. This much-discussed trial, which has achieved "mythic status" (Hare 1995: 237), and whose proceedings were eventually edited and triumphantly published by Penguin in book form (Rolph 1961), hinged largely on the fact that the book was published in cheap paperback form. The infamous address by the prosecution demonstrated clearly that the provocation caused by the publication was one of *access* to content as much as content alone:

> You may think that one of the ways in which you can test this book, and test it from the most liberal outlook, is to ask yourselves the question, when you have read it through, would you approve of your young sons, young daughters – because girls can read as well as boys – reading this book. Is it a book that you would have lying around in your own house? Is it a book that you would even wish your wife or your servants to read? (Rolph 1961: 17)

In Steven Connor's analysis, the significance of this comment "lies in its acknowledgement of the huge and troubling power of an immoderately enlarged readership for fiction, and the incipient collapse of the ideally homogenous culture of the past" (Connor 1996: 14). Indeed, the expansion of the reading public brought about by educational reforms had the effect of widening culture to a mass audience. In *The Intellectuals and the Masses* (1992), John Carey argues that one effect of this expansion of readers was a retrenchment by modernist writers in order "to exclude these newly educated (or 'semi-educated') readers, and so to preserve the intellectual's seclusion from the mass" (Carey 1992: vii). The fear of the masses apparent in the modernists' reactions would modulate in subsequent decades into a fear of the deleterious effects of mass readership on literature. In her survey of Britain's reading patterns, *Fiction and the Reading Public* (1932), Q. D. Leavis declared that "novel-reading is now largely a drug habit" (Leavis 1932: 19), while the publisher Geoffrey Faber was vociferous in 1934 in his condemnation of the new reading public's impact on his industry:

> Literature now is in the hands of the mob; and the mob is stampeded. It moves in a mass, this way or that, and all its thinking is done for it. For those who will hit the taste of the masses the reward is very large. Hence an ever growing temptation to write for the herd, to publish for the herd, to buy for and sell to the herd. . . . The whole nation reads to order. Books are, increasingly, written to order. (Faber 1934: 29)

Faber's polemic is couched in very unsympathetic terms, but his argument about the impact of market-focused publishing became widely shared. Hoggart, whose analysis in *The Uses of Literacy* is more sympathetic to the working classes, is nonetheless deeply concerned about what he calls "mass-publications": books, newspapers, and magazines (Hoggart 1957: 193). Effective distribution networks augment this trend:

> Popular reading is now highly centralized; a very large body of people choose between only a small number of publications. This is a very small and crowded country; today almost everyone can be supplied at almost the same time with the same object. The price paid for this in popular reading is that a small group of imaginatively narrow and lamed publications are able to impose a considerable uniformity. (Hoggart 1957: 196)

As publishing changed in both culture and shape after the Second World War, these debates around the desirability of market-based publishing and the marketing activity that surrounds it would only intensify.

To defend themselves against the accusations of corrupting the new mass readership, Penguin summoned a glittering array of literary and establishment figures to the defence of *Lady Chatterley's Lover*, including E. M. Forster, Richard Hoggart, Rebecca West, and the Bishop of Woolwich. The "not guilty" verdict was unanimous. Penguin had 200,000 copies printed and ready for distribution, and the book went on to become a multimillion seller that solidified Penguin's reputation as a modern publisher at the vanguard of society. In business terms, it was also thoroughly advantageous to Penguin: the following year the company was floated on the stock market, oversubscribing 150 times, and making Allen Lane a millionaire (Hare 1995: 249). The *Lady Chatterley's Lover* trial did not mark the end of censorship and prosecution, however. The 1960s may have been the era of liberation, but in the book world this was hard fought, with prosecutions of John Cleland's *Fanny Hill* in 1963, Alexander Trocchi's *Cain's Book* and William Burroughs's *Naked Lunch* in 1964, and Hubert Selby Jr.'s *Last Exit to Brooklyn* in 1968, and into the 1970s with the sentencing to jail of the editors of *OZ* magazine in 1971 (Bloom 2002: 73; Sutherland 2002: 51).

In Ireland the postwar period was also one of censorship. Liberalization, however, was less apparent, and legislation had an extremely adverse effect on Irish writers. The

Censorship Board combined with unofficial censorship by booksellers and the wider society, whereby "writers whose books were banned immediately became stigmatised and were regarded as legitimate targets for harassment" (Carlson 1990: 11). In *Banned in Ireland*, Carlson reports an "increasing bitterness and alienation" among writers, with a consequent turn towards Britain and the US (p. 12). Many writers were subject to censorship, including Benedict Kiely, John Broderick, Edna O'Brien, and Lee Dunne. John McGahern, whose novel *The Dark* was banned in 1965, also lost his job as a teacher and experienced his censorship as a "social disgrace" for himself and his family (Carlson 1990: 55). This, as McGahern makes clear, led to his turn away from Ireland:

> It would have been very, very difficult for me to have lived in Dublin at that time because ... I was recognized everywhere ... I was in the newspapers every day. My photograph was all over the place. I stayed in London for several years after that; I just had to make a living. One was very lucky that one could actually go to England and that one's books sold in England. (Carlson 1990: 61)

The impact of harsh censorship and repressive social attitudes was to cripple the novel-producing sector of the Irish industry in the postwar period, and to confirm the trend for Irish writers to seek primary publication – and even their homes – abroad.

Social movements in the 1970s in both Britain and Ireland brought the advent of feminist publishers. At the forefront of these was the Virago Press, established in 1972 by Carmen Callil, which included such writers as Angela Carter, Zoe Fairbairns, and Micheline Wandor on its Advisory Group. Virago prioritized women writers and women's issues through the publication of works of social history and political ideology and through the creative work of writers such as Carter and Pat Barker. The Modern Classics supplemented the publication program by recovering out-of-print works by women, performing the political function of enlarging the canon, and making much forgotten writing easily available to students and general readers. Although Virago suffered accusations from more radical feminist presses that it was not sufficiently separatist – Callil claimed that the mission of the company was both "ideological" and "commercial" (1998:185) – the publisher was an example of a politically engaged company, which had a symbiotic relationship with the profound social changes wrought by second-wave feminism.

In the decades following its establishment, Virago would undergo a complex history of ownership that reflected and resisted the patterns of conglomeration of the later 1970s, 1980s, and 1990s. Merged with the Chatto, Bodley Head, and Cape Group in 1982, it became independent again via a management buyout in 1987, before being bought out once more by Little, Brown (later renamed Time Warner Books in accordance with conglomerate identity), in 1995. Whether it is possible to retain a publishing program with a political mission under such swings of ownership is questionable, and the history of Virago demonstrates the fate of radical publishing practices under the pressures of conglomeration.

Conglomeration and Competition

The greatest transition in postwar publishing has been in its changing patterns of ownership. At the beginning of the twentieth century, the British publishing industry was largely run by mid-sized, family-owned businesses, including such houses as Chatto and Windus (established 1876), Hodder and Stoughton (established 1868), The Bodley Head (established 1887), and the long-established John Murray (1768). At the end of the Second World War, this pattern remained largely the same, though with the addition of several new companies, including Penguin, Victor Gollancz, and Mills and Boon. By the end of the 1990s, however, this pattern had been completely overturned, with all market sectors being dominated by a very small number of multinational, multimedia companies. Mergers and acquisitions in the publishing industry before the war were not unheard of – Stanley Unwin bought the flagging George Allen to form George Allen & Unwin in 1914, for example, and the nineteenth-century companies of Methuen, and Chapman and Hall, came together in 1938 – but they proliferated from the late 1960s onwards. The 1990s continued this trend, with significant mergers and acquisitions including Bertlesmann's takeover of Random House, in 1998.

The deregulation of the financial markets in the US and UK in the 1970s and 1980s was crucial to the intensification of publishing conglomeration. As Clark explains in *Inside Book Publishing*, deregulation "led to increased availability of long- and short-term equity and debt financing allowing large publishers or their parents to take over medium-sized publishers, and small publishers to expand or start-up" (2001: 15). The implications of this for the publishing industry were manifold. First, by the end of the 1990s, economic power was controlled by an oligopoly of large publishers. By 2001, five companies (Bertelsmann, Pearson, HarperCollins, Hodder Headline, and Hachette) had just over 50 percent of market share in the UK, thus controlling over half the market (Gasson 2002: 88–9). Given the enduring importance of books in society, it necessarily follows that significant cultural and political power was invested in the hands of the same small group of conglomerates. The prevention of HarperCollins's publication of Chris Patten's book on Hong Kong, *East and West: The Last Governor General of Hong Kong on Power, Freedom and the Future* (1998), is frequently cited as an example of conglomerate intervention in editorial decisions; Rupert Murdoch (head of News Corporation, HarperCollins's owner) infamously suppressed the book, as it was deemed detrimental to his business interests in China and the Far East. Less overt forms of control over conglomerate publishing are described by André Schiffrin in *The Business of Books*, where "market censorship" – governed by profitability rather than politics – is as effective as ideological controls in curtailing the range of publishing activity (2000: 103). The political and cultural autonomy of a nation's publishing industry is inevitably under duress when controlled by a small number of large agents, a recurrent theme in analyses of the late-twentieth-century trade. Nonetheless, as Clark's analysis of the impact of the deregulation of the financial markets emphasizes, money was also made available to small companies to be established or expand, and new technologies, including desk-top publishing software (DTP), print on demand (POD), and Internet publishing, cut down on costs and on the need for traditional production skills for entrants into the market. The biggest problem for small companies lay rather in the supply chain: the preferential discounts offered by large publishers to major retailers, and demanded of small publishers by retailers, meant that new independents were forced to sell to larger companies (such as Fourth Estate's sale to HarperCollins in 2000) in order to access their negotiating power and distribution channels.

A second implication of conglomeration on the publishing industry is structural. In the transformation from mid-sized family-run businesses to large multinationals, many once independent publishers became incorporated into conglomerates. Publishers are thus both vertically integrated (publishing in hard- and paperback) and include previously independent houses as imprints. Random House now includes a host of previously independent houses as imprints, including Jonathan Cape, Secker and Warburg, Chatto and Windus, The Bodley Head, Hutchinson, and the Harvill Press. Imprints are then used within publishing companies to signal list identity and to demarcate genre divisions: Jonathan Cape, and Secker and Warburg, as literary imprints, for example, and Hutchinson as a mass-market one.

A third implication of conglomeration is the increased money made available to large publishers. As Clark makes clear, increased equity accelerated mergers and acquisitions, but also made money available to conglomerate publishers to spend on advances and marketing. The late twentieth century saw rapid rises in advance levels for the select few, a parallel rise in marketing spend, and a consequent intensification of marketing and promotional activity surrounding certain books and market sectors. The concentration of resources on lead titles has also had the effect of increasing competition. The eventual demise of the Net Book Agreement (NBA) in 1995 – following its successful legal defence in 1962 (see Barker and Davies 1966) – after several major publishers and retailers broke its terms by offering books at discount, is another indicator of the intensely competitive nature of the more recent literary marketplace. The wild discounting practices that ensued suggest, as do the high advance levels and marketing spend on some books, that by the end of the 1990s the market had not yet found its equilibrium between protectionism and competition.

The decades between 1945 and 2000 also marked the irresistible rise of television, and, in later decades, the appearance of new technologies in the form of CDs, DVDs, home computers, and computer games. However, far from the book as a product and reading as an activity being edged out by these competing forms of cultural production and consumption, the twentieth century marked the continuing presence and relevance of the print-based publishing industry, through the corporate partners it acquired under conglomeration. Publishers became subsumed into multimedia conglomerates: companies with interests in newspapers and magazines, film, television and radio, and new communications technologies. For example, News Corporation, besides HarperCollins, has newspaper, magazine, satellite and terrestrial television, and film production and distribution interests. Viacom, owner of Simon and Schuster, has cable and broadcast television, film and television production, music, video, theme parks, and cinemas. Publishers, therefore, came to operate with other cultural and media industries for whom "content" and intellectual property rights are central to their business. The possibilities for cross-media re-use of content were thus intensified, with books turned into films (and vice versa), merchandise produced alongside television shows and spin-off books, and electronic games giving print- or audio-based characters a repurposed form of life. J. K. Rowling's Harry Potter character and stories are a prime example of this. Clark describes how the publishing industry has thus become "part of the larger media leisure industry" as a result of patterns of ownership, and the competition and synergy between books and other leisure products and their producers (2001: 15). Moreover, the possibilities of content repurposing opened new revenue channels, in which the author, as content creator, can play a vital role. The consolidation of publishing companies into multimedia conglomerates has therefore occurred alongside the diversification of rights sales, content re-use, and the ascendancy of the literary agent, as well as the intensification of marketing.

The Changing Culture of Publishing

One of the most striking transitions in the treatment of novels in the twentieth century has been in marketing terms. Although intensified by the late-twentieth-century arrival of conglomerate finance, the culture of marketing had developed substantially throughout the century. Each new generation of publishers caused consternation to the previous one by their market-based activities. Allen Lane came to regret the direction his company, and publishing generally, was taking in the 1960s, thinking, as he explained in an interview in 1967, that his conception of Penguin was being undermined:

> 'My idea when I started was to produce cheap books that were aesthetically pleasing.'
>   He didn't approve of the way those bright young marketing people in London were jazzing up the covers. 'Quite vulgar, some of them, and quite misleading. . . .
>   'So much dignity was going out of my books. Some of the frightful young marketing whizz-kids just wouldn't realise a book is *not* a tin of beans.' (Batt 1967)

Lane felt that the book's uniqueness as a product was under attack from a new wave of market-oriented publishers. His choice of a most prosaic comparison is done for comic effect, but tellingly insists on the disparity between beans and books. Yet as units manufactured for profit, sustaining the distance between one and the other was not always so easy or, in fact, desirable, as Lane's own shrewd distribution of Penguin through Woolworth's demonstrated (Hare 1995: 7). Ironically, the growth of supermarket sales of books in the 1990s would place books and beans in adjacent aisles, and in the same shopping trolley. By 1999, the clashing values of the literary marketplace were encapsulated by Catherine Lockerbie in a *Scotsman* article on World Book Day, which drew on Lane's earlier assertion:

> Yes, yes, books are uniquely transfiguring, soul-saturating artistic artefacts; they are also commodities to be bought and sold as surely as baked beans . . . Yes, yes, readers may clasp literary enlightenment in their trembling hands and feel the shift in their very synapses; they are also fools to be parted from their money. The two aspects of this strange business of the book trade dovetail neatly in World Book Day. (Lockerbie 1999: 10)

Lockerbie summarizes the paradox at the heart of publishing – "this strange business of the book trade" – which struggles to combine, and justify, economic and cultural imperatives. The perceived difference of publishing is still upheld in the UK through the taxation system (VAT – Value Added Tax – is not applied to books), and is the cause of recurrent debate about the tension between commerce and culture in the industry.

In 1963, E. V. Rieu encountered the new generation in the forceful shape of Tony Godwin, who wanted the Penguin Classics to be redesigned. Rieu wrote to Lane to express his anxieties: "'I find it hard to believe that you would allow a newcomer to the firm, without discussion with me, its editor, to mutilate a series that you and I had created in 1944 and have since made world famous'" (Hare 1995: 189). Rieu's language of mutilation suggests that the battles over the definition of publishing could indeed be bloody. The publishing industry that Fredric Warburg, the founder of Secker and Warburg, cherished was founded on the concept of the "gentleman publisher," after which he entitled his memoirs *An Occupation for Gentlemen*. Incensed by the advertising trends of Victor Gollancz, Warburg set the gentleman publisher in direct opposition to the "tradesman":

> A publisher, if he is not to be a wholly commercial operator, must put a lot of his own personality into his firm. It must reflect him directly or indirectly, and if it does it will have a recognizable character. . . . No doubt my view of a publishing house as having a personality can be regarded as highbrow. It will be said that a publisher is a tradesman who is not in business for his health; his job is to take a book that in his view has a sales potential and boost it to the skies, regardless of its merits or lack of them. This view I understand, respect, and profoundly disagree with. (Warburg 1959: 14–15)

The cult of personality as Warburg saw it, and the ability of the publisher to make his mark on his company, would inevitably dimninish in the transition from small to mid-sized companies to globalized conglomerates; but "recognizable character" is something that publishers still attempt to retain through the preservation of imprints. Tony Godwin would take up the debate over the direction of the trade in a talk given to the Society of Young Publishers in 1967, after leaving Penguin. His talk was summarized in *The Bookseller*:

> The reason why publishing has been regarded as an occupation for gentlemen, [Godwin]
> suspected, had been because the upper class considered themselves – possibly they still
> did – as the custodians of culture ... However, as a result of the education acts raising
> the school leaving age and the steady 'democratization' of culture, the distinguished
> amateur in publishing was, he liked to think, being supplanted by the passionate
> professional. (Hare 1995: 263)

Godwin's passionate advocacy of professionalism in publishing is an assault on the class-based cult of the "distinguished amateur." The establishment of feminist publishers, with their policies of female work forces and revised editorial and gate-keeping policies, also worked to remove the gendered construction of the "gentleman publisher."

In the claim Godwin went on to make for professionalism, though, he quite specifically clung to the notion of the book's uniqueness and role in society, while calling for a holistic view of the publishing process (Hare 1995: 263). The primacy of the editorial function was thus undermined, but only – in Godwin's vision – to the extent of ensuring that the commissioning process was integrated into and supported by the other publishing functions. The transition from editorial primacy to a holistic view of publishing has continued to provoke controversy, however, particularly in the emphasis this has placed on sales and marketing, and the corresponding shift in perspective from production to consumption. As Michael Lane identified in *Books and Publishers: Commerce against Culture in Postwar Britain*, this has entailed both an economic and an ideological shift. In opposing "traditional" and "modern" models of publishing, he analyses the "golden age myth of the editor as cultural entrepreneur" as incorporating "the idea of intuitive and individual decisions," whereas the "modernist" approach (his terminology is not be confused with modernist artistic movements) is one of "enlarging the book-buying public," requiring "a more active approach to that audience" (Lane 1980: 77, 112). Lane goes on to describe the attributes of the modernist publisher:

> Such publishers believe that the sectors of the population they want to convert do not
> go into bookshops at all, so they have made some efforts to market their books where
> this public does go. The ideological shift entailed in this secularisation of the book is at
> least as important as the structural and institutional changes that have occurred. (Lane
> 1980: 112)

Writing in 1980, Lane had yet to see the extent to which the modern publisher would go, with heavy selling through supermarkets, e-commerce, and other non-traditional outlets. The book retail environment is one of the clearest indicators in the change in book trade philosophy: from a culture of independent, sometimes intimidating bookshops, to the rise of the attractively designed chain bookstores such as Dillons, Waterstone's, Hammicks, Ottakar's, and Books Etc. The further development of book retailing has seen bookshops, led by the US chain Borders, offering a range of products, including books, CDs, videos, DVDs, newspapers and magazines, and with late opening hours, cafés, and social events.

To claim that the development of new models of publishing practice has meant a steady progression towards a better, more effective publishing industry would be controversial, however. The switch from an editorial emphasis to a sales and marketing one has arguably elevated the principle of commerce above that of culture. The rise of the conglomerates has, as the suppression of Patten's book exemplified, brought in a greater fear of global control of communications media and a decline in politically-engaged and radical publishing. The homogenization of publishing – and of culture – may result. Moreover, if market-based publishing comes to mean an emphasis on sales figures and the bottom line at the expense of innovation, a meaningful future for the novel is severely compromised. Some commentators on the book trade at the turn of the twentieth and twenty-first century already think that time has come. Schiffrin's *The Business of Books*, a book tellingly subtitled *How International Conglomerates Took Over Publishing and Changed the Way We Read*, argues:

> Publishers have always prided themselves on their ability to balance the imperative of making money with that of issuing worthwhile books. In recent years . . . that equation has been altered. It is now increasingly the case that the owner's *only* interest is in making money and as much of it as possible . . . The standards of the entertainment industry are . . . apparent in the content of best-seller lists, an ever-narrower range of books based on lifestyle and celebrity with little intellectual or artistic merit. (Schiffrin 2000: 5–6)

The vision Schiffrin has of the contemporary industry is a depressing one. Quantitative data and interpretive analysis are both much needed in order to assess whether this vision is already a reality. Yet, as Schiffrin himself remarks, this is a difficult thing to do: there is a paucity of information other than anecdotal to clarify the arguments for or against the deterioration of publishing practice under conglomerate rule. Recent publishing history is undoubtedly an area that demands more attention from researchers in order to determine the current condition of the industry and its future effects on culture and society.

The Commodification of Fiction

It is undeniable, despite the need for substantially more data about and interpretation of the postwar publishing industry, that shifting publishing practice and philosophy have affected novelistic production. The novel has always been a market-based literary form, but the period of 1945–2000 witnessed an intense period in the commodification of fiction. The reversal of the traditional book economy of long-termism and the backlist towards a short-term, mass-market logic has been profound. Increasing advance levels have meant that publishers make greater initial financial outlay, which demands to be quickly recouped. The shelf life of books is short – worryingly so to many. Short-termism encourages novelty, and the late twentieth century has seen a growing pressure on novelists to produce works of fiction with greater regularity, to counteract short shelf lives and the threat of returns. The advent of EPOS (Electronic Point of Sale) in the early 1990s enabled booksellers, through the reading of bar codes, to monitor sales and stock closely; it also allowed publishers to have instant access to sales information both of their own and of their competitors' titles, and indications of themes and trends in publishing. The use of EPOS figures has been contentious, with some publishers and literary agents maintaining that it encouraged further short-termism, whereby "publishers and booksellers are losing confidence in authors when their early works fail to set the charts alight." Others say that sales figures are "never allowed to obstruct [our] fiction acquisitions," and that they rely instead on the foresight of the editor and the effectiveness of marketing and publicity depart-ments. One commentator argues that over-reliance on EPOS was "catch-up publish-ing. The role of the editor is to be ahead of the beat, whereas the role of BookTrack [the chief provider of sales data] is to be behind the beat" (Rickett 2000: 21). The recuperation of the role of the editor and his or her individual talent despite the sophistication of sales data is an interesting development, though whether it can countermand the trend for short-term reward remains to be seen.

Short-termism and the emphasis on novelty have also led to rapidly rising produc-tion figures in the period between 1945 and 2000. In 1945, 6,747 new titles were published. The year 2000 saw 116,415 new books (Norrie 1982: 220; *Book Facts 2001*: 17). Advance levels and marketing spend have also increased, though they are harder to quantify. Evidence would suggest, though, that the increase in production, promotion, and financial reward has not benefited every writer equally. In 2000, the Society of Authors published the results of a survey in which responding writers were asked to give their "approximate total gross income arising directly from their freelance writing in the previous year." The average overall figure was £16,600, with 75 percent earning under £20,000 (in other words, under the national average wage), and 46 percent under £5,000. Despite a few high earners (5 percent earning over £75,000), the overwhelming response to the survey suggested that as a profession in 2000 writing was badly remunerated, even poverty-stricken; as the survey suc-cinctly phrased it, half earned "less than an employee on the national minimum wage." The survey closes with the pessimistic aphorism, "Authorship is clearly much more than a job, but it too frequently pays less than a living wage" (Pool 2000: 58–66). The 1998 update of Cyril Connolly's original "Questionnaire: the cost of letters" (1946), *The Cost of Letters: A Survey of Literary Living Standards*, paints a picture of the economics of authorship as gloomy as that of its predecessor (Holgate and Wilson-Fletcher 1998). In the 1998 version, the novelist Jonathan Coe, offering advice to "young people who wish to earn their living by writing," suggests that they "Pay no attention to fairytales about new authors' multi-million pound windfalls" (Holgate and Wilson-Fletcher 1998: 23). As Coe concludes, large advances are as much a media phenomenon as a publishing one, and that the "multi-million pound windfall . . . happens occasionally, and for some reason is the only kind of literary story the newspapers are interested in reporting" (Holgate and Wilson-Fletcher 1998: 23).

The variable degree of attention paid to authors and their books in time and marketing results in the creation of a hierarchy of marketability. "Journalistic capital," to use James English's phrase, is conferred on a few "valuable" authors, making them, and their books, highly visible in the marketplace, while the rest are condemned to what Karl Miller calls a "painful soundlessness in the utterance of authors" (Miller 1989: 192; English 2002: 123). A concentration on celebrity and marketability has resulted in a squeezing of the mid-list. For the authors high in the hierarchy of marketability, the authorial role is expanded far beyond that of writer of the text. In a culture of increasing commodification of the novel, authors give readings in bookshops, attend events at literary festivals, appear in the media, and embark on promotional tours that can last months. Literary prizes – and particularly the Booker Prize for Fiction – increase this commodification and celebritization, with their success in directing media attention to the book world. This, then, is the "promotional circuit"; and for those writers who have achieved this level of promotional activity, it is the creator of their literary celebrity. Joe Moran's study of the phenomenon of literary celebrity, *Star Authors* (2000), comments on the ubiquity of writers in the late twentieth century, noting that excess publicity can cause anxiety amongst cultural commentators, who adversely compare the "hype" of the promotional circuit to a system of judgment based on perceived literary value.

In her essay on literary journalism, "Living on writing" (1998), Lorna Sage also discusses the place of the author in the late-twentieth-century media environment. She notes the increasing prevalence of the "feature" alongside the more traditional review, and analyses how this extends the role of both author and book:

> Zest, curiosity, voyeurism, vicarious *paper*-living enter into book reviewing, there's no real boundary around the books, and indeed book pages merge more and more into features, and there's a constant rearguard action being fought by literary editors to keep their space, and to find ways of allowing books to look like books without losing their 'living' appeal. (Sage 1998: 264)

The result of all this attention to the "living" appeal of the book is, according to Sage, a renewed emphasis on "the life of the author," supplemented by the array of author-centered promotional events (pp. 266–7). The argument Sage makes is more subtle than seeing the extension of the authorial role simply into the realm of literary gossip. Rather, it is a debate engaged with both the life and death of the author – the trope of celebrity and literary biography on the one hand, and the interrogation of the "author-function," in Foucault's terms, on the other. Thus this is a period that has seen the "rise and rise of literary biography," "life-writing," and the memoir, as well as a fictional inscription of the debate "*inside* many contemporary novels" (pp. 265, 267). Writers respond to the contextual "*paper*-living," Sage argues, by an internalization of the authorial voice. The author is resuscitated not only as author-promoter, then, but also in the act of writing itself. For some writers this textual negotiation results in overt inscriptions of the authorial life, such as Martin Amis's parable of authorship, promotion, and literary rivalry in *The Information* (1995), or J. K. Rowling's *Harry Potter and the Goblet of Fire* (2000), in which Harry is besieged by the investigative journalist Rita Skeeter, a character presaged by the media fascination with Rowling herself. For Zadie Smith, one of the most hyped, but also critically and commercially successful young novelists of the late twentieth century, the forces of marketing and branding are satirized at the end of *White Teeth* (2000), in the dystopic "new British" Perret Institute.

Lockerbie's comments on World Book Day in *The Scotsman* refer to the inescapability of promotion, in which the social practices of reading are inextricably caught up with the economic imperatives of the companies that produce reading matter. As Andrew Wernick states in "Authorship and the supplement of promotion," there is now no space that is "hors-promotion": outside the promotional circuit (1993: 101). As Wernick goes on to explain:

> The well-founded suspicion . . . that behind every public act of communication someone is trying to sell us something, multiplies its effects by rebounding from the reader on to the writer: a cynicism which at once sows self-suspicion, and confronts the writer with a resistance to writing that writing itself must find a way to overcome. (1993: 101–2)

This vision of readerly and writerly cynicism in the face of the market is bleak; yet while authors still struggle to communicate with their readers, despite the quandaries of textual production and the vagaries of textual consumption, their work will continue to provide metaphors of escape and eloquent reminders of humanity's capacity for imagining the world and its systems otherwise.

References and Further Reading

Athill, Diana (2000) *Stet: A Memoir*. London: Granta Books.

Barker, R. E. and Davies, G. R. (1966) *Books Are Different: An Account of the Defence of the Net Book Agreement Before the Restrictive Practices Court in 1962*. London: Macmillan.

Batt, Anne (1967) "A book is not a tin of beans . . . ," *Daily Express*, May 8, 1967.

Bloom, Clive (2002) *Bestsellers: Popular Fiction Since 1900*. Basingstoke: Palgrave Macmillan.

Book Facts 2001: An Annual Compendium (2001). London: Book Marketing Ltd.

Brown, Richard H. (1981) "Books and bombs," *Publishers Weekly*, January 23: 81–6.

Callil, Carmen and Simons, Judy (1998) "Women, publishing and power," in Judy Simons and Kate Fullbrook (eds.) *Writing: A Woman's Business: Women, Writing and the Marketplace*. Manchester: Manchester University Press.

Carey, John (1992) *The Intellectuals and the Masses*. London: Faber and Faber.

Carlson, Julia (ed.) (1990) *Banned in Ireland: Censorship and the Irish Writer*. London: Routledge.

Clark, Giles (2001) *Inside Book Publishing*, 3rd edn. London: Routledge.

Connolly, Cyril (ed.) (1946) "Questionnaire: the cost of letters," *Horizon*, 14/ 81: 140–75.

Connor, Steven (1996) *The English Novel in History 1950–1995*. London: Routledge.

Davis, Kenneth C. (1981) "Ireland: a new flowering," *Publishers Weekly*, January 23: 63–80.

English, James (2002) "Winning the culture game: prizes, awards, and the rules of art," *New Literary History*, 33/1: 109–35.

Faber, Geoffrey (1934) *A Publisher Speaking*. London: Faber and Faber.

Feather, John (1991) *A History of British Publishing*. London: Routledge.

Gasson, Christopher (2002) *Who Owns Whom in British Book Publishing*. London: Bookseller Publications.

Hare, Steve (1995) *Penguin Portrait: Allen Lane and the Penguin Editors 1935–1970*. London: Penguin.

Hill, Alan (1988) *In Pursuit of Publishing*. London: John Murray.

Hoggart, Richard (1957) *The Uses of Literacy*. London: Chatto and Windus.

Holgate, Andrew and Wilson-Fletcher, Honor (eds.) (1998) *The Cost of Literary Living Standards*. Brentford: Waterstone's Booksellers Ltd.

Kinane, Vincent (2002) *A Brief History of Printing and Publishing in Ireland*. Dublin: National Print Museum.

Lane, Michael (1980) *Books and Publishers: Commerce Against Culture in Postwar Britain*. Lexington, MA: Lexington Books.

Leavis, Q. D. (1932) *Fiction and the Reading Public*. London: Chatto and Windus.

Lewis, Jeremy (1995) *Kindred Spirits: Adrift in Literary London*. London: HarperCollins.

Lockerbie, Catherine (1999) "Return of reading's red letter day," *The Scotsman*, April 10: 10.

Miller, Karl (1989) *Authors*. Oxford: Oxford University Press.

Moran, Joe (2000) *Star Authors: Literary Celebrity in America*. London: Pluto Press.

Norrie, Ian (1982) *Mumby's Publishing and Bookselling in the Twentieth Century*, 6th edn. London: Bell and Hyman.

Penguins Progress: 1935–1960 (1960) Harmondsworth: Penguin.

Pool, Kate (2000) "Love, not money: the survey of authors' earnings," *The Author*, 111/2: 58–66.

Rickett, Joel (2000) "Publishing by numbers?," *The Bookseller*, September 1: 20–2.

Rolph, C. H. (ed.) (1961) *The Trial of Lady Chatterley*. Harmondsworth: Penguin.

Sage, Lorna (1998) "Living on writing," in Jeremy Treglown and Bridget Bennett (eds.) *Grub Street and the Ivory Tower: Literary Journalism and Literary Scholarship from Fielding to the Internet*. Oxford: Clarendon Press.

Schiffrin, André (2000) *The Business of Books: How International Conglomerates Took Over Publishing and Changed the Way We Read*. London: Verso.

Sutherland, John (2002) *Reading the Decades: Fifty Years of the Nation's Bestselling Books*. London: BBC Worldwide.

Warburg, Fredric (1959) *An Occupation for Gentlemen*. London: Hutchinson.

Wernick, Andrew (1993) "Authorship and the supplement of promotion," in Maurice Biriotti and Nicola Miller (eds.) *What is an Author?* Manchester: Manchester University Press.

13

The Novel and the Rise of Film and Video: Adaptation and British Cinema

Brian McFarlane

The phenomenon of adapting literary and theatrical works into film is almost as old as the cinema itself. It was especially prominent in the history of British cinema, which tended to highlight connection with the antecedent text as a basis for the respectability of the new medium. If Shakespeare and Dickens were being adapted to film, and they profusely were from early days, then surely the cinema might solicit audiences more cultivated than those associated with end-of-pier peepshows.

Adaptation was, of course, also endemically associated with Hollywood cinema, but there were always identifiable differences of approach to the processes of transposition in the two major English-speaking cinemas. It used to be held that British film-makers were more respectful of their precursors and that this was a good thing: there was less critical talk of "tampering" with the original, more praise for the "fidelity" of the transfer, the very terms suggesting morally reprehensible possibilities as well as implying not merely the antecedence but also the primacy of the literary text, as the standard against which a film version would be measured. This was perhaps one of the reasons that Britain's became known, certainly from the 1940s on, as a "literary cinema." But this term implies not just a predilection for adapting literary works but also a cinema that depended much on dialogue as a means of exposition, on detailed novelistic character-drawing, on the concern for representational realism recalling the great tradition of the middle-class English novel. Realism was the most persistently admired strand and mode of British cinema and it provided the context for films that drew heavily on adaptation. British cinema also favored classic or middlebrow popular fiction, with very few exceptions eschewing Hollywood's often very productive dealings with pulp fiction. The major exception to this generalization is the prewar passion for adapting the plays and crime novels of Edgar Wallace, and the 1950s short films adapted from them, though there is in postwar British cinema a smattering of films derived from thriller writers such as John Creasy and Peter Cheyney. More characteristically, though, British cinema would be drawn to, say, Dickens or Francis Brett Young, rather than the profitable dime-novel underbelly of the literary world.

It is possible to identify several key periods in postwar British cinema's traffic in adaptation. Immediately after the war, much of the newfound prestige was associated with adaptations from novels and plays, with Dickens, Shakespeare, and Graham Greene to the fore. In the late 1950s and early 1960s, there was a very unusual congruence between British cinema's quality output and changes in the literary scene, with a parallel sense of chafing under traditional class constraints, on which they looked back in anger. All-star adaptations of Agatha Christie dominated the 1970s and early 1980s, gradually ceding ascendancy to the alliance of adaptation and heritage cinema in the 1980s and 1990s, producing films that seemed to cater for the generation of filmgoers who no longer went to the cinema, perhaps the very people who had admired, say, *Brief Encounter* or *Great Expectations* in the 1940s. The rest of this essay will consider how these key periods came to establish their responses to their literary predecessors.

More often, though, this middle-class, educated audience was, in these later decades, likely to be attracted to the television serial versions of novels, especially of classic novels, which perhaps were attractive to filmmakers because they were out of copyright as well as offering opportunities for the display of decorative production values. Up to a point, it might be argued that the four- or six-episode television serial enabled the filmmaker to provide a narrative experience nearer to that of reading the antecedent novel. It allowed time for developing the subplots usually, perforce, shorn away in a two-hour film; and it corresponded more closely to the experience of reading a novel with breaks enjoined by other demands on the reader's time. Often, though, the classic serial tended to give an impression of filming by numbers. "Ah, today we do Lady Catherine's dinner party," one can almost hear the BBC producers saying as they set about the business of making their hugely popular version of *Pride and Prejudice* (1996); "Let's segue into it with a gallop through the Kentish countryside." A controversial transformation, such as Patricia Rozema's *Mansfield Park* (1999) or the feminist-inspired television serialization of *Great Expectations* (1999), seemed to some people at least to offer a more stimulating challenge than the meticulously researched, but somehow embalmed, Sunday-night serial we counted on to get us through the winter.

As to the effect of television serialization on novel-writing, Malcolm Bradbury once suggested in a television interview that it influenced the structuring of novels. Authors were now more apt to have in mind the dictates of the serial format in which each episode, though clearly part of a larger whole, needed to have its own sense of shaping, of moving towards some sort of semi-autonomous climax, while at the same time leaving the viewer anxious to resume acquaintance with the set of characters and their ambience in seven days' time. Among recent writers on the subject, Sarah Cardwell (2002) has been the most perceptive in her discussion of what she sees to be a new mode of adaptation, the intertextuality of which includes the television serial format itself and its by now imposing list of exemplars. The television serial has provided a different context for the study of adaptation; I am concerned in this essay essentially with adaptation for the cinema, but it is important to keep in mind that the cinema is not necessarily the most popular viewing forum for films derived from literary sources in the early years of the twenty-first century.

And the rapid rise of the video cassette recorder (now about to be superseded by the DVD player) has enabled comparative studies more accessible and more rigorous than were available to earlier generations of adaptation scholars. The pause button means that one can now be precise about such matters as length of shot or segment or about the recurrence of effects of *mise-en-scène*, editing and sound, thus obviating the previously unreliable impressionistic and subjective responses. So much earlier writing about adaptation arrived at conclusions that favored the novel, because it was easier to be exact about what was going on in the novel than in the film in relation to which the best guide a critic might have was notes jotted down during a screening.

It is not possible in the scope of this essay to detail the full range of literary borrowings; I want certain key trends to emerge, one of the chief of which has been the continuing fascination with the classics, despite the challenges involved in producing visualizations of what has already been powerfully (and, of course, differently) visualized by every reader and of what has been canonized in the nation's cultural heritage. This is not to say that the modern British novel was ignored (think of authors such as Daphne Du Maurier, Anthony Burgess, Nicholas Monsarrat, Rumer Godden, Nevil Shute, or Richard Gordon, whose "Doctor" novels spawned a successful series), but the prestige of British cinema in the postwar period has depended enormously on the adaptation of classic fictions. I turn now to the major periods of adaptation in postwar British cinema.

The Latter Half of the 1940s

The World War II period itself was the least prolific in terms of adaptation, British cinema finding other more pressing contemporary topics, especially in relation to representations of the home front as well as to celebrations of the various branches of the services. It may be argued that the British cinema came of age during the war years, engaging for perhaps the first time in any sustained way with the circumambient realities of British life. The critic Dilys Powell wrote: "The war both encouraged a new seriousness of approach by British producers and directors, and drove them to look nearer home than before in their themes," praising a film for "the native truth of its characterisation and setting" (1948). Home-front films such as *Millions Like Us* (1943) and *Waterloo Road* (1944) and such depictions of service life as *In Which We Serve* (1942), *The Gentle Sex* (1943), *San Demetrio, London* (1943), and *The Way Ahead* (1944) were enthusiastically welcomed by critics and audiences alike. In them, British cinema was held to have found a subject it could handle better than anyone else, and they in varying degrees embraced a realist aesthetic that owed something to the achievements of the documentary movement. There was a sense of obvious seriousness about them that was at odds with the Gainsborough melodramas that were adapted from melodramatic novels (*The Man in Grey*, 1943, from Lady Eleanor Smith's Regency romance led the way) and which, *critically* excoriated, only the public loved. These novels, though, would scarcely qualify as "literature," as critics then understood it, and the challenges they offered to adaptors were different from those derived from, say, Dickens. In some ways, the popular fictions freed the adaptors from a slavish respect for the original and liberated filmmakers to exercise visually imaginative approaches to their material. It would, however, be several decades before the value and importance of these popular films would be seriously assessed, and, when it was, this would not have much to do with their precursor novels (Aspinall and Murphy: 1983). During the actual war years, the very few critically respectable novels filmed included A. J. Cronin's *Hatter's Castle*, made into a powerful melodramatic film in 1940, and Michael Sadleir's *Fanny by Gaslight*, handsomely filmed by Gainsborough in 1944, as was Osbert Sitwell's ghost story, *A Place of One's Own*, in 1945.

However, it was the period immediately after the war that produced some of the most striking instances of adaptation. Not only novels, but plays as well, notably those of Shakespeare, Noël Coward, and Terence Rattigan. The wartime ascendancy of British film had been, as suggested above, essentially a realist triumph, and in being so it laid the ground for critical appreciation of a different attitude to adaptation: that is, it now seemed important, after the wartime realism, to bring some of this approach to films adapted from novels, either classic or contemporary, realism having become invested with moral as well as aesthetic value. Some of the most admired films of the time combined the twin prestige strands of British filmmaking: the realist and the literary. It is safe to say that some of the most important of these films could not, or would not, have been made as they were before the war. John Ellis writes of "The quality film adventure" (1996) in relation to the critically well-regarded films of this period, and that "quality" most often comprehended the literary and/or the realist.

Our concern here is with those films that came bearing the status of "adaptation" and from 1946 to 1950 almost all major British films were derived from novels. It is surprising that Dickens, with his flamboyant gothic tendencies, should be favored by a cinema drawn to restraint, but *Great Expectations* (1946) and *Oliver Twist* (1948) achieved a remarkable degree of the author's extravagance as well as taking on board the wartime predilection for realism – and compressing plot-thick novels into cinematic length. The "quality" arm of British Film production at this time was undoubtedly the group of filmmakers operating as Independent Producers – Cineguild, Archers, Individual Pictures, Wessex – and Two Cities, all under the Rank umbrella. Cineguild was the prestige leader, and *Brief Encounter* and *Great Expectations* were the watershed films. Both were critically admired and both derived from literary sources: from Coward's one-act play (*Still Life*) and from Dickens's sprawling *bildungsroman*. Both chimed with the critical ideal of "quality cinema" for Britain, a cinema that distanced itself from Hollywood by its concern for literary-style virtues and for representational realism.

One of the strengths of David Lean's *Great Expectations* is the way in which it embeds its gallery of Dickesian grotesques in a convincing cinematic world. John Bryan's masterly production design is no doubt crucial to this enterprise: the physical world of the marshes, where the film begins and to which it will return, and the bustling life of London to which Pip ventures in pursuit of his "expectations" are realized with attention to what Henry James called "felt life." As well, though, Lean has understood that, if the film is not to be overwhelmed by such wonderfully larger-than-life characters as Martita Hunt's reclusive Miss Havisham, Francis L. Sullivan's lawyer Jaggers, and Finlay Currie's convict Magwitch, the central character of Pip must be firmly rooted in a recognizable reality. Lean's way of keeping Pip in virtually every sequence and John Mills's careful, detailed, naturalistic performance as the adult Pip (Anthony Wager is a finely watchful, sometimes alarmed young Pip) helps to ensure that this is so. Another element of interest perhaps peculiar to the latter 1940s is the way in which its last scenes, as well, of course, as the whole story of a poor boy's upward mobility, seem to hint at a new Britain in the postwar world. As Pip rips down the curtains of Satis House to let in the light, it is not too fanciful to see this as a renunciation of a moribund class system. From this point of view, the film may be seen as inheriting the more democratic tenor that had made itself felt in the wartime films themselves.

Two years later the Cineguild team did a very skillful pruning job on *Oliver Twist*, as a result of which the eponymous hero, who all but disappears for the novel's final third, is kept at the forefront of the viewer's attention. Lean and Bryan again catch some of Dickens's dark vision, as well as imbuing it with a physical realism not commonly found in prewar British cinema, in its representation of provincial work-house, London streets, and Fagin's thieves' kitchen. Contact with none of these stains the saintly, beautifully spoken Oliver, who, in John Howard Davies's performance, as in Dickens's characterization of him, is more an idea of innocence than a realistically drawn figure. Other Dickensian adaptations of the period included Ealing's tonally less certain *Nicholas Nickleby* (1947, directed by Alberto Cavalcanti), in which the picaresque plot and its somewhat pallid hero lack the persuasive rooting in the real that characterizes the Lean films from Dickens, and Brian Desmond Hurst's *Scrooge* (1951), which has an eye-catching title-role performance from Alistair Sim, and a certain charm, but which encourages the greeting card and old-coaching-inn version of Dickens, rather than the tougher, more gothic actuality.

Of the other authors to whom British filmmakers were attracted in this period, three rough categories are discernible. There are sturdily popular middle-range authors like Francis Brett Young (*A Man About the House*, 1947; *My Brother Jonathan*, 1948, the most popular British film of its year; *Portrait of Clare*, 1950), Howard Spring (*Fame Is the Spur*, 1947), Rumer Godden (*Black Narcissus*, 1947; *The River*, 1951, UK/US), Nigel Balchin (*Mine Own Executioner*, 1947; *The Small Back Room*, 1948); and Eric Ambler (*The October Man*, 1947). More obviously "prestige" authors adapted at this time included Graham Greene (*The Man Within* and *Brighton Rock*, 1947; *The Fallen Idol*, 1948, from a novella; *The Third Man*, 1949, written with the screen in mind), D. H. Lawrence (*The Rocking-Horse Winner*, 1948 – a short story, Lawrence's novels being too sexually challenging for 1940s cinema), Somerset Maugham (novels and plays much filmed in Hollywood, his short stories memorably in three British portmanteau films: *Quartet*, 1948; *Trio*, 1950; and *Encore*, 1951, and his novel, *Vessel of Wrath*, refilmed as *The Beachcomber*, in 1954), H. G. Wells (*The History of Mr Polly* and *The Passionate Friends*, both 1948) and Hugh Walpole (*Mr Perrin and Mr Traill*, 1948; *Kind Lady*, 1951, UK/US). There was also a sprinkling of crime fiction from the likes of Hammond Innes (*Snowbound*, 1948), Vera Caspary (*Bedelia*, 1946), Georges Simenon (*Temptation Harbour*, 1947; *Midnight Episode*, 1950; *The Man Who Watched Trains Go By*, 1952); and Gerald Kersh (*Night and the City*, 1950, UK/ US). These three categories, along with the film versions of such plays as *The Winslow Boy* (1948) and *The Browning Version* (1951) produced some of the more notable and best-remembered films of the postwar period, in which British cinema achieved a new reputation for "quality" films.

Much of this reputation clearly derived from its dealings with literature. Not just in the sense that so many of the resulting films were adaptations, but also because of the involvement of authors in screenwriting. "I have somehow in the last years lost all my interest in films, and I don't think I've seen one for the last nearly ten years," Graham Greene wrote in 1990 (in a letter to the author). This statement has a melancholy ring in relation to the British novelist who, perhaps more than any other, had such memorable relations with the cinema in the mid-century decades. Not merely was he more frequently adapted than any other modern author, in both British and American films of widely varying quality, he was also a film reviewer, for *The Spectator* and the short-lived *Night and Day,* which collapsed after Greene's "outrage" against Shirley Temple attracted a libel suit. As well, and most important, he was associated with several of the defining British films of the later 1940s. He took over from Terence Rattigan when the Boulting brothers were dissatisfied with Rattigan's screenplay for their version of Greene's drama of prewar racetrack and protection rackets in *Brighton Rock* (1947). He also wrote the screenplay for two of the films that accounted for the ascendancy of director Carol Reed at this time: *The Fallen Idol* (1948), adapted from Greene's own novella, *The Basement Room*, and *The Third Man* (1949), voted No. 1 in the British Film Institute's list of the top 100 British films (2000). For the latter, Greene first wrote a novel that he then reduced to a screenplay, set in war-ravaged Vienna, then occupied by the four Allied powers, and the result was one of the most seductive films ever made. Greene and Reed's combined talents and sensibilities were less noticeably challenged by the film of *Our Man in Havana* (1959), and adaptations of his work continue apace to this day (see below), but he remains above all a key figure in the prestigious heyday of British films.

Eric Ambler's association with director Roy (later Roy Ward) Baker, whom he had met while on war service, produced the tense thriller *The October Man* (1947), with its war-disordered protagonist, and a decade later Ambler wrote the screenplay for

Baker's (to date) definitive account of the sinking of the *Titanic, A Night to Remember*
(1958). In between, he had written the screenplay for Baker's Cold War comedy-
thriller, *Highly Dangerous* (1950), and adapted other men's novels for such films as *The
Passionate Friends* (1948, from H. G. Wells), *The Card* (1952, from Arnold Bennett),
The Cruel Sea (1952, from Nicholas Monsarrat), *Rough Shoot* (1953, from Geoffrey
Household), and *The Purple Plain* (1954, from H. E. Bates). The very eclecticism of
these films and novels and their overall success rating (in particular, *The Cruel Sea* is
one of the most moving of all British war films) points to Ambler's protean involvement in the film medium, going well beyond the status of adapted author, though
several of his novels had been filmed in both the US and Britain, and the spy thriller,
Journey into Fear, was indeed filmed twice, in 1942 (US) and 1975 (Canada/US).
Greene and Ambler are but the two most prominent novelists who took serious
interest in the postwar cinema, but others were involved in the writing of screenplays.
For instance, Nigel Balchin, whose *Mine Own Executioner*, which dealt intelligently
with psychiatry and postwar problems, was filmed by Anthony Kimmins in 1947,
also wrote the screenplays for the Boulting brothers' version of Spring's *Fame Is the
Spur*, skillfully compressing a very long saga into a rigorous account of the rise and
moral fall of a Labour politician, and for Ronald Neame's version of Ewen Montagu's
true-life story, *The Man Who Never Was* (1955). This kind of coal-face involvement of
literary figures in British cinema is not limited to this period; it has been an ongoing
aspect of British cinema, sometimes referred to as a writer's and actor's cinema, rather
than a director's, and not without some reason.

The New Wave

Much was made of the notion that a new spirit was abroad in British cinema from the
late 1950s, the result of films that drew on kinds of working-class life hitherto
marginalized in the popular genres of the preceding decade. It is significant that all
the films that constitute the British cinema's new wave (the term was a riposte to the
French *nouvelle vague*) were adapted from literary or theatrical texts. It is also significant that the kinds of novels and plays adapted constituted various strands of "radical"
writing; and there was, as noted, an unusual overlap between what was critically
accepted and praised in both writing and filmmaking. For once, the kinds of novels
that were being praised were made into films that were also praised – and for the same
virtues. Surely, though, there is something very un-radical as far as film is concerned
in the fact that all these movies *did* derive from literature; that their newness was
more a matter of location and class setting rather than the stylistic breakthrough of
the *nouvelle vague*, that they were all made by middle-class men with Oxbridge
backgrounds, and that they almost all focused on the plight of *male* protagonists
rebelling against the constrictions of their lives. In general, they kept closely to the
plots and sympathies of their precursor texts and even to the narrative modes (*vide* the
series of flashbacks in which *This Sporting Life* is revealed).

The men associated with this new wave were more than usually articulate about what they were doing and had found influential forums in which to expound their views. None more so than Lindsay Anderson, who, to the end of his life, maintained his allegiance to the views he expressed in a famous essay he wrote in 1957, "Get out and push!":

> What sort of cinema have we got in Britain? First of all it is necessary to point out that it is an *English* cinema (and Southern English at that), metropolitan in attitude and entirely middle-class. This combination gives it, to be fair, a few quite amiable qualities: a tolerance, a kind of benignity, a lack of pomposity, an easy-going good nature. But a resolution never to be discovered taking things too seriously can soon become a vice rather than a virtue, particularly when the ship is in danger of going down. To counterbalance the rather tepid humanism of our cinema, it must also be said that it is snobbish, anti-intelligent, emotionally inhibited, wilfully blind to the conditions and problems of the present, dedicated to an out-of-date, exhausted national ideal. (Anderson 1957: 157)

Anderson goes on to claim:

> The number of British films that have ever made a genuine try at a story in a popular milieu, with working-class characters all through, can be counted on the fingers of one hand; and they have become rarer, not more frequent, since the war. (p. 158)

Whatever limitations may now be adduced against the body of films, all of them adaptations, that constitute the British new wave, it has to be allowed that they did fly in the face of some of the prejudices and predilections Anderson was identifying. And perhaps it is worth adding that he came from an upper-class background himself (military officer father, Cheltenham College, Oxford), so that his dissatisfactions may be granted at least the virtue of detachment in relation to the aspects of the national life he finds missing from the contemporary cinema. Not only Anderson, but other key directors of the period were similarly articulate about what they wanted of film. Tony Richardson wrote in 1959: "I should certainly like British films to be different from what many have been in the past" (Richardson 1959: 9), and thirty-five years later Karel Reisz recalled that

> the writers – novelists and playwrights – were taking note of the changes [in postwar society]. The cinema *followed*. We felt our pictures should reflect more of what was in the air. (in McFarlane 1986: 476)

The films are derived from forebears that were shaking up the literary and theatrical scene in the latter 1950s, and film, characteristically perhaps, was trailing in the wake of what quickly became known as the "angry young man" syndrome. Richardson felt at the time that it was "absolutely vital to get into British films some sort of impact and sense of life that, what you can loosely call the Angry Young Man cult, has had in the theatre and literary worlds" (Richardson 1959: 9). In the theater John Osborne's *Look Back in Anger* (1956) marked a decisive turning away from the long-standing West End fare provided by Coward and Rattigan (they would return to favor several decades later); its atrabilious attacks on every aspect of British establishment life had the invigorating quality of a gust of wind from the North, and its articulate antihero, Jimmy Porter, became the template for a whole slew of disaffected young protagonists. Among novels, new voices included most strikingly John Braine's in *Room at the Top* (1957) and Alan Sillitoe's in *Saturday Night and Sunday Morning* (1958). Four decades later, John Sutherland wrote: "Those two novels . . . dramatised the dilemma of the young man coming of age at the end of the 1950s" (*The Sunday Times*, February 1, 1998). Add to these Sillitoe's *The Loneliness of the Long Distance Runner* (1959), Keith Waterhouse's *Billy Liar* (1959), Stan Barstow's *A Kind of Loving* (1960), David Storey's *This Sporting Life* (1960), and the plays, Osborne's *The Enter-tainer* (1957) and Shelagh Delaney's *A Taste of Honey* (1959), and you have accounted for the immediate forerunners of most of the new wave films. (The other novelist who made his name at this time for his satirical tilts at bourgeois life was Kingsley Amis, but he was less happily filmed: *Lucky Jim* (1954, film 1957) settled for easier, sunnier laughs than Amis's hapless hero did on the page; *Only Two Can Play* (from *That Uncertain Feeling*, 1955, film 1962) missed the novel's sourer undertones; and *Take a Girl Like You* (1960, film 1969) was scarcely seen, though it made a sharply witty television mini-series in 2000.)

Not that they – the films or the directors who made them – were all alike, and the above summary may tend to elide their differences; but they do "[translate] to the cinema some of their generation's revolt against the complacency of the older generation and the metropolitan bourgeoisie . . . finding in the northern working class a vitality and toughness" (Caughie 1996: 38) not found in other reaches of postwar British cinema. To keep the distinctions clear, look briefly at the protagonists of the films that emerged. Joe Lampton (Laurence Harvey), upwardly mobile hero of Jack Clayton's *Room at the Top* (1959), nearly achieves emotional adulthood but remains locked in adultery instead and is forced to settle for marriage to the daughter of "the top." Osborne's ranting Porter has a barely concealed romantic streak, a yearning for the Edwardian certainties whose relics he seems so to despise in *Look Back in Anger* and whose "anger" feels compromised in Richardson's film by the star-casting and too-mellifluous tones of Richard Burton. In Richardson's *Loneliness of the Long Distance Runner* (1962), Colin Smith (Tom Courtenay) is a pinched and resentful iconoclast, thumbing his nose at the Establishment's attempts to rehabilitate him, while Courtenay in John Schlesinger's *Billy Liar* (1963) finally swops mild rebellion for the safe confines of his rich fantasy life. In Schlesinger's *A Kind of Loving* (1962), Vic Brown (Alan Bates) traps himself into stultifying lower-middle-class mores when he marries his pregnant girlfriend, and, in settling with some degree of integrity for "a kind of loving," sacrifices the prospects his intelligence might have opened up to him. Arthur Seaton (Albert Finney), the hedonistic lathe-worker hero of Karel Reisz's *Saturday Night and Sunday Morning* (1960), is similarly trapped by marriage and can't be said to maintain the aggression implied in his credo of "Don't let the bastards grind you down." Finally, the emotionally inarticulate footballer, Frank Machin (Richard Harris) acquires an almost tragic stature as his casually bruising persona is forced to give way to some sense of self-realization in Anderson's *This Sporting Life* (1963), last and perhaps greatest of the new wave films.

There may be a common denominator of dissatisfaction with the social organization in which they find themselves, but these men cross a broad spectrum in such matters as how far each is in charge of his life, how articulate they are about their discontents, and the kinds of prospects that seem open to them. The fact that the future for all of them is in varying degrees and ways bleak may well constitute a comment on how far British society really had changed since the war. For one thing, with the exception of Jo (Rita Tushingham) in Richardson's *A Taste of Honey*, 1961, these protagonists are all men and the directors are all men, though there are some remarkable roles for women in them; but it might have taken different (women?) directors to move them closer to the center. Formally, there are some serious disparities to be observed between, say, the classic narrative pattern of *Room at the Top* and the intricate structure of flashbacks and memory sequences in *This Sporting Life*; but they are not works of great formal daring as the films of the French *nouvelle vague* were. In terms of style, they now seem characterized by long panning shots of rows of terraces or what Andrew Higson has called "That Long Shot of Our Town from That Hill" (1996: 150), the latter usually motivated by a brief respite for the protagonist from the suffocations of the working-class world below, with belching chimneys and threadbare popular culture.

It is not to disparage the effect of these adapted works at the time, when they seemed be shaking the cobwebs of the 1950s conventional British cinema, to say that they now appear both less adventurous than they did and less different in tone from other films being made at the time. The amount of attention, largely *positive* attention, they received at the time in itself proclaims a real level of innovation, and perhaps also testifies to the unusual eloquence of their makers in promoting their works. However, in turning their attention away from the kinds of novels adapted in the preceding decades (classics, middle-brow fictions) to much rawer regionally-set fictions they paved the way for bringing a lot of important new talents into British cinema when they were urgently needed. Directors such as Anderson, Richardson, Schlesinger, and Reisz, who came from backgrounds in Free Cinema documentary and/or the theater, especially of London's Royal Court; actors such as Finney, Tushingham, Courtenay, Bates, and David Warner; and cameramen such as Freddie Francis and Walter Lassally gave a new look to British cinema. There were no more than ten of these films before the wave broke on the wreck-strewn shores of "swinging sixties" cinema, but they offered a sternly admonishing challenge to the pretty-pretty Rank comedies and endless war heroics of the 1950s.

Coinciding roughly with the new wave was the phenomenon of the Hammer horror industry, set going by the success of *The Quatermass Experiment*, adapted from Nigel Kneale's television serial, but sustained by the mutations wrought on such celebrated fictions as Mary Shelley's *Frankenstein* and Bram Stoker's *Dracula*. *The Curse of Frankenstein* and *Dracula*, both released in 1957, were both directed by Terence Fisher, whose name would become synonymous with Hammer horror; both were produced by Anthony Hinds, written by Jimmy Sangster and starred Christopher Lee, who was joined in *The Curse of Frankenstein* by Peter Cushing. These two films laid the basis for one of the most successful production enterprises in British film history. Critically excoriated at the time by genteel critics such as C. A. Lejeune, these films and many of their successors, the ties to Shelley and Stoker loosening, were subsequently praised for their wit and style, and explored productively as a sort of "return of the repressed" in British cinema. They are less notable as adaptations of literary texts than as a Technicolored echo of the Gainsborough melodramas of the mid-1940s, as a *showing* rather than merely suggesting of the source of the horror. As David Pirie writes (1973: 40–1), they belong to a Gothic tradition "which precisely *depends* on the clear visual portrayal of every stage of the action." As well as the two main strands, Hammer also produced versions of Robert Louis Stevenson's *Dr Jekyll and Mr Hyde* (Fisher's *The Two Faces of Dr Jekyll*, 1960, Lance Comfort's parodic version, *The Ugly Duckling*, 1959, and Roy Ward Baker's *Doctor Jekyll and Sister Hyde*, 1971), and a genuinely alarming version of Conan Doyle's *The Hound of the Baskervilles* (1959).

However, neither the new wave nor the Hammer assembly line, notable as both were, accounted for more than a trickle in the steady stream of adaptations that emanated from British studios from the later 1950s to the 1970s. They are merely the most coherent bunches of literature-derived films of the period. There were other more or less isolated adaptations of distinction, including several from D. H. Lawrence, taking advantage of increasingly relaxed censorship in sexual matters: Jack Cardiff's *Sons and Lovers* (1960), undermined by a miscast American lead (Dean Stockwell), Ken Russell's flamboyant, ambitious, and passionate go at the dauntingly discursive *Women in Love* (1969), Christopher Miles's lower-key but intelligent *The Virgin and the Gypsy* (1970), and the US/Canadian version of the novella, *The Fox* (1968), a then-daring depiction of a lesbian couple whose lives are disrupted by a stranger. There were further dealings with Dickens, including Ralph Thomas's *A Tale of Two Cities* (1958) and Ronald Neame's *Scrooge* (1970, from *A Christmas Carol*), none of them rivaling David Lean's 1940s triumphs; Jack Clayton's magisterial ghost story, *The Innocents* (1961) drew brilliantly on Henry James's *The Turn of the Screw*; and Tony Richardson's rollicking, wildly popular *Tom Jones* (1963) prompted both his *Joseph Andrews* (1977) and, at some remove from author Henry Fielding, Cliff Owen's *The Bawdy Adventures of Tom Jones* (1976). For the rest, there were prestige adaptations of superior modern authors such as L. P. Hartley (*The Go-Between*, 1971; *The Hireling*, 1973) and Graham Greene (*Our Man in Havana*, 1960; *The Comedians*, 1967, US/Bermuda/France; the very 'Greenean' *England Made Me* and *Travels with My Aunt*, both 1972), and such popular fictions as Ian Fleming's James Bond stories, starting with *Dr No* (1962) and still going forty commercially productive and culturally revealing years later; and Agatha Christie's detective stories. The latter included the four made with Margaret Rutherford as Miss Marple (1962–5). Although engaging enough, it must be said that two decades later Joan Hickson's Marple on television was both nearer to the original and more invincibly intelligent in the role of spinster sleuth. As well, there were several plushy all-star Christie thrillers, set in motion by the 1974 success of Sidney Lumet's *Murder on the Orient Express* and grinding to an overdue halt with Michael Winner's *Appointment with Death* (1988), but television proved the true home for Christie and others of her ilk (P. D. James, Ruth Rendell, Dorothy Sayers), providing cosy entertainment in attractive settings and with casts of ageing film stars for nostalgia value.

The "Heritage" Film, Television and Adaptation of the 1980s and 1990s

The final batch of adaptations of the postwar decades, especially since the early 1980s, that I want to consider comprises, above all, films made from the classier end of the literary spectrum. As television increasingly commanded the audiences who once found film their chief narrative mode, two main developments can be observed: television serials based on classic novels; and film versions of classic novelists, in films that made much of the listed buildings before which their distinguished casts disported themselves. The films made for both media found favor not merely in Britain but throughout the English-speaking world, in spite of the sometimes disparaging attitudes taken to them by critics who want British cinema to engage itself (exclusively it often seems) with rawer aspects of contemporary British life. Such critics are more likely to champion the works of, say, Ken Loach or Shane Meadows or Mike Leigh, but this bias can lead them to overlook the solid virtues of the "heritage" film. Not every film that comes under this vague and often patronizingly used heading is a literary adaptation, but the overwhelming majority are.

The authors most commonly adapted in this period include Henry James, E. M. Forster, Jane Austen, Charles Dickens, Thomas Hardy, and Virginia Woolf, with more modern fiction represented by Graham Greene, Hanif Kureishi, Kazuo Ishiguro, Helen Fielding (of *Bridget Jones's Diary*, 2001), and others.

It is the classic authors who, by and large, excite the "heritage" instincts of filmmakers, none more so than the Merchant Ivory company, which after a dozen or more years of modestly attractive, idiosyncratic work had a major commercial breakthrough with *A Room with a View* (1986). This version of Forster's vision of the emotions struggling for expression in middle-class England and finding release in sunny Italy offered a critique of the very beauties of the home counties the film so lovingly recreates. Other Forster adaptations followed: *Maurice* (1987) and *Howards End* (1992), both evincing the Merchant Ivory fastidiousness in period recreation and both alert to the conflict between the emotional needs and social demands faced by their characters. (The Forster oeuvre, hitherto largely ignored, was ransacked during the period: David Lean did his least ponderous work for two decades with *A Passage to*

India, 1984, and Charles Sturridge, who had made his name on the television serialization of Evelyn Waugh's *Brideshead Revisited*, 1981, directed *Where Angels Fear to Tread*, 1991, and would also direct a lesser Waugh adaptation, *A Handful of Dust*, 1987). The Merchant Ivory team had made an intelligent, low-key version of James's *The Europeans* in 1979 and moved on to more demanding James with *The Bostonians* (1984, UK/US) and, especially, the famously difficult *The Golden Bowl* (2000, Fr/UK/US), in which a surprising amount of complexity and subtlety survived the sumptuous production design. As the popularity of Merchant Ivory increased, among art-house audiences, and was sometimes more widespread than that implies, they began to attract a predictable, only partly deserved critical backlash. Higson sums up the conflicting responses they excited:

> For many, their films are wonderfully refined, boast superb performances, and display production values that far supersede what might be expected from such modestly budgeted films. But others dismiss the films as overly nostalgic, middlebrow and reverential, the Laura Ashley of contemporary cinema. (Higson 2003: 449)

They undoubtedly appealed to older, middle-class audiences, possibly those familiar with the famous novels on which they drew, but this should not, of itself, lead to their blanket dismissal as retrograde exercises in middlebrow culture.

Whereas television had worked its way through Jane Austen with conscientious versions of most of the novels, the 1961 version of *Emma* staying in the mind as unusually rigorous, it was not until the mid-1990s that the Austen cinematic drought was broken. Not since the MGM version of *Pride and Prejudice* (1940), which outraged some Austen purists, had her novels been adapted to the cinema. Even then, the most popular version was probably the television serialization of *Pride and Prejudice* (1996), which quite properly made the relationship between Elizabeth and Darcy a sexually charged affair – and made a star of Colin Firth, who became a thinking woman's sex object. Also made for television but screened in cinemas in some countries was Roger Michell's *Persuasion* (1995), a subdued, intelligent reading of Jane Austen's autumnal romance, and there was a telemovie version of *Emma* (1996), with Kate Beckinsale as the endearingly interfering heroine. On the big screen, *Emma*, almost simultaneously with the preceding, was a sunny UK/US co-production, starring Gwyneth Paltrow, complete with convincing accent, but skimming so swiftly over some of the plotting as to make it scarcely intelligible to those unfamiliar with the novel. This was perhaps the result of a misguided "fidelity" principle: that is, it is as if the makers felt it is not *Emma* if you leave out, say, Jane Fairfax, but what she means in this version is surely hard to fathom. A more ruthless approach might have made a tougher film. *Sense and Sensibility* (1995) was also a UK/US co-production and its lavish production testified to its budget. Its overtly feminist approach to this lesser Austen gave it a witty contemporary gloss, but despite the overall excellence of its casting, direction (by Ang Lee, bringing an outsider's perception to bear on its enclosed world) and production design, it seemed to cut less rawly to its repressed emotional life than Michell's physically much less ambitious production, and to be less inventive as adaptation than Patricia Rozema's idiosyncratic, feminist *Mansfield Park* (1999, UK/US).

In this later period, Iain Softley directed a very assured, austerely shorn version of James's demanding *The Wings of the Dove* (1997, UK/US), focusing hard on the central trio of this remorseless drama of opportunism and redemption; and there were two stimulating brushes with Virginia Woolf, a novelist who always seems to have been influenced by the cinema which has, curiously, had little to do with her. Sally Potter, with a record of feminist filmmaking, procured international financial support for her version of Woolf's century- and gender-spanning *Orlando* (1992, UK/Fr/It/Neth/Russ), and the result was both epic and personal. On a smaller scale, Marleen Gorris's *Mrs Dalloway* (1997, UK/Neth/US) was irradiated by a beautiful performance from Vanessa Redgrave as the party-giving eponym whose carefully crowded day keeps threatening to unnerve her. The Irish James Joyce, another whose work showed traces of the cinema, was several times filmed in the latter decades of the century: there was a doomed and daring version of *Ulysses* (1967, UK/US), a very decent attempt on the less demanding *A Portrait of the Artist as a Young* Man (1977), with both "heritage" elements as it celebrated Georgian Dublin and surprisingly large chunks of the novel's dialectic; and John Huston, by now living in Ireland, made a sublimely elegiac version of Joyce's story, *The Dead* (1987, UK/Ger/US). And Graham Greene, of all British novelists perhaps the one most tenaciously associated with cinema, was twice more (re-)adapted to the screen around the turn of the century: in Neil Jordan's *The End of the Affair* (1999, UK/Ger/US), recreating wartime London and with the magnificent Julianne Moore as the fulcrum of its action; and Philip Noyce's careful, intelligent version of *The Quiet American* (2001), its release delayed because of its anti-American sentiments in relation to interference in the affairs of foreign countries, and with a subtle central performance from Michael Caine.

There was much more sense of "fidelity" about the adaptations of this period than those of earlier decades and indeed they helped to consolidate the heritage genre as a recognizable entity. Perhaps the more leisurely approach of a four- or six-part serial has accustomed audiences to a closer regard for the original, and this in turn seems like a continuation of the British approach to the filming of novels since World War II. That reckless and sometimes hugely successful Hollywood gutting of classic and popular novels was never — for better and worse — the British way. Some novelists, such as Anita Brookner and Ivy Compton-Burnett who have been filmed with distinction for television, have resisted the screen; J. K. Rowling and J. R. R. Tolkien have been made with largely US money; offbeat authors such as Kureishi have usually reached the art-houses rather than the mainstream, but the British mainstream, insofar as there is one, is still markedly literary.

If no author has been so much associated with the screen in more recent times as Greene once was, Kureishi may yet rival his involvement. He wrote the screenplays for *My Beautiful Laundrette* (1985) and *Sammy and Rosie Get Laid* (1987), two films that took an invigorating look at contemporary Britain and were both directed by Stephen Frears, wrote and directed *London Kills Me* (1991), and provided story and screenplay for *My Son the Fanatic* (1997) and for the well-regarded television mini-series, *The Buddha of Suburbia* (1993). In controversial vein, stories by Hanif Kureishi were adapted by Patrice Chéreau in *Intimacy* (2001), groundbreaking in its mainstream (more or less) depiction of sexual activity. Playwright Harold Pinter has written or adapted screenplays for such films as *The Servant* (1963), *Accident* (1967) and *The Go-Between* (1971), all for Joseph Losey, and *The French Lieutenant's Woman* (1981) and *The Comfort of Strangers* (1990, UK/It), adapted from novels by, respectively, Robin Maugham, Nicholas Mosley, L. P. Hartley, John Fowles, and Ian McEwan. The last-named wrote several screenplays in the 1980s, including the state-of-the-nation piece, *The Ploughman's Lunch* (1983) and, apart from *The Comfort of Strangers*, other films adapted from his novels include *The Innocent* (1993, UK/Ger), for which he also wrote the screenplay, and *The Cement Garden* (1993, UK/Fr/Ger). Ruth Prawer Jhabvala has been associated almost exclusively with the Merchant Ivory output, adapting both her own novel, *Heat and Dust* (1982), Kazuo Ishiguro's Booker Prize-winner, *The Remains of the Day* (1993), and those of Henry James and E. M. Forster among others. The tradition of British novelists' affiliations with the screen clearly is in no danger of extinction.

There have been some interesting developments in relations between novel and film. *Dreamchild* (1985) examines connections between *Alice in Wonderland*, the real Alice, the nature of narrative and the idea of narrative as a gift of love. In the Jane Austen craze of the 1990s, the US-made *Clueless* (relocating *Emma* to teenage LA and the world of computer-generated wardrobe coordination and mobile phones) and *Mansfield Park* (drawing on Austen's diaries and other works, as well as history) were the most interesting, and least "faithful." There was an inventive tussle with Virginia Woolf in David Hare's 2002 adaptation of Michael Cunningham's *The Hours*; Michael Winterbottom, addressing Hardy, made his own masterwork of *Jude* and relocated *The Mayor of Casterbridge* to the Rockies in *The Claim* (2001); and Danny Boyle took Irvine Welsh's invigorating and foul-mouthed *Trainspotting* and made, in 1996, one of the hit films of the decade, becoming as few British films do an instant cult success.

More conventional were Anthony Minghella's pictorially indulgent *The English Patient* (1996), which languorously smoothed out the complexities of Michael Ondaatje's novel, and his more restrained but still too pretty version of Patricia Highsmith's *The Talented Mr Ripley* (1999, US); Kenneth Branagh's overwrought, underthought *Frankenstein* (1994, UK/US); and Gillian Armstrong's inert version of Sebastian Faulks's *Charlotte Gray* (2001, UK/Aust/Ger). But "conventional" needn't always be a defect: in this same period, Sharon Maguire had a box-office success with her good-humored, funny adaptation of *Bridget Jones's Diary* (2001, UK/Fr/US), its provenance as a working-girl's *Pride and Prejudice* underlined by the casting of Colin Firth as another Darcy.

Nothing stems the flow, whether of classics or recent novels, whether made in the UK from British novels or by British and other filmmakers working elsewhere. British television would scarcely have become the admiration of the English-speaking world and British cinema would hardly have existed without its roots in the novel.

REFERENCES AND FURTHER READING

Anderson, L. (1959) "Get out and push,"in T. Maschler (ed.) *Declarations*. London: MacGibbon and Kee.

Aspinall, S. and Murphy, R. (eds.) (1983) *Gainsborough Melodrama: BFI Dossier 18*. London: British Film Institute.

Cardwell, S. (2002) *Adaptation Revisited: Television and the Classic Novel*. Manchester: Manchester University Press.

Cartmell, D. and Whelehan, I. (eds.) (1999) *Adaptations: From Text to Screen, Screen to Text*. London: Routledge.

Caughie, J., with Rockett, K. (1996) *The Companion to British and Irish Cinema*. London: Cassell and the British Film Institute.

Ellis, J. (1982) "The literary adaptation: an introduction," *Screen*, 23/1 (May–June): 3–5.

—— (1996) "The quality film adventure: British critics and the cinema, 1942–1948," in A. Higson (ed.) *Dissolving Views: Key Writings on British Cinema*. London: Cassell.

Falk, Q. (1984) *Travels in Greeneland*. London: Quartet Books.

French, P. (1966–7) "All the better books," *Sight and Sound*, 36/1 (Winter): 38–41.

Higson, A. (1996) "Space, place and spectacle: landscape and townscape in the 'kitchen sink' film," in A. Higson (ed.) *Dissolving Views: Key Writings on British Cinema*. London: Cassell.

—— (2003) "Merchant Ivory Productions," in B. McFarlane, *The Encyclopedia of British Film*. London: Methuen and the British Film Institute.

Klein, M. and Parker, G. (eds.) (1981) *The English Novel and the Movies*. New York: Frederick Ungar.

McFarlane, B. (1986) "A literary cinema? British films and British novels," in C. Barr (ed.) *All Our Yesterdays: 90 Years of British Cinema*. London: British Film Institute.

—— (1996) *Novel to Film: An Introduction to the Theory of Adaptation*. Oxford: Clarendon Press.

—— (2001) "The more things change . . . British cinema in the 90s," in R. Murphy (ed.) *The British Cinema Book*, 2nd edn. London: British Film Institute.

Orr, C. and Nicholson, C. (eds.) (1992) *Cinema and Fiction 1950–1990: New Modes of Adapting*. Edinburgh: Edinburgh University Press.

Pirie, D. (1973) *A Heritage of Horror*. London: Gordon Fraser.

Powell, D. (1948) "Films since 1939," in *Since 1939: Ballet, Films, Music, Painting*. London: Readers Union and British Council.

Reisz, K. (1997) "Karel Reisz," in B. McFarlane, *An Autobiography of British Cinema*. London: Methuen and the British Film Institute.

Richardson, T. (1959) "The man behind an angry young man," in *Films and Filming*, 5/5 (February): 9, 32.

Sinyard, N. (1986) *Filming Literature: The Art of Screen Adaptation*. London: Croom Helm.

14

The English Heritage Industry and Other Trends in the Novel at the Millennium

Peter Childs

Two key publishing changes of the 1990s have impinged on British literary fiction. The first of these embraces the various takeovers and mergers among publishing houses and their parent organizations, which have increasingly resulted in conglomerates who perceive literature as they might any other part of their business: as a source of profit and prestige, generating cultural capital if not always financial capital. The other major, but now familiar, factor is the collapse of the net book agreement, by which booksellers in the UK voluntarily sold books only at prices decided by publishers. Its cessation has meant that today's consumers need only pay the full price for a "reader-friendly" novel if they choose to, and may benefit by a 50 percent discount from a promotional offer, even on some literary fiction such as those works on the Booker Prize short list. The number of works of fiction published each year doubled between 1950 and 1990, such that well over one hundred new novels have been published each week during the last decade of the century. Around 130 of them are submitted for the Booker Prize each year.

The 1990s have been considered from one perspective as the decade of book prizes, promotional tours, and literature festivals. These years also saw a marked growth in genre fiction. For example, popular sci-fi novelists (such as Brian Aldiss, Michael Moorcock, and J. G. Ballard) and disparate fantasy writers (such as Iain Banks, Douglas Adams, Clive Barker, Neil Gaiman, and Terry Pratchett) continued to push their genres into new realms of philosophical and psychological extremity, while retaining undercurrents of social comment. Several of them also gained cult status alongside the growth of SF, fantasy and horror movies, games, and television series – products of the mainstream mass-consumer culture that was widely and wrongly anticipated to bring about the commercial failure of the novel. Instead literary fiction has adjusted once more to the new science, giving rise to diverse texts which attempt to come to terms with current theories and technologies, from

Jeanette Winterson's *The PowerBook* (2000), which employs cyberspace to explore gender roles and identities, to Bo Fowler's *Scepticism Inc.* (1998), in which a microchip of consciousness is implanted, including a belief in God, into a supermarket trolley.

Literary fiction at the turn of the millennium is also experiencing a boom, in quantity if not necessarily quality, fuelled by reading groups, media interest in celebrity authors, creative writing courses, television and newspaper "best of" lists, as well as the new marketing and promotional industry that now surrounds high-profile novels. Writing about the novel at the millennium, one of the instigators of university creative writing courses, Malcolm Bradbury noted:

> Fiction is in fact in a state of plenitude, its stories coming from many directions. Certain themes have become routine diet: apocalyptic cities, gender wars, gay and lesbian relations, marital collapse, feminist self-discovery, football fever, serial killers, child abuse, New Age consciousness, laddish girls and girlish lads. (Bradbury 2001: 539)

In this chapter, with an emphasis on the most recent trends, I will discuss four broad categories that allow a review of new fiction from the 1980s onwards.

Heritage

In Julian Barnes's *England, England* (1998) a powerful business magnate develops the Isle of Wight into a colossal theme park, so that tourists will not have to traipse from Dover to London to Stratford-on-Avon to Chester to sample olde England. In Barnes's novel the small island off the south coast becomes "England, England," importing all the main cultural-commercial aspects of the mainland, which is itself transformed into "Anglia," a backward nation that gradually regresses into its own past, finally becoming a rural country dominated by Celtic culture and pagan ceremonies. Though Barnes's novel was published at the end of the century it parodied a nostalgic repackaging of the history of post-imperial England that had been happening for twenty years. In literature, the most commented-upon aspect of this trend was "Raj revivalism." Important books set in India won the Booker prize in 1973 (J. G. Farrell's *The Siege of Krishnapur*), 1975 (Ruth Prawer Jhabvala'a *Heat and Dust*), 1977 (Paul Scott's *Staying On*), and 1981 (Salman Rushdie's *Midnight's Children*), but were followed by more prominent and more nostalgic television and film adaptations that generated further cultural interest in Anglo-India, including *The Jewel in the Crown*, *The Far Pavilions*, and *A Passage to India*. These texts can be seen from one perspective as precursors to the welter of prominent postcolonial novels on India and Indians in Britain that have figured on prize short lists more recently, from Vikram Seth's *A Suitable Boy* (1993) through Arundhati Roy's *The God of Small Things* (1997), to Monica Ali's *Brick Lane* (2003).

The contemporary meaning of the word "heritage" came to the fore in the 1980s to describe a drive towards reappropriating the past in the cause of national pride across both culture and politics. As Andrew Higson points out, this new meaning differs from the dictionary definition in which heritage is deemed to be "received or inherited" (Higson 2003: 50). Indeed "heritage" is now no longer that which is handed down from the past to the present, but that which is superimposed on to the past by a present generation. National heritage acts in 1980 and 1983 gave a new philosophy to the work of archivists, filmmakers, politicians, and also novelists interested in not just preserving or restoring aspects and images of the past but reorienting their (re)production and consumption. English Heritage was established to maintain nationally important buildings and monuments while the Heritage Educational Trust was set up in 1982 to encourage the exploitation of their social and educational value. Film was the most obvious medium in which the new heritage movement reached the national consciousness, but it did so through the adaptation of culturally significant narratives from national history and classic fiction, especially Austen, the Brontës, James, Forster, and Hardy. The director/producer team most associated with heritage films are James Ivory and Ismail Merchant, who adapted Forster's *A Room With A View* (1986), *Maurice* (1987), *Howards End* (1992), and Ishiguro's *The Remains of The Day* (1993). To this can be added Hugh Hudson's *Chariots of Fire* (1981), whose enormous success was one of the catalysts for the genre, Charles Sturridge's films of Forster's *Where Angels Fear to Tread* (1991) and Waugh's *A Handful of Dust* (1987), and even the adaptations of Woolf in Marleen Gorris's *Mrs Dalloway* (1997) and Sally Potter's *Orlando* (1992). For some critics the films offer liberal critiques of class and gender stereotypes, but for most they accentuate a golden, frequently Edwardian past and evince a profound nostalgia for a bygone imperial England, tapping into a Thatcherite agenda that advocated the sharp return to hierarchical Victorian/ Edwardian values and a reverse of the radical social changes associated with the 1960s and 1970s.

Sturridge also directed *Brideshead Revisited* (1981), which is the first prominent television example of the genre, and as a novel is itself a self-conscious literary exercise in nostalgia, just as *The French Lieutenant's Woman*, filmed in the same year and with the same star, Jeremy Irons, became in John Fowles's original text the template for British postmodern historiographical metafiction. One writer who made the historical turn twenty years after Fowles's novel appeared is A. S. Byatt, whose work is particularly associated with the reinscription of Victorian Britain in works such as *Possession* (1990), *Angels and Insects* (1992), and *The Biographer's Tale* (1999). However, unlike many writers, Byatt is also concerned with a dialogue between experimentalism and the traditions of realism behind contemporary fiction. She writes in one of her essays:

> I believe that postmodern writers are returning to historical fiction because the idea of writing the Self is felt to be worked out.... We like historical persons because they are unknowable, only partly available to the imagination, and we find this occluded quality attractive. (Byatt 2001: 31)

Byatt is referring to authors writing in a fabulist European tradition, such as Lawrence Norfolk, Penelope Fitzgerald, Peter Ackroyd, and Tibor Fischer, but her comments about a return to history apply to a wide range of literary production in the period. She notes that in the 1950s the historical novel was frowned on as "escapist" or pigeon-holed as "pastoral," but that it has proved more durable than the majority of "urgent fictive confrontations of immediate contemporary reality" despite the more recent tags of "nostalgic" and "costume drama" (2001: 9). Byatt notes that this renaissance is at least coincident with, if not in part due to, the reconsideration of history's relation to narrative by historians themselves, from Hayden White to Simon Schama, and also the imaginative, inventive and speculative approach to literary biography in such works as Peter Ackroyd's *Dickens* (1990) and D. J. Taylor's *Thackeray* (1999).

It is often felt that an unprecedented number of writers turned to history in the late 1980s and 1990s; even the work of the most well-known chronicler of the contemporary, Martin Amis, returned to the past in his 1991 book *Time's Arrow; Or, The Nature of the Offence,* which reversed causation as well as its narrative from the present back to the holocaust. Like A. S. Byatt in *Possession* (1990), Graham Swift interleaved a modern story with a Victorian back-history in *Ever After* (1992), building on his more successful weaving of personal, local, natural, and political history in *Waterland* (1983). Angela Carter's baroque *Nights at The Circus* (1984) is an exploration of ideas about gender and sexuality set in London, St Petersburg and Siberia at the end of the nineteenth century, while Beryl Bainbridge's *Master Georgie* (1998) concentrates on the Crimean War. Peter Ackroyd has mined London's history in works such as the Victorian psycho-thriller *Dan Leno and the Limehouse Golem* (1994), and Sarah Waters's reputation has been built on ludic post-realist takes on Victorian Britain in *Tipping the Velvet* (1998) and *Fingersmith* (2002). Carter's final novel, *Wise Children* (1991), is a review of the twentieth century, recounting the adventures of two "stage girls" born on New Year's Day, 1900, as is Liza Jarrett Wright, the heroine of Pat Barker's *The Century's Daughter* (1986) (later republished as *Liza's England*).

The First World War and its aftermath was a major reference point as the century turned, revisited in a range of novels, from Barker's *Regeneration* trilogy (1991–5), initially built around the real-life meeting at Craiglockhart of the psychiatrist W. H. R. Rivers with Siegfried Sassoon and Wilfred Owen, through Sebastian Faulks's popular story about the Western Front, *Birdsong* (1993), to Adam Thorpe's *Nineteen Twenty-One* (2001).

The interwar years and the Second World War formed the backdrop to Ian McEwan's first novel mostly set before his own birth, *Atonement* (2001), and also to Kazuo Ishiguro's *When We Were Orphans* (2000), as well as Louis de Bernières' *Captain Corelli's Mandolin* (1995), Faulks's *Charlotte Gray* (1998), and Rachel Seiffert's *The Dark Room* (2001). Older historical moments were the subject of Jim Crace's story of Christ in the wilderness *Quarantine* (1997), Barry Unsworth's *Morality Play* (1995), set in the years following the Black Death, Lawrence Norfolk's *Lemprière's Dictionary* (1991), about an eighteenth-century lexicographer, Penelope Fitzgerald's final novel

The Blue Flower (1995), a fictionalization of the life of Novalis, Mick Jackson's *The Underground Man* (1997), about the agoraphobic fifth duke of Portland, and Rose Tremain's redemptive picaresque *Restoration* (1989), about a selfish and loveless medical student who has to survive his own personal revolution when sent away from the court of Charles II. One explanation of this turn to the past is intimated in a review of McEwan's *Atonement* by John Updike, who suggested that

> Compared with today's easy knowingness and self-protective irony, feelings then had a hearty naïveté, a force developed amid repression and scarcity and linked to a sense of transcendent adventure; novels need this force, and must find it where they can, if only in the annals of the past. (Updike 2002: 82)

A British novelist who herself tried to assess this phenomenon is Jane Rogers, one of the editors of the 2003 British Council *New Writing* volume. Speaking for herself, she has said

> When I was working on *Promised Lands*, and on my previous novel, *Mr Wroe's Virgins* which is set in 19th century Lancashire, I did feel that using historical material was a route into exploring and addressing contemporary ideas, whilst leaving behind the prejudices and knee-jerk responses that I as a writer, and that my readers, might bring to such material if set in the present. (Rogers 1999)

This stance is in some ways a development but in others a considerable shift from the preoccupation with historiography that characterized many prominent novels of the 1980s, from Salman Rushdie's *Midnight's Children* (1981) and Swift's *Waterland* (1983), to Julian Barnes's *Flaubert's Parrot* (1984) and Peter Ackroyd's *Hawksmoor* (1985).

In the 1990s, novelists have also turned more often to a range of different countries, in Europe and beyond. A few of the better received authors and books have been Hilary Mantel's novel of the French Revolution, *A Place of Greater Safety* (1993), Andrew Miller's *Casanova* (1998), Tibor Fischer's *Under the Frog* (1992), about postwar Hungary, and Giles Foden's Boer War novel *Ladysmith* (1999), which followed his study of Idi Amin, *The Last King of Scotland* (1998).

A similar engagement with the past, usually focused on the British Isles or Europe, has been evident in Irish writing. Both before and after the huge success of the Dublin writer Roddy Doyle up to his Booker Prize win in 1993 for *Paddy Clarke Ha Ha Ha*, Irish literature was both strikingly diverse and deeply concerned with questions of history in a number of well-received novels since John Banville's *Kepler* (1981): Bernard McLaverty's *Grace Notes* (1997), Glenn Patterson's *Black Night at Big Thunder Mountain* (1995), Robert McLiam Wilson's *Eureka Street* (1996), Deidre Madden's *Remembering Light and Stone* (1992), and Seamus Deane's *Reading in the Dark* (1996).

Another significant development to note in this section is the vogue since the 1990s for sequels to classic novels such as *Wuthering Heights* (both Jeffrey Caine's *Heathcliff,*

1992 and Lin Haire-Sargeant's *Heathcliff: The Return to Wuthering Heights,* 1992) and *Rebecca* (both Sally Beauman's *Rebecca's Tale,* 2001 and Susan Hill's *Mrs De Winter,* 1998). A postmodern variant on this is Christine Brooke-Rose's *Textermination* (1991), which features a cast of "real" fictional characters, from Emma Woodhouse to Gabriel Farishta, gathered at a literary convention. The experiment found its more populist incarnation in Jasper Fforde's *The Eyre Affair* (2001), about a female detective who rescues characters kidnapped by terrorists from novels.

The vogue for historical novels has not passed with the turning of the millennium, and it is likely to continue until a sharper vision of postcolonial Britain comes into focus, identifying a richer vein of contemporary experience for novelists to explore. There is perhaps a new trend emerging that revisits the more recent past, exemplified in the novels of Jonathan Coe, such as *What a Carve Up!* (1994) and *The Rotters' Club* (2001). In the meantime, British novels all too often shy away from the contemporary and in doing so appear to feel keenly the shadow of American and to a lesser extent European fiction, such that, for some critics at least, there are almost no British writers who engage with the present as persuasively as Don DeLillo or Philip Roth, on the one hand, or Milan Kundera and Michel Houellebecq on the other.

Lad, Chick, and Children's Lit.

From the British media's point of view, the time from 1993 to 2001 was most marked by the emergence of post-Amis "lad lit.," in novels from John King, Nick Hornby, Mike Gayle, Tim Lott, and Tony Parsons, alongside notable media-friendly successes in "chick lit.," including celebrated work by Helen Fielding, Jessica Adams, and Allison Pearson. There has even arisen a hybrid form of the subgenres, epitomized by the several works of the husband-and-wife co-authors Josie Lloyd and Emlyn Rees, who compose such modern romances as *The Boy Next Door* (2001) in alternating male and female first-person narratives.

"Lad lit." ostensibly sought to redefine masculinity, in various forms ranging from violence to sensitivity, in the post-feminist era (Showalter 2002). The genre generated huge sales by appealing to a readership that had found little reflection of itself in fiction before 1990. The archetypal new-lad author was Nick Hornby, whose eminently filmable books of the 1990s (*Fever Pitch,* 1992, *High Fidelity,* 1995, and *About a Boy,* 1997) portrayed solitary "kidult" males alienated from the norms of heterosexual pairing by the pressures and temptations of the media age, which had arrested them in an adolescent world of football, pop music, and gadgetry.

By contrast, "chick lit." appeared to offer the authentic voice of contemporary women in one way or another disillusioned with similar questions to do with marriage and romance that preoccupied Jane Austen's heroines two hundred years earlier – self-consciously foregrounded by Helen Fielding's use of the plot from *Pride and Prejudice* in the seminal work in the genre: *Bridget Jones's Diary* (1996). More serious revaluations of contemporary women's experience appeared from Jackie Kay in

Trumpet (1998), Lesley Glaister in *The Private Parts of Women* (1996), Anna Maxted's *Running in Heels* (2001), and Lucy Ellmann in *Man or Mango?* (1998).

Before post-feminist chick lit, feminist novelists such as Zoë Fairbairns, Minette Walters, Frances Fyfield, and Sarah Dunant had remodeled masculinist genres such as the sci-fi novel, detective fiction, and crime thrillers. Fairbairns also founded the very productive Feminist Writers group with Sara Maitland, Michelene Wandor, and Michèle Roberts, and a number of new women's presses were founded in the 1970s and 1980s after the success of Virago. From the momentum gained by an increasingly militant movement in the 1970s, gay writing came into the limelight in the 1980s with prominent novels from Jeanette Winterson, Maureen Duffy, and Alan Hollinghurst, followed by well-received fiction with gay protagonists by many others, including Oscar Moore, Paul Magrs, Patrick Gale, Sarah Waters, Jamie O'Neill, and Jackie Kay. Gender criticism, body politics, queer theory, and media interest in (usually food-related) "hysterical illnesses" all led to increased emphasis on sexuality and identity, though by the millennium "gay writing" was increasingly a part of the mainstream.

To an extent it could be said that some of the popularity of traditional "literary" fiction (generally but not exclusively, this means work by authors whose novels are not discussed in terms of genre) was lost to works of authors such as Hornby and Fielding, which appealed to a new market and sold in record shops or supermarkets, while the novel as a genre also appeared to be losing a little of its popularity alongside history, science, or (auto)biography. An alternative way of stating this is to say that differences between literary and genre fiction started to erode towards the end of the last century at the same time as distinctions between fiction and history or life-writing were questioned from both sides. It is therefore all the more interesting that early twenty-first century criticism of the vibrancy of contemporary British fiction coincided with a promotion of history, especially via the television programs of "media dons" such as Simon Schama and David Starkey, as though literature and history were not only disconnected but also opposed: a startling impression after the call "to historicize" became the rallying-cry of university literature departments in the 1990s. Yet, for many people, science and history have stolen some of the narrative power traditionally associated with fiction.

Lastly, the largest book-marketing phenomenon at the millennium has been the remarkable success in the late 1990s in children's literature of J. K. Rowling's *Harry Potter* novels, alongside the more literary works of Philip Pullman, especially the *His Dark Materials* trilogy. With success that has matched that of favourite children's authors such as Roald Dahl and Jacqueline Wilson, both series have been read nearly as avidly by adults. Rowling's novels appear in two formats, identical except for covers aimed at the different age markets. Consequently, the trade magazine *Booklist* now has a category, Crossovers, for titles that appeal to both children and adults. Alongside the widely-praised Melvin Burgess, another children's author who passed into the adult mainstream in 2003 was Mark Haddon, whose *The Curious Incident of the Dog in the Night-Time* utilizes a barrage of diagrams, fonts, pictures, and mathematical puzzles to filter its narrative through the mind of a 15-year-old with Asperger's. Though it narrowly failed to make the Booker Prize shortlist, Haddon's novel was a favorite of the chair of judges, John Carey, and went on to win the Whitbread Prize.

Nonfiction and the Confessional

Asperger's, a form of autism, is also invoked by Pat Barker in her 2003 novel *Double Vision*. One character explains it to another:

> It's basically a sort of difficulty in seeing people as people. . . . So you can't change your perspective and see the situation from another's point of view, because you can't grasp the fact that they have their own internal life, and they might be thinking something different from you. (2003: 83–4)

In the wake of the 9/11 terrorist attack on the World Trade Center in New York in 2001, this is a metaphor for Barker's view that to injure others intentionally is effectively to deny that they possess the same internal life. Barker thus finds herself in accord with the points of view put across by other British authors in September 2001. It is notable that the events of September 11, 2001 were, for many people, most affectingly considered in the UK by novelists. The broadsheets turned to writers such as Martin Amis and Salman Rushdie to best express what many others were feeling. Of these articles, two of the most praised were written by Ian McEwan for *The Guardian* on September 12 and 15. McEwan argued for a sensibility similar to that advocated by Barker and spoke up for the qualities of compassion and empathy that have often been at the heart of the ethical vision promoted by the novel:

> we remember what we have seen, and we daydream helplessly. Lately, most of us have inhabited the space between the terrible actuality and these daydreams. Waking before dawn, going about our business during the day, we fantasize ourselves into the events. What if it was me? . . . This is the nature of empathy, to think oneself into the minds of others. These are the mechanics of compassion. . . . It is hard to be cruel once you permit yourself to enter the mind of your victim. Imagining what it is like to be someone other than yourself is at the core of our humanity. It is the essence of compassion. . . . The hijackers used fanatical certainty . . . to purge themselves of the human instinct for empathy.

Also writing in *The Guardian*, on September 18, Martin Amis echoed McEwan's view: "Our best destiny, as planetary cohabitants, is the development of what has been called 'species consciousness' – something over and above nationalisms, blocs, religions, ethnicities."

Like Pat Barker and a growing number of British writers, Amis himself has attempted to fashion a post-9/11 novel, *Yellow Dog* (2003), yet his formal project as a novelist is aimed at illustrating the predicament in which the novelist at the millennium is caught:

> realism and experimentation have come and gone without seeming to point a way ahead. The contemporary writer, therefore, must combine these veins, calling on the strengths of the Victorian novel together with the alienations of post-modernism. (2002: 78–9)

If, for Amis, the novelist is still at a crossroads where realism and experimentalism meet, in more general terms the place at which modern British fiction has arrived might be described in terms of a number of tendencies or cultural dominants. For example, the majority of novels published in the twenty-first century are likely to be written in the first person. Belief in the appropriateness of the omniscient narrator declined over the last century and many novelists, such as Kazuo Ishiguro for example, prefer to use one consciousness or narrator and not to write in the third person: a way of rendering the world that they might see as antithetical to everyday experience. The critique of realism from this angle has perhaps been most vociferously fought by the experimental novelist B. S. Johnson, who advocated that to avoid being totally eclipsed by film, the novel had to concentrate on its ability to render individual consciousness (Johnson 1990). Johnson therefore is placed in a different camp from Byatt, who feels that the novel has little more to say on the subject of the Self, as noted above, though there is perhaps a middle ground.

This can best be considered in terms of an increase in "life-writing." The first-person narrator has very commonly been an individual in many ways similar to the author. Such books use the autobiographical mode and are written in a meditative, confessional style, while their authors often seek neither to equate the narrator with themselves nor to pretend that the narrator is simply a fictional character. Books in this mode range from Martin Amis's literary "autobiography" *Experience* (2000), to semi-autobiographical novels such as V. S. Naipaul's *The Enigma of Arrival* (1987).

In many instances, contemporary fiction over the last half of the twentieth century has also eschewed the novel's traditional attempt to render depth, preferring to tell a story which, instead of attempting to offer metaphysical truth, philosophical meaning, or moral belief, depicts myriad aspects of the modern world refracted through the life experience of individuals. With works such as *The Enigma of Arrival* in mind, the Nobel citation for Naipaul referred to his invention of a new kind of writing: one that collapses boundaries between the novel and life-writing. He himself has argued that the traditional novel is moribund. His tribute on winning the Nobel Prize in *The Times*, written by the editor of *The New Statesman*, Jason Cowley, glossed this as follows:

> he means the novel as practised by most professional novelists as a preformed mould of plot, character and event into which one pours his or her cheap slurry of words. Naipaul's own novels are novel in the true sense of the word: new, mould-breaking,

experimental, a hybrid of autobiography, social inquiry, reportage and invention. (Cowley 2001: 15)

Yet it is perhaps Naipaul's postcolonial perspective over fifty years that has injected something new into the British novel. His books, alongside works by many other non-English writers, have introduced into the mainstream of fiction a new emphasis on questions of ethnicity, nationalism, and the politics of identity and belonging. These questions, alongside ones of gender and sexuality, history and apocalypse, science and the New Physics, have multiplied both the form and the content of the literary novel, transforming its production and reception since the discussion of the "literature of exhaustion" in the 1960s and 1970s. Those pronouncements on the death of the novel proved to be revealingly premature because they marked an end, not to fiction, but to the model of the English novel with which critics were working. Since the 1980s, fiction has had a remarkable resurgence, though its cultural centrality, seemingly self-evident mid-twentieth century, has come into question. The much-vaunted "crisis" in the novel in the 1970s has resulted not in ossification but in rejuvenation, much of it achieved by individuals born outside of Britain, as will be discussed in the next section.

One of the most notable successes of the 1990s was Dava Sobel's *Longitude* (1999), the story as much as the history of the clockmaker John Harrison. Other novels, such as Poet Laureate Andrew Motion's *Wainwright the Poisoner* (2000), turned real life into fiction. Many books used the real life of the author or others to tell their stories: Blake Morrison's *And When did you Last See your Father* (1992), Iain Sinclair's *Downriver* (1991), and John Banville's *The Untouchable* (1997) (based on Anthony Blunt and the Cambridge spies), or the novels of the journalist Gordon Burn, who has fictionalized the life of *Alma Cogan* (and Myra Hindley, 1991) but has also written factual accounts informed by fictional techniques in his story of Fred and Rosemary West in *Happy Like Murderers* (1998), and of the Yorkshire Ripper, Peter Sutcliffe, in *Somebody's Husband, Somebody's Son* (1984).

The increase in factual-fictional life-writing since the early 1990s has been paralleled by a rise in the autobiographical-confessional novel. In Hanif Kureishi's *Intimacy* (1998) the narrator Jay watches his family move about their business while he reviews in his mind the fact that he is about to leave them. Jay's partner Susan is seen by him as a hard and charmless woman but in the narrative she appears quite differently, and *Intimacy*, though most often read as a simple confessional, teases away repeatedly at the separation between perception and reality, the complexity of human emotions, and the tensions created by alternative impressions. It is a study in simultaneous bad faith and authenticity, about the contradictions, paradoxes and (self-)delusions involved in trying to be true to oneself but not to others. A concern to challenge the social constructions of gendered identity underpins another prominent example of the confessional novel, Jeanette Winterson's *Written on the Body* (1992), which explores connections between autobiography and fiction as well as between the material existence of the other and the writing of the self. The book is in essence the story

of the obsession that the narrator, whose sex is unknown, has for Louise, who is
married to a doctor called Elgin. When Louise develops cancer, a kind of appropriation of the body that threatens to overtake the narrator's desire, it is only Elgin who
can treat her. The narrator's response to this putative double-loss, of Louise to cancer
and to Elgin, is to explore Louise's body in and through writing: to anatomize love
and to celebrate its beauties. "Written on the body is a secret code ... so heavily
worked that the letters feel like braille. ... I didn't know that Louise would have
reading hands. She has translated me into her own book" (Winterson 1992: 89).
Also questioning generic as well as gender boundaries, Winterson's *Art & Lies: A Piece
for Three Voices and a Bawd* (1994) has the refrain "There's no such thing as autobiography, there's only art and lies."

New and Postcolonial Novelists

The first literary movement of the new millennium was known as the "new puritanism"; it published a self-promoting ten-point manifesto and short-story collection
from fifteen young writers: *All Hail the New Puritans* (2000) edited by Nicholas
Blincoe and Matt Thorne. After the fashion of the Danish *Dogme* school of filmmakers,
the writers pledged themselves to the core ingredients of plot and narrative, clarity
and moral purpose, over the experimental excesses of the modernist and postmodernist writers who had respectively sought to explore the qualities of consciousness
and the possibilities of metafictional technique. The adherents included Bo Fowler,
Alex Garland, Geoff Dyer, Candida Clark, and Scarlett Thomas.

Of more importance for signalling possible names of the future was the 2003
Granta list of "best young novelists." The list prominently features several rising
writers, such as Zadie Smith, David Mitchell, and Sarah Waters, but has generally
been considered inferior to the two previous lists of 1983 and 1993. However, this
perception is at least in part due to the fact that there is now a plethora of young
talent, whereas when Amis and McEwan broke through in the 1970s, they were
singled out for attention almost by default, as McEwan has acknowledged. The
novelists on the 2003 list were Monica Ali, Nicola Barker, Rachel Cusk, Susan
Elderkin, Peter Ho Davies, Philip Hensher, A. L. Kennedy, Hari Kunzru, Toby
Litt, David Mitchell, Andrew O'Hagan, David Peace, Dan Rhodes, Ben Rice, Rachel
Seiffert, Zadie Smith, Adam Thirlwell, Alan Warner, Sarah Waters, and Robert
McLiam Wilson. The most famous name of the list is that of the then 24-year-old
Zadie Smith: the first British literary celebrity of the twenty-first century. Her debut
novel *White Teeth* (2000) was met with a barrage of publicity. Her writing has been
compared to that of many writers, but most regularly to the novels of Salman Rushdie
and Hanif Kureishi. *White Teeth* is similar in its use of repetitions, digression,
and hyphenated constructions to Rushdie's work, but is closer to Kureishi's in its
extensive use of social satire rather than methods that could be likened to those of
magic realism. Against social and genetic engineering of any kind, the novel is

a snapshot of postcolonial London from the 1970s to the millennium, and satirizes a simple view of race relations moving from a tense past to a future perfect "happy multicultural land." Similar critical praise if less commercial success greeted Hari Kunzru's *The Impressionist* (2002). Kunzru, son of a Kashmiri father and an English mother, went on to cause controversy when, after winning the Betty Trask and Somerset Maugham awards for his first novel, he rejected the award of the 2003 John Llewellyn Rhys prize, the second oldest literary award in Britain, on the grounds that its sponsors, the *Daily Mail*, had a hostile editorial policy towards non-white Britons and asylum-seekers.

In terms of racial politics, there was a noticeable shift in the 1990s to a concern with reclaimed histories, the "black Atlantic," and ethnic and religious differences. While powerfully explored by writers such as David Dabydeen and Caryl Phillips, some of this was also recognized in white writers, notably in Barry Unsworth's Booker Prize-winning novel *Sacred Hunger* (1992): an affecting condemnation of the eighteenth-century slave trade that exemplified the gradual shift from novels with an element of "Raj nostaligia," as Rushdie had seen it, to a more overt concern with the legacy of colonialism.

Indeed, the fiction of the 1990s can be characterized overall in terms of cultural diversity and postcolonial themes such as decolonization and diaspora. For example, Indian fiction concerned with migrant identity and colonial relationships has revealed some of the most exciting writers of the last decade or so of the century: Amitav Ghosh (e.g. *The Shadow Lines*, 1988), Shashi Tharoor (*The Great Indian Novel*, 1989), Bapsi Sidhwa (*The Ice-Candy Man*, 1992), Sunetra Gupta (*The Glassblower's Breath*, 1993), Vikram Seth (*A Suitable Boy*, 1993), Amit Chaudhuri (*Afternoon Raag*, 1993), Vikram Chandra (*Red Earth and Pouring Rain*, 1995), Arundhati Roy (*The God of Small Things*, 1997), Rohinton Mistry (*A Fine Balance*, 2001), and Monica Ali (*Brick Lane*, 2003). In parallel with the emergence of these authors, many of whom either do live or have lived in Britain, has developed a strong range of British writers with roots in the Caribbean or Africa, including Caryl Phillips (e.g. *Cambridge*, 1992), Fred D'Aguiar (*Feeding the Ghosts*, 1998), Ben Okri (*The Famished* Road, 1990), Bernadine Evaristo (*The Emperor's Babe*, 2001), Joan Riley (*The Unbelonging*, 1995), Buchi Emecheta (*Joys of Motherhood*, 1979), Courttia Newland (*Society Within*, 1999) Abdulrazak Gurnah (*Paradise,* 1994), and Diran Adebayo (*My Once Upon a Time*, 2000).

The late 1990s in particular has seen a noticeable shift in dominance from writing that has looked at Britain from the point of view of the migrant's experience to fiction that has opened up new black British urban perspectives, in for example the work of Newland and Adebayo. Alongside these are also the excellent writers whose work is informed by other national traditions like the Sri Lankan-born Romesh Gunesekera, the British-Chinese Timothy Mo and the British-Japanese Kazuo Ishiguro. One of the most celebrated writers at the millennium had been resident in Britain for thirty years at his death in 2001, but wrote in German: W. G. Sebald, whose four "novels," including *Austerlitz* and *Vertigo*, have been widely praised as among the best published in Europe since the early 1980s. Sebald worked very closely with his

English translators Michael Hulse and Anthea Bell on his prose works, which are part-fiction, part-memoir, part travelogue. He is one of those, like Naipaul, for whom the traditional novel, with its emphasis on personal relationships and its clumsy narrative devices, has become an outmoded form.

Postcolonial British writers have been among those authors who have most vividly retold the past. The Guyanese poet David Dabydeen's *A Harlot's Progress* (1999) focuses on the slave Mungo while reinventing William Hogarth's famous series of 1732, which tells the story of a whore, a merchant, a magistrate and a doctor, bonded by avarice and lust. In the earlier *Disappearance* (1993) Dabydeen charts the brief relationship between a young Guyanese engineer and the old woman he lodges with while building sea defences for a cliff-top village near Hastings. Reminding the reader of Shelley's "Ozymandias," the novel uses the poetic metaphors of making and building to reconsider the memory of the transient empire alongside the erosive powers of time and nature.

Scottish literature has also enjoyed a renaissance since its traditions were rejuvenated by the publication of Alasdair Gray's *Lanark* (1984). It was given a shot in the arm by the success of Irvine Welsh's 1993 debut *Trainspotting*, while the following year James Kelman became the first Scottish novelist to win the Booker Prize with *How Late It Was, How Late*. Following the lead of Muriel Spark, Gray, and Kelman, Welsh is now one of the established names of the Scottish new wave, alongside such writers as the poet John Burnside, Janice Galloway, Jeff Torrington, Andrew O'Hagan, Andrew Greig, Iain Banks, Alan Warner, and A. L. Kennedy. *Trainspotting* marked an important literary shift for the British novel because it was a new best-seller that was distinctly Scottish as well as distinctly working-class; it dealt with a subject and with an underclass that both society and fiction had largely chosen to ignore, in a demotic language and a dialect it had also largely chosen to ignore.

Contemporary Welsh literature has had less prominence, but modern Welsh fiction has continued to explore the collapse of the traditional foundation of the country, especially the mining industry, for example in Gwyn Jones's *Times Like These* (1979) and Gwyn Thomas's *Sorrow for My Sons* (1986). A major talent has emerged in the 1990s with the first novels published by Swansea-born Russell Celyn Jones (e.g. *The Eros Hunter*, 1998), while other notable Welsh prize-winners of this period are Niall Griffiths (*Sheepshagger*, 2001), John Evans (*Giants*, 2000), and Stephen Knight (*Mr Schnitzel*, 2001).

Two final trends can be noted here, both of which apply to Knight, an established poet and now an experimental prose-writer, in that *Mr Schnitzel* is composed of seven cleverly interwoven fairy stories with a parallel commentary. The first trend to note is the significant increase in poets turning to the novel; and so, for example, the post-1990 years have seen fiction appearing from John Burnside, Simon Armitage, Fred D'Aguiar, E. A. Markham, David Dabydeen, and Lavinia Greenlaw. A second trend is the continued use into the twenty-first century of experimentation among younger writers, though many of them have adopted more accessible forms than the writers of earlier generations: Jonathan Tulloch's use of Geordie dialect in *The Bonny Lad* (2001),

Ali Smith's haunting multiple narration in *Hotel World* (2001), Will Self's posthumous narrator of *How the Dead Live* (2000), Dan Rhodes's sudden-fiction vignettes in *Anthropology: and a Hundred Other Stories* (2000), David Mitchell's cyber novel *Number9dream* (2001), and Jim Crace's culinary, sensual, sixty-part *The Devil's Larder* (2001), reminiscent of one of the best debut-novels of the 1990s: John Lanchester's *The Debt to Pleasure* (1996).

Conclusion

David Lodge in the prefatory essay to his collection entitled *The Practice of Writing* considers pluralism to be the foremost characteristic of contemporary fiction by the 1990s. He says: "The astonishing variety of styles on offer today, as if in an aesthetic supermarket, includes traditional as well as innovative styles, minimalism as well as excess, nostalgia as well as prophecy" (Lodge 1996: 11). Without a dominant literary mode or any consensus about aesthetic value, as Lodge believes there was in the 1930s or 1950s, some other value system may take over. He argues therefore that "given the nature of our society it is not surprising that a somewhat materialistic notion of success, as measured by sales, advances, prizes, media celebrity etc., has filled the vacuum" (p. 11). Lodge thinks that commercial success has supplanted the fashions of literary judgment. In revising his essay, first written in 1991, for publication in *The Practice of Writing* in 1996, Lodge considers the economic recession earlier in the decade. He sees publishing houses streamlining their lists as well as their staff, reviews dedicated to hyped rather than innovative fiction, and the mass-marketing of competent writers alongside the downward spiral of sales of less accessible novels. Lodge observes that today "novelists with a reputation do not send off a manuscript for publication but enter into negotiations between agent and publisher, with the prestigious novel itself possibly even going up for auction" (1996: 14). He decries the "contamination of literary values by considerations of fame and money," observing that the majority of novelists are embarking on a career as much as if not more than a vocation (Fay Weldon's *The Bulgari Connection* (2001) was the first novel to be sponsored). In an expression which itself fixes Lodge's essay in our time, he remarks that a major repercussion of this situation is that the modern novel, even an experimental one, will be "reader-friendly."

A consequence of this is that the traditional distinction between popular and serious literary fiction will continue to fall away. The democratic impulse of the novel may thus hold sway once more as the less accessible experiments of modernism fade further into the past. However, fiction continues to operate as a radical cultural force, especially in the novels that are written from Scotland, Wales, Ireland, or by that diverse range of writers inadequately described as black British. Tibor Fischer and Lawrence Norfolk, joint editors of the 1999 *New Writing* volume published by the British Council, reveal another side to this. They note a general reduction in stories set in England, adding:

Britain has become more of a launch pad than terrain in its own right, because its writers have actively chosen to seek out new challenges; a sign of writerly confidence. In turn, the diversity of what they have surveyed and logged speaks well of this country as a cultural entrepot, a place of flux and reflux, differently but intricately connected to both Europe and the US, historically and more problematically to the Indian subcontinent and to Africa. Plenty of grist still passes through this mill called Britain. (quoted in Rogers 1999)

Amid this diversity, there are still occasional pronouncements of the death of the British novel as the primary imaginative means of debating and disseminating ideas in society. These may sometimes seem to hold some credence because they do not engage with authors that largely go unnoticed by the mainstream. Since the 1980s British fiction has been in robust health and continues to produce strong work from prominent writers such as McEwan and Ishiguro, but also excellent writing closer to the margins, which is perhaps the principal place from which socially important novels have always been written.

REFERENCES AND FURTHER READING

Amis, Martin (2002) *The War Against Cliché*. London: Vintage.

Barker, Pat (2003) *Double Vision*. London: Fontana.

Bradbury, Malcolm (ed.) (1990) *The Novel Today*, 2nd edn. London: Fontana.

——(2001) *The Modern British Novel*, rev. edn. Harmondsworth: Penguin.

Brannigan, John (2003) *Orwell to the Present: Literature in England 1945–2000*. London: Palgrave.

Byatt, A. S. (2001) *On Histories and Stories: Selected Essays*. London: Vintage.

Connor, Steven (1996) *The English Novel in History 1950–95*. London: Routledge.

Corner, John and Hardy, Sylvia (eds.) (1991) *Enterprise and Heritage: Crosscurrents of National Culture*. London: Routledge.

Cowley, Jason (2001) "V. S. Naipaul," *The Times*, October 12.

Head, Dominic (2002) *The Cambridge Introduction to Modern British Fiction, 1950–2000*. Cambridge: Cambridge University Press.

Higson, Andrew (2003) *English Heritage, English Cinema: Costume Drama Since 1980*. Oxford: Oxford University Press.

Johnson, B. S. (1990) "Introduction to *Aren't You Rather Young to be Writing Your Memoirs?*," in Malcolm Bradbury (ed.) *The Novel Today*, 2nd edn. London: Fontana.

Lane, Richard J., Mengham, Rod, and Tew, Philip (eds.) (2003) *Contemporary British Fiction*. Cambridge: Polity.

Lodge, David (1996) *The Practice of Writing*. Harmondsworth: Penguin.

Luckhurst, Roger and Marks, Peter (eds.) (1999) *Literature and the Contemporary: Fictions and Theories of the Present*. Harlow: Longman.

Mengham, Rod (ed.) (1999) *An Introduction to Contemporary Fiction*. Cambridge: Polity.

Morrison, Jago (2003) *Contemporary Fiction*. London: Routledge.

Rogers, Jane (1999) "Contemporary British literature," Moscow: British Council. <http://www.britishcouncil.ru/britlit/rogetalk.htm>

Showalter, Elaine (2002) "Lad lit.," in Zachary Leader (ed.) *On Modern British Fiction*. Oxford: Oxford University Press.

Taylor, D. J. (1993) *After the War: The Novel and England Since 1945*. London: Chatto and Windus.

Todd, Richard (1996) *Consuming Fictions: The Booker Prize in Britain Today*. London: Bloomsbury.

Updike, John (2002) "Flesh on Flesh," *The New Yorker*, May 13: 80–2.

Waugh, Patricia (1995) *Harvest of the Sixties*. Oxford: Opus.

Winterson, Jeanette (1992) *Written on the Body*. London: Jonathan Cape.

PART II
Reading Individual Texts and Authors

15

Samuel Beckett's *Watt*

S. E. Gontarski and Chris Ackerley

Samuel Beckett's third but second-published novel, *Watt*, gives the appearance of an incomplete, unfinished project, which, in a sense, it is – or perhaps has to be. One need only thumb through its pages to notice gaps in the text and what look to be omissions, absences, authorial queries, or compositional notes, all of which suggest that the work was stopped (temporarily or permanently) rather than completed. The 37-item "Addenda" with which the novel "ends" (if that is the word) seems to confirm that suspicion as a footnote informs readers that "Only fatigue and disgust prevent its incorporation" into the body of the text. Despite such authoritative (if not authorial) subversion, these unincorporated fragments remain crucial to the narrative, extending it, often backwards and thus bridging many an archeological gap in the novel, even as such entries emphasize the irremediable persistence of gaps. Such textual anomalies and the signals of incompletion that characterize this text emphasize its openness, its inability to achieve closure either in rational thought or its textual transmission. They suggest irresolution and negation, textual and thematic, and so anticipate the epistemological crisis that characterizes Beckett's postwar French fiction, particularly *Molloy, Malone Dies*, and *The Unnamable*, and the drama. *Watt* thus remains enthymematic; it is about those lacunae, and so it anticipates a body of work that will help define the postwar literary era and receive the validation of the Nobel Prize committee in 1969. Hidden among the disparaged "Addenda" is an emblematic poem that Beckett published separately as "Tailpiece" to conclude (if that is the word) the 1984 *Collected Poems, 1930–1978*. The short poem raises the conundrum of enclosing "nothingness in words."

While the poem's tone and parallel interrogatories seem decidedly inconclusive, the rhetorical questions evasive, suggesting the epistemological uncertainties of postmodernism, its metaphysical enigmas emerge from biblical mysteries. In a manuscript notebook for the novel Beckett identified their source as Isaiah 40: 12, "Who hath measured the waters in the hollow of his hand, and meted out heaven with a span, and comprehended the dust of the earth in a measure, and weighed the mountains in scales, and the hills in a balance?" Words like "meted" and "span" echo the King James rhetoric, and the last two lines of the poem become an afterimage of Isaiah 40: 17: "All nations before him are as nothing, and they are counted to him less than nothing, and vanity." In Isaiah the interrogatories imply yet another interrogatory: Who can claim to have God's perspective? Thus conclusions about the nature of existence from a limited number of examples (or accidents), the amount of water one can contain in the hollow of one's hand, say, are mere vanity and so nothing. These philosophical and theological problems are glossed shortly thereafter: "limits of part's equality with whole."

Watt was written, Beckett told various critics, to occupy himself through the ennui of his World War II exile in the south of France. He later disparaged it as "just an exercise" or an "unsatisfactory book," a paradigm of waiting he would later exploit more thoroughly in his most famous play, but he also told friend and literary agent George Reavey just after the war (but before the novel's completion), "it has its place in the series, as will perhaps appear in time" (May 14, 1947). It was begun in Paris, written mostly in Roussillon in the south of France, and completed on Beckett's return to Paris in 1948. Beckett had the usual difficulties with publication. Routledge rejected it, unable to feel "the same whole-hearted enthusiasm" they had for his first published novel, *Murphy* (1938), their enthusiasm shaken by its lack of sales. Nothing happened until after the success of *Waiting for Godot* (1953) when American Richard Seaver of the Paris-based literary magazine *Merlin* wrote to Beckett requesting a text of some kind and was given the manuscript of *Watt*. Subsequently, an excerpt was published in *Merlin* and a contract made with Maurice Girodias of Olympia Press, who advertised it on a publicity leaflet with works by the Marquis de Sade and Henry Miller.

The novel was published by Olympia Press (Collections Merlin) on August 31, 1953 in a small edition of 1,125 copies. Beckett abhorred its magenta cover and despaired at its typographical errors. In 1953 Beckett also found an American publisher willing to publish the whole of his output, and the first American edition (errors and all) appeared from Grove Press in 1959. It was distributed in the UK by publisher John Calder, whose own edition would finally appear in 1963 as a Calder Jupiter Book. The original edition, uncorrected, was reprinted by Olympia in 1958 in The Traveller's Companion series, and an extract printed in *The Olympia Reader* (Grove Press, 1965: 213—20).

If "Watt" is the ultimate question, then "Knott" is the only possible answer. The novel is a metaphysical quest, or parody thereof, whereby Watt, applying logic and reason in accordance with the Cartesian "Method," finds that his rational attempts to understand his master Mr Knott by means of his phenomena (his accidents, the preferred term of the scholasticist philosophers with whom Beckett was working) leads not to any substantive knowledge of him but ultimately to the asylum. This accords with the Augustinian precept that we cannot know God directly, but, in what becomes the doctrine of Negative Theology, only what he is not. In the words of Watt: "For the only way to speak of nothing is to speak of it as though it were something, just as the only way one can speak of God is to speak of him as though he were a man, which to be sure he was, in a sense, for a time" (p. 77). There is a further twist to the question of the perception of "God" (subject and object genitive), whereby it is less true that his servants need to witness Mr Knott to know that they exist, than that Mr Knott needs his servants to witness him, or he might not exist.

The novel begins indirectly, with an episode concerning Mr Hackett, "his" seat, a lady and a gentleman occupying it, and a policeman who sees no indecency. The perspective changes to that of the Nixons, Goff and Tetty, who greet Mr Hackett, hear him recite the poem, "To Nelly," and remember the night when Larry was born – a comic scenario that encapsulates Beckett's personal memories of the "woom." Watt appears and is approached by Goff, to whom he owes five shillings, "that is to say, six and ninepence." A conversation about this strange creature ensues, of which the conclusion is Mr Nixon's angry outburst (p. 21): "I tell you nothing is known." The opening pages thus encapsulate the theme of the whole book: if nothing can be known of Watt, then how can he, Watt, expect to know anything of Knott?

Watt has arrived, by tram, to what, in Beckett's world, was the Harcourt Street Station in Dublin, from which he will take a train to what is, in Beckett's world, Foxrock, whence he will walk to Mr Knott's house, the model for which, ditto, is Cooldrinagh, Beckett's family home. En route he encounters Mr Spiro, editor of the popular Catholic monthly, *Crux*, who expounds to him knotty points of religion, of which Watt hears nothing (p. 29) because (here follows the first of the logical paradigms, which in the manuscripts are grounded in a truth-table, the author ticking them off to insure his being inclusive) of other voices, singing, crying, stating, murmuring, in various combinations of these modes, things intelligible, in his ear. He gets down from the train, making his way to Mr Knott's house in a "headlong tardigrade" (p. 30), a sigmoidal movement not unlike that of a fish or reptile, and attracting the attention of Lady McCann, who throws a stone at Watt's hat, a cause of as little resentment to Watt (to take a simple example) as if a bomb had fallen on his bum (p. 32).

After a short interval in the ditch, where he hears from afar a mixed choir, Watt arrives at Mr Knott's house, finding it in darkness, the front door locked, the back door locked, the front door locked, the back door, somehow, open. No explanation is offered, and Watt never knows how he got into the house. If he cannot comprehend such minor matters, what chance has he of understanding more complex ones? But he crosses the threshold, into the kitchen, to sit beside the fire to watch the ashes redden and greyen. The rest of Part I is made up of Arsene's "short statement" beginning with the sense of the old ways and winding to the "celebrated conviction" (echoing Voltaire's satire of Leibniz) that all is for the best (p. 41). That was challenged one beautiful October afternoon, when "something slipped" (p. 42). There follows a critique of the Proustian moment, the epiphany: "What was changed was existence off the ladder...the reversed metamorphosis. The Laurel into Daphne" (p. 44). Arsene insists the experience was not an illusion, though he is buggered if he can understand how it could have been anything else. His words should warn Watt of the futility of his quest, but they do not. Arsene celebrates the seasons, the crocuses, and the larch that turns green and brown a week before the others, the pastures red with uneaten sheep's placentas (see the short story "Walking out" (1970a: 109)), and the whole bloody business starting all over again.

A new note is struck with the three-fold paradigm of the laugh: the bitter, the hollow, the mirthless, corresponding to successive excoriations of the understanding and culminating in the dianoetic laugh, the laugh that laughs at that which is unhappy (p. 48). This is the guffaw of the Abderite, or Democritus, revisited from *Murphy*. For Arsene it is the only response possible to his perception of his role at Knott's house, the realization that he, and thus Watt, are but one in a series of servants and witnesses who gather about Mr Knott and watch over him: before him, Vincent and Walter and others unknown; and after him, Erskine and Watt and Arthur and Micks. When Arsene came in, Walter went up and Vincent went out; when Erskine came in, Arsene went up and Walter went out; now that Watt has arrived, Erskine goes up and Arsene goes out; when Arthur comes, Watt will go up and Erskine out; and when Micks comes, then Arthur will go up and Watt will go out. Yet the portrait of Knott's father, and Arthur's story as told in the "Addenda" (pp. 250–3), suggests that he, too, may be serial, but in an order imperceptible to his servants. Mr Knott remains unchanged throughout, apparently immortal, but an immortality based on one's perspective on time, like the gardener to the rose. Beckett picked up the image from Diderot's "Le Rêve de d'Alembert" (1769) and used it in the short story "Draff": "No gardener has died, comma, within rosaceous memory."

Part II consists of several episodes, during what is presumably (for Watt does not know) the first year of employment, but in no strict narrative order. The principle of composition is the set-piece, and the principle within that logical disjunction is the heavy use of the comma and qualifying phrase: "Mr Knott was a good master, in a way" (p. 67). The opening pages detail the daily routine, such as emptying the slops, the first "incident of note" being the visit of the Galls, father and son (pp. 71–80), come to "choon the piano." The episode irritates Watt, at first, for it frustrates his inquiry into what such incidents mean, "oh not what they really meant, his character was not so peculiar as all that, but into what they might be induced to mean" (p. 75). The narrator, making his first appearance, is scathing of such vexations: "One wonders sometimes where Watt thought he was. In a culture-park?" (p. 77).

Watt's next semantic (mis)adventure concerns the pot (pp. 81–4), the tragedy being that the object, or pot, resists the linguistic formulation, "pot," if only by a hairsbreadth. But at this point, the text insists (p. 85), Watt's words and thus his world had not yet begun to fail him, as they later would. He copes with his routine, such as preparing the weekly "poss" (pp. 87–8), yet this simple task generates complexities that are beyond him. For instance (pp. 89–90), the decisions concerning mealtime give rise to queries concerning (1) responsibility for the arrangement, (2) knowledge of the responsibility, (3) knowledge of the arrangement, (4) knowing "he" was responsible vs. knowing "who" was, and (5) being content. Of the permutations outlined in a manuscript truth-table, twelve occur to Watt, but others are possible and the paradigm excludes negations of "was content." This attempt at exhaustive logic leaves Watt exhausted, to say nothing of the reader, and foreshadows others more complex in the pages to come, the cumulative effect of which will be to drive Watt insane.

More frustrating is the following parable, the satire on pre-established harmony and proofs of the existence of God from cause, the story of the Lynch family and their famished dog (pp. 90–117). This scenario is the excrescence of scholastic logic working from the simple premise that if the dog's dish is put outside at evening full or partly so, and is brought in the next morning empty, then something must have brought about that change of state. And so the series begins. A dog. A famished dog. A dog kept famished so that it wants to eat the food. A family who owns the dog. A family who (of necessity) must breed dogs so that there is always a famished dog. And so on, each premise begets fresh premises, until, from the simple statement that "it was necessary" (p. 91) that a dog from outside call at the house, and a series of propositions in the conditional mood, there comes into being a declaration in the indicative that the name of this dog "was" Kate, and that of the family "was" Lynch (p. 100). The reification is purely linguistic, nominalist, but by the end of the sequence Watt has made to comfort himself "a pillow of old words," and the image of Kate eating from her dish with the dwarfs standing by has assumed substantial being (p. 117).

For much of his time (pp. 117–31), Watt is preoccupied with Erskine's movements and the problem of getting into his room to resolve the mystery of what makes Erskine run and the bell that is heard but not seen. Eventually he gets into the room by a ruse ("Ruse a by") which is never explained. The narrator, later named as Sam, enters the text in person for the first time (p. 125), as witness to what Watt has said. When Watt gets into the room he finds a bell, yes, but it is broken. So much for the bell. The other "object of note" in Erskine's room (the phrase echoing the Galls, the earlier "incident of note") is the picture of the circle and point (its point?), which fascinates Watt, who tries to determine the relationship of the two, wondering how it might look upside down, with the point west and the breach north, or in various other directions (p. 129). The givens of left and right, up and down, do not correspond with the coordinates of north, south, east and west, until one realizes that the perspective is not that of the subject, Watt, but of the object, the picture. The normal relationship between perceiver and perceived is thus subverted. The picture is an emblem of the relationship of Knott (the circle) and Watt (the point), and as such is a source of infinite wonder to Watt, but as he is about to depart the comment is made: "The painting, or coloured reproduction, yielded nothing further. On the contrary, as time passed, its significance diminished" (p. 208).

What preoccupies Watt during his stay on the ground floor is his sense of the seriality of all things, except apparently Mr Knott, his sense of the pre-established arbitrary (p. 134), as imaged immediately in the comings and goings of various servants. A series is established, but the sequence of elements is not necessarily *because* they are related (design need not imply cause); and with that complication in mind Watt "laboured at the ancient labour" (p. 136) to dubious effect: Watt, "having opened this tin with his blowlamp, found it empty." Seriality gives way to periodicity, as Watt recalls the song of the three frogs, croaking Krak!, Krek!, and Krik! at intervals, respectively, of eight, five, and three, a Fibonacci sequence, beginning together but not croaking in unison again until after 120 bars. The Olympia Press edition made a mess of this, but Beckett insisted, whatever the cost of resetting the type, that they get it right.

At this point (p. 138) there is an abrupt change, and the text concerns itself with less philosophical matters; first, the *amours* of Watt and Mrs Gorman, the fishwoman (pp. 138–42); then, his conversations with Mr Graves, the gardener (pp. 142–5); and finally Watt's occasional glimpses of Mr Knott (pp. 145–7), whom he does not see face to face. The chapter ends, after a telephone call to Mr Knott, asking how he was, to Watt's frustration. What had he learned? Nothing. What did he know of Mr Knott? Nothing. Of his anxiety to improve, understand, get well, what remained? Nothing. He is asked, "But was that not something?" Might not this be a first step to wisdom? All that happens, however, is that one morning, on arising, he finds Erskine gone and a strange man in the kitchen, Arthur. A new point in the series has been reached.

Part III is set in an asylum, metaphorically the station at the end of the line. The sequence thus violates logical order, and the explanation vouchsafed on p. 215 is only partially satisfactory: "Two, one, four, three, that was the order in which Watt told his story." The narrative, however, has not quite followed that sequence. Suitably in this setting, the narrative assumes irrational form, and the reader's security with respect to this dislocated world is undermined. The presence of Sam, intimated earlier, is now marked. The narrative as a whole purports to be that recounted by Watt to Sam, on those odd occasions (the wind high and the sun bright) when they met, coaxed from their mansions (Boswell's word for the cells of Bedlam) into the little garden, where they pursue birds with stones and clods, and cherish their friends, the rats, perhaps feeding a plump young one to one of its family (p. 156). On such occasions, Sam and Watt agree, they came nearest to God.

Despite impediments to communication (the weather, Watt's deterioration (p. 159), and the hole in the fence (pp. 160–3)), Sam is able to walk and talk with Watt and to construe an imperfect narrative (which the book purports to be) from what is said. Watt's language undergoes several inversions (pp. 164–9). These affect the order of the sentences, the letters of the words, and the sentences in the paragraph; the three are combined in orders of increasing complexity until the "sense" is almost unintelligible (a "translation" is offered in Ruby Cohn's *Comic Gamut* (1962: 309–10)). Beckett went to considerable trouble with these passages. Each is associated with other permutations, as: "Thus I missed I *suppose* much I *suspect* of great interest touching I *presume* the *first* or initial stage of the second or closing period of Watt's stay in Mr Knott's house." The refrain is constant, but the italicized words form an erratic paradigm, neither exhaustive nor matching the manuscripts, which indicate that

Beckett was considering a series such as: 123, 132, 231, 213, 312, 321, then back to 123 again (there are eight, not seven variations, a basic incommensurability). There is a more logical sequence of *first* to *eighth* (only six permutations are possible, but eight are needed – a basic incommensurability). The particulars are demented, but (Sam insists) it is to such conversations that the following elements of the narrative are indebted.

These are a motley collection. The first concerns the problems of Mr Graves, the gardener, with respect to potency, Arthur's solution being "Bando," which has had such a restorative effect that he has become vivacious, restless, a popular nudist, regular in his daily health, almost a father, and a lover of boiled potatoes (pp. 169–71). And, one might add, a teller of tales, for this is but foreplay to the extended story of his old friend (pp. 171–98), whose dissertation *The Mathematical Intuitions of the Visicelts* forms a sustained satire on Trinity College, the academic industry, and the Gaelic or Antiquarian revival. The obsessive rendering of the movements of Louit's examiners, Messrs Fitzwein, MacStern, de Baker, Magershon and O'Meldon, reaches the point where even the most dedicated reader cannot tease out everything (Beckett's method is exhaustive, the manuscripts listing all the permutations), which is a pity, as there are gems within the deliberately turgid prose. In the end, having mentioned the bitter stout porter, Power, Arthur tires of his story, and even Watt is thankful.

The ending of Part III differs only in its complexity from that of Part II: "Of the nature of Mr Knott himself Watt remained in particular ignorance" (p. 199). That simple statement derives from an even more exhaustive listing of the attributes of Mr Knott that Watt has been able to discern: his dress (pp. 200–1); his furniture (pp. 203–7); and the "important matter" of his physical appearance (pp. 209–11). The lists get longer and more complex, Beckett again creating exhaustive truth-tables, ticking off each permutation in such a way as to cover every possibility. The method has been present in the text from the outset, but at first the number of variables was small, and thus the combinations were limited. As the variables increase their combinatory total expands factorially. The intent is not simply to frustrate the dedicated reader, although that is part of it, but to parody the Cartesian methodology of complete enumeration, and, in particular, the theological impasse that arises from attempting to derive the essential from its phenomena, its accidents. The consequence is that Watt, when the time comes for him to depart, first from the house of Mr Knott (p. 208) and then from Sam (p. 213), does so in ignorance. The final image of the issuing smoke signifies not so much a reconciliation, as at the end of episode 9 of *Ulysses*, but a coming together, only to vanish, having reached no conclusion.

Part IV is the shortest, dealing with the departure of Watt. Inevitably, of necessity, Watt comes down one evening to find Micks sitting in the kitchen, and knows that his time has come to go. He puts on his greatcoat and hat, his shoe and his boot, but before he leaves his face assumes an expression of such vacancy that Micks recoils (p. 220). The night is of unusual splendor, with no wind; but on his way to the station (p. 223) Watt feels on the nape of his neck the cold air: an intimation, imperfectly understood, of the Dream of Descartes, which does nothing to confirm him in the path that henceforth he must take. There is a second manifestation, a figure perceived (pp. 225–8), like the experience of the disciples on the road to Emmaus, or Eliot in *The Waste Land*, a hint of Providence unrecognized. Although Watt is lacerated with curiosity (the "old error") it comes no nearer and finally fades. Watt prevails on Mr Case to stay the night locked in the train station, despite a problem with the keys. The manuscripts sketch the three rooms and their geometrical proportions, each formed from the dimensions of the other in the ratio of the golden rectangle. After much logical agonizing Watt is admitted to the waiting-room, and droops sigmoidal (p. 253). He spends the night in darkness, until it lightens, and he is able to distinguish a chair, and, on the wall, a large colored print of the horse, Joss (p. 236). There are also flies, of skeletal thinness, pressed against the window, as in the poems "Serena I" and "La Mouche."

When Mr Nolan arrives, he unlocks the waiting-room door with such vigor that Watt is knocked unconscious, and, in this state, becomes an object of note to others present, who determine to revive him by sousing him with the contents of the muck-bucket (p. 239). This is a process that Büttner likens to an obscene birth (1984: 136–7). Watt, who was perhaps a uiversity man (p. 23), distinguishes fragments of Hölderlin's "Hyperions Schicksalslied" and Farquar's *The Beaux' Stratagem* as the slime engulfs him. The scene is excruciating because the vulnerability of Watt has rendered him an object of pity, a sentiment alien to those who work on the platform (Mr Gorman, Mr Nolan, Mr Case), or arrive there (Lady McCann, Arsy Cox, Herring-gut Waller, Cack-faced Miller), to whom he remains an object of scorn and derision. Watt buys his ticket to the end of the line, the round end or the square (p. 244); and when charged one and three instinctively tenders three and one. The train arrives, and although the text says that not a single passenger was taken up Watt is not obviously included thereby, for without further comment he is gone. The novel ends in the early morning light, Messrs Nolan, Case, and Gorman looking at each other in a reciprocal paradigm, preceded by one last image of Watt, "the long wet dream with the hat and bags" (p. 246). In the words of Frank Doherty (1971: 20), a metaphysical farce of cruelty is taking place in the midst of an unconcerned and smugly self-satisfied Irish world, which can claim on its penultimate page that "Life isn't such a bad old bugger."

The "Addenda"

The 37 fragments attached to *Watt* as "Addenda" were all considered at some point in the genesis of the novel, but their continued presence in the text suggests a set of epistemological crises that parallel those of the novel itself. Are they finally a part of the novel or apart from it? As enigmatic fossils they bear witness to earlier states of creation even as they retain the emphasis on the novel's incompletion. The "Addenda" thus take us back to the novel's origins. Most feature Quin, the proto-Knott, but, like the novel itself, they raise questions about whose voice they represent: Watt's, that of the purported narrator, Sam, or that of the author?

1. *her married life one long drawsheet*: "Leda, née Swan, demi-mondaine, of Enniskillen"; mother of James Quin (the original of Mr Knott), and wife to Alexander; a faded and dejected woman who passes away after the death of her fourth Willy, her last-born, who (like the family of Mahood in *The Unnamable*) has died of sausage-poisoning. A *drawsheet*, on the natal bed, is one that can be drawn without disturbing the patient (as in *Footfalls*). Of Mrs Quin's eleven children (besides James: Willy, Willy, little Leda, Willy, Agnes, Lawrence, Prisca, Zoe, Perpetua, Willy), James – his place in the sequence unspecified – is the sole survivor.

2. *Art Conn O'Connery*: forbear of Art and Con, and painter of the second picture in Erskine's room, that of Alexander Quin (in early drafts, in Quin's dining room). His premature death at 81 from heart failure brought on by the downfall of Parnell or a surfeit of corned beef and cabbage was a loss to Rathgar. While "black velvet" denotes a standard backdrop to a portrait, it is also a mixture of stout and champagne. George Chinnery (1774–1852), born in England, resided in Dublin from 1797 until 1802, when he sailed for India never to return; he painted landscapes and portraits, the Dublin National Gallery owning since 1918 his *A Portrait of a Mandarin*. John Joseph Slattery was a portraitist active in Dublin between 1846 and 1858.

3. *the Master of the Leopardstown Halflengths*: one Matthew David McGilligan, priest and artist, whose dissertation on the *Mus Exenteratu McGilligani* (the rat that swallowed the consecrated host) appears in transubstantiated form in *Watt* (p. 280).

4. *who may tell the tale*: words attributed to the author's executrix, Madame Pompedur de Videlay-Chémoy ("Pompette"), 69 ter rue de Vieux Port, Cette; a form formerly divine, recalling, in old age and in solitude, the tale of an old has-been who might-have-been.

5. *judicious Hooker's heat-pimples*: in an early draft "we" (the narrator) meets Arsene and Eamon at the foot of the stairs, in a dark passage-way (see #37); and they remain some time in mutual affection and content. Arsene comments: "You said that what warmed you to Hooker was his heat-pimples and his habit of never looking a person straight in the face, and that for these endearing traits you were willing to forgive him the rest." The reference is to Izaak Walton's *The Life of Mr. Richard Hooker, the Author of those Learned Books of the Laws of Ecclesiastical Polity* (London, 1675), in which Walton, having sung the praises of "Judicious Hooker," suggests that visitors to the Parsonage of Bourne might find: "his Face full of Heat-pimples, begot by his unactivity and sedentary life."

6. *limits to part's equality with whole*: the conversation takes a mathematical turn, the point being that the relationship between life, experience, and the lamentable tale of error, folly, waste, and ruin works for 0 and 1 but for nothing else. It thereby confounds the Euclidean axiom that the whole is greater than the part.

7. *dead calm . . . to naught gone*: the talk then turns to "the unconscious mind! What a subject for a short story," and the attempt to go "perhaps deep down in those palaeozoic profounds, midst mammoth Old Red Sandstone phalli and Carboniferous

pudenda...into the pre-uterine...the agar-agar...impossible to describe... anguish...close eyes, all close, great improvement, pronounced improvement."

8. *Bid us sigh*: as Harvey notes (1970: 391), these lines are from James Thomson's "To Fortune." They anticipate the paean to the Seasons in the novel *Watt* (p. 47). Beckett drops Thomson's question mark, thus turning the quatrain into an imperative.

9. *Watt learned to accept*: Watt's growing ability to accept the concept of Nothing. This refers back to a passage on p. 80: "Watt learned towards the end of this stay in Mr Knott's house to accept that nothing had happened."

10. *Note that Arsene's declaration gradually came back to Watt*: Beckett's instruction to himself, recorded at the end of Notebook 5. It marks the decision to tell the tale erratically through Watt, a perspective not originally present.

11. *One night Watt goes on roof*: this he does not do in the novel, but in the drafts Quin's house is described: "There was a ground floor, a first floor, and a second floor. And access to the roof was provided by a skylight in its midst, for those who wished to go on the roof."

12. *Watt snites*: from the Anglo-Saxon *snytan*, to pull or blow the nose. Beckett wrote in the manuscript: "Part IV. Watt snites in his toilet paper." The word is eliminated from the description of Watt's nasal masturbation (pp. 234–5).

13. *Meals*: the drafts comment: "Out of sheer Schadenfreude simply to annoy the table, Quin changed his seat at each repast. He even carried this disposition so far, on days of ill-humour, as to change his seat between courses." Beckett changed "Quin" to "Knott," and introduced Watt, whose activity with the chalk may reflect Horace's "Creta, an carbone notandi?" ("Are they to be marked with chalk or charcoal?"), i.e., is he sane or mad? (*Satires* 2. 3. 246).

14. *the maddened prizeman*: Arsene, who, but for the boil on his bottom (p. 46), might have been the recipient of the Madden Prize, an academic award at Trinity College, Dublin. Mr Quin's servants, Arthur and Erskine, were once maddened prizemen.

15. *the sheet of dark water*: in early drafts, a silence in the midst of a conversation between Quin and his valet, Arthur, concerning Quin's difficulties in finding his way about the house, in particular the location of the lavatories (compare p. 203). Quin, about to descend the stairs and meet a strange man (Hackett), is listening to the empty echo of his own words and the nothingness behind them.

16. *never been properly born*: testifying to an early impulse behind the novel, Quin's sense of the nothingness of his own being: "The plain fact of the matter seems to be, that Quin had never been properly born. / The five dead little brothers support this view, as do the five dead little sisters. / His relatively great age, and comparative freedom from grave bodily disease, confirm this conception. / For all the good that frequent departures out of Ireland had done him, he might as well have stayed there." The sentiment was one of Beckett's favorites, and echoes his sense of the unborn embryonic self, that *être manqué*; and his fascination with the comment made by Jung

after one of the Tavistock lectures (1935), about a little girl whose dreams of death revealed that "She had never been born entirely."

17. *the foetal soul is full grown*: the themes of the unborn soul and nothingness continue in the drafts: "The feeling of nothingness, born in Quin with the first beat of his heart, if not before, died in him with the last, and not before. And between these acts it waned not, neither did it wax, but its strength at its beginning was as its strength at its end, and its strength at its middle as its strength at its beginning. The foetal soul is full-grown (Cf. *Cangiamila's Sacred Embryology* and *the De Synodo Diocesana*, Bk. 7, Chap. 4, Section 6, of Pope Benedict XIV)." Francesco Emanuele Cangiamila (1702–63) was a Sicilian theologian whose most celebrated work, *L'Embriologia sacra*, was published in 1745. It concerns such matters as Caesarian birth and the problems of salvation in difficult circumstances, teachings noted approvingly by Benedict. It is unlikely that Beckett had read the *Embriologia sacra* or Benedict's *De Synodo diocesana libri tredecim* (1748), a summa of ecclesiastical traditions from the Synod of 1725, for his learned reference is wrong: the reference to Cangiamila and the problem of uterine baptism may be found at XL.vii.xiii in that tome, with further discussion at VII.v.iv, in a tone not unlike that of the Messrs de la Sorbonne in *Tristram Shandy* I.xx.

18. *sempiternal penumbra*: darkness having a beginning but no end. Compare the "rosa sempiterna" of *Paradiso* XXX.124 that Dante uses to describe the light of Paradise (I.76). In the drafts the phrase is applied to Mr Quin's coal-hole.

19. *for all the good that frequent departures out of Ireland had done him, he might just as well have stayed there*: see #16, above.

20. *a round wooden table*: this mahogany table, described extensively in the drafts, is like Quin's round bed, which survives into the novel (p. 207); first in the bed and later, as a child under the table, "Quin began the fatal journey towards the light of day."

21. *zitto! zitto! das nur das Publikum nichts merke!*: It. and Ger. "Hush, hush, so that the public may notice nothing." From Schopenhauer's *Über die vierfache Wurzel des Satzes vom zureichenden Grunde* ("Concerning the four-fold root of the Principle of Sufficient Ground").

22. *on the waste, beneath the sky*: a passage that goes back directly to the sense of nothingness (the sky above, the waste below) which was Quin's first awareness and of which his life partook. This is the primal scene of the novel to be.

23. *Watt will not / abate one jot*: the poem exists in the typescript, in a form virtually identical save for initial capitalization, the substitution of "Johnny" for "Watt," and the phrase "Naught's habitat" in line 7 ("Knott" had not yet materialized). The narrator was then a small man called Johnny, who visits Quin's establishment and converses with Arsene in the hall. The record of this meeting was to be published in a book called *A Clean Old Man*, destined to become Book of the Week in 2080, the praises of which are sung in the leap-year song, "Fifty two point two eight five seven one four two," in the novel transferred to the indifferent mixed choir (pp. 34–5). The

sentiment derives from Milton's second sonnet to Cyriack Skinner: "Yet I argue not / Against Heaven's hand or will, nor bate a jot / Of heart and hope."

24. *die Merde hat mich wieder*: a parody of Goethe's "die Erde hat mich wieder" ("the earth has me again"), from *Faust* 1.784, as Faust listens to the choirs of angels and disciples, and hears their summons to return to life.

25. *pereant qui ante nos nostra dixerunt*: L. "let those who used our words before us perish," a dictum attributed to St Jerome (his commentary on *Ecclesiastes*), who took it from Aelius Donatus (a fourth-century grammarian), who based it on a line from Terence. Beckett perhaps found it in Bartlett's *Familiar Quotations,* attributed to an anonymous author.

26. *Second picture in Erskine's room*: that of Alexander Quin, father of James (see #2). The fragment crucially suggests that Quin/Knott, like all around him, may equally be serial (see #29).

27. *like a thicket flower unrecorded*: this echo of Gray's *Elegy*, "Full many a flower is born to blush unseen," appears in the drafts as part of an elaborate discussion about the mating possibilities between Irish Setters and Palestine Retrievers, to produce the right kind of famished dog; leading to an enormous spectacle mounted (as it were) by the Lynch family, charging spectators for admission; and speculating as to where such customs may have originated (Eire? Pelasgia? the Hardy country?); only to conclude: "Nothing is known, as far as can be ascertained."

28. *Watt's Davus complex (morbid dread of sphinxes)*: in Terence's *Andria* (194) a slave quips: "Dáuos sum, non Oédipus" ("I am Davus, not Oedipus"), as he feigns ignorance of amorous matters.

29. *One night Arthur came to Watt's room*: the most important of the Addenda, as it encapsulates many of the earliest details from the notebooks and touches lightly on the novel's central themes. The episode, with minor variations, is present in all the early drafts: an encounter between Quin and an old man in Quin's garden, with some of the dialogue later given to Mr Hackett. A revised typescript adds a crucial reference to the Knott family and its serial nature. The passage anticipates Watt's encounter with Knott in the garden (p. 145); permits the joke about the passing shrub, or bush, which proves to be a hardy laurel; and offers a further arabesque upon the theme of relative immortality, expressed in *Proust* (1970b: 21) in terms of the whisky's grudge against the decanter, and in "Draff" (1970a: 175) as the words of the rose to the rose, that "No gardener has died, comma, within rosaceous memory."

30. *Watt looking as though nearing end of course of injections of sterile pus*: this cheerful vision appears nowhere in the notes or manuscripts, but echoes the inoculation of anthropoid apes hinted at in *Murphy* (1957: 50).

31. *das fruchtbare Bathos der Erfahrung*: Ger. "the fruitful bathos of experience." From Kant's *Prolegomena zu einer jeden künfigen Metaphysik die als Wissenschaft wird auftreten können* ("Prolegomena to Any Future Metaphysics that Will Be Able to Present Itself as a Science"), in which Kant attacks a reviewer who had misunderstood his earlier work. Kant uses "Bathos" in its Greek sense of a deep place, in contrast with "High towers, and metaphysically tall men like them, round both of which there

is commonly a lot of wind"; and suggests that the citation can easily be misread (as Beckett perhaps intended) in terms of the more usual "Pathos," or suffering.

32. *faede hunc mundum intravi, anxius vixi, perturbatus egredior, causa causarum miserere mei*: L. "in filth I entered this world, anxious I lived, troubled I go out of it, cause of causes have mercy on me" derives from Lemprière's *Dictionary* ("Aristotle," said to be his dying words), but the mistranscription (*faede* for *fœde*) seems to be Beckett's own.

33. *change all the names*: in the manuscript, the instruction is written: "Walterize selon p. 81," i.e., change all the names, e.g., from "Walter" to "Vincent"; and in the passage that follows Beckett does so.

34. *descant heard by Watt on way to station (IV)*: no such mention of a descant is made in the novel. Originally included in the drafts at a much earlier point, it was attributed to a "Distant Mixed Fifth-rate Choir," as heard by those waiting in Quin's passage-way for anything "of note."

35. *parole non ci appulcro*: It. "I will add no words to embellish it." This derives from Dante's *Inferno* VII.60, the irony being that Virgil, by describing the corruption of avaricious cardinals, is unable to remain silent. In the drafts the phrase appeared near a song to be sung by Erskine and Watt (or Johnny, as he then was) after they have prepared the poss of Mr Knott (as by then he was). The words so bravely sung are the celebrated ones from Voltaire's *Candide*: "O che sciagura d'essere senza coglioni!" ("Oh what a shame, to be without balls").

36. *Threne heard by Watt*: one of the few "Addenda" with a direct relation to the final text (cf. the footnote on p. 33).

37. *No symbols where none intended*: on p. 80 of the Grove edition Watt thinks about Arsene, and wonders what has become of the duck, the only mention of such a bird. This is a truly magnificent fossil, in a state of perfect preservation, but one that disappeared (at Beckett's instigation) from the Calder edition. It is explicable only with reference to the manuscripts, the encounter between the narrator (Johnny Watt, who refers to himself as "we") and two bipeds: one featherless, a maddened prize-man named Arsene; the other feathered, an India Runner Duck named Eamon (see #5–8). A long conversation ensues in the darkened hallway of Mr Quin's house, of which this is the conclusion: on the uttering of the sentiment, "Each in his own way, all are in the dark," a match is struck, and burns bravely, until its fire reaches the fingers and it is dropped; whereupon "it continued for a little while bravely to burn, till it could burn no longer, bravely or otherwise. Then it went out." In that brief light, much is revealed: "the dark in which we were, each in his or her own way, and Eamon and Arsene and the passage and the stairs and the bells and the newell – and we." It is too easy: a little light in the big dark; a feathered and featherless biped; a dark passage; purgatorial stairs; hints of the Eucharist in distant bells. But "we" remains in the dark. In a context so insistently demanding symbolic interpretation, in the presence of details so often used to translate consciousness into meaning, all Watt can say is: "No symbols where none intended." That phrase, by a strange synecdoche, stands for the entire novel, even as it shifts interpretation to authorial intentionality.

REFERENCES AND FURTHER READING

Ackerley, C. J. and Gontarski, S. E. (2004) *The Grove Companion to Samuel Beckett: A Reader's Guide to His Works, Life, and Thought*. New York: Grove Press.

Beckett, Samuel (1957) *Murphy*. New York: Grove Press.

——(1959) *Watt*. New York: Grove Press.

——(1970a) *More Pricks than Kicks*. New York: Grove Press.

——(1970b) *Proust*. New York: Grove Press.

——(1984) *Collected Poems, 1930–1978*. London: John Calder.

Büttner, Gottfried (1984) [1981] *Samuel Beckett's Novel* Watt, trans. Joseph P. Dolan. Philadelphia: University of Pennsylvania Press.

Cohn, Ruby (1962) *Samuel Beckett: The Comic Gamut*. New Brunswick: Rutgers University Press.

——(2001) *A Beckett Canon*. Ann Arbor: University of Michigan Press.

Doherty, Francis (1971) *Samuel Beckett*. London: Hutchinson.

Harvey, Lawrence (1970) *Samuel Beckett, Poet and Critic*. Princeton: Princeton University Press.

Knowlson, James (1996) *Damned to Fame: The Life of Samuel Beckett*. New York: Simon and Schuster.

O'Brien, Eoin (1986) *The Beckett Country: Samuel Beckett's Ireland*. Dublin: Black Cat Press.

Seaver, Richard (1974) Introduction, in *"I can't go on, I'll go on": A Selection from Samuel Beckett's Works*. New York: Grove Press.

Wheatley, David (1995) "'He is a University Man, of course': sourcing Quinn," *Journal of Beckett Studies*, 4/2: 93–5.

16
George Orwell's Dystopias: *Animal Farm* and *Nineteen Eighty-Four*

Erika Gottlieb

Both utopian and dystopian fiction – visions of the best and the worst of all possible worlds – belong to the genre of political satire. In this genre the reader plays an active role. Through the satirical devices of indirection – irony, allusion, the reversal of cause and effect relationships, apposition, overstatement – the satirist prepares us to recognize the flaws of our own society. When reading utopian fiction, we are invited to see the rationality of bringing into reality the vision of the best of all possible worlds, the society without the flaws of our own. In reading dystopia, we are expected to see the rationality of preventing the nightmare vision of the future – a monstrous world that could develop from the flaws rampant in our own society – from becoming reality. Orwell was familiar with these genres, particularly with dystopias, although, like his contemporaries, he did not yet use the term "dystopia" and called all kinds of speculative literature "utopian." Undoubtedly, he was closely familiar with *Brave New World* (1931) and *Darkness at Noon* (1940), and after he read Zamiatin's *We* (1920), he wrote: "I am interested in that kind of book and even keep making notes for one myself that may get written sooner or later" (III: 8). In his 1946 review of *We*, Orwell praised Zamiatin's "intuitive grasp of the irrational side of totalitarianism – human sacrifice, cruelty as an end in itself, the worship of the Leader who is credited with divine attributes – that makes Zamiatin's book superior to Huxley's" (IV: 98). He also reviewed, favorably, Koestler's *Darkness at Noon*, a work that describes Stalin's betrayal of the Revolution.

The betrayal of the socialist utopia is a theme central to *Animal Farm*. A masterpiece of satirical invention, here the political allegory works as an extended metaphor, where the activities of animals on an English farm represent the activities of historical figures and classes in the Russian Revolution. Demonstrating the betrayal of the goals of the Revolution in Russia by the very leaders of the Revolution, Orwell's satire is addressed to the satirist's adversary, the western intellectual on the Left, who is unaware of the falsehood implied in worshiping Soviet Russia as a model of socialism.

By the time Orwell wrote *Animal Farm* he had already completed four naturalistic novels: *Burmese Days* (1934), *A Clergyman's Daughter* (1935), *Keep the Aspidistra Flying* (1936), and *Coming Up for Air* (1939), as well as three works of documentary realism that laid the foundation for his reputation, *Down and out in Paris and London* (1933), The *Road to Wigan Peer* (1937), and *Homage to Catalonia* (1938). Today, he is recognized as among the greatest English essayists of his time, as witnessed by the four volumes of his lively, controversial, often highly provocative prose written between 1920 and 1950. Even so, Orwell would not have won the international reputation he has today were it not for his last two novels, *Animal Farm* (written in 1943 and published in 1945) and *Nineteen Eighty-Four* (written in 1948 and published in 1949).

That said, many of Orwell's critics argue that his final two works are flawed because they represent what Isaac Deutscher called a "cry of despair" about the human predicament. I believe, however, that Orwell's final vision does not express a "cry of despair," nor is it flawed by any standard of mature, tragic humanism. Indeed, Orwell's first four novels are all representatives of the genre of psychological realism. Of course, no one would deny that they are recognizably "Orwellian" in tone and texture; the narrative technique combines an extremely close observation of the environment and the revealing nuances of the individual's psychological response. Still, these early works are, on the whole, the reliable, respectable works of a not-yet-major writer: the imagination is restrained, the vision is private, the insights and observations have a tendency towards not only the specific, but also the minuscule or the eccentric. *Animal Farm* is a significant new departure for Orwell, showing a hitherto entirely unexpected dimension of his imagination: the visionary perspective of an original, imaginative structure, finding embodiment in sustained, brilliant political allegory, in the universality and compelling vision of an undeniably major writer whose language is satire.

I believe this new compulsion to write satire had much to do with Orwell's powerful twofold experience in the Spanish Civil War. Although he always felt great sympathy for the underdog, it was only in 1937 in Barcelona, while taking part in the fight against fascism, that he suddenly felt fully committed to socialism. It was only at this point that he announced: "I have seen wonderful things and at last really believe in Socialism, which I never did before" (I: 301). But we have to recognize that his commitment to socialism was also simultanenous with his experience of socialism being betrayed in Spain by the Stalinist faction. Fighting against Franco in the POUM (Partido Obrero Unificación Marxista, The United Marxist Workers' Party), Orwell was shot through the throat by a fascist sniper. While he was in hospital, the Communists, allegedly the strongest party on the Left, came to power. Their first move was to liquidate the rival parties on the Left such as the POUM, whom they denounced as Trotskyists and pro-fascist. Orwell had to run for his life, in danger of being thrown in jail, tortured, and executed by those who were, ideologically, the most obvious enemies of fascism. On his return to England, Orwell's personal experience of this betrayal was reinforced by his reading in the western papers about the atrocities in the USSR: Stalin's purges against the old Bolshevik leadership, rigged trials, torture, public confessions to phantasmagorical charges, mass denunciations, deportations, and executions. In fact, as Orwell came to realize (and Raymond Williams never forgave him for this insight), the Soviet system had little to do with democratic socialism. As a regime of terror, Orwell wrote, it "does not seem to be very different from fascism . . . The G.P.U. [the Soviet secret police] are everywhere, everyone lives in constant terror of denunciation, freedom of speech and of the press are obliterated to the extent we can hardly imagine . . . Meanwhile the invisible Stalin is worshipped in terms that would have made Nero blush" (I: 370). Outraged by the Big Lie of Stalin's propaganda, Orwell was even more alarmed by the attitude of western intellectuals on the Left who complacently believed in the preposterous charges against the accused in Stalin's purges, uncritically accepting the party line determined by the USSR and spread by the Comintern all over the world. It is this twofold experience of a deeply felt moral commitment to the cause of socialism, combined with the bitter recognition that it is thwarted, deliberately betrayed by the Stalinists, and that this betrayal is denied or simply overlooked by Stalin's duped western followers, that lends Orwell's voice the great satirist's powerfully focused "generous anger."

Both *Animal Farm* and *Nineteen Eighty-Four* are examples of dystopian fiction, dealing with the vision of the worst of all possible worlds, a world readers should recognize as a serious parody of the totalitarian dictatorship in Stalin's Russia – the kind of society, Orwell warns, that could come about in the west, in Britain in particular, should the satirist's Adversary fail to see the truth behind the "Soviet myth." My point is that it is in his last two novels that Orwell hits his stride, driven by a satirical passion that is distinctly different from political or personal despair (although the political situation gave good reason for anxiety, and when writing his last novel he was indeed an ailing man and often in pain). Political satire, built on a dramatic contrast between darkness and light, real and ideal, the way things are and the way they ought to be, is not expressive of the passivity or complacency associated with despair; on the contrary, it serves to prevent complacency. Orwell's desire to enlighten the western public and militate against the Stalinist betrayal of socialism is central to *Homage to Catalonia*, "Spilling the Spanish beans" (1937), and "Looking back on the Spanish War" (1942), and with even greater dramatic impact, it will become essential to the political allegory of *Animal Farm*. Yet it took Orwell several years after his return from Spain in 1937 to find the central conceit, the organizing metaphor that led, almost immediately, to the writing of his first major satire. He came upon it, he tells us, quite inadvertently:

> On my return from Spain I thought of exposing the Soviet myth in a story that could be easily understood by almost everyone and which could be easily translated to other languages. However, the actual details of the story did not come to me for some time

until one day (I was then living in a small village) I saw a little boy, perhaps ten years old, driving a huge cart-horse along a narrow path, whipping it whenever it tried to turn. It struck me that if only such animals became aware of their strength we should have no power over them, and that men exploit animals in much the same way as the rich exploit the proletariat. (III: 458–9)

The metaphor of the little boy controlling the powerful carthorse with a whip immediately establishes where Orwell's sympathies lie: just as the Russian Revolution against the exploiter was fully justified, so the animals on Manor Farm are fully justified in overthrowing their cruel human master and in establishing Animal Farm. However, when Orwell shows us that this human exploiter with a whip is soon supplanted by pig Napoleon, who gradually begins to walk on his hind legs and also carry a whip, this metaphor by itself could carry the full weight of Orwell's intention of "exposing the Soviet myth." In *Animal Farm* Orwell compels us to see that the USSR is not a socialist country; under Stalin's reign a new ruling class, just as exploitative and even more oppressive than the pre-revolutionary ruling class, comes to power.

Orwell's satire takes the form of political allegory, an animal fable, where every detail of life among the animals on Manor Farm serves as a vehicle. The target is the central events in the Russian Revolution, a historical process beginning with old Major's awakening of the masses to the egalitarian dream of socialism. Old Major is a composite character: like Karl Marx, he implants a dream of equality and prosperity among the masses; he draws the animals' attention to their ill-treatment by the human exploiter whose prosperity is built upon their hard and unpaid labor. Old Major also represents Lenin at the beginning of his career, when he worked underground to prepare the Revolution. The animals are established in the allegory as the working class, and Farmer Jones represents the regime of the tsar, their cruel and neglectful master. When the master fails to feed the animals (when, after the loss of millions of lives in World War I, the survivors returned to face poverty and starvation) the animals revolt. Once the human master – that is the old ruling class – is chased away, the animals have an opportunity to establish an egalitarian system where all animals are equal, and where no animal can exploit another animal, or behave in any way resembling the human exploiter of the past. (For this reason the animals' seven commandments make clear that no animal should walk on two legs, live in a house, sleep in a bed, drink alcohol, or exploit or murder other animals.) However, soon after the euphoria of the Revolution, Orwell shows us the intellectuals among the animals, the pigs, emerging as a new ruling class. (The socialist dream is betrayed by the new leadership of Stalin and his cohorts, whose hunger for power creates a ruthless, violent dictatorship aided and abetted by the Big Lie of the propaganda machine.)

Orwell also shows us the hostility between two potential leaders, Napoleon and Snowball (Stalin and Trotsky). Undoubtedly, Orwell reveals a great deal more sympathy for Snowball, who is exceptionally bright and has excellent results in writing and in teaching the animals to read; it is Snowball who composes the seven commandments and writes them laboriously on the wall of the barn for all animals to see. Snowball is also an excellent military planner whose strategy, coupled by personal courage and heroism, repels the attack by Jones and his neighbors at the victorious Battle of the Cowshed (a representation of Trotsky's role in organizing the Red Army, becoming its leader during the Civil War, and leading the young Soviet Union to victory against the old regime and its foreign defenders). At the same time, Orwell also shows us that old Major's dream (the Marxist dream of equality) is being betrayed almost from the outset not only by dictatorial Napoleon, but by Snowball himself. Both Napoleon and Snowball agree upon a decision that only the pigs, the intellectual leaders of Animal Farm, are privileged to drink the milk and consume the fallen apples, favorite components in many animals' diet. Should the other animals object to this decision, they are soon pacified by Squealer's explanation that if the pigs did not get the milk and apples that help them in their mental work as leaders of the victorious revolution, Jones would come back. This decision forms a turning point in the development of the new regime, because it legitimizes a way of thinking that gradually introduces an unstoppable line of privileges for the new ruling class.

In the meantime, the hostility between Napoleon and Snowball develops further (alluding to the rivalry, after Lenin's death, between the new leaders, Stalin and Trotsky). Napoleon uses underhand methods to develop his ferocious bodyguard and secret service, the dogs he took away from their mothers and indoctrinated in secret. Unaware of Napoleon's secret power, Snowball is eager to present his plan to all for the building of the windmill; he argues that a heavy industry is essential to face the technically more advanced enemies abroad, and also to ensure prosperity and comfort for the animals on the farm. (Here Snowball represents Trotsky's position on the importance of heavy industry, versus Stalin's emphasis on agriculture.) Napoleon rejects Snowball's plans, and at the animals' public meeting he unexpectedly summons his secret service, the ferocious dogs, to tear Snowball apart. Snowball runs away from the farm, where, from then on, Napoleon becomes the all-powerful dictator all animals fear. Soon Napoleon takes credit for initiating the idea of the windmill, and starts blaming the absent Snowball for all the possible errors or mishaps on the farm. Like that infallible dictator, Stalin, Napoleon also forbids public discussion; he simply cannot accept criticism.

This, in turn, means that he needs a scapegoat on whom to blame any mistakes. In fact, Orwell shows Stalin's unceasing hostility against the exiled Trotsky in the mind-boggling process of rewriting official history. To begin with, Squealer, Napoleon's propaganda chief, succeeds in convincing the animals that in the war against foreign intervention, Snowball had only a minor role compared to Napoleon. Then, going even further, Squealer announces that Snowball, whom we have seen repelling Jones and his neighbors at the Battle of the Cowshed, was only pretending to fight for the animals and was instead actually on Mr Jones's side, fighting not to defend but to defeat Animal Farm. Squealer also convinces the animals that Snowball is hiding on Pilkington's Farm, conspiring with Pilkington (Britain and the capitalist democracies) against Animal Farm. Then, when the other treacherous and aggressive dictator, Frederick (Hitler) appears on the scene, Orwell skillfully allegorizes the story of the Soviet alliance with the West *against* Nazism. The allegory also shows how, to the surprise of everyone, this alliance is suddenly broken by Stalin, who signs a Non-Aggression Pact with Hitler in 1939. Shortly after, in 1941, this pact is also broken, this time by the treachery of Hitler: unexpected by Napoleon, Frederick attacks and invades Animal Farm. Without reproaching Napoleon for his gullibility over Frederick, all the animals now pit their strength against the foreign conqueror, who violently destroys the windmill, the heavy industry built with the self-sacrifice of the working class, represented by Boxer, the exceptionally powerful but rather slow-witted carthorse (the same animal Orwell suddenly felt for when he saw him attacked by the human oppressor's whip). At this point, Napoleon finds it appropriate to make the animals turn their pain and frustration into a new hate campaign against Snowball who, they are now told by Squealer, was instrumental in the destruction of the windmill; in fact Snowball had been conspiring with Frederick all along to destroy Animal Farm. (In his essays Orwell frequently expresses outrage at the proliferation of lies in Stalin's propaganda machine, which engaged in the continuous rewriting of the official history of the Soviet Union, focusing on the shameless scapegoating of the exiled Trotsky.)

After the battle the undernourished and overworked animals start rebuilding the windmill, driven by their unshakeable faith in the Revolution. Quite unabashedly, Napoleon treats the animals as his slaves, to serve the increased pig population (Stalin's bureaucracy) and the equally increased army of the ferocious dogs (Stalin's secret police). Orwell also introduces here the entire machinery of terror under Stalin's totalitarian dictatorship, represented by Napoleon's purges, the witch hunts, the hysterical confessions of the animals who are then torn apart by the dogs, and the desperate bitterness vented upon the archetypal scapegoat, Snowball, and upon any of his alleged followers on the farm.

Particularly moving in the story of the animals' betrayal is Boxer's final illness and death. Boxer represents the working class that was used ruthlessly by Stalin during and after the war (there is even an allusion here to those millions of Russian prisoners of war captured by the Germans at the beginning of World War II, who were then returned to the USSR after the war only to be sent to labor camps or killed by the dictator). Ever since the victorious uprising against Jones, Boxer has been told that he will spend the last years of his life in the well-earned comfort of a state-supported retirement. Instead, when he receives his last injury as a result of overwork, his pig masters simply have him taken away by the "knacker" to be butchered, in exchange for a huge crate of whisky. By now all seven of the commandments that started the Revolution have been altered, with the effect of changing their meaning entirely. The pigs learn to walk on two legs, live in the house, sleep in beds, consume alcohol, and exploit and rule violently over the other animals. The most important of the commandments – that summarizes the purpose of all seven of them – is that all animals are equal. By the end of the novel Napoleon and the pigs – the new ruling class – have developed an undeniable, conspiratorial relationship with the human beings outside the farm, and they claim, shamelessly, that "some animals are more equal than others" (p. 63). In an allusion to the Teheran Conference at which Stalin hosted a final pact with his capitalist allies, Napoleon and his pigs host a feast in the farmhouse for their human allies. The other animals, peeking in at the window, are amazed to see that the pigs look and behave like human beings. Napoleon has become as greedy and aggressive as any other "human" exploiter of his own masses.

In his "Preface to the Ukrainian edition of *Animal Farm*" (1947) Orwell explained his purpose:

> I would not interfere with Soviet domestic affairs . . . But on the other hand it was of the utmost importance to me that people in Western Europe should see the Soviet regime for what it really was. And so for the past ten years I have been concerned that the destruction of the Soviet myth was essential if we wanted a revival of the Socialist movement. (III: 458)

Emphasizing his commitment to the fight against totalitarianism and for democratic socialism, he wrote that "the whole point is the effect of the Russian mythos on the Socialist movement here. One cannot build up a healthy Socialist movement if one is obliged to condone no matter what crime when the USSR commits it" (III: 443). Completed in February, 1944, *Animal Farm,* an anti-Stalinist satire, was not an easy thing to publish, given the wartime alliance between England and the USSR and the cultural influence of the satirist's pro-Soviet adversary. However, by August, 1945, that is, right after the war, when Secker and Warburg undertook to publish it in England, and Harcourt Brace in the United States, *Animal Farm* suddenly became a resounding success. Between 1946 and 1949 it sold 460,000 copies and soon became a runaway best-seller (Rodden 1989: 44).

It is worth asking why in *Nineteen Eighty-Four,* written in 1948, Orwell felt it important to repeat the message of *Animal Farm,* written only five years earlier. For undoubtedly the structure and the target of the allegory are the same in both novels; both are parodies of the betrayal of the Russian Revolution (see, for example, the connection Orwell establishes between Napoleon and Big Brother (Stalin); between Snowball and Goldstein (Trotsky); and between Squealer and the Ministry of Truth (Stalin's propaganda machine that attempted to rewrite history)). Both novels demonstrate that the totalitarian dictator's popularity is based on the ritual public sacrifice of his scapegoats – a clear reference to Stalin's public purges (and an allusion to Hitler's need for an inexhaustible supply of victims). In fact, if we look at the structure and basic attributes of totalitarianism, it becomes clear that *Nineteen Eighty-Four* contains *Animal Farm.*

By 1948 (the time of writing *Nineteen Eighty-Four*) Orwell took it for granted that the atom bomb, seen in its full effect in August 1945, could be manufactured only by the richest powers to emerge after World War II, the same superpowers controlling a world split into "zones of influence." He also noted with alarm that in the thirties and forties the world became quite willing to accept totalitarian dictatorships; after fascism was defeated, those on the Left, more than ever clung to their faith in the Soviet Union. In fact, they were duped by the "Stalingrad syndrome," in which the western world's gratitude and admiration for the millions of Soviet citizens who died in the war against Hitler was transferred, uncritically, to the Soviet leadership (who did, in effect, send further millions of their own citizens to the Gulag). Ready to respect, even emulate, the Soviet system, many a westerner was ready to deny or simply overlook Stalin's personality cult, in which human bonds were repressed by the Party, so as not to interfere with people's loyalty to, and indeed worship of, the semi-divine leader. This is the aberrant mentality of the totalitarian state, which Orwell also refers to as "protective stupidity," "black-white," "controlled insanity," "mental cheating," a strikingly "schizophrenic way of thinking" originated by the dictator's propaganda machine but also swallowed uncritically by the people. This is the way of thinking that, Orwell fears, could allow the coming to power of a new ruling class in the West, a class more ruthless in its hunger for power than any other in history. In fact, Orwell wrote in 1948, the world of the near future could very easily be split into three gigantic dictatorships, each developed from within and ruled by terror and a total disregard for objective truth. Then, because of the force of the atom bomb as a final deterrent of war, the three power blocks could remain in perfect equilibrium, a structure forever unchangeable by the superpowers without and the smaller nations within.

Goldstein's book, the secret document Winston is so eager to get hold of, explains that the slogan "War is peace" implies that the three world dictators participate in the "imposture" of war in order to mislead their own population. Only when presented with the fiction of a ceaseless war can each population be kept overworked, under-nourished, and hysterically adulating Big Brother, the Savior against the archetypal Satan figure of the Enemy. In fact, in the "secular religion" of totalitarianism, this mythical Enemy and the equally mythical Traitor allow the government to keep each citizen in constant fear of being singled out, quite randomly in fact, to be victimized by the dictatorship as a conspirator with the Traitor. This is the world system of terror brought to reality in *Nineteen Eighty-Four*. Goldstein's book is a significant element of the dystopian novel: it explains in detail how "our" flawed world of the present in 1948 (the world of the satirist and his readers) could change into "our" future in 1984. Its implication is that we should not allow this process to take place.

Orwell introduces here another significant change from his animal fable. By using a major character, Winston Smith, as a central human consciousness with whom we can readily identify, Orwell makes us sense, as if in our own skin, what it is like to be living in the worst of all possible worlds in Oceania. Consequently, Orwell could also reintroduce here the other aspects of his consummate skill as a master of detailed, closely observed naturalistic texture, honed to perfection in his first four novels. In *Nineteen Eighty-Four* Orwell the visionary and Orwell the naturalist finally come together.

Hence the complexity of Orwell's genre, a composite he defines as "in a sense a fantasy, but in the form of the naturalistic novel. That is what makes it a difficult job"

(IV: 378). There is no doubt that the book was intended as a horrifying "fantasy of the future" (IV: 378, 536), what we call today a dystopian satire. As such, Orwell tells us, it is a parody – a word he uses as a synonym for satire – about the splitting up of the world by the superpowers (IV: 520); about the effect of the atom bomb on the divided world; and about the perversions of a centralized economy (IV: 564) aiding and abetting the centralized powers of dictatorship. But most importantly, and in a way that summarizes all of these genres, the book was to be a bitter parody of the "intellectual implications of totalitarianism"; that is, a satire on the totalitarian mentality (IV: 520, 564).

Despite the novel's international success as an all-time bestseller, critics have been confused by its composite genre; that is, by the unprecedented combination of political allegory and psychological realism. They have been largely split as to whether to read the novel as an exclusively naturalistic novel of depth psychology (Fiderer 1970, Roazan 1978, Smyer 1979, Sperber 1983) or a work with exclusively political concerns (the larger camp). Few, however, ask the question why Orwell felt it necessary to go on with the "difficult job" of combining psychological verisimilitude with political allegory. Yet, as a careful reading of the novel makes clear, Orwell the satirist makes his most significant statement here about the nature of totalitarianism by demonstrating that the greatest political disaster brought forth by the totalitarian regime is psychological: the final, irrecoverable disintegration of the individual psyche.

The striking combination of political allegory and psychological verisimilitude is obvious right from the novel's start. Within the space of the first few pages of the novel we get to know Winston, the middle-aged central character climbing the stairs to his seventh-floor apartment, not only in terms of his physical characteristics (his varicose ulcer, and nervous cough), but also in terms of his intellectual and psychological attitudes (his instinctive sense of protest, his fear, his recurring nightmares). As a result, the unfolding political allegory touches us with an intimacy unknown in other novels of this genre. Through Winston we sense what it is like to be living under the ever-watching eyes of the police state, as if it were our own first-hand, personal experience.

As the first scene leads unobtrusively to Winston's overview of the sprawling gray city of London dominated by the overpowering structures of the four ministries, we come face-to-face with the source, and the eventual explanation of, the contrast between so many "Victories" (he enters the slum-like Victory Mansions, swallows a slug of an atrocious Victory gin, and takes out a badly-made Victory cigarette) and the conspicuous economic failure of Oceania. Guided by the convincingly realistic detail, we are scarcely aware of Orwell's mastery: by now the casually naturalistic description has imperceptibly turned into the scaffolding of the political allegory. Still on the same flight of stairs, we pick up Winston's growing uneasiness as he observes the Party's incessant vigilance: the ever-watching eyes of Big Brother on the posters, the helicopters snooping through the windows, the omnipresence of the Thought Police, and the telescreen in the very center of his own apartment. Without the use of any explicit comment, Orwell the satirist prepares us to recognize the ironic contrast between Big Brother's world and the word used to describe it. Having understood that victory stands for failure, we can now proceed to solve the next puzzle: what is the true meaning of the Newspeak names, Minitrue, Minipax, Miniluv and Miniplenty (p. 9)? As we are enabled to see, Minitrue (small truth) represents the ministry of lies, of propaganda; Minipax the ministry of war; Miniplenty the ministry in charge of creating shortages, a scarcity economy; while Miniluv represents the overpowering ministry of hate and torture. (Arendt (1951), Friedrich and Brzezinsky (1956), and Kirkpatrick (1982), among others, outline the structure of totalitarianism similarly to Orwell: the one-party system, with its semi-divine leader, rules in the name of an ideology; the Party taking "total" control over the machinery of constant war, a scarcity economy, and the propaganda machine in charge of education, entertainment, and the news; and, most important, the elaborate system for the punishment of the "heretic" – in the face of any conceivable challenge to government authority.)

Through Winston's fate at the Ministry of Love, we become fully aware of the gratuitous cruelty involved in this state religion that worships God as power. By the end of Winston's trial in the various torture chambers enwombed within the Ministry of Love, O'Brien declares himself the priest serving the god of power and reveals that "the object of persecution is persecution. The object of torture is torture. The object of power is power" (p. 227). Here Orwell's brilliant insight into the dynamics of the totalitarian dictatorship coincides with the diagnosis of Hannah Arendt, who argues that the "real secret, the concentration camps, fulfill the function of laboratories in the experience of total domination" (1951: 436), and that the system relies on the deliberate perpetration of terror as the style, "the very essence of government" (1951: 344).

Since his work in the Ministry of Truth consists of doctoring the documents of the past in order to make them agree with the ever-changing pronouncements of Big Brother in the present, Winston is obsessed with the need to find out the truth in a society where "everything faded into mist. The past was erased, the erasure was forgotten, the lie became truth." This is why he feels compelled to explore simultaneously the political history of Oceania and his own personal history, why he purchases a diary. Winston knows, the moment he opens his diary, that he is committing "thoughtcrime" and that his act cannot remain undetected by the Thought Police. Having seen in his twenties the victims of the public trials, "outlaws, enemies, untouchables, doomed with absolute certainty to extinction," Winston knows that "No one who had once fallen into the hands of the Thought Police ever escaped in the end" (p. 69). Still, Part I ends on a note of mystery: "When once you had succumbed to thoughtcrime it was certain that by a certain date you would be dead. Why then did that horror, which altered nothing, have to be embedded in future time?" Speculating about the nature of that mysterious horror, his attention wonders to the three Party slogans that are phrased like riddles asking for a solution: "WAR IS PEACE. FREEDOM IS SLAVERY. IGNORANCE IS STRENGTH." He knows all his questions relate to his desire to understand not only the methods but also the motivation for the Party's actions – "I understand how – I don't understand why" – and intuitively he turns to the omnipresent portrait of Big Brother for an answer. He is, however, confronted only with yet another aspect of the same puzzle: "The face gazed up at him, heavy, calm, protecting: but what kind of smile was hidden beneath the dark moustache?" (p. 92).

To appreciate Orwell's unique achievement in combining depth psychology with political satire in his analysis of totalitarianism, we must answer the following questions: Why in Room 101 does the Party require from Winston that he offer up Julia as a human sacrifice to be devoured by the starved rats in their cage? And why are the rats the inevitable choice for Winston's final, humiliating breakdown?

Answers to these questions spring from the fact that the scene in Room 101 is, in effect, the re-enactment of a previous crisis. It relates to that significant childhood "memory that [Winston] must have deliberately pushed out of his consciousness over many years" (p. 142), a repression that for almost thirty years made him suffer from recurring guilt dreams and a number of psychosomatic symptoms. After his "break-through dream," he remembers and re-lives this painful, shameful scene in detail, when, as a starving child, he snatched the last piece of chocolate out of his starving sister's hand "and was fleeing for the door... His mother drew her arm round the child and pressed its face against her breast. Something in the gesture told him that his sister was dying" (pp. 144–5). It is the mother's protective gesture around her dying child that Winston has seen in a "flick" that triggers the first vague memory that compels him to start writing in the diary. The process of writing activates his dream-life, until the repressed memory gradually surfaces and he realizes its significance. As he discusses this memory with Julia in their hide-away, he realizes that, although he could not have caused his mother's death – it was the Party that vaporized her – he was nonetheless guilty. When, in his uncontrollable hunger, the child Winston snatched away the last piece of food from his starving mother and sister, he betrayed them by willing their death, as if willing to devour them to appease his own hunger. Just as important, he realizes that with Julia he has another chance to forge an emotional and spiritual bond based on private loyalty and devotion. To liberate himself from the past and expiate his guilt, he seeks this second chance through Julia. The lost paradise of childhood can be re-gained by re-entering paradise with her in the Golden Country.

When in Room 101 O'Brien presents him with a mask-like cage of the starved rats, Winston is forced to break through the walls of darkness, until he faces another, by now final breakdown and re-enacts his childhood betrayal. When he screams, "Do it to Julia! Not me, Julia!", he once more offers up the body of the person he loves as a surrogate for his own. By allowing himself to be degraded to the level of the starving rats, he has become what he most abhors. O'Brien's laboratory experiment in the science of domination has been successful. Winston is turned into a will-less, obedient instrument in the hands of the Party.

Room 101 is the center of the psychosis of betrayal: it is here that any victim can be broken down and turned into the victimizer of others, forced to give up his private bond of loyalty, his private conscience. Winston is ready to join in the collective insanity imposed upon the population by Big Brother, as if joining all the other starved rats in their cage. Ultimately the real face behind the mask-like cage is the face of Big Brother, the god of power (Gottlieb 1992: 74–84). In the moment Winston betrays his loved one, he becomes one with the godhead, acting out the horrible yet inevitable mystery, the loving union between victim and victimizer. It is only now, following the Room 101 incident, that Winston understands the third slogan: "Ignorance is strength." Having learnt to practice doublethink, he chooses to deny, to be ignorant of the private self he has to give up during his interrogation. Having lost his private self, he draws strength from the hysterical worship of the Party: he has come to love Big Brother. This is the horror that had to lie embedded in the future all along, the secret behind Big Brother's smile hiding behind the dark moustache.

Winston's final disintegration after Room 101 can be most clearly demonstrated by the changes in his dream life. Originally, the light-flooded dream landscape of the Golden Country represented Winston's violent effort "to wrench his head away from the pillow," to tear himself away from the nightmare of Oceania; first to find freedom with Julia away from the world of Big Brother, then, in the diminishing versions of the Golden Country envisioned in the interrogation cells, to rescue whatever was left of his inner self. By the end of the novel Winston is totally enslaved: nothing remains of the former self to compel him to get away or to seek shelter. He dismisses the past as a "false memory" and has a vision of walking toward his execution, "as if he walked in sunlight." Not only does he accept, he anticipates and celebrates the bullet in the back. It is the nightmare world of Oceania that has taken the place of his dream of paradise. In fact, our most harrowing discovery in the novel consists of the recognition that in a totalitarian system one can no longer be "free inside," that there is absolutely no hiding place for the inner self. Bit by bit Winston has to give up the freedom of keeping a diary, of the "few cubic centimetres within his skull," of his "inner heart," and, finally, even the freedom of his last place of refuge: his dreams.

There is no doubt that Winston's psychological fate is tragic. His loss of Julia and loss of his private self and private memory are irrevocable and tragic losses. Yet the novel's composite genre demands not only that we identify with Winston's tragic fate but that we examine it from the intellectual distance created by satire. "What happened had to happen" is the recognition reached at the end of tragedy. Only by confronting the darkness of evil and suffering can we liberate ourselves from it. In tragedy, liberation comes as a result of and following the catastrophe. In satire, the catharsis consists of another kind of recognition: that we are still in front of the catastrophe and therefore are in possession of the freedom to avert it. When asked to read Goldstein's book and the Dictionary of Newspeak, dealing, respectively, with Oceania's past (in the 1940s) and its future (in 2050), we are reminded that Winston's moving story, which we have just been reading, has not yet happened. Unlike Winston, we still have the freedom to shape the future according to our higher understanding and according to our free choice. In other words, we can still stop the alarming trends of power-worship and self-deception around us that could lead to an invincibly demonic world in the future. Seen in this light, Orwell's last work is not a product of despair; rather, *Nineteen Eighty-Four*, the twentieth century's dystopian novel *par excellence*, is a powerful warning to the reader not to allow the worst of all possible worlds, that of totalitarian dictatorship, to come into being.

REFERENCES AND FURTHER READING

References to George Orwell's *Animal Farm* and the first four novels are to *The Penguin Complete Novels of George Orwell* (1983); references to *Nineteen Eighty-Four* are to the novel's 1984 Penguin edition.

All quotations from George Orwell's essays, articles, and letters are from *The Collected Essays, Journalism and Letters of George Orwell* in 4 volumes, ed. Sonia Orwell and Ian Angus, Penguin Books, in association with Secker and Warburg, 1970. Page references are in brackets immediately after the quotation and include both volume and page number.

Arendt, Hannah (1951) *The Origins of Totalitarianism*. New York: Harcourt, Brace and World.

Bonifas, Gilbert (1984) *George Orwell: L'Engagement*. Paris: Didier.

Buitenhuis, Peter and Nadel, Ira (eds.) (1988) *George Orwell: A Reassessment*. London: Macmillan.

Calder, Jenni (1987) *Animal Farm and Nineteen Eighty-Four: Open Guides to Literature*. Philadelphia: Open University Press.

Crick, Bernard (1980) *George Orwell: A Life*. London: Secker and Warburg.

Davison, Peter (1996) *George Orwell: A Literary Life*. London: Macmillan.

Deutscher, Isaac (1955) "1984 – the mysticism of cruelty," in *Heretics and Renegades*. London: Hamish Hamilton.

Fiderer, Gerald (1970) "Masochism as literary strategy: Orwell's psychological novels," *Literature And Psychology*, 20: 3–21.

Friedrich, Carl and Brzezinsky, Zbigniev (1956) *Totalitarian Dictatorships and Autocracy*. New York: Praeger.

Gottlieb, Erika (2001) *Dystopian Fiction East and West: Universe of Terror and Trial*. Montreal: McGill-Queen's University Press.

——(1992) *The Orwell Conundrum: A Cry of Despair or Faith in the Spirit of Man?* Ottawa: Carleton University Press.

——(1995) "The satirical masks of utopia and dystopia: a discussion of the two film versions of Orwell's *Nineteen Eighty-Four*," *The Texas Review*, 26/1–4: 83–94.

Hitchens, Christopher (2002) *Orwell's Victory*. Harmondsworth: Penguin.

Kirkpatrick, Jeane (1982) *Dictatorship and Double-standards*. New York: Simon and Schuster.

Myers, Jeffrey (2003) *Orwell: Wintry Conscience of a Generation*. New York: W. W. Norton.

Patai, Daphne (1984) *The Orwell Mystique: A Study of Male Ideology*. Amherst: University of Massachusetts Press.

Roazan, Paul (1978) "Orwell, Freud and 1984," *Virginia Quarterly Review*, 54: 675–95.

Rodden, John (1989) *The Politics of Literary Reputation: The Making and Claiming of St. George Orwell*. New York: Oxford University Press.

Smyer, Richard (1979) *Primal Dream and Primal Crime: Orwell's Development as a Psychological Novelist*. Columbia: University of Missouri Press.

Sperber, Murray (1980) "Gazing into the glass paperweight: the structure and philosophy of Orwell's *Nineteen Eighty-Four*," *Modern Fiction Studies*, 26: 213–16.

Stansky, Peter (ed.) (1983) *On 1984*. New York: Freeman.

Williams, Raymond (1970) *George Orwell*. Modern Masters Series. London: Fontana.

Woodcock, George (1982) *The Crystal Spirit: A Study of George Orwell*. New York: Schocken.

17

Evelyn Waugh's *Brideshead Revisited* and Other Late Novels

Bernard Schweizer

I

There's an evocative scene in *Brideshead Revisited* (1945), depicting the nostalgic narrator, Charles Ryder, at dinner with a modern vulgarian. In the course of their meal, Ryder muses about the wine they are drinking: "I rejoiced in the Burgundy. It seemed a reminder that the world was an older and better place than Rex knew, that mankind in its long passion had learned another wisdom than his" (1988: 169). Charles Ryder, Waugh's alter ego in the novel, expresses an opinion dear to the author himself. According to Waugh, the world acquired a satisfactory degree of substance and value only if it was aged and preserved. To stay within this analogy, the upstart Rex Mottram might have reached the metaphorical level of a Beaujolais nouveau – a cut above the pedestrian beer, but still unripe, insipid, and undeveloped by comparison with the deep, full-bodied, aged Burgundy. What the wine metaphor fails to reflect is the ideological basis of Ryder's (and Waugh's) idealization of the past. Indeed, Waugh's nostalgia was underwritten by distinctly illiberal, anti-industrial, aristocratic, and chivalric values. In keeping with this reactionary sensibility, Waugh's novels are all meditations on one congregate theme: the decline of British culture from its medieval and aristocratic heights; the encroachment of "barbarism" and anarchy from the periphery to the sophisticated centers of civilizations; and the search for spiritual reassurance in a progressively secular, materialistic, and egalitarian world.

Judged from today's viewpoint, this may strike one as a dated project. To extend the wine analogy, the "idiosyncratic Tory Catholicism" (Davis 1989: x) of Waugh's vintage is now past its prime. So, why is Waugh still admired, read, and studied today? Surely, his eccentric personality and eventful life contributed to the ongoing popularity of his work. At the time of this writing, no less than four and a half Waugh biographies are on the table, three of them published in the 1990s within six years (the "half" biography would be Frederick Stopp's *Evelyn Waugh: Portrait of an Artist,* 1958). Another full biography, written by Waugh's grandson, Alexander, is to be released shortly. Besides biographical excitement, Waugh has generated formalist interest, indicated in titles like *The Ironic World of Evelyn Waugh* (1992), *Evelyn Waugh and the Forms of his Time* (1989), and *The Satiric Art of Evelyn Waugh* (1966). These studies rightly emphasize Waugh's superior skills as an ironist, his talent as a constructor of farcical plots, his love of caricature, and his mastery of a spare, precise prose-style. Not surprisingly, biographic-formalist scholars tend to be tolerant or openly apologetic of Waugh's ideological premises. Consider Robert Murray Davis's summary of Waugh's

> central theme: the individual, to be saved as an individual, must retreat from modern society; institutions are finally not worthy of loyalty, though ideals and people are; power in the world inevitably corrupts, but renunciation of the world and of power entails a real cost; the pressure is toward greater confusion, increasing drabness, and vitiation of energy; and private salvation cannot be shared. (1989: 67)

This ideologically sanitized algorithm bypasses the direct political relevance of Waugh's agenda.

Surprisingly, the number and stridency of Waugh's critics has diminished rather than grown over the years. A writer who had been hounded for his reactionary views by progressive writers such as J. B. Priestley, Rose Macaulay, and Rebecca West during his lifetime now manages to incite very little controversy, even among leftists. Take Christopher Hitchens's article on the centennial of Waugh's birth. He finds Waugh's unabashed polemicism appealing, admonishing readers to look beyond the obvious point that "moral courage may be shown by reactionaries or good prose produced by snobs," and appreciating the fact that "Waugh wrote as brilliantly as he did precisely *because* he loathed the modern world" (2003: 107). But this is a problematic proposition. Does Waugh's resolute trashing of the Welfare State, his contempt for non-white races, women, and the "Common Man," and his lampooning of liberal democracy not at all interfere with the leftist intellectual's enjoyment of consummate artistry? Perhaps Hitchens's appreciation is a function of his status as a white middle-class male rather than a reflection of his politics. By the same token, readers hailing from different subject positions, notably women, non-whites, or workers, as well as academic critics with a feminist, Marxist, or postcolonial persuasion might think very differently about Waugh's contemporary relevance.

Waugh's misogyny is a case in point. To observe that "the world of Mr. Waugh's novels is essentially a male world" (Stopp 1958: 119) is to say the least. When the focus is on individual women, rather than on "a rabble of womankind" (Waugh 1988: 23), his female characters tend to belong to what Stopp characterized as "the long line of vapid and predatory females descending from Brenda Last and Lucy Simmonds" (p. 119). In *The Loved One* (1948), Waugh's mordant farce of California's funeral industry, the female protagonist is described as "the exquisite dim head in the corner" (2002: 115), whose "heart was broken perhaps, but it was a small inexpensive organ of local manufacture" (p. 109). The picture is filled out by a detailed description of Aimee's cosmetic "instruments and chemicals which are the staples of feminine well-being . . . [and] the brown tube of barbiturates which is the staple of feminine repose" (pp. 119–20). In keeping with an old sexist tradition, most of Waugh's female characters fall either under the heading of the dangerous temptress or the childlike (and therefore insignificant) woman. As for the latter category, Kerstie, in the *Sword of Honour* trilogy, "was a good wife to Ian, personable, faithful, even-tempered and economical" (2000b: 180); she is a proper Angel in the House and, together with her two friends Brenda and Zita, she "giggled and gossiped about their customers like real waitresses (p. 181). But Kerstie is also "point by point . . . the antithesis of her friend Virginia Troy" (p. 180). And that would make Virginia a prototypical femme fatale. Uncle Peregrine muses that "Virginia was a Scarlet Woman; the fatal woman who had brought about the fall of the house of Crouchback" (2000c: 169) and his brother pushes the analogy further, explaining that she was named "Like Helen of Troy" (p. 170). In this manner, Virginia comes across as a promiscuous, sexually rapacious, and profiteering woman in the tradition of Chaucer's Wife of Bath, except that Waugh doesn't have a shred of sympathy for her. She is merely the canvas on which Waugh paints his image of misogyny.

But Waugh's negative depiction of women has another significance. In *Brideshead Revisited*, the best of Waugh's non-satirical novels, Brideshead Castle displays architectural features defined as variously feminine and masculine. Charles Ryder, the I-narrator, comments on the difference as follows:

> I closed the door behind me, shutting out the *bondieuserie*, the low ceiling, the chintz . . . [of] the intimate feminine, modern world and was back under the coved and coffered roof, the columns and entablature of the central hall, in the august, masculine atmosphere of a better age. (1988: 133)

Here, Waugh's alter ego not only contrasts the (supposedly feminine) intimacy of Lady Marchmain's room with the masculine appeal of the grandiose architectural designs in the main hall, he also asserts in the same breath that modernity is a function of effeminacy, whereas aristocracy pertains of a declining era of masculine vigor. Thus, Ryder's discourse codes modernity as feminine *and* bourgeois, a combination that he blames for the cultural decline of his age.

But while femininity and modernity are conspiring to destroy masculine aristocratic virtues within England, "barbarism" is, in Waugh's logic, the equivalent of such a decline on a worldwide scale. In this context, non-white races parallel the role of English women as the symptoms *and* the instruments of this creeping degradation. As I have shown in *Radicals on the Road* (2001), Waugh's travel books (and the novels inspired by them) consistently link the advance of "barbarism" with the growth of anti-colonial resistance, and Abyssinia's attempt to constitute a government independent of western tutelage elicits only contempt. This politically motivated rejection of non-white rule is paired with an unapologetic form of racist denigration. But the comedy inspired by racial superiority no longer seems in good taste now: "[The missionaries] don't stand any nonsense from the natives. None of that 'me velly Clistian boy got soul all same as white boss'" (2000a: 90). Such jokes, made at the expense of "natives" rather than of the people expressing such stereotypes, may have worked better in bygone days; but today they are likely to cause more embarrassment than mirth.

Waugh's elitist conservatism also colors his depiction of lower-class members. Workers hardly figure in his fiction, and the scenes in *Brideshead* that are set during England's General Strike of 1926 lack a single believable portrait of a striker. Waugh even implies that the whole rebellion was a feeble, silly protest: "Next day the General Strike was called off and the country everywhere, except in the coal fields, returned to normal. It was as though a beast long fabled for its ferocity had emerged for an hour, scented danger, and slunk back to its lair. It had not been worth leaving Paris" (1988: 199). But while his treatment of the working classes is generally dismissive and scornful, characters holding elitist social views are portrayed sympathetically. Take, for instance, Guy Crouchback's father, who declares his love of social hierarchy: "[Mr. Crouchback] saw the whole intricate social structure of his country divided neatly into two unequal and unmistakable parts. On the one side stood the Crouchbacks and certain inconspicuous, anciently allied families; on the other side stood the rest of mankind" (2000a: 38). Although the reader is invited to chuckle over such crass attitudes, it is clear that Waugh half believed in Mr Crouchback's social creed. Not only was Waugh compulsively trying to fashion himself as a country squire, thereby "improving" on his bourgeois upbringing, he also expressed warm tribute to nostalgic ideas of inborn virtue, heritable power, pedigree, and white supremacy. These ideological constants of this outlook never changed throughout his career.

What changed are Waugh's use of satire and his weighing of autobiographical materials. One critic argued:

> with *Brideshead Revisited*, the first of Waugh's novels to depict a Catholic rather than a neopagan environment, the change becomes profound. The enunciation of a positive spiritual norm, absolute and unequivocally expressed, offers an alternative to mundane disorder and obliges the author, through a highly subjective first-person narrator, to utter moral pronouncements that are irreconcilable with irony on a philosophical plane. (Beaty 1992: 8)

Though this is likely to be an overstatement, given that Waugh kept producing satires after *Brideshead Revisited* and that his religious outlook remained implicit rather than didactic, his later work was indeed more mellow, serious, and self-searching. In tow with this, there is an increasing reliance on autobiographical materials in Waugh's later fiction.

While many incidents and personages in *Decline and Fall* (1928), *Vile Bodies* (1930), or *Scoop* (1938) are traceable to Waugh's experiences as a novice teacher, a member of London's "Bright Young People," or a war correspondent, there are many more story elements that are pure inventions. But as Waugh aged, his own life became an obsessive and almost exclusive source of inspiration for his fiction. Much of *The Ordeal of Gilbert Pinfold* (1957) is straightforward, unapologetic autobiography:

Mr Pinfold is an ailing, ennui-ridden, Catholic novelist of celebrity status. Sounds like Waugh. We are told, moreover, that

> he was not what is generally meant by the appellation a "philanthropic" man; he totally lacked what was now called a "social conscience." But apart from his love of family and friends he had a certain basic kindliness to those who refrained from active annoyance. And in an old-fashioned way he was patriotic. (*1979:* 140–1)

No biographer could come up with an apter description of Waugh's character. Or take Guy Crouchback, the protagonist of Waugh's *Sword of Honour* trilogy (1952, 1955, 1961), who is active in the same theaters of World War II to which Waugh was dispatched (West Africa, Crete, and Croatia), shares Waugh's opinions about Churchill's policies, and by and large undergoes the same fate that befell Waugh during the war, down to the detail of an injury incurred after a parachute jump. It is not surprising, then, to learn that Guy Crouchback's birth date is given as October 29, 1903, the same as Waugh's. This aspect of Waugh's work mesmerized his friends and acquaintances who would set straight about puzzling out the key to his novels the moment they were published. But such a fixation can be a liability.

Although most fiction can be traced in one way or another to the author's own life, Waugh's heavy reliance on autobiographical data raises some basic questions of creativity and literary merit. For instance, *The Ordeal* comes across as a joint-venture of private exorcism and apologia pro vita sua – a work so self-involved as to almost shunt aside the reader. The story is about a Waugh-like character in the throes of schizophrenic delusions. The voices that torment Mr Pinfold on board a ship bound for Ceylon are conspiring to humiliate, expose, or even kill him. But rather than being the kind of postmodern fancy that blurs the dividing line between "reality" and hallucination, *The Ordeal* comes to resemble a case study in actual psychopathology. For any reader aware of Waugh's personal problems with drunkenness, insomnia, ennui, and depression, it is impossible not to succumb to the biographical "fallacy" of mentally substituting "Waugh" every time he reads "Pinfold." But the self-importance of Pinfold/Waugh, a man who believes that the passengers of a large cruise ship have nothing better to do than to spend their entire time conspiring against him, takes on the quality of an obsessive narcissism. By the same token, the reader is willy-nilly turned into a psychiatrist, tracking the protagonist's progressive mental illness in a self-interpreting novel that excludes more open-ended ways of reading.

Still, as a discursive platform for Waugh's personal weaknesses and anxieties, the book holds interesting clues to the author's inner life, notably his world-weariness, his emotional distance to his children, even hints of sexual dysfunction. More significantly, the book turns into a justification of Waugh's religious and political views. The "voices" in Pinfold's head argue that "he doesn't really believe in his religion, you know. He just pretends to because he thinks it aristocratic" (1979: 148). As a self-fashioned aristocratic parvenu and a Catholic convert, Waugh must have faced this accusation again and again. On the subject of Pinfold's politics, the voices are unequivocal: "all I know is that he is a fascist. I have heard him speak ill of democracy" (p. 151). Again, it is a reasonable inference to make with regard to Waugh, and Pinfold's self-defense is revealing: "I had every sympathy with Franco during the Civil War.... [But] I never had the smallest sympathy with Hitler... Once I had hopes of Mussolini. But I was never connected with Mosley" (p. 159). If Waugh's strategy was to take the wind out of his detractors' sails, such passages may very well have succeeded in stealing their thunder. After all, what can one say to someone who declares his admiration for Franco and Mussolini? But then, I agree with Robert Murray Davis's estimation that *"The Ordeal of Gilbert Pinfold* will interest only specialists" (Davis 1989: 61), because the work is deficient in imagination and too closely resembles a cat and mouse play between author and contemporaneous critics.

II

What ultimately saves Waugh's later novels from being disguised memoirs and political mouthpieces is the fact that the best of them approach their protagonists and subjects in an ironic, playful, and self-deflating manner. The *Sword of Honour* trilogy is a good case in point. Guy Crouchback, Waugh's fictional stand-in, sees himself as a "lonely and ineffective man – the man he so often thought he saw in himself, past his first youth, cuckold, wastrel, prig" (2000a: 184). While Waugh's earlier fiction often involved his fictional alter egos in various wish-fulfillment scenarios, his later fiction is more resigned. Crouchback, whose very name is a word-play on regression and defeat, is the divorced, melancholy, self-doubting, and inept son of an impoverished member of the Catholic gentry. Although the family's estate had been "held in uninterrupted male succession since the reign of Henry I" (p. 16), declining incomes forced Mr Crouchback to let it. Mr Crouchback lives out his last years as a lodger in a small seaside hotel where he serves the community as a pedantic Latin teacher. In keeping with the downward turn of the Crouchback family's fortunes, Guy's brother, Ivo, goes mad, his uncle, Peregrine, settles into perpetual bachelorhood, and his nephew, Tony, turns into a dotty religious fanatic.

Significantly, Guy's personal fortune starts to unravel in Kenya, a place Waugh had visited in 1930 and found to be as close to heaven as anything. Similarly, Guy Crouchback enjoyed "Kenya, living it seemed to him afterwards, in unruffled good-humour beside a mountain lake where the air was always brilliant and keen and the flamingoes rose at dawn first white, then pink, then a whirl of shadow passing across the glowing sky" (2000a: 16). But the paradisal state is disrupted when Guy's wife, the above-mentioned promiscuous Virginia, deserts Guy during his stint as a gentleman farmer in colonial Kenya. Ever since that fateful year, it seemed Guy "had suffered a tiny stroke of paralysis; all his spiritual faculties were just perceptibly impaired" (p. 10). This is clearly meant as a reference to Waugh's own desertion by his first wife, Evelyn Gardner, in 1929. Like Guy, Waugh agonized over his wife's infidelity and re-enacted the pain again and again in his fiction, inventing a series of unfaithful women.

But there is a strange dissociation between the reported torment of Guy's haunted psyche and the degree to which that predicament is made accessible to the reader: "into that wasteland where his soul languished he need not, could not enter. He had no words to describe it. There were no words in any language" (p. 10). This is more than a description of Guy's state of mind – it is a programmatic statement of Waugh's fictional method. Throughout the trilogy, as in most other novels by Waugh, the reader is almost never allowed to glimpse into the character's soul, to partake of his thoughts, or to ride along his "stream of consciousness." Such lack of introspection prompted Frederick Stopp to invoke a cinematic analogy, identifying "two Mr. Waughs, the one who delivers the film, and the one who cuts it" (1958: 187). In *Sword of Honour,* the camera-like perspective is quite fitting, since it reduces Guy to the imponderable, fate-buffeted, mysterious entity that he sees himself as being. Moreover, Douglas Patey argued, rather convincingly, that the "'external,' un-subjective presentation [of Waugh's characters] accurately captures their modern lives," and that "the literary form in which such limited characters' are most at home is satire" (1998: 57). Thus Waugh's external narrative perspective is simply an expression of his overall rejection of modernity and his satirical aim. But Waugh's reluctance to reveal the inner workings of his characters has yet another implication. Waugh not only rejected artistic and literary modernism, he also abhorred the psychological interests of other modernists. Contrary to writers such as Graham Greene and W. H. Auden, who worked Freud's theories into their texts, Waugh denounced psychoanalysis as a sham. Patey sheds a revealing light on this view, too, insisting that "such hostility to 'psychology' was widely shared among the devout, especially Catholics suspicious of all speculative systems that undermined belief in the soul, will and divine purpose" (1998: 36).

Seen from this perspective, it is paradoxical that one of the most memorable scenes in all of Waugh's work, the descent of Major Hound (dubbed Fido) in *Officers and Gentlemen* from starvation, to delirium, to desertion, to death, is worded precisely in the language of psychological symbolism. In a beautifully evocative scene, Waugh depicts Major Hound enacting an archetypal return to the womb. Impelled by the raw instinct for survival, Fido first crawls into a drainpipe under the road, where he curls up in fetal position, contemplating Edenic visions at the end of the tube. Later, he falls down a ravine, loses consciousness, and is stripped of all his military accoutrements by a looting native. The regress is completed when he staggers almost naked into a strange, psychedelic cave full of humanity at its most basic – a womb of kinds featuring a large, steaming cauldron at its center. There, closing the symbolical cycle of life and death, he is dispatched by his enemy in the ranks, Corporal Ludovic.

The descent of Fido, narrated from the characters' internal perspective and saturated with psycho-imagery, might simply be a spoof on the methods of symbolism and psychological realism. That is the spin Waugh himself tries to put on the episode. In *The End of the Battle,* Waugh turned Fido's nemesis, Corporal Ludovic, into a pseudo-modernistic author, whose successful first novel is titled "The Death Wish." Ludovic, who is paradoxically modeled on Waugh himself, also tries his hand at poetry, and in so doing fills his poems with instance upon instance of "Cave image" (2000c: 57). This causes one acquaintance to ask: "You must have read a lot of Freudian psychology?" Although Ludovic protests that "there was nothing psychological about the cave," the critic reassures him that his poems reveal "a spontaneous liberation of the unconscious" (p. 57). In my judgment, the archetypal nature of Fido's descent is too sincere to be considered a spoof, and its literary qualities are far above burlesque. More likely, Waugh was trying to exorcise the "demon" of psychological realism that had tempted him while imagining Fido's demise.

This argument is bolstered by the superior quality of the entire Cretan episode in *Officers and Gentlemen*, which can pass as a small masterpiece in its own right. The harrowing rendition of shock, despair, fear, chaos, and violence lend color, depth, and drama to this often too sprawling, discursive, jargon-ridden, and slow-paced sequence of novels. Once Guy lands on enemy territory and gets involved in belligerent action, the real meaning of the war, which had remained largely in the background till then, reveals itself uncompromisingly. The euphemistically termed "tactical dispersal" of allied forces soon turns into an open rout, as German warplanes pound the retreating columns: "The procession shuffled dismally past and was still in sight when the first aeroplane of the day roared down on them. Some stood their ground and waved their white flags; others scattered. These were the wiser. The German fired a line of bullets through them; several fell; the remainder scattered for cover as the airman returned and fired again" (2000b: 260). The reality of death, which is masked in such mass scenes, is touchingly revealed when Guy contemplates the body of a fallen British soldier:

> Why was he lying here? . . . Guy would never know. It remained one of the countless unexplained incidents of war. . . . Guy knelt and took the [identity] disc from the cold breast. He read a number, a name, a designation, *R.C.* . . . Guy stood. The bluebottles returned to the peaceful young face. Guy saluted and passed on. (2000b: 279–80)

The perspective remains camera-like, the style almost laconic. Once again, however, the narrative distance serves a purpose, foregrounding the exhaustion and desperation that have reduced Guy almost to an automaton. Waugh's bleak, spare, style conveys another message too: the war is not about heroism; fighting does not build character; and the allied armies are not instruments of superior politics.

Already in the first installment of the trilogy, Guy muses glumly that "he was engaged in a war in which courage and a just cause were quite irrelevant to the issue" (2000a: 192). From there, things get only worse. As can be expected, Guy's wartime experience parallels that of Waugh's in many ways: "The Halberdiers offer Crouchback many of the values which the novelist himself passionately admires: tradition, continuity, order, ritual" (Carens 1966: 42). Though an enthusiastic conscript who left no stone unturned to get himself an appointment in the army, despite his prohibitive age (36), Waugh gradually turned into a cynical critic of the British military. His disgust was sharpened by British inaction when Catholic Poland and Finland were gobbled up by the Nazis and the Russians.

Waugh's criticism of British wartime policy translates directly into *Sword of Honour*. Recovering in Cairo from the tribulations of his Cretan expedition, Guy muses "that was early in the morning of June 22 – a day of apocalypse for all the world for numberless generations" (2000b: 324). On June 22, 1941, Germany launched its offensive against Russia, rescinding the Molotow–Ribbentrop pact and forcing the allied nations to accept Stalin as a partner against Nazi Germany. To Waugh, Churchill's decision to side with Stalin was equivalent to treason, making Britain an accomplice of Stalin's crimes against humanity, signs of which began to emerge in the late 1930s. Thus, the eponymous sword on display in Westminster Abbey, designed as a gift from King George IV to Stalin, is ironically named "Sword of Honour." To Guy, the sword is a badge of dishonor and the symbol of the Allies' betrayal of Eastern Europe and its Catholic population, who could expect nothing but brutal repression from the Soviet Union.

As far as Guy Crouchback is concerned, "half an hour's scramble on the beach near Dakar; an ignominious rout in Crete. That had been his war" (2000c: 220). The same goes, with minor adjustments, for Waugh himself. Waugh's sardonic portrait of Guy as a quintessential naïf, the humoristic depiction of eccentrics like Apthorpe, and the ridiculous efforts of the Secret Service to prove Guy to be a fascist infiltrator, lend themselves well to Waugh's satirical talents. But the war was no laughing matter, and sometimes Waugh's efforts to make it seem so are contrived. While describing a rollicking guest-night at the Halberdiers' boot camp, Waugh reminds the reader how "immeasurably far" this scene was "from the frontier of Christendom where the great battle had been fought and lost; from those secret forests where the trains were, even then, while the Halbierdiers and their guests sat bemused by wine and harmony, rolling east and west with their doomed loads" (2000a: 98). Waugh's juxtaposition of banality with deportation and mass murder risks devaluing the immensity of the human tragedy, while failing to augment the humor. Waugh wants to have it both ways: the trilogy is ostensibly an historical novel with all the trappings of verisimilitude and didacticism; but then it is also a farcical fantasy intended to entertain. The contrary impulses set up a tension that threatens to undermine the work's formal coherence and to dislodge its moral center.

III

It has been argued that Guy becomes a "new man" in *The End of the Battle*, owing to his pro-active behavior in rescuing Jews, re-marrying Victoria, and adopting her illegitimate son. I am not so sure. Although there is a hint of development in his character, the change is patchy and comes very late in the trilogy. By comparison, *Brideshead* is clearly a *Bildungsroman* rather than a satire, with developing figures and an I-narrator who allows the reader access into his consciousness, thereby lending the novel greater range and depth. This alone would make *Brideshead* a better novel than the trilogy; but the reader is further rewarded by an exciting dialectic, where the novel's central intelligence is actually a credible anti-Catholic, at least during the larger part of the story. This distance from the customary autobiographical perspective lifts Waugh's art to a new level. Here Waugh's nostalgia finds an appropriate outlet, without being cranky, and his satirical streak is tamed for the benefit of subtler depictions of character, belief, and motivation. Finally, the framed, dispersed, interrupted narrative technique is genuinely innovative, and Waugh's style, too, is particularly assured, inspired, and vividly colored.

If the basic recipe for modernistic fiction includes the absence of an omniscient narrator, arbitrariness and chance, as well as a focus on the individual's inner struggles, then the same applies to some degree to the Catholic concept of grace. According to St Augustine, constant introspection and contrition are ways to make oneself available for grace, although ultimately God's will is beyond human comprehension, as he unpredictably saves whomever he chooses, regardless of apparent merits. In a preface for the revised 1959 edition of *Brideshead*, Waugh announced that the novel's central theme is "the operation of divine grace on a group of diverse but closely connected characters" (1988: 7). This strikes one as a programmatic Catholic premise liable to ruin the book. Fortunately, this theme is much less obvious than Waugh makes it appear, except at the very end when Waugh manufactured a graphic instance of grace. But, overall, the operation of grace is more evident structurally than thematically: for one thing, the narrator of *Brideshead* is not omniscient, which reflects the author's unwillingness to become God's surrogate; next, the plot is far from giving a semblance of revealed destiny, which is God's own domain; rather, the narrative twists and turns in flash-backs, flash-forwards, and multiply-framed metanarratives; also, the set of dramatis personae never remains quite stable, with some characters rocketing off in brilliant displays to the margins of the story, while others suddenly materialize out of nowhere. All this can be perfectly reconciled with the concept of grace, of which Sebastian Flyte is a fitting allegory. Indeed, the precise reasons for his descent from the heights of vitality at the beginning of the novel to senile decrepitude in the end are shrouded in mystery. Is he a recandescant Catholic? A repressed homosexual? A man burdened with hereditary depression and alcoholism? Waugh seems to give his destiny over to divine grace, and in the course of doing so, he writes a modernistic tale.

Over and above Waugh's optimistic aim to explore the operations of grace, *Brideshead* is first and foremost concerned with the pessimistic implications of decline, which figure on three separate levels in the narrative: personal, familial, and cultural. First, there is the fate of Sebastian, Lord Marchmain's teddy-bear-toting son, who becomes Charles Ryder's lover. Being chronically misbehaved, academically disinclined, and progressively alcoholic, he is sent down from Oxford after only one year. When his drinking turns pathological, Sebastian escapes from his paternalistic reformers to live as a homeless dipsomaniac, drifting through North Africa. The second level of decline is adumbrated by the aristocratic family's dwindling fortunes, as evidenced in the accumulated debt of the Marchmains, which forces them to sell some of their outlying property for cash and shut down the estate's private chapel. Intertwined with this material decline is the decay of the family's emotional bonds, epitomized by the separation between the Lord and Lady Marchmain – she living in England, he in Venice. Being Catholics, they cannot divorce each other, and they live out a life of alienation and mutual resentment. The last level of decline, finally, is cultural. Interspersed throughout the book are clues about the advance of barbarism: "It's just another jungle closing in" (1988: 221) muses Charles Ryder when questioned by his wife about the future of his career as a painter. But the trope of encroaching chaos is double-headed.

Ironically, Waugh's imagination (and hence, his income) thrived on the universal decline he lamented. *Brideshead* contains a shrewd meditation on that very paradox. Waugh's stand-in, the narrator Charles Ryder, makes a fortune by painting country houses before they are torn down.

> In such [ancient aristocratic] buildings England abounded, and, in the last decade of their grandeur, Englishmen seemed for the first time conscious of what before was taken for granted, and to salute their achievement at the moment of extinction. Hence my prosperity, far beyond my merits.... My success ... was, indeed, itself a symptom of the decline. (1988: 215–16)

If one substitutes writing for painting and exchanges country houses with their inmates, this description can serve as an (albeit self-deprecatory) outline of Waugh's own professional project. Waugh, too, captured the country-house culture at the moment of its demise, and he also traveled to Latin America in his thirties, only to witness that barbarism was advancing there as well: "we had overtaken civilization in its retreat" (*1991:* 172), he writes about British Guyana. But is this a cause for celebration or despair? One of Ryder's art critics comments that "by focusing the frankly traditional battery of his elegance and erudition on the maelstrom of barbarism, Mr Ryder has at last found himself" (1988: 218). The same applies, with minor adjustments, to Waugh, whose satire depended on the presence of chaos, anarchy, and barbarism, all of which he seemed to have enjoyed as much as deplored.

Thankfully, *Brideshead* moves beyond these and other mainstays of Waugh's imagination. There is little racial commentary, and although *Brideshead* has its share of silly, weak, insignificant female characters ("My wife seemed to make a sacred, female rite even of seasickness" (p. 239)), the novel also features a spirited, intelligent, and dignified woman –Julia. Sadly, though, it turns out that her dignity is propped up by her religious function in the narrative. She believes in mortal sin and laments "Christ dying with [our sin], nailed hand and foot ... no comfort except a sponge of vinegar and the kind words of a thief" (p. 274). So, when she lashes Ryder across the face after an altercation in the park, leaving behind two cuts in the shape of a cross, she appears to be exorcising the evil of atheism in him. Indeed, Ryder had denounced the Catholicism of the Marchmains as "a lot of witchcraft and hypocrisy," as well as mere "mumbo-jumbo" (pp. 310, 312), excoriating at great length the logical fallacies of the Catholic doctrine. But when the dying Lord Marchmain, a fervent anti-cleric and dissenter, makes the sign of the cross, Ryder begins the change: "Then I knew that the sign I had asked for was not a little thing, not a passing nod of recognition, and a phrase came back to me from my childhood of the veil of the temple being rent from top to bottom" (p. 322).

Although the religious dispute eventually causes Ryder's break-up with his fiancée, Julia Brideshead, Ryder appears to be fully converted to Catholicism by the time he returns to Brideshead Castle as an officer during World War II. He goes into the chapel to say "a prayer, an ancient, newly-learned form of words" (1988: 330), and receives solace from the flame burning anew in the tabernacle. But Ryder is far from being saved, he is not even happy: "I'm homeless, childless, middle-aged, loveless" (p. 330) he confesses to Hooper, of all people. Although his conversion makes him eligible for divine grace, the pagan Ryder was a much more lively, likable, and interesting character than the resigned, brooding entity we encounter in the framing narrative. If that is the operation of grace then so be it, but it is not a strategy likely to convert many to the tenets of Catholicism. But this could very well be the ultimate triumph of *Brideshead* – its refusal to yield to any doctrinaire religious complacency and instead to elevate the "fierce little human tragedy in which [Ryder] played" (p. 331) to the level of great secular art.

References and Further Reading

Beaty, Frederick L. (1992) *The Ironic World of Evelyn Waugh*. DeKalb: Northern Illinois University Press.

Carens, James F. (1996) *The Satiric Art of Evelyn Waugh*. Seattle: University of Washington Press.

Davis, Robert M. (1989) *Evelyn Waugh and the Forms of His Time*. Washington, DC: Catholic University of America Press.

Hitchens, Christopher (2003) "The permanent adolescent," *Atlantic Monthly*, 291/4 (May): 107–16.

Patey, Douglas (1998) *The Life of Evelyn Waugh*. Cambridge, MA: Blackwell.

Schweizer, Bernard (2001) *Radicals on the Road*. Charlottesville: University of Virginia Press.

Stopp, Fredrick J. (1958) *Evelyn Waugh: Portrait of an Artist*. Boston: Little, Brown.

Waugh, Evelyn (1979) *The Ordeal of Gilbert Pinfold*. New York: Little, Brown.

—— (1988) *Brideshead Revisited*. Harmondsworth: Penguin.

—— (1991) *Ninety-Two Days*. London: Methuen.

—— (2000a) *Men At Arms*. New York: Little, Brown.

—— (2000b) *Officers and Gentlemen*. New York: Little, Brown.

—— (2000c) *The End of the Battle*. New York: Little, Brown. (Published in UK as *Unconditional Surrender*).

—— (2002) *The Loved One*. Barnes and Noble Modern Classics.

18

Modernism's Swansong: Malcolm Lowry's *Under the Volcano*

Patrick A. McCarthy

One of the two framed artworks hanging side by side in my living room is a 1986 linocut entitled "Under the Volcano," by the Miami poet and artist Laurence Donovan. With its intricate design, fine attention to detail, and overlapping, repetitive patterns it resembles Malcolm Lowry's *Under the Volcano*, which inspired the Donovan print. Looking closely at the print, we can see other similarities, some of them obvious (the volcano looming over the Mexican buildings) and others less so: the numerous circles, for example, as well as the various paths leading downward, perhaps to the barranca.

Were it not framed, the other piece, consisting of two color photocopies, would hardly be regarded as a work of art. One sheet is a menu in Spanish listing "servicio a la carta" prices at "El Petate" and bearing a large picture of a woman holding tickets for the Mexican national lottery; the other reproduces the back of the same menu. The two sides are packed with writing in Lowry's hand, some from 1938 (the date on the menu), some from the mid-1940s. The menu, with its scribblings and drawings, represents various aspects of Lowry's life in, and involvement with, Mexico. Among the 1938 scribblings are a bar tab for three drinks totaling 2 pesos 10 centavos, an unfinished poem entitled "A Curse," and two drafts of another poem, one bearing the title "The Comedian." Those from the 1940s include a long note beginning "full length a buxom and dowdy Mexican girl" as well as several brief notes: "Number should be number of Hugh's passport"; "Get Margie to describe the colors"; and, most tellingly, "Reprint in *full*."

The original menu, now housed in the Malcolm Lowry Archive at the Main Library, University of British Columbia, is familiar to readers of *Under the Volcano*, for as the note "Reprint in *full*" indicates, the menu reappears in the novel, transformed from part of Lowry's life into an element of his art. In the novel the verso scribblings are written by "the Consul," Geoffrey Firmin, the alcoholic ex-British Consul to Quauhnahuac, Mexico, who is the novel's quasi-autobiographical protagonist. In Chapter 11, Yvonne and Hugh – Geoffrey's estranged wife and his brother – stop at the Hotel y Restaurant El Popo and have drinks before starting out again to look for the Consul. Hugh suddenly appears with the menu/bar tab, having paid Geoffrey's bill, and when Yvonne looks at the menu, she sees representations of herself on the front and of the Consul on the back. I will return later to the menu's role in the novel. For now I will simply note that placing the menu and the Donovan print side by side on the wall sets up a contrast between a document that fed into *Under the Volcano* and a print inspired by the novel. In a pattern typical of modernist fiction and poetry, the menu, the novel, and the print all demand to be read intertextually.

Lowry's life (1909–57) was to some extent the basis of all of his fiction. *Under the Volcano* (1947), his one clear success, grew out of his stay in Mexico from November 1936 to July 1938, a particularly turbulent period in his life. With his first wife, Jan Gabrial, Lowry entered Mexico full of hope that the visit could save their marriage, but his drinking made that impossible, and after a year Jan left him; later, he was arrested, having aroused suspicion by claiming to have fought in Spain against Franco. By the time Lowry departed Mexico, however, he had begun the long process of writing *Under the Volcano*. Moving to British Columbia in 1939, he was joined by Margerie Bonner, who became his second wife. There, he obsessively wrote and rewrote *Under the Volcano*.

What emerged from those innumerable revisions is a complex, symbolic narrative. Lowry explained some of his novel's themes, symbols, and techniques in a remarkable letter to his British publisher Jonathan Cape (1995–6, I: 498–528). The twelve chapters form a cyclic narrative, Chapter 1 taking place on the Day of the Dead in 1939, Chapters 2–12 on the same day a year earlier, when the Consul and Yvonne died. The four main characters are the Consul, Yvonne, Hugh, and Jacques Laruelle, an expatriate French film director. In the first chapter, Jacques remembers his friend's life, then discovers (and ultimately burns) a letter the Consul had written but never sent to Yvonne. This chapter ends with the image of a backwards-turning Ferris wheel, which for Lowry had many meanings: "it is Buddha's wheel of the law . . . it is eternity, it is the instrument of eternal recurrence, the eternal return, and it is the form of the book." It is also the wheel of time returning us to the Day of the Dead 1938.

Lowry called *Under the Volcano* "a prophecy, a political warning, a cryptogram, a preposterous movie, and a writing on the wall." Above all it is a novel, one whose meanings are both universal and particular: the Consul's fate, he said, is related to "the ultimate fate of mankind." "There are," Lowry proclaimed, "a thousand writers who can draw adequate characters till all is blue for one who can tell you anything new about hell fire. And I am telling you something new about hell fire." Finally, "the book was so designed, counterdesigned and interwelded that it could be read an indefinite number of times and still not have yielded all its meanings or its drama or its poetry." Lowry's claims for his fiction might sound exaggerated, but it is clear that he meant to produce a work that is not only "new" in its revelations about hell fire but new each time it is read, in part because its intricate patterns reveal (or perhaps assemble) themselves only on re-reading.

The basic plot of Chapters 2–12, in which Geoffrey and Yvonne are called back to life for a day, is simple. Having left the Consul nearly a year earlier, Yvonne returns unexpectedly and finds him at the Bella Vista bar, drinking at seven in the morning. Later Geoffrey, Yvonne, and Hugh take a bus ride that is interrupted when the bus driver spots a dying Indian by the side of the road; one of the other riders on the bus steals the Indian's money. They head to the bull ring in Tomalín, then to the Salón Ofélia, where the Consul drinks mescal before Hugh and Yvonne arrive. At dinner Hugh and the Consul quarrel about politics, and Geoffrey runs out, heading for Parián and another cantina, the Farolito. Hugh and Yvonne take a longer path to Parián, stop for drinks at El Popo (where Hugh finds the menu with Geoffrey's bar tab), then make their way through the forest toward Parián; but at the end of Chapter 11 Yvonne is trampled to death by a horse with the number seven on its rump – the horse of the dying Indian.

The action of Chapter 12 is simultaneous with that of Chapter 11: both occur roughly between 6:00 and 7:00 p.m. Moving from the end of Chapter 11 to the beginning of Chapter 12, we are therefore taken back an hour, to a past when Yvonne was alive, much as the movement from Chapter 1 to Chapter 2 takes us back a full year. In Chapter 12, at the Farolito, the Consul drinks mescal again, has sex with a prostitute, and becomes embroiled in an argument with members of a fascist militia. At the end he is shot as he releases the horse that a few minutes later (but a chapter earlier) tramples Yvonne.

This précis omits crucial events whose function is primarily symbolic or revelatory of character: for example, Geoffrey's misreading of a sign in a public garden as a threat that those who destroy will be evicted. Moreover, this discussion cannot do justice to the poetry of the novel's descriptive passages, its complex symbolic patterns, its richness of observation, its humor. Here, I will briefly illustrate Lowry's handling of perspective, dialogue, and allusions before returning to the menu of Chapter 11.

Aspects of Perspective

In general, Lowry filters each chapter through the consciousness of one of the main characters: Chapter 1 through Jacques's mind, 2, 9, and 11 through Yvonne's, 3, 5, 7, 10, and 12 through the Consul's, and 4, 6, and 8 through Hugh's. Lowry never uses the same character's perspective in two sequential chapters, a technique that sets up a "dialogue" among the fundamental perspectives of the chapters. In turn, those perspectives are often disrupted by alternative voices or discourses. In Chapter 2, for example, the voice of an unseen man intrudes on the conversation between Yvonne and Geoffrey, and part of Chapter 10 alternates between what Geoffrey hears and his reading of a Tlaxcalan tourist brochure.

At times, however, as in the expansive opening paragraphs of Chapter 1, before Jacques makes his appearance, *Under the Volcano* presents material to us independently of the consciousness of any individual character. One example is the set of three epigraphs that precede the narration; another is the corrected sign in the garden that appears on the end page. The first epigraph, from Sophocles' *Oedipus at Colonus*, comments on mankind's wonderful ability to master the world; the second, from Bunyan's *Grace Abounding for the Chief of Sinners*, describes a state of despair so extreme that, Bunyan says, he cannot "desire deliverance"; the third, from Part II of Goethe's *Faust*, tells us that Faust is saved from Mephistopheles because he "unceasingly strives upward." Yet all three epigraphs are ambiguous and may be read in ways contrary to their dominant meaning (McCarthy 1994: 78–9). Sophocles' Chorus knows that the one exception to man's wonderful ability to control his world is the most important of all: "only against Death shall he call for aid in vain"; Bunyan's state of desolation is countered by his title, which announces that grace abounds even for him; and if the angels can save those, like Faust, who strive upward, they cannot save those, like the Consul, who strive downward.

The sign that the Consul sees in the garden in Chapter 5 is the most prominent of the many "texts" that intrude on *Under the Volcano*. Here it appears as the Consul sees it:

¿Le gusta este jardín? it asked . . .
                    ¿LE GUSTA ESTE JARDIN?
                    ¿QUE ES SUYO?
                    ¡EVITE QUE SUS HIJOS LO DESTRUYEN!
The Consul stared back at the black words on the sign without moving. You like this garden? Why is it yours? We evict those who destroy! Simple words, simple and terrible words, words which one took to the very bottom of one's being . . . (1971: 128)

Like the menu of Chapter 11, this sign is based on Lowry's own experiences. In the 1930s he copied down the threatening sign, hoping to use it in his novel; returning to Mexico in late 1945, however, he found that he had miscopied it, since the first two lines should be one question rather than two. Moreover, the sign has nothing to do with eviction: it really means "You like this garden that is yours? Don't let your children destroy it." In a scene in Lowry's posthumous novel *Dark as the Grave Wherein My Friend Is Laid* that probably recreates his own experience (1968: 140–1), his character Sigbjørn Wilderness discovers that he has made the same mistake in his own novel, but he realizes that by transferring the mistake to the character he can make it thematically significant.

Lowry told Jonathan Cape that the words on the sign are "the most important theme of the book," adding that although Geoffrey "slightly mistranslates" them, "the real translation can be in a certain sense even more more horrifying" (1995–6, I: 514). Five months later, writing to his editor, Albert Erskine, Lowry described his problems in introducing the sign into his narrative, and a month after that he wrote again to Erskine about the sign, noting that the sign's errors in Chapter 5 are the result of the Consul's hallucination (pp. 585–7, 613–14). In all, the text of the sign makes four appearances, its form and meaning changing each time. Initially, the meaning is also dependent to some extent on whether or not the reader knows that the sign probably could not read as the Consul first imagines it, and that his translation is wide of the mark.

Yet while the sign *should not* have the meaning Geoffrey assigns to it, to some extent it does, for *Under the Volcano* never simply dismisses the Consul's paranoid symbolic readings of the external world. Instead, it arranges a dialogue between the Consul's vision and that of other characters, portraying external reality as both a projection of his mind and a world of phenomena that he misinterprets. The Consul admits that "Perhaps the sign didn't mean quite that – for alcohol sometimes affected the Consul's Spanish adversely (or perhaps the sign itself, inscribed by some Aztec, was wrong) – but it was near enough," adding shortly thereafter that the sign "certainly seemed to have more question marks than it should have" (1971: 129). Moving from doubt that he has interpreted the sign correctly (either because of his drinking or because the sign itself is written incorrectly), to assurance that his translation is "near enough," to further doubts about the text of the sign itself, given its excess of question marks, this passage hardly challenges the Consul's reading of the sign, although it leaves open the possibility of later corrections and additional readings.

Two chapters later the sign reappears just after the Consul imagines that Laruelle calls him a self-deceiving fool who has brought on his own suffering, adding, "I can see the writing on the wall." Suddenly, Geoffrey realizes that

> M. Laruelle wasn't there at all; he had been talking to himself. The Consul stood up and finished his tequila. But the writing was there, all right, if not on the wall. The man had nailed his board to the tree:
> ¿LE GUSTA ESTE JARDIN? (p. 219)

Once again the sign, or part of it, is portrayed as it appears in Geoffrey's mind, unless there are in fact two signs with the errant question mark after "JARDIN." Rather than indicate that the sign has a meaning independent of the ominous one the Consul previously gave it, this passage reinforces the earlier reading, as the phrase "the writing on the wall," with its echo of the writing that foretold the death of Belshazzar (Daniel 5), suggests. The sign's appearance here may also suggest that on some level the words Geoffrey attributes to Laruelle are true: he does bring about, perhaps even wills, his own suffering.

In Chapter 8, as the Consul, Hugh, and Yvonne ride the bus to Tomalín, Hugh asks, "How are the rajah shakes?" and in reply the Consul points to an undertaker's sign reading "*Inhumaciones*" (Burials), joking that his alcoholic shakes will be the death of him (1971: 232). The light tone is undercut somewhat by another of the undertaker's signs, "*Quo Vadis?*" In the Latin Bible (John 13: 36), after the Last Supper, Peter asks Jesus "Quo vadis?" (Where are you going?). Jesus responds that Peter cannot follow where he is going right now, and that Peter will deny him three times. We might assume that the undertaker chose this Latin phrase to suggest the inevitability of death rather than to evoke the theme of betrayal suggested by its biblical context. Still, for alert readers, the sign is ominous, especially since it is followed by the third appearance of the garden sign, this time not as Geoffrey sees it but as it is seen by a narrator who generally reports events from Hugh's perspective:

> In the garden under the trees were doves and a small black goat. ¿Le gusta este jardín, que es suyo? ¡Evite que sus hijos lo destruyen! Do you like this garden, the notice said, that is yours? See to it that your children do not destroy it!
> ... There were no children, however, in the garden; just a man sitting alone on a stone bench. The man was apparently the devil himself, with a huge dark red face and horns, fangs, and his tongue hanging out over his chin, and an expression of mingled evil, lechery, and shame. (1971: 232–3; ellipsis in text)

Three major changes in the presentation and interpretation of the sign are obvious. First, the sign's text is no longer distinguished typographically from the surrounding narration, even to the extent of its being italicized (like *Inhumaciones* and *Quo Vadis?*), much less being presented entirely in capitals, like the earlier garden signs. Thus it does not loom out of the text: for the Consul, the sign has a physical presence that it loses in Hugh's consciousness. Second, its punctuation is corrected so that the sign makes sense. Finally, someone (the narrator or Hugh) correctly translates the sign. Yet the Consul's earlier misreading is hardly erased by this passage, which places the garden sign between another sign suggestive of Christ's crucifixion and betrayal and a man dressed as a devil, presumably part of a Day of the Dead celebration.

Given Lowry's confusion over the correct form of the garden sign, it is perhaps understandable that in some editions of *Under the Volcano* the sign is erroneously reproduced at the end of the book, after the Consul's death, just as it is when the Consul first sees it, extra question marks and all. Yet Lowry insisted that the sign be printed correctly on the end page, where, he noted, its "two meanings should explode simultaneously" (1995–6, I: 614). Despite frequent hints about the sign's "two meanings," Lowry never specified what it means, apart from the interpretation the Consul gives it; but we can now see it as a plea to take responsibility for the world – our garden – rather than seeing ourselves as victims of fate. Lowry underscores the point by allowing the sign to stand on its own at the end, separated both from the narration and from the consciousness of any individual character.

Double Dialogue, Implied Dialogue, Internal Dialogue

In his study of how *Under the Volcano* evolved through years of revision, Frederick Asals has called attention to the novel's "multidimensionality," which he observes is the result of its having been "so deliberately constructed ... that it will respond at different frequencies, contain within itself conflicting perspectives that forestall resolution." The multiple meanings of the garden sign are one example of this multidimensional, and to some extent indeterminate, character that Lowry made possible by telling his story from the viewpoints of several characters – perspectives that the narrative in turn reveals as "limited, partial, dubious in their constructions of the world beyond the self" (Asals 1997: 369–70). Further examples may be seen in Lowry's handling of dialogue.

Lowry's dialogue is hardly the transparent medium of realistic fiction: rather, it includes examples of doubled or cross-dialogue, implied dialogue, and internal dialogue that are always thematically significant. Doubled dialogue is an important technique in Chapter 2, where the Consul's and Yvonne's words in the Bella Vista bar are played off against another conversation in a part of the bar separated from theirs by a partition. The other dialogue, as we hear it, is actually a monologue, perhaps because only one of the participants speaks loudly enough to be overheard; moreover, it is fragmentary but potentially ominous. Thus Yvonne's description of how she returned to Quauhnahuac is interrupted:

> "From Acapulco, Hornos . . . I came by boat, Geoff, from San Pedro – Panama Pacific. The *Pennsylvania*. Geoff –"
> "– bull-headed Dutchmen! The sun parches the lips and they crack. Oh, Christ, it's a shame! The horses all go away kicking in the dust! I wouldn't have it. They plugged 'em too. They don't miss it. They shoot first and ask questions later. You're goddam right. And that's a nice thing to say. I take a bunch of goddamned farmers, then ask them no questions. Righto! – smoke a cool cigarette –" (1971: 47; ellipsis in text)

On second reading, these references to people who shoot first and ask questions later and to horses kicking in the dust seem almost to predict the Consul's and Yvonne's deaths a few hours later.

Under the Volcano also abounds in potential or implied dialogue, which is accorded almost the same status as words the characters actually speak. Laruelle, for example, recalls that when the Consul lent him a collection of Elizabethan plays he did so with

> a diabolical look . . . that seemed now to have said: "I know, Jacques, you may never return the book, but suppose I lent it you precisely for that reason, that someday you may be sorry you did not. Oh, I shall forgive you then, but will you be able to forgive yourself? Not merely for not having returned it, but because the book will by then have become an emblem of what even now it is impossible to return." (1971: 27)

Reality is so unfailingly subjective in the novel that a character's look, recalled a year and a half later, may well be understood as a prediction of his own death and its consequences for those left behind.

Chapter 2 includes one of the most effective instances of implied dialogue, as Yvonne converses in her mind with the Consul. " 'God knows I've seen you like this before,' her thoughts were saying, her love was saying, through the gloom of the bar," and she goes on to plead with him not to retreat into darkness and drunkenness, only to be answered by what "the Consul seemed to be saying in reply to her" (pp. 49–50). His "reply" is a defense, an argument that his life is "not altogether darkness," that it has compensations: "how, unless you drink as I do, can you hope to understand the beauty of an old woman from Tarasco who plays dominoes at seven o'clock in the morning?" In another novel the specificity of that question would insure that it comes from the Consul, for surely Yvonne, who just arrived in town, has no way of knowing that the old woman is from Tarasco. In *Under the Volcano*, however, the words are entirely unspoken, yet they emanate from the Consul's mind and are understood by Yvonne, who finally notices the woman playing dominoes as she imagines the Consul speaking to her.

Implied dialogue often demonstrates the thin line between the Consul's own "reality" and that around him, for example in Chapter 3, when Geoffrey "either thought or said" that he would reduce his drinking, soon either "thinking or saying" that he could imagine reviews of the book on Atlantis that he might just write (p. 86). The same chapter introduces his "familiars," voices that speak within him. First, as he and Yvonne walk to his house, the Consul imagines hearing the tragedy of his dying garden "reviewed and interpreted by a person walking by his side suffering for him" (p. 65). Although this voice might just articulate his self-pity, it also appears to be one of his familiars, as indicated by its references to "how strange, how sad, *familiar* things may be" and to "the plantains with their queer *familiar* blooms." Other familiars emerge after Geoffrey, hoping to justify his drinking, offers Yvonne a drink:

> "– She might have said yes for once," a voice said in the Consul's ear at this moment with incredible rapidity, "for now of course poor old chap you want horribly to get drunk all over again don't you the whole trouble being as we see it that Yvonne's long-dreamed-of coming alas . . . has in itself created the most important situation in your life save one namely the far more important situation it in turn creates of your having to have five hundred drinks in order to deal with it," the voice he recognized of a pleasant and impertinent familiar, perhaps horned . . . (pp. 68–9)

This familiar is soon countered by another, who threatens to "kick your face in, O idiot!" if Geoffrey persists in rationalizing his drinking. As Ackerley and Clipper observe, these familiars, "like the good and bad angels in Marlowe's *Doctor Faustus*, do battle for [the Consul's] soul" (Ackerley and Clipper 1984: 108).

The ambiguous and unstable status of the novel's dialogue is among other things an aspect of the Consul's precarious hold on reality. He constantly retreats to the interiors of cantinas or of his own imagination in hopes that there he will be protected, in control; likewise, in Chapter 12 he imagines that his dark glasses disguise him so fully that he might easily escape those who threaten him, if only he did not first need one drink for the road. Lowry's handling of dialogue and consciousness also reveals his attempt to *present*, rather than merely to *state*, the novel's mental action. Asals points to a note Lowry copied for himself in capital letters:

ABJURE THE PLATITUDE OF STATEMENT. FOR IN ART WHAT IS MERELY
STATED IS NOT PRESENTED, WHAT IS NOT PRESENTED IS NOT VIVID,
WHAT IS NOT VIVID IS NOT REPRESENTED, AND WHAT IS NOT REPRE-
SENTED IS NOT ART. (Asals 1997: 5)

Although the Consul is beset by demons, and he and Yvonne often say only to
themselves what they would most like to say to one another, direct representation
of consciousness allows Lowry to bring what is unspoken into full light – for the
reader if not, tragically, for the characters themselves.

Borrowings, Echoes, Design-governing Postures

Among the more important features of *Under the Volcano* is its (inter)textuality: not
only do the characters often encounter and assimilate the "texts" of everyday life –
signs, announcements, advertisements, newspaper headlines, brochures – but the
novel itself often depends on other literary works for its meaning. This second sense
is typical of modernist novels and poems, which may involve extensive allusions to
other literary works: Eliot's *The Waste Land*, Joyce's *Ulysses* and *Finnegans Wake*,
Pound's *Cantos*, and Beckett's *Murphy*, are examples. In *Under the Volcano*, allusions
pervade and even shape the narration.

An early example, from Chapter 1, is the simple statement, "Darkness had fallen
like the House of Usher" (1971: 22). Appearing to come directly from the narrator,
the line gives voice to Laruelle's perception of the sudden and ominous fall of
darkness. Since Laruelle is a French film director, it seems likely that he is thinking
not of Poe's original story but of the 1928 silent film by Jean Epstein *La chute de la
maison Usher* (*The Fall of the House of Usher*), in which, Sigbjørn remembers in *Dark as
the Grave*, "the entombed was Usher's wife and not his sister [who] came back in
time ... to save him" (1968: 249). In *Under the Volcano*, of course, a wife also comes
back; but rather than saving her husband, as in Epstein's happy ending, she is killed
by a horse that represents her husband's self-destructive impulses. The Poe/Epstein
simile, introduced directly into the narration, has a resonance that is typical of
Lowry's allusions.

An important set of allusions derives from Dante's *Inferno*. At several points,
Dante's poem is related to the world of Lowry's novel, whose central symbol, the
volcano itself, seems an inversion of Dante's cone-shaped hell. In the second paragraph, a "fine American-style highway" leads to Quauhnahuac from the north
but narrows to "a goat track" headed south (1971: 3): a narrowing related both to
Dante's circles of hell and to the rooms of Lowry's Farolito, "each smaller and darker
than the last" (p. 200). Cantinas are the Consul's favorite version of hell, and one, the
Hotel Casino de la Selva, stands at the outset of the novel, its name echoing
the opening lines of *Inferno*, where Dante finds himself lost "per una selva oscura" –
in a dark wood. Hugh slightly changes Dante's opening at the outset of Chapter 6,

where he finds himself "nel mezzo del bloody cammin di nostra vita . . . in the middle of the bloody road of our life" (p. 150). At the end of that chapter there is another road, portrayed on a picture postcard from Yvonne to the Consul. Turning it over, Hugh finds a desert scene with a "road [that] turned a little corner in the distance and vanished" (p. 193), replicating the narrowing road of the book's opening and suggesting somewhat more distantly Dante's road of our life and his straitening circles of hell.

Lowry's art resided less in his invention than in his ability to revise and assimilate what he found in his reading and his life, reworking phrases until they had precisely the effect he wanted. He might well have based the Consul's final vision of worldwide conflagration ("the world itself was bursting, bursting into black spouts of villages catapulted into space, with himself falling through it all, through the inconceivable pandemonium of a million tanks, through the blazing of ten million burning bodies, falling, into a forest, falling —" (p. 375)) on a similar passage in Liam O'Flaherty's *The Black Soul* (1924): "He saw millions of dying men, worlds falling to pieces, continents being hurled into the air . . . the wails of women, the bodies of children transfixed on spears. Over all came the noise of the guns, millions of guns, rising and falling and intermingling. . . . His brain began to expand. It covered the earth and then the universe, and then it burst, hurting his forehead" (O'Flaherty 1996: 47–8). If so, however, Lowry might easily justify his rewriting of O'Flaherty by noting that the Consul's vision is prophetic of the horrors of World War II, a fact that makes it universal and apocalyptic to an extent that O'Flaherty could not have imagined when he created the original scene.

Yet while Lowry enriched *Under the Volcano* considerably by allusions to and rewritings of other authors, he was concerned that his work might not be sufficiently original, that he might be entangled in the nets of other writers rather than fully in control of his appropriations. Lowry told Albert Erskine that he once considered "appending a list of notes to the book," both to explain some of its "deeper layers" of meaning and "to acknowledge in these notes any borrowings, echoes, design-governing postures, and so on" (1995–6, I: 595). Later he assured Erskine that "There are really no echoes etc that I do not myself really consider to be absolutely justifiable & assimilated, *absorbed*" (p. 599). Despite this reversal, concerns that he might be accused of plagiarism troubled Lowry all his life.

Works by other authors were both grist for Lowry's mill and a source of anxiety, but in using materials drawn from his own life, like the El Petate menu, he must have seemed on safer ground. The overwritten menu of Chapter 11 is part of Lowry's ongoing effort both to transmute life into art and somehow to separate himself from that life, or at least give him some measure of control over it, by transferring the words on the menu to his character. Holding the menu, Yvonne first looks at the printed side, with its picture of lottery tickets "on each of which a cowgirl was riding a bucking horse and (as if these ten minute figures were Yvonne's own reduplicated and half-forgotten selves waving good-bye to herself) waving her hand" (1971: 329). The passage is sinister in ways that Yvonne cannot guess: she associates the horses with her own past as an actress in Western movies, not knowing that in less than an hour she will be killed by a horse.

When she turns the menu over, it becomes more ominous. In Chapter 1, as if the Consul is speaking from the dead, we "hear" him through Jacques's unexpected discovery of a letter Geoffrey wrote to Yvonne but never posted; now, Yvonne will "hear" him through his poem, a meditation on his own suffering. Surrounded by drawings that suggest the Consul's sense of entrapment, the poem describes the largely self-inflicted torments of a "poor foundered soul/ Who once fled north," unaware that there was no reason for him to flee, since he is no longer pursued. He has indeed fled from Yvonne and Hugh, this time to the Farolito and death.

Despite its tragic conclusion, *Under the Volcano* is at times remarkably funny: the Consul's excuses for his drinking, his indignation when Yvonne implies (correctly) that he is not sober, his belief that there are drinks that "he both had and had not drunk: had drunk in fact, had not drunk so far as the others [Hugh and Yvonne] were concerned" (p. 303) – all of these are sources of comedy for Lowry. Moreover, as the Consul seems to tell Yvonne, "it is not altogether darkness." For *Under the Volcano* does more than tell us "something new about hell fire." Ironically, through its portrayal of someone who imagines himself "suffering the tortures of the damned and the madhouse . . . for fully twenty-five minutes on end without having a decent drink," *Under the Volcano* reveals what the Consul calls "the perils, the complications, yes, the *importance* of a drunkard's life!" (p. 85).

Postscript

Under the Volcano is one of the last great modernist epics, a complex, allusive, often self-referential work that, like *Ulysses* and *To the Lighthouse*, may be read on many levels. Like other modernists, Lowry was concerned with the presentation of mind in relation to world, and at the same time he hoped to make his novel universally significant. Both through a proliferation of symbolic meanings and correspondences and through an encyclopedic array of cultural references (mythic, literary, historical, and so forth), Lowry aimed at a totalizing vision of human life. Even so, he often treated his own search for symbolic meaning ironically, as when the Consul claims that "Everything is to be found in Peter Rabbit" (p. 175), or when, suspended upside down in a carnival ride called La Máquina Infernal, the Consul imagines that his position "was symbolic, of what he could not conceive, but it was undoubtedly symbolic" (p. 222).

The publication of *Under the Volcano* led to critical praise that faded when Lowry failed to produce another masterpiece; a decade later, when he died, he was largely forgotten. Beginning in the 1960s, posthumous publication of a series of works in various stages of completion led to a revival of his reputation, which today seems stronger than ever. It remains, however, a reputation based largely on one book, which is perhaps why Lowry is less often read than, say, Conrad, Woolf, or Forster, even though *Under the Volcano* merits comparison with their finest novels. Still, it is hard to ignore the tribute paid to Lowry's masterpiece by Samuel Beckett, who called it "a very great book" (Cronin 1996: 479). Few novels of the 1940s deserve that accolade so much as *Under the Volcano*.

REFERENCES AND FURTHER READING

Ackerley, Chris and Clipper, Lawrence J. (1984) *A Companion to "Under the Volcano."* Vancouver: University of British Columbia Press.

Asals, Frederick (1997) *The Making of Malcolm Lowry's "Under the Volcano."* Athens and London: University of Georgia Press.

Asals, Frederick and Tiessen, Paul (eds.) (2000) *A Darkness That Murmured: Essays on Malcolm Lowry and the Twentieth Century*. Toronto, Buffalo, and London: University of Toronto Press.

Binns, Ronald (1984) *Malcolm Lowry*. London: Methuen.

Bowker, Gordon (1993) *Pursued by Furies: A Life of Malcolm Lowry*. New York: St Martin's Press.

Bradbrook, M. C. (1974) *Malcolm Lowry: His Art and Early Life*. Cambridge: Cambridge University Press.

Cronin, Anthony (1996) *Samuel Beckett: The Last Modernist*. London: HarperCollins.

Cross, Richard K. (1980) *Malcolm Lowry: A Preface to His Fiction*. Chicago: University of Chicago Press.

Day, Douglas (1973) *Malcolm Lowry: A Biography*. New York: Oxford University Press.

Gabrial, Jan (2000) *Inside the Volcano: My Life with Malcolm Lowry*. New York: St Martin's Press.

Grace, Sherrill E. (1982) *The Voyage That Never Ends: Malcolm Lowry's Fiction*. Vancouver: University of British Columbia Press.

——(ed.) (1992) *Swinging the Maelstrom: New Perspectives on Malcolm Lowry*. Montreal and Kingston: McGill-Queen's University Press.

Lowry, Malcolm (1961) *Hear Us O Lord from Heaven Thy Dwelling Place*. Philadelphia: J. B. Lippincott.

——(1962) [1933] *Ultramarine*. London: Jonathan Cape; rev. edn. Philadelphia: J. B. Lippincott.

——(1968) *Dark as the Grave Wherein My Friend Is Laid*, ed. Douglas Day and Margerie Bonner. New York: New American Library.

——(1970) *October Ferry to Gabriola*, ed. Margerie Lowry. New York: World.

——(1971) [1947] *Under the Volcano*. New York: Reynal and Hitchcock; repr. New York: New American Library.

——(1975) *Malcolm Lowry: Psalms and Songs*, ed. Margerie Lowry. New York: New American Library.

——(1992) *The Collected Poetry of Malcolm Lowry*, ed. Kathleen Scherf. Vancouver: UBC Press.

——(1994) *The 1940 Under the Volcano*, ed. Paul Tiessen and Miguel Mota. Waterloo: MLR Editions Canada.

——(1995–6) *Sursum Corda!: The Collected Letters of Malcolm Lowry*, 2 vols., ed. Sherrill E. Grace. Toronto and Buffalo: University of Toronto Press.

——(1996) *Malcolm Lowry's "La Mordida": A Scholarly Edition*, ed. Patrick A. McCarthy. Athens and London: University of Georgia Press.

McCarthy, Patrick A. (1994) *Forests of Symbols: World, Text, and Self in Malcolm Lowry's Fiction*. Athens and London: University of Georgia Press.

McCarthy, Patrick A. and Tiessen, Paul (eds.) (1997) *Joyce/Lowry: Critical Perspectives*. Lexington: University Press of Kentucky.

O'Flaherty, Liam (1996) [1924] *The Black Soul*. London: Jonathan Cape; repr. Dublin: Wolfhound Press.

Tiessen, Paul (ed.) (1990) *Apparently Incongruous Parts: The Worlds of Malcolm Lowry*. Metuchen, NJ and London: Scarecrow Press.

Vice, Sue (ed.) (1989) *Malcolm Lowry Eighty Years On*. New York: St Martin's Press.

Wood, Barry (ed.) (1980) *Malcolm Lowry: The Writer and His Critics*. Ottawa: Tecumseh Press.

19

The Heart of the Matter and the Later Novels of Graham Greene

Cedric Watts

By 1948, Graham Greene had already gained the reputation of a major novelist. His first novel, *The Man Within*, had appeared in 1929; *Stamboul Train* (1932) and *Brighton Rock* (1938) had been successful; and, above all, *The Power and the Glory* (1940), which won the Hawthornden Prize and became a best-seller, had confirmed his reputation as an author who could dextrously combine the popular appeal of a graphic, exciting, sexually-frank narrative with the intellectual appeal of ideological conflict and moral-theological paradox. He could write thrillers which set religious and political problems; recurrently he deployed moral shock-tactics and perplexing outcomes. Though he was known as a Catholic writer, the religious ideas voiced in his novels were often unconventional and heterodox. Comfortable orthodoxy, respectable conformity, decent secular middle-class conduct: these antagonized him. Separated from his wife Vivien, the mother of his two children, he alleviated his dark moods of depression and boredom by means of travel, adulteries, and a huge output of creative work. Ironically, it was the wish to marry Vivien (herself a convert) which had led him to be received into the Roman Catholic Church in 1926. Previously, as an Oxford undergraduate, he had briefly joined the Communist Party. The tension between Catholicism and Communism provided thematic material for numerous novels and tales by him.

His literary range included not only novels but also poems, travel books, critical essays, tales, *novelle*, biographical works, and screenplays. He admired fiction-writers who variously spanned the adventurous and the subtle: Rider Haggard, Joseph Conrad, Henry James. A knowingly cinematic writer who was an incisive film-critic, Greene was doubly influenced by films: his descriptive montages displayed the panache of well-directed camera-work, and his narratives were aimed towards possible screen adaptation. (Already, by the time of *The Heart of the Matter*, nine of his works had been filmed, his strategy having proved remarkably effective.) Since 1940, he had been known as the creator of "Greeneland": a distinctive imaginative terrain, characterized by the seedy, sleazy, and corrupt. He resisted the term (conferred by Arthur Calder-Marshall and enshrined later in the *Oxford English Dictionary*), claiming that he was merely an accurate reporter of what others preferred to ignore; but repeatedly his fictional locations, whether in Britain or in distant lands, seemed to be tainted by the debased and even by the hellish or purgatorial. "Why, this is Hell, nor am I out of it," said Mephostophilis in Marlowe's *Doctor Faustus*; "Why, this is Hell, nor are we out of it," says Prewitt in *Brighton Rock*. Furthermore, one of Greene's boldest achievements was to incorporate God and the metaphysical as active agents in the narrative. Even readers with secular beliefs could find themselves speculating about the kind of afterlife to which a character might be destined, the nature of that destinal force, the arrogance of certitude, and the perils of skepticism.

The publication in 1948 of *The Heart of the Matter*, which became a best-seller, consolidated his fame and prestige. (The first film version would appear five years later, with Trevor Howard, Maria Schell, and Peter Finch among its leading actors; and in 1983 there would be an adaptation for German television.) In this novel, the setting is Freetown in Sierra Leone, where Greene had worked as a wartime secret agent from 1942 to 1943. The locality is superbly evoked, and, inevitably, the fictional Sierra Leone merges with Greeneland, as we encounter oppressive humidity (blotting-paper soaks sweat from Scobie's wrist as he writes), tedium, moral corruption, tropical diseases, garbage, vultures on tin roofs and a dead dog in the gutter, while the narrator provides numerous intelligently pessimistic generalizations about human nature. Henry Scobie, the protagonist, is a scrupulous and sensitive police officer whose marriage is failing and who becomes gradually ensnared in corruption. To give his wife, Louise, a long holiday from the area that she finds tedious, Scobie accepts a bribe to turn a blind eye to smuggling. Next, he commits adultery with Helen Rolt, a woman young enough to be his daughter, and is consequently blackmailed, so that he himself becomes a smuggler. A devout Catholic, he yet takes Mass in a state of mortal sin, being unable to repent his adultery. Later, he arranges for his African servant (who knows too much of his corruption) to be "silenced" – actually murdered. Finally, Scobie commits suicide, another mortal sin for a Catholic, attempting to disguise this as a heart attack. He believes that he is undertaking the suicide partly out of pity for his wife and Helen, and partly out of pity for Christ, who (he imagines) would be repeatedly wounded by his protracted impenitence if he lived. Here the imagery reaches its most shocking extreme:

> He had a sudden picture before his eyes of a bleeding face, of eyes closed by the continuous shower of blows: the punch-drunk head of God reeling sideways... He thought, 'And again at Christmas,' thrusting the Child's face into the filth of the stable. (Greene 1948: 246, 247)

The "heart of the matter," it seems, is pity; but Scobie's pity is compromised, to a greater extent than he ever fully recognizes, by an irresponsibility entailing cruel consequences.

The ending has multiple ironies. Louise, it is revealed, has been well aware of her husband's adultery, in spite of all his endeavors to conceal it. Scobie's attempt to conceal the fact of suicide fails, too. A crowning irony occurs when Father Rank, the Catholic priest, talks to Scobie's widow. Scobie believed that in committing suicide he was damning himself. Like the priest who, in *Brighton Rock*, consoled Rose after Pinkie's death, Father Rank says:

> For goodness sake, Mrs. Scobie, don't imagine you – or I – know a thing about God's mercy... The Church knows all the rules. But it doesn't know what goes on in a single human heart. (Greene 1948: 297)

Thus, as in previous works by Greene, the text suggests that, after all, the sinner may be saved: God may take Scobie's love (of God, or of fellow humans) as a redemptive quality. As so often, Greene offers the prospect of a redeemed (if not sanctified) sinner, of the salvation of a man who, by orthodox standards, has been corrupt and destructive. The Romantic tradition, advocating sympathy with the rebel against convention, deeply permeated the culture of the twentieth century; and Greene (who claimed to be "a much better Catholic in mortal sin") certainly knew T. S. Eliot's wicked paradox:

> [T]he recognition of the reality of sin is a New Life; and the possibility of damnation is so immense a relief... that damnation itself is an immediate form of salvation – of salvation from the ennui of modern life, because it at last gives some significance to living. (Eliot 1932: 375)

Some commentators on *The Heart of the Matter* (notably Edward Sackville-West and Raymond Mortimer) even considered the possibility that Scobie was a saint, but Greene denied any such intention. Various Catholics condemned the work strongly. Ronald Brownrigg said it gave the impression that what Christ taught was: "If you love me, break my commandments." The Reverend John Murphy remarked that Scobie "despaired when he should have repented." In addition, George Orwell complained that if Scobie really believed in Hell, he would not risk going there, and that Scobie was too sensitive to be a colonial police officer (Hynes 1973: 108). Orwell's comments indicate that the demands of the plot seem to have twisted the central characterization into self-contradiction. If Scobie is indeed a man of "pity," his readiness to acquiesce in the murder of his young servant seems implausibly pitiless. Greene himself remarked later: "I don't like the book much... Freetown is well described, but the dilemma of Scobie seems to me an exaggerated one" (Parkinson 1993: 555).

The Heart of the Matter was controversial, much publicized, banned in Eire, and chosen by the Book of the Month Club. It became an international best-seller. In Britain *The Ministry of Fear*, his previous novel, had sold 18,000 copies; within three years, *The Heart of the Matter* sold nearly 300,000. Publishers promptly reissued his earlier novels, swelling Greene's royalty-earnings.

Three years later, *The End of the Affair* made God an even more conspicuous presence in a novel of adultery. Maurice Bendrix, an atheistic author, loves Sarah Miles, who is married. Suddenly, after a bomb-explosion during an air raid, she discontinues their relationship. Bendrix suspects that she has taken another lover, and becomes obsessed by the need to identify this rival. Eventually, after her death, he discovers that her other lover is actually God. What had happened was that when Bendrix seemed to have been killed in the explosion, Sarah had made a pact with God: "I'll give him up for ever, only let him be alive." Furthermore, it appears that Sarah had thereafter become a tutelary saint, performing miracles in life and after death. Her kiss heals a strawberry-mark on a rationalist's cheek (thus also curing him of his skepticism). A boy with a grave stomach complaint dreams that she touches his stomach, and he is promptly cured. Bendrix prays to her to save him from taking another woman as his mistress, and his prayer is answered by the intervention of Sarah's mother, who incidentally reveals that Sarah was baptised a Catholic. The more Bendrix defies God, the greater the reality that God gains for him. Eventually his tone is that of the weary believer: "O God, you've done enough." Bendrix, a fiction-writer, has become a character in God's plot; and that plot comes dangerously close to specifying sin (rather than repentance for sin) as a medium of exchange for grace.

This novel exhibits a familiar tension in Greene's work. The setting is convincing, as is the rendering of the stresses, guilts and jealousies of lovers; but the complications of the plot are far less so. The novel's suggestion that adultery may lead, via a bargain with God, to sainthood for an erring wife is a characteristic Greenian paradox. Never before, however, had Greene written a novel in which God intervened so directly and manifestly in the ordination of events: here religion resembles endorsed superstition. Even a believer might flinch at the extent to which the outcome appears to depend on supernatural intervention. If the evidence for Sarah's virtual canonization had been more ambiguous, it would have been more plausible. Greene himself recognized this: "I realised too late how I had been cheating – cheating myself, cheating the reader" (Greene 1974: ix). Accordingly, *The End of the Affair* became one of numerous works by Greene which he revised, so that some later printings differ significantly from the first printing. For instance, the rationalist's strawberry-mark becomes urticaria or nettle-rash, making its cure seems less miraculous. Once again, though, Greene had provided a story so graphic, and fraught with such potent sexual tension, that film versions followed: one in 1955 (directed by Edward Dmytryk, with an excellent performance by the beautiful Deborah Kerr), another in 2000 (directed by Neil Jordan, its stars including Ralph Fiennes and Julianne Moore).

Revealingly, Greene remarked that "every novelist has something in common with a spy" and that "a writer is even more like a double agent than he is like God" (Greene 1971: 141; Allain 1983: 161). One of the most extensive paradoxes of Greene's career was that, although he served in the SIS, the British Secret Intelligence Service, for many years, his writings and public utterances indicated not only protracted hostility to the USA and to what Greene deemed its broadly reactionary politics, but also considerable sympathy with Communism and the USSR; indeed, he hoped, somewhat ingenuously, for cooperation between atheistic Communism and the Catholic Church. His perennial sympathy with the underdog led him into hostility to the "upper dog" in the modern political world. He said:

> I would go to almost any length to put my feeble twig in the spokes of American foreign policy...Some time ago there was an article in *The Spectator*...which said that it made little difference whether I inclined to the Right or the Left, since what I detested was American liberalism. That wasn't far wrong. (Allain 1983: 90)

Liberalism, however, nurtures democracy. Repeatedly Greene seemed to undervalue the democratic tradition which gave him the freedom of speech to voice his criticisms; he overlooked the sacrifices made by the USA to liberate Europe from fascism; and, meanwhile, in his enjoyment of brothels, strip-clubs, abundant alcohol and occasional opium, he contributed to the western decadence which evoked his scorn. He met, and was impressed by, such revolutionary dictators as Fidel Castro and Ho Chi Minh.

The Quiet American (1955) drew on his personal experiences as a journalist and agent in Vietnam during the time when the French were losing their battle against Communist and nationalist insurgents. The protagonist, Fowler, is a skeptical British journalist; like Greene, he is separated from a Catholic wife who declines to grant him a divorce. Fowler is eventually drawn into political collaboration with the left-wing insurgents: he instigates the murder of Pyle, an American agent of the CIA. Fowler's motives are mixed. By removing Pyle he is removing a rival for the love of Phuong, his local mistress. But he also believes that he is removing a dangerous "innocent," a well-meaning but ignorant American whose schemes to establish a "Third Force" in Vietnam have entailed the killing of civilians by plastic bombs. Suspiciously mixed motives, in which public concern is entangled with private desire, had preoccupied Greene from his first novel (*The Man Within*) onwards. Whether as an adulterer or as an employee of the British state, he knew personally the wiles of the double agent. In him, loyalty and treachery were interwoven, as they had been ever since the troubled school-days at Berkhamsted where his father was the headmaster.

The Quiet American was widely praised by British reviewers, but, predictably, there were some hostile reviews in the USA, notably from *Newsweek*, which said that Greene had played into the Communists' hands. As time passed, this novel was increasingly regarded as an astutely prophetic warning against the burgeoning US involvement in Vietnam. (The 1957 film, which reduced the anti-American element, proved less successful than the 2002 film, directed by Phillip Noyce.)

Pre-revolutionary Cuba, with its nightclubs, strip-shows, and lotteries, forms the setting of *Our Man in Havana* (1958). Here Greene mocks his employers in the SIS by depicting them as absurd and incompetent. Wormold, the hero, is recruited as an agent, and responds by recruiting imaginary informants so that he can collect their pay. For a while, he is drawn into a dangerous arena of violence, but fortunately he escapes; and finally, though his deception is recognized, it is hushed up by his employers, and Wormold can look forward to a happy future with his partner,

Beatrice. The whole novel works proficiently as a comedy-thriller. The narrator's view of the world is broadly benign, the satire almost genial. This is a lightweight among Greene's novels, and seems to be an anticipation of the lightening of mood which was to find fuller expression in, for example, *Travels with My Aunt* and *Monsignor Quixote*. (A film of *Our Man in Havana*, directed by Carol Reed, appeared in 1959, and in 1962 Malcolm Williamson made an operatic version of the novel.)

In the meantime, however, came one of his most sombre and searching works, *A Burnt-Out Case* (1961). In this, Querry, a famous ecclesiastical architect, travels into the Congo to a leper colony organized by Catholic priests. He is befriended by a doctor there and permitted to assist the treatment of the lepers. "A burnt-out case" is, we are told, the name given to a leper in whom the disease has run its course: he or she is extensively mutilated and lacks feeling in various areas. Querry is a moral and psychological burnt-out case: depressed and rootless, he has lost his Catholic belief, his ambition, his sexual desire, and his interest in everyday humanity. Gradually, however, he becomes involved in the work of the colony, and, eventually, he even begins to experience contentment. An absurd reversal ensues: Querry's innocently helpful involvement with a young woman is misconstrued by her husband, Rycker, who jealously shoots and kills him.

This novel is thoroughly researched: the African setting is as convincing as any in Greene's fiction, and the work of the leper colony is described in vivid and persuasive detail. The accounts of the modes of leprosy are unsparing and compassionate. The characterization of Querry is problematic: the autobiography of Greene seems to be infiltrating the portrayal of the ecclesiastical architect when, for instance, we are told that commentators on Querry's work write such articles as "The Toad in the Hole: the Art of Fallen Man" or "From Easter Egg to Letters of Marque: the Jeweller of Original Sin." As for Querry's loss of religious conviction, this too was happening to Greene: in his later life, his views were modulating unevenly towards the agnostic, and, eventually, he would term himself "a Catholic agnostic" and remark "With age ... doubt seems to gain the upper hand" (Allain 1983: 172). Nevertheless, like Querry, Greene sometimes entertained the idea that, in an individual, loss of belief might coexist with faith, the loss being construed as a mode of divine punishment. Evelyn Waugh remarked that *A Burnt-Out Case* displayed Greene's exasperation at his reputation as a Catholic writer; and the novelist himself remarked:

> I would not claim to be a writer of Catholic novels, but a writer who in four or five books took characters with Catholic ideas for his material. Nonetheless for years – particularly after *The Heart of the Matter* – I found myself hunted by people who wanted help with spiritual problems that I was incapable of giving. Not a few of these were priests themselves ... I was already beginning to live in the skin of Querry, a man who had turned at bay. (Waugh 1976: 779)

In 1966 appeared *The Comedians*, a political comedy-thriller set in Haiti during the era of the ghoulish dictator, Dr François Duvalier: an era in which the people experienced tyranny, corruption, voodoo, and poverty. Greene had visited the island several times, most recently in 1963. One of the main characters in the novel is a familiar Greenian type: Jones is yet another likable English middle-class confidence-trickster. After various shady and farcical escapades, he emerges as a hero in reality, dying while defending a group of rebels against the harsh regime. A Marxist idealist, Dr Magiot, opposes the dictatorship and proposes that recurrent Greenian scheme: an alliance of Catholics and Communists against tyranny. Magiot is killed by Duvalier's henchmen, the Tontons Macoutes, to reassure the USA that Haiti is a bastion against Communism. The novel finally hints that the narrator, Brown, may be led from disillusioned detachment to left-wing political commitment.

The Comedians sold well. The ensuing film, however, though served by an impressive cast (including Alec Guinness, Richard Burton, Elizabeth Taylor, James Earl Jones, and Peter Ustinov), proved to be an expensive failure: "negligible," said the *New Statesman*, criticizing the script; "Elizabeth Taylor was a disaster," remarked Greene (Watts 1997: 76). Nevertheless, the publicity provided by the film industry continued to sustain and increase the sales of his fictional works.

Another strongly political novel with related themes was *The Honorary Consul* (1973). Again, one of its main political targets was US foreign policy, particularly the Cold War policy of supporting right-wing dictatorships – in this case, the dictatorship of General Stroessner in Paraguay. Set on the Argentinian side of the border with Paraguay, the novel tells how guerrillas attempt to kidnap a US ambassador in the hope that some Paraguayan political prisoners will be released in exchange. Incompetently, they capture not the ambassador but Charley Fortnum, an alcoholic British Honorary Consul. The guerrillas include a Marxist and a former Catholic priest, and they are aided by Dr Plarr, a sympathizer who has been enjoying an adulterous relationship with Fortnum's young wife. Eventually Plarr and the kidnappers are surrounded and ruthlessly shot. Fortnum is rescued and returns to his wife; he knows of her infidelity but forgives her.

This novel could have been improved by editorial pruning. The ratio of ethical debate to action, particularly in the last third of the novel, is too high: suspense wilts as discussion extends. (The discussion includes the heretical claim that God may be a mixture of good and evil, struggling to evolve towards a better state.) Nevertheless, Greene deemed *The Honorary Consul* "perhaps the novel I prefer to all the others" (Watts 1997: 77); and the 1983 film (directed by John Mackenzie, and featuring Michael Caine and Richard Gere) was passably proficient.

Between the last two political novels had appeared a radically new kind of novel for Greene. *Travels with My Aunt* (1969) was a comic picaresque in which Aunt Augusta is the *pícara* and her son, swept along by her irrepressible panache, becomes a middle-aged Pooterish apprentice in various forms of lawbreaking. Greene explained:

> If *A Burnt-Out Case* in 1961 represented the depressive side of a manic-depressive writer, *Travels with My Aunt* eight years later surely represented the manic at its height – or depth. (Greene 1980: 286)

Greene associated this manic mood with his decision to leave England and settle permanently in France, where he enjoyed the sexual company of Yvonne Cloetta, a vivacious married woman whom he called "HHK" – "Happy Healthy Kitten." Lively and episodic, *Travels with My Aunt* is a saturnalia of self-referentiality, abounding in literary allusions to delight Greene's loyal readers. There's a scene in Brighton, a journey on the Orient Express, a friend called Mario in honor of Greene's flamboyant friend Mario Soldati, and a lover called Visconti (termed "a viper") as homage to Marjorie Bowen's *The Viper of Milan*, the historical romance which had crucially influenced the young Greene. The author said that *Travels with My Aunt* simply unfolded without planning: "I felt like a rider who has dropped the reins"; and that's how it reads: loose, galloping, entertaining enough, though death enters even this Arcadian racecourse. The serious and black-comic elements are nevertheless encompassed by the comic and nostalgic, inflected by whimsy and fantasy. The older that Greene became, the more he was prepared to relax and contemplate life with a smile rather than a scowl. The film of *Travels with My Aunt* (directed by George Cukor) was well served by the acting of Maggie Smith, who, as Aunt Augusta, admirably combined the imperious with the mischievous. Stage adaptations have proven popular. Greene has sometimes been criticized for his presentation of relatively shallow or unconvincing female characters, but Augusta is certainly memorable in herself and the occasion of memorability in her interpreters.

One of Greene's wartime bosses in the Secret Intelligence Service had been Kim Philby, who was eventually exposed as a traitor working for the USSR. Having caused the deaths of British agents abroad, Philby defected to Moscow in 1963 before he could be arrested. The Philby defection is an important part of the background to *The Human Factor* (1978). In *Our Man in Havana*, Greene had depicted the SIS (which he termed "the best travel agency in the world") as bungling and incompetent. In *The Human Factor*, it is depicted as Machiavellian, ruthless, and collaborative with the apartheid regime in South Africa. The hero, Castle, employed by the SIS, has a black wife and adopted son. In gratitude to Communists, who had helped the woman and her son to escape from South Africa, Castle has been passing British secrets to the Russians. His office comes under suspicion, and a colleague, wrongly thought to be the traitor, is murdered by his own employers. Castle then escapes to Moscow. In a bitter ending, he learns there that his information was regarded as of minor importance: it was being passed back to London by a Russian agent in order to fool London into trusting the Russian. So Castle has merely been helping to establish the credentials of a triple agent. Furthermore, although he had been promised that his wife and son would soon be joining him, the promise is not kept. Castle, it seems, will have a lonely existence in a bleak Moscow for a long time to come. In the game of political chess, this "castle" proves to be a mere pawn. The world of spying is depicted as one of bluff and double bluff, of multiple treachery and profound cynicism.

The Human Factor lacks the imaginative intensity of the best of the earlier novels, and there are some implausibilities (notably when Castle feigns blindness during his escape). Nevertheless, the novel was, in its day, a proficient espionage-thriller, deservedly a best-seller. The subsequent novel or novella, *Doctor Fischer of Geneva* (1980), was, understandably, far less successful, for it is short (little more than a protracted short story), slight, and contrived. As a satire on the greed of the rich or as an allegory of materialistic corruption, it remains unconvincing, being so unlikely in its plot and characterization. Paradoxically, whereas *The Human Factor* yielded a disappointing film, *Doctor Fischer of Geneva* became, thanks largely to the sardonic acting of James Mason, an effective film for television.

Far more enjoyable as a novel was *Monsignor Quixote* (1982), a genial comic work set in Spain, in which the modern counterpart to Don Quixote is a benevolently innocent old priest. A Marxist ex-mayor is his Sancho Panza, a battered Seat car his Rosinante. There are some debts to Miguel de Unamuno and Giovanni Guareschi. That old preoccupation of Greene's – the argument between Communism and Catholicism, and the possibility of some compromise between them – underlies the story of this comical pilgrimage. Greene offers ingenious present-day equivalents, variously whimsical, farcical, and satiric, to scenes in Cervantes' novel, concluding with a death scene rather more sentimentally pietistic than the original. In 1985, a beguiling televised version of *Monsignor Quixote* made apt use of Alec Guinness as Quixote and Leo McKern as his Marxist friend.

The last of Greene's novels to be published in his lifetime was *The Captain and the Enemy* (1988), an uneasy mixture of familiar ingredients. Once again, as in *It's a Battlefield* and *The Human Factor*, Greene's home town, Berkhamsted, is a setting; once again, as in his first novel, *The Man Within*, the hero is rescued from school by an older male; again, this older male is of the raffish gentleman-trickster type (like Jones in *The Comedians*); and, as in *The Comedians*, the trickster is vindicated by a heroic death. In this case, he dies during an attempt (betrayed, predictably, by the CIA) to bomb President Somoza, dictator of Nicaragua. As in *The Man Within*, the young protégé becomes an informer against his mentor. The setting of the later part of the novel is Panama: Greene draws on his (regrettable) involvement there with the dictatorial General Torrijos and his henchman José Martínez; indeed, Greene even enjoyed the patronage of the notoriously corrupt Colonel Noriega. The structure of *The Captain and the Enemy* is loose, and the work as a whole resembles a recycling of previous materials. It gives the sense that a social narrative of an earlier decade (concerning the Captain, Liza, and Jim as a boy) is being grafted on to a tale of up-to-date politics. Though lucidly readable – for Greene was virtually incapable of writing a boring page – *The Captain and the Enemy* makes an anti-climactic conclusion to the sequence of his novels.

When we look back over his career as a novelist, we see that after some weak, derivative early work (e.g. *The Name of Action* and *Rumour at Nightfall*), and after some modernistic technical experimentation (in *Stamboul Train* and *It's a Battlefield*), Greene reached his maturity in the period 1938 to 1951. Here he gained his distinctive literary character, again and again dealing with people's treachery to each other and with the apparent betrayal of God by men, while repeatedly he displayed marked left-wing sympathies, offering resourceful defences of the social underdog and the rebel against authority. He also gained a distinctive style: graphic, with an eye for the tellingly unexpected, absurd or sordid detail, and recurrently enlivened by what he called his "leopards": similes that leap at you, as in the following examples from *The Heart of the Matter*: "Round the corner... stood the law courts and the police station, a great stone building like the grandiloquent boast of weak men"; "He watched her go out of the dark office like fifteen wasted years"; "When he called her name he was crying like Canute against a tide – the tide of her melancholy"; "His wife's absence was like a garrulous companion in the room." (In *Ways of Escape*, while criticizing such similes, Greene nevertheless refers to a Scandinavian visitor who brought him hope, "carrying it like a glass of akvavit down the muddy lane.") Provocative generalizations are offered with almost casual ease or arrogance: "Comfort, like the act of sex, developed a routine"; "He felt the loyalty we all feel to unhappiness – the sense that that is where we really belong"; "When the damage was done[,] adultery became as unimportant as friendship." On the large scale, his treatment of Catholicism was such as to challenge both the skeptic and the devout, while his treatment of politics questioned notions of the superiority of capitalist democracy to imperialistic Marxism. His paradox-loving intelligence enlivened his renderings of the particular and the general. In short, like other major writers, he gained that special literary identity which derives from a combination of strong thematic preoccupations, descriptive verve, and stylistic distinctiveness. (Naturally, recent political and cultural changes have retrospectively given some of his concerns a dated, historically-localized character.)

After 1948, his range widened as he experimented with plays, *novelle*, children's tales, biographical studies, and autobiographical works, while his novels, as we have seen, gradually became more variable (sometimes markedly lighter) in mood and tone, and their style became relatively "transparent" and less rich in similes and skeptical aphorisms. His international fame and cultural influence were augmented by the many films (the finest being *The Third Man*, directed by Carol Reed, based on a "treatment" or tale for adaptation). His eminence was acknowledged by the awards that he garnered over the years. He had been appointed a Companion of Honour in 1966 and enrolled in the Order of Merit in 1986. Balliol, his old college, had made him an Honorary Fellow in 1963. Honorary doctorates were conferred by the universities of Cambridge (1962), Edinburgh (1967), Oxford (1979), and Moscow (1988). Prizes awarded to him included the Shakespeare Prize (Hamburg, 1969), the John Dos Passos Prize (1980) and, in spite of the anti-Semitism of some of his early works, the Jerusalem Prize (1980). In France, he was made a Chevalier de la Légion d'Honneur (1967) and a Commandeur des Arts et Lettres (1984). He was elected an Honorary Citizen of Anacapri (where he had enjoyed adultery with Catherine Walston) in 1978, and was awarded the Medal of the City of Madrid in 1980, the Grand Cross of Panama's Order of Vasco Núñez de Balboa in 1983, and Nicaragua's Order of Rubén Darío in 1987. In his lifetime, his novels were translated into at least twenty-seven languages, and more than 20 million copies of them were sold. Seldom in literary history has a fiction writer achieved such international prestige and critical acclaim together with a vast popular readership and consequent financial wealth. By the time of his death, in 1991, Greene was widely recognized as a great literary spokesman for a century's concerns. Among the obituary tributes came a telling observation from Sir William Golding:

> Graham Greene was in a class by himself... He will be read and remembered as the ultimate chronicler of twentieth-century man's consciousness and anxiety.

REFERENCES AND FURTHER READING

Allain, Marie-Françoise (ed.) (1983) *The Other Man: Conversations with Graham Greene.* London: Bodley Head.

Eliot, T. S. (1932) *Selected Essays.* London: Faber and Faber.

Greene, Graham (1948) *The Heart of the Matter.* London: Heinemann.

——(1971) *A Sort of Life.* London: Bodley Head.

——(1974) Introduction to the Collected Edition text of *The End of the Affair.* London: Heinemann and Bodley Head.

——(1980) *Ways of Escape.* London: Bodley Head.

Hynes, Samuel (ed.) (1973) *Graham Greene: A Collection of Critical Essays.* Englewood Cliffs, NJ: Prentice-Hall.

Parkinson, David (ed.) (1993) *The Graham Greene Film Reader: Mornings in the Dark.* Manchester: Carcanet.

Watts, Cedric (1997) *A Preface to Greene.* Harlow: Longman.

Waugh, Evelyn (1976) *The Diaries of Evelyn Waugh*, ed. Michael Davit. London: Weidenfeld and Nicolson.

20

William Golding's
Lord of the Flies and Other
Early Novels

Kevin McCarron

When William Golding died in 1993, at the age of 81, he was one of only five British authors to have been awarded the Nobel Prize for Literature. Nevertheless, it was clear from the obituaries that he was considerably more highly regarded by his fellow novelists than by either educated general readers, most of whom were familiar only with *Lord of the Flies* and *Rites of Passage*, or by the very large majority of academic critics. The general reader found the formal experimentation of novels such as *The Inheritors* and *The Spire* uncongenial, while academics found his pessimism, determinism, interest in religion, and, perhaps above all, his apparent lack of interest in contemporary society, unforgivable. Moreover, throughout his career, but particularly in the first phase of it, Golding had little sympathy for the pervasive twentieth-century view that saw human nature as culturally determined, created by social circumstances. In his review of Golding's *Pincher Martin*, Kingsley Amis criticized its author for failing "to turn his gifts of originality, of intransigence, and above all of passion to the world where we have to live" (Watson 1991: 70). However, there is no logical link between the mode of representation Amis inferentially endorses here (a mode we might call "realism") and a direct engagement with society; and the fabular, or allegorical mode of representation, which Golding clearly favored, may comment on a culture, if more obliquely, with equal, or indeed more, perceptiveness. While Golding's early novels are indeed pessimistic, religious, and deterministic, and while of his fourteen published novels only four are located in a recognizably contemporary setting, his lack of engagement with his own society is only apparent. When compared to the British neo-realist writers of the 1950s, with their depiction of a recognizably changing contemporary England, Golding's work does indeed seem deliberately unfashionable, and provocatively ahistorical; but despite the geographically and historically isolated settings of his novels, Golding was always very much a novelist of his times, and in his early fiction his chief preoccupations were fiction itself, masculinity, and religion.

Golding was 43 when *Lord of the Flies* was published; he was not a young man, but he was angry – not in the class-preoccupied manner of writers such as Allan Sillitoe, Amis, and John Braine, but angry with the writers, all male, and the texts that he believed misrepresented the actuality of human experience. All of Golding's early novels are "rewritings" of earlier texts and Golding is actually closer in spirit to the iconoclastic cultural revisionism of later women writers such as Jean Rhys and Angela Carter than he is to Braine, Amis, and Sillitoe. The sociologist David Morgan writes: "Of all the sites where masculinities are constructed, reproduced, and deployed, those associated with war and the military are some of the most direct" (1995: 165). *Lord of the Flies* could not have been written, or perhaps even published, without the historical actuality of Auschwitz, Bergen-Belsen – and Dresden; indeed *Lord of the Flies* is not only a response to these historical horrors, it begins as a conventional war novel. All four of Golding's 1950s novels have war and masculinity as their central subject.

In an appraisal of 1960s feminist criticism George Watson writes that "male writers like Amis and Osbourne have portrayed man in his essential ruthlessness and selfishness with a more withering accuracy than any feminist would dare or wish to do" (1991: 180). However, Golding is even more critical of conventional notions of masculinity than are such writers as Amis, Stan Barstow, Sillitoe, and Braine, all of whom equate masculinity with conflict, aggression, possession, attainment, and, particularly, material success. While these writers depict specific men living their lives in 1950s England, Golding evaluates the entire concept of masculinity, quite aware that while to be male is a biological fact, masculinity is a cultural construction. Golding's principal characters in *Lord of the Flies*, *The Inheritors*, and *Free Fall* reject the aggressive ethos of masculinity so prevalent in the literature of the period. Moreover, the punishment inflicted upon Pincher Martin, who is a greedy and violent woman-izer, is immeasurably more severe than any meted out by Golding's peers to their delinquent protagonists. Golding's searching evaluation of masculinity throughout his 1950s novels makes him one of the most radical writers of the immediate postwar years. Strikingly, the *telos* of Golding's fiction is centered in revelation, not attainment or acquisition. None of Golding's favored protagonists could say what Braine's principal character innocently says in *Room at the Top*: "I wanted an Aston-Martin. I wanted a three-guinea linen shirt, I wanted a girl with a Riviera suntan – these were my rights, I felt, a signed and sealed legacy" (Braine 1985: 29). In Golding's fiction "success" for his male protagonists is always presented as a moment of revelation, an epiphany, never as a material acquisition or as a favorable advance in society.

Watson maintains that "Post-war British fiction is rootedly secular, its heroes as unbelieving of a world beyond the grave as they are insecure in the only world they know" (1991: 13). Watson disregards here the postwar fiction of, among others, Graham Greene, Evelyn Waugh, and Muriel Spark, as well as, most strikingly, the early fiction of William Golding, whose writing is preoccupied with the religious and the supernatural. Golding's early novels consistently imply the existence of a spiritual power, external to humanity, which in its numinous intangibility is directly opposed to a rational, scientific worldview that is conventionally gendered in our culture as masculine. Throughout his early fiction Golding suggests that the supernatural forces at the center of existence, which his protagonists are eventually compelled to recognize, are capricious and irrational, generating horror and fear as much as joy and peace. Although religion is a central issue in Golding's fiction, it rarely manifests itself as conventional, contemporary Christianity. Golding's religious vision is an integration of the harshness of the Old Testament and the redemptive possibilities suggested by the New Testament, though at times it seems determinedly pre-Christian. Overall, while his representation of religion often incorporates traditional Christian imagery, it is considerably less morally focused than most contemporary understandings of Christianity. Religion, in Golding's work, is often depicted as a force, morally neutral and even capricious. Golding's primary religious concern is the nature of evil and, in particular, its often ambivalent causes and manifestations. His early fiction, however, suggests that any understanding of evil that sees it as simply opposed to good is severely limited. Golding endorses the view expressed by the anthropologist David Parkin: "Evil fits the ontological description of inexplicably human, inhuman monsters, and so is not simply a term opposed to 'good'" (Parkin 1985: 13). Golding's depiction of evil is not grounded in this conventional understanding of evil as the second part of the good/evil dichotomy. William Ray cites Derrida: "an opposition of metaphysical concepts (e.g. speech/writing, presence/absence etc.) is NEVER the confrontation of two terms, but a hierarchy and the order of a subordination" (Ray 1984: 173). Golding rejects the depiction of good and evil as a "hierarchy and the order of a subordination"; instead he invariably illustrates the ways in which these two concepts are interwoven rather than in opposition. Perhaps Golding's principal achievement in his early fiction was to develop innovative formal techniques that enabled him to incorporate his unique religious vision into the traditional forms of the English novel.

During the period 1954–64, Golding published five novels, all densely textured, fable-like narratives, employing brutally limited and strikingly unconventional narrative perspectives. He demonstrated throughout this period an unmatched ability to infuse pragmatic and minutely observed detail with a visionary significance. In these novels Golding depicted isolated men, stripped of social encumbrances, indeed usually *in extremis*, while alluding throughout to, and usually subverting, his literary predecessors, who included H. G. Wells, Ambrose Bierce, and Dante. While his peers were describing parochial communities of considerable limitations, Golding was writing aggressively bold fables, which claimed for themselves a universal and an eternal applicability. In particular during this period, Golding's was an art of essences; he strove to depict what lay beneath, or above, the observable surface of life. If contemporary society had no fictional interest for him, it was because, unfashionably, he prioritized what he perceived as humanity's eternal spiritual struggle, its craving for religious enlightenment, over its desire for social cohesion.

In 1930, aged 19, Golding began reading Science at Oxford University, but changed to the study of Literature in 1932. Although *Lord of the Flies* is popularly believed to be his first book, while at Oxford he published a small volume of poetry in Macmillan's Contemporary Poets series. *Poems* (1934) contained twenty-nine poems, and, although in later life he was dismissive of this volume and of his abilities as a poet, the collection anticipates some of the concerns that were to become central to his early fiction. In the best-known of these poems, "Mr Pope," Golding uses Alexander Pope as a spokesman for the Age of Reason and mocks the rationalist's desire for perfect order and control; this distrust of rationalism is a feature of all of Golding's early novels. In 1939 Golding married and began teaching at Bishop Wordsworth's school in Salisbury, but upon the outbreak of war he joined the Royal Navy, in which he served until 1945. Clearly, World War II, considerably more than Oxford, was Golding's most significant educative experience. What he saw and experienced during those years forced him to query even more forcefully than he had done at Oxford his scientific, rationalistic, and ultimately optimistic picture of the universe. He later wrote in his essay "Fable":

> Before the second world war I believed in the perfectibility of social man; that a correct structure of society would produce goodwill; and that therefore you could remove all social ills by a reorganisation of society...but after the war I did not because I was unable to. I had discovered what one man could do to another...I must say that anyone who moved through those years without understanding that man produces evil as a bee produces honey, must have been blind or wrong in the head. (Golding 1984: 86–7)

These words could serve as an epigraph to all of Golding's early fiction. The war not only changed Golding's moral and political outlook, but also broadened his intellectual perspective. While at sea, to pass the dull hours on watch, he began to study Greek; and Greek myth was to play a significant role in shaping his literary imagination: Euripides' *The Bacchae* is an obvious influence on *Lord of the Flies*, his *Ion* influenced the posthumously published *The Double Tongue* (1995), and Aeschylus' *Prometheus* influenced *Pincher Martin*. Golding's early fiction, in particular, is underpinned by Greek myths, legends, and drama, echoing their rhythms and vision. The importance of Greece and classic Greek Literature, however, went further with Golding than specific textual influences. Greek art formed the basis for his own metaphorical statements about the nature of humanity, but he also used Greece as a contrast to the idea of Egypt, contrasting the rationality and light associated with the Greek tradition with the mystery and darkness of the Egyptian tradition.

In 1945 Golding returned to Bishop Wordsworth's School to teach English and Classics. While teaching he wrote several novels, all of which were rejected, and, in Golding's later opinion, deservedly so. The book that was to make him a household name was itself rejected by twenty-one publishers, until Faber published it, in September of 1954. In *Lord of the Flies* a group of boys, the oldest of whom is 12 and the youngest 6, are marooned on an idyllic desert island, and almost immediately a battle for supremacy takes place among the principal characters. Violence and death follow. *Lord of the Flies* is as fine an adventure story as any published in the second half of the century, demonstrating an impressive ability to employ language that both provides narrative impetus and also evokes profounder, more theological implications: "Taking their cue from the *innocent* Johnny, they sat down on the *fallen* palm tree and waited" (Golding 1982b: 18; my emphasis). The novel is spare and deliberate in its intentions; and certainly Golding himself had little hesitation in referring to it as a "fable." In the essay "Fable," he writes: "It is worth looking for a moment at the great original of boys on an island. This is *The Coral Island*, published a century ago, at the height of Victorian smugness, ignorance and prosperity" (1984: 88). *Lord of the Flies* is usually read as Golding's commentary upon human evil, but a crucial aspect of the novel, and of the majority of its successors, was its indebtedness to an earlier literary source.

In R. M. Ballantyne's *The Coral Island* (1858), evil lies firmly outside the English schoolboys and is made manifest by savage, black cannibals. Throughout *Lord of the Flies*, Golding overturns Ballantyne's optimistic portrait, which equates Englishness with good and foreignness with evil, and suggests that evil is more likely to reside within humanity and that external evil is in reality a projection of an inner evil. Golding uses the same names for his central characters as Ballantyne does for his trio of brave, clean, young Englishmen, which assists the comparison and eventual subversion of the beliefs central to Ballantyne's book. Golding's characters are used to portray sharply differing points of view on the nature of evil, and the means of placating this powerful force. For Piggy, there is no such thing as evil, which is just people behaving irrationally; for Jack, evil resides outside humanity and must be placated by various forms of sacrifice; and for Simon, evil expresses itself in the words of the Lord of the Flies: evil is inside humanity. Conversely, the depiction of evil in *The Coral Island* is strikingly simplistic, revolving about a specifically Christian/pagan dichotomy. Ballantyne offers a solution to the problem of evil at the end of *The Coral Island* that Golding has introduced at the beginning of his novel, and it is, significantly, no solution at all. *The Coral Island* insistently suggests that the cruelty and savagery of the pagans are due to their unfortunate ignorance of Christianity, and it is precisely this optimistic view that Golding seeks to subvert in *Lord of the Flies*. Golding makes his characters Christian from the novel's beginning and, strikingly, it is the choir, ostensibly the most pious group, who become the most cruel and violent of all the boys on the island. In *Lord of the Flies*, therefore, we find an adumbration of the disturbing connection between religion, violence, and blood sacrifice that Golding examines in close detail throughout the first phase of his career, and which is realized most powerfully in *The Spire*. As Golding's first novel moves toward its grim conclusion, the reader must wonder if Jack and his choir become hunters and sacrificers of other human beings despite their obvious Christian origins, or because of them.

When the hunters place the severed head of a pig in a clearing they are performing an act of propitiation; they have projected evil outside themselves. Simon, however, realizes that the severed head is an ineradicable part of humanity: "At last Simon gave up and looked back; saw the white teeth and dim eyes, the blood – and his gaze was held by that ancient, inescapable recognition" (1982b: 152). When Simon attempts to communicate his knowledge that the parachutist is only a pathetic victim of a larger war and that evil is internal, he is torn to pieces by Jack's tribe. Similarly, when Piggy tries to reason with the boys he also is killed. Ralph himself is on the point of being killed when a naval officer arrives to save him. Golding often described the ending as a "gimmick," but, strictly speaking, it is a shift in perspective; it is a device he also uses at the end of *The Inheritors* and *Pincher Martin*. As a technique it is clearly indebted to the Greek device of the *deus ex machina*, a supernatural intervention, and in *Lord of the Flies* the effect of this shift in perspective is considerable. Most importantly it reminds the reader that the characters we have been seeing as hunters and killers are only children, while the officer's patronizing air alerts us to the fact that precisely the same horrors are being re-enacted in the adult world. Ralph's bitter understanding of the evil that resides within humanity both anticipates what is to be a consistent theme in Golding's early novels and provides a darkly ironic counterpoint to the officer's comment: "I know. Jolly good show. Like the Coral Island" (p. 223). Golding's island is nothing like Ballantyne's Coral Island – it is a hundred years and two world wars away from the earlier writer's callous optimism, and such intertextual subversion remains a constant feature of Golding's early fiction.

Lord of the Flies was well received by the reviewers, and several very influential writers, including E. M. Forster, C. S. Lewis, and T. S. Eliot, were highly enthusiastic about the novel. Eliot, for example, described it as "not only a splendid novel but morally and theologically impeccable" (Carey 1986: 63). It began to sell well and was soon reprinted. In America it made little impression at first, but by 1957 the paperback edition had attracted a huge cult following among university students, following which it moved rapidly into the mainstream. Over the next thirty years the novel became a "set text" at secondary and tertiary level in America and Europe, and by the end of the twentieth century it had been translated into over thirty languages, including Russian, Icelandic, Japanese, Serbo-Croat, and Catalan, with worldwide sales estimated at well over 10 million copies. *Lord of the Flies* brought Golding fame and financial security, but he was deeply ambivalent about the book, often claiming the same irritated relationship with his first novel as Rachmaninoff had with his famous C-sharp minor Prelude, which, Golding often bleakly observed, his audience insisted on his playing throughout his career. The novel was made into a memorable film by Peter Brook in 1963, and was filmed again, less memorably, in 1990. *Lord of the Flies* was adapted for the stage by the novelist Nigel Williams, and was first produced by the Royal Shakespeare Company at Stratford-upon-Avon in the summer of 1995.

Just as *Lord of the Flies* "rewrites" *The Coral Island*, its successor, *The Inheritors* (1955), Golding's own favorite among his novels, written in twenty-eight days while the author was still a teacher, rewrites H. G. Wells's short story "The grisly folk" (1921). The plot of Golding's second novel is as straightforward as that of *Lord of the Flies* and indeed is similar to it: a small group of Neanderthalers is systematically killed by a larger and more powerful group of "New Men," *Homo sapiens*, the

"Inheritors" of the title. The difficulty some readers experience with *The Inheritors* is generally traceable to the novel's point of view. The nature of perception, the way in which we see, is central to *The Inheritors* and remains a constant issue throughout all of Golding's fiction. The novel is far more easily understood once we accept that we are observing the Neanderthalers' primitive and violent world through eyes that cannot comprehend what they are seeing. In *The Inheritors*, Golding makes us see through a perspective so limited and simple that the novel appears, perhaps paradoxically, difficult and complex.

In *The Inheritors*, so much of the narrative is refracted through the uncomprehending perceptions of Lok that it becomes impossible to separate Golding's manipulation of an extraordinarily limited point of view from the novel's thematic structure. With this, Golding does something remarkable. Normally when we read fiction we are pleased at our own ability to comprehend, and particularly to anticipate; for example, we are pleased at having worked out for ourselves where Pip's money comes from in Dickens's *Great Expectations*. But *The Inheritors* does not offer us this sense of superiority over the text. This is not because the novel is too complex to understand, far from it, but because, forced to view shocking events – which we understand – through uncomprehending eyes, we are manipulated into a position of complicity with guilt, and our knowledge does not flatter us, it condemns us. Although we are inclined to sympathize with Lok's people, Golding's narrative technique forces us to realize that we belong with the New Men; that we are the Inheritors. The novel also calls into question precisely what it is we have inherited, and suggests that chief among our legacies is guilt.

From the novel's beginning, the New Men are associated with disruption, violence, and death. The title contains a somber pun on "Blessed are the meek, for they shall inherit the earth" (Matthew 5: 5), as throughout the course of this novel the meek do not inherit the earth; rather, we, *Homo sapiens*, do – and the meek are completely destroyed. In Wells's book *Outline of History*, from which Golding takes the epigraph to *The Inheritors*, Wells writes: "As the Fourth Glacial age softened towards more temperate conditions, a different human type came upon the European scene, and it would seem, exterminated Homo Neathanderlis." The equanimity of Wells's tone here is complemented by the narrative voice of "The grisly folk" itself. In this story, Wells describes the adventures of a group of our remote ancestors, a tribe of hunter-gatherers whom Wells refers to throughout as the "true men." This tribe have one of their children stolen by the "grisly folk," a tribe with cannibalistic tendencies whom Wells also refers to as the "pre-men," and whom he persistently reduces to animal status. In "The grisly folk" the "true men" have one of their children abducted by the "pre-men." Golding inverts Wells's scheme: in *The Inheritors* it is the "true men" who do the kidnapping and it is they who are the cannibals, while Lok's tribe, who think of themselves as "The People," are the victims.

The New Men murder any of the People they encounter, and then abduct two of their children, in this reversal of Wells's plot. When Lok and the only remaining woman, Fa, follow the New Men to their camp they observe their actions from the vantage point of a dead tree, another characteristic example of Golding's ability to integrate the pragmatic with the symbolic. The reader sees, through Lok's mainly uncomprehending eyes, the New Men's rutting, masculine Stag God, and their violent, drunken, sexually orgiastic behavior – and a mute comparison between the two tribes underlies the whole sequence of events. While the religion of the New Men is aggressively patriarchal, the religion of Golding's Neanderthalers is strikingly matriarchial. Lok' s People are innocent. Their lives are hard and mundane, but we see their sense of tribal communion, their gentleness, their physicality and love of play, and their worship of a female deity, Oa, who abhors bloodshed. Oa is fecund and protective; she inspires joy, not fear. Oa is clearly the opposite of the rutting, bellowing Stag God of the New Men, yet the reader is forced to accept that any culture based upon Christianity has more in common with this violent being than with the gentle Oa. Another clear distinction is drawn when we see that among Lok's People it is the women who control the tribe's religious life. When Lok follows the women into the cave of ice where Oa is worshipped, and which is to melt while Lok dies alone in a poignantly symbolic episode near the end of the novel, he is terrified by the sense of religious power he feels and Fa is forced to comfort him by saying, "It is too much Oa for a man" (Golding 1981: 85). The life-affirming vision of the People embodies a set of values that cannot comprehend blood sacrifice, a practice that is, as is revealed while Lok and Fa are in the tree, central to the religion of the New Men. No postwar English novelist dramatizes the tragic consequences of an unchecked patriarchy with the imaginative intensity Golding employs in *The Inheritors*.

One of Golding's principal interests in his early fiction is to examine the ways in which humanity projects an inner evil on to something, or someone, external. It is this issue of "projection" that accounts for the stress Golding lays in these early novels upon the scapegoat, human sacrifice, and, in *The Inheritors*, cannibalism. The acts of sacrifice and propitiation that are so important in *Lord of the Flies* are equally important in *The Inheritors*; they are a way of projecting, and then of attempting to appease, an evil that is actually internal. Lok and Fa, for example, find "presents" which have been left for them by the New Men. These gifts are an act of propitiation similar to the one that is made in *Lord of the Flies* when Jack's hunters leave out their gift for "the beast." To the New Men, Lok and Fa are devils and must be placated, even to the extent of offering the child Tanakil as a blood sacrifice. *The Inheritors* is a novel as deeply concerned as its predecessor with humanity's persistent attempt to locate evil outside itself and to offer it blood, in the doomed hope that, in Jack's words in *Lord of the Flies,* "Then it won't bother us, maybe" (1982b: 147).

While both *Lord of the Flies* and *The Inheritors* consider the projection of evil on a grand scale, and assess its implications for humanity and for history, Golding's third novel, *Pincher Martin* (1956), focuses on one unique individual, Christopher Martin, known as "Pincher" Martin. Again, the plot is extremely simple; the difficulty readers often experience with the novel is, as with *The Inheritors*, due to its complex form of expression. During World War II, Christopher Martin, a lieutenant in the navy, is thrown from the bridge of his ship when it is hit by a torpedo, and the novel opens with him struggling in the water. The novel describes him finding a small rock in the middle of the ocean and then recounts, in extraordinary detail, his grim struggle for survival on the rock. Consistent with his early practice, Golding here rewrites an earlier text; in this case a novel by Henry Dorling, *Pincher Martin OD* (1916). However, instead of drowning when he is shipwrecked, Golding's character refuses to die. As Martin struggles in the sea we are given his thoughts:

> I won't die.
> I can't die.
> Not me.
> Precious. (Golding 1972: 18)

The final chapter offers us, as did the two earlier novels, a shift in perspective, but this is the most dramatic of them all, because at this point in *Pincher Martin* we discover that the protagonist has been dead since the opening pages of the novel. *Pincher Martin* investigates greed so intense and a pride so enormous that death becomes unthinkable.

Although *Pincher Martin* is the first of Golding's novels to take place in the contemporary world, it is also a book set on an island, and one that is concerned with survival and isolation, those perennial Golding themes. Similarly, just as the boys in *Lord of the Flies* project their fears and horrors on to "the beast," and the New Men in *The Inheritors* turn the gentle Neanderthalers into demons, so Martin in this novel transforms an aching tooth in his own mouth into an island in the middle of the ocean, and creates from his egotistical and perverse refusal to die a heroic struggle for survival. Again, like its predecessors, *Pincher Martin* is a deeply moral fable, as it becomes apparent that Martin's punishment is directly proportionate to the life he had led. Our knowledge of his previous life is revealed in a series of flashbacks; and one of the novel's dominant structural devices is this alternation between past and present, between the world and the rock. As the novel progresses our admiration for Martin's epic fight for life is undermined by our increasing knowledge of his viciousness and greed. The language of drama permeates the novel: the opening reference to a stage is succeeded by memories of Martin's career as an actor and, ultimately, by his attempts to play the great tragic roles. As the illusory nature of his survival becomes inexorably more apparent to Martin, he even turns to the great figures of myth, re-creating himself as Ajax and Prometheus, in order to keep reality from intruding. When he realizes that he cannot maintain this fantasy, Martin shows characteristic cunning in deciding that he is mad, preferring this to death. It is significant, however, that when he adopts the role of Lear he misquotes, underlining his inability to play the part. Remorselessly, Martin is made to see the truth: he is not a king, transformed by suffering into a tragic figure, but a dead man who refuses to die.

Pincher Martin parodies the Genesis myth of creation and for six days and six nights Martin creates his world: the rock, the sea, the sky, night, day, the seaweed, the gulls, and the shell fish. Finally, it seems that he creates God, who is in his own image, wearing an oilskin and sea boots, and who asks him, "Have you had enough, Christopher?" (1972: 198). But Martin refuses to admit that he has had enough, and screams defiance to the end. Finally he is metonymically reduced to a pair of claws (pincers) and is annihilated by the black lightning that is the only conception of an afterlife that he possesses. Although the parallels with Genesis might prompt the reader to assume that the figure who speaks to Martin is God, it is also possible that this is the voice of the author. As Martin begins to disintegrate in the face of the black lightning, references that could clearly refer to the act of writing begin to appear: "The sea stopped moving, froze, became paper, painted paper that was torn by a black line. The rock was painted on the same paper" (p. 204). There are few novels that cannot be re-read profitably, but to re-read *Pincher Martin* with the knowledge that the protagonist has been dead throughout the novel is to encounter a radically different book. The densely textured and graphically detailed descriptions of the rock and physical landscape that, on a first reading, persuaded us of the realism of Martin's plight are now seen as deeply ironic. What the reader now recognizes is the appalling strain Martin experiences in maintaining the fantasy that the rock is real, a demand that clearly has an analogue with the creative process, and perhaps not only with writing but also with reading. *Pincher Martin* can also, therefore, be read as a metafictional text, openly commenting on its own fictional status, rather than as a purely theological fable. Golding's interest in the process of artistic creation itself is further developed in his use of the painter, Samuel Mountjoy, the protagonist of his next novel, *Free Fall*.

Like the previous novels, *Free Fall* (1959) is indebted to an earlier literary source; it is a parody of Dante's *La Vita Nuova* (*The Poems of Youth*, c.1290), a collection of thirty-one lyrical poems celebrating the beauty and virtue of Dante's beloved Beatrice. However, Golding's use of Dante's poem signals a shift in his practice up to this point. The earlier novels had incorporated literary analogues as a way of demonstrating the partiality, or even incorrectness, of the beliefs central to these texts; but throughout *Free Fall* Golding uses Dante's poem to suggest that Mountjoy's desire for his Beatrice, Beatrice Ifor, is inferior to Dante's devotion to his Beatrice. Mountjoy, as indeed his name indicates, is only interested in sex with his Beatrice, and her surname, "I-for," emphasizes her object-status for him. Generically, *Free Fall* can be read as a *Künstlerroman*, an "artist novel"; and Golding's use, for the first time, of a first-person narrator enables him to use Mountjoy's profession as an artist to comment on the nature of art – all art. As an artist, Mountjoy selects and arranges his materials in order to create a pattern, something recognizable. This is what he hopes to find as he re-examines his life – a pattern that will give meaning to his life. The chronological structure of *Free Fall* is inseparable from the novel's central concerns. In the opening pages Mountjoy writes: "For time is not to be laid out endlessly like a row of bricks. That straight line from the first hiccup to the last gasp is a dead thing. Time is two modes" (Golding 1982a: 6). This dualism is anticipated by the novel's title. The phrase "free fall" can be used scientifically, to describe an object obeying the law of gravity and falling through space; but it also has religious connotations, implying the theological fall of humanity.

The protagonist's name is also one that sets up dualities: "Samuel" is the name of an Old Testament prophet, while "Mountjoy" clearly possesses sexual connotations. This tension between the religious and the carnal, the spirit and the flesh, provides the central dynamic of *Free Fall*. These different perceptions are personified in the characters of Mountjoy's schoolteachers, Nick Shales and Rowena Pringle. Shales, an amiable and friendly man, is a scientist, a rationalist, while Pringle, an unpleasant and bitter woman, teaches Scripture, and tells the children of a world in which a bush can catch fire and yet be unconsumed by the flames. Despite his liking for Shales, Mountjoy sees the limitations inherent in the rational, mechanistic, and thoroughly masculine world of Shales and succumbs to the enchantment of Pringle's irrational universe. Mountjoy's attempts throughout the novel to find a way to reconcile these two visions, to find a bridge between the two worlds, ends in failure, and he acknowledges in the closing pages, "There is no bridge" (p. 253). Mountjoy's failure, of course, is not Golding's. *Free Fall* can be seen as a book that is concerned not only with the attempt to find the truth, but also with the desire to communicate that truth. Early in the book, Mountjoy notes: "To communicate is our passion and our despair" (p. 8). *Free Fall* ceaselessly investigates the ways in which we select the material we wish to communicate, and the nature of the language we use for this communication.

Golding's fifth novel, *The Spire* (1964), is also structured around the act of communication, in this case a vision and a command from God. Like *Free Fall*, *The Spire* is an investigation of the two differing worlds of the flesh and the spirit; but unlike its predecessor *The Spire* moves toward an emphatic resolution. Jocelin, Dean of Barchester Cathedral, believes that he has been chosen by God to build a 400-foot-high spire on top of the cathedral. It quickly becomes apparent that the foundations under the cathedral will not support such a weight, and yet, against all sound practical advice, Jocelin persists with his dream. The novel has an omniscient narrator, yet virtually every event within it is seen through Jocelin's eyes. This creates a perspective that is both ambivalent and circumscribed, and this latter quality is paralleled in the claustrophobic, fourteenth-century setting of the novel. Similarly, the continuous blurring of the two narrative perspectives parallels the movement of the story toward the reconciliation of two worlds, an event most spectacularly realized in Jocelin's deathbed epiphany.

During the course of the novel the workmen murder Pangall, a deformed cathedral factotum, and Jocelin eventually realizes that Pangall has been sacrificed in an attempt to appease the dark powers, which the workmen worship. Sacrifice is interwoven throughout *The Spire* with revelation and vision; and, as the novel progresses, we witness the appalling personal price Jocelin is prepared to pay as well as the price he inflicts upon the innocent. In *The Inheritors*, too, we are made aware of cost – of the awesome price the New Men have to pay in order to surmount their origins. One of Golding's most persistent themes, and one as grimly embedded in the text of *The Spire* as Pangall himself is embedded in the foundations of the cathedral, is the necessity of acquiring knowledge. The movement from ignorance to revelation is a continual process in Golding's early fiction: Ralph's recognition of human evil on the beach in *Lord of the Flies*, Lok's realization that Liku has been eaten in *The Inheritors*, Martin's final knowledge that he is indeed dead in *Pincher Martin*, and Mountjoy's understanding that his lust and selfishness have driven Beatrice insane in *Free Fall*. Jocelin also moves from ignorance to knowledge and, as in Golding's first two novels, it is an act of murder that causes the revelation.

However, in certain respects, *The Spire* has more in common with *Pincher Martin* than with the first two novels: both depict the slow, intensely detailed growth of a structure in stone. Simultaneously, because both novels are concerned with portraying a central act of construction, they can be seen as self-reflexive, commenting on their own status as texts. While *The Spire* and *Pincher Martin* share a minutely detailed attention to the act of construction, their protagonists also share a characteristic which, paradoxically and probably against the author's intentions, sweeps the reader along with them. Despite the realization that Pincher Martin is a greedy and vicious man, the reader cannot help marveling at, and perhaps even admiring, his cornered courage, his relentless will, and his refusal to die. Similarly, while it is made clear from the opening of *The Spire* that Jocelin stands convicted of hubris, the reader marvels at the dean's faith and is overwhelmed by its power and splendor. The results of Jocelin's actions cannot change the intensity of the faith, which he so obviously possesses, and it is the power of this conviction that we are being asked to witness. Golding writes of a faith so strong that its destructive powers amount to what is virtually a blasphemous travesty of faith, yet still remains superior to its antithesis, reason. What appears to be a simple dichotomy between faith and reason, however, is complicated when we realize that faith in this novel has two guises. The historical setting allows the proximity of Stonehenge to challenge the authority of the cathedral, and this allows Golding to depict a destructive collision between pagan beliefs and Christianity – and to suggest the deep and cruel similarities between them. At the novel's conclusion, when all the principal characters are dead or dying, the spire still stands. Disturbingly, the reader is asked to consider whether the spire stands despite the sacrifice of Pangall, or because of it. The final moments are a technical triumph for Golding; the highly charged language and the splintered chronology brilliantly evoke the dying moments of Jocelin. In his last moment of life Jocelin discovers something of immense importance, and simultaneously discovers that what he understands cannot be communicated. Language is an ineffective medium for the communication of what Jocelin has to say, and he is reduced to simile:

> In the tide, flying like a bluebird, struggling, shouting, screaming to leave behind the words of magic and incomprehension –
> *It's like the appletree!* (Golding 1983: 223)

In this final moment, Jocelin realizes that, like the spire itself, life is a miracle, rooted deeply in both innocence and guilt, in beauty and in blood.

In its extraordinary control and ingenious use of narrative perspective Golding's early fiction extended the formal boundaries of fiction and made a significant contribution to Britain's literature. Golding returned to the past in search of the stories that still reverberate through our culture, which he then used to create myths for a modern age. Golding's characters are never helpless victims of socioeconomic forces beyond their control. They live in a world in which tragedy is not just present but actively inscribed in the nature of things, a world in which one must choose and in which the consequences of a wrong choice can be fatal. In his later novels, particularly in *The Pyramid* (1967), *Rites of Passage* (1980), *The Paper Men* (1984), *Close Quarters* (1987), and *Fire Down Below* (1989), Golding demonstrated a previously unsuspected gift for comedy; but to the end of his life and career his mythic and allegorical universe remained one where damnation and salvation are still possible, and where the actions of a single individual can have an effect on the world.

REFERENCES AND FURTHER READING

Boyd, S. J. (1988) *The Novels of William Golding*. Brighton: Harvester.

Braine, J. (1985) *Room at the Top*. Harmondsworth: Penguin.

Carey, J. (ed) (1986) *William Golding: The Man and His Books – A Tribute on his 75th Birthday*. London: Faber and Faber.

Gindin, J. (1988) *William Golding*. London: Macmillan.

Golding, W. (1972) *Pincher Martin*. London: Faber and Faber.

—— (1981) *The Inheritors*. London: Faber and Faber.

—— (1982a) *Free Fall*. London: Faber and Faber.

—— (1982b) *Lord of the Flies*. London: Faber and Faber.

—— (1983) *The Spire*. London: Faber and Faber.

—— (1984) *The Hot Gates*. London: Faber and Faber.

Gindin, J. (1988) *William Golding*. London: Macmillan.

Hodson, L. (1969) *William Golding*. Edinburgh: Oliver and Boyd.

Johnston, A. (1980) *Of Earth and Darkness: The Novels of William Golding*. Columbia: University of Missouri Press.

Kinkead-Weekes, M. and Gregor, Ian (1984) *William Golding: A Critical Study*. London: Faber and Faber.

McCarron, K. (1995) *The Coincidence of Opposites: William Golding's Later Fiction*. Sheffield: Sheffield Academic Press.

Morgan, D. (1994) "Theater of war: combat, the military, and masculinities," in Harry Brod and Michael Kaufman (eds.) *Theorizing Masculinities*. Thousand Oaks, CA: Sage.

Page, N. (ed.) (1985) *William Golding: Novels, 1954–67*. London: Macmillan.

Parkin, D. (ed.) (1985) *The Anthropology of Evil*. Oxford: Blackwell.

Ray, W. (1984) *Literary Meaning: From Phenomenology to Deconstruction*. Oxford: Blackwell.

Redpath, P. (1986) *William Golding: A Structural Study of His Fiction*. London: Vision Press.

Tiger, V. (1974) *William Golding: The Dark Fields of Discovery*. London: Calder and Boyers.

Watson, G. (1991) *British Literature Since 1945*. London: Macmillan.

21

Amis, Father and Son

Merritt Moseley

In 1989 John Hayes, the Director of the National Portrait Gallery in London, wrote to Kingsley Amis inviting him to sit for a joint portrait with his son Martin Amis. The elder Amis's reply (K. Amis 2000: 1066–7) declared the request

> one of the most amazingly inept and tactless suggestions that has ever been made to me. Martin fully agrees with this judgement. Whoever put it forward originally is obviously waiting for a vacancy at Harpers & Queen or Tatler [fashionable magazines].
>
> If this refusal leaves your artist with time on his hands, you might get him to knock up a picture of the Two Ronnies [a team of popular comedians].
>
> Yours sincerely
>
> Kingsley Amis

This incident provides a peculiarly rich insight into the two novelists, father and son, going well beyond its glimpse of Kingsley Amis's famously waspish public personality. It shows how highly visible both father and son were: being chosen for the National Portrait Gallery is a rare recognition for a living celebrity. And both were very newsworthy. Kingsley turned over both Hayes's letter and his response to journalist Peregrine Worsthorne, who printed them in a front-page story in the *Sunday Telegraph*.

Hayes's suggestion demonstrates the way the two of them were linked. A joint portrait is an odd choice, but in this case it undoubtedly made sense to John Hayes because Kingsley and Martin Amis are, as a father-son pair of distinguished novelists, unparallelled. Martin Amis has commented, "there's Mrs. Trollope as well as Anthony, and Dumas *père et fils*, and that's about it" (M. Amis 2000: 23). And it demonstrates the complicated relations between the two men. Kingsley is the one indignantly rebuffing the invitation – and indeed it is likely that, for a much admired 67-year-old novelist, it may have been an insult to include his 40-year-old son as part of a package deal. Yet Martin agreed with his father's indignation.

Much of the discussion of Kingsley and Martin Amis, and their relations with each other, falls into the field of literary chat. This reached peak volume when Kingsley Amis's *Letters* and Martin Amis's memoir, *Experience*, were published in the space of six weeks in the spring of 2000. Martin's book strongly reinforced his love and respect for his father, who had died in 1995. He acknowledged the fact, evident from previous interviews and public comment by Kingsley, that his father did not care for Martin's fiction, the fiction of those he admired (Nabokov, Bellow, Joyce, Roth), or his politics. Rather pitifully, he seemed to express gratitude to his father because, despite a strong aversion to experimentalism, he did read *some* of his son's books. In fact, as he reveals elsewhere, Kingsley finished three of them (M. Amis 2001: 110).

Kingsley's *Letters* provided a richer source of comment on the two men's relationship. In correspondence with his oldest friend, Philip Larkin, Kingsley comments, with apparent envy (though perhaps it is at least partly ironic) on his son's success: "Did I tell you Martin is spending a year [1979] abroad as a TAX EXILE? Last year he earned £38,000. Little shit. 29, he is. Little shit" (K. Amis 2000: 871). In 1984 he compares the Public Lending Right payments – payments in lieu of royalties for authors' books borrowed from public libraries – earned by the two of them and writes that "Martin Amis is more famous than I am now" (p. 969). As for his son's work, he lumps it with that of other (to him) unreadable modernists: "[H]ave you actually tried to *read* Clive Sinclair and Ian MacEwen (mcewan?) and Angela Carter and M**t** *m**?" (pp. 950–1). About *Money*, Martin Amis's brilliant 1984 novel, he wrote to Larkin:

> I laughed heartily at your excellent jest about Martin's book. You almost had me believing you sort of, well, *enjoyed* it or something, ha ha ha. If I didn't know you better I'd, etc. I hated its way of constantly reminding me of Nabokov. But of course I'm very old-fashioned. Set in my ways, what? I expect you read a lot of Saul Bellow and Philip Roth and Norman Maaaaghgh [. . .] (p. 989)

The two major topics of disagreement between the two men were politics and literary practice. Kingsley regularly denounced Martin's fashionably "lefty" politics; just as regularly he denounced his approach to fiction, which he thought too attention-getting because of the complexity of Martin's sometimes experimental style, and such ways of "buggering about with the reader" as introducing a character called "Martin Amis" into *Money*. A closer look at these two issues sheds some light not only on the relations between father and son but also on the more important issues of the trajectory of a literary career in postwar Britain.

By the time he was criticizing his son's left-wing views, in the 1960s, Kingsley Amis had become a crusty, even cranky, conservative; he supported the American war in Vietnam (unlike almost every other British literary figure), he worried about the Communist threat, and he was distinctly uneasy about feminism, the Labour Party, and the Welfare State. But he had begun his public career as a radical himself, and his radicalism went back to his teenage years. Biographer Richard Bradford links this to the young Kingsley's rebellion against his own father, William (who had *himself* migrated from left to right):

> William was once a Liberal who turned into an arch-Tory after the Great War, an affiliation strengthened by the General Strike and the emergence of the Labour Party as a serious contender for power. Amis himself, summarizing his father's view of him, became a 'bloody little fool of a leftie' and an avid supporter of Joseph Stalin. (Bradford 2001: 23)

He continued to support the Communist Party until some time in the middle 1950s, when the Hungarian invasion completed his rejection of that god that failed. In *Lucky Jim* (1954) the protagonist Jim Dixon espouses no developed political program but does argue strongly for the redistribution of wealth and suggests that rich people are a doomed breed.

Martin Amis, then, was following an Amis family pattern, not to say a nearly universal one, when as a young man he irritated his father with his politics. And, though he may not have followed his father all the way across the spectrum to the right wing, it is worth noting that his book *Koba the Dread: Laughter and the Twenty Million* (2002) is a nonfiction account of the horrors of Stalinism, which includes sharp criticism of various socialists for their too-sanguine acceptance of Stalin. His father is one of the thinkers he criticizes for his protracted toleration of Stalinism. Youthful political naivety is now deplored in the reverse direction.

Kingsley's distaste for Martin's literary practices is evident in his letters to Larkin quoted above. Martin told interviewer Claudia Fitzherbert about his father's reaction to *Money*:

> There were bits of my novels which I know he would have liked very much, but really his whole attitude is expressed in his reaction to . . . *Money*: he read the first chapter, and liked it, but as soon as the "Martin Amis" character appeared, he threw the book across the room. Because that came under the heading of buggering the reader about. (Fitzherbert 2001: 17)

The introduction of the author under his own name may seem one of those self-referential, attention-drawing, playful tricks that social-realist Kingsley would necessarily deplore. But he clearly knew the temptation. Not only was his first, never published, novel *The Legacy*, written in the late 1940s, the story of a character called Kingsley Amis trying to write a novel; but in the first stages of writing his third novel *I Like It Here* (1958), he "toyed with the idea of bringing back Jim Dixon who would be sent to Portugal by his employer, Gore Urquhart, and there meet an author called Kingsley Amis" (Bradford 2001: 140-1). He rejected this thought. But the idea of engineering an encounter between Jim Dixon and a character called Kingsley Amis is not so different from the plot development in *Money*, which produces unsettling meetings between John Self and "Martin Amis." The extent to which Jim Dixon is to be identified with his author is an old controversy. Amis did nothing to end it when he published a pamphlet called *Lucky Jim's Politics* in 1968 or entitled an essay about his own political transformation, "Why Lucky Jim turned right," in *What Became of Jane Austen* (1970).

All this shows that Martin Amis was more like Kingsley than Kingsley ever suspected or admitted, and that there is something paradigmatic about the career paths the two men established. What recognizing these similarities does not fully include is how unusual the Amises, father and son, are – *because* they are father and son. Kingsley was the author of scores of books, including the twenty-four novels covering the forty-one years between *Lucky Jim* (1954) and *The Biographer's Moustache* (1995). He published five books of literary criticism, including both single-topic books such as *New Maps of Hell: A Survey of Science Fiction* (1961) and *The James Bond Dossier* (1965) and collections of his reviews and journalism. Throughout much of his career, and especially in its first two decades, he was an active and vivid reviewer, notable for his iconoclasm. Other books were political or polemic, including *Socialism and the Intellectuals*, published by the Fabian Society in 1957, when he was still a left-winger, and *Lucky Jim's Politics*, published by the Conservative Political Centre in 1968, when he had swung dramatically to the right. In 1991 he published his *Memoirs*.

Martin has probably been more famous than Kingsley ever was, in part because of changes in the media in his lifetime. For instance, his sex life has received much more coverage in newspapers than his father's; he was regularly referred to in print as one of the most sexually successful and enviable men of his time, while Kingsley's own tireless seductions – which followed rather than preceded (as Martin's had) his marriage – came to public view only at the end of his life. This fame has been something of a curse. Many reviewers have blamed him because, as the son of an established and successful writer, he had it too easy. Artistically, Kingsley had come from nowhere; his son, unsympathetic observers were free to conclude, was born into a writer's privileged life and a good contract with Jonathan Cape. A 2003 profile explains:

> The mantel of Britain's Greatest Living Novelist settled on Amis young and has grated and gratified ever since. McEwan has won more awards; Rushdie more notoriety, Ishiguro greater success in Hollywood. Murdoch was arguably brainier, Spark funnier. But it is with Amis that the press and the reading public have chosen to enact "keeping dad in his place." (Brockes 2003)

Though Kingsley earned a great deal of money, Martin may have been even more successful in worldly terms. He famously received an advance of £500,000 for *The Information*, though it is equally famous that the book did not earn its advance. He is less prolific. His ten novels are his major accomplishment, though he is also the author of two books of short fiction, the memoir/history/polemic *Koba's Dread*, three books of collected journalism, and his own memoir, *Experience* (2000). The publication

of *The War Against Cliché: Essays and Reviews, 1971–2000*, in 2001, made it possible
to recognize his major stature as a literary critic. His reviews can be as sharp and fluent
as his father's, but are informed by a more serious approach to criticism. As a critic
Kingsley rejoices to concur with the common reader, or with what the common reader
would believe if he were not misled by reputation or by lack of confidence. Martin's
criticism is, if not more academic (unlike his father he was never an academic), more
scholarly, more intellectual. Martin is both more honest about his own complicated
feelings toward his contemporaries and more generous toward other writers. Kingsley's criticism too often takes the form of insisting that someone critically admired –
Dylan Thomas, Philip Roth, or John Keats, for example – is really no good; though
he is also ready to insist that someone in critical disrepute (say, Rudyard Kipling or
Ian Fleming) or some genre considered inferior (for instance, jazz, science fiction,
detective novels) is really good. If Kingsley Amis's poetry is enough to have earned
him a reputation without the fiction, so is Martin Amis's criticism and journalism.

The major difference between the bodies of work belonging to these two men of
letters may be that Martin is not a poet. Though Kingsley was primarily a novelist,
his early writing was in poetry, his first published book was poetry, and over
his lifetime he wrote a substantial body of verse, much of which is first rate. If he
had never written fiction he would have earned a modest but firm reputation as a
postwar poet, for work less profound than that of his friend Philip Larkin but in
a similar tonal range.

His first book was *Bright November* (1947), a slim volume of verse published by the
Fortune Press. Before long he was working on what was first called "Dixon and
Christine" and later became *Lucky Jim*. The idea for setting it at a university, Amis
said, came from a visit to Philip Larkin at Leicester, where he was a university
librarian, though his own circumstances as a young lecturer at University College,
Swansea undoubtedly played a role. The appearance of *Lucky Jim* in 1954 immediately
announced a new voice in the postwar fictional conversation. Amis felt ill-suited as
the voice of youth (he was 32) and was impatient with the journalistic conceit of the
"Angry Young Men," which lumped him, John Wain, John Osborne, Colin Wilson,
and Iris Murdoch together in the public mind. Amis always insisted that fiction was
not the proper vehicle for a social or political argument. Jim Dixon is a poorly
qualified history lecturer at an unimpressive regional university, teaching on a
short-term contract. His twin predicaments are his job and his love life. To keep
his job, he needs to impress the awful Professor Welch, who is an anthology of
appalling tastes and proclivities. In particular he is wedded to an idea of culture that
Jim finds alien and false; nevertheless Jim believes he must pretend to care about such
things as a madrigal evening and "Merrie England." The second predicament is an
entanglement with another lecturer, Margaret Peel, which Jim cannot seem to end
though he finds her unattractive (she is both physically plain and full of affectations of
behavior and dress) and she treats him badly. The explanation for his helpless
attachment to Margaret against his own desires seems to be his shyness and a good
heart, which makes him pity her. She has recently attempted suicide and is recovering

at the Welches' home, so befriending her may also be a way of ingratiating himself with Welch.

Jim rebels against these conditions, sometimes privately (he makes faces to himself and sings vulgar songs about Professor Welch under his breath), sometimes more publicly: getting drunk, setting his bed on fire at the Welches' house, and so forth. His rebellion becomes more active when he meets Christine Callaghan, a beautiful woman from London unfortunately linked with Professor Welch's egregious son Bertrand. Jim eventually secures Christine for himself, beats up Bertrand, destroys his chances to continue in his teaching position, but gets a better (non-teaching) job with Christine's uncle. He is indeed "lucky"; the novel is a male Cinderella story.

Its emblematic quality, if it has one, comes from its placing Jim, who at least internally is honest and sensible, in opposition to a range of older, stuffier, phonier representatives of academic inanity and bourgeois false consciousness. But Amis's great talent, as David Lodge pointed out long ago, is a linguistic one, and the memorable parts of *Lucky Jim* are not so much its plot events as its language: for instance, Jim's feeling, in response to some emotional manipulation by Margaret, that he "wanted to rush at her and tip her backwards in the chair, to make a deafening rude noise in her face, to push a bead up her nose" (K. Amis 1954: 160). Or his impatient reflections on country folk who are delaying his bus to the station to detain Christine:

> Dixon's head switched angrily to and fro in vain search for a clock; the inhabitants of this mental, moral, and physical backwater, devoting as they had done for years their few waking moments to the pursuits of offences against chastity, were too poor, and were also too mean ... (p. 250)

Jim also speaks for a common-sense view of life, as when he reminds Christine that "nice things are nicer than nasty ones" (140).

Lucky Jim is the best of Amis's novels of the 1950s, the others of which are *That Uncertain Feeling* (1955) and *I Like It Here* (1958). A change arrived with *Take a Girl Like You* (1960), which tells a dual story; instead of one male protagonist, this novel has a male and a female; and the woman, Jenny Bunn, is given considerably more development than the women who figured in the first three novels. Christine Callaghan had complained to Jim Dixon that men were always trying to seduce her, "And I didn't want to be seduced, you see, and as soon as I'd convinced them of that, they were off" (K. Amis 1960: 141). Jenny is the same sort of woman and, for the first time in Amis's fiction, there is a serious attempt to understand and sympathize with the point of view of a woman resistant to seduction. Northern, relatively unsophisticated schoolteacher Jenny loves sophisticated but unreliable southern Lothario Patrick Standish; eventually, he rapes her, and the novel ends with an accommodation between the two of them. She tells him, "those old Bible-class ideas have certainly taken a knocking, haven't they?," to which he replies, "It was inevitable" (K. Amis 1960: 320). *Take a Girl Like You* is not without comedy, but its overall tone is darker (the model is Richardson's *Clarissa*). Amis returned to Patrick and Jenny Standish in one of his late novels, *Difficulties With Girls* (1988).

Though most of Kingsley Amis's novels are set in the contemporary or recent world and take a social-realist comic approach, he also contributed to a variety of popular or demotic genres (as he was always eager, in his criticism, to defend "genre" fiction against the excessive claims of the "literary novel"). These include *Colonel Sun* (1968), a James Bond novel written under the pseudonym of Robert Markham; *The Green Man* (1969), a fantasy of the supernatural; *The Riverside Villas Murder* (1973) and *The Crime of the Century* (1987), detective fictions; *Russian Hide-and-Seek* (1980), a dystopia of life in Britain under a Russian occupation; and *The Alteration* (1976), a "time romance" developing an idea of what life in Europe would have been like if the Protestant Reformation had not occurred.

Amis's career passed through a sort of crisis between 1978 and 1986. In the former year he published *Jake's Thing*, which in some ways is a sequel to *Lucky Jim*. Protagonist Jim Richardson (i.e. Dick's son, Dixon) is an aging academic who teaches at Comyns College, Oxford, and lives in London. The academic content of the novel concerns efforts to admit women to men's colleges at Oxford, a development that Jake, who takes a reactionary distaste to a great many modern developments, opposes; the personal content is to do with his loss of interest in and capacity for sex, after a lifetime as something of a sexual athlete. Jake undergoes a variety of comically-rendered treatments, some by ridiculous American therapists; eventually he loses his wife, through indifference, and, when he is informed that his condition can be cured by medication, reflects on what he knows about women and decides to remain impotent.

Stanley and the Women (1984) took a major step forward into full-blown misogyny. Martin Amis calls this his father's "hate novel" (M. Amis 2000: 309). Stanley Duke's troubles begin with his deranged son, but soon turn into a series of false accusations and wounding persecutions by his wife, his former wife, and a woman psychiatrist. There is a circling-of-the-wagons among the well-meaning men in the novel, all of whom recognize the awfulness of women. For the first time, Amis had some trouble finding an American publisher for *Stanley*, because of the unpleasantness of the attitudes it seemed to endorse.

But with *The Old Devils* (1986) Amis returned to his strongest form. Martin Amis, who believes this is "the book he will be remembered for" (2000: 257), identified its strength as a *"a surrender of intransigence.... he had forgiven love..."* (2000: 258). An ensemble piece about nearly a dozen old people living in Wales, it combines sharp satirical observation of such phenomena as pretentious Welshness (Dylan Thomas comes in for attack under the name Brydan) and the heartlessness of the lifelong seducer with a humane sympathy for the ravages of age and the emotional needs of ordinary people. The three most sympathetic characters (as Kingsley pointed out in a letter) are two women and a homosexual man.

Stanley and the Women reflected the bitterness of Amis's second divorce and his animosity toward his ex-wife, generalized to an indictment of women; *The Old Devils* incorporated some of his experience of Wales as well as his personal knowledge of what it means to be old, including dental problems, drinking too much, and getting fat. Generally speaking Kingsley Amis is not an autobiographical novelist in important ways, despite the use of people he knew from time to time (Professor Welch is based on his first father-in-law). An exception is his penultimate novel, *You Can't Do Both* (1994). It was written at a time when he was cooperating with biographer Eric Jacobs and reflecting more mellowly on his early life, including relations with his parents and his first wife Hilly. (Amis and Hillary separated in 1963; in 1981, after the breakup of his second marriage, he moved into a house where he lived with Hilly and her third husband until his final hospitalization. His *Memoirs* (1991) are dedicated to Hilly, along with their children and her third husband and stepson, and conclude with a moving poem to her.) *You Can't Do Both* explores the choices, good and bad, that had determined Amis's life. In particular it embodies a recognition – announced in the title – that the determination to have a wife and family and at the same time to carry on a joyously unfettered sex life with other women is unrealistic and vain. *You Can't Do Both*, though not one of his finest novels, is the fitting climax to his career, despite the later lightweight *The Biographer's Moustache*.

Jake's Thing appeared when Kingsley Amis was 56, and thus mid-career (nine more novels followed). Martin published *Koba the Dread* at 53 and presumably in the middle of his own career. He began younger – he was only 24 when *The Rachel Papers* came out – and, as the son of a writer famous at the time, was not obscure even at that age. The similarities between father's and son's first novels should not be exaggerated, though the description of Jim Dixon ("on the short side, fair and round-faced, with an unusual breadth of shoulder that had never been accompanied by any special physical strength or skill" (K. Amis 1954: 9)) does remind one of Martin's first-person narrator, who begins, "My name is Charles Highway, though you wouldn't think it to look at me. It's such a rangy, well-travelled, big-cocked name and, to look at, I am none of these" (M. Amis 1973: 7).

The Rachel Papers is the story of Highway's coming of age, no less deft because he is hyper-conscious that he is recounting, while living, his own coming of age, and has set himself a series of tasks that includes seducing the Rachel of the title by his twentieth birthday. For a first novel, it is a comic masterpiece; it is also much franker (on masturbation, for instance) than anything Kingsley ever published; and the first-person narrator provides ample opportunity for taking the measure of the excesses and pomposities of youth. And the style is fresh and vivid: Charles Highway considers how to present himself to Rachel:

> What clothes would I wear? Blue madras shirt, black boots, and the old black cord suit with those touching leather elbow-patches. On the two occasions I had seen her last August I underwent several complete identity-reorganizations, settling finally somewhere between the pained, laconic, inscrutable type and the knowing, garrulous, cynical, laugh a minute, yet something demonic about him, something nihilistic, muted death-wish type. Revamp those, or start again? (1973: 45)

The Rachel Papers received the Somerset Maugham Award for the best first novel, as *Lucky Jim* had done twenty years earlier.

Amis quickly became known as the possessor of a strong new voice who wrote daringly about squalor, sex, drugs, youth. His second novel, *Dead Babies* (1975), reinforced this perception, recounting a house party among vicious and amoral young people. In *Success* (1978) he told a dual story of two foster brothers, one apparently as suave and successful as the other is blundering and futile. Successful Gregory and hapless Terry take turns in narrating accounts of the same events, and this study in alternate perspectives develops surprising depths. It is stylistically brilliant, particularly in the voice of Gregory, which is baroque and witty as well as inhumane.

> *Terence* thinks – he doesn't actually dare say it – that my life is in some sense a gloating parody of the huff-and-puff of his own quotidian dreads, slumped where he is now in his days and days. All my gifts – social, monetary, physiognomic – take on monstrous shape, loom large, like muscle-clouds, in his sallow mind.... Do I mind – do I mind the guaranteed dazzle of my days, the way I surge from one proud eminence to another, the way my life has always pounded through the unequal landscape about us on arrow-straight, slick silvery rails? (M. Amis 1978: 48–9)

These novels of the 1970s are all short, nervous, brilliant; arguably aggressively masculine; very contemporary in concerns and language (though Amis *creates* contemporary style and is undoubtedly the most imitated prose writer of his generation). With *Other People: A Mystery Story* (1981) he changed gears; this is the story of an amnesiac who takes the name Mary Lamb, and her efforts to understand a world made strange. His other ventures into what might be called genre fiction, or deviations from the main lines of the modern British "literary novel," include *Einstein's Monsters* (1985), a collection of short fictions united by a concern for the nuclear threat; *Night Train* (1997), a detective story in the voice of a female American investigator; and, most ambitiously and most controversially, *Time's Arrow: or, The Nature of the Offense* (1991), a serious treatment of the Holocaust and the guilt of one of its perpetrators. Its treatment is experimental: time moves backward. Eating, for instance, is described this way: "Various items get gulped up into my mouth, and after skilful massage with tongue and teeth I transfer them to the plate for additional sculpture with knife and fork and spoon" (M. Amis 1991: 19). This device was considered by some critics a gimmick that trivialized the Holocaust and Amis was accused of anti-Semitism.

Martin Amis's major works are *Money: A Suicide Note* (1984); *London Fields* (1989); and *The Information* (1995). They are all ambitious, subtle, morally serious books. Both *London Fields* and *The Information* have a strong, brooding, anxious tone. *London Fields* is set slightly in the future and part of its background condition is the threat of nuclear winter. The male characters are all in some way involved with Nicola Six, called a "murderee" because she is convinced that she will be murdered by either Keith Talent, a yob, or Guy Clinch, a nob. One of its great strengths is the strong feeling it conveys for London and particularly the more louche sections of it, for instance in passages like this one:

> And God – look out! – the Portobello Road, the whole trench scuffed and frayed, falling apart, and full of rats. Guy could feel the street frisking him – to see what he had and what he might give up. A queue of tramps had formed at the gates of the Salvation Army Hostel, waiting for soup or whatever was offered, the troops of the poor, conscripts, pressed men, hard pressed. Tall, and with clean hair, clean teeth, Guy moved past them painfully, the tramps and their tickling eyes. All he saw was a montage of preposterous footwear, open at the toes like the mouths of horses, showing horse's teeth. (M. Amis 1989: 149)

The Information, as a work of fiction, was almost completely overshadowed by journalistic curiosity about Amis's life, including the money he had received for it, his falling-out with old friend Julian Barnes (whose wife had been Amis's agent until he employed another one to negotiate his contract for *The Information*), and the condition of his teeth. It is a study of contrasting men (like Gregory and Terry in *Success*, like Keith and Guy in *London Fields*). They are both novelists. Unsuccessful Richard Tull increasingly resents his successful old friend Gwyn Barry and makes increasingly elaborate plans to destroy him and his career. The novel is much concerned with the effects on men of middle age, which, along with failure, generates considerable misery. It is full of Martin Amis's sardonic humor:

> Of the pressure facing the successful novelist in the mid-1990s Richard Tull could not easily speak. He was too busy with the pressures facing the unsuccessful novelist in the mid-1990s – or the resurgent novelist, let's say (for now): the *unproved* novelist. (M. Amis 1995: 211)

The cosmological scene-setting ("the sun is very old, but the sun has *always* lied about its age. The sun is older than it looks: eight minutes older" (p. 342)) seems less functional than the heat-death of the universe in the background of *London Fields*. This may be because turning 40 and not being a successful novelist are less dreadful than being murdered, or murdering, and Amis always risks trivializing his foreground by bathetically grand background. But he is a daring novelist and in *The Information* he justifies the risks.

Martin Amis's masterpiece is *Money*. It is brilliantly representative of the 1980s, with this decade's mixture of greed and ambition and cultural coarsening. The narrator is John Self, a vulgarian who is a success in advertising and is moving into filmmaking. Self is nearly illiterate, a creature of immense appetites (for alcohol, tobacco, pornography, violence, masturbation, reassurance). We see him in what at first he cannot recognize as a downward spiral; the book shows him being destroyed by a combination of forces, some of them his own fault, others implacable and cruel and beyond his control or even understanding.

Despite his frequent obtuseness (or even ignorance of what is going on because of his drunkenness and blackouts and crippling cultural illiteracy), Self is an exciting narrator. His first day in New York he is walking south on Broadway:

> I strode through meat-eating genies of subway breath. I heard the ragged hoot of sirens, the whistles of two-wheelers and skateboarders, pogoists, gocarters, windsurfers. I saw the barrelling cars and cabs, shoved on by the power of their horns. I felt all the contention, the democracy, all the italics, in the air. These are people determined to be themselves, whatever, little shame attaching. Urged out from the line of shufflers and idlers, watchers, pavement men, a big blond screamer flailed at the kerb, denouncing all traffic. His hair was that special mad yellow, like an omelette, a rug omelette. (M. Amis 1984: 12)

John Self's alter ego is Martin Amis, whom he meets in London, and who explains things to him. For instance, Martin tells him that "The distance between author and narrator corresponds to the degree to which the author finds the narrator wicked, deluded, pitiful or ridiculous" (p. 233). John Self is all these things, though Amis is able to arrange that, by the end, he is mostly pitiable, because, as he painfully comes to know, he was in over his head from the beginning. A brawler, he is no match in ruthlessness for the other people in his life.

Money is the book Kingsley Amis threw across the room unfinished because of its "buggering about the reader." He lacked a tolerance of or curiosity about other people's writing, and other *kinds* of writing – of the sort which Martin admirably demonstrates. As the son comments,

> The only contemporary novelist that gave him any pleasure was Anthony Powell, then next would be Dick Francis. I remember him saying proudly, 'I'm never going to read another novel that doesn't begin with the words, "A shot rang out."' (Brockes 2003)

A longer view reminds us of how much Kingsley and Martin have had in common. Each was *avant-garde*; *Lucky Jim*, in 1954, was as shocking to conventional expectations in its way as *Dead Babies* was in 1975. Each has been a primarily comic novelist with deep and powerful moral interests and a determination to write importantly on what is important in the times in which he lives. Each has become for his time the highly visible and versatile man of letters, writing critical, political, and social analysis in a way continuous with the novels that are the primary achievement. Each would be a distinguished and estimable novelist if the other had never existed. Considered together – the brilliant novelist father of a brilliant (possibly more brilliant) novelist son, two remarkable careers spanning over fifty years – the Amises represent a unique continuity of artistic accomplishment.

REFERENCES AND FURTHER READING

Amis, Kingsley (1954) *Lucky Jim*. London: Gollancz.

——(1960) *Take a Girl Like You*. London: Gollancz.

——(1971) *Girl, 20*. London: Jonathan Cape.

——(1984) *Stanley and the Women*. London: Hutchinson.

——1986) *The Old Devils*. London: Hutchinson.

——(1991) *Memoirs*. London: Hutchinson.

——(2000) *The Letters of Kingsley Amis*, ed. Zachary Leader. London: HarperCollins.

Amis, Martin (1973) *The Rachel Papers*. London: Jonathan Cape.

——(1978) *Success*. London: Jonathan Cape.

——(1984) *Money: A Suicide Note*. London: Jonathan Cape.

——(1989) *London Fields*. New York: Harmony Books.

——(1991) *Time's Arrow: or, The Nature of the Offence*. London: Jonathan Cape.

——(1995) *The Information*. New York: Harmony Books.

——(2000) *Experience*. London: Jonathan Cape.

——(2001) *The War Against Cliché: Essays and Reviews 1971–2000*. New York: Hyperion.

Bradford, Richard (2001) *Lucky Him: The Life of Kingsley Amis*. London: Peter Owen.

Brockes, Emma (2003) "Even the praise is bad for you," *The Guardian* (August 29): Features pages, 2.

Fitzherbert, Claudia (2001) "Amis on Amis," *The Daily Telegraph* (November 12): 17.

22

Dame Iris Murdoch

Margaret Moan Rowe

"*What's the difference between me and an old soak in the Bayswater Road except the memories that we trail behind us?*"

(*The Flight from the Enchanter*)

"*What is history? A truthful account of what happened in the past. As this necessarily involves evaluation, the historian is also a moralist.*"

(*The Green Knight*)

Dame Iris Murdoch (1919–99) had a distinguished career as a philosopher and novelist. She published six books of philosophy: *Sartre: Romantic Rationalist* (1953), *The Sovereignty of Good* (1970), *The Fire and the Sun: Why Plato Banished the Artists* (1977), *Acastos: Two Platonic Dialogues* (1986), *Metaphysics as a Guide to Morals* (1992), and *Existentialists and Mystics: Writings on Philosophy and Literature*, ed. Peter J. Conradi (1997). And no less an intellectual mandarin than George Steiner praises her considerable philosophical contributions. Herein, however, I want to look at her work as novelist. The trajectory of her long and impressive career, beginning with *Under the Net* in 1954 (and her inclusion among the "Angry Young Men" of the fifties) and ending with *Jackson's Dilemma* forty-one years later, reveals a writer of significant stature. Her prominence was secured by the cleverness of such early works as *Under the Net*, *The Flight from the Enchanter*, *The Bell* (1958), and *A Severed Head* (1961), and assured by the "big" novels of the 1970s: *A Fairly Honourable Defeat* (1970), *The Black Prince* (1973), *The Sacred and Profane Love Machine* (1974; winner of the Whitbread Prize), *A Word Child* (1975), *Henry and Cato* (1976), *The Sea, The Sea* (1978; winner of the Booker Prize), and *Nuns and Soldiers* (1980). The 1970s novels clearly demonstrate the serious task Murdoch set for the novel, well described by Dominic Head: "The novel, with its imaginative range, and its freedom from 'factual' codes, becomes an important focus for the society's alternative, redemptive, and connective thought" (2002: 25).

History as "connective thought" is central to Iris Murdoch's fiction. Historians – amateur or professional – and their attempts to record history, personal or public, are a recurring population in her novels. From Peter Saward, "a historian of the empires which rose and fell before Babylon" (1976: 20) in *The Flight from the Enchanter*, through Ludwig Leferrier, "the young ancient historian" (1979: 72) in *An Accidental Man*, to Rosalind Berran, a "swot" with an "ambition to study art history" in *Jackson's Dilemma*, historians as rememberers are ubiquitous. History as a way of recovering and knowing the past promises continuity and connection in Murdoch's fictional world.

But not all promises are kept, and Murdoch, child of a century awash in the horrors of war, also understood the threat of discontinuity and displacement. She knew human identity to be a fragile possession. Her own sad terminal battle with Alzheimer's Disease dramatically enacted a battle between continuity and discontinuity – with discontinuity emerging victorious. Neurological displacement annihilated the memories that Murdoch, the individual, trailed behind her and claimed her life. But one way to read her fiction is as a trail of historical memories important to Iris Murdoch, the author.

Murdoch's interest in history is not surprising in someone who declared "there was a time when I thought I wanted to be an archaeologist and art historian, when I was at Oxford. I couldn't go on with art history because I was conscripted as soon as I left Oxford" (Haffenden 1985: 199). After securing her First at Oxford in 1942, Murdoch went to work in the Treasury (many of her experiences there would color *A Word Child*). By 1944, she was working for UNRRA (the United Nations Relief and Rehabilitation Administration) in Brussels, helping refugees and becoming interested in Existentialism. The war not only redirected Murdoch's career plans but also, and more importantly, led to a central preoccupation in her fiction, a preoccupation with displacement – physical, psychological, and historical – and its effect on human beings. Who more than displaced people are concerned with a record of past events, either as something to preserve, something to suppress, or something to retrieve? As Salman Rushdie observes:

> All migrants leave their past behind, although some try to pack it into bundles and boxes – but on the journey something seeps out of the treasured mementoes and old photographs, until even their owners fail to recognize them, because it is the fate of migrants to be stripped of history, to stand naked amidst the scorn of strangers upon whom they see the rich clothing, the brocades of continuity. (1983: 60)

Rushdie's two phrases, "the fate of migrants" and "the brocades of continuity," provide a useful way to capture a fascinating doubleness in Murdoch's relationship to her own identity and history. On the one hand, she is an Oxford graduate, a product of continuity, a wearer of the "rich clothing" of class and culture. Recollect that this chapter is titled "Dame Iris Murdoch"; she was invested as a Dame of the British Empire in 1987. Murdoch is clearly comfortable wearing "the brocades of continuity." Born in Dublin into a middle-class family (her father was a civil servant), Murdoch was brought to England as an infant and sent to private schools. She completed her education at Oxford, where she returned to teach philosophy in 1948. Not without reason has James Atlas called her "the supreme chronicler of the literary journalist/ academic/civil-servant class" (1988: 80).

But there is another side to Murdoch's work as chronicler: her interest in the migrant's fate, an interest linked to her philosophy, her experience in World War II, her Irish family, and her Jewish mentors. Throughout her long career as philosopher and as novelist, Murdoch came more and more to appreciate Plato. As late as in *Metaphysics as a Guide to Morals*, Murdoch takes issue with Nietzsche, Heidegger, and other philosophers who have in her view misinterpreted Plato. According to Murdoch, it is "the Platonic view of the cosmos which speaks to our age" (1992: 181). That Platonic view invites identification with exile; in fact, Murdoch's Platonism might well be termed a philosophy of exile. We are displaced persons in the Platonic world, forever hungering for connection with the ideal.

Displacement, too, was central to Murdoch's experience in World War II – her career plans redirected – and to her work in refugee relief at the end of the war. In *Patterned Aimlessness*, Barbara Stevens Heusel writes convincingly of the profound effect of World War II on Iris Murdoch:

> Perhaps Murdoch's past helps account for her commitment to otherness. Reaching maturity during a world crisis and then beginning her independence by attempting to relieve the horror of World War II marked Murdoch as a deeply moral person. (1995: 86)

That same war brought a wave of Jewish intellectuals to Britain, many of whom became Murdoch's mentors. Reviewing Conradi's *Iris Murdoch: A Life*, Stuart Hampshire refers to those mentors as "magical foreigners, all genuinely gifted men . . . loved by her for their individuality and eccentricity, each being in different degrees wounded and scarred by history and by circumstance" (2001: 3). They were exiles, and, by her own account, so was Murdoch.

Speaking of her own family history, she told John Haffenden: "I feel as I grow older that we [her parents and herself] were wanderers, and I've only recently realized that I'm a kind of exile, a displaced person. I identify with exiles" (Haffenden 1985: 200–1). Murdoch's fiction is replete with exiled characters. Many are Eastern Europeans who have been "stripped of history." In *The Time of the Angels* (1967), Eugene Peskov, displaced by the Russian revolution and World War I, concludes that "The world was just a transit camp. The only certain thing was that one was not in it for long" (1978b: 222). Peskov's is not an isolated view in Murdoch's fictional world, which is peopled by a myriad of displaced persons.

But of all the displaced groups affected by the historical turmoil of the twentieth century, the Irish and the Jews have the most prominent places in Murdoch's chronicles of exile. As Patrick Fenman, the Irish poet, seemingly restored to life by Marcus Vallar, the Jewish polymath, in *The Message to the Planet* (1989) avers,

"Marcus and I understand each other, we are the folk of the frontier" (1991: 131). For both the Irish and the Jews, the image of the frontier underscores their unsettled status, a status reinforced by two historical traumas: the Easter uprising and the Holocaust.

I

From Jake Donaghue, the narrator-protagonist of *Under the Net* (and his cousin Peter O'Finney) to Lewen Dunarven, "a distinguished scholar in the history of Ireland" (1996: 96) whose dead presence looms in *Jackson's Dilemma*, Irish characters find their way into many of Murdoch's novels. And for the Irish, history is mother's milk, albeit often sour. In *An Accidental Man*, Murdoch sets a scene that underscores just how important historical resonance is for the Irish. The engaged couple Gracie Tisbourne and Ludwig Leferrier, the historian, are vacationing in Ireland and Ludwig suggests buying a cottage there, a suggestion that prompts the following dialogue:

> "No, Ludwig. This is lovely, but I don't think I could really live in Ireland. There's too much trouble all the time." "Trouble, yes." Ludwig had forgotten about trouble.
> "Ireland is like Austin. Nice to look at, and one's sorry for it, but it's somehow – awful.""Poor Austin again!"
> "And one would have to know so much history. I hate history. Sorry.""Yes I know. Everyone talks history here." (1979: 288)

Murdoch's own relationship with Irish history is a complex one. She saw herself as a member of the Anglo-Irish ascendancy, no longer ascendant; its "brocades of continuity" had become threadbare. Or did she? In *A Life*, Peter Conradi devotes considerable discussion to "Iris's willingness to mythologise her own origins" (2001: 26). Irish-born she certainly was, but from a maternal family long removed from the trappings of gentry. Still, the self-created memory of that identity stayed with Murdoch to the end.

Not surprisingly, then, when Murdoch wrote her only orthodox historical novel she turned to the trauma of the Easter uprising, though with an Anglo-Irish slant. In *The Red and the Green* (1965), she focuses primarily on the Anglo-Irish community in Dublin in the days before the action on Easter Monday. As Peter Kemp notes, "The Anglo-Irish family... suits itself to Miss Murdoch's needs, being sufficiently wide-spread for her to include the attitudes of most ranks and sympathies towards the rebellion, and sufficiently tightly-knit to concentrate, as she likes to do, upon a small group of people trapped together under a web of emotion" (1969: 404–5). Like so much of Murdoch's fiction, *The Red and the Green* is a family saga built around secrets. But the sexual and generational secrets that structure many of Murdoch's narratives are joined to the political and generational secrets that surround the planning for a civil uprising, one that will sever the family ties between the Irish and the English. The plot of *The Red and the Green* centers on the interrelationship of the Anglo-Irish Dumay and Chase-White families, some of whose members have crossed over as Catholic converts and Fenian sympathizers and activists.

The novel opens with the arrival of an English soldier in Dublin. Before leaving for France, Second Lieutenant Andrew Chase-White of King Edward's Horse comes to spend some time with his mother, Hilda, in Dublin. Both Andrew, who is described as "a confused soldier" (1965: 8), and Hilda, who has resettled in Dublin because of "the Zeppelin raids on London" (p. 10), see Ireland as a place of safety in a world at war. The Chase-Whites and some of their friends and relatives spend much of their time arguing about the responsibilities of the Anglo-Irish, discussions that lead Hilda to exclaim: "Why do people in Ireland always talk about *history*? . . . My head's always swimming with dates when I'm over here. English people don't talk about English history all the time"(p. 37).

For Pat Dumay, Andrew Chase-White's cousin, the time for talk of history is over. Committed to the cause, the Catholic Dumay is at odds with superiors inordinately concerned with uniforms that will legitimize their military action. While preferring "a cleaner, straighter fight," Dumay recognizes "his choice and his justification would be lonely and secret, and the killing he would do would look like murder. But that was how it had to be" (p. 89). Dumay is the embodiment of the lonely fanatic, the precursor of the ideologue/terrorist we have come to know too well in recent years. He is a remarkable presentation in *The Red and the Green*.

Remarkable, too, is Murdoch's feminization of Ireland and the political struggle. Years before postcolonial theorists connected the position of the colonized with issues of gender, Murdoch created Frances Bellman, engaged to Andrew Chase-White but secretly in love with Pat Dumay. Early in *The Red and the Green*, Hilda Chase-White, Frances, and her father, Christopher Bellman, engage in a discussion of Millicent Kinnard, another relative:

> "She certainly has plenty of energy," Hilda conceded. "I sometimes think she really might have been somebody if she had been born a man.""Can't one be somebody if one's born a woman?" asked Frances.
> "Well hardly in that way, dear. Though in plenty of other ways which are just as important," said Hilda vaguely.
> "I think being a woman is like being Irish," said Frances, putting aside her work and sitting up . . . "Everyone says you are important and nice, but you take second place all the same."
> "Come, come, women have always had Home Rule!" Christopher always jestingly set aside his daughter's sometimes rather ferocious attempts to turn conversation into serious channels.
> "The emancipation question is certainly a grave one." said Hilda. "I am not at all hostile to the idea myself. But there are so many values – And I'm afraid your Aunt Millicent's idea of emancipation is wearing trousers and firing a revolver in her own house." (1965: 30)

I quote the dialogue at length because it encapsulates the linkage of gender, class, and colonization that pervades *The Red and the Green*.

Throughout the novel, both being a woman and being Irish lead to second place. For all of his anger about English domination, Pat Dumay sees Dublin as a woman to be dominated; he conflates military and sexual prowess:

Now they were hard, well-trained troops, real soldiers as good as their enemy and better. They had felt their power. This year on St. Patrick's Day they had taken the city over... Dublin stood and watched them like a breathless, enchanted girl. Pat felt they could have taken Dublin that day. (p. 89)

Pat Dumay and other male characters, particularly Andrew Chase-White, Christopher Bellman, and Barnabas Drumm, Pat's history-loving stepfather, dominate the action of the novel. In an enormous sexual confusion, all four men have an interest of sorts in Millicent Kinnard, Murdoch's portrait of gender frustration. Knowing only a male model of freedom, Millicent becomes the parody of the sexual predator and man of action.

Frances Bellman is a more subtle female characterization. Patronized by her father, her temporary fiancé Andrew, and her unidentified English husband, Frances is the Anglo-Irish exile at novel's end. Indeed, for all the questioning of the cost of the "terrible beauty" born in 1916, Murdoch allows Frances's view to close the "Epilogue." Now living in London and facing the possibility of her "tall son" fighting in the Spanish Civil War, Frances looks back to the men of 1916:

They, those others, had a beauty which could not be eclipsed or rivaled. They had been made young and perfect forever, safe from the corruption of time and from those ambiguous second thoughts which dim the brightest face of youth. In the undivided strength of their first loves they had died, and their mothers had wept for them, and had it been for nothing? Because of their perfection she could not bring herself to say so. They had died for glorious things, for justice, for freedom, for Ireland. (1965: 311)

The Red and the Green exhibits sympathy toward the uprising that, while predominantly Catholic in its leadership, was connected, at least in sentiment, to the rich Anglo-Irish past of revolutionary fervor. Robert Emmet and Wolfe Tone still hover over the Dublin of 1916. Murdoch saw no "glorious things" in the troubles that wounded Northern Ireland later in the century.

John Bayley, Iris Murdoch's husband, describes a lecture at Maynooth seminary outside Dublin when Murdoch's host assumed everyone in the audience was pro-IRA. According to Bayley:

She told me later that she had been hardly able to contain herself and maintain her usual civil and smiling demeanour. I am sure the priests would have had no idea of the passion they had unwittingly unleashed, assuming in their bland way that Iris, like all London intellectuals, would have the fashionably correct attitude toward Irish unity. She did not. It was the one political topic on which the presbyterian atavism of her Northern Irish ancestors completely took over. (1999: 180–1)

"Presbyterian atavism" might not have been the way Murdoch would herself have described her response. She aligned herself more closely with the view Honor Tracy expressed in a letter: "It is the Stone Age ferocity of the native Irish Catholics in the north which brings these ferocious deeds about" (quoted by Conradi, *2001: 465*).

Indeed, her depiction of the historian Emmanuel Scarlett-Taylor (Emma by nickname) in *The Philosopher's Pupil* (1983) captures Murdoch's unambiguous second thoughts about Irish militarism. Emma "hated with all his heart and soul, Ireland, the Irish, and himself"(1984: 122). That intense response is occasioned by the trauma in Ulster. Admiring of the heroes of 1916, Emma can find nothing to praise in the masked men of the eighties:

> He saw with unutterable grief the emergence of Protestant murderers, as vile as their foes. He felt guilt and misery and rage. A bomb placed in the sad little main street with its white houses and its six pubs blew the little town near his mother's family house apart. Protestants and Catholics died together. He visited Belfast and saw the handsome city wrecked, its public buildings destroyed, its abandoned streets turned into bricked-up tombs. As it seemed to him nobody cared much, not even the decent English taxpayers who paid the bill, not even the Protestants in the South. So long as the bombs stayed in Ulster, there was even a mild satisfaction in hearing about them. (1984: 123)

The use of the word "emergence" in the first line offers the code for the passage: the Protestant murderers are to be condemned but must be seen as products of "the Stone Age ferocity of the native Irish Catholics."

Yet Emma's disgust with the Irish does not lead to an acceptance of the English part of his hyphenated identity: "he was utterly utterly not English. When people said (for his voice, damnably, betrayed him), 'You're Irish?', and he replied, 'Anglo-Irish', and they said, 'Oh, so you're not real Irish,' Emma Scarlett-Taylor smiled faintly and said nothing" (p. 124). In *Iris Murdoch: The Saint and the Artist*, Peter Conradi calls "The Anglo-Irish . . . a peculiar people, from whose stock some most gifted writers have come, but also a people with a dual identity, seeing themselves in some sense as both the true Irish *and* the true English, while being regarded by everyone else as neither, and as outsiders" (1986: 10). Or, as Patrick Fenman would suggest, the Anglo-Irish are "folk of the frontier," at least, in the family history Murdoch created in her fiction.

II

Jews have an even longer and more troubled history as "folk of the frontier" than the Irish, and they, too, play significant roles in Murdoch's novels about personal and public history. Much like George Eliot in *Daniel Deronda*, Murdoch often sanctifies Jewish identity by linking it to concerns with questions about truth, justice, and morality. That linkage owes much to Murdoch's relationships with Jewish exiles, among them Eduard Fraenkel and Elias Canetti, who were her mentors, "the magical foreigners" of Stuart Hampshire's description. And what was the magic? Perhaps

Peter Conradi best answers that question when he writes: "she came to see that the Jewish expatriates whom she loved, who fought as expatriates will, who had undergone the worst their century had to offer, carried within themselves, as it were, an understanding that she and other British people lacked" (*2001:* 371). She saw Jews as more intellectual and more worldly-wise than the Irish, and they became for her another family to which she wished to belong.

The world of books also supplied Murdoch with significant connections to the family of Jewish intellectuals. In an article in *The Times* about his preparations to sell Murdoch's library, John Bayley is described as recalling "Dame Iris's passion for authors such as Freud, Wittgenstein and Simone Weil who are well-represented in the collection" (Alberge 2003: 5). These and other Jewish writers had enormous influence on Murdoch's thinking. As Bayley claims,"'Their work had, to use an expressive phrase of Emily Brontë, gone through and through her and altered the colour of her mind'" (1999: 5).

In Murdoch's chronicles, Jews are not just other people or at least not just any other people. They are a chosen people. Valentine Cunningham rightly notes that the Holocaust "is for her the largest, most looming and oppressive moral problematic of her time"(2002: 163). For Murdoch, the Holocaust is not just an historical episode or event; it is a deep historical wound that must be examined and re-examined. Attention must be paid, and the Holocaust must be remembered. In *Metaphysics as a Guide to Morals*, Murdoch underscored the need to remember the Holocaust, even if it meant making it the subject of what she termed "bad art":

> The Holocaust on television seems a blasphemous impossibility; and when a TV film was made about a Jewish family in Hitler's Germany many people protested at the prettified inadequacy of the presentation. Yet the blunted art did convey some conception of *the facts* to a large audience, and according to some critics did so more effectively because the film resembled the other sorts of TV films with which the viewers were familiar. This may be worth reflecting on. (1992: 94)

Reflection is an important activity in Murdoch's aesthetic and ethical practice, and the novel as a site for reflection was central to her view of the novel's importance in the contemporary world. In *Metaphysics as a Guide to Morals*, she declares: "We read great novels with all our knowledge of life engaged, the experience is cognitive and moral in the highest degree" (p. 97). It is no accident that Dominic Head closes *The Cambridge Introduction to Modern British Fiction, 1950–2000* with a section called "Murdoch and morality." According to Head, "the social novel, in the post-war years, has consolidated its claim to being the privileged form of moral discourse in a secular world" (2002: 251). In *The Sovereignty of Good*, Murdoch maintains that "A moral philosophy should be inhabited" (1980: 47), a spatial metaphor recalling her oft-repeated metaphor of the novel as a house. Murdoch's novels, like her works of moral philosophy, "make new and fruitful places for reflection" (p. 45), particularly as she grapples with ways of presenting the Holocaust.

Time and again in her fiction, Murdoch approaches the central historical event of
Jewish displacement in the twentieth century: the Holocaust. I want to stress the
importance of "approaches" when looking at Murdoch's presentations of the Holocaust. I use the verb in the sense of "coming near or nearer" to suggest the way
in which examining the Holocaust has been a series of steps – indirect and direct – in
Murdoch's fiction. It is as though the Holocaust became Murdoch's tabernacle or holy
of holies that she never gazed on directly. She never represented the reality of the
camps and the murders; rather, she dealt with memories of or speculations about the
Holocaust in a range of novels.

Willy Kost of *The Nice and the Good* is a "refugee scholar" (1978a: 17) who describes
himself as "a past with no present" (p. 353), a man haunted by his own feelings of
guilt not just as survivor but as betrayer: "I betrayed two people because I was afraid
and they died . . . They were gassed. My life wasn't even threatened," he tells his friend
Theo. The experience, according to Willy, is "not even like a memory. It's all just
there . . . And there's no machinery to shift it. No moral machinery. No psychological
machinery." There is, however, spiritual "machinery" in the person of Theo, who
invites Willy to "tell me the whole thing after all" (p. 354). At this point Murdoch's
narrative moves away from any direct representation of Willy's experience in Dachau.
Encouraged to tell his story Willy does, but Theo determines not to listen: "He fixed
his eyes upon the dazzling window. The sunlight seemed to have got inside the glass
and the blue sky was visible through a sparkling screen of splintered light. As Willy's
voice murmured on, Theo tried hard to think about something else" (p. 354). Willy's
story can have only Willy as audience.

Another camp survivor, Julius King, the celebrated biologist, never tells his story
in *A Fairly Honourable Defeat*. Indeed, it is not until near the end of the novel that
King's identity as a survivor is confirmed – by a tracing of sorts. Like E. M. Forster,
Murdoch teatables a crucial scene. Two men are washing dishes in a shabby kitchen
when Tallis Browne discovers "a blue tattoo mark" on Julius's arm, only to be told by
Julius: "I spent the war in Belsen" (1972: 430). Nothing is directly shown of the
experience; once more silence about the reality of the camps prevails.

It is the spirit of Simone Weil that hovers over *A Fairly Honourable Defeat*:
"Whoever is uprooted himself uproots others" (p. 48). And Julius King's uprooted-
ness manifests itself in his seeing himself as "an instrument of justice" (p. 431)
exposing hypocrisies. The answer to King's willingness to set in motion the destruction of others is found in Auden's explanation in "September 1, 1939": "Those to
whom evil is done / Do evil in return." In *A Fairly Honourable Defeat*, Murdoch refuses
to sentimentalize the effect of the Holocaust: Julius King does not emerge an
innocent victim from the camp. This depiction of Julius King caused some problems
for Murdoch as she noted in the "Closing debate" in *Rencontres*:

[Some people] thought it was anti-semitic because Julius King was Jewish – which
stunned me because I'm pro-semitic and the idea of being accused of anti-semitism is so
alien to me that I couldn't imagine how anyone could see it that way, but I think some

people were offended by the fact that this character was Jewish. I should say that Jews, in my novels, always appear as spiritual figures and tend to gather the spirit of the novel toward themselves and this is usually the case of good spiritual people; in this case it was a bad spiritual person. (Chevalier 1978: 75)

Interestingly enough, it is to the child of an anti-Semite that Murdoch gives the dream of the Warsaw ghetto, her most direct approach to Jewish life during the war, but outside the actual camps. The Polish "Count" in *Nuns and Soldiers* is described as doing "constant penance" (1982: 4) for his father's ferocious anti-Semitism. That penance seeps into his dream life where Murdoch stages a detailed war scene of the collapse of the Warsaw ghetto. Imagining himself as a Polish Jew, the Count watches the end:

> The ghetto burns. The Count runs. The machinegun is silent. A voice is speaking in Hebrew. 'Behold happy is the man whom God correcteth: therefore despise not thou the chastening of the Almighty.' But it is too late for such wisdom, and there is nobody left to hear it. The gunfire ends, the flames subside. There is silence. The ghetto does not exist any more. They have taken the Count and put him onto the train for Treblinka, Warsaw is *Judenrein*. (1982: 254)

Through the Count's dream, Murdoch shapes a Kaddish for the end of a Jewish way of life.

The Message to the Planet is Murdoch's most complex approach to the Holocaust; yet here, too, direct description of the camps is never attempted. Alfred Ludens, a privileged consciousness in the novel, is the descendent of Warsaw Jews but his ties to Judaism are at best tenuous: "Ludens, becoming as he grew up aware of Judaism as a historical phenomenon, attempted to feel Jewish, but usually preferred to say that he had no sense of identity" (1991: 6). His circle of friends is formed around his university days and they are not Jews: Gildas Herne, former Anglican priest, Jack Sheerwater, a successful painter, and Patrick Fenman, "a penniless poet from Ireland" (p. 5). All had at one time been influenced by Marcus Vallar, who appears in their early lives only to vanish before the novel opens.

At the beginning of the narrative, Ludens's professional life, too, reflects nothing of his Jewish identity; he feels more connected to the Italian Renaissance than to any Jewish past. Ludens is described as belonging "firmly to the old school of historians who believed that a historian must know the whole of history" (p. 6), although knowledge of Jewish history is not part of his historian's universe. By the novel's end, Ludens is speaking of the Midrash and "a kind of continuous making of history" (p. 560). The change in Ludens comes through his renewed relationship with Marcus Vallar, his former teacher, and Vallar's responses to the Holocaust. Vallar is not himself a camp survivor; his daughter Irina declares:

> He got it all out of books . . . His grandparents were bankers in Switzerland, his parents had a luxury home on Lake Geneva and later on they had a flat in London and another in

Paris. I daresay his ancestors were slaughtered in various pogroms somewhere or other, but so what? Do the Jews have a monopoly of suffering? (p. 159)

Irina Vallar's cavalier dismissal of "various pogroms somewhere or other" captures one Jewish response to Jewish suffering, a response Ludens initially shares.

Ludens sees Jewish suffering, significantly the Holocaust, as "an object of historical study like any other. Of course we feel it as a wound. But other people have their wounds too" (p. 166). For Marcus Vallar, the Holocaust is not "like any other" event; it is "That concentrated evil, that supreme almost supernatural cruelty " (p. 166). Vallar concludes: "The camp, too, in its own terms, is without why, it has put itself beyond the reach of human justifications or causes, it cannot be questioned, it is outside rational human discourse. It cannot be described, scarcely thought about" (p. 381). So overpowering is Vallar's meditation/obsession on the Holocaust that his death seems a re-enactment of it: "He [Ludens] had at once on entering been aware of a strange smell. The door of the gas oven was open. Marcus's head was not in the oven but lying beside it on the floor" (p. 468). I say "seems" because Vallar's death, like his life, is subject to the interpretation of the individual perceiver. One important interpretive strand is of course Vallar's identification with the Holocaust. Ludens's friend Christian, another historian, raises the question, "are we to see him as one of Hitler's victims. When will the lethal effects of that monstrous crime ever end?" (p. 484).

For Murdoch, attempting to answer that question ended with the publication of *Jackson's Dilemma*. Here Murdoch once again turns to the Holocaust. For Thomas Abelson (called Tuan), the Holocaust is an event that has directly affected his family history. Son of a Jewish father who escaped the Holocaust, Tuan feels survivor's guilt when he thinks "of *them* – millions, tens of millions –" (1996: 167). Ultimately, buttressed by a happy marriage and someone who listens to his survivor's grief, he resolves to "devote myself to holy things, my Maimonides, my Spinoza, my Scholem" (p. 235).

Yet an even more intriguing shadow of the Holocaust is present in the novel in the work on Heidegger being written by Benet Barnell, retired civil servant and amateur philosopher. Barnell's work parallels Murdoch's last philosophical work in progress. As George Steiner notes: "It is poignant to know that Dame Iris's most recent and incomplete work was to bear on Heidegger" (1998: xiii). Commentary on Heidegger and the Holocaust might well have been Murdoch's most involved look at that historical wound. I have come to wonder if Benet Barnell's anxiety about approaching that connection in Heidegger's life was not also Dame Iris's:

What on earth does he mean, thought Benet, or what do *I* mean? I thought it would be an escape – instead I am just involving myself in a dark spider's web, the web of *his mind*. And did dear good Celan, they say, visit him in his mountain hut – and Hannah Arendt forgive him – and he dare to take over great Hölderin, as well as the Greeks? Alas, that awful darkness is there, but for me it is *my* darkness, it is *my* neighbour and *my* heavy chain. I am small and I do not understand. (1996: 47)

In a review in the *New York Times*, Michiko Kakutani noted, "there is a fatigued feeling to this entire book" (B2). That fatigue, obviously, emanated from Murdoch's Alzheimer's, diagnosed in 1997. What is remarkable in this flawed, final novel is to see how enduring a familial and cultural memory the Holocaust was for Murdoch, even as her own ability to remember was leaving her and her own history was closing.

References and Further Reading

Alberge, Dalya (2003) "Iris Murdoch's husband sells 1000-book library," *The Times*, April 28: 6.

Atlas, James (1988) "The abbess of Oxford," *Vanity Fair*, 51/3 (March): 70, 76, 80, 86.

Bayley, John (1999) *Elegy for Iris*. New York: St Martin's Press.

Chevalier, Jean Louis (ed.) (1978) *Rencontres avec Iris Murdoch* (Encounters with Iris Murdoch). Caen: Centre de Recherches de Litterature et Linguistique des Payes de Langue Anglaise.

Conradi, Peter (1986) *Iris Murdoch: The Saint and the Artist*. New York: St Martin's Press.

——(2001) *Iris Murdoch: A Life*. New York: W. W. Norton.

Cunningham, Valentine (2002) "Shaping modern English fiction: the forms of the content and the contents of the form," in Zachary Leader (ed.) *On Modern British Fiction*. New York: Oxford University Press.

Haffenden, John (1985) "Iris Murdoch," in *Novelists in Interview*. London: Methuen.

Hampshire, Stuart (2001) "The pleasures of Iris Murdoch," *New York Review of Books*, November 15: 1–6. <http//www.d.umn.edu/revans~>.

Head, Dominic (2002) *The Cambridge Introduction to Modern British Fiction, 1950–2000*. Cambridge: Cambridge University Press.

Heusel, Barbara Stevens (1995) *Patterned Aimlessness: Iris Murdoch's Novels of the 1970s and 1980s*. Athens: University of Georgia Press.

Kakutani, Michiko (1996) "A hidden social turmoil amid bucolic charms," Review of *Jackson's Dilemma*, by Iris Murdoch. *New York Times*, January 9: B2.

Kemp, Peter (1969) "The fight against fantasy: Iris Murdoch's *The Red and the Green*," *Modern Fiction Studies*, 15 (Autumn): 403–15.

Murdoch, Iris (1965) *The Red and the Green*. New York: Viking.

——(1972) [1970] *A Fairly Honourable Defeat*. Harmondsworth: Penguin.

——(1976) [1956] *The Flight from the Enchanter*. London: Triad/Granada

——(1978a) [1968] *The Nice and the Good*. New York: Penguin.

——(1978b) [1966] *The Time of the Angels*. London: Triad/Granada.

——(1979) [1971] *An Accidental Man*. London: Triad/Granada.

——(1980) [1970] *The Sovereignty of the Good*. London: Routledge and Kegan Paul.

——(1982) [1980] *Nuns and Soldiers*. New York: Penguin.

——(1984) [1983] *The Philosopher's Pupil*. New York: Viking Penguin.

——(1989) *The Message to the Planet*. New York: Penguin.

——(1992) *Metaphysics as a Guide to Morals*. New York: Penguin.

——(1994) *The Green Knight*. New York: Viking Penguin.

——(1996) *Jackson's Dilemma*. New York: Viking Penguin.

Rushdie, Salman (1983) *Shame*. New York: Picador.

Steiner, George (1998) "Foreword," in Peter Conradi (ed.) *Existentialists and Mystics* by Iris Murdoch. New York: Penguin.

Weil, Simone (1952) *The Need for Roots*. New York: Putnam.

23

Academic Satire: The Campus Novel in Context

Kenneth Womack

The campus novel enjoys a long and distinguished history in the annals of literary studies. A review of academic fiction's emergence as a literary form, particularly during the nineteenth century, accounts for its archly satirical manifestations during the latter half of the twentieth century, the era in which academic satire enjoyed its most fruitful period, with forays into a variety of creative spheres, including fiction, poetry, drama, and film. The analysis of exemplary works by Kingsley Amis, Malcolm Bradbury, David Lodge, A. S. Byatt, and Jane Smiley demonstrates the nature of campus fiction's abiding influence.

"As a literary genre," Mortimer R. Proctor writes in *The English University Novel*, the academic novel "has always reflected conditions within Oxford and Cambridge far more closely than it has followed any literary trends or movements" (1957: 185). The universal conceptions of Oxford and Cambridge as unique intellectual societies – in short, the fictive terrain of "Oxbridge" – inspired centuries of fictions devoted to university life, from Chaucer's Clerk of Oxford through the romanticized academic novels of the early nineteenth century. While these narratives poked occasional fun at the ineffectuality of university faculty or the unreality of college life, their plots generally involved sentimental, often melodramatic portrayals of Oxford and Cambridge. The genre of English university fiction finds its more satiric origins, however, in the various educational reform movements of the mid-nineteenth century, as well as in the admission of women to the sacred groves of Oxford and Cambridge in the latter half of the nineteenth century. During this era, Oxford and Cambridge witnessed a significant decline in the hegemony of their influence upon English society and culture. Their fictional portrayals, once predicated upon more lofty elements of esteem and erudition, now languished in narratives about "university lecturers who did not lecture, and undergraduates who freely enjoyed all the pleasures of depravity" (Proctor 1957: 11).

The acts of reform experienced by Oxford and Cambridge found their roots in the 1850s, when a series of reports commissioned by the British government revealed a set of institutions that operated on an outmoded classical curriculum and blatantly catered to the needs of the socially privileged. In "From Narragonia to Elysium: some preliminary reflections on the fictional image of the academic," Richard Sheppard notes that for universities this era in English history also marks the shift from their function as clerical institutions devoted to producing educated priests to their emergence as the precursors of our modern research institutions (Bevan 1990: 11). While a set of statutes during the 1870s virtually redesigned the governance of both institutions, reform acts in 1854 and 1856 had already abolished religious tests at Oxford and Cambridge, respectively, thus providing access to the universities for students outside of the Church of England (Proctor 1957: 56–7). This movement against exclusion ultimately resulted in the momentous events of 1879, when Somerville College first opened its doors to female students at Oxford. As Janice Rossen observes in *The University in Modern Fiction: When Power Is Academic*, the exclusion of women from the university community continues to resonate within the pages of academic fiction. "There has been nothing else like the wholesale resistance to the admission of a particular, coherent group to the University in Britain, and this is part and parcel of the subject," Rossen writes. "The two facts are inextricable – women got into the University, and women were bitterly opposed in their efforts to do so. The powerful initial resistance to their inclusion in the University would certainly have affected how they saw themselves and their place in that community for some time to come" (1993: 34).

In addition to increasing the public's interest in the business of higher education, the nineteenth-century reform acts at Oxford and Cambridge succeeded in establishing a social landscape ripe for narrative consideration. "Reform," Proctor observes, "brought new causes to urge, and a new cast of characters to add to the traditional rakes. With reform, it became more plausible to take an interest in the success of scholars; examination halls became the scenes of triumphs and disasters in which good very nearly always triumphed over evil" (1957: 59). As with their English antecedents, American novels about academic life find their modern origins in the nineteenth century, an intense era of social change and industrial growth that destabilized the prodigious cultural influences of privileged institutions of higher learning such as Oxford and Cambridge, and in America, Harvard. The emergence of the American academic novel can be traced to Nathaniel Hawthorne's *Fanshawe*, published in 1828. Set at Harley College in the wilderness of New England during the eighteenth century, Hawthorne's novel – which he later attempted to suppress – explores a number of themes endemic to modern academic fictions, including Hawthorne's depiction of the eccentric Dr Melmoth, an absent-minded and ineffectual scholar who later becomes the institution's president. In his examination of the American evolution of the academic novel, John Lyons remarks:

> The advance of industrial capitalism during the nineteenth century is another cause for the popular suspicion of the academy. The mechanical sciences which fathered and made this advance possible were eminently practical ones. It was engineering which laid the

rails and built the bridges and designed the mills, not philosophy. And the money which engineering made possible was used to buy and sell engineers, so it was unlikely that the capitalist businessman should even respect the engineer when his knowledge brought him so little power. (Lyons 1962: 4)

The "popular suspicion of the academy" that Lyons ascribes to the industrialized societies of the latter nineteenth century underscores the emergence of the brand of satire endemic to the Anglo-American novels about university life. Satire, by its traditional definition, functions as a critique of the follies of humankind. Yet Lyons astutely differentiates the modern incarnations of satire in university fiction from the texts of the great satirists of the Augustan age who invariably situated themselves on the side of "Reason . . . tempered by humanity and common sense." The satirists of the Augustan era, Lyons notes, often hinted at solutions to the dilemmas depicted in their narratives. Satiric novels of academic life, however, provide no such answers (Lyons 1962: 162–3). Further, in his essay, "Inside jokes: familiarity and contempt in academic satire," Brian A. Connery observes that academic satire – in contrast with neoclassical satire, which only attacks the vices and follies of an absent or unknowing target – also aims its satiric barbs at the reader. In this way, he argues, academic novelists deny their readers the ironic, self-congratulatory pleasures of neoclassical satire because the readers themselves, often academics, function as the texts' ultimate targets (Bevan 1990: 124–6).

Their nostalgia for the ivory towers of their pre-nineteenth-century cultural and social supremacy prevents academic fictions from positing solutions in a pragmatic world where the idealism of the academy lacks viability and significance. In the first half of the twentieth century, then, when the world demanded answers to even more complicated social and political predicaments – from the calamities of the First and Second World Wars to the Great Depression and beyond – the academy once again lacked practical answers to the human community's most vexing problems. Hence, the interconnections between the satiric ambitions of the Menippean writers and the motivations of twentieth-century academic novelists merit particular attention. As W. Scott Blanchard notes in *Scholar's Bedlam: Menippean Satire in the Renaissance*, "Menippean satire is a genre both for and about scholars; it is an immensely learned form that is at the same time paradoxically anti-intellectual," he writes. "If its master of ceremonies is the humanist as wise fool, its audience is a learned community whose members need to be reminded . . . of the depravity of their overreaching intellects, of the limits of human understanding" (1995: 14). In short, modern academic satire began to share in a richly developed and lengthy satiric tradition. And academic novels flourished as never before.

Campus novels have seen an enormous growth in Britain and the United States since the 1950s. Richard G. Caram usefully describes these works as *Professorromane*, "a term of my own coining, in the tradition of slightly-pompous Germanic scholarship," he writes. "The *Professorroman* has distinctive features which qualify it as a sub genre of literature similar to the *Künstlerroman* or the *Bildungsroman*" (1980: 42). The genre's evolving presence in contemporary British fiction finds its origins in the proliferation of provincial "redbrick" universities, which, like the reform acts of the nineteenth century, undermined the formerly exalted influence of Oxford and Cambridge and expanded appreciably the public's access to institutions of higher education in England. For the first time, academic novels – through their explicit use of satire – seemed to offer solutions for the problems that confront modern readers far beyond the hallowed walls of the university. As Ian Carter remarks in *Ancient Cultures of Conceit: British University Fiction in the Post-War Years*, the answers lie in "taking culture seriously, and taking universities to be important bastions of culture. But the notion of what constitutes culture," he cautions, "must be transformed from that typical of British university fiction" (1990: 277). In this way, the academic novel proffers – through its satiric depiction of the institutional states of malaise inherent in its fictive representations of contemporary universities – a means for both implicitly and explicitly advocating positive value systems. In short, contemporary academic novels, by postulating a kind of anti-ethos in their narratives, ultimately seek to enhance the culture and sustain the community through a more ethically driven system of higher education. This anti-ethos, which I describe as a "pejorative poetics" in *Postwar Academic Fiction: Satire, Ethics, Community* (2001), underscores the satirical motivations of the authors of academic fiction and the manner in which their narrative ambitions function as self-conscious ethical correctives.

A thematic analysis of various works of postwar academic fiction sheds considerable light on the remarkable rise of the campus novel during the latter half of the twentieth century. Rossen identifies a "dynamics of power" that undergirds postwar manifest-ations of English and American academic novels during this era. "We should begin to read these novels less in terms of their actual brilliance or success," she argues, "and more in terms of what they reveal about the dynamics of power between the contem-porary novelist and his audience" (1993: 188). Rossen's paradigm for interpreting academic fiction's vast output reveals the various structures of power that simultan-eously manipulate the life of the individual scholar and the life of the university community. These power structures, she argues, ultimately problematize campus life through their creation of a philosophical paradox that scholars ultimately cannot escape. As Rossen observes, "The scholarly life inevitably consists of life in commu-nity, though it is fundamentally predicated on a principle of individualism" (p. 9). Modern universities, by virtue of their tenure and research requirements, maintain, at least for the benefit of their non-tenured members, the explicit threat of expulsion. The ominous power of this vestige of professional affiliation creates "an imposing façade" in favor of the university, Rossen writes, "which suggests a powerful presence through its ability to exclude potential members" (p. 30).

The politics of exclusion – the threat of ultimate severance from the community – functions as a menacing obstacle in the path to institutional success for the individual scholar. For this reason, the nature of academic scholarship receives particular attention in university fictions. As Rossen observes, "All novels about academic life and work exploit the tension between these two poles of idealism and competition, or scholarship as a means to an end and as an end in itself" (p. 140). This tension presents scholars with an emotional dilemma of staggering proportions: in one sense, campus life purports to offer them an arena to engage their colleagues in free intellectual discourse, while in another sense it necessitates that they confront their colleagues in a high-stakes competition based upon the quality and proliferation of their intellectual capabilities in order to ensure their professional security. "The emotional dimension of such work can lead to heightened battles between scholars," Rossen remarks, "and in a way which brings their powerful intellectual abilities and skills to bear on what is fundamentally an emotional issue" (p. 145). Rossen's contentions regarding the highly competitive nature of contemporary academic life can be ascribed to the experiences of students as well. Through the necessity of entrance requirements and performance standards, students endure similar threats of expulsion from the university community. Undergraduates must also conform to a form of communal disruption each term as their lives redefine themselves around new course schedules and holiday breaks. "What undergraduates in all of these novels seem to experience primarily is an intensely intimate, private world with their peers – and one in which they suffer from either ambitions to be included ... or yearning to find love and acceptance," Rossen observes. "The unique feature of community life for undergraduates is that the small world which they create for themselves vanishes when the students disperse at the end of their University terms" (p. 118). Thus, a number of novels treat the undergraduate experiences of students in the academy, including Martin Amis's *The Rachel Papers* (1973), Clare Chambers's *Uncertain Terms* (1992), and Bret Easton Ellis's *The Rules of Attraction* (1987), among others.

Many scholars attribute the origins of postwar academic fiction to the landmark publication of Kingsley Amis's *Lucky Jim* in 1954. In addition to its widely acknowledged place as the quintessential campus novel of the twentieth century, *Lucky Jim* illustrates the peculiar dilemmas experienced by young scholars in their efforts to achieve selfhood and find acceptance within the larger academic community. Often characterized as an unabashedly comic novel, *Lucky Jim* offers a moral landscape that confronts the novel's protagonist, Jim Dixon, with a variety of ethical predicaments. Amis utilizes the *métier* of comedy in the novel as a means for delivering his judgments regarding the problematic moral state of academic life during the remarkably fractious era in which his novel first appeared. His satiric attacks on the university community find their targets in those privileged individuals who endeavor to maintain the academic status quo in their favor through the exploitation of junior colleagues, and, ultimately, through the threat of expulsion from the seemingly sacred groves of campus life. As Amis's novel so stridently reveals, the very threat of severance from the scholarly community poses as a powerful obstacle in the young academic's path to self-knowledge.

Lucky Jim finds its textual roots in Amis's 1946 visit to the Senior Common Room at Leicester University, although it also owes its genesis to the confluence of three historic moments in twentieth-century British social and literary history: the passage of the Education Act of 1944, the expansion of redbrick universities in Britain during that same era, and the subsequent apotheosis of *Lucky Jim* as the master-text of the "Angry Young Man" phenomenon in the 1950s. In 1946, Amis visited Philip Larkin at Leicester University, where Larkin, Amis's friend from their scholarship days at Oxford, worked as an assistant librarian. "He took me into the Common Room there," Amis later remarked, "and after about a quarter of an hour I said, 'Christ, someone ought to do something about this lot'" (McDermott 1989: 17). Amis's experiences during the late 1940s as a junior lecturer at University College, Swansea, only served to confirm his initial impressions about the ethical inequalities of academic life. In addition to his personal observations of the university community, Amis found the inspiration for his novel in the social and political turmoil that followed the passage of the Education Act of 1944, an article of legislation that, for the first time since the landmark educational acts of the mid-nineteenth century, attempted to undermine the place of university education as an exclusive privilege of the upper classes. The Education Act required students to pursue their secondary education to at least the age of 15, while also creating a system of free secondary education consisting of distinct kinds of school, largely "grammar" and "secondary modern" schools.

During the decades that followed, the Education Act accomplished its intended goal of producing a greater quantity of college-bound working-class students. Accommodating this influx of grammar-school students likewise necessitated the wholesale expansion of the British university system and resulted in the construction of an assortment of provincial redbrick institutions and new universities across Great Britain. Despite the Act's intention of assimilating a larger working-class student population into English university life, it "gave rise to a significant number of deracinated and disoriented young men, no longer at home in their working- or lower-middle-class attitudes and environments, but at the same time not feeling accepted by the social system into which their education appeared to be pushing them" (Gardner 1981: 24). This culture of alienation in the 1950s ultimately produced the "Angry Young Man," that peculiar social manifestation of cultural angst and intellectual derision depicted in such works as John Wain's *Hurry on Down* (1953), *Lucky Jim*, and John Osborne's *Look Back in Anger* (1956), among others. The figure of the angry young man as a fictive persona reveals himself as a literary character simultaneously oppressed by the hypocritical value system of the same society whose standards and traditions he so desperately strives to oblige.

In *Lucky Jim*, Amis traces the life and times of Jim Dixon, a fledgling academic who must negotiate his way through a maze of ethical choices. In addition to his satiric characterizations of Dixon's senior colleagues, particularly the unforgettable Professor Welch, Amis addresses the perils of scholarly research and publication, as well as the peculiar, unforgiving nature of university politics. Focalizing the narrative through Dixon's working-class eyes allows Amis to dramatize the uneasy relationships that develop between the privileged upper-class denizens of the university community and their disoriented and insecure junior counterparts. A graduate of Leicester University, Dixon secures a temporary adjunct position at an unnamed provincial redbrick university after besting an Oxford candidate at his job interview. Like the other angry young working-class men who struggle to find acceptance and self-sufficiency in the groves of academe, Dixon hungers for job security amidst a world that both bores and bewilders him. A probationary junior lecturer in medieval history – a subject that he detests, yet that seems to offer him the promise of secure employment that he so covets – Dixon confesses in the novel that his policy "was to read as little as possible of any given book" (Amis 1954: 16–17). He harbors little regard for academic research and scholarly publication, although he realizes their esteemed places in the competitive campus arena.

As one of the most notorious figures in the genre of campus fiction, Professor Welch serves as Dixon's primary nemesis in *Lucky Jim*, as well as the target of many of the novel's satiric barbs. In Welch, Amis proffers a blistering portrayal of academic pretension and indifference, what Gardner calls "a devastating portrait, incidentally, of a certain type of British academic" (1981: 27). For Dixon, Welch represents everything that he finds troubling about academic life: from snobbery and cultural affectation to vocational ineffectuality and self-indulgence. "No other professor in Great Britain," Dixon muses, "set such store by being called Professor" (Amis 1954: 7). Dixon finds himself equally perplexed by the disparity between Welch's academic standing and his vague qualifications: "How had he become Professor of History, even at a place like this?" Dixon wonders. "By published work? No. By extra good teaching? No in italics" (p. 8). Yet, because Welch possesses the power to decide Dixon's ultimate fate at the university, he remains unable to express his dismay at the inequities of his precarious position as a probationary lecturer. For this reason, he accedes to all of the professor's demands for his service, while secretly imagining the violent acts to which he would subject Welch.

When Dixon prods Welch for reassurance regarding the state of his uncertain position in the department, moreover, the professor refuses to show any compassion for his adopted "protégé" and nervously avoids Dixon's glance while stammering unintelligibly. Despite all of his efforts to curry Welch's favor, Dixon essentially lacks any palpable identity in the professor's eyes, for Welch frequently refers to him as "Faulkner," the name of a previous temporary assistant lecturer. He is counseled by Welch that an effective public lecture on behalf of the department might save his job at the university, and gives a talk on "Merrie England," which is the novel's hilarious climax, as well as Dixon's supreme, inebriated moment of ethical judgment. Well fortified with alcohol, Dixon delivers a protracted and forceful parody of the academy, scholarship, and his senior colleagues. During his "Merrie England" speech, Dixon effects a series of cartoonish faces along with drunken imitations of the voices of Welch, the university Principal, and, finally, a Nazi stormtrooper. In this way, he posits his final, blistering attack upon the untenable foundations of the academic world of his experience. When Dixon effects his own expulsion from university life at the novel's conclusion, his sense of humanity soars when he finds solace and acceptance in a bona fide community of genuine friends and truly conscientious mentors. "It is no accident," Rossen argues, "that many of the best University novels are about someone leaving academe at the end of the book" (1993: 188).

Malcolm Bradbury's *Eating People Is Wrong* (1959) provides a tragicomic look at the interpersonal conundrums inherent in academic life. The novel traces the experiences of the inexorably earnest Professor Stuart Treece, the Head of an English department at a provincial, redbrick university located, ironically enough, in the city's former lunatic asylum. Through Treece, Bradbury's novel asks complex questions about the nature of liberalism as a philosophy connoting tolerance, decency, and moral liberty. Bradbury complicates this issue via Treece's relationships with two students, including an older, mentally disturbed man, Louis Bates, and Mr Eborabelosa, an African student who violates academic – indeed, social – decorum at nearly every turn. The manner in which Treece responds to their difficulties leads to disastrous results, especially when he considers his liberal impulses in comparison with the choices that he must inevitably make when confronted with Bates's and Eborabelosa's convoluted interpersonal issues. Treece's love affair with Emma Fielding, a postgraduate student at the university, also suffers from the dichotomy between his liberal ideals and the vexing ethical realities of contemporary life. As the novel comes to its disheartening close, Treece feels utterly betrayed by his value systems – especially his ethical devotion to the precepts of responsibility and goodness – and ends up in a mental hospital with little hope for the future. In this way, Bradbury postulates a damning critique of the academy's capacity for engendering genuine educational and social change when its most cherished principles evince little practical application.

Scholars of academic fiction often identify novelist and critic David Lodge as the genre's most significant practitioner. Lodge's trilogy of academic novels – *Changing Places: A Tale of Two Campuses* (1975), *Small World: An Academic Romance* (1984), and *Nice Work* (1988) – satirizes academe's convoluted nuances with playful abandon. In *Changing Places*, Lodge traces the intellectual and sexual lives of Philip Swallow and Morris Zapp, the academic characters whose professional and social intersections grace each of the narratives in Lodge's academic trilogy. An introverted and ambitionless lecturer at an English redbrick university, Swallow distinguishes himself among his peers at the University of Rummidge because of his superior skills as an examiner, rather than because of his reputation as a literary scholar. "He is a mimetic man," Lodge writes, "unconfident, eager to please, infinitely suggestible" (1975: 10). In sharp contrast with Swallow's ineffectual scholarly career, Zapp enjoys considerable scholarly renown for his numerous well-received studies of Jane Austen. A full professor of English at the State University of Euphoria in the United States, Zapp plans to embark upon an ambitious critical project that would treat each of Austen's novels from every conceivable hermeneutic perspective: "historical, biographical, rhetorical, mythical, Freudian, Jungian, existentialist, Marxist, structuralist, Christian-allegorical, ethical, exponential, linguistic, phenomenological, archetypal, you name it." In this way, Zapp plans to exhaust Austen's canon of novels for future critical study. "There would be simply *nothing further to say*," Lodge remarks, "periodicals would fall silent, famous English Departments [would] be left deserted like ghost towns" (1975: 44–5). Swallow and Zapp's lives collide in 1969 when they agree to participate in an annual professorial exchange scheme that exists between their respective institutions. During their transatlantic experiences, the two scholars not only exchange their students and colleagues, but their wives and families as well. The manner in which they literally swap their entire worlds with one another underscores Lodge's satiric critique of his academic characters and the ease and alacrity with which they exchange the emotional and sexual discourses of their respective lives.

As the narrative of *Small World* unfolds, we find Zapp and Swallow once again ensconced in the comfortable scholarly and interpersonal inroads of their respective worlds. While their private lives seem to follow a rather predictable course – Swallow returns to married life with Hilary and Désirée delivers on her promise to divorce Zapp – the worldwide reinvigoration of their profession in the late 1970s irrevocably alters their academic experiences through the auspices of international conferences and global scholarly trends. "The day of the single, static campus is over," Zapp triumphantly announces in *Small World*, and with its demise arrives a new generation of globe-trotting scholars equally beset by the professional and interpersonal contradictions inherent in academic life (Lodge 1984: 72). In *Small World*, Lodge traces the international scholarly and romantic exploits of Zapp, Swallow, and a wide range of other intellectuals bent on exerting their professional and erotic wills upon one another. A rousing keynote address delivered by Zapp at a conference hosted by Swallow at the University of Rummidge inaugurates the novel's thematic exploration of erotic love and its narrative possibilities for interpersonal fulfillment. Entitled "Textuality as striptease," Zapp's lecture discusses the inadequacy of language and scholarship as mechanisms for communication. Because it fundamentally encourages the act of interpretation, language necessarily denies itself the capacity to articulate any singular meaning with precision and exactitude. Scholarship suffers from a similar interpretive malady. As Zapp astutely remarks, "Every decoding is another encoding" (1984: 29). As does the text, which contains so many convoluted layers of unattainable meaning, the striptease, Zapp argues, entices the viewer by arousing curiosity and desire while ultimately defying possession. This struggle for erotic authority motivates the quests for love embarked upon by Lodge's academics in *Small World*, and its consummate elusiveness challenges their capacity for finding self-satisfaction in the competitive community of scholars.

In addition to detailing once again the sexual and professional exploits of Swallow and Zapp, Lodge traces in *Small World* the erotic quests of such fictive critical luminaries as Arthur Kingfisher and Fulvia Morgana, as well as the romantic experiences of the naive lover and scholar, Persse McGarrigle, a fledgling young academic from University College, Limerick. In the novel, Persse's search for the elusive independent scholar, Angelica Pabst, functions as a framing device for the erotic quests of Lodge's other intellectual characters. He crisscrosses the globe, exhausting his savings in a wild international pursuit of the evasive Angelica while sporadically encountering Lodge's other protagonists in such disparate locales as Rummidge, Amsterdam, Geneva, Los Angeles, Tokyo, Honolulu, Jerusalem, and finally, New York, where Lodge's entire coterie of academics reconvenes for the annual meeting of the Modern Language Association. Perhaps even more importantly,

Kingfisher acts as Lodge's most corrosive example of academic dysfunctionality. Secluded in his penthouse suite high above Chicago, Kingfisher lies naked in bed with a scattered selection of critical quarterlies and his delectable Korean research assistant, Song-Mi Lee, by his side. An emeritus professor of Columbia and Zurich Universities, Kingfisher spends his days writing reviews of the latest monographs of hermeneutics while watching pornographic movies on television. "A man who has received more honorary degrees than he can remember, and who has at home, at his house on Long Island, a whole room full of the (largely unread) books and offprints sent to him by disciples and admirers in the world of scholarship," Kingfisher, Lodge writes, can unfortunately no longer "achieve an erection or an original thought" (Lodge 1984: 105). His unsavory depiction of Kingfisher consuming pornography while simultaneously engaging in the act of literary criticism underscores Lodge's exacting critique of the academy via one of its most cherished mechanisms for professional advancement.

As the final installment in Lodge's academic trilogy, *Nice Work* examines the uneasy relationship that often exists between the academy and the "real world," between the competitive forces of the intellect and the free-market forces of industry. In addition to questioning the relevance of literary theory to the problems that plague the world beyond the halls of the academy, the novel attempts to give a sense of reconciliation regarding the tenuous relationship between industry and academe. It does so through the medium of an erotic affair between the novel's protagonists, Victor Wilcox, the managing director of an engineering firm, and Robyn Penrose, a temporary lecturer at the University of Rummidge. The dramatic consummation of their relationship seems to offer the possibility of mutual understanding between these remarkably disparate characters, yet the instability of love and language depicted in the novel's closing pages ultimately undermines their genuine attempts at ideological compromise. In the novel, Robyn agrees to participate in the "Shadow Scheme" that eventually draws her into Vic's orbit on the advice of Swallow, still chair of the department at Rummidge, although he is succumbing to incipient deafness. The brainchild of the university's vice-chancellor, the Shadow Scheme endeavors to enhance the university's understanding of the commercial world by requiring a faculty member to "shadow" a senior managerial figure in the local manufacturing industry, and vice versa. Swallow believes that Robyn's participation in the exercise might allow her to keep her Rummidge lectureship beyond her current three-year allotment. A gifted and well-published scholar, Robyn remains unable to secure a position in England's depressed academic job market, despite her extraordinary professional credentials.

Vic, Robyn's industrial counterpart and the managing director of J. Pringle and Sons Casting and General Engineering, harbors disdain for the value of higher education and views the university as a "small city-state" characterized by its "air of privileged detachment from the vulgar, bustling city in which it is embedded" (Lodge 1988: 14–15). Robyn possesses a similar distrust for members of the private sector and their commercial activities. Her ideological and social differences with Vic likewise manifest themselves on a number of occasions throughout their association during the Shadow Scheme. Robyn reacts in horror, for example, when she visits the factory's dark, inner recesses: "It was the most terrible place she had ever been in her life," Lodge writes. "To say that to herself restored the original meaning of the word 'terrible': it provoked terror, even a kind of awe" (p. 90). Her revulsion at the squalid conditions in the factory later results in a spontaneous strike after she warns one of the laborers of his imminent dismissal.

The Shadow Scheme reaches its dramatic climax when Robyn agrees to accompany Vic on a business trip to Frankfurt, where her knowledge of German allows Vic to negotiate the purchase of a machine for the factory at an exceptional price. Elated by the success of their cooperative effort as business negotiators, Robyn and Vic retire to her suite for a sexual encounter: "The captain of industry at the feet of the feminist literary critic – a pleasing tableau," Robyn muses to herself (p. 207). Back in England, their relationship deteriorates rapidly. "When Wilcox screwed you, it was like the factory ravished the university," Robyn's friend Penny observes (p. 212). Robyn and Vic only achieve reconciliation after he visits the university as her "shadow," after the factory has discharged him from his position as managing director. Using the proceeds of her inheritance from the estate of a recently deceased relative in Australia, Robyn salvages their relationship when she good-naturedly offers to invest in Vic's plans to design a revolutionary spectrometer. In this manner, Vic and Robyn opt for a working relationship rather than the semiotic and interpersonal struggles of romance. Robyn's own professional fortunes eventually soar after Zapp fortuitously arrives in Rummidge – about to embark upon his annual European conference tour, of course – and negotiates the American rights of her second monograph for Euphoric State's university press. The novel's *deus ex machina* conclusion reaches its fruition when Swallow finally, almost predictably, locates the funding to extend Robyn's contract for another year at the University of Rummidge. In this manner, *Nice Work*'s hopeful denouement allows Lodge to establish a state of reconciliation between industry and academe.

A. S. Byatt's acclaimed *Possession: A Romance* (1990) adopts the detective form in a labyrinthine campus novel about the complicated nature of love and possession, as well as about the primacy of the text in academic circles. In the novel, Byatt narrates the interconnected stories of two, historically disparate couples: Roland Mitchell and Maud Bailey, a pair of contemporary literary scholars on a quest to authenticate a love affair between two Victorian poets; and the poets themselves, Randolph Henry Ash and Christabel LaMotte. As a postmodern pastiche, *Possession* features a panoply of textual voices, ranging from scholarly articles and autobiographical texts to Ash and LaMotte's correspondence and verse. While Christine Brook-Rose draws upon the textual nuances of postmodern pastiche in her novel *Textermination* (1991), the result hardly compares to the quality and nuance of Byatt's achievement. With *Possession*, Byatt succeeds in both satirizing academic life and yet managing to venerate its capacity for generating viable textual research – and engendering romance, no less – at the same time. Byatt's most exacting critique of the scholarly world emerges via her treatment of Professor James Blackadder, Roland's avaricious employer and the curator of a vast museum of holdings related to Ash's life and work. Byatt similarly derides the unchecked ambitions of two caustic American characters, rival collectors Mortimer Cropper, the representative of a wealthy New Mexico foundation, and Leonora Stern, an influential feminist scholar who longs for Maud's affections. In many ways, the most effective aspect of Byatt's satire involves the manner in which Roland and Maud become so obsessed with their subject that they can hardly begin to consummate the romantic feelings that blossom during their time together. Although *Possession* ends by suggesting that they might eventually enjoy a fulfilling romantic connection, Roland and Maud conclude their quest by only solving the mystery of Ash and LaMotte's affair. The novel's sad irony is that they fail to unravel the equally complex and intriguing mystery about the bond that has come to exist between themselves. The rigors and demands of scholarship, it seems, have established barriers rather than fomenting the interpersonal bridges that the university champions in workaday life.

While Amis's and Lodge's narratives illustrate the vexing world of British higher education, Jane Smiley's *Moo* (1995) focuses a sharp, satiric eye upon the political machinations and ambitions of the administration and faculty of Moo U., a large midwestern university well known for its agricultural department. Rife with social and scholarly intrigue, Smiley's novel admonishes the bankrupt value systems of a powerful American institution of higher learning obsessed with its agenda for technological and financial superiority. Smiley allots conspicuous attention to all of the competing voices that comprise Moo U.'s political maelstrom: from the contentious professoriate in the Horticulture and English departments to the institution's dubious administration, an often bemused and vacant student population, and a giant hog named Earl Butz who resides in an abandoned building in the middle of Moo U.'s campus. In addition to her penetrating critique of university life's economic circle – an endlessly negating system of consuming and being consumed – Smiley addresses the interpersonal motivations exhibited by an array of administrative, professorial, and undergraduate characters. Smiley's self-conscious retelling of consumerism's cautionary tale – of what happens when a beast like Moo U. is permitted to gorge itself at the trough of other, ethically dubious creatures – affords us with one of academic fiction's most compelling narratives.

In addition to the aforementioned paradigmatic campus novels by Amis, Bradbury, Lodge, Byatt, and Smiley, the tragicomic world of academic literature increasingly includes works of detective fiction, nonfiction, poetry, drama, film, and textual experimentation. Academic novels frequently employ the conventions of the murder mystery, as evidenced by such texts as Amanda Cross's *Death in a Tenured Position* (1981), P. D. James's *An Unsuitable Job for a Woman* (1972), D. J. H. Jones's *Murder at the MLA* (1993), and Estelle Monbrun's *Meurtre chez Tante Léonie* (1995). In the nonfictional *Masterpiece Theatre: An Academic Melodrama* (1995), Sandra M. Gilbert and Susan Gubar consider the ethical implications of the "culture wars" of the early 1990s by fashioning a loosely veiled account of the political machinations by a host of international academic and political figures. With *Recalcitrance, Faulkner, and the*

Professors: A Critical Fiction (1990), Austin M. Wright offers one of the genre's more innovative works. In his quasi-nonfictional study, Wright satirizes contemporary literary criticism through his reproduction of two imaginary essays on Faulkner's *As I Lay Dying* (1930) by a pair of feuding instructors, whose students subsequently meet at "Phil's Pub" in order to critique the quality of their professors' divergent arguments. In addition to poet Galway Kinnell's satirical look at literary studies in "The deconstruction of Emily Dickinson" (1994), the academy receives attention in such plays as Susan Miller's experimental *Cross Country* (1977) and David Mamet's controversial *Oleanna* (1992). Produced as a film in 1994, *Oleanna* concerns a professor and his student's inability to communicate with each other on any genuinely meaningful level. Their utter incapability of comprehending the nature of their obligations and responsibilities, both to each other and to higher education, predicates Mamet's brutal musings on sexual harassment and political correctness. The academic novel reaches its experimental apex in Alexander Theroux's *Darconville's Cat* (1981), a work that features stylistic forays into such genres as blank-verse drama, the sermon, the diary, the fable, poetry, the essay, and formal oration, among a host of others.

There is little question that the campus novel will continue to resound as one of literature's most satirical genres. While their forebears in the academic fictions of the late nineteenth and early twentieth centuries languished under the specter of "Oxbridge," contemporary academic characters must contend with the whimsy of global economic slumps and university budget cuts, the fashionable nature of structuralist and poststructuralist literary criticism, growing social and racial divisions on college campuses, and an increasingly hostile academic job market, among a range of other issues. Indeed, there seems to be no end to the ways in which the practitioners of Anglo-American university fiction can utilize academic characters and institutional themes as a means for exploring, through the deliberately broad strokes of their satirical prose, the ethical and philosophical questions endemic to their genre.

References and Further Reading

Aisenberg, Nadya and Harrington, Mona (1988) *Women of Academe: Outsiders in the Sacred Grove.* Amherst: University of Massachusetts Press.

Amis, Kingsley (1954) *Lucky Jim.* New York: Penguin.

Begley, Adam (1997) "The decline of the campus novel," *Lingua Franca*, 7: 39–46.

Bevan, David (ed.) (1990) *University Fiction.* Amsterdam: Rodopi.

Blanchard, W. Scott (1995) *Scholar's Bedlam: Menippean Satire in the Renaissance.* Lewisburg, PA: Bucknell University Press.

Bradbury, Malcolm (1959) *Eating People Is Wrong.* Chicago: Academy Publishers.

——(1985) [1975] *The History Man.* New York: Penguin.

Byatt, A. S. (1990) *Possession: A Romance.* New York: Vintage International.

Caram, Richard G. (1980) "The secular priests: a study of the college professor as hero in selected American fiction (1955–1977)," Dissertation, Saint Louis University.

Carter, Ian (1990) *Ancient Cultures of Conceit: British University Fiction in the Post-War Years.* London: Routledge.

Gardner, Philip (1981) *Kingsley Amis.* Boston: Twayne.

Inness, Sherrie A. (1995) *Intimate Communities: Representation and Social Transformation in Women's College Fiction, 1895–1910*. Bowling Green, OH: Bowling Green State University Popular Press.

Johnson, Lisa (1995) "The life of the mind: American academia reflected through contemporary fiction," *Reference Services Review*, 23: 23–44.

Kramer, John E., Jr. (1982) *The American College Novel: An Annotated Bibliography*. New York: Garland.

Leonardi, Susan J. (1989) *Dangerous by Degrees: Women at Oxford and the Somerville College Novelists*. New Brunswick: Rutgers University Press.

Lodge, David (1975) *Changing Places: A Tale of Two Campuses*. New York: Penguin.

——(1984) *Small World: An Academic Romance*. New York: Penguin.

——(1988) *Nice Work*. New York: Penguin.

Lyons, John (1962) *The College Novel in America*. Carbondale: Southern Illinois University Press.

——(1974) "The college novel in America, 1962–1974," *Critique*, 16: 121–8.

Marchalonis, Shirley (1995) *College Girls: A Century in Fiction*. New Brunswick: Rutgers University Press.

McDermott, John (1989) *Kingsley Amis: An English Moralist*. London: Macmillan.

Proctor, Mortimer R. (1957) *The English University Novel*. Berkeley: University of California Press.

Rossen, Janice (1993) *The University in Modern Fiction: When Power Is Academic*. London: Macmillan.

Siegel, Ben (ed.) (1989) *The American Writer and the University*. Newark: University of Delaware Press.

Womack, Kenneth (2001) *Postwar Academic Fiction: Satire, Ethics, Community*. London: Palgrave.

24

Lawrence Durrell's
Alexandria Quartet

Julius Rowan Raper

"After all, people sometimes get stuck like an old disc and can't move out of a groove."
(*Clea*)

When Clea expresses the opinion above in the last book of Lawrence Durrell's *Alexandria Quartet*, she captures the theme that from the start dominates the series, a psychological complex summed up by the Check (1961b: 69). When Durrell in 1985 chose a half sentence from Wordsworth – " ... must itself create the taste by which it is to be judged" – as the epigraph for *Quinx*, the last novel of the *Avignon Quintet*, he, in effect, applied the Check to the novelistic form itself and, in the same move, indicated how an experimental author like himself might break that Check. With this gesture, he turned the human drama of the *Quartet* into a subtle metaphor for his efforts to push fiction out of the grooves in which it had become stuck by the 1950s; at the same time, he nudged it in postmodern directions that his *Quintet* would exploit, including devices that already in the *Quartet* anticipated metafiction. In form and content, each volume in the *Quartet* illustrates the Check or breaks it.

When Clea, herself an artist, uttered her simple words in a work published in 1960, postmodern fiction as we have come to know it was not yet properly born. The modernist experiments of James Joyce and his contemporaries lay decades in the past. British fiction, in revolt against the internationalism of the recent world war, had fallen under the nativist, often neo-naturalist spell of Kingsley Amis, John Braine, Alan Sillitoe, and John Wain. In America, J. D. Salinger, Vladimir Nabokov, and Saul Bellow were perfecting the late modernist novel, while writers elsewhere had begun violating the limits of realist and naturalist fiction: Jorge Luis Borges in Argentina and Paris, Italo Calvino in Italy, Alain Robbe-Grillet, Michel Butor, and other New Novelists in France. Even in America, John Barth was constructing the liberating parodies of realist-existential conventions found in his first three novels. Nabokov had not yet published *Pale Fire* (1962), nor had John Fowles finished *The Magus* (1966).

Born, in 1912, in India, of an English father and an Irish-English mother, and later a resident of England (briefly), Greece, Egypt, Yugoslavia, Argentina, and France (for thirty-five years), Lawrence George Durrell was not drawn by experience or interests to write often about the British Isles. He belongs instead to the tradition of expatriate authors that in the twentieth century included major experimenters with the novel in English, especially Joseph Conrad, James Joyce, and D. H. Lawrence. Internationally (more than in Britain), his *Quartet*, a critical and commercial success from the start, continues to rank among the most important fictions produced in the twentieth century, and especially during its second half.

Justine: The Novel Bound

Standing on its own in 1957, the first novel in the *Quartet* appeared, at its deep structural level, to be another effort by an experienced novelist to lift the conventions of modernism to a further level of excellence. Admittedly, compared to nativist novels then dominant, *Justine's* setting seemed exotic inasmuch as Egypt was considered oriental. Similarly, its diction was lush, even lyrical in places, and its characters appeared borrowed from the traditions of the Romance: a Coptic prince, a Jewess as fascinating as Scott's Rebecca, a sensitive poet-teacher, a blond painter in her solitary tower, a prostitute with a heart of gold – all surrounded by assorted grotesques. Otherwise, the novel compares favorably with other works produced between 1947 and 1963 by the best late modernists, including Malcolm Lowry, Salinger, Nabokov, Bellow, and John Updike.

As late-modernist fiction, *Justine* is an undauntingly short and expertly crafted book, one that shares the modernists' respect for the power of language, whether vernacular, symbolic, or mythic, to capture reality, whether that reality is external and physical, internal and psychological, or even transcendental and metaphysical, as would be the *fons signatus* of the psyche and the "inherent order in the universe" of which the as yet unnamed narrator of *Justine* (Darley) speaks (1969: 85–6). Such novelists generally avoid fantasy materials except in dreams or in deranged states of consciousness; the novels instead rely heavily on verisimilitude, as the Note to *Justine* suggests when it asserts that *"Only the city is real."*

Late-modernist novels also frequently employ fragments rather than construct clearly plotted stories. The fragments may come together following the associative logic of streams of consciousness, as when Darley informs us that he is deploying his memories not in chronological order "but in the order in which they first became significant" for him (1969: 100). Or the fragments may cohere only at a subterranean level of which readers but not the characters become aware, a device that increases the possibility of dramatic irony and multiple levels of interpretation. Despite, perhaps due to, such fragments, one finds in *Justine*, as in many modernist novels, an intense rage for an order often hidden, deep, and abstract. While early modernists frequently revealed an Eliot-like eagerness to accept external systems of order based on traditional authorities, other modernist novels look, as does *Justine*, to the newer system based on the inward knowledge that Freud and Jung discerned in dreams and in the unconscious.

As the reader becomes drawn by Darley into a search for pattern and order, the reader may feel as swamped as Darley by confusing events that memory dredges up. This disorientation can grow so compelling that it distracts readers from raising essential questions about the protagonist's reliability and the authority on which the character bases his or her assumptions about the nature of reality. This is precisely what happens in *Justine*, but as long as the reader remains between the covers of the volume, he or she shares this error with Darley. In a sense, this blindness represents the checked nature of those late-modernist fictions grounded in a dominating subjectivity, like that of Darley who, despite his best efforts, limits the vision created by *Justine*.

To illustrate such blindness, Durrell provides the dramatic situation shaping *Justine*. In the section that defines that situation, Darley contrasts his view of order in fiction, and seemingly in life, with that of Arnauti, who was his predecessor both as novelist and as lover of Justine. In *his* novel about Justine, Arnauti contends that the imagination of the artist gives form to "real people" who exist like all of life only *in potentia* without the strong artist's intervention. Darley objects: "But of course one cannot escape so easily from the pattern which he [Arnauti] regards as imposed but which in fact grows up organically within the work and appropriates it" (p. 61). Thus informed by Darley, the reader is encouraged to wait for the pattern of the novel to reveal itself by appropriating the various fragments and making sense of them. In anticipating a structural epiphany the reader is simply using lessons learned from exploring a string of modernist novels famous for hidden but firm and deep structures, including *Ulysses*, *To the Lighthouse*, and *The Sound and the Fury*. It is difficult to overestimate the aesthetic delight of finally comprehending the pattern of such works.

In *Justine*, the whole the reader ultimately discovers has at its foundation the famous Check that Justine struggles against. Immediately after Darley's assertion of an organic pattern, Darley informs the reader of Arnauti's determination to break the Check placed on Justine's capacity to love her husband (at the time Arnauti) or any man passionately, because as a street urchin she was "raped by one of her relations" (pp. 63–4). When Daley confesses that he is repeating Arnauti's impossible relationship with Justine, the reader, conscious that this is the end of the first third of the novel, grows acutely aware that this moment has to be the defining one in the action of the novel and that the organic pattern that narrator and reader both seek is manifesting through the fragments of the work. And at the end of part two, just short of the two-thirds mark, when Justine announces that "something is happening" to Nessim, her current, hitherto complacent and much cuckolded husband, and that for "the first time [she] is afraid," the reader may feel reassured that not only is Darley following Arnauti into a checked relationship with Justine but that a screw is being turned in that familiar pattern (p. 127). For this time a husband is involved who may not be amused by the possibility that Darley will do what all Arnauti's psychoanalysts from Freud down could not do: that is, Darley may break the Check.

The shooting of Capodistria and the simultaneous defection of Justine provide sufficient drama to create the catastrophic climax the novel requires. And when the alert reader places the obligatory clues about Capodistria's eye-patch matching that of Justine's assailant along side Clea's report that Justine associated her youthful viola-tion with Washington DC as echoed by Da Capo's initials, the organic pattern of the novel appears unmistakable. To an aggressive reader trained on modernist fiction, the rumor appears true that claims Nessim planned Capodistria's death. The reader willing to follow the emerging pattern to the spaces between the lines also knows Nessim's motive must have been to take revenge on his wife's violator and thereby break the Check so that she can love Nessim. Nessim's discovering the initiator of Justine's problem has, the trained reader may infer, saved Darley from the jealous husband's violence.

The reader buys the unifying pattern the Check seems to provide, not only because he or she has practiced deep-pattern-seeking techniques on all the modernist texts from late Henry James novels onward, but also because the structure Darley's associations produce matches the second most common psychological pattern employed by modernist fiction. As one of Darley's epigraphs suggests, Justine's relationship with Capodistria provides a screen memory of the Electra complex that Jung proposed as the female version of the Oedipus complex; the latter, Freud believed, put "four persons" in bed during "every sexual act," the intruders being the opposite-sex parent of each sexual partner. In this deep sense, every man or woman struggles with the Check – in ways the subsequent *Quartet* volumes will illustrate.

Because a lack of boundaries between street urchins and wealthy male relatives, even between fathers and daughters, appears to be a mainstay of Alexandria, the deep structure uncovered clearly illustrates another pillar of modernist fiction: the stress on environmental determinism that post-naturalist writers borrowed from the scientific novelists of the previous century. Darley restates this determinism when he assures readers that his friends are the flora of the city that has "precipitated in us conflicts which were hers" and when he creates impressionist word-paintings of settings with enough force to dominate characters (p. 3). In his conviction that the city is all-powerful, Darley echoes Georg Groddeck's *The Book of the It* (1927) as he excuses the actions he and his friends took in Alexandria. For Groddeck pushed the naturalist assumptions about the power of place to an extreme by arguing for the "It" (Freud's Id, the German *Es*) as a Schopenhauer-like libidinal Cosmic Will that manifests itself in the world at large. In this fashion, Durrell shows that the novel Darley has created is as bridled by Darley's modernist conventions as Justine is checked by larger forces working within and around her. This limit on the novel occurs despite Darley's apparent sharing of Arnauti's desire to *"set my own book free to dream"* (p. 61). Such freedom, Darley admits, cannot coexist with his own expectation that an organic pattern will rise up and appropriate his novel.

Balthazar: Free to Dream

Darley's discovery of a true, organic pattern for *Justine* is chiefly hogwash, as the subsequent volumes in the *Quartet* show. For Darley's desire to have Justine love him largely creates the structure that emerges, and, as Balthazar reports in the second volume, she loved someone else. In short, the pattern in *Justine* is too much a product of a lover's inflated volition to shape a true dream-novel. The process that produces dreams dispenses with objective spatial, temporal, and causal order. More so even than memory, it generates fresh creations, including condensations and displacements of persons, places, things. Many of these powers of imagination Darley finds his way to in the second volume of the *Quartet*.

In *Balthazar*'s framing narrative, the title character informs Darley that his first effort contains significant fallacies and loose ends, the most important of which must be that elegant Justine did not love the shabby little teacher and poet, and that his manuscript fails to explain Pursewarden's bitterness or the "obscure political ends" that Nessim pursues. Taking local newsman John Keats as his model, a deflated Darley first responds by abandoning the memory-work of the modernist novelist and resorting to a realism built on photographs, physical descriptions, and notes left him by Balthazar. At the same time he realizes that the city he presents is "half-imagined" though still "wholly real" (1961a: 13).

As Darley enters the middle third of his new account, however, he recalls what Balthazar has said about imagination: that it is not necessarily "invention." Balthazar has challenged him to work backwards from the actions of their friends to uncover the feelings out of which one assumes their deeds grow "as leaves grow out of a branch" (p. 98). In this way a brave novelist might fill the gaps in their actions with his own interpretations. This is precisely the creative work Darley avoided in *Justine* by depending on organic form and by documenting his sources in the diaries of Justine, the folio of Nessim, the autobiographical novel *Moeurs* by Arnauti, and his memories of scattered comments and behaviors of his Alexandrian friends – all incomplete, some falsified sources. Trusting in memory, documents, and the fatal power of the city, Darley allowed his first novel to be checked by realist-naturalist conventions that modernist novelists generally accepted.

How then is Darley to know what went on in Nessim's or in Justine's mind? This Balthazar does not explain. Darley, however, has the additional example of the novelist Pursewarden to draw upon. In words Darley now recalls in the book's frame, Pursewarden has transcended all morality-ridden monistic, dualistic, and tripartite models of personality associated with theology, romanticism, and Freudian theory. According to the older novelist, our lives are selected fictions because personalities are always conditioned, like Einstein's train and Heisenberg's electrons, by our and their positions in time and space. Far from fixed, each psyche is "an ant-hill of opposing predispositions." In his aphoristic fashion, Pursewarden has discovered that in "the end ... everything will be found to be true of everybody" (p. 15).

Such variability hardly makes Darley's attempt to understand his friends less difficult, and he would founder once more – except for an inkling that slips out. In the first pages of the novel, Darley despairs that his friends have ceased to live for him but have in his pages become "coloured transfers of the mind" (p. 14). He has in mind "tapestry figures" that begin as cartoons and are transferred to fabric. More useful for Darley, however, is the psychoanalytic use of the word "transference" to designate the critical moments when individuals undergoing analysis transfer unresolved problems with parents, siblings, and others from their past onto the relatively blank screen provided by their analyst. These constitute moments of creation, revelation, and possible understanding. Between themselves, the patient and the analyst, in effect, create a third party who consists of both the sender and the receiver of the transference. Like the Alexandria Darley describes in *Balthazar*, this third being is half-imagined yet wholly real – psychologically true, that is. It is so real, in fact, that the analyst may use the transference to "reconstruct" the client's repressed *emotional* past. As a second royal road to the unconscious, it becomes an avenue to valuable empathetic knowledge. This provides a tool that Darley, like other brave novelists, can use to fill gaps by looking into his own feeling and intuiting what goes on in the minds of lovers, friends, and acquaintances.

In affirming Darley's rediscovery of imagination, Durrell is showing novelists of the future a way to transcend the check of modernism, its often passive, even fatalistic limit as a literature of memory. In this transformation, Darley has recovered the secret of storytelling: first-person omniscience, the point of view of Homer and all who successfully invoke the muse.

Darley's muse goes by modest names – extrapolation, interpolation, inference, speculation, interpretation – the daughters of imagination too often ignored during the century that left imagination an outcast in a realm ruled by observation, journalism, natural science, social sciences, and the other offspring of positivism who were the muses of realism, naturalism, and modernism. Even early in *Balthazar* when Darley employs the tools of correspondent John Keats, in this case a photograph, he says of the newsman that his profession has so taught him to "stay on the superficies of real life (acts and facts about acts)," that he suffers from "the typical journalist's neurosis," a "haunting fear of missing a fragment of reality" no matter how "trivial, even meaningless" (p. 26).

While Darley could have partially reconstructed many passages in the first third of *Balthazar* from Balthazar's interlinear, those that follow Balthazar's challenge to imagine what Nessim, Justine, and others were thinking demonstrate Darley's increasing ease with first-person omniscience. To comprehend the importance of this shift readers have to remain aware that these are Darley's *inventions* (not his reports) even as they allow themselves to become *engrossed* by episodes that rank among the most convincing, yet exotic, in twentieth-century fiction.

Without recognizing the fictional, "first-person," frame of these richly verisimilar scenes, we cannot comprehend Durrell's contribution to postmodernism. Such scenes both affirm and deny the verity of what they assert. This paradox – that one can simultaneously experience an event emotionally and deny it intellectually – remains one of the great powers of self-proclaimed fictions. In affirming its true nature, *Balthazar*, like subsequent postmodern fictions, differs importantly from realist, naturalist, and most modernist novels; and Durrell has used the first three chapters to remind the (careful) reader that much that follows – Narouz's encounter with the Magzub and certain carnival scenes, for example – will be "mere" fiction, no matter how convincing the materials may appear. For Balthazar's "words in green ink have detonated in [Darley's] imagination," setting him free to dream such remarkable events into being (p. 151). In short, like the domino worn in carnival, fictions known as fictions allow readers to face the truths of the collective unconscious that they may not acknowledge in the light of common day (p. 188).

Entering the realm of the imagination and its concomitant denials carries Darley into a fictional space where, in Balthazar's words, Truth is far more likely to "just slip out" of the unconscious than it is when one bears down on it trying to utter it "in full consciousness" (p. 146). At the same time, however, he has subverted the modernists' demand for wholeness and abstractly classical order. Since the novel's middle, built around Pursewarden's death, chronologically occurs before its ending, the murder of Toto de Brunel, this volume lacks the dramatic structure that *Justine* provided. In his new-found field of free imagination, Darley has neither discovered nor imposed a supposedly organic pattern on his materials, nor has he borne down excessively on them. In place of a logical dramatic pattern, Darley offers a strong emotional structure built upon the engagement of Justine to Nessim, the death of Pursewarden, and the murder of Toto de Brunel, all centered seemingly on Nessim's honor and jealousy.

If we follow the emotions, we find that, rather than the expected aesthetic order, the novel offers a different but equally profound structure: a psycholgically "deep" structure marked by Pursewarden's emergence as a major figure. In the first volume Darley was able to merge so regressively with Justine because Nessim was too compliant to separate Darley from her, the way an effective oedipal father figure might. In contrast, Pursewarden becomes the "Third Party" required to divide a developing individual from a clinging mother figure. Pursewarden's detached wit masters Justine's mind, thereby reducing Darley to Justine's "decoy." As Pursewarden writes, love allows an individual to fill the emptiness of oneness and momentarily "enjoy the illusion of completeness." But, he continues, love ultimately separates "us most thoroughly from" that with which we felt it had joined us: "Love joins and then divides. How else would we be growing?" (p. 234). Breaking intolerable checks appears to be one important function of third parties in novels where, as Darley infers, "One always falls in love with the love-choice of the person one loves" (1969: 183).

Mountolive: True to Art

One of the supreme ironies in a series in which so many realities prove to be mere appearances must be Durrell's playful description, in the "Note" to *Balthazar*, of the next volume as a "straight naturalistic novel," a label implying factual accuracy and scientific "omniscience." In truth, *Mountolive* is the most artificial or "purely imaginary" novel in the *Quartet*. It moves with ease from mind to mind, continent to continent, present to past, in order to establish motives for actions and, as Balthazar instructed in the previous volume, to cement actions with authorial interpretations. Because its nature is pure artifice, it convincingly demonstrates a major axiom of the *Quartet* and of postmodern fiction: that our natural(istic) reality may be one of the most deceptive fictions those in the postmodern world must learn to frame and thereby limit.

Having separated the emotional structure of *Balthazar* from the dramatic structure – in effect having deconstructed the novel – Durrell through Darley used the free play of the imagination thus liberated as his faculty for discovering a deeper psychological structure that, while confounding the logical mind in its quest for chronological and causal order, nonetheless satisfied the need of the emotions for deep mirroring. In the third volume Darley reconstructs the novel by recombining the dramatic and psychological structures. In the process, he demonstrates the power of the imagination available to a novelist mature enough to accept the truth of artifice as more penetrating than the truth of life that Darley sought in assembling *Justine*. In this way Darley fulfills the promises of liberated imagination he groped toward through the second half of *Balthazar*.

In reconstructing the inner worlds of his friends in *Balthazar*, Darley used, for several vital episodes, the perspective of Narouz, the most elemental, the least British- and Darley-like major character in the series. To round out the vision of Alexandria while building on the imaginative momentum generated in *Balthazar*, Darley now elects to explore the inward space of the character farthest removed from Narouz culturally, David Mountolive. As Britain's ambassador, Mountolive stands at the head of English culture in Egypt, and his story symbolizes the tragedy of the British empire's endeavor in its "oriental" sphere of influence. In choosing Mountolive as his central figure, Darley has freed himself well enough from his former subjective realism to employ the artifice of high tragedy in dramatizing the psychological catastrophe of British colonialism.

The public life of Mountolive generates the very visible dramatic structure of the book. It traces his rise from a junior foreign officer in Egypt befriended by Nessim, Leila, and the Hosnanis, up through the ranks and the snows of Eastern Europe, to knighthood and his return as ambassador to Cairo. There he finds himself having to choose between the credibility of his government's military intelligence and that of his political secretary, Pursewarden, who feels as loyal to the Hosnanis as Mountolive chiefly because both have benefited from (or have been seduced by) the patronage of Nessim's family. After Pursewarden's suicide of conscience underscores the discovery that has changed Pursewarden's mind about Nessim's political activities, Mountolive feels honor-bound to take action: he informs the Egyptian foreign minister, Nur, of the Hosnanis' threat. Nur, however, can act only through the Egyptian minister of the interior, Memlik, whom Nessim now bribes (shamelessly employing the Koran).

A chess-like stalemate follows; it is, in fact, a naturalistic balance of competing forces, one that to Mountolive feels like "destiny" (1961c: 214, 270–1). Memlik uses this period of suspended action to decide where his personal benefit lies. It appears to be in Memlik's interest – and Nessim's, Justine's, Leila's, perhaps Mountolive's and the Coptic community's as well – to offer Narouz up as scapegoat for the Hosnani family's political ambitions. After Narouz's sacrifice, the novel ends with a lamentation worthy of Kazantzakis or the Homer who created the *Iliad*.

The emotional structure of the novel is not as obvious as the dramatic, but it is one familiar from the psychological naturalism of the 1920s. It tells the story of Mountolive's buried life. Leila (as "Egypt") so thoroughly bewitched Mountolive during his first stay in Egypt because his early life prepared him for this seduction. With his scholarly father absent in India, young Mountolive became a mother's boy given to neurotic earaches that left him physically dependent on her ministrations, a pattern that will continue even after he is appointed ambassador. Leila simply sexualized his unconscious need for the absent mother. When he leaves Egypt and Leila, his "real" emotional life goes underground to become a "buried stream." After he returns to Egypt but Leila refuses to see him, "Egypt itself [cannot] fully come alive for him" (pp. 56, 148). All along, his public role has kept him from his private self, but after he reads Pursewarden's secret exposure of the Hosnanis, the public Mountolive destroys the private and the dramatic structure of the novel swallows the psychological: "Unwittingly... Pursewarden had, he reflected, separated him forever from Leila" (p. 190). In this way, Mountolive feels as checked as Justine was by her violator, Darley by his love for Justine, Pursewarden by his eroticized tie to his sister Liza, Narouz by his unrequited affection for Leila, the Copts by Islamic Egypt and the British.

The dramatic and pychological patterns have dovetailed as they failed to do in *Balthazar* and more clearly than in *Justine*, where the psychological pattern obscures, and almost buries, the dramatic architecture. In this convergence, the many checks of the series receive a new emphasis as they are mirrored and refocused by the fate of the ranking Englishman in the Middle East.

The way Mountolive attempts to transcend his stymied return to Egypt parallels Pursewardern's response to his final problems (as it both foreshadows and echoes Darley's answer in *Clea* to his own blocked existence). To Pursewarden's contention in *Balthazar* that the divisions brought about by love are necessary for growth, the older novelist adds a new dimension: just hours before he dies, he observes that "Growing up means separation in the interests of a better, more lucid joining up" (p. 160). Both Mountolive and he, however, attempt unwittingly to deny this insight, which is the great corollary in the series to the often iterated idea of the Check. For both men attempt instead to regress to unions like those they enjoyed in the past, unions that have trapped them.

Following his uneasy triumph over his military rival, Pursewarden descends at dusk into Alexandria on a quest for enjoyment that leads him at last to a substitute sister, Melissa. After she reads his hand, hears his confession of incest and makes love with him, Melissa allows the truth about Nessim's political goals to slip out, thereby forcing both Pursewarden and Mountolive to perform their public duties. Mountolive tries to restore his unity with his lost Egypt by accepting an urgent plea to meet Leila – an encounter that completes his alienation from her family – and then by disguising himself as a Muslim to descend into the Arab quarter of Alexandria. The latter attempt ends with him smothered by child prostitutes, reliving both the ordeal of Gulliver among the Lilliputians and his excessive closeness to his own mother who would read him the picture-book of Swift's story as she gave him comfort. Neither Englishman has escaped his trap in past relationships. Rather, Pursewarden falls a suicide to his past mistakes, and his ambassador ends his novel as companion to a loathsome, urinating "sausage-dog" named Fluke (p. 298).

Durrell, in effect, has nearly accomplished what Borges proposed in "Pierre Menard, Author of Don Quixote" (1939). Durrell has not rewritten *Don Quixote* word for word while producing a totally different novel because the context has changed. He has, however, written a premodern, naturalist novel framed front and back by modernist and (post)modern fictions that show where the facts and feelings in *Mountolive* originated. In doing so, he has rendered the pretense of the latter novel to naturalistic (that is, scientific) "omniscience" – and all such pretenses to omniscience – merely relative. Being merely relative, however, does not leave the "omniscience" and pure artifice of *Mountolive* without its uses. Darley, Pursewarden, Mountolive – the fates of such westerners in the reaches of their beloved and lost empire seem more dire when seen in sequence than does that of any protagonist taken alone. Therefore, the truth to personal memory that Darley attempted in *Justine* cannot capture such fates; nor can the parallax vision he and Balthazar provided in the early parts of the second volume. Only the particulars of life reshaped by the high artifice of the imagination and placed in the service of art can create a vision of such tragic misalliances as the temptations of empire generate. Mountolive's story, seen in its multiple mirrors, stands as a warning to public men who serve the aspirations of empire.

Clea: **Alexandria Unbound**

By the time Durrell was composing the fourth volume, he had deviated sufficiently from the dominant realist assumptions of modernist fiction that it was appropriate to explain what he was about in order to justify his aesthetic of fiction. He had, of course, been doing this, in bits and pieces, all along. In the center of *Clea*, however, he embeds a thirty-page chapter, titled "MY CONVERSATIONS WITH BROTHER ASS." It consists of the now dead Pursewarden's opinions on the state of the British novel and culture as well as his prescription to Darley for a four-volume novel as a continuum or prism of human personality "embodying not [Proust's] *temps retrouvé* but a *temps délivré*" – a work providing an apparent freedom from memories as determinants, one that moves into indeterminacy (1961b: 126). In addition, *Clea*

is rife with the now familiar sort of remarks about fiction and Truth – especially
Darley's all important "psychographic" truth – sufficiently so to warrant placing it
among the most important early "metafictions" that played a central role in the
postmodern movement (p. 64).

One may object initially to designating it a metafiction because the self-conscious
fictional passages about the fiction that we are reading do not frame the events of the
novel and thereby limit the verisimilitude, the (potentially dangerous) illusion that
what we are reading presents, or represents, reality. Along with the need postmodern
novels have to explain the unconventional moves they make – as Wordsworth had in
the quotation that opens this essay – framing reality and breaking frames has been a
major function of metafictional passages. Metafictional deliverance from the seduction
of, and return to the deniability of, fiction is hardly necessary, however, in a series
whose essence consists of overturning realities as when one moves from *Justine* to
Balthazar to *Mountolive*. Like Darley, the reader has been spun around often enough
to learn to distrust all available representations of "reality," or at least to treat them as
hypotheses based on individual experiences, not as revelations. In contrast to many
metafictions, Durrell's commentaries on fiction turn up embedded in the drama itself
as opinions of central characters, and not as authorial comments in the manner
pioneered by Henry Fielding's critical-interpretative chapters in *Tom Jones*.

While frame-breaking throughout the series repeatedly overthrows truths based on
relative facts, certain psychographic truths survive the deconstructive process; the two
most important may be the Check as a general emotional block and the complementary personality cycles Durrell dramatizes time and again in *Clea*. After Darley
returns from his Greek island to war-battered Alexandria and Justine once more offers
herself to him, Darley tells Balthazar that despite "factual falsities" in the *Justine*
manuscript the portrait there was "somehow poetically true – psychographically" so
(1961b: 64). Balthazar concurs that in a world of overdetermined facts each fact can
have "a thousand motivations, all equally valid." The "all multiplicity" that Balthazar
envisions here strongly suggests the possibility that Justine loved Darley as well as
Pursewarden. At the same time, as Darley reports on writing *Mountolive* "in the
[nineteen-] fifties," she still loved Nessim and served his conspiratorial ends by taking
the two Englishmen for lovers (1961c: 254). If, as Pursewarden contends in *Balthazar*,
"everything will be found to be true of everybody," or, in Balthazar's version, "Truth is
what most contradicts itself in time," one must cease to view "truths" in monistic,
dualistic, or dialectical forms (1961a: 15, 23). It would be better to visualize truth
perhaps as an all-inclusive spherical hologram with a here and there, a front and back,
a left and right, and a relativistic up and down – all dimensions changing in time the
way a hologram changes as an observer moves around it.

In *Clea*, Durrell embodies the series' principles of multiplicity in the many
characters that have altered radically during Darley's absence. The early pages catalogue Darley's friends who have changed by embracing their own contradictions. The
most remarkable transformation, and symbolically the most suggestive, may be that
of Capodistria. Having "died" in *Justine*, he turns up here in both a photograph and

long letter indicating he is very much alive. His mutation serves as a Gidean *mise en abyme* that underscores the meaning of the great catalogue of similar alterations. Of these, the most important structurally and thematically are the cycles that Clea and Darley pass through.

Capodistria's renewed state, transformed from dead to alive once again, also raises the possibility that Durrell has left "reality" behind altogether and has entered, not the kingdom of imagination, but a fantasy world where "everything" literally is possible. Such is not the case. For as the novel shows, Pursewarden was correct in *Mountolive* when he theorized that the psyche, no matter how like an anthill or rainbow in its mutability, has something like a king as "a biological necessity" of its "very constitution" (1961a: 141; 1961c: 63–4). Additionally, as Pursewarden wishes for his sister Liza in *Clea*, each person may encounter a *dominant* external figure that mirrors an inner stabilizing force (1961b: 105). Balthazar, for example, has devolved from his former wisdom, poise, and dignity into a gray-haired, love-wounded self-mutilator; yet he returns to his dominant self when Mountolive, Amaril, Pombal, and Clea take him to a restorative dinner with twenty friends.

To Darley, Clea seems to transcend the rule of change through time as she paints deliberately in her tower as detached as Artemis. When he comes to know her better, he discovers that she only appears a stable point, for the obsession Narouz felt for her wounded her deeply and still tugs at her conscience. More importantly, an affair she had while in Syria – with Amaril – delivered her from her virginity but left her with a child she felt she had to destroy. Amaril thus served as the Third Party who broke Clea's bond to her old father as well as her narcissistic (because same-sex) tie to Justine; the affair has made her available, in Pursewarden's terms, for "a better, more lucid joining up" – with Darley. To become a more inventive artist, however, she will have to sacrifice another part of her being.

Nor is Darley yet ready for either a better union or to write a novel of pure artifice like *Mountolive*. Pulled by the many attractions of Justine from his early symbiosis with Alexandria and honey-sweet Melissa to a more grandiose love, Darley dropped, after Justine's defection and *Balthazar's* interlinear, into a (Mountolive-like) deflation, which left him ineffective as lover, writer, and thinker – the "first great fragmentation of [his] maturity" (1969: 7). He has attempted to heal himself by putting the pieces back together in *Justine* and *Balthazar*, but he remains checked. His return to Alexandria brings him back to Clea, the former Artemis, who has taken on some of the Aphrodite generosity in love associated with Melissa, in whose place Darley finds her sitting.

Although Darley has now abjected Justine from his emotions, he cannot yet prove himself completely worthy of Clea. This requires a symbolic act, one in accord with the cycles of transformation through which his friends, including Capodistria, Balthazar and Clea, even Mountolive, are passing. Only when he imposes his own will by defying the seeming will of the city – embodied in Clea's pinned hand, the sea, the tug of death itself – as he cuts away her painting hand, drags her unbreathing from the deeps of the sea, breathes new life into her, and delivers her into the next stage of her evolution as artist, can Darley himself be reborn as artist, lover, and man. For as a thinker his boldness has repudiated the fatalism to which he submitted in *Justine*, where he affirmed organic form, dramatized the Check, and assumed that his friends and he were the passive flora of "the city which used us" (1969: 3).

Darley's rebirth and Clea's thus occur in the same event and dovetail brilliantly with all the other returns to dominant form found in the final novel of the *Quartet*. With the Check, this cycle that breaks the Check constitutes a second major psychographic truth embodied in the series. Determined by forces larger than the city, this universal cycle generates the form of comedy, whether human or divine, as the Check created the shape of tragedy; thus it rounds out Durrell's classical tetralogy. Both patterns are sufficiently dominant to rank among the great symbols that constitute Pursewarden's heraldic reality, and, as archetypes of nature, psyche, and the arts, each form can strike any time from any direction. More even than the city, they rule our lives. Seldom do they strike as forcefully as they do in Durrell's evolving novels.

References and Further Reading

Bowen, Roger (1995) *"Many Histories Deep": the Personal Landscape Poets in Egypt, 1940–45.* Teaneck, NJ: Fairleigh Dickinson University Press.

Cox, Shelley (1988) *As Water into Language Flowing: The Lawrence Durrell Papers at Southern Illinois University, Carbondale.* Carbondale: Friends of Morris Library.

Dasenbrock, Reed Way (1987) "Lawrence Durrell and the modes of modernism," *Twentieth Century Literature*, 33 (Winter): 515–27.

Durrell, Lawrence (1961a) [1958] *Balthazar.* New York: E. P. Dutton.

—— (1961b) [1960] *Clea.* New York: Giant Cardinal.

—— (1961c) [1958] *Mountolive.* New York: E. P. Dutton.

—— (1969) [1957] *Justine.* New York: Pocket Books.

Durrell, Lawrence and Aldington, Richard (1981) *Literary Lifelines: The Richard Aldington–Lawrence Durrell Correspondence,* ed. Ian S. MacNiven and Harry T. Moore. New York: Viking.

Durrell, Lawrence and Miller, Henry (1988) *The Durrell–Miller Letters: 1935–1980,* ed. Ian S. MacNiven. New York: New Directions.

Friedman, Alan Warren (1970) *Lawrence Durrell and "The Alexandria Quartet": Art for Love's Sake.* Norman: University of Oklahoma Press.

Friedman, Alan Warren (ed.) (1987) *Critical Essays on Lawrence Durrell.* Boston: G. K. Hall.

Herbuchter, Stefan (1999) *Lawrence Durrell: Postmodernism and the Ethics of Alterity.* Amsterdam: Rodopi.

Kaczvinsky, Donald P. (1997) *Lawrence Durrell's Major Novels: The Kingdom of the Imagination.* Cranbury, NJ: Associated University Presses.

Lillios, Anna (1997) Brief biography of Lawrence Durrell, International Lawrence Durrell Society site: <http://www.lawrencedurrell.org/bio.htm>

MacNiven, Ian (1998) *Lawrence Durrell: A Biography.* London: Faber and Faber.

Pine, Richard (1994) *Lawrence Durrell: The Mindscape.* New York: St Martins Press.

Raper, Julius Rowan (1992) "Lawrence Durrell's *Mountolive* (1958): merger, abjection, and a better union," in Frederico Pereira (ed.) *Literature and Psychology: Proceedings of the Ninth International Conference on Literature and Psychology.* Lisbon: Instituto Superior de Psicologia Aplicada.

—— (1993) "Lawrence Durrell's *Balthazar* (1958): breaking the modernist mold," *Deus Loci: The Lawrence Durrell Journal,* ns 2: 69–84.

—— (1999–2000) "Durrell's *Justine* and Fowles's *The Collector* as late modernist novels: why the postmodern?," *Deus Loci: The Lawrence Durrell Journal,* ns 7: 93–100.

Raper, Julius Rowan, Enscore, Melody L., Bynum, Paige Matthey (eds.) (1995) *Lawrence Durrell: Comprehending the Whole*. Columbia: University of Missouri Press.

Scholes, Robert (1979) *Fabulation and Metafiction*. Urbana: University of Illinois Press.

Thomas, Alan G., Brigham, James A. (1983) *Lawrence Durrell: An Illustrated Checklist*. Carbondale: Southern Illinois University Press.

Vander Closter, Susan (1985) *Joyce Cary and Lawrence Durrell: A Reference Guide*. Boston: G. K. Hall.

Weigel, John A. (1965) *Lawrence Durrell*. New York: Twayne.

25

The Oxford Fantasists: J. R. R. Tolkien and C. S. Lewis

Peter J. Schakel

The immense popularity of fantasy literature in the latter half of the twentieth century is directly attributable to the influence of two friends who lived, taught, and wrote in Oxford: J. R. R. Tolkien and C. S. Lewis. Each wrote highly successful fantasy stories and each contributed in a significant way to the theoretical understanding of the genre. Their lives, intertwined through the positions they held during the same decades at the University of Oxford, led them to the fantasy genre and shaped their understandings of the relation of fantasy and culture.

Lives

The backgrounds of the two men were very different. Tolkien was born in 1892 in South Africa, but was raised – after the death of his father when Tolkien was 4 – in Birmingham, England. He entered King Edward's School, where his aptitude for languages, and his interest in the nature of language, emerged. Here he began to read the literature – *Beowulf*, *Sir Gawain and the Green Knight*, and *Pearl* – that later became central to his scholarship. His interest in language itself led him to make up words and alphabets, and eventually to invent a complete language, with its own phonology, grammar, lexis, and history. He entered Oxford in 1911 to read classics, but later switched to the English School to study philology, earning First Class Honours in 1915.

After serving in World War I, he was appointed Reader in English Language at the University of Leeds, and in 1925 was elected to the Professorship of Anglo-Saxon at Oxford. In 1945 he became Merton Professor of English Language and Literature there, a position he held until his retirement in 1959. His knowledge of languages – particularly the history and development of Old and Middle English – was unparalleled in his generation. Among his scholarly publications are an edition of *Sir Gawain and the Green Knight* (co-edited with E. V. Gordon) that remains in use today; several superb and still influential essays, such as his acclaimed British Academy lecture "*Beowulf:* the monsters and the critics"; and translations of *Pearl, Sir Gawain and the Green Knight*, and *Sir Orfeo*. Many other scholarly projects were left incomplete when he died, partly owing to the great amount of time he spent on his invented languages and fantasy worlds.

He had begun, as an undergraduate, to compose poems dealing with fairies and elves, some of them in the fairy language he had carried to near perfection. This led to writing legends that supplied the history behind his invented languages and accounted for their development. Part of his motivation was the desire to create an epical mythology for England, to be for it what the *Iliad* and *Odyssey* are for Greece, the *Aeneid* for Italy, and the *Nibelungenlied* for Germany. To this end, he worked on these legends, influenced by the Celtic, Germanic, and Finnish literature he absorbed in his study of languages, throughout his life. In them he describes the creation of the universe and lays out the history of Middle-earth, that is, our world, but "in a purely imaginary (though not wholly impossible) period of antiquity," the First and Second Ages (quoted in Carpenter 1977: 91). *The Hobbit* and *The Lord of the Rings* occur during the Third Age of his historical scheme; we live in the Fourth. The vast scope of the world he created is indicated by the posthumous publication of manuscripts and notes that remained unfinished at his death, edited by his son Christopher: *The Silmarillion* (1977), *Unfinished Tales of Númenor and Middle-earth* (1980), and *The Book of Lost Tales* (1984), comprising the first two volumes of the twelve-volume *History of Middle-earth* (completed in 1996).

Shortly after he returned to Oxford from Leeds, Tolkien met a newly appointed fellow at Magdalen College, who would become a close friend who appreciated and encouraged his fantasy writings. Clive Staples Lewis was born in Belfast in 1898 to parents who valued education and loved to read. Lewis's love of fantasy was sparked by Edith Nesbit's recently published *Five Children and It* (1902) and *The Story of the Amulet* (1906). Influenced by these and the Beatrix Potter books, he began writing illustrated fantasies with "dressed animals" as characters – some have been published in *Boxen: The Imaginary World of the Young C. S. Lewis* (1985).

Lewis attended boarding schools in England and was awarded a scholarship in classics by University College, Oxford, where (after military service in France) he compiled a brilliant academic record, gaining three first class degrees: in Honour Moderations (Greek and Latin texts), Greats (classical philosophy), and English Language and Literature. He became a fellow in English at Magdalen College in 1925 and held that position until his election to the Professorship of Medieval and Renaissance Literature at Cambridge in 1955.

Lewis became widely known as a literary scholar, publishing such influential works as *The Allegory of Love* (1936), *A Preface to Paradise Lost* (1942), *English Literature in the Sixteenth Century, Excluding Drama* (1954), *An Experiment in Criticism* (1961), and *The Discarded Image: An Introduction to Medieval and Renaissance Literature* (1964), as well as many articles and reviews. While Tolkien's approach to fantasy was shaped by his interest in languages, Lewis's approach reflects his work as a literary historian.

In his teaching and his scholarly writings, Lewis tried to enable students and readers to enter, to some extent, the imagination and world – both very different from ours – of someone living in the Middle Ages or the Renaissance, and to read their literary works as closely as possible in the way they read them. In his fantasies he sought to achieve a similar effect: to enable readers to enter other worlds and imagine what life in those worlds was like for their inhabitants.

After his conversion (or re-conversion) in 1931, Lewis also became widely known as a spokesperson for the Christian faith. During World War II he delivered talks about Christianity on BBC radio, and thereafter wrote numerous books explaining and defending Christian beliefs, among these *The Screwtape Letters* (1942), *Miracles* (1947), and *Mere Christianity* (1952).

Tolkien and Lewis first met at a gathering of the English faculty on May 11, 1926. In his diary Lewis describes Tolkien as "a smooth, pale, fluent little chap...thinks language is the real thing in the school...No harm in him: only needs a smack or so" (1991: 393). Only several years later did a close connection emerge, when Lewis invited Tolkien to his rooms after an evening meeting in December 1929 and they talked into the wee hours about Norse gods and mythology and their shared interest in "northernness" (Lewis 1979: 317). Out of that meeting developed one of the best-known and most influential literary friendships of the twentieth century.

Theory

Tolkien and Lewis held similar ideas about fantasy, but used different approaches in arriving at them. Lewis's reflections on fantasy focus on readers and on the effects that stories have on them. In *An Experiment in Criticism* Lewis defined literary fantasy as "any narrative that deals with impossibles and preternaturals ... [with] the fantastic" (1961: 50). Fantasy enables readers to leave the narrow confines of their own lives and enter a totally different world, not because they want to escape from reality or indulge in fantasizings, but because they seek an enlargement of their being: "We want to see with other eyes, to imagine with other imaginations, to feel with other hearts, as well as our own" (p. 137). Lovers of fantasy respond to "an imaginative impulse as old as the human race," that is, "to visit strange regions in search of such beauty, awe, or terror as the actual world does not supply." Such stories are "actual additions to life," giving us "sensations we never had before" and enlarging "our conception of the range of possible experience" (1966: 68, 70).

Tolkien's discussions of fantasy focused more on the writer than on the reader, and more on the essence of the form than on its literary effect. His clearest and fullest exploration of the form – one of the most important contributions to the theory of fantasy anywhere – appears in his essay "On fairy-stories," published in 1947 in a book of essays edited by Lewis. In it, Tolkien affirms the status of a writer of fairy stories – that is, stories about the world of Faërie, of magic, enchantment, and elves (not "fairies" as thought of today). Those who write about Faërie are "sub-creators": their creating of new worlds in a sense parallels God's creating of the world.

At its best, he believed, fantasy achieves the level of Enchantment – that is, a Secondary World of such artistic and imaginative power that both the writer and the reader can give it not just Secondary Belief (a willing suspension of disbelief), but Primary Belief, the kind we extend to the Primary World, the reality that surrounds us. For an imagined story to achieve Primary Belief requires abundance and total consistency of detail. As Tolkien put it, the story-maker as successful sub-creator "makes a Secondary World which your mind can enter. Inside it, what he relates is 'true': it accords with the laws of that world. You therefore believe it, while you are, as it were, inside" (1947: 60).

Such fantasies offer their readers Recovery, Escape, and Consolation, all of which children need, but adults need even more. Recovery – regaining a clear view – involves seeing things not as they appear but as they are, as we were meant to see them. In a successful fantasy the Secondary World enables us, when we return to the Primary World, to see it afresh, to recognize its richness and potential. By Escape, Tolkien means the desire to escape the ugliness and evil of contemporary life by returning to the more permanent and fundamental things that fairy stories and myths concern. And by Consolation he means the Consolation of the Happy Ending, what he labels *Eucatastrophe* (*Eu*= "good"), the sudden joyous turn which "denies (in the face of much evidence, if you will) universal final defeat and ... [gives] a fleeting glimpse of Joy, Joy beyond the walls of the world, poignant as grief" (1947: 81).

Neither Tolkien nor Lewis subscribed to the conventional twentieth-century view that realistic fiction is the acme of narrative art. Because the fantasy writer is creating something new – a world with the potential to achieve Primary Belief – Tolkien regarded fantasy as "a higher form of Art," perhaps the highest form, the "most nearly pure form, and so (when achieved) the most potent." To write fantasy is among the most difficult tasks a human can undertake, one that demands special skill, "a kind of elvish craft." But when the task is "attempted and in any degree accomplished, then we have a rare achievement of Art" (Tolkien 1947: 67, 68).

Practice

It was in the achievement of such art, not in theorizing about it, that Tolkien and Lewis made their greatest contributions to fantasy. The first of their fantasy works to appear in print was *The Hobbit, or There and Back Again,* which began, Tolkien said, when on an empty page in an examination booklet he "scrawled 'In a hole in the ground there lived a hobbit.' I did not and do not know why" (quoted in Carpenter 1977: 177). He gave no date for this. At some point, probably in the late 1920s, he told adventures of a hobbit to his children as bedtime stories and, in the early 1930s, began to write them down. He showed a typescript of most of the story to Lewis in 1932, but he did not complete it until several years later. It was published in

September 1937 and was an immediate success, with the first printing selling out before Christmas.

Scrawling the word "hobbit" started Tolkien on the path toward writing his most brilliant fantasy creations. Hobbits are short, plump beings, about half the height of humans, who have no need for shoes because their feet have leathery soles and are covered with brown, curly hair. At first the hobbits were not related to the mythology Tolkien had long been developing; but as he wrote about them, he began to see a connection: Bilbo Baggins, the title character, lives in a small corner of Middle-earth, the Shire, in the Third Age, later than the First and Second Ages of the earlier chronicles. He is persuaded by the wizard Gandalf to accompany thirteen dwarves on a quest to reclaim their treasure from the dragon Smaug. The tale is structured as a journey to the Lonely Mountain (under which is the treasure trove) and back to Bag End, with a series of adventures along the way. In the most important adventure, Bilbo, lost in a cave, finds a magic ring that has the power to make its wearer invisible, and escapes with it (to the anguish of its previous owner, the diminished hobbit Gollum).

From here on the story gradually begins to deepen in seriousness and complexity, and the character of Bilbo begins to develop, though the tale remains – in tone, diction, and use of obtrusive narrator – a story for children. Bilbo saves the dwarves by killing a giant spider with his sword, which makes him feel "a different person, and much fiercer and bolder" (Tolkien 1937: 167). He then uses his wits, his ring, and his new-found courage to help the dwarves escape from a company of wood-elves. By the time they reach the Lonely Mountain, Bilbo is "a very different hobbit from the one that . . . [left] Bag-End long ago" (p. 225). He becomes the leader of the company, with "ideas and plans of his own" (p. 232). He enters the dragon's cave alone to steal a golden cup and later returns to discover Smaug's vulnerable spot, which enables Bard, a heroic archer, to kill the dragon. The dwarves regain their treasure, and Bilbo returns to Bag End, rich and more mature: "not the hobbit that you were," as Gandalf puts it (p. 311).

The Hobbit develops several themes meaningful to adults as well as children. One is the confrontation with evil. In this book, evil (except in its milder, comic version of the Sackville-Bagginses) does not enter the Shire. Outsiders come into the Shire and ask Bilbo to leave with them; when he does so, Bilbo encounters evil, and does not back away from it. Closely related to that is heroism. Bilbo is a most unlikely hero, very different from the heroes found in the literature Tolkien dealt with in his scholarly work – Beowulf, for example – who possessed the strength of thirty men. Bilbo lacks the size, strength, and experience to be physically heroic, and significantly it is not he who slays the dragon. Heroism in this book takes on properties other than physical strength and aggressiveness. Bilbo emerges as a hero because of the way he changes and develops on his journey. Initially indolent, fearful, and wishy-washy, he ends up exhibiting prudence, justice, fortitude, and magnanimity. Thorin, on his deathbed, sums up Bilbo's type of heroism: "There is more in you of good than you know, child of the kindly West. Some courage and some wisdom, blended in measure.

If more of us valued food and cheer and song above hoarded gold, it would be a merrier world" (Tolkien 1937: 299). The qualities exhibited by Bilbo are those that will be required to confront and defeat the much greater evil that the world will face in Tolkien's later work.

The success of *The Hobbit* led to requests for a sequel. Tolkien offered *The Silmarillion* to his publisher, but it seemed too different to attract the same readers as the earlier book. So Tolkien set about writing a new hobbit book, starting with the idea, "Make *return of ring* a motive" (quoted in Carpenter 1977: 186). He then began to realize that the "ring of power," which in *The Hobbit* only had the power of making the wearer invisible, might have other properties: that it was, in fact, a very dangerous ring that could dominate the life of one who used it. From this kernel the story expanded to a length (around 500,000 words) and depth Tolkien had not dreamed of, creating a Secondary World of unsurpassed richness and detail that turned out to be closely related to the earlier mythology, as the end of the Third Age of Middle-earth.

Geographically, its scope and complexity required maps of regions from the Shire in the west to the realm of Mordor in the east. Within that world are individual locales of haunting beauty and appeal, such as the house of Elrond in Rivendell and the elven forest of Lothlórien, and fearsome places like the Old Forest and the Mines of Moria. Tolkien populated this world with characters ranging from those inherited from the world of Faërie – elves, dwarves, wizards, trolls, and the living dead – to ones of his own invention, such as ents (sentient, mobile tree-herds), orcs, worgs, balrogs (ferocious beasts), and of course hobbits. He also created individuals such as Tom Bombadil, the ageless master of wood, water, and hill; Galadriel, the deathless Lady of Lórien; and the evil Sauron, whose symbol is a lidless eye. And he filled in the countryside – plants, trees, streams, plains, and mountains – through abundant description. It is a perfectly self-contained world: there can be no reference to the Primary World that we know, because the story occurs in our world though in an earlier age, forgotten except in Tolkien's mythic recreation.

The publisher's hopes that the new story would be completed within two or three years were to be disappointed. Tolkien was busy with preparation for college lectures and scholarly work. He was dilatory by nature, easily diverted, and a perfectionist, constantly rewriting to make sure that every detail in the ever-growing geography, history, and body of characters and names was consistent with the rest. And he found himself encountering dead ends, as his stock of ideas temporarily ran dry. The book was not finished until 1949, twelve years after he started it; and concerns about its length delayed publication another five years, until August and November of 1954. Volume 3, held up further because Tolkien was still composing appendices, finally appeared in October 1955. The work sold well and was translated into all of the major European languages, but it became a best-seller only when issued in paperback, in 1965. Then it quickly attained cult status, and Tolkien gained worldwide fame.

Publication in three volumes was necessary because of the work's length, but Tolkien always insisted that it was not a trilogy. He conceived of *The Lord of the Rings* as a single unified and continuous story, divided like other epics into books: six books – half the number in the *Aeneid* and *Paradise Lost,* one fourth of the number in Homer. The individual titles of the three volumes, *The Fellowship of the Ring, The Two Towers,* and *The Return of the King,* were not part of Tolkien's original conception of the work, but were added at the point of publication; Tolkien insisted on retaining *The Lord of the Rings* as the overall title.

Like *The Hobbit, The Lord of the Rings* sends a hobbit on a quest that seems beyond his strength and ability, but at which perhaps only a hobbit could succeed. The only way to prevent the ring from being misused, by Sauron or anyone else who possesses it, is to destroy it by returning it to the place where it was made and hurling it into the Crack of Doom in the fiery mountain Orodruin, inside the evil kingdom of Mordor. That mission Frodo undertakes.

The background of the story lies in earlier ages of Tolkien's mythology. In the Elder Days the evil tyrant Sauron (the Lord of the Rings) had tricked elves into fashioning many rings of power: seven dwarf-rings and nine rings of mortal men. Then Sauron himself made the One Ring (that which Bilbo gave to Frodo) to control the others. Isildur, the King of Gondor, defeated Sauron in battle at the close of the Second Age, and cut the ring from his finger. Now, thousands of years later, Sauron has returned to the kingdom of Mordor, determined to regain the ring and through it to acquire dominance over the whole of Middle-earth.

The complex plot of the story is tightly constructed. Book 1 follows Frodo on his way from the Shire to Rivendell, accompanied at first only by three other hobbits: his servant Sam Gamgee and their friends Meriadoc (Merry) Brandybuck and Peregrin (Pippin) Took. They are joined by a mysterious ranger named Strider (later revealed to be Aragon, descended from Isildur and heir of the ancient Kings of the West). The story moves from one peril to another with Frodo escaping uninjured until he is wounded in the battle of Weathertop by a Black Rider (one of the Ringwraiths, nine men reduced through possession of lesser rings to shadowy extensions of Sauron's will), a wound he carries with him the rest of his life.

In Book 2 Frodo is nursed back to health by the elves at Rivendell and learns the history of the ring, as summarized above. Here the challenge Gandalf put before him in Book 1 is reaffirmed: at the great council of Elrond, Lord of Rivendell, it is decided that he shall continue his journey to Mount Doom. And the company which began to form in Book 1 is enlarged into a "fellowship": Frodo, the other three hobbits, and Strider are joined by an elf (Legolas), a dwarf (Gimli), a man from the southern kingdom of Gondor (Boromir), and Gandalf. However, the fellowship soon begins to break apart. Gandalf is swept into a fiery pit in the Mines of Moria, and Frodo and Sam decide to set off without the others after Boromir attempts to take the ring from Frodo.

With the company divided, the plot also divides, following different hobbits, giving each the opportunity for personal growth and individual heroic deeds. Book 3 relates the adventures of Merry and Pippin, from being carried off by and escaping from a band of orcs to witnessing the fall of the powerful fallen wizard Saruman at the tower Isengard. Book 4 follows Frodo and Sam as they cross the wastelands and reach the tower Minas Morgul on the outskirts of Mordor. The book ends with Frodo drugged and carried off by Orcs, and Sam in possession of the ring, but unable to help Frodo.

As Sam and Frodo are parted at the end of Book 4, so the other two hobbits separate in Book 5, Pippin accompaning Gandalf to Gondor, and Merry joining Theoden, King of Rohan; and both perform notable deeds of valor. They are reunited as all the armies of the west march toward Mordor to assault its gates, hoping to divert Sauron's attention from Frodo and Sam. Likewise Frodo and Sam are reunited in book 6, as Sam finds Frodo and releases him from the Orcs. The two travel on, followed by Gollum, and reach the Crack of Doom. Here Frodo, despite the strength and courage that have enabled him to travel this far and resist the ring's power, finally succumbs to it. Instead of throwing the ring into the fire, he puts it on his finger, and catastrophe threatens. But catastrophe turns to eucatastrophe, as Gollum knocks Frodo down and bites off his ring finger, but in doing so stumbles and falls into the Crack of Doom, taking the ring with him and destroying Sauron's power.

Book 6 ends where book 1 began. The four hobbits who started out from the Shire return to it, only to find that it has been turned into a police state during their absence. These are not the same hobbits who left the Shire many months before: they organize a rebellion, overthrow the tyrant, and undertake a rebuilding process. But Frodo, weary from his journey and the burden he carried, and no longer content in his beloved Shire, departs with Elrond, Gandalf, and the elves for the Grey Havens, and the Third Age comes to an end.

The Lord of the Rings explores many of the same themes as *The Hobbit,* but in a much more complex way. The need to confront evil is present again, but the threat of Sauron is enormously more serious than that embodied in Smaug. Nothing in *The Hobbit* even approaches the evil intensity of the Dead Marshes: "Here nothing lived, not even the leprous growths that feed on rottenness, [it was] a land defiled, diseased beyond all healing" (Tolkien 1954: 239). This killing field, this hell on earth, provides a powerful image of what would have been in store for the world had Frodo failed. Much of *The Lord of the Rings* occurs in a darkness that is both literal and symbolic of death and despair. Countering this is the theme of *hope*: the word occurs well over one hundred times, as hope wanes and then rises. Central to the spirituality of the story is the hope, in the Christian sense of a firm assurance, that good ultimately will triumph over evil, no matter how dire the circumstances may seem at any given moment.

The theme of the unlikely hero also carries over from *The Hobbit.* As Bilbo accomplished unexpected deeds and grew in stature and maturity, so does each of the four hobbits in *The Lord of the Rings.* In a world containing great heroes, such as Aragorn and Faramir (Boromir's brother), the most difficult task is left to creatures half their size with a quarter of their physical strength. Destruction of the ring could be accomplished only by a hobbit, for the task requires not physical strength but strength of character: someone without regard for personal glory or even recognition, someone able to endure great hardship, someone with unbending will, dedication, patience, and self-control, someone able to face enormous temptation but remain uncorrupted. Sauron had prepared to defeat strong heroes and great armies, but he did not prepare for halflings, since he saw no threat in them and could not imagine anyone willingly giving up the ring instead of using it to gain power over others. These are heroes new to epic; in them lies much of the originality of *The Lord of the Rings,* and a great deal of its appeal.

Critics differ on the degree to which Tolkien's Christian faith (he was a devout Catholic) appears in the story; some maintain that he excluded Christianity from the work and others conclude that the work is thoroughly Christian. Perhaps the soundest position lies between these extremes. The setting of *The Lord of the Rings*, in the Third Age, is pre-Adamic. Thus no fall in the Genesis sense has occurred. The larger myth, however, as recounted in *The Silmarillion,* begins with a tale analogous to the fall of Lucifer and recounts many other examples of perverse behavior in the First and Second Ages. Fallenness is evident in *The Lord of the Rings* as well: evil abounds in these latter years of the Age. The Age is in need of redemption, which comes through figures with affinities to Christ. Although no one character should be identified as Tolkien's Christ-figure, several exhibit Christ-like traits: Aragorn is a conquering king; Gandalf died in his fight with the balrog in Moria and came back to life; and Frodo willingly sacrificed himself for the salvation of others.

Artistically, *The Lord of the Rings* sets the standard for the genre. It is written in the high, dignified style of an epic, becoming more archaic and solemn in manner as the story proceeds. Its greatness lies in the scope of its vision, its vast, complete Secondary World, its independence from our world, the richness of the detail that fills it with life and energy, the variety of its characters, familiar and strange, and the consistency with which every aspect is worked out. The work attains what Tolkien called the level of Enchantment; readers are able to give to it not suspension of disbelief but Primary Belief: readers enter its world and accept it as real for as long as the book lasts.

Some readers have attempted to make connections between its Secondary World and the Primary World: between the Shire and England in World War II, for example, and between the ring and the bomb. To claim that a book dealing with powerful evil forces and written during the depths of that war does not reflect contemporary events would be foolish: the darkness of the tone and setting and the sense of eminent defeat surely were influenced by what Tolkien and the British at large were experiencing. Tolkien, however, maintained that the book was not intended to be read allegorically: were it allegory, were one-to-one correspondences to exist between its world and events outside it, the independence of its Secondary World would be violated. The principle of Primary Belief requires a separate, self-contained Secondary World, and Tolkien claimed that sense of separation as a key artistic principle of his fantasies, as Lewis did for the same reasons for his fantasies.

Lewis's first fantasy, *Out of the Silent Planet* (1938), was published a year after *The Hobbit.* It grew out of his love of early science fiction writing, especially the works of

H. G. Wells; but it is more profitably treated as an example of fantasy than of science fiction. Rather than emphasizing science or technology, it deals with the impossible (a journey to Mars) and preternaturals (hrossa, sorns, pfifltriggi, eldils (angels), and Oyarsas (ruling angels of a planet)), and it enables readers to experience a Secondary World.

Out of the Silent Planet introduces the main characters of this and the two following books. A middle-aged professor, Elwin Ransom, who combines characteristics of Lewis and Tolkien, is kidnapped by a scientist and an adventurer (Edward Rolles Weston and Richard Devine) and is taken with them on a space vehicle to Mars (though they initially give only its name in Old Solar, "Malacandra"). After escaping from his captors, he lives for several months with some of the inhabitants of the planet and, before returning to Earth, learns much about their society and about the spiritual structure of the universe: about spiritual hierarchies, about the pervasiveness of spirit life throughout the heavens (which, he discovers, is the proper name for what we call "outer space"), and about a war in heaven in which the Oyarsa of our planet, the "Bent One" (Satan), rebelled against the Old One (God), was defeated, and was hurled back to Earth, or Thulcandra – thereafter called the "silent planet" because, to prevent contagion, it was quarantined from the rest of the universe.

In *Perelandra* (1943) Ransom is whisked to Venus (Perelandra) in a coffin-like container by supernatural power and finds himself in a world utterly unlike ours. Perelandra is Lewis's most imaginative and beautiful Secondary World, a planet totally covered with water, with floating islands moving about its surface; a world covered by a golden dome, as the sun causes the dense atmosphere to glow warmly; a world of fresh, vibrant colors and unfamiliar, delightful smells. Ransom discovers that this is a new world – not that the planet is new, but that sentient life on it is. It is a paradisal world, a global Garden of Eden, and he has been sent to help its Eve, an unfallen woman, human in form but green in color, defend herself against diabolical powers that have taken over Weston's body and have used it to travel to Perelandra on a space ship. With Ransom's help, the green lady resists the temptations of the Un-man (Weston) and tragedy is averted. This planet, unlike ours, will remain unfallen, obedient, and Edenic.

Having defeated Weston on Perelandra, Ransom does battle with Devine on Earth in *That Hideous Strength* (1944), which describes the attempt to seize control of Earth by a large, powerful, supremely evil socio-scientific organization (the National Institute for Coordinated Experiments, known mostly by its acronym NICE.). The story traces the steady expansion of the control and influence of the NICE as it takes control of Edgestow University, the media, and the police and seems well on its way toward turning England into a totalitarian state. The story ends in eucatastrophe rather than catastrophe, however, thus tacking a key element of fantasy on to what was up to that point a dystopia. The forces of good, headed by Ransom, with the help of several preternaturals – the wizard Merlin (awakened from the sleep he has enjoyed since Arthurian times) and the Oyarsas of the planets we call Mercury, Venus, Mars, Saturn, and Jupiter – are able to destroy the NICE and retard the progress of evil.

The book ends with the warning that evil has not been defeated; the struggle against what the NICE epitomizes must continue if freedom and what we think of as civilized life are to survive.

In contrast to Tolkien's subtle and indirect way of treating Christian ideas, Lewis was explicit and direct about including Christian themes in his stories. In an August 1960 letter Lewis said that in writing *Out of the Silent Planet* he was "trying to redeem for genuinely imaginative purposes the form popularly known in this country as 'science-fiction' . . . just as . . . *Hamlet* redeemed the popular revenge play" (1988: 492). But the redemption was not only literary. His references to the Old One, Maleldil (Christ), the Bent One, and a war in heaven embed core Christian beliefs in a story taking place on another world. In an earlier letter he took great satisfaction in the way he had been able to include Christian ideas subtly in the book: "Out of about sixty reviews, only two showed any knowledge that my idea of the fall of the Bent One was anything but a private invention of my own! . . . Any amount of theology can now be smuggled into people's minds under cover of romance without their knowing it" (1988: 322). Christian ideas are even more prominent in *Perelandra,* which develops themes of divine sovereignty and of redemption, the latter imaged in Ransom and reflected in his name: he is sent to Perelandra to rescue the Green Lady, and in doing so becomes a surrogate for Christ. Likewise, adoration appears throughout *Perelandra* in the response to the planet's natural beauty, but particularly in the final chapter's Litany of the Great Dance.

The trilogy also explores social issues with a directness not found in Tolkien. *Out of the Silent Planet* is, in part, a critique of the competitive, materialistic nature of Western society: unlike the inhabitants of Earth, the Malacandrians – though very different from each other – live in perfect peace and harmony. *That Hideous Strength* asks if the human race as a society of free, responsible individuals can survive against the "hideous strength" of totalitarian movements that are opposed to the traditional moral values of the ages. Like George Orwell's *Nineteen Eighty-Four,* published four years later (1948), it issues a powerful warning against the dangers inherent when the knowledge, skills, and authoritativeness of science and the social sciences are united with nefarious political structures and powers.

Several years after the publication of *That Hideous Strength,* Lewis began writing his best-known and most influential fantasy works, the seven Chronicles of Narnia. The first was published the year after Tolkien finished writing *The Lord of the Rings,* and the last came out a year later than the third volume of Tolkien's masterpiece. Lewis therefore was receiving worldwide acclaim for his series before Tolkien's far greater achievement was known to the public, which became a source of tension in their friendship.

The earliest books in Lewis's series focus on the four Pevensie children. In the first and most famous, *The Lion, the Witch and the Wardrobe* (1950), Peter, Susan, Edmund, and Lucy enter the land of Narnia through a magic wardrobe. They lead the Narnians (who include good creatures such as talking animals, fauns, centaurs, dwarfs, and giants) to victory over the White Witch, who for years has made it always winter, but never Christmas, in Narnia. They are assisted by the great lion Aslan, the Narnian incarnation of Christ, who sacrifices himself when Edmund is condemned to death as a traitor. Aslan comes back to life, however, joins in a great battle being led by Peter and Edmund, and slays the White Witch. The four children rule over Narnia for many years as joint kings and queens before returning to our world, where no time has passed while they were away.

In *Prince Caspian* (1951) the Pevensie children return more than a thousand years later (a year later in Earth time) to help save Narnia from the evil King Miraz and to place Prince Caspian on the throne that rightly belongs to him. In *The Voyage of the "Dawn Treader"* (1952) Edmund and Lucy join Caspian on an odyssey to the ends of the world in search of seven lords who were exiled from Narnia by Miraz. In *The Silver Chair* (1953) two other children, Eustace Scrubb and Jill Pole, are brought to Narnia to rescue Caspian's son, Prince Rilian, from the Queen of the Deep Realm. *The Horse and His Boy* (1954) follows two talking horses, Hwin and Bree, and two children, Aravis and Shasta, as they discover a plot against Archenland, a small country next to Narnia, and race across the desert to warn of the approaching danger. *The Magician's Nephew* (1955) treats the beginning of Narnia. Polly Plummer and Digory Kirke watch Aslan bring Narnia to life, though its innocence and purity are immediately threatened by the arrival of the evil queen Jadis (the White Witch of the first book). *The Last Battle* (1956) describes the demise of Narnia. Eustace and Jill are brought back to Narnia to help King Tirian resist invaders from Calormene, but the King's forces are vastly outnumbered and all are lost in a decisive last battle. They pass through a door into a new world, a New Narnia (heaven), where they truly live happily ever after.

The Chronicles of Narnia have been immensely popular, with millions of copies in print. They are read and loved by college students and other adults as well as by children and adolescents, and seem the most likely of Lewis's works to continue to be read in the future. They have succeeded in large part because of their Secondary World, which, though not as complex, detailed, and consistent as *The Lord of the Rings,* creates an immensely appealing idyllic, pastoral paradise, populated with lovable talking animals and intriguing creatures like Dufflepuds and Marsh-wiggles. Part of their appeal, and the appeal of Tokien's fantasies, is nostalgic, as they take us not just to other worlds but to worlds that have a quality of life very different from the modern, industrialized, urbanized one to which we have become accustomed.

The Chronicles have succeeded also because Lewis tells stories well – these are exciting, suspense-filled adventures – and because of the mythical dimensions he weaves into them. And they have succeeded, at least with some readers, because of their connections with Christianity. Lewis did not intend his stories to be taken as allegories and did not regard them as such himself. To be sure, when Aslan dies in Edmund's place, the episode clearly parallels the death of Christ on the cross; and the creation scene in *The Magician's Nephew* is strongly influenced by the Bible. Yet Lewis was not seeking to repeat biblical accounts in different settings; rather, he was interested in telling new stories of the biblical type: a new creation story, a new sacrifice story. He was interested in writing stories that could stand on their own, adventure stories that would echo other stories, classical and Christian, and that would enrich the imaginative experience of his readers.

The appeal and the influence of the fantasies of Tolkien and Lewis are indisputable. Both are worldwide best-selling authors and both have spawned countless followers and imitators. Their work has given rise to an important twentieth-century genre, with hundreds of works being advertised as written in the tradition of the Chronicles of Narnia or *The Lord of the Rings*. Yet the infrequency with which these works approach the level of the originals underscores the uniqueness of Lewis's and Tolkien's achievement.

References and Further Reading

Carpenter, Humphrey (1977) *J. R. R. Tolkien: A Biography*. Boston: Houghton Mifflin.

Downing, David C. (1992) *Planets in Peril: A Critical Study of C. S. Lewis's Ransom Trilogy.* Amherst: University of Massachusetts Press.

Flieger, Verlyn (1983) *Splintered Light: Logos and Language in Tolkien's World.* Grand Rapids, MI: Eerdmans.

Hillegas, Mark R. (ed.) (1969) *Shadows of Imagination: The Fantasies of C. S. Lewis, J. R. R. Tolkien, and Charles Williams.* Carbondale: Southern Illinois University Press.

Hooper, Walter (1996) *C. S. Lewis: A Companion and Guide.* London: HarperCollins.

Lewis, C. S. (1961) *An Experiment in Criticism.* Cambridge: Cambridge University Press.

—— (1966) [1955] "On science fiction," in *Of Other Worlds: Essays and Stories,* ed. Walter Hooper. London: Geoffrey Bles.

—— (1979) *They Stand Together: The Letters of C. S. Lewis to Arthur Greeves (1914–1963),* ed. Walter Hooper. New York: Macmillan.

—— (1982) [1954–5] "Tolkien's *The Lord of the Rings*," in *On Stories and Other Essays on Literature,* ed. Walter Hooper. New York: Harcourt Brace Jovanovich.

—— (1988) *Letters.* Revised and enlarged edition, ed. Walter Hooper. London: Fount.

—— (1991) *All My Road Before Me: The Diary of C. S. Lewis 1922–1927,* ed. Walter Hooper. London: HarperCollins.

Lobdell, Jared (1982) *England and Always: Tolkien's World of the Rings.* Grand Rapids, MI: Eerdmans.

Manlove, C. N. (1975). *Modern Fantasy: Five Studies.* Cambridge: Cambridge University Press.

—— (1993) *The Chronicles of Narnia: The Patterning of a Fantastic World.* New York: Twayne.

Purtill, Richard L. (1974) *Lord of the Elves and Eldils: Fantasy and Philosophy in C. S. Lewis and J. R. R. Tolkien.* Grand Rapids, MI: Zondervan.

Sayer, George (1988) *Jack: C. S. Lewis and His Times.* San Francisco: Harper and Row.

Schakel, Peter J. (ed.) (1977) *The Longing for a Form: Essays on the Fiction of C. S. Lewis.* Kent, OH: Kent State University Press.

—— (1979) *Reading with the Heart: The Way into Narnia.* Grand Rapids, MI: Eerdmans.

—— (2002) *Imagination and the Arts in C. S. Lewis: Journeying to Narnia and Other Worlds.* Columbia: University of Missouri Press.

Schakel, Peter J. and Huttar, Charles A. (eds.) (1991) *Word and Story in C. S. Lewis.* Columbia: University of Missouri Press.

Shippey, T. A. (1992) [1983] *The Road to Middle-earth,* 2nd edn. London: Grafton.

—— (2000) *J. R. R. Tolkien: Author of the Century.* London: HarperCollins.

Tolkien, J. R. R. (1937) *The Hobbit, or There and Back Again.* London: George Allen and Unwin.

—— (1947) "On fairy-stories," in *Essays Presented to Charles Williams,* ed. C. S. Lewis. Oxford: Oxford University Press.

—— (1954) *The Two Towers.* London: George Allen and Unwin.

Tyler, J. E. A. (1976) *The Tolkien Companion.* New York: Avon Books.

Urang, Gunnar (1971) *Shadows of Heaven: Religion and Fantasy in the Writing of C. S. Lewis, Charles Williams, and J. R. R. Tolkien.* Philadelphia: Pilgrim Press.

26

Muriel Spark's *The Prime of Miss Jean Brodie*

Bryan Cheyette

Born in 1918, Dame Muriel Spark was nearly 40 years of age when she completed *The Comforters* (1957), her first novel. Over the next five decades, she published twenty-two novels, three volumes of short stories, and the occasional play, collection of poetry, and children's work. The phenomenal success of Spark's sixth novel, *The Prime of Miss Jean Brodie* (1961) – as a stage-play, feature film, and television series – has ensured that she retains a popular appeal. After gaining innumerable literary prizes and academic awards, she is now widely considered one of the most enthralling writers of her generation. What is extraordinary about Spark's achievement is that as well as having a large international readership she manages to engage with many of the most serious intellectual issues of her time. It is typical of her work that it both gestures towards and acknowledges many of the debates and concerns of the age without, ever, being wholly reliant on them.

Spark gained a good deal from avant-garde movements such as the French *nouveau roman* of Alain Robbe-Grillet and the British "experimentalism" of B. S. Johnson and Christine Brooke-Rose in the 1950s and 1960s; the feminist writing of the 1970s; and postmodern and magical realist fiction of the 1980s and 1990s. At the same time, she has continued the long tradition of British social realism and literary satire in much of her work and has placed these more conventional modes alongside the avant-garde ones. But what is clear from even a cursory reading of Spark's dazzling and cunning fictions is that she only ever engages with these various literary modes insofar as they can be subsumed by her unique vision. Spark's quirky and playful voice refuses to be contained by any single doctrine. Her abiding doubleness, above all, places a sense of history, tradition, and the avant-garde next to an irreverent and whimsical sense of the absurdity of all human philosophies.

Spark's ability to subsume in her fictions the larger cultural questions of her day is in part a consequence of her formative years as a literary critic. Along with a collection of poetry, her books in the early 1950s consisted of a tribute to William Wordsworth; a reassessment of Mary Shelley and a selection of her letters; editions of the poems and letters of Emily Brontë; and an account of John Masefield. Spark might well have continued as a critic and occasional poet if it were not for the publication of "The seraph and the Zambesi" (1951), which won the *Observer* short story prize. This story made such a profound impact that it literally transformed Spark's life. After it was published, she was immediately introduced to the editor and staff of *The Observer* and began writing occasionally for the newspaper. Because she was poverty-stricken and unwell at the time, Graham Greene offered to support her financially and was an influential patron. More importantly, "The seraph and the Zambesi" attracted the attention of Alan Maclean, the fiction editor of Macmillan, who commissioned her to write a novel and a collection of short stories, which subsequently became *The Comforters* and *The Go-Away Bird and Other Stories* (1958), respectively. Such was Spark's meteoric rise as a writer of fiction.

Spark's twenty-two novels reflect her competing fictional identities as both an unchanging moralist and a playfully anarchic one. The reason that she is equally well known as a Scottish-Jewish writer, Catholic convert, and poetic modernist is that she has managed to defy all of these categories. Her fictions are tantalizing precisely because they are able to sustain such radically different readings, and this applies especially to her most accomplished achievements, such as *The Prime of Miss Jean Brodie*. The key to understanding Spark's fiction is to recognize that it is constantly in dialogue with itself, and that each of her novels, or groups of novels, zigzags between her converted and unconverted selves. After initially descending into the murky world of private emotions and unconverted history in her first two novels, she eventually found refuge behind an impersonal and godlike narrator in her neoclassical third novel, *Memento Mori* (1959). This pattern was continued throughout her career.

More unruly books, *The Ballad of Peckham Rye* (1960) and *The Prime of Miss Jean Brodie* quickly followed her early didactic tales such as *Memento Mori*. If her novels became too impersonal – as in *The Driver's Seat* (1970) and *Not to Disturb* (1971) – she wrote anarchic works such as *The Abbess of Crewe* (1974) and *The Takeover* (1976), or ostensibly autobiographical books such as *Loitering with Intent* (1981) and *A Far Cry from Kensington* (1988). Spark's abundant gifts are such that she has refused to rest on her laurels. Always shifting in time, from the 1940s to the 1990s, her fiction has encompassed Rhodesia, Edinburgh, and Jerusalem, and has rotated between London, New York, and Rome. But no one time, place, or culture has been allowed to delimit Spark's imagination. It is in these terms that Spark's hybrid background – part English, part Scottish, part Protestant, part Jewish – has enabled her to become an essentially diasporic writer with a double vision (Cheyette: 2000).

The Prime of Miss Jean Brodie remains one of Spark's finest achievements and, although the film and play tend to flatten out the complexity of the written text, it remains one of her most compelling works. While the novel has been frequently read for a single, didactic meaning, it should be placed in the context of the self-questioning and doubleness that characterizes her best works. The book that most closely resembles *The Prime of Miss Jean Brodie* is, in many ways, the largely unsung *The Ballad of Peckham Rye* (1960), with its antihero Dougal Douglas or Douglas

Dougal. This comparison is often obscured by the phenomenal success of Spark's sixth novel. But both works have deceptively attractive and forceful protagonists whose Scottishness defines their difference from convention and helps proclaim their anarchic presence. These determinedly amoral figures paradoxically act as a catalyst to elicit the spiritual life of others. They both exist as witty and alluring personalities who, in a skillful sleight-of-hand, appear to elude the author's narrative control. Such rampant singularity means that Dougal Douglas and Jean Brodie attempt, not unlike their author, to determine reality. The fact that the figure of Jean Brodie can be so easily extracted from an elaborate and closely textured story-line points to Spark's overpowering fascination with her. That Brodie exists so completely beyond the written text is especially startling when we remember that the novel, more than any other that she had written to date, is distinguished on the page, as opposed to the stage or screen, by a fragmented and continually shifting narrative.

Yet as soon as one compares her later and earlier works it becomes clear that *The Prime of Miss Jean Brodie*, along with *The Girls of Slender Means* (1963) and *The Mandelbaum Gate* (1965), achieve a level of literary sophistication that eclipses much of what has gone before. Unlike her previous novels, Spark now takes seriously the question of locale and historical context. If her first five novels could easily have been situated anywhere at just about any time, *The Prime of Miss Jean Brodie* could only have been set in Edinburgh in the 1930s. As with *The Girls of Slender Means* and *The Mandelbaum Gate*, *The Prime of Miss Jean Brodie* is also directly related to the history of fascism and the aftermath of war. Unlike these contemporaneous works, however, *The Prime of Miss Jean Brodie* also introduces the first sustained use of Spark's distinctive flash-forward technique, to accompany her more conventional use of flashbacks, which complicates any straightforward reading of the novel. As her narrative style becomes more complex, so does the range and depth of her interests.

Continuity between Spark's earlier and later writing is found in her abiding sense of death-in-life or of suffering as the foundation of creativity. An important link with both *Memento Mori* and *The Bachelors* is the often-stressed fact that Brodie, as a result of the carnage of the First World War, is one of a large number of Edinburgh spinsters.

> It is not to be supposed that Miss Brodie was unique at this point in her prime... She was alone, merely, in that she taught in a school like Marcia Blaine's. There were legions of her kind during the nineteen-thirties, women from the age of thirty upward, who crowded their war-bereaved spinsterhood with voyages of discovery into new ideas and energetic practices in art or social welfare, education or religion. (Spark 1961: 42)

Instead of showing humility in the face of death on a mass scale, Brodie acts as if she were immortal, not unlike many of the benighted septuagenarians in *Memento Mori*. What is more, she also weaves unreal fantasies out of her spinsterly solitude, which leads to solipsism and the creation of a private dream world. But Spark, needless to say, did not call this novel *The Spinsters* after *The Bachelors*. While Brodie might not be "outwardly odd...inwardly was a different matter"; it is her deformed "nature" (p. 43) that separates her from the legions of lonely Edinburgh spinsters. Her singularity is confined to her internal health, and this book, above all else, becomes Brodie's spiritual biography. Even her support for Mussolini and Hitler, in the end, indicates that she was a "born Fascist" and that her politics, when compared to her inner deformity, is a "side interest" (p. 125).

Half way through the novel, Sandy Stranger and Jenny Gray, two of Brodie's students, gain a crucial insight into her true character when they listen to yet another account of her "felled fiancé" (p. 13) Hugh, who died in the Great War at Flanders Field. After six years of being taught a spectrum of subjects by Brodie, from age 10 to age 16, the girls begin to realize that the story of her dead fiancé has been successively modified over the years. Hugh was always interested in music, reflecting her affair with Gordon Lowther, the school's music teacher. But in this final retelling Hugh has suddenly become an aficionado of art because of her deeper affection for the school's art master, Teddy Lloyd, who himself lost an arm during the First World War. Once Jenny and Sandy comprehend that Brodie is "making her new love story fit the old" (p. 72), they listen with "double ears" and become "fascinated by this method of making patterns with facts" (p. 72). Sandy's gradual distrust of Brodie, and the reason for her eventual "betrayal" (p. 60) of her beloved teacher, stem from this moment. In the end, Sandy coldly rejects the "excesses" of Brodie's prime because, in an extreme rendering of Scottish Presbyterianism, she had "elected herself to grace...with more exotic suicidal enchantment than if she had simply taken to drink like other spinsters who couldn't stand it any more" (p. 109).

On one level, Brodie's main offence is that she is a mythomaniac who fictionalizes everything she does as well as those she encounters. This can be seen mainly in her egocentric belief that the six students who form "the Brodie set" (p. 5) can be shaped by her romantic fantasies and fit into her predetermined categories for them. She thus adopts the oft-stated Jesuit belief, which Spark herself deplores, that children are essentially malleable: "Give me a girl at an impressionable age, and she is mine for life" (p. 9). This reference to the Jesuits is paradoxical in that Brodie is most closely identified with the confining predestination of the Scottish "God of Calvin, who sees the beginning and the end" (p. 120). But while Catholicism and Calvinism are contrasted in the novel as Sandy Stranger and Jean Brodie, Rome and Edinburgh, they are not straightforward oppositions. For one thing, we are told that Brodie is "by temperament suited only to the Roman Catholic Church," which she "could have embraced, even while it disciplined, her soaring and diving spirit" (p. 85). Brodie's romanticized love for Rome, albeit in secular terms, is an obvious counter to the dour rationalism of the Marcia Blaine School at which she teaches and the Presbyterian Edinburgh in which she lives. Sandy Stranger, although a convert to Catholicism, is repeatedly pictured as being imprisoned in her convent, clutching at the "bars of her grille" (p. 128). What is more, in a parodic version of Spark's usual heroines, Sandy is portrayed as being unpleasantly cerebral and analytical, not unlike a stereotypical Presbyterian, which Teddy Lloyd deems "unnatural in a girl of eighteen" (p. 122).

As with much of Spark at her best, the paradoxes of her characters counter overly dogmatic readings of her books.

The comic version of Calvinistic determinism can be found in the self-classifications that each of her students promotes. Monica Douglas is famous for mathematics and her temper; Rose Stanley is famous for sex; Eunice Gardner is famous for gymnastics and swimming; Jenny Gray is famous for her beauty; Mary Macgregor is famous for being a nobody; and Sandy Stranger is famous for her vowel sounds and "merely notorious for her small, almost non-existent eyes" (p. 7). Such categories are amusing when they are merely "unreal talk," but become dangerous when Brodie is no longer "game-planning" (p. 119) and actually believes her own godlike pretensions. In terms of the God of Calvin, Brodie "thinks she is Providence" (p. 120) and that she can therefore mould other people's lives. She thus urges the "mad" (p. 118) Joyce Emily Hammond, another student, to fight in the Spanish Civil War, where she is killed, and encourages Rose Stanley to sleep with Teddy Lloyd as her surrogate lover. At this point Sandy decides to put a "stop" (p. 125) to Brodie because the teacher is confusing, with lethal consequences, her romantic fantasies with reality.

Yet the condemnation of Brodie for "making patterns with facts" (p. 72) also has a hollow ring to it. After all, such pattern making is the very essence of the art of fiction. As a writer and artist, respectively, both Sandy and Teddy Lloyd also aestheticize reality or "transfigure the commonplace," according to the title of Sandy's "odd psychological treatise" on the "nature of moral perception" (p. 35). To be sure, Brodie does falsely categorize her girls, and much of the plot is about the assertion of their free will, often successfully, in relation to Brodie's intended plans for them. It is also true that her beliefs are often simply an extension of her ego, as can be seen by her typical contention that the "greatest Italian painter" is Giotto; "he is my favourite" (p. 11). But all of these traits – classifying people, transforming life into art, and confusing the self with the world – turn Brodie into a peculiar double of the novelist Muriel Spark. After all, Sandy Stranger is immediately limited and predetermined by her surname – as are so many of Spark's characters – which indicates that she is inevitably estranged, an outsider who is never fully at home in the Brodie set. And the book's narrator, who constantly sees the future and looks back into the past, is more godlike than ever, even though such omniscience is wittily particularized by the use of a rather prim Edinburgh voice.

In the end, what distinguishes this novel is its refusal to make easy moral judgments. David Lodge overstates the case when he describes this "largely comic novel" as containing a "severe and uncompromising dogmatic message" (1971: 135). In this reading, Brodie is a bogus Christ figure and the Brodie set is a caricature of the "chosen" (Spark 1961: 79) or the Christian apostles. According to Lodge, the Church as the mystical body of Christ is travestied when Sandy looked back at her companions and "understood them as a body with Miss Brodie as a head" (p. 30). Teddy Lloyd is aware of this symbolism when he paints all of the Brodie girls as if they were versions of Jean Brodie. When he offers to paint a group portrait, Sandy comments tellingly that the girls would "look like one big Miss Brodie, I suppose" (p. 102).

Such specious messianism leads to fascism, which is an extreme account of a single body with the head of a redemptive leader. In *Memento Mori* the eleven "grannies" in the Maud Long Medical Ward lie "still and soundless breathing like one body" (Spark 1959: 116) and, as completely spiritual beings, are a sympathetic instance of the same theological symbolism. But, unlike in her earlier work, in *Brodie* Spark now leaves it to the reader to negotiate her ambiguous moral universe.

The abiding problem with Lodge's orthodox reading of *The Prime of Miss Jean Brodie* is that it fails to account sufficiently for the many paradoxes in the novel, which are reinforced by its dislocated narrative. On a didactic level, Sandy rejects Brodie as a false Christ-figure and converts to the real thing by becoming a Catholic nun called Sister Helena of the Transfiguration. The shift from Calvinist predestination to the centrality of free will within Catholicism points to a blunt theological divide. Nevertheless, as we have seen, such easy oppositions are subverted in this work because Spark sets up many possible readings of her main characters, with each interpretation being equally plausible. Both Brodie and Sandy have strong and competing elements of Calvinism and Catholicism within them. It is misleading, in these terms, to place Sandy at the moral center of this work as so many critics have done. Much of the action is seen through Sandy's narrow "little pig-like eyes" (Spark 1961: 66), which are repeatedly described as "almost non-existent" (p. 7). While Brodie has an excess of vision Sandy, in stark contrast, almost literally lacks vision.

To be sure, one aspect of Miss Jean Brodie eventually culminates in Spark's inhuman writers manqués, such as Lise in *The Driver's Seat* (1970) or Lister in *Not to Disturb* (1971), who mistakenly think that their myth-fictions can determine reality. For this reason, she has routinely exposed those dangerously attractive mytho-maniacs, such as Brodie, who think of their lives, and those under their sway, as having a single destiny. In her short story, "The fortune-teller" (1985), Spark distinguishes crucially between having a "destiny" and a "destination" (1994: 335). Once her character's life story is thought of as a foregone conclusion, determined by a single destiny, then other potential destinations are of necessity excluded and diminished. This determinism, which Michael André Bernstein has called "foreshadowing," is precisely what Spark's fictional practice works against (Bernstein 1994). By setting up Brodie, and her later counterparts Lise and Lister, as examples of the false novelist or mythomaniac, Spark is by implication constructing an ideal "Catholic writer" in her fiction. It is in these terms that Spark has been misguidedly seen as belonging to the neoclassical "Catholic novelists of detachment, like Joyce, whose God-like writer is indifferent to creation, paring his fingernails" (Bradbury 1987: 271). Her often cool aesthetic surface and narrative indifference, coupled with her supposed commitment to a god-given truth, has resulted in many of her critics, such as David Lodge and Malcolm Bradbury, viewing her mainly through her apparently secure identity as a Catholic writer.

Yet Spark, as we will now see in *The Prime of Miss Jean Brodie*, is often aware of the dangers of coldly expunging an uncontrollable emotional life from her fiction. One way of reading her sixth novel, for instance, is precisely as a way of questioning the values of clarity and order that are personified by Sandy Stranger. In her contemporaneous story, "Bang-bang you're dead" (1961), Spark's protagonist Sybil asks, "am I a woman . . . or an intellectual monster?" (1994: 85) and the same question can be asked of Sandy Stranger. For all of her crypto-fascist control of her girls, Brodie, on the other hand, hates anything that smacks of "the team spirit" (1961: 78), which is authoritarian and diminishes human individuality. After all, Brodie's definition of education is "a leading out," "from *ex* out and *duco*, I lead" (p. 36). This is an essentially liberal version of education from below as opposed to the imposition of knowledge on her pupils from above. But, *ex duco*, of course, is similar to Il Duce, the title that Mussolini adopts. Brodie, in these terms, is paradoxically both a liberal and a fascist cliché – the freethinking schoolteacher who both inspires and dominates her pupils – and Spark clearly wanted to subvert such easy approval or disapproval.

The unattractive Sandy, on the other hand, is a rather one-dimensional figure, as suggested by her allegorical surname, Stranger, even though she is ostensibly supposed to embody the novel's truths. While Sandy's crisis of belief and coming of age drive the action of the plot, we gain very little insight into her reasons for her conversion and we know absolutely nothing about her "odd psychological treatise" (p. 35), except that it finally made her famous. As Bernard Harrison rightly argues, the story-line might well be organized around Sandy but she remains "enigmatic and incomplete" and is treated throughout the novel as if she were a peripheral figure (Harrison 1991: 154). In Spark's previous works, mono-dimensional characters without any inner life are automatically dismissed as moral degenerates. Sandy, however, is both a disagreeable caricature and close to being an authorial mouthpiece. She is half-English, like Spark, a "stranger" to Edinburgh, and has a "creeping vision of disorder" (Spark 1961: 86) that her conversion is meant to resolve. Although she shares a portion of Spark's life history, she is the most unlovable of heroines and, when she dismisses Brodie as a "tiresome woman" (p. 60), the reader's sympathy is undoubtedly on the side of her more seductive and nuanced teacher.

It is in relation to Sandy's conversion to Catholicism that the conventional orthodox reading of *The Prime of Miss Jean Brodie*, and Spark's fiction as a whole, can be challenged. Spark's anti-determinism, in response to Calvinism, is especially troubling when placed next to the conversionist narrative that surrounds both her and Sandy as a "Catholic writer" and convert to the Catholic faith. The convert, in this orthodox reading, is meant to close off one set of possibilities, and one version of the self, and to embrace a radically new and all-encompassing *weltanschauung*. Spark's fiction has, as a consequence, been read as a "spiritual autobiography" that distinguishes, above all, between the self before and after conversion. Each novel, according to this interpretation, becomes a kind of ongoing conversion, transforming the author anew, and distancing her from her previous self (Whittaker 1982; Randisi 1991). The abiding problem with thinking of Spark in this way is that it tends to set up an overly simple model of conversion that unproblematically splits the self into old and new, before and after, inner and outer. Conversion, that is, is turned into another form of determinism, or merely a self-congratulatory act of redemption. Sandy's abiding

memory of the irresolvable presence of Miss Jean Brodie and the influence that she has
had on her is especially subversive, in these orthodox terms, after she has been
"transfigured" through her conversion. Although Sandy's new self is meant to have
transcended her old self, she remains, paradoxically, enraptured with her past.

Those critics who have noted Spark's double conversion – to Roman Catholicism
and to novel writing – have argued mistakenly that these coexisting transformations
are somehow equivalent (Bradbury 1987). Instead of assuming that there is an organic
coherence between her religion and her art, Gauri Viswanathan has maintained that
religious conversion, far from being a unitary form of exchange, is a model of
"dissent." In her reading, conversion is primarily a form of doubleness that "destabil-
izes" modern society as it "crosses fixed boundaries between communities and
identities" (1998: xvii). According to this argument, the mixing of two different
religions or cultures inevitably creates a sense in which any one ideology can be
viewed from an estranged or defamiliarized perspective. This is precisely what Sandy
Stranger does in *The Prime of Miss Jean Brodie*. In these heterodox terms, far from
merely superseding the past, conversion is seen primarily as an interpretative act that
perceives one world through the eyes of another. Sandy, for instance, reinterprets the
presence of Miss Jean Brodie as a parodic form of spiritual transfiguration, while
her Catholicism is observed with an artist's skeptical eye. Rather than being an
all-encompassing orthodoxy, conversion in the novel becomes a form of heterodoxy
that multiplies endlessly the official or didactic version of Miss Jean Brodie.

As with the doubled and redoubled Dougal Douglas or Douglas Dougal, Brodie is
equally attractive and dangerous and impossible to pin down according to a self-
evident moral schema. Such uncertainties are initially resolved by identifying her
with her famous ancestor, Deacon William Brodie, a respectable "man of substance"
who was a "night burglar," a bigamist, and died "cheerfully on a gibbet of his own
devising" (p. 88). As Velma Richmond has noted, William Brodie was the historical
source for Robert Louis Stevenson's *The Strange Case of Dr Jekyll and Mr Hyde* (1886),
which is also centrally concerned with the doubleness of its protagonist (Richmond
1984: 26). For this reason, unlike in Spark's earlier fiction, there is no simple
redemptive closure in *The Prime of Miss Jean Brodie*, even when Edinburgh is viewed
in passing as a "floating city when the light was a special pearly white" (p. 111). This,
as the narrator makes clear, is just one of a large number of versions of the city and of
Brodie, who looked "beautiful and fragile" in this light (p. 111). Thus Sandy ends the
novel by repeating the refrain that "Miss Jean Brodie in her prime" (p. 128) was an
important influence on her life. But we know from what has gone before that Brodie's
prime – "Prime what?" (p. 27) – is a particularly vague notion, as this word is both a
noun and an adjective. In a typical paradox, Brodie herself objects to exactly this kind
of linguistic vagueness: "Social what?," she responds, when one of her girls says that
she is going to "a social" (p. 62).

The Prime of Miss Jean Brodie is a deliberately uncertain rendition of a figure who
is defined *par excellence* by her astonishing, if misplaced, certainties. The reason
why Sandy's famous treatise, "The transfiguration of the commonplace," is left

unexplained is that Spark allows her readers to tease out the truth about Brodie and engage in an act of aesthetic transformation themselves. Like Brodie, Spark does not wish to impose meaning from above, but leaves "the nature of moral perception" (p. 35) to her individual readers. The Marcia Baine School provided Spark with a circumscribed social grouping that she could simultaneously document, mythologize, and debunk. But the same could be said of Sandy Stranger's conversion into a Catholic nun called Sister Helena of the Transfiguration. In the context of such spiritual transformation, "Miss Jean Brodie in her prime" (p. 128) is a peculiarly ambiguous influence. Is this a reference to Brodie's moral prime, as it should be, or to her pedagogic or mythomanical prime? It is this unresolved clash of two different kinds of transformation – one aesthetic, one religious – that is to be found not only in *The Prime of Miss Jean Brodie* but in Spark's fiction as a whole.

REFERENCES AND FURTHER READING

Bernstein, Michael André (1994) *Foregone Conclusions: Against Apocalyptic History.* Berkeley: University of California Press.

Bradbury, Malcolm (1987) *No, Not Bloomsbury.* London: Arena.

Cheyette, Bryan (2000) *Muriel Spark: Writers and Their Work.* Tavistock, Devon: Northcote House.

Harrison, Bernard (1991) *Literature and the Limits of Theory.* New Haven: Yale University Press.

Lodge, David (1971) *The Novelist at the Crossroads.* London: Routledge.

McQuillan, Martin (ed.) (2002) *Theorising Muriel Spark: Gender, Psychoanalysis, Deconstruction.* London: Macmillan.

Randisi, Jennifer Lynn (1991) *On Her Way Rejoicing: The Fiction of Muriel Spark.* Washington, DC: Catholic University of America Press.

Richmond, Velma Bourgeois (1984) *Muriel Spark.* New York: Frederick Ungar.

Spark, Muriel (1951) *Child of Light: A Reassessment of Mary Wolstonecraft Shelley.* Hadleigh: Tower Bridge Publications.

——(1952) *The Fanfarlo and Other Verse.* Aldington, Kent: The Hand and Flower Press.

——(1953) *John Masefield.* London: Peter Nevill.

——(1957) *The Comforters.* London: Macmillan.

——(1959) *Memento Mori.* Harmondsworth: Penguin.

——(1960a) *The Bachelors.* London: Macmillan.

——(1960b) *The Ballad of Peckham Rye.* London: Macmillan.

——(1961) *The Prime of Miss Jean Brodie.* Harmondsworth: Penguin.

——(1963) *The Girls of Slender Means.* London: Macmillan.

——(1965) *The Mandelbaum Gate.* London: Macmillan.

——(1968) *The Public Image.* London: Macmillan.

——(1970) *The Driver's Seat.* London: Macmillan.

——(1971) *Not to Disturb.* London: Macmillan.

——(1974) *The Abbess of Crewe.* London: Macmillan.

——(1976) *The Takeover.* London: Macmillan.

——(1981) *Loitering with Intent.* London: Bodley Head.

——(1988) *A Far Cry from Kensington.* London: Constable.

——(1994) *The Collected Stories of Muriel Spark.* Harmondsworth: Penguin.

Spark, Muriel and Stanford, Derek (eds.) (1950) *Tribute to Wordsworth: A Miscellany of Opinion for the Centenary of the Poet's Death.* London: Wingate.

——and——(eds.) (1953) *Emily Brontë: Her Life and Work.* London: Peter Owen.

Whittaker, Ruth (1982) *The Faith and Fiction of Muriel Spark.* London: Macmillan.

Viswanathan, Gauri (1998) *Outside the Fold: Conversion, Modernity, and Belief.* Princeton: Princeton University Press.

27

Doris Lessing's
The Golden Notebook

Judith Kegan Gardiner

Prescient, prolific, cranky, and now canonical, Doris Lessing, like her masterpiece *The Golden Notebook* (1962), continues both to provoke and defy categorization. She may well be the greatest English novelist of the postwar period, and *The Golden Notebook* one of the best-loved and most influential novels. Despite her bemusement that it was received both as a volley in the "sex war" and as the "'Bible' of the Women's Movement," she is pleased the book is widely translated and taught, especially in Africa where she grew up (Lessing 1997: 338, 339). Contributing to the genres of feminist novel, satire, and postcolonial fiction, and immersed in both realist and modernist traditions, it has been hailed as a postmodern masterpiece.

Lessing was born to English parents in Persia, now Iran, in 1919. From 1924 to 1949 she lived in Southern Rhodesia, now Zimbabwe, where she left school early, married, divorced, remarried, and had three children before coming to England with her younger son and the manuscript of her first novel. Her publications now comprise over fifty volumes. Before *The Golden Notebook* she published *The Grass Is Singing* (1950), which sets a distraught white African housewife in collision with her black male servant; the Communist novel *Retreat from Innocence* (1956), which she later repudiated; plays and short stories; and three of the five autobiographical fictions in "The Children of Violence" series (1952–69). Her writings after *The Golden Notebook* describe women and men in contemporary life, often using older female protagonists. They critique the English class system and extol the Sufi way explicated by Idries Shah. They explore social and mental breakdown on earth and imagine alternative societies in space. In addition to novels, they include short stories, essays, children's literature, operas, and vivid autobiographies. *The Golden Notebook* forecasts many of her later themes and remains her most daring, original, and engaging fiction.

In the widely quoted Introduction to the 1971 edition, Lessing claims, "my major aim was to shape a book which would make its own comment, a wordless statement: to talk through the way it was shaped" (1999: xix). The long, garrulous novel is hardly "wordless," but its structure, originally perceived as chaotic, is now understood as a triumph. The novel is built of interlocking parts that are apparently unified by a single consciousness, that of the autobiographical character Anna Freeman Wulf. Among Anna's major preoccupations are the patterns of history and the myths of ideology; the responsibilities of writing fiction in a chaotic world; the relationships among writing, experience, and memory; the psychologies of conformity, madness, love, and obsession; and the compulsive, often destructive attachments between men and women, parents and children. A writer herself, Anna frequently denounces the inadequacy of words: "the real experience can't be described," and "a row of asterisks" might be better "or a symbol of some kind, a circle, or a square" (p. 604). *The Golden Notebook* is carefully built of such geometrical shapes, a kind of square within a circle, though each construction transmutes into the next. Within these forms, Lessing claims that the novel describes "the matrix of emotions...the flavour of a time in a way formal history cannot" (p. viii).

Lessing's 1971 Introduction identifies the novel's central themes as "the end of fragmentation," "unity," and "breakdown" rather than the more obvious motif of the "sex war" (p. xii). Anna's first sentence declares, "The point is, that as far as I can see, everything's cracking up" (p. 3). This opening signals dissolution and new directions in the political environment of England in 1957 and in the characters' mental health. The structure of the novel satisfies readers' desires both for unified completion and for open possibilities. It fulfills realist expectations for a specific and richly detailed historical context, modernist criteria for the development of individual interiority, and postmodernist undermining of such coherence. Anna is introduced as a once-published novelist unable to write a new novel; instead she fills up four notebooks (p. xi). These notebooks are color coded: black for her experiences in Africa during World War II and the novel based on them; red for her relationship to the Communist Party; yellow for story ideas, which feature the romances of her alter-ego Ella; and blue for her diary entries. The five sections of "Free Women," which Lessing characterized as together comprising a "conventional short novel," are interleaved by selections from the four notebooks and a fifth, golden notebook near the book's end (p. xi). The characters in "Free Women" are variants of the notebooks' characters, often with repeating or similar names, as in the sons and lovers named Paul, Saul, and Michael. Although "Free Women" can be read as a complete novella, the notebooks give it depth by indicating the kind of materials from which fiction may be shaped, even as they reveal such coherence as distorting. The Anna of "Free Women" differs in some respects from the various Annas in the notebooks, from Ella, and from the authorial persona. Anna both is and is not the author of the entire *Golden Notebook*, creating a structure where inside undecidably blends into outside: "I see Ella....I, Anna, see Ella. Who is, of course, Anna. But that is the point, for she is not" (1999: 439–40).

The five sections of "Free Women" are labeled like a nineteenth-century novel with teasing plot summaries. "Free Women" is also a Jungian narrative of psychological development, which begins with the line, *"The two women were alone in the London flat"*

(p. 3). We later learn that Anna received this sentence from her lover Saul Green and that it refers to "the two women" of Anna's divided personality (p. 610). Everything begun in this novella is already at an ending, so that it assumes a circular form. As "Free Women" starts, the close friendship between Anna and the actress Molly Jacobs is already unraveling. Anna is years past the most significant love affair of her life and has left the Communist Party. She has become disgusted with literary and film people seeking to commercialize her novel, *Frontiers of War*, and her income from the book is running out. "Free Women" also resembles a five-act play, with scenes among a few quarrelsome and interconnected actors set in a few London interiors. The crisis of this ironic melodrama is the off-stage attempted suicide of Tommy, Molly's young adult son, after he reads Anna's notebooks. The novella acts, too, as a denunciation of British society like those of England's Angry Young Men of the time. And, despite Lessing's reputation for humorlessness, "Free Women" is also a comedy of contemporary manners.

In *A Room of One's Own* Virginia Woolf said that it would revolutionize English letters if women wrote about friendships between women. "Free Women" appears to answer Woolf's call, Anna's last name echoing Woolf's. However, it is unclear both how much Anna and Molly are separate people and how solid is their friendship. To other people, the two women are "practically interchangeable," playing "the same role," though they are physical opposites, as different as "chalk and cheese," one fair and one dark, one actress and one writer, one Jewish and one gentile (pp. 4, 8). Yet both are "a completely new type of woman": unmarried, working mothers who are politically and sexually active, "prepared to experiment" with their lives, and, as they repeatedly and ironically insist, "free women" (pp. 5, 25, 4). The duet of women is quickly triangulated by a man, Molly's rich ex-husband Richard, and then complicated by additional characters who parallel, echo, and replace each other in "Free Women" and the notebooks – Richard's and Molly's son Tommy and Richard's second wife Marion, all worrying about Tommy's future and, implicitly, the future of England.

The mobile dynamics among the characters of "Free Women" prefigure the apparently neat but fraying divisions of *The Golden Notebook* as a whole. In the course of the novel, all opposites collapse, and shapes shift: "Men. Women. Bound. Free. Good. Bad. Yes. No. Capitalism. Socialism. Sex. Love…" (ellipsis original, p. 43). The first four sections of "Free Women" are followed by selections from the four notebooks in color and chronological sequence, although the arrangement increasingly breaks down until the fifth, golden, notebook incorporates the themes and characters of the rest. It is written collaboratively by Anna and Saul Green, whose character seems mixed from yellow notebook story ideas and blue notebook incarnations of them. In the transformative symbiosis between Anna and Saul, the two blur together, then separate, like Anna and Molly at the end of the novel: "The two women kissed and separated" (p. 635).

The first notebook entries following the "Free Women" sections come from the black notebook. The black notebook looks back on Anna's sojourn in Africa during

World War II, the novel she wrote about this time, and her encounters with the literary establishment. *Frontiers of War* portrayed a white British airman in a tragic affair with a married black African woman that ends with the woman's prostitution and the man's going off to battle. Contrasted with this novel, which Anna now rejects because of its nostalgic attraction to death, are revisions proposed by filmmakers and publishers who want to sweeten and whiten the story. Anna then details the events that inspired the novel. These memories center on the Mashopi Hotel, a bastion of Britishness in tropical Central Africa during the war. There men from the Royal Air Force gather with African white leftists and displaced Europeans such as the doctrinaire German Communist Willi. They flirt and argue about politics. A white trade unionist anguishes over his clandestine affair with the hotel cook's wife. Meanwhile, the upper-class British airman Paul Blackenhurst infuriates the white woman hotelkeeper by chatting amiably with Jackson, the black cook. She fires the cook, dispersing his family, including the mixed-race "cuckoo" born of the wife's affair (p. 124). Thus, while the white leftists talk about bringing down the color bar, they make life worse for the only black Africans they contact. Racist Central Africa supports England's distant anti-Nazi struggle, but "the black masses hadn't begun to stir," and the white leftists are completely cut off from those black nationalists who will later win independence from Britain (p. 65).

In her *African Stories*, Lessing draws incisive portraits of white colonials and more stereotyped, though sympathetic, black characters. In *The Golden Notebook* she chooses not to invade blacks' privacy by attempting to describe their inner life. Jackson the cook appears briefly, while his wife Marie remains silent and off-scene, corroborating the Soviet criticism of Anna's novel that its "representative" black woman "remains shadowy, undeveloped, unsatisfying" (p. 426). For Anna, the virtuous Mr Mathlong represents the ideal black African political leader. However, she cannot imagine his thoughts, whereas in mad moments she does project herself into the paranoid psyche of the future dictator Charlie Themba.

One break from the black notebook's political conversations at the Mashopi Hotel is the scene in the African bush where the white visitors shoot birds for a pigeon pie. Here a lush, teeming nature reverberates with the novel's color symbolism. "A million white butterflies" delight the eyes, though they are as doomed as the white airman Paul Blackenhurst or the emotionally dead "unattainable beauty" Maryrose (pp. 397, 79). Later, when Anna struggles with the "burden of re-creating order out of the chaos" of her life, she describes her memory and invention joining in an "orderless dance, like the dance of the white butterflies" (p. 591). The African landscape also displays hordes of copulating grasshoppers that comically mirror the white characters' erotic pairings, while colonies of industrious black ants, like the black population, are attacked by their imperialists, the anteaters. Nature's cycles of sex and death appear unfazed by human actions, though Paul accurately prophesies the eventual transformation of the bush into cheap housing for newly independent Africans. Anna says that her novel based on these African experiences addresses "the colour problem" but that "the emotion it came out of was something frightening, the unhealthy, feverish illicit excitement of wartime, a lying nostalgia, a longing for license, for freedom, for the jungle, for formlessness" (p. 61). This formulation shows Anna's conflation of the African "jungle" with "freedom," "formlessness," and death (p. 61).

Though sometimes allegorizing Africa, *The Golden Notebook* insists on its status as a historical document chronicling the British place in European history in the 1940s and 1950s. Anna dates her diary entries and tries to grasp the significance of historical events, especially in 1956 and 1957, in her obsessive newspaper clippings about atomic bomb tests, national independence movements, Communist victories, and Stalinist atrocities. The red notebook addresses the ideology of this period through the characters' waning beliefs in Communism, although they retain their skepticism toward free enterprise and their frustrated idealism. Maryrose is disconsolate because "only a few months ago we believed that the world was going to change and everything was going to be beautiful and now we know it won't" (p. 125). Though the characters in the novel grow cynical about both establishment and left politics, they still believe that good people strive toward a better social organization. Anna wistfully admires selfless Comrade Jack, who dedicates his life to the improvement of humanity despite his party's corruption. In a recurrent metaphor, Ella's psychiatrist lover Paul Tanner says, "we are both boulder-pushers" against human ignorance and social injustice (p. 199). Similarly, Anna tells Tommy she believes that in every century "A well of faith fills up, and there's an enormous heave forward in one country or another, and that's a forward movement for the whole world. Because it's an act of imagination . . . . the dream gets stronger" (p. 263). This conversation immediately precedes Tommy's suicide attempt.

Unlike Christina Stead's *I'm Dying Laughing* (1987) or Lessing's own *A Ripple From the Storm* (1958), *The Golden Notebook* describes little of internal Communist maneuvering. The only time the characters engage in Communist organizing is when Anna does electoral canvassing in a working-class neighborhood. She finds many lonely women but hardly any Communist voters – a relief because the Communists don't really want to split the Labour Party vote. The sense of a greater mission permeates the novel, even when belief in its achievement is lost. Yet most of the Communists in the novel are lying or deceived, naively believing in good Papa Stalin and regurgitating socialist realist critiques of Anna's writing. In a prefiguring of the feminist belief that the personal is political, Anna claims, "If Marxism means anything, it means that a little novel about the emotions should reflect 'what's real' since the emotions are a function and product of a society" (p. 41). Although Lessing herself was active during the 1950s in left journalism and anti-nuclear protests, Anna grows discouraged with organized politics and turns increasingly inward, striving to understand rather than to change history. Communism in *The Golden Notebook* thus becomes simultaneously a set of false beliefs, a hypocritical facade over Stalinist anti-Semitism and butchery, and a repository of social ideals. In 1993 Lessing claimed that Communism began "as a genuine dream for a better world" and that the "remarkable vitality" of the novel sprang from the "energy of conflict. I was writing my way out of one set of ideas, even out of a way of life, but that is not what I thought while I was doing it" (p. ix).

The Red and the Black of Anna's notebooks, like much of European nineteenth-century fiction, place individual destinies in contexts of national upheaval where ideas are transformed by events and events by ideas. These notebooks dominate the earlier portions of *The Golden Notebook*, but they become less salient as the novel progresses. In the later yellow, blue, and golden notebooks, the novel moves from historical realism to modernist interiority in its focus on Anna as a writer who analyzes sexual and emotional relations between women and men.

Lessing early expressed annoyance that "the sex war" was the only theme originally noticed in the novel (p. xii). The book became enormously popular, especially among American women during the Women's Liberation Movement of the 1960s and 1970s, owing to its "filter which is a woman's way of looking at life" (p. xvi). As Lessing noted in 1971, "This book was written as if the attitudes that have been created by the Women's Liberation Movement already existed" (p. xiv). She said then that most women were "cowards" because they had been "semi-slaves for so long," while claiming that "the whole world is being shaken into a new pattern" that will make the "aims of Women's Liberation . . . look very small and quaint" (p. xiii). Anna and Molly call themselves "free women" largely because of their sexual autonomy. (Although the novel does not mention it, the greater accessibility of birth control at the time aids this freedom.) Yet Anna's happy sexual relationships are described only briefly, and then she attributes her happiness as much to naivety as to emotional compatibility. For example, after her one-night stand with the previously homosexual Paul Blackenhurst, she exclaims, "I have never, in all my life, been so desperately and wildly and painfully happy" (p. 142). This encounter is immediately followed by hostile sex with Anna's normally cool partner Willi. Even with the one great love of her life, Michael, their sexual harmony is overshadowed by jealousy. With Saul in the golden notebook, Anna almost comically recapitulates this downward emotional progression: "I lay on the bed, happy. Being happy, the joy that filled me then was stronger than all the misery and the madness in the world, or so I felt it. But then the happiness began to leak away . . ." (p. 568). Ella's affairs in the yellow notebook exaggerate the masochistic, passive, dependent, and deluded aspects of Anna's relationships. There Ella says she is "completely happy" with her lover Paul Tanner, but this happiness requires that she "drifted along on a soft tide of not-thinking" (p. 189). Lessing doesn't show men as thinking more deeply, but simply as less emotionally committed. The "real" men in the novel are compulsive philanderers, while other men are unmanned or unmanly, like the sexually dysfunctional capitalist Richard or the caricatured gay couple Ivor and Ronnie (p. 375).

Despite Lessing's dismissals of feminism, which are perhaps legacies of Communist scorn for bourgeois women's movements, *The Golden Notebook* fits many feminist values and has been hailed as a feminist novel (Greene 1994: 98). From this perspective, the book breaks new ground in portraying the complex subjectivity of a strong, positive, female main character who is a writer, an intellectual, and a mother, and who acknowledges her body, her desires, and her anxieties. Feminist readers appreciate the friendship between Anna and Molly, their sexual frankness, economic independence, and understanding of women's subordination. Saul becomes Anna's "brother" because at least he can recognize that he enjoys a "society where women are second-class citizens" and because he can "name" and understand her feelings (pp. 612, 577). In their period of mutual breakdown, Saul defines himself through his country, the United States, while Anna becomes "the position of women in our time" (p. 553). The breakthrough they experience consists in understanding, not changing, their stereotyped national and gendered behavior, though the novel implies that by reaching the lowest point of individual madness and dissolution, the characters are ready for reintegration at a higher level. Anna and Molly know that women isolated as housewives and mothers are often miserable, suffering "the problem that has no name," as Betty Friedan would describe it in *The Feminine Mystique* (1963), but which Anna calls "the housewife's disease," "the woman's emotion: resentment against injustice, an impersonal poison" (Friedan 1963: 11; Lessing 1999: 318). Yet Anna also internalizes the misogyny around her: she dislikes women for "not thinking when it suits us" (p. 465). As "Free Women," Anna and Molly regularly sleep with married men and share the men's disregard for their wives. Anna tells Richard that his callous treatment of Marion has turned her into a miserable alcoholic, although Lessing makes the simpering, whining, and politically naive character more contemptible than sympathetic. In the yellow notebook, Ella begins by feeling superior to her lover's wife but later envies her. Finally she realizes that "the shadow of the third" in this triangle is not the neglected wife at all but rather a Jungian projection, "her own shadow, everything she is not" (p. 196). And since Ella is in some sense Anna's shadow side, it makes sense that Anna titles her incomplete novel about Ella "The Shadow of the Third" (p. 429).

The blue notebook of Anna's diaries records her venture into psychoanalysis and also her political and sexual relations, but it also continues the theme of the writer developed throughout the book and especially in the yellow notebook. The yellow notebook includes Anna's stories about Ella while demonstrating the writer's choices in character, plot, and point of view, most obviously when it ceases continuous narrative and instead consists of numbered story ideas about heterosexual relations. These numbers appear parenthetically in the blue notebook, where they explain the situations that gave rise to the story ideas or show how the stories might be written. The single day that Anna chooses to chronicle in her blue notebook is September 16, 1954. It begins with the attempt "to write down, as truthfully as I can, every stage of a day" but ends illustrating the incommensurability of art and life and the inevitable fractures in subjectivity (p. 316): "who is that Anna who will read what I will write?" (p. 335). On this day she starts her menstrual period and worries about her irritability, her moods, and her "bad smells" (p. 325). She reflects on "a major problem of literary style, of tact," like that faced by James Joyce describing "his man in the act of defecating" (p. 325). Anna's literary concern about "being truthful in writing (which is being truthful about oneself)" blends into her concerns about the lies in the Communist Party and her own erotic illusions (p. 325). Cooking for her lover Michael makes her happy, but "Being happy is a lie. . . . The fight with my various forms of dissatisfaction tires me; but I know this is not a personal fight" (pp. 348–9); rather, it is one common to women. The diary account is written in a "flowing and untidy" handwriting, she reports, like the flow of her body, but then she judges her account "a failure as usual" (p. 351). The day she records is the day she leaves the Communist Party and the day her long-term lover breaks off their affair, so that the menstruation works symbolically with these events as an emblem of sterility, the loss at once of red blood, Red beliefs, and a fruitful sexual relationship.

In Lessing's first autobiographical novel, her protagonist Martha Quest defines herself through antagonism to her mother. In *The Golden Notebook*, an "impossible, bullying, embarrassing mother" is assigned to another character, Maryrose (p. 98). Anna's mother is long dead, and Anna's daughterly efforts at autonomy are played out against maternal figures who are easy to outgrow: her older friend Molly, her analyst Mother Sugar, and Ella's editor Patricia Brent, all women envious of the writer's creative powers. Thus Anna's decision in "Free Women" not to write more fiction can be seen as an adolescent victory in thwarting such maternal desires. Anna may also be treating her readers as an adolescent does her parents, protecting her sense of self by never giving a straightforward account of her affairs. Anna's decision in "Free Women" not to write more fiction can be read as a self-defeating anticlimax, or, conversely, as a demonstration of the character's difference from her successful author. The day Anna completes her analysis with Mother Sugar in the blue notebook is April 23, 1954 (p. 241). Auspiciously enough, this is Shakespeare's birthday, a promise that this Anna will write again. None of the incarnations of Anna is a reliable narrator, and some of the reader's pleasure in the novel comes from noting its echoes and discrepancies and solving its puzzles.

If the novel sometimes acts like a rebellious adolescent, however, it also sympathizes with the trials faced by single mothers. It records the ambivalence conventionally simplified into either sentimentality or misogynous anti-Mommism. Anna professes devotion to her young daughter Janet but finds her boring: "no more than a charming, conventionally intelligent little girl" (p. 518). Anna assumes she understands Janet's emotions as echoes of her own, but Janet's character remains undeveloped, as does the relationship between mother and child. Anna recreates Janet's days in bedtime stories, but Janet prefers to see herself mirrored as the spunky heroine of a girls' school novel. Anna admits she has "no time for people who haven't experimented with themselves" (p. 518), and when Janet does go away to school, Anna feels relieved: "An Anna is coming to life that died when Janet was born" (p. 523).

Tommy, the pivotal figure in "Free Women's" plot, is both another double for Anna, criticizing her divisions and her diaries, and, like Janet, an alienated child eager for a conformity that Anna condemns. Although he seems little more than a confused young man, Anna describes him in portentous terms: "his blunt dark obstinate face was twisted into a mask of smiling spite" (p. 249). He thus becomes an example of that destructive but potentially creative "joy in spite" that Anna later recognizes in herself (p. 456). Tommy is close to three mother figures in "Free Women": his mother Molly, Anna, and his stepmother Marion. He attempts suicide, like the hero of Ella's novel. Instead of killing himself, however, he is stricken blind, ironically incarnating the incestuous Oedipus. After his injury, he inhabits his mother's house like an ominous oracle, "dominating it, conscious of everything that went on in it, a blind but all-conscious presence" (p. 361). Here, too, he resembles Anna, who claims that when she is writing, "I seem to have some awful second sight" (p. 546).

The Golden Notebook both relies on and rejects Freudian and Jungian psychologies. The Jungian Mrs Marks, nicknamed Mother Sugar for her complacent faith in art, teaches Anna to control her dreams, turning to creativity the malevolent, sado-masochistic power of "joy in spite" that appears in her fantasies as an old dwarf or bejeweled crocodile (p. 457). "Joy in spite" might also be seen as the death instinct that Freud after World War I decided was as basic to human nature as sexual desire. The characters in *The Golden Notebook* believe Freud's theories. The men interpret their psyches through Oedipal dynamics, which separate desirable young women from maternal and therefore undesirable wives, whom they accuse of trying to castrate them. The lowest point of the relationship between Saul and Anna is reached when he curls into her like a baby seeking his mother and declares "Ise a good boy" (p. 611). Anna heightens the psychological drama of "Free Women" by converting the married Tommy of the blue notebook into "Free Women"'s repulsive, quasi-incestuous blind seer. And, figuratively at least, Lessing does "castrate" many of her male characters by making them sexually impotent. More literally, she kills airman Paul Blackenhurst when he walks into an airplane propeller: "His legs were cut off just below the crutch and he died at once" (p. 75).

Ella writes a novel about a man who doesn't realize he has decided to commit suicide until he does so – one example of the Freudian death wish, and also an indication of *The Golden Notebook's* relationship to another European ideology of the mid-twentieth century, existentialism. Existentialists such as Albert Camus and Jean-Paul Sartre pondered how one could live freely and why one should live at all. In *The Second Sex,* the pioneering existentialist feminist Simone de Beauvoir foreshadows Lessing in showing the dire effects that male-dominated society has on women's self-esteem. Beauvoir also shares Lessing's unease at the way women get trapped by love in comparison with men's rational disengagement. In this context, *The Golden Notebook* can be read as an existentialist novel that asks its characters to choose freedom over both conformity and attachment. The word "free" echoes constantly throughout the book, from political slogans to Anna's birth name, "Freeman," to Anna's and Molly's insistence that they are new social phenomena, "Free Women," who can use men's language, share their sexual adventures, and flout bourgeois marriage. The title "Free Women" is thus both ironic and self-congratulatory, while the novella skewers social and psychological limitations on women's freedom. Whereas Anna gives up her literary career in "Free Women", however, the author of *The Golden Notebook* revels in her freedom to critique social pieties and revise literary forms.

Lessing is a notoriously uneven writer. *The Golden Notebook* contains diverse passages of beauty and power, for example those describing the African bush or the mutual breakdown of Saul and Anna. These passages contrast with perfunctory pastiches and dull denunciations of corrupt publishing practices. Compared to the style of other great novelists, Lessing's prose is unusually flat, yet she is fascinated by the power of language. Like the poststructuralists, she emphasizes its slipperiness and the non-congruence of names and things. Her characters overlap, often exchanging names, so that, for example, Michael is the name of Anna's lover and also of Ella's son. Lessing also shares with poststructuralist thought a tendency to see subjectivity as fluid and multiple for each person both over time and at the same time, and she implies a performative perspective on character as evoked by social circumstances rather than as emanating from within a person's essence. Anna also dwells on such poststructuralist themes as the unreliability of memory, the contingencies of history, and the failure of the totalizing grand narratives of Communism, free enterprise, democracy, or psychoanalysis. The novel thus becomes "the history of an effort to understand history and the fiction of the effort to understand fiction" (Gardiner 1989: 144).

One of the jokes of *The Golden Notebook* is that Anna in "Free Women" suffers from writer's block while scribbling away in the notebooks, including the yellow notebook in which her surrogate Ella completes a novel. The notebooks contain a medley of literary genres and parodies of contemporary writing styles, from women's magazine gush to macho prose, Communist realism, and the phoney exoticism of "Blood on the banana leaves" (p. 421). These parodies are heavy-handed, though they emphasize Anna's attention to language. Language cannot become a mere formal system for her because her horror of Communist lies underscores the value of truth. Yet the truth of experience escapes language. She believes that the "fragmentation of everything" is connected to "the thinning of language against the density of our experience" (p. 288). Perhaps, she thinks, film can transmit experience better, and she pictures her unconscious mind as a series of films, even though she rejects all proposals to turn her book into an actual movie.

Like much of Lessing's fiction, *The Golden Notebook* is clearly autobiographical. For example, Anna says she will write a psychological play featuring a tiger, and Lessing simultaneously produces *Play with a Tiger* (Klein 2000: 186). She insists that she has generalized the facts of her past to depict the emotions of an era, but she also feeds the biographical impulse by naming some names and withholding others. Her autobiographies confirm that Saul Green was modeled on the American leftist novelist Clancy Sigal, whose own novel about their affair is *The Secret Defector* (1992). Lessing describes her friend Joan Rodker and Joan's son Ernest Rodker as the people on whom Molly and Tommy are roughly based. However, Anna, unlike Lessing, is British by birth, has only one child, and is less politically active than her author.

Lessing has been commenting ambivalently on *The Golden Notebook* and its success for decades. In 1993 she said, "I was writing my way out of one set of ideas, even out of a way of life, but that is not what I thought while I was doing it. Inside that tight framework is an effervesence" (p. ix). She still describes the book as a "failure" because it did not change people's "tendency to think like computers"

(Lessing 1997: 338). Although this language of "failure" recalls Lessing's presumably outgrown Communist illusions about a literature that can transform the world, it is precisely its "failure" of closure that makes the novel a success for many readers today. Several books help teachers and students understand the novel (Singleton 1977; Kaplan and Rose 1989; Pickering 1990). While earlier criticism focused on the structure of the novel and its relationship to feminism (Rubenstein 1979; Draine 1983; Schweickart 1985; Sprague 1987; Sprague and Tiger 1988; Gardiner 1989; Greene 1994), more recent approaches concern such issues as Lessing's relationship to race and national identity, to the literary tradition, and to spiritual transformation (Sprague 1990, Saxton and Tobin 1994, Yelin 1998, Perrakis 1999). *Doris Lessing Studies*, formerly the *Doris Lessing Newsletter*, is a periodical dedicated entirely to Lessing's work.

In *The Golden Notebook* Lessing changes the narrative structure of the woman's novel, working against the traditional marriage plot and allowing Anna an open-ended and self-critical quest (DuPlessis 1985). Self-centered and generous, opinionated and open-minded, she is one of the major characters of twentieth-century literature. When she claims, "yet I am incapable of writing the only kind of novel which interests me: a book powered with an intellectual or moral passion strong enough to create order, to create a new way of looking at life," the reader may well feel that *The Golden Notebook* succeeds where Anna failed, even when the order created is the recognition of the collapse of order (1999: 59). The novel works as a brilliant ensemble, a powerful identificatory experience for many readers, a record of a period of history, an intellectual puzzle, and a very satisfying read – a whole marvellously greater than the sum of its parts.

REFERENCES AND FURTHER READING

Draine, B. (1983) *Substance under Pressure: Artistic Coherence and Evolving Form in the Novels of Doris Lessing*. Madison: University of Wisconsin Press.

DuPlessis, R. (1985) *Writing Beyond the Ending: Narrative Strategies of 20th-Century Women Writers*. Bloomington: Indiana University Press.

Friedan, B. (1963) *The Feminine Mystique*. New York: Dell.

Gardiner, J. K. (1989) *Rhys, Stead, Lessing, and the Politics of Empathy*. Bloomington: Indiana University Press.

Greene, Gayle (1994) *Doris Lessing: The Poetics of Change*. Ann Arbor: University of Michigan Press.

Kaplan, C. and Rose, E. C. (eds.) (1989) *Approaches to Teaching Lessing's "The Golden Notebook."*

New York: Modern Language Association of America.

Klein, C. (2000) *Doris Lessing: A Biography*. London: Duckworth.

Lessing, D. (1965) *African Stories*. New York: Popular Library.

—— (1997) *Walking in the Shade: Volume Two of My Autobiography, 1949 to 1962*. New York: HarperCollins.

—— (1999) *The Golden Notebook* (including "Introduction 1993" and "Introduction 1971"). New York: HarperCollins.

Perrakis, P. S. (ed.) (1999) *Spiritual Exploration in the Works of Doris Lessing*. Westport, CT and London: Greenwood.

Pickering, J. (1990) *Understanding Doris Lessing*. Columbia: University of South Carolina Press.

Pratt, A. and Dembo, L. S. (eds.) (1974) *Doris Lessing: Critical Studies*. Madison: University of Wisconsin Press.

Rubenstein, Roberta (1979) *The Novelistic Vision of Doris Lessing: Breaking the Forms of Consciousness*. Urbana: University of Illinois Press.

Saxton, R. and Tobin, J. (eds.) (1994) *Woolf and Lessing: Breaking the Mold*. New York: St Martin's Press.

Schweickart, P. (1985) "Reading a wordless statement: the structure of Doris Lessing's *The Golden Notebook*," *Modern Fiction Studies*, 31/2 (Summer): 263–79.

Sigal, C. (1992a) " 'You can't do it!' I shouted, 'Oh, can't I?' she shouted back," *New York Times Book Review*, April 12: 13–14.

——(1992b) *The Secret Defector*. New York: HarperCollins.

Singleton, M. A. (1977) *The City and the Veld: The Fiction of Doris Lessing*. Lewisburg, PA: Bucknell University Press.

Sprague, C. (1987) *Rereading Doris Lessing: Narrative Patterns of Doubling and Repetition*. Chapel Hill and London: University of North Carolina Press.

——(ed.) (1990) *In Pursuit of Doris Lessing: Nine Nations Reading*. New York: St Martin's Press.

Sprague, C. and Tiger, V. (eds.) (1988) *Critical Essays on Doris Lessing*. Boston: G. K. Hall.

Taylor, J. (ed.) (1982) *Notebooks/ Memoirs/ Archives: Reading and Rereading Doris Lessing*. London: Routledge and Kegan Paul.

Yelin, L. (1998) *From the Margins of Empire: Christina Stead, Doris Lessing, Nadine Gordimer*. Ithaca and London: Cornell University Press.

28

Jean Rhys's *Wide Sargasso Sea*

John J. Su

Jean Rhys's critical rewriting of Charlotte Brontë's *Jane Eyre* (1847) has become a canonical text of postcolonial studies; it has also figured significantly within scholarly debates over feminism and literary modernism. Yet the status *Wide Sargasso Sea* currently enjoys could hardly have been foreseen when it was first published in 1966. It was written by an author whose four earlier novels had long since fallen out of print; the most recent of them was published in 1939. Rhys herself had fallen into such obscurity that when actor Selma Vaz Dias sought to locate her in the late 1940s in order to get permission to perform a dramatic adaptation of her novel *Good Morning, Midnight* for BBC radio, it was necessary to publish an open advertisement in newspapers.

The hundreds of books, dissertations, and scholarly articles that have been produced about Rhys since the publication of *Wide Sargasso Sea*, however, testify to the impact the novel has had. Embraced and repudiated in turn by theorists of postcolonialism, feminism, and modernism, the novel and its author continue to be sources of fierce critical debates. On the one hand, *Wide Sargasso Sea* has become emblematic of postwar literary critiques of Victorian social mores and British colonial policies. By giving voice to the silenced Bertha Mason, the "madwoman in the attic" and first wife of Rochester in *Jane Eyre*, Rhys succeeds in "breaking the master narrative" of patriarchal and imperialist Englishness, according to Ellen G. Friedman (1989: 117). On the other hand, Rhys's novel has been criticized for its depictions of Afro-Caribbean populations, and Veronica Gregg condemns its "racialist usurpation" of their voices and culture (1995: 114). The wide range of interpretations that Rhys's work provokes has led Barbadian poet and critic Kamau Braithwaite to describe her as "the Helen of our wars," a figure whose work provides the grounds on which broader ideological battles are waged among British and Caribbean scholars (1995: 69).

Rhys's own liminal status as a Dominican-born Creole whose adult life was spent in Paris, Vienna, and England defies easy categorization, and her work has likewise frustrated definition. The ambiguities of identification are made explicitly apparent in the first lines of *Wide Sargasso Sea*, as the narrator notes: "They say when trouble comes close ranks, and so the white people did. But we were not in their ranks" (1966: 17). Her statement attests to a moment of dis-identification, as Antoinette Cosway Mason discovers that her European ancestry does not guarantee her whiteness, as she previously assumed. Birthplace and social class figure in definitions of race as much as skin color, and Antoinette and her fellow Creoles are considered racially "impure" for being born and raised outside of Britain. Nor are the Creoles accepted by the Afro-Caribbean populations, for Creoles were slave-owners before the Emancipation Act was passed in 1834. As a girl, Antoinette painfully learns that her feelings of attachment to a black playmate, Tia, are not reciprocated. After Antoinette's childhood home is set ablaze by rioting former slaves, Antoinette flees to Tia rather than joining her own parents and family. Longing to identify with Tia, Antoinette fantasizes, "I will live with Tia and I will be like her" (p. 45). Yet Tia responds by throwing a stone at Antoinette as Tia's mother looks on approvingly.

The struggle for self-identification in the novel foregrounds the crucial epistemological implications of identity categories, and suggests that debates over how to label *Wide Sargasso Sea* are not merely abstract academic concerns but efforts to address basic issues about how human experience is interpreted. The identity categories with which Antoinette and Tia have been raised shape the ways in which they can understand their interactions with each other. When Antoinette is frustrated with her playmate during a game and applies to her the term she has been taught, "cheating nigger," this act transforms their relationship. The two girls subsequently avoid each other, and their past experiences are recast in terms of prejudicial racial categories. Tia responds by calling Antoinette a "white nigger," further limiting the possibility for them to discover common ground. Hence, both are startled when they later experience a moment of identification with each other. After Tia hits Antoinette with a stone, they sense commonality, not difference: "I looked at her face and I saw her face crumple up as she began to cry," Antoinette notes. "We stared at each other, blood on my face, tears on hers. It was as if I saw myself. Like in a looking-glass" (p. 45). Momentarily separated from her parents and their interpretations of Afro-Caribbeans, Antoinette becomes capable of identifying with Tia and thereby knowing her in a way that was not previously possible.

The crucial implication here is that by redefining identity and identity categories individuals can learn to perceive themselves and their surroundings differently. It is this recognition that motivates Rhys to rename Bertha Mason in her novel. According to *Wide Sargasso Sea*, Antoinette Cosway is the "true" name of the woman who becomes Rochester's first wife. The name Mason was given to her by her stepfather after her mother remarries; the name Bertha was imposed on her by her husband Rochester. Antoinette's struggle to retain her name is desperate because husband and wife alike recognize that the terms of their relationship will be shaped by the result. Indeed, Antoinette more self-consciously recognizes the consequences of Rochester's actions than he does. She likens his renaming of her to the local form of voodoo, obeah, practiced by Afro-Caribbeans: "Bertha is not my name. You are trying to make me into something else, calling me by another name. I know, that's obeah too" (p. 147). Changing her name will "make [her] into something else" because her identity is the product of her experiences and the ways in which she and others interpret them. This shift in names away from the French-influenced Creole "Antoin-ette" to the English "Bertha" indicates how Rochester wishes to redefine who she is. His efforts are apparent throughout Part Two of *Wide Sargasso Sea*, in which he is the primary narrator. The re-categorization of her *vis-à-vis* Englishness emphasizes her racial "impurity," her inability to be "truly" English and, therefore, a legitimate wife. From his very first description of her, he contests her purported English ancestry, noting her "[l]ong, sad, dark alien eyes" (p. 67). By recasting her in terms of his own standards and identity categories, he effaces her past and her efforts to define herself. This erasure of her past, according to Rhys, enables him to define how she is perceived by others; and ultimately he will portray her as insane in order to rationalize imprisoning her in the attic of Thornfield Hall.

Rhys's critique of *Jane Eyre*, then, targets the novel's unwillingness to grant Bertha Mason the same right of self-representation that Jane herself enjoys. Indeed, it is intriguing that a novel so preoccupied with the struggle for women to find a voice within patriarchal Victorian society would find it unnecessary ever to quote directly Rochester's first wife. From the first pages of Brontë's novel, Jane is acutely aware of human cruelty and the restraints placed upon her own freedom. She invokes the language of slavery and tyranny to describe her situation, referring to herself as a "rebel slave" of a different "race" from her adoptive family, the Reeds (1985: 44, 48). She refers to John Reed, Mrs Reed's eldest son, as a "slave-driver" and a "tyrant" (p. 43). Yet, despite her feelings of pity for Bertha Mason, Jane seeks neither to converse with her nor to question Rochester's descriptions of her past. As a result, characterizations of Bertha's past come to readers thirdhand. Rochester alone narrates Bertha's past, a narrative that is filtered in turn through Jane's own narration. Rochester rationalizes his authority over her by means of a set of descriptions that undermine Bertha's capacity and right to self-representation. Rochester insists that Bertha Mason is incapable of language, and the animalistic metaphors with which he describes Bertha foreclose any efforts Jane might make to reach out to her. Indeed, when Rochester finally takes Jane to see Bertha Mason, Jane imitates Rochester's characterization of his first wife, referring to her as a "clothed hyena" (p. 321). Rochester further insists that his wife is insane, and that she therefore lacks the rational faculties to describe her experiences in her own terms. Thus, Bertha Mason's violence toward those around her appears to lack rational motivation, the result of a violent animal nature rather than a legitimate response to her imprisonment.

By casting Rochester's first wife as the initial narrator of *Wide Sargasso Sea*, Rhys provides a literary space for describing Bertha Mason's history in her own terms. This intention is explicitly stated in Rhys's correspondence during the 1950s and 1960s. In a letter to Selma Vaz Dias, for example, Rhys laments the absence of Bertha's voice in Brontë's novel. "[Bertha is] necessary to the plot," Rhys writes, "but always she shrieks, howls, laughs horribly, attacks all and sundry – *offstage*. For me (and for you I hope) she must be right *on stage*" (1984: 156). By providing the "lost history" of Bertha Mason, Rhys provides a rationale for understanding her violent behavior. According to this account, she is seduced by the money-obsessed Rochester, deceived by her stepbrother Richard Mason, and cruelly abandoned to a life of misery and loneliness in the attic of Thornfield Hall. When perceived from this perspective, even Bertha Mason's most irrational actions demonstrate a sad though compelling logic. In *Jane Eyre*, Bertha sets Thornfield Hall ablaze and throws herself to her death from the rooftop out of pure self-destructive spite toward Rochester. Despite his valiant attempt to rescue her from the burning house, Rochester cannot prevent her death, though he will certainly benefit from it; Bertha's suicide removes the final obstacle to his marriage to Jane. In *Wide Sargasso Sea*, by contrast, Antoinette's apparent suicide leap is motivated by the fantasy of restored communion with her lost past. Looking down from the rooftop of Thornfield Hall, Antoinette perceives an image of Tia and her childhood home reflected in the garden pool. Her leap, then, represents an effort to rejoin her sometime childhood friend, to return to the moment before she forever transformed their relationship by her use of the racial epithet; indeed, she fantasizes experiencing a sense of community she never felt before – a community untainted by prejudicial racial categories. If Antoinette's action is directed toward realizing an impossible fantasy, it is nonetheless neither unmotivated nor the product of malice.

Rhys's novel does not simply provide an alternative explanation for the motivations behind Bertha Mason's actions; rather, it recasts how readers can interpret Brontë's novel. For the revelation of Bertha's "true" name represents only the most salient example of Rhys drawing attention to gaps in Jane Eyre's narrative. Rochester's attitude of benevolent endurance toward his first wife appears, in light of *Wide Sargasso Sea*, to be a more sinister effort to control the woman from whom his fortune derives. The lucidity and thoughtfulness of Antoinette's narrative further undermine Rochester's accusations of his wife's insanity. The absence of any medical basis for his accusation, not to mention his curious unwillingness to seek out a "cure" for her, reminds readers that applying the category of insanity to women has historically been a means of enforcing cultural and religious values on them as much as a diagnosis of physiological or psychic pathology. Simply by casting her actions as irrational, Rochester can deny to Bertha the right to participate in civil society. And the absence of any sustained interrogation of Rochester's actions by Jane casts doubt on her faith both in him and in the Christian Victorian society to which she so desperately wishes to belong. For in the process of cementing her role within this society, Jane must ultimately relinquish her narrative voice. The final words of the novel are not her own, but a quotation from a letter sent by St John Rivers, Christian missionary to India: "Daily He announces more distinctly, 'Surely I come quickly!' and hourly I more eagerly respond, 'Amen; even so, come, Lord Jesus!'" (Brontë 2003: 502).

St John's acquiescence to the benevolence and mercy of divine authority becomes a model not only for his religious vocation but also for her role as a British subject, who must learn to acquiesce to purportedly benevolent social strictures in ways she never has previously. Thus, Jane herself can be read as suffering in a much less extreme way from the same patriarchal system that allowed Bertha to be imprisoned in the attic of Thornfield Hall.

Rhys's engagement with Victorian social and cultural mores in *Wide Sargasso Sea* anticipates the central theoretical and philosophical concerns that increasingly pre-occupy contemporary British literature toward the end of the twentieth century. The so-called "neo-Victorian" novels of A. S. Byatt, Peter Ackroyd, John Fowles, and others arise from a sense that engagement with the Victorian past is crucial to the redefinition of British national identity. Such literary texts depart from the modernist tendency to reject all things Victorian. Whereas the protagonists of Joseph Conrad, Ford Madox Ford, and Virginia Woolf struggle against static and even claustrophobic social roles inherited from the nineteenth century, protagonists in postwar British novels more typically turn to the past as a source for guidance and meaning. In A. S. Byatt's *Possession* (1990), for example, the characters' fascination with Victorian heritage arises out of their profound disappointment with the unimaginative and often draconian policies of Thatcherite Britain and the willingness of government officials to subject national heritage to the whims of "Market Forces" (1991: 431). Only after literary scholars Roland Michell and Maud Bailey begin to pattern their own lives in terms of the Victorian poets they study are they able to experience a mutually satisfying romance. This is not to suggest that neo-Victorian novels such as *Possession* promote an uncritical endorsement of Victorian ideals. Though Byatt's protagonists imitate the romance plot established by the Victorian poets for almost the entirety of the novel, they ultimately diverge from it in search of "a modern way" to balance professional and personal demands (p. 550); Fowles's narrator in *The French Lieutenant's Woman* (1969) is obsessed with locating the "moment [that] overcame the age," the moment when the modern age emerges from the Victorian past (1970: 199). Yet these novels share Rhys's sense that engagement with the Victorian era and Victorian writings is crucial to addressing present social ills.

While Rhys does not employ the elaborate pastiche of Victorian writing styles characteristic of many neo-Victorian literary texts, she does embody in Antoinette and Rochester attributes that she associates with the Victorian era more broadly. Antoinette possesses many of Jane Eyre's most positive traits, including courage, the desire for emancipation, and an eagerness to explore the world. At the same time, Rhys is clearly critical of nineteenth-century ideas about positivism and the mastery of the natural world through empirical inquiry, insisting that such notions enable Rochester to rationalize his abominable behavior toward Bertha Mason. From the moment of his arrival in the Caribbean, Rochester demonstrates a keen interest in acquiring knowledge about the island and its inhabitants. His first spoken words are a question about the historical source of the name of the village, Massacre. Rochester poses similar questions throughout his narrative, and he reads voraciously in an effort to gain specifically western, empirical forms of knowledge about cultural practices such as obeah. Rochester believes that such knowledge is crucial to controlling his environment. This is apparent as he becomes obsessed with the idea that the island contains a "secret," knowledge that is being deliberately kept from him. "What I see is nothing – I want what it *hides* – that is not nothing," he thinks to himself (Rhys 1966: 87). Knowledge here is intimately linked with possession; to learn about the unknown, for Rochester, is to gain power over it. And this leads to his irrational possessiveness of Antoinette after he associates her with the secret of the island. In one of his most terrifying reflections, Rochester insists: "She's mad but *mine, mine*" (p. 166). He objectifies not only his surroundings but even his wife.

Rochester's failure to acquire the knowledge he desires points to Rhys's critique of positivism more generally. For if Rochester continually tries to acquire knowledge about the island, his inquiries consistently fail. He never learns of the event to which "Massacre" refers; he never discovers the "secret" of the island. Perhaps more significantly, he comes to realize that he lacks crucial knowledge about himself and his own psychology. At several moments he refers to "blanks in my mind that cannot be filled up" (p. 76). These "blanks" refer to psychically repressed knowledge about his motivations and actions, and the recognition of them points to the limits of positivism and its purported goal of acquiring objective, transparent knowledge. As Rhys makes clear, Rochester's pursuit of knowledge is guided by his desires, and these desires define what kinds of knowledge are available to him and how he interprets his surroundings. Rochester fails to sustain even the more modest claim that his method of acquiring knowledge produces more objectively accurate results than Antoinette's. In an exchange between the two, Rochester and Antoinette take turns claiming that their own homeland is real and the other person's – England or the West Indies – is simply a dream. The debate ends unsatisfactorily because neither can claim an epistemological basis for knowledge that the other accepts. Rochester may have the final word in this exchange because he is the narrator of Part Two, but his failure even in his own terms to demonstrate adequately the superiority of his knowledge challenges the idea that any single viewpoint can arrive at an accurate truth. As Antoinette comments at one point, "There is always the other side, always." Taken to its logical conclusion, such a critique applies to the narrative structure of *Jane Eyre*, which is organized exclusively around the narrative voice of Jane herself. Whereas *Wide Sargasso Sea* provides multiple narrators, each of whom interprets the world according to his or her subjective location, *Jane Eyre* establishes a single narrative voice that excludes the thoughts and perceptions of others such as Bertha Mason.

Wide Sargasso Sea itself can be subject to a similar critique, however. While Rhys demonstrates a great deal of sympathy for Antoinette and even Rochester, her descriptions of the Afro-Caribbean characters lack subtlety and border at times on caricature. Tia is reduced to little more than a marker of Antoinette's fantasy. Antoinette's final dream of a reunion with her sometime childhood friend is not motivated by anything having to do with Tia herself, but instead with Tia as the representation of Antoinette's lost childhood. As a result, Gayatri Spivak's reading of

Rhys as reproducing the very colonial ideologies she was challenging continues to occupy a central position within scholarly discussions of *Wide Sargasso Sea*. From Spivak's perspective, Rhys's project of giving voice to Bertha Mason is ideologically compromised because she fails to question the foundational discourse of self-and-other that continues to guide British literary texts even after the collapse of the British empire. As a result, Rhys's novel repeats the error of *Jane Eyre*: establishing the subjectivity of its emancipated female narrator at the expense of another character, Tia, whose existence is defined solely with respect to her.

While Spivak's reading points to an ideological inconsistency in *Wide Sargasso Sea*, it does not nullify the overall force of Rhys's novel. Indeed, Spivak's case may be somewhat overstated. She argues: "No perspective *critical* of imperialism can turn the Other into a self, because the project of imperialism has always already refracted what might have been the absolutely Other into a domesticated Other that consolidates the imperial self" (1985: 253). The understanding of the "project of imperialism" presented here grants to it a monolithic stability that may not be justifiable without more evidence than Spivak provides. Certainly, Rhys denies such stability in her novel. Her depiction of Rochester demonstrates him as consistently failing to consolidate his subjectivity. His desperate possessiveness of Antoinette, as indicated earlier, points to the contingency rather than the stability of his identity. He cannot relinquish control over her even after he has seized her fortune because she provides the alien "other" against which he may define his own Englishness. Moreover, Rochester's own position within the imperial economy is anything but secure given his position as a second son. Primogeniture leaves him without any guaranteed financial prospects; hence, to the extent that he can be seen as a representative of the colonial project in the British West Indies, his participation is motivated by a belief neither in the glory of the empire nor in the need for evangelization of the world. Rather, he simply desires economic gain to ensure his class standing within Great Britain. His letters to his father reveal his tenuous position, negotiating between the need to appease this authority figure and to express his deep resentment. The oscillation between these feelings frequently occurs over the course of only a few sentences. "I will never be a disgrace to you or to my dear brother the son you love," Rochester begins in one of his letters (Rhys 1966: 70). But only three sentences later he desperately tries to rationalize away his resentment at being sent to the Caribbean for an arranged marriage: "I have sold my soul or you have sold it, and after all is it such a bad bargain?"

Rochester's narrative in Part Two of the novel thus clarifies not only his cruelty toward Antoinette but also the consequences of British colonial policies on even purported beneficiaries such as himself. His sense of helplessness is apparent in the grammatical construction of his very first sentences: "So it was all over, the advance and retreat, the doubts and hesitations. Everything finished, for better or for worse" (p. 65). The tense of the verbs and the absence of active verbs or direct references to himself in the first person indicate the degree to which Rochester feels unable to affect his circumstances. Even his name, Rochester, is never directly mentioned in the novel by him or anyone else. This is significant because, as mentioned earlier, Rhys links identity to epistemology. Antoinette's desperate struggles to reclaim her name represent efforts to redefine for herself how she might interpret her experience. The absence of Rochester's name indicates his inability to interpret his experience in ways that differ from his father, the absent voice of authority who presumably names him. As a result, Rochester never directly confronts his father or rejects his father's plans for him. Instead, he redirects his repressed anger toward Antoinette to compensate for impulses he feels unable otherwise to express. Hence, his insistence on Antoinette's rampant promiscuity late in the novel. Projecting his own fantasy of disobedience on to his wife, Rochester thinks: "Sneer to the last, Devil. Do think that I don't know? She thirsts for *anyone* – not for me" (p. 165). Rochester cannot address such patently false charges directly to her, but in his mind he constructs a series of fantasies of her betrayal and the need for her punishment.

While Part One of *Wide Sargasso Sea* describes Antoinette's childhood from her perspective, and Part Two describes her marriage from Rochester's point of view, Part Three follows her experiences after she is locked away within Thornfield Hall. Once again Antoinette becomes the narrator; however, the narrative voice has changed dramatically from that of Part One. Whereas Part One demonstrated an articulate and self-conscious narrative style, Part Three is characterized by a fragmented, halting narrative voice that rambles and digresses. The cruelty and isolation to which Antoinette is submitted, in other words, affect her ability to represent herself and her surroundings. Perhaps the most interesting feature of this section occurs in the final two scenes. In the penultimate scene, Antoinette describes her apparent arson and suicide leap from the rooftop of Thornfield Hall. While the motivations for her actions differ from those of Bertha Mason in *Jane Eyre*, the actions themselves appear to follow fairly closely those detailed in Brontë's novel. The final scene, however, reveals that these events were only a dream. Upon waking up, Antoinette gains a new sense of purpose and clarity. "Now at last I know why I was brought here and what I have to do," she thinks (p. 190). This newfound clarity leads her in the final moments of the novel to attempt an escape from her attic prison.

The deliberate refusal to provide an unambiguous conclusion to the novel shapes the kind of alternative history that Rhys offers. For if Antoinette gains clarity, this clarity is not shared with the reader. Antoinette may now know what she needs to do, but the reader does not. The narrative ends before it is revealed whether Antoinette will attempt to live out her dream, and thereby replay the events of *Jane Eyre*, or attempt to return to the Caribbean and find Tia, or seek out for herself some different life within England. The possibility that Antoinette's future is not necessarily determined by the narrative of *Jane Eyre* challenges the positivist certainty that Rhys associates with the Victorian mindset and that she embodies in Rochester. As Gary Saul Morson has noted in another context, historical narratives as conceived by nineteenth-century historians and writers such as Brontë have the tendency to portray events as if they were inevitable. And this sense of historical determinism can discourage marginalized groups from feeling that they have the capacity to effect social change in the present. By recovering a sense of historical contingency, Morson argues, historians and literary authors can encourage such groups to feel that they can significantly alter their circumstances. According to this logic, *Wide Sargasso Sea* would be an early postwar example of a broader effort by Kazuo Ishiguro, Hanif Kureishi, Jeanette Winterson, and other authors in the 1980s and 1990s to conceive of a more culturally and racially inclusive British identity by giving voice to groups typically excluded from previous historical accounts. And indeed Antoinette challenges the idea of England as conceived by Rochester. She denies that the "cardboard world" to which Rochester takes her is England (p. 181), and she describes a single afternoon in which she is allowed to travel to the English countryside – a journey that provides the source for her own vision of what England truly is: "This, I thought, is England" (p. 183). The idea that multiple conceptions of England exist opens up the possibility that national identity need not necessarily be understood solely in terms of the Victorian heritage associated with Brontë's vision of the world. And it is perhaps this alternative England, one not yet fully articulated, that Antoinette in the final lines of the novel hopes to find.

While the place of *Wide Sargasso Sea* within the study of contemporary literature has proved as difficult to locate as the England about which Antoinette fantasizes, the novel's significance is not to be underestimated. Its critical engagement with one of the canonical works of Victorian fiction anticipates many of the significant issues that will be central to novels in the last decades of the century: neo-Victorianism, the critique of patriarchy, the redefinition of Englishness, and, to a lesser degree, postmodernism. For the epistemological uncertainty of the novel's conclusion has affinities with so-called postmodern novels, including Fowles's *The French Lieutenant's Woman*. *Wide Sargasso Sea* avoids any direct metacommentary on the artifice of narrative, which will become a distinguishing feature of Fowles's work and that of subsequent authors associated with postmodernism, including Salman Rushdie, Angela Carter, and Julian Barnes. Rhys shares with these authors, however, the sense that literary fictions have a unique capacity to prompt critical reassessments of social mores and normative codes of behavior that are taken for granted. Rhys's effort to bring Brontë's madwoman in the attic "onstage" and to the attention of the British public provides a model for redrawing the boundaries of public discourse and for attending to the implications of identity constructions, whether personal or collective.

REFERENCES AND FURTHER READING

Braithwaite, Kamau (1995) "A post-cautionary tale of the Helen of our wars," *Wasafiri*, 22: 69–81.

Brontë, Charlotte (2003) *Jane Eyre*. Harmondsworth: Penguin.

Byatt, A. S. (1991) *Possession: A Romance*. New York: Vintage.

Ciolkowski, Laura E. (1997) "Navigating the *Wide Sargasso Sea*: colonial history, English fiction, and British empire," *Twentieth Century Literature*, 43: 339–59.

Emory, Mary Lou (1990) *Jean Rhys at "World's End": Novels of Colonial and Sexual Exile*. Austin: University of Texas Press.

Fowles, John (1970) *The French Lieutenant's Woman*. New York: Signet.

Friedman, Ellen G. (1989) "Breaking the master narrative: Jean Rhys's *Wide Sargasso Sea*," in Ellen G. Friedman and Miriam Fuchs (eds.) *Breaking the Sequence: Women's Experimental Fiction*. Princeton: Princeton University Press.

Gregg, Veronica Marie (1995) *Jean Rhys's Historical Imagination: Reading and Writing the Creole*. Chapel Hill: University of North Carolina Press.

Huggan, Graham (1994) "A tale of two parrots: Walcott, Rhys, and the uses of colonial mimicry," *Contemporary Literature*, 35: 643–60.

Joseph, Margaret Paul (1992) *Caliban in Exile: The Outsider in Caribbean Fiction*. New York: Greenwood Press.

Le Gallez, Paula (1990) *The Rhys Woman*. London: Macmillan.

Morson, Gary Saul (1994) *Narrative and Freedom: The Shadows of Time*. New Haven: Yale University Press.

O'Connor, Teresa F. (1986) *Jean Rhys: The West Indian Novels*. New York: New York University Press.

Ramchand, Kenneth (1976) *An Introduction to the Study of West Indian Literature*. Sunbury-on-Thames: Nelson Caribbean.

Rhys, Jean (1966) *Wide Sargasso Sea*. New York: W. W. Norton.

——(1984) *The Letters of Jean Rhys*, ed. Francis Wyndham and Diana Melly. New York: Viking Penguin.

Savory, Elaine (1998) *Jean Rhys*. Cambridge: Cambridge University Press.

Spivak, Gayatri Chakravorty (1985) "Three women's texts and a critique of imperialism," *Critical Inquiry*, 12: 243–61.

Su, John J. (2003) "'Once I would have gone back...but not any longer': nostalgia and narrative ethics in *Wide Sargasso Sea*," *Critique*, 44/2: 157–74.

Thomas, Sue (1999) *The Worlding of Jean Rhys*. Westport, CT: Greenwood Press.

29

John Fowles's *The French Lieutenant's Woman*

James Acheson

John Fowles has the distinction of being both a best-selling novelist and one whose work has earned the respect of academic critics. Why his novels are best-sellers is clear enough. Fowles has tremendous narrative drive, the ability to compel his readers' attention from the beginning of his novels to the end. Fowles so beguiles us with uncertainty in his fiction, so tantalizes us with a variety of possible outcomes, that we read his novels and short stories eagerly to find out what happens in the end. Will Frederick Clegg, the twisted clerk in *The Collector* (1963), rape Miranda, the attractive young woman he has taken captive? Alternatively, will he take pity on her and let her go? Will Nicholas Urfe, the main character of *The Magus* (1965), make his way safely through the "godgame" that the mysterious Maurice Conchis has chosen to play with him? Will Charles Smithson, one of the main characters in *The French Lieutenant's Woman* (1969), leave his fiancée, Ernestina Freeman, for Sarah Woodruff, a woman whose haunting eyes draw him to her, just as the sirens' songs lured sailors to shipwreck? And what about Sarah, the novel's other main character? After making love to Charles in an Exeter hotel, will she drift into prostitution in London, or survive in some more respectable situation? Such questions as these arise in all of Fowles's novels, and the reader's curiosity about the answers does not always stop short of prurience.

Fowles includes the erotic in his novels because, he has said, "I teach better if I seduce" (Sage 1974: 35). What he seeks to teach us, in large part, is the importance of striving to understand ourselves better, and of founding relationships on friendship and trust rather than merely on sexual attraction. The right kind of relationships, he emphasizes in his fiction, can be highly educational, and especially so for the male of the species, since men, in his view, are more likely than women to need help in coming to terms with their sexuality. For Fowles, masculinity is an "appalling crust" that filters everything men hear and see. This "crust" is especially rigid, Fowles told Sarah Benton in a 1983 interview (Benton 1983: 19), in those who went through a single-sex school and served in the military, as he did. What intelligent, sensitive men need to do, he stressed, is to penetrate the crust to discover the feminine element within themselves, the element that Jung referred to as "the anima."

Fowles almost made a career of the Royal Marines, but on the advice of Isaac Foot, Lord Mayor of Plymouth, went to Oxford instead, where he graduated with a degree in French literature, in 1950. At Oxford he became familiar with the work of Sartre and Camus; he was attracted to their views on authenticity and personal freedom. For Fowles, just as it is important that sensitive, intelligent men explore the feminine component within themselves, so it is important that such men throw off the shackles of convention and freely discover their authentic selves – the people they really are. "This," Fowles told James Campbell in 1976, "is the sort of existential thesis of [my] books – that one has to discover one's [true] feelings" (Campbell 1976: 465). In *The French Lieutenant's Woman*, we observe the novel's two main characters, Charles Smithson and Sarah Woodruff, striving to do just this. In an essay written while *The French Lieutenant's Woman* was still in progress, Fowles commented that Sarah and Charles are "existentialist[s] before [their] time" (Fowles 1977b: 141). "It has always seemed to me," he says in this essay,

> that the Victorian age, and especially from 1850 on, was highly existentialist in many of its personal dilemmas. One can almost invert the reality and say that Camus and Sartre have been trying to lead us, in their fashion, to a Victorian seriousness of purpose and moral sensitivity. (p. 140)

The French Lieutenant's Woman is not only an existentialist novel but a postmodern one as well; and if it is the novel's erotic content that made it a best-seller, it is its postmodern complexity that has appealed to the many academic critics who have written on it. Postmodern novels present the world as a place that is endlessly complex and uncertain, often mirroring it by way of their self-conscious arbitrariness and constructedness. Fowles seeks in *The French Lieutenant's Woman* to show how uncertain life can be by providing us with three possible endings to the novel, in Chapters 44, 60, and 61. Each ending shows us a different way in which the lives of the characters might have developed, and emphasizes that there are always too many variables in day-to-day existence for any single ending to be the only possible one. Another example of the novel's self-consciousness is found in Chapter 13, in which Fowles objects to conventional omniscient narration on the grounds that the omniscient narrator is an analogue to God, and as such is inappropriate to an age in which God's existence has fallen into doubt. Fowles includes the chapter, ironically enough, in a novel in which he pretends to be omniscient, flaunting his ability to enter the minds of some of his characters, but pointedly refusing to reveal the workings of the mind of one of them, the enigmatic Sarah Woodruff. Fowles thus demonstrates his mastery of omniscient narration, including the device of limited omniscience – of withholding from the reader information that the narrator possesses but prefers not to disclose – while at the same time objecting to novelists who write novels in the mid-twentieth century that adopt an omniscient viewpoint. He also appears in his own person (or, more accurately, as two caricatured versions of himself) in Chapters 55 and 61 – to remind us that his assumption of omniscience is only a pretence.

Omniscient narration is not only inappropriate in an age of declining faith, but also in the light of research in experimental psychology, which shows that all-encompassing knowledge of the world lies beyond human reach. In the early years of the twentieth century, the Danish psychologist Edgar Rubin performed experiments to show how the mind makes sense of sense data. He discovered that in every act of perception the mind distinguishes between "the figure, the substantial appearance of objects, and the ground, the . . . environment in which the [objects are] placed" (Watson 1968: 439). The figure–ground relationship is best illustrated by the black and white drawing found in many psychology texts: a drawing in which we may discern either a white vase on a black background, or two black faces, facing each other, on a white background. What we perceive in the drawing depends on which part we assign the primary status of figure and which the secondary status of ground.

Experiments performed by Rubin's contemporaries show that the figure–ground distinction is invariably a simplification of what is perceived. "[Experienced] perceptual wholes," they found, "tend toward the greatest regularity, simplicity, and clarity possible under the given conditions" (Asch 1968: 168). The world as we know it through perception is merely a simplification (because a series of simplifications of sense data in different situations) of the world as it really is. Moreover, it is a *subjective* simplification, since our every act of perception is colored by considerations that are unique to us as individuals.

Literary texts are, of course, a part of our world, and when we read them we make figure–ground distinctions, ultimately arriving at a subjective simplification of the material the text provides. If our every act of reading were *not* a subjective simplification of the text, we would all agree that there is a single, definitive way in which every text is to be interpreted. In *The French Lieutenant's Woman* Fowles invites us to view the narrative as the tragedy, to see Sarah Woodruff as the tragic protagonist and Victorian society as the antagonist; then to change our figure–ground standpoint and regard Charles as the protagonist and Sarah as the antagonist. He asks us, in other words, to apply two different figure–ground distinctions to the novel and to consider why it is that to view *The French Lieutenant's Woman* as a tragedy in both cases is to simplify our experience of it.

Fowles complicates matters by providing three endings to his novel. Charles Scruggs has observed that the last two serve as an invitation to "retrospective patterning" (Scruggs 1985: 98), to the formation of two quite different patterns of interpretation where the main characters are concerned. Scruggs is right about retrospective patterning; in fact, however, the novel contains four potential tragic actions (with four endings) involving Sarah as protagonist, and three (with three endings) involving Charles – presenting us with a total of seven different patterns of interpretation altogether. The first action, with Sarah as the main character, centers on her relationship with Varguennes, and ends tragically; the second, third, and fourth, which end in Chapters 44, 60, and 61, respectively, concern her relationship with

Charles. Chapter 44, the novel's first ending, may be tragic, but Chapters 60 and 61, its second and third endings, are clearly not. When we alter the figure–ground relationship and view Charles as the protagonist, we see that he escapes a possibly tragic fate in Chapter 44, when he decides to marry his fiancée, Ernestina Freeman. Chapter 60 also ends well for him, but Chapter 61 ends equivocally, suggesting that he may or may not come to a tragic end on "the unplumb'd, salt, estranging sea" (1972: 399) of life. Thus, although it contains tragic elements, *The French Lieutenant's Woman* is only partly tragic: to describe it as a tragedy overall, as at least three critics have done (Evarts 1972; Rose 1972; Johnstone 1985), is to simplify its complexities.

The fact that Fowles refers to Sarah as the novel's "protagonist" (348) suggests that she is, more obviously than Charles, the central character in a tragic action, although, as we will see later, Charles has a claim to being the protagonist, too. In the four actions in which Sarah (or "poor Tragedy," p. 12) is involved, the antagonist is the society against whose stifling conventionality she struggles to establish a place for herself as an individual in her own right. Fowles emphasizes that, as the protagonist, Sarah is superior to the majority of her contemporaries, though in intelligence rather than in social class.

[Sarah's] intelligence belonged to a rare kind; one that would certainly pass undetected in any of our modern tests of the faculty. It was not in the least analytical or problem-solving, and it is no doubt symptomatic that the one subject that had cost her agonies to master was mathematics . . . It was rather an uncanny – uncanny in one who had never been to London, never mixed in the world – ability to classify other people's worth: to understand them, in the fullest sense of that word. . . . She could sense the pretensions of a hollow argument, a false scholarship, a biased logic when she came across them; but she also saw through people in subtler ways . . . [She] saw them as they were and not as they tried to seem. (pp. 49–50)

This statement is problematic. At times Sarah *does* see through people – she sees, for example, that Mrs Poultney is a hypocrite – but at other times she makes significant mistakes. She is mistaken, for example, about Varguennes, following him to Weymouth on the understanding that he will marry her, only to find that he is already married.

Why does Fowles tell us that Sarah is a good judge of character when she clearly misjudges the perfidious lieutenant? Part of the answer lies in the fact that Sarah is, prior to meeting Varguennes, desperate to get married, for she finds it distressing to experience the happiness of family life as an onlooker – as a governess – rather than as a wife and mother. Originally from an undistinguished agricultural family, she has been educated to a point where no man of her background would seek to marry her; at the same time, she is too poor to attract a husband of the middle or upper classes. Varguennes offers her an escape from the dreariness of spinsterhood, and she jumps at it rashly. In terms of classical tragedy, she is an essentially good person whose miscalculation leads to a tragic end.

Yet there are at least two other ways of explaining the mistake she makes over Varguennes. At one point Sarah tells Charles that "some deep flaw in my soul wished my better self to be blinded" (p. 150): in terms of Renaissance tragedy, Sarah falls because she suffers from a character flaw akin to Othello's jealousy, Macbeth's ambition, or Hamlet's vacillation. Alternatively – and here there is another link to Hamlet – she may be mad. Certainly this is what Dr Grogan thinks: he tells Charles that she suffers from "obscure melancholia" (p. 134), "a cholera, a typhus of the intellectual faculties" (p. 194). Sarah's madness, is, however, never established beyond a reasonable doubt. Charles reflects at one point that "her mind . . . was very far from deranged" (p. 122), and, indeed, much of Sarah's behavior seems rational, though she herself is aware that it is not always so. She tells Charles, for example, of a day when "I was nearly overcome by madness" (p. 126), and later of an occasion when "[a] madness was in me" (p. 383). By her own testimony, Sarah seems intermittently mad, or, as Hamlet has it, mad "by nor' nor' west."

In any case, it is clear that her dealings with Varguennes contain some important elements of tragedy. As she tells Charles the story of her pursuit of the lieutenant to Weymouth, we experience, just as he does, feelings of pity and fear in anticipation of the outcome. Sarah experiences tragic recognition (in classical terms, *anagnorisis*), when she sees that Varguennes is a "worthless adventurer" who had "appeared far more a gentleman in a gentleman's house" (p. 151), and a reversal in her fortunes (a classical *catastrophe*), when she discovers that the lieutenant is married. What follows is her fall from good fortune: she leaves Lyme Regis as a governess with an unsullied reputation and returns as a fallen woman.

All this is consistent with tragedy: what seems odd is that she takes delight in her new status, telling Charles that she now has "a freedom" that the people of Lyme Regis "cannot understand. No insult, no blame, can touch me. Because I have set myself beyond the pale. I am nothing. I am hardly human any more. I am the French Lieutenant's Whore" (p. 153). Charles (and indeed, the reader unfamiliar with Fowles's longstanding interest in existentialism) finds this difficult to understand. What Sarah is saying is that it is important to live outside convention, for once outside it, the individual can experience the freedom to begin discovering the truth about him- or herself: to go beyond the conventional role he or she plays and discover the person he or she really is. ("It [is] as if we [are] all acting players," Fowles once remarked to Katherine Tarbox. "What we've lost is the trick of seeing through these public roles and discovering the actor's true self underneath . . ." (Tarbox 1988: 183)). Sarah's first tragic fall, from governess to social outcast is, then, matched by an increase in personal awareness: outside convention, she takes her first steps towards attaining to existential authenticity.

Her second tragic fall, in Chapter 44, takes place without any such compensation. Here, despite his extended conversations with Sarah and apparent willingness to help her, Charles decides to abandon her and return to his fiancée, Ernestina Freeman. "And so ends the story," comments Fowles. "Whatever happened to Sarah, I do not know – whatever it was, she never troubled Charles again in person, however long she may have lingered in his memory. This is what most often happens. People sink out of sight, drown in the shadows of closer things" (p. 292). In this, the novel's first ending to the story of Charles and Sarah, Sarah simply vanishes into obscurity. She may find another position as a governess, but the fact that she is no longer well enough to look after Mrs Talbot's children, and that she has been a less than satisfactory companion to Mrs Poulteney, suggests that she will have difficulty finding further employment and may drift into London to become a prostitute. Fowles foreshadows such a possibility three chapters earlier when Charles picks up a prostitute named Sarah after leaving his London club. That Sarah Woodruff will suffer this fate, however, is only a possibility: we cannot say that she comes to a definitely tragic end in Chapter 44, because Fowles refuses to tell us what happens to her.

Nor does she come to a tragic end in either of the novel's remaining endings, Chapters 60 and 61. In Chapter 60 we discover that, after disappearing from her Exeter hotel, she has made her way to London and the household of Dante Gabriel Rossetti, where she has been working as the artist's amanuensis. Far from being a tragic ending, Chapter 60 is one in which she exchanges her position of governess for one that is far more advantageous. It is a position in which she has maintained her integrity (she emphasizes to Charles that she is not Rossetti's mistress), and in which she has become aware of having made some all-too-human mistakes. In the course of their conversation, she confesses that, in Lyme Regis, "I . . . abused your trust, your generosity, I, yes, I [threw] myself at you, forced myself upon you, knowing very well that you had other obligations. . . . I believe I was right to destroy what had begun between us. There was falsehood in it . . ." (p. 383). It is because she has attained a greater degree of existential authenticity and independence of mind that she expresses a reluctance to marry Charles, to continue a relationship she believes is founded on "falsehood." Sarah emerges from the novel's second ending not as a tragic heroine but as someone whose existential self-awareness has allowed her to see that she need not be married in order to be fulfilled.

In Chapter 61, Sarah is again found in the Rossetti household; and although this ending is somewhat darker than the Chapter 60 version, it is still short of tragic. Here she tells Charles that she is only interested in his friendship; and his reaction is to storm out of the house without discovering that the baby held by another occupant of the house is his daughter. The family is not united as in Chapter 60, but things have still worked out well for Sarah; she has improved her station in life and is able to live, as in the previous chapter, authentically and in the company of intelligent, creative people. Some feminist readers may object that Sarah is in both Chapter 60 and Chapter 61 left financially dependent on a man (see, for example, Goscilo 1993: 64), but such dependence is not necessarily tragic. On the contrary, prostitution would be tragic, Fowles suggests, while financial dependence is the best a woman in Sarah's position could hope for in mid-Victorian England.

Thus, in the four potential tragic actions in which Sarah appears as the protagonist, there is only one tragic ending. Her association with Varguennes ends badly for her, in that she becomes the French Lieutenant's Whore in the eyes of provincial Lyme Regis;

however, there emerges from it a new sense of existential freedom and self-knowledge. In the second action, ending in Chapter 44, it is unclear what happens to Sarah after Charles abandons her, and therefore it is equally unclear whether she fares tragically or not; while in the third and fourth actions, she emerges in an advantageous position, ensconced in the Rossetti household. To conclude that *The French Lieutenant's Woman* is a tragedy in which Sarah serves as the protagonist and Victorian society as the antagonist is to deny the significance of these latter endings.

The fact that Sarah is referred to as the protagonist does not alter the fact that Charles, too, has a claim to this status. In an interview with Melvyn Bragg, Fowles commented that "practically everyone's assumed the central character is the heroine Sarah. But for me the book was always equally about Charles" (quoted in Woodcock 1984: 85). Fowles makes a central character of Charles by entering his mind repeatedly, and by presenting most of the action of the novel from this young man's point of view.

Sarah, as the antagonist, is a quintessential female temptress: Charles thinks of her as being a "siren" and a "Calypso" (p. 125) at one point, and Grogan comments later that she has "eyes a man could drown in" (p. 195). What Grogan fears is that Sarah is an hysteric who poses a serious threat to Charles, and it is with this in mind that he gives him the story of Lieutenant Emile de La Roncière to read. Charles is horrified to learn how a young woman, Marie de Morell, brought charges against de La Roncière, and how a trial that was largely a travesty of justice ended in his being sentenced to ten years in prison (see Shields 1995 for a full account of this case). Afraid that he might come to a similar end, he decides to abandon Sarah in the novel's first ending, Chapter 44. This is not a tragic ending, for Charles as protagonist escapes the threat posed by Sarah by ending their relationship.

Nevertheless, Fowles emphasizes that Chapter 44 is "a betrayal of Charles's deeper potentiality" (p. 295), by which he means that Charles would have done better, in existential terms, to remain with Sarah. The life he will lead married to Ernestina will be a conventional Victorian life, characterized by an unwillingness to question what societal norms dictate. By contrast, Fowles implies, the life Charles would spend with Sarah would be one in which convention would be eschewed in the interests of attaining to existential authenticity. However, Chapter 44 exists only in Charles's imagination: in actuality, he visits Sarah in Exeter and makes love to her, but discovers to his surprise that she is a virgin – that she lied to him about sleeping with Varguennes. Later she will tell him that she cannot explain why she lied: "I cannot explain it. It is not to be explained" (pp. 308–9). Although this statement is open to a number of interpretations, it is above all reminiscent of Iago's statement that he is governed by "motiveless malignity" in his behavior to Othello. In the Exeter hotel, we are led to believe that Sarah is a destructive figure.

Here Charles experiences, in existential terms, the "anxiety of freedom – that is, the realisation that one *is* free and the realisation that being free is a situation of terror" (p. 296). Now that he has made love to Sarah, Charles can see that he is free to choose between living a conventional life with Ernestina, or breaking off his engagement to her and taking up with Sarah. "You know your choice," Charles reflects to himself. "You stay in prison, what your time calls duty, honour, self-respect, and you are comfortably safe. Or you are free and crucified. Your only companions the stones, the thorns, the turning backs; the silence of cities, and their hate" (p. 314). Charles does not, of course, imagine that he is a Christ figure, or that he will be literally crucified: he simply sees that making choices without reference to any established conventions or sets of values will be a lonely business, filled with anxiety and self-doubt. It is then that he sees that Sarah's role is to "uncrucify" (p. 315) him, to help relieve his anxiety by serving as a mentor and friend. "The false version of her betrayal by Varguennes, her other devices, were but stratagems to unblind him; all she had said . . . was but a test of his new vision" (p. 318).

The visionary experience to which Sarah gives rise enables Charles to see her no longer as a temptress figure but as a savior who might help him to enjoy a life of existential freedom. When he returns to her hotel room, however, she has departed without leaving a forwarding address, and he is left to face a life of existential anxiety on his own. We now begin to experience the pity and fear of the audience attending a tragedy: we pity Charles because he has been abandoned, and fear that his new vision may lead not to a sense of existential authenticity but to a tragic fall. Charles employs a private detective to find Sarah; but after the search has dragged on for some time he begins to doubt her status as savior, distinguishing "between the real Sarah and the Sarah he had created in so many such dreams: the one Eve personified, all mystery and love and profundity, and the other, a half-scheming, half-crazed governess from an obscure seaside town" (p. 367).

For Charles, Sarah's status is uncertain, and each of the novel's two remaining endings, Chapters 60 and 61, resolves it in a different way. At the start of Chapter 60, Fowles hints that Charles will find himself ultimately in the position of Oedipus at the end of *Oedipus Rex*, aware that, although he has believed himself to be free, he is in fact subject to forces beyond his control. Thus, the chapter begins with Charles's solicitor, Montague, comparing Sarah to the Sphinx and warning him to "bear in mind what happened to those who failed to solve the enigma" (p. 376). Fowles furthers our expectation of this kind of outcome by commenting that Charles must pass through the "fatal gate" of the house (p. 377) in which she is now living, and by adding that in his conversation with Sarah, "[what] cried out behind [his words] was not melodrama, but tragedy" (p. 388). Charles finds that she has been living and working in the home of the Rossettis, that she now has the appearance of a self-supporting "New Woman" (p. 379), and that she is apparently uninterested in marriage and children. She is an intimidating figure and causes Charles to reflect that "Some terrible perversion of human sexual destiny had begun; he was no more than a footsoldier, a pawn in a far vaster battle; and like all battles it was not about love, but about possession and territory" (p. 387). Here Charles appears to experience a moment of tragic awareness similar to Oedipus' final recognition that he is a pawn of fate.

Yet, as in Chapter 44, the novel's first ending, Fowles here raises our expectations of a tragic outcome only to disappoint them. In producing Lalage, the child Charles has fathered, Sarah reveals that she has not participated in some "terrible perversion of human sexual destiny" – has not refused a traditional maternal role – and the chapter ends happily with a family united. Rather than conclude as a tragedy, Chapter 60 ends as a Providential melodrama, with Charles convinced that the family's reunion "had been in God's hands, in His forgiveness of their sins" (pp. 392–3). Earlier he thought of Sarah as a savior who might "uncrucify" him – who might relieve him of the existential "anxiety of freedom." Now he assigns responsibility for his reunion with Sarah to a benevolent Providence. In existential terms, Charles is behaving as though he were subject to the will of God: as though, after emerging from the church in Exeter, he had turned away from his conviction that he was "shriven of established religion for the rest of his life" (p. 318). In invoking a benevolent God to explain his situation, Charles denies himself the role of existential hero.

In Chapter 61, the last ending, Charles and Sarah meet as before, though by accident rather than by Providential design. "There is," says Fowles, "no intervening god" (p. 398) in this chapter, beyond what can be seen in its first epigraph, an epigraph stating that evolution "is simply the process by which chance . . . co-operates with natural law to create living forms better and better adapted to survive" (p. 394). Charles is now convinced of something he only suspects in Chapter 60: that Sarah is a manipulative schemer who habitually makes victims of the men in her life. Though she refuses to marry him, Sarah hints that she might be willing to continue their relationship as a "Platonic – and [eventually] . . . more intimate, never consecrated – friendship" (p. 397).

Although Charles, who is filled with a sense of his "own true superiority to her," here pictures himself melodramatically as "the last honourable man on the way to the scaffold" (p. 397), in fact it is unclear that he is necessarily proceeding to a tragic fate. It may be that what he is to experience after leaving Sarah is a better life than the one he has known, and, if that is the case, it would be inappropriate to think of him as a tragic protagonist who has come to a disastrous end, or to think of Sarah as his antagonist. In the novel's closing sentences, Fowles suggests that in fact Charles has become a better person and can look forward to a better life. His decisiveness about no longer needing Sarah to bolster his freedom indicates that he has, Fowles says,

> at last found an atom of faith in himself, a true uniqueness, on which to build; has already begun . . . to realise that life, however advantageously Sarah may in some ways seem to fit the role of Sphinx . . . is not one riddle and one failure to guess it, . . . but is to be, however inadequately, emptily, hopelessly into the city's iron heart, endured. And out again, upon the unplumb'd, salt, estranging sea. (p. 399)

The last sentence in this passage, the last in the novel, echoes a line from Matthew Arnold's "To Marguerite" (1853), a poem Charles has "committed to heart" (p. 365). Arnold's poem tells how the ancient continents were joined together, only to be divided by the seas, and suggests that people are like those continents, wanting to be reunited in love. Clearly, Charles has memorized this poem because, prior to Chapter 61, he has yearned to resume his romantic involvement with Sarah. In the last stanza, quoted in Chapter 58 of the novel, Arnold asks:

> Who order'd, that their longing's fire
> Should be, as soon as kindled, cool'd?
> Who renders vain their deep desire? –
> A God, a God their severance ruled;
> And bade betwixt their shores to be
> The unplumb'd, salt, estranging sea. (p. 366)

Fowles's use of the last line of this poem in the concluding sentence of his novel might suggest that he intends Chapter 61 to be a conventionally tragic ending, with God intervening malevolently at the last moment to separate Charles and Sarah. What seems more probable, however, is that Fowles echoes the line from Arnold for the sake of suggesting that however hard he has tried to make his characters seem free, as their author he is ultimately the God who separates them. He separates them in Chapter 61 for the sake of emphasizing that true existential freedom is only to be found in solitude (not in the company of a savior figure) on the "unplumb'd" sea of life, with the sea representing life's unfathomed depths, its flux and hidden mysteries. Charles may perish tragically on the voyage, but Fowles "think[s] not": having acquired a certain "faith in himself" (p. 399), he will more probably attain to increasing existential authenticity.

For all of the narrative complexity of Fowles's novel, we might object that *The French Lieutenant's Woman* does an inadequate job of representing the world's complexity, a job that could only be done by a novel of endless length, with an infinite number of endings. But such a novel could never be written, for it would take forever to complete; and it could never be read to the end, since it would take forever to read it. But this is Fowles's overall point. When he objects, in Chapter 13, to the convention of omniscient narration, he makes it clear not only that it is inappropriate for the novelist to mimic God's omniscience in a century characterized by widespread loss of faith, but (by extension) that the world is far too complex to be represented fully in any but a novel that would be impossible for any human being to write. Instead, a novel such as *The French Lieutenant's Woman*, whose several endings are an extended reminder that tragedy, like all other literary forms, is an all-too-obvious simplification of the world's infinite complexity, must of necessity serve in its place.

REFERENCES AND FURTHER READING

Asch, Solomon E. (1968) "Gestalt theory," in David Sills (ed.) *The International Encyclopedia of the Social Sciences*, vol. VI. London: Macmillan and the Free Press.

Benton, Sarah (1983) "Adam and Eve," *New Socialist*, 11 (May–June): 18–19.

Campbell, James (1976) "An interview with John Fowles," *Contemporary Literature*, 17 (Autumn): 455–69.

Evarts, Prescott, Jr. (1972) "Fowles's *The French Lieutenant's Woman* as tragedy," *Critique: Studies in Modern Fiction*, 13/3: 57–69.

Foster, Thomas C. (1994) *Understanding John Fowles*. Columbia: University of South Carolina Press.

Fowles, John (1972) [1969] *The French Lieutenant's Woman*. London: Panther.

——(1977a) "Hardy and the hag," in Lance St John Butler (ed.) *Thomas Hardy After Fifty Years*. London: Macmillan.

——(1977b) "Notes on an unfinished novel," in Malcolm Bradbury (ed.) *The Novel Today*. Manchester: Manchester University Press.

Goscilo, Margaret Bozenna (1993) "John Fowles's Pre-Raphaelite woman: interart strategies and gender politics," *Mosaic: A Journal for the Interdisciplinary Study of Literature*, 26 (Spring): 63–83.

Johnstone, Douglas (1985) "The 'unplumb'd, salt, estranging' tragedy of *The French Lieutenant's Woman*," *American Imago*, 42 (Spring): 69–83.

Lovell, Terry (1984) "Feminism and form in the literary adaptation: *The French Lieutenant's Woman*," in Jeremy Hawthorn (ed.) *Criticism and Critical Theory*. London: Edward Arnold.

Rose, Gilbert(1972) *"The French Lieutenant's Woman*: the unconscious significance of a novel to its author," *American Imago*, 29: 165–79.

Sage, Lorna (1974) "John Fowles: a profile," *New Review*, 1 (October 7): 31–7.

Scruggs, Charles (1985) "The two endings of *The French Lieutenant's Woman*," *Modern Fiction Studies*, 31 (Spring): 95–114.

Shields, Ellen (1995) "Hysteria, sexual assault and the military: the trial of Emile de La Roncière and *The French Lieutenant's Woman*," *Mosaic: A Journal for the Interdisciplinary Study of Literature*, 28 (September): 83–108.

Tarbox, Katherine (1988) *The Art of John Fowles*. Athens and London: University of Georgia Press.

Watson, Robert I. (1968) *The Great Philosophers from Aristotle to Freud*. Philadelphia: J. B. Lippincott.

Woodcock, Bruce (1984) *Male Mythologies: John Fowles and Masculinity*. Brighton: Harvester.

30

Angela Carter

Nicola Pitchford

Since about 1990, Angela Carter (1940–92) has become an unassailably canonical contemporary writer. By the mid-1990s, she was the single most popular subject of PhD theses in English Literature at British universities (Sage 1994b: 3). The predictable irony is that such fame and status came essentially after her death, although she had been enjoying increasing critical and commercial success in the decade preceding it. Her massive posthumous reputation obscures the fact that Carter was always somehow slightly tangential to the mainstream of British literary writing, never quite welcomed into the innermost circles of the lauded and glamorous. She certainly had many influential literary friends – most visibly in the 1980s, Salman Rushdie – and never a shortage of outlets for her essays or her fiction. Her early novels won prizes and her last novels and short-story collections became instant feminist classics. But even the most positive reviews of her work tended to hesitate subtly, to reveal amid their praise a note of reserve or bewilderment, usually directed at what they saw as Carter's stylistic excess. Carter herself felt that she never quite *arrived* as a major British writer, seeing as evidence the fact that none of her novels even got so far as the shortlist for the Booker Prize.

From the outside, it is hard to see Angela Carter's career as anything but successful. She was born during World War II, a fact that contributed to her eclectic upbringing: her middle-class family left South London to escape the Blitz, retreating to her grandmother's mining village in Yorkshire. The no-nonsense, working-class matriarchy of her grandmother's household was as enduring an influence on her personality and her writing as was her parents' bookishness (Carter 1982; Sage 1994a: 5–6). After leaving school, Carter briefly followed her father into journalism; she married young (eventually divorcing), then earned a degree in English from Bristol University. She published her first novel, *Shadow Dance*, in 1966. Between that first book and her early death from lung cancer, she published eight more novels; three collections of short stories; plays for radio and for stage; children's books; regular essays and reviews for *New Society* and other publications (enough for two collections); and screenplays for the movie versions of both her story "The company of wolves" and her second novel, *The Magic Toyshop* (the former directed by Neil Jordan in 1984; the latter made for television by David Wheatley in 1987). Further collections of her shorter works appeared after her death. She was a founding member of the advisory board of the feminist publishing house Virago, for which she produced a controversial book-length rumination on feminism and pornography (*The Sadeian Woman*) as well as editing three collections of fairy tales and women's short stories. She was also influential as a university writer-in-residence, holding visiting positions in creative writing programs in the US and Australia as well as the UK.

Yet, for much of her career, Angela Carter seemed not to fit with whatever writing or writers were in vogue. She happened to be female, but she never produced the sort of tightly wound domestic realism favored by the foremost women writers in Britain in the 1960s and 1970s (with the exception of Doris Lessing, who has also often been overlooked). Instead, her work was dark and Gothic and coyly self-reflexive. The forward movement of plot tended to be disrupted by stylized tableaux and by Carter's suffocatingly rich language, which constantly called attention to itself. Most of her early novels did have recognizable domestic settings, and three of them – the so-called *Bristol Trilogy*, comprising *Shadow Dance*, *Several Perceptions* (1968), and *Love* (1971) – were widely praised for capturing the decadent, volatile atmosphere of late-1960s youth subculture in England's faded provincial cities. But as her writing grew more experimental in the following decade – often taking place in futuristic and apocalyptic worlds – reviewers found it, and her, increasingly hard to place. Despite Carter's public feminism, her perversely elaborate representations of female characters caught in situations of sexual domination and violence seemed at odds with the dominant wing of the Women's Liberation Movement, which rejected pornography and the eroticization of oppression. In addition, her work from the 1970s apparently struck many British readers as excessively intellectual and suspiciously continental, with its richly layered allusions to French and German literature and film as well as psychoanalytic and poststructuralist theory. As her friend, the critic Lorna Sage, summed up, "experiment was un-English, somehow" (Sage 1994a: 2).

The mid-1980s brought Carter major critical and commercial success but still not the level of acknowledgment she might have anticipated. Ironically, now that having an internationalist sensibility had suddenly become fashionable in British literary circles under the umbrella of multiculturalism, Carter suspected she was considered *too* English, too white and middle-class to satisfy the new vogue for exotic tokenism among influential critics and prize judges (Walsh 1992). By this point, Rushdie's *Midnight's Children* (1981) had enjoyed tremendous success and Gabriel García Márquez was gaining a broad readership in Britain after winning the Nobel Prize (1982), opening the doors for non-realist or magical realist writing. Also, a kind of highly stylized and conspicuously erudite postmodern writing that resembled Carter's had become the "next big thing." Yet she was a crucial few years too old to be included among the under-40 talents championed by *Granta* magazine as the "Best Young British Novelists" in its landmark 1983 issue, or to be touted alongside the brash "New Lads" like Martin Amis – and, again, she was female. Many younger writers, and the critics who championed them, bought into a retrospective vision of the British novel of the 1960s and most of the 1970s as an unrelieved wasteland of dull realism and resistance to innovation; they tended to cite iconoclastic (male) American writers as their inspiration.

Given this evidence, it is tempting to make up a story about Carter's career based on the myth of being "ahead of one's time." Indeed, a number of critics have pointed to the ways in which her writing, both fictional and critical, seemed to predict major intellectual and aesthetic trends: the vogues for poststructuralist theory, magic realism, transgender and gender studies, as well as the heated debates within feminism over pornography and female desire (Bristow and Broughton 1997: 14; Gamble 2001: 74, 88). On occasion, critical claims of Carter's prescience have unfortunately led to reductive readings of her novels as mere fictionalized treatments of emergent ideas. She has seemed, in such readings, either impressive or misguided as a thinker, but dismissible as a novelist. (To be fair, Carter herself once proclaimed that her 1977 novel *The Passion of New Eve* had been "conceived as a feminist tract" about the construction of gender (1998: 25).) Aside from this risk, there is authorial intention to consider: Carter was a committed socialist and therefore a fierce opponent, both in her fiction and in her published comments, of such convenient and ahistorical myths as being ahead of one's time. She described herself, in a much-quoted 1983 essay, as someone thoroughly shaped by and squarely situated in her place and time: "I simply could not have existed, as I am, in any other preceding time or place. I am the pure product of an advanced, industrialized, post-imperial country in decline" (1998: 27).

It seems important to focus on the ways in which Carter's fiction *does* reflect its own location in history, in order to understand how it offers not only an increasingly critical commentary on the state of late twentieth-century Britain but also a minority perspective on the political role of literature in this context. If her writing seemed, for most of her career, atypical of contemporary British writing and even un-English, that says a lot about the narrowness of dominant notions of Englishness and British writing at the time and about the ways in which Carter's work resisted such narrowness.

History and Recycling: Working Backwards from the Late Novels

Reading Carter's fiction as historical is not always easy. Her novels and short stories tend to have such strong components of fantasy, allegory, surrealism, the lurid, and the grotesque that many readers have understandably downplayed their other side: insistent social criticism, careful historical grounding, and the frequent interjection of a down-to-earth narrative voice that debunks the text's own rhetorical glamour and glitter. These two elements, the spectacular and the pragmatic, exist side by side in all her fiction, and the contrast between them is often more or less dramatized by pairs of opposing characters: for example, Buzz and Lee in *Love*; Dr Hoffman and the Minister of Determination in *The Infernal Desire Machines of Doctor Hoffman*; Fevvers and Lizzie in *Nights at the Circus*. In these pairings, neither character consistently represents the authorial viewpoint.

The extravagantly imaginative, self-consciously arty side of Carter's fiction has often seemed to render its overall political purposes slippery and obscure. There was never much debate over the fact that Carter *had* political or satirical intentions, but the spectacular element tended to be more striking and its presence confusing. It was certainly less familiar to British readers in the 1960s and 1970s, who could draw on a strong twentieth-century tradition of politically dissident high culture but less so on a native tradition of self-conscious stylistic decadence. For a "serious" novelist to convey socialist sentiments in his or her work was not so unusual; but to do so in a frivolously non-realist novel was.

However, beginning with her popular short-story collection based on European folk-tales, *The Bloody Chamber* (1979), and continuing through her final novel, *Wise Children* (1991), Carter's late fiction seemed suddenly to place political critique and arch showmanship in a much more understandable relation to one another. Her new writing still breached the boundaries of realism, but its flights of fancy became more playful and cheerful, less dark and bizarre. Critics proposed that in her last two novels particularly, she altered her dominant mode from the Gothic – preoccupied with danger, sexual perversity, spatial confinement, concealed identity, and intimations of the supernatural – to the carnivalesque, a mode based on the joyful anarchy of the carnival, which temporarily sanctions the ridiculing of authority and the celebration of "coarse" bodily desires (Bakhtin 1968). And in doing so, Carter focused less on women as victims of eroticized violence and started producing more liberating, positive models of female identity, desire, and power (Palmer 1997: 31). This lightening-up of her approach, perhaps as much as a growing general fashion for postmodernism and magic realism, may account for the new enthusiasm with which her work was received – especially by feminists – in the 1980s and afterwards. Carter's politics could more easily be reconciled with her free use of the imagination as a tool of subversion, now that both were apparently channeled into the recognizable form of empowering feminist fables.

Carter's 1984 novel *Nights at the Circus*, with its larger-than-life heroine, Sophie Fevvers, is the most celebrated example of the ways in which her penchant for stunning invention and her self-conscious recycling of previous texts and styles came together with an obviously feminist message. However, I want to discuss this novel not as an example of her new approach but, rather, in order to highlight how readings of her late works as empowering feminist fables may obscure both their continuity with her earlier writing and also the scope of the political issues her fiction touched upon.

Carter's protagonist, Fevvers, is a popular celebrity in *fin de siècle* London, a vulgar but dazzling circus star who has captivated the public by apparently being equipped by nature with a massive pair of wings. These wings may or may not be the secret of her success as a trapeze artist; "Is she fact or is she fiction?" is the tantalizing catchphrase supplied by her savvy nineteenth-century publicity machine. The first part of the novel is dominated by Fevvers's own irreverent Cockney voice as she tells her colorful life story to a skeptical young (male) American journalist eager to debunk her as a "humbug"; he soon joins the circus as a clown in order to observe her, incognito, during a series of performances (and hair-raising adventures) at the Tsar's Imperial Circus in St Petersburg. Then, in the novel's third and final section, the circus travels on towards America across Siberia, where it is attacked by bandits and the characters scattered in the wilderness for another series of self-contained adventures. The action culminates with Fevvers – accompanied as ever by her Marxist-anarchist foster mother, Lizzie – triumphantly rescuing the young American from peril and claiming him as her husband, just as the clock strikes for the twentieth century to begin.

Nights at the Circus is an immediately appealing novel, in the familiar, bawdy tradition of picaresque narratives like *Tom Jones* and *Moll Flanders*. And it is hard to see Fevvers as anything but a wholly positive feminist icon, a winged symbol of the New Woman and the new century itself, with all its potential: "the New Age in which no women will be bound down to the ground," as one character proclaims (Carter 1985: 25). She is a woman of intimidating size, sharp intelligence, intuitive generosity, fierce physical strength, and unapologetic appetites, from her thirst for champagne to her carefully manipulated but ultimately joyous sexuality. (Because of her wings, she tells her dumbstruck beloved, she must always be "on top" (pp. 82, 292).)

The change in *tone* from most of Carter's writing before 1979 to *Nights at the Circus* is undeniable. Nevertheless, it is worth questioning the idea that this novel consolidates a profound shift in her *approach*, toward either a more utopian or a more pragmatic feminism (although Fevvers is certainly both a utopian and a pragmatic figure). Despite creating female characters who can cast off their oppression and soar heavenward as winged giantesses or transform themselves into tigers (as in *The Bloody Chamber*), Carter herself had no patience with the idea that she had begun writing new feminist myths. As she half-joked in an interview, "I'm a socialist, damn it! How can you expect me to be interested in fairies?" (Harron 1984). Her late novels remain as eager as ever to reveal the dangers involved when people produced by specific historical circumstances – like Fevvers – get turned into myths. But it would also be a mistake to focus only on the pragmatism and commitment to "good old common sense" that are much in evidence in *Nights at the Circus*, or on its more restrained narrative style. Rather, the thread that runs through *Nights at the Circus* and connects it to all of Carter's work is the idea that it is impossible to separate fantasy from pragmatism, substance from style, or old stories from new visions if one is to understand the real political power of fictions. Emphasizing this idea highlights the real continuity between her late novels and her earlier work, and provides a framework for understanding those more bewildering and problematic earlier novels. It also makes clear that while feminism became central to Carter's political outlook, her commitments also extended well beyond feminism per se.

Carter's sense of how aesthetic texts inevitably also perform *political* functions remained remarkably consistent throughout her career. For her, politics depends on recognizing the fact that history proper (by which I mean events, facts, economic realities) is always intertwined with fictions (meaning stories, images, myths). We construct ourselves and understand our place in history through fictions. Carter talked about the canonical cultural tradition of the West, in which she read so widely and on which she drew so extensively, as "a vast repository of outmoded lies" that remain important not only because many of them are also genuinely beautiful, but because they have provided "the social fictions that regulate our lives" (1998: 29, 25). This belief underlies the "excessive" allusions to and borrowings from other texts in her work; they are how we learn to imagine ourselves in history, and also how we are misled.

Despite its gleefully winking implausibility, *Nights at the Circus* has one foot firmly on the ground of history proper. Carter situates Fevvers's fantastical adventures in a particular historical moment freighted with significance. The most obvious references to the conflicts of the time are Fevvers's concern with the fight for women's suffrage in Britain and the setting of two-thirds of the novel in pre-revolutionary Russia, with its grotesque disparities of wealth and poverty and its widespread injustice. Lizzie and Fevvers, we eventually discover, are themselves part of an international revolutionary underground: Fevvers's hefty income has been funding the struggle and Lizzie has been sending secret dispatches from Russia back to none other than Karl Marx in London (1985: 292). There is another epochal shift also already underway in Carter's 1899: while her narrative notes the lingering oppressive power of the British empire – there are passing mentions, for instance, of the Irish question and the contemporaneous Boer War – the global balance of power is clearly beginning to shift toward the USA, symbolized rather obviously here by Colonel Kearney, the Barnum-like circus entrepreneur in his stars-and-stripes suit.

So the turn of the twentieth century is figured not only as a moment of great potential for women's rights and for socialist revolution; it is also the dawn of the American century, of amoral capitalism's triumphant hegemony, and Carter is offering an elegy for "those last, bewildering days before history, that is, history as we know it, that is, white history, that is, European history, that is, Yanqui history... that final little breathing space before history itself extended its tentacles to grasp the whole globe" (p. 265). The third-person narrator tells us that the Siberian shaman who adopts Walser, the American journalist, is unknowingly living out the last days of his timeless tradition; in real life, the American-led Jesup Expedition (1897–1902) introduced Siberian shamanism to western anthropology just at the same moment as Carter's fictional encounter, and soon such customs were all but eradicated by Soviet policies. The whole novel hovers on the cusp of two very different possibilities for history – one full of hope for democratic progress, the other full of revulsion at the unprecedented forms of global domination the twentieth century will bring – but in either event, it suggests that coming to terms with the forward movement of history itself is unavoidable.

A history of fictions (a vision of history *as* fiction) is also deeply embedded in the very style and structure of *Nights at the Circus*. Carter's style here may be less overwritten but, as in her previous fiction, it remains packed with literary and cultural allusions: her profligate borrowings encompass everything from the picaresque form itself to snippets of Shakespeare, Goethe, Yeats, the *Arabian Nights*, *Don Quixote*, classical mythology, and the Christian Bible, not to mention *lieder* and music-hall tunes. One of the aspects of Carter's work that can usefully be seen as postmodern (highlighting its connections to the work of such contemporaries as Martin Amis and Rushdie) is its mingling of canonical high culture with popular culture. Part of Fevvers's subversive power comes precisely from the fact that she is able to cross the boundaries between the high-culture world and the nascent sphere of mass culture. She mingles with aristocrats and royalty as well as street urchins and "women of the *worst class*" (p. 21), but also, the social strata meet in the very language of both Fevvers and the third-person narrator. For instance, Carter stretches the bounds of realism to give the self-educated Fevvers access to an extensive body of high-cultural reading from which to quote. In this, Fevvers is as much a figure of *class* subversion as of gender fluidity. A similar class critique is even more central to the working of allusions in Carter's other "cheerful" late novel, *Wise Children*, which draws most heavily on Shakespeare but also on popular culture from the 1920s to the 1980s. Contrasting the working-class Chance sisters, who are music-hall dancers, with their more wealthy and aristocratic relatives the Hazards, who are "legitimate" stage actors, *Wise Children* examines the unjust and ironic mutual construction of culture and class in supposedly classless modern Britain.

In *Nights at the Circus*, the extensive interweaving of references produces a sense that Fevvers herself is not only a character poised at a turning-point in history, she is also a textual construction, a patchwork of already existing images: she is seen, at various moments in the story, as Helen of Troy, Cupid, "the Cockney Venus," the Winged Victory, the New Woman, and the Angel of Death, among others. However, Fevvers is also an active *reader* of those many images, putting them to her own uses as new situations arise. She is always aware of herself as a performer with a script, or with a whole library of scripts and characters among which she can switch around. She draws on the stock associations she raises in others to pass herself off as an avenging angel or a cheeky Cockney with a heart of gold, as the occasion demands.

Walser too is a reader, who at first serves as a surrogate for the novel's real readers as he listens to Fevvers's story and is sucked in by it. Not knowing what to make of Fevvers, he then undergoes an intensive program of *un-learning* how to read: learning that his strategies for reading the world will not suffice if he wishes to be a fit companion for a New Woman like Fevvers. He finds himself constantly confounded and bamboozled (not to mention subjected to physical danger and ultimately amnesia). Whereas he has previously always remained detached and has never considered the effect on his experience of how others see *him*, he now develops self-awareness and ultimately recognizes that he will need to "start all over again" if he is to find a way to make sense of his own, transformed life story (pp. 293–4).

So Carter's concern with history in *Nights at the Circus* is, at least in part, to show that history is made up of texts, and to teach us the necessity of *actively reading* history, of approaching it as something both materially real (and constraining) and yet somewhat open to being manipulated and reinterpreted, as it is by Fevvers. Reading, in the broadest sense, becomes a way to recognize and to make the most of one's situation. Carter's writing style, that excessive layering of allusions and stylized gestures, and her political "message" are in fact interdependent rather than being two sides of her fiction in tension with one another; and this remains consistent throughout her career, not only in her carnivalesque novels but also in her earlier, more disturbing ones.

The Dangerous Dreams of the 1960s and After

If Carter's tone changed while her strategy remained consistent, that may have a great deal to do with the changing political climate of Britain in the 1960s, 1970s, and 1980s. When she added a new epilogue to the 1987 reissue of her novel *Love*, she wrote, "I've changed a lot since 1969 [when *Love* was written], and so has the world; I'm more benign, the world is far bleaker" (Carter 1988: 113). Margaret Thatcher's Conservative government had come to power in 1979; soon not just Britain but much of the West was undergoing a neoconservative transformation that dismayed Carter and many British intellectuals. It is possible to read the "benign" tone of her later works not as sturdy cheerfulness – as expressed in the resilient, World War II spirit of *Wise Children*'s Chance sisters, who sing and dance their way through most of the twentieth century despite a constant awareness of death and disenfranchisement – but as ironic fatalism. (Claire Hanson (1997) makes this argument, suggesting that Carter's ongoing balancing act between faith in the imagination and political anguish tips toward nihilism in her last novels.) Either way, Carter's writing during the Thatcher years was part of a larger groundswell among producers of culture in Britain: a massive, desperate flowering of oppositional creative energy that was evident in literature and in independent film, popular music, and visual art. In addition, many leftist intellectuals at the time shared with Carter a desire to "reclaim" from right-wing ultranationalists a kind of traditional, distinctly English, working-class robustness – as embodied by both Fevvers and the Chance sisters – which had historically been associated with socialism and the Labour Party. In that sense, Carter did perhaps engage, despite her protestations, in *reaffirming* some myths in her later work.

During the late 1960s and 1970s, exploring and *attacking* the allure of myths, literary and otherwise, was an approach more suited to the times. Carter personally shared in much of the revolutionary optimism now associated with the phrase "the sixties" and there are moments of utopian hope in her work from that decade, such as the cathartic Christmas Eve party that ends *Several Perceptions*. But even her earliest novels illuminated more frequently the period's dangerous glamorization of mental instability and violence – a romanticization especially hazardous for women. In *Shadow Dance*, *The Magic Toyshop*, and *Love* (and, less centrally, in *Several Perceptions*), young women fall prey to violence wrapped in arty trappings, or almost do; they are lured into seeing themselves as Ophelia or Leda or doomed vampires. Their complicity with their own fate, which bothered many subsequent feminist readers, varies in degree – they resist suffering but believe they deserve it, or they actively court it – but Carter's lush, stifling style implicitly attributes this complicity to the women's habit of swallowing whole the "repository of outmoded lies."

The gender roles are reversed in *Heroes and Villains* (1969), the first of Carter's three speculative or science-fiction novels (with *The Infernal Desire Machines of Doctor Hoffman* and *The Passion of New Eve* (1977)), but it continues her exploration of the deadly allure of romantic myths. The protagonist, Marianne, is a harsh realist and it is her husband, the gorgeous barbarian warrior, Jewel, who is destroyed by the romantic fictions woven around him. Jewel is a post-apocalyptic "noble savage," perhaps redolent of some of the doomed male beauties of the contemporary 1960s counterculture. Carter was taken to task for her depiction of rape in this novel – Jewel rapes Marianne, then she grows sexually obsessed with him – but in fact the incident shows that Jewel's attempt to master Marianne through force is futile. Such violent, physical power, born of fear, is finally nothing compared to the power to manipulate myths and ideas (possessed first by Jewel's "mentor," a former professor, and ultimately by the literate and clever Marianne). Jewel's glorious, sacrificial death is preordained and he knows it; he is little more than a helpless character in a text written for him by others who know all the possible variations on his story.

The casting of a man in the "female" role of glamorized victim in *Heroes and Villains* points forward to Carter's growing interest in the social construction of gender and in transgender performance, the focal concerns of *The Passion of New Eve*. (These issues also surface in *Doctor Hoffman*, each subsequent novel, and many of Carter's short stories.) *New Eve*'s narrative is darkly picaresque, chronicling a cynical Englishman's journey across a futuristic, war-torn and factionalized USA, during the course of which he gets kidnapped and undergoes forced surgical transformation into a woman. She/he then meets and falls in love with a legendary Hollywood movie actress, Tristessa, who turns out to be a cross-dressing man. The novel incorporates satirical representations of just about every fringe group of the American 1970s, from Manson-like cults to Aryan Christian paramilitaries to radical separatist feminists. No matter how dissimilar, each group bases its worldview on a bizarre collage of available myths and icons, from those supplied by Hollywood and *Playboy* magazine to fragments of the Bible, Blake's visionary poems, and classical mythology. "Eve" and Tristessa, neither of them an "authentic" biological woman, are themselves perfect imitations of a female ideal that never existed, but which nevertheless seems to appear in almost every text of western culture, sacred or profane. Both learn to equate their femininity with suffering and victimhood, although Eve struggles to break this pattern. Despite the novel's satire, Carter does not suggest that there is any easy way to escape this overwhelming legacy of cultural imagery.

The Passion of New Eve, along with *The Infernal Desire Machines of Doctor Hoffman* (which follows a similar narrative pattern of a nightmarish journey through a series of scenarios based on received fantasies), adjusts its sense of politics toward the moment in which it was written, despite its fantastical setting. The 1970s were a very unsettled period of social fragmentation in Britain, with a major economic recession and widespread labor unrest contributing to a rapid turnover of governments and a series of policy reversals from the Labour and Conservative Parties alike. To many younger Britons like Carter who had built up great hopes in the 1960s, the following decade brought profound uncertainty about where their dreams would lead and whether they had any real potency or relevance. Carter's fiction from the period, the least positively received of her career, struggles at its core with the significance of utopian dreams. Its lurid, downward-spiraling narratives suggest that most, if not all, utopian visions are inescapably bound up with the very traditions they seek to reject. Specifically, they are doomed to reproduce the violence and the racial and gender oppression of the mainstream culture precisely because they think they are innocent of it. While the racial politics of these novels could be debated as much as their gender politics have been – because Carter is so often reproducing stereotypes, albeit with a satirical eye – both *New Eve* and *Doctor Hoffman* address racial conflicts in ways that reflect critically back on to British society and its failure to develop new, genuinely post-imperial images of racial identity.

Carter's vision in these novels is not, however, completely closed and hopeless. When she reproduces in her own narratives compelling phrases or images from Baudelaire, Tennyson, *Gulliver's Travels*, the golden age of Hollywood cinema, or even the obscene works of the Marquis de Sade, Carter recognizes also their beauty and allure. They are sources of social regulation but also of potentially subversive power. The most hopeful characters in the apocalyptic novels are those, just as in the later, "benign" novels, who know how to manipulate existing images rather than investing them with sincere belief or attempting to escape them entirely. Thus Leilah, the hyper-sexy, black exotic dancer whom the male narrator uses and discards early in *New Eve*, reinvents herself as Lilith, the armed guerrilla leader in fatigues – an image straight out of news footage about Third World liberation struggles. Both versions of herself are secondhand fictions of a sort, although Carter is very clear that Leilah becomes indistinguishable from the clichéd erotic image she constructs elaborately in the mirror before going out to dance for money; in that sense, there is no true self separate from these fictions. Nevertheless, the fictions can be chosen, to a certain extent, from among the various compromised images of "the charismatic black woman" in Carter's fictionalized America.

In her attempt to juggle available images, Leilah/Lilith is not so far removed from Fevvers; Fevvers's juggling act is simply more complex and confident. Perhaps by the mid-1980s Carter's fiction put aside any lingering, unresolved desire for an escape from the "outmoded lies" and settled down to have as much fun with them – and to instigate as much subversion with them – as possible. The neoconservative transformation of British society in the 1980s had certainly proved that genuinely novel political formations could arise out of old images and rhetoric.

Political theorists such as Stuart Hall have proposed that the Thatcherite revolution was built on bringing together existing images of social identity in ingenious new combinations that seemed to offer solutions to nagging social and economic problems (Hall 1988): for instance, the familiar figures of the working man threatened by rising industrial unemployment and the plucky Briton proud of having seen off the Germans in the last war were brought together by neoconservative rhetoric in the image of the blue-collar racist demanding that the government defend his job from immigrants; or the woman struggling to earn equal pay in a pink-collar position and the timeless image of the loving mother as the heart of the family coalesced in the new figure of the "family first" Conservative woman who has seen through feminism's promise that she can have it all and has chosen instead to return to the home.

Again, Carter was not so much ahead of her time as highly attuned to it when her novels moved toward a stubborn (or fatalistic) "making do" with the cultural materials available. It is simply that the politics of *her* new uses for familiar stereotypes were diametrically opposed to those of Thatcherism. And apparently, her fundamentally anti-Thatcherite aesthetic struck a chord with many readers and fellow writers who were also feeling the need for a new vibrancy of the imagination, even in a supposedly postmodern and cynical moment.

REFERENCES AND FURTHER READING

Bakhtin, M. M. (1968) [1965] *Rabelais and his World*, trans. H. Iswolsky. Cambridge, MA: MIT Press.

Bristow, J. and Broughton, T. L. (eds.) (1997) *The Infernal Desires of Angela Carter: Fiction, Femininity, Feminism*. London: Longman.

Carter, A. (1982) "The mother lode," in *Nothing Sacred: Selected Writings*. London: Virago.

——(1985) [1984] *Nights at the Circus*. New York: Penguin.

——(1988) [1987] *Love*, rev. edn. New York: Penguin.

——(1998) [1983] "Notes from the front line," in L. Tucker (ed.) *Critical Essays on Angela Carter*. New York: G. K. Hall.

Day, A. (1998) *Angela Carter: The Rational Glass*. Manchester: Manchester University Press.

Gamble, S. (ed.) (2001) *The Fiction of Angela Carter: A Reader's Guide to Essential Criticism*. Cambridge: Icon Books.

Hall, S. (1988) "The toad in the garden: Thatcherism among the theorists," in C. Nelson and L. Grossberg (eds.) *Marxism and the Interpretation of Culture*. Urbana: University of Illinois Press.

Hanson, C. (1997) " 'The red dawn breaking over Clapham': Carter and the limits of artifice," in J. Bristow and T. L. Broughton (eds.) *The Infernal Desires of Angela Carter: Fiction, Femininity, Feminism*. London: Longman.

Harron, M. (1984) "I'm a socialist, damn it! How can you expect me to be interested in fairies?": interview with writer Angela Carter, *The Guardian*, September 25. Retrieved July 24, 2003, from LexisNexis Academic database.

Lee, A. (1997) *Angela Carter*. New York: Twayne.

Jordan, E. (1990) "Enthralment: Angela Carter's speculative fictions," in L. Anderson (ed.) *Plotting Change: Contemporary Women's Fiction*. London: Edward Arnold.

Kendrick, W. (1993) "The real magic of Angela Carter," in R. E. Hosmer, Jr. (ed.) *Contemporary British Women Writers: Narrative Strategies*. New York: St Martin's Press.

Palmer, P. (1997) "Gender as performance in the fiction of Angela Carter and Margaret Atwood," in J. Bristow and T. L. Broughton (eds.) *The Infernal Desires of Angela Carter: Fiction, Femininity, Feminism.* London: Longman.

Peach, L. (1998) *Angela Carter.* New York: St Martin's Press.

Pitchford, N. (2002) *Tactical Readings: Feminist Postmodernism in the Novels of Kathy Acker and Angela Carter.* Lewisburg, PA: Bucknell University Press.

Gass, J. M. (ed.) (1994) Special issue: "Angela Carter," *Review of Contemporary Fiction*, 14/3.

Sage, L. (1994a) *Angela Carter.* Plymouth: Northcote House in Association with the British Council.

——(ed.) (1994b) *Flesh and the Mirror: Essays on the Art of Angela Carter.* London: Virago.

Schmidt, R. (1989) "The journey of the subject in Angela Carter's fiction," *Textual Practice*, 3/1: 56–75.

Tucker, L. (ed.) (1998) *Critical Essays on Angela Carter.* New York: G. K. Hall.

Walsh, J. (1992) "Muscular prose," *Sunday Times*, September 13. Retrieved August 6, 2003, from LexisNexis Academic database.

31

Margaret Drabble

Margaret Moan Rowe

Made a Commander of the British Empire (CBE) in 1980, Margaret Drabble has established a formidable record as a novelist, biographer, literary scholar, and public intellectual. Her biographies of Arnold Bennett in 1974 and Angus Wilson in 1995, as well as a short study of Wordsworth in 1966, underscore her interest in fiction and poetry. Those works, along with her editorship of *The Oxford Companion to English Literature* (5th edition, 1985; 6th edition, 2000) and a bevy of introductions to works by Jane Austen, George Eliot, and Herman Melville among others, have established her considerable scholarly credentials. But a larger audience of readers, particularly female readers, has been engaged by Margaret Drabble the novelist who, thus far, has written fifteen books, beginning in 1963 with *A Summer Bird-Cage*.

Much of Drabble's early celebrity, especially among female critics, resulted from her giving voice to the significance of maternity. Valerie Grosvenor Myer highlights that contribution when she writes: "The area she has made her own is that of motherhood: pregnancy, birth, lactation and maternal care . . . Motherhood is a central experience in the life of Margaret Drabble's characters and maternal love a means to salvation" (1974: 14). Readers of her 1960s novels find themselves in agreement with Myer. Motherhood and its salvific possibilities are central themes in *The Garrick Year* (1964), *The Millstone* (1965; winner of the John Llewelyn Rhys Prize), and *The Waterfall* (1969), novels that prompt Ann Rayson to declare: "Margaret Drabble ushers in a new era for the woman writer in which the relationship between a mother and her children is catalytic rather than destructive" (1978: 43).

Emma Evans, the first-person narrator of *The Garrick Year*, meditates on a friend's suicide and concludes: "Indecision drowned him. I used to be like Julian myself, but now I have two children, and you will not find me at the bottom of any river. I have grown into the earth: I am terrestial" (1977a: 252). *The Waterfall* focuses on the affair between Jane Gray and James, her cousin Lucy's husband. The affair begins just after Jane gives birth to her second child, and Drabble deftly underscores the maternal eroticism that leads to Jane's sexual birth. If motherhood makes Emma Evans "terrestial," then I would argue that it makes Rosamund Stacey, the narrator of *The Millstone*, practically celestial. Pregnant after a single sexual encounter with George, a bisexual acquaintance, Rosamund finds her life changed utterly. An intellectual who obsessively prizes her independence and emotional isolation, Rosamund is forced to make some connections as she writes her dissertation and prepares for her baby's birth. She is literally transformed by maternity: "She put her [Octavia, Rosamund's daughter] in my arms and I sat there looking at her, and her great wide blue eyes looked at me with seeming recognition, and what I felt it is pointless to try to describe. Love, I suppose one might call it, and the first of my life" (1998: 114). But that love proves to be problematic for the reader of *The Millstone*, especially a feminist reader. Rosamund concludes her narrative with a note of triumph: "Love had isolated me more securely than fear, habit or indifference. There was one thing in the world that I knew about, and that one thing was Octavia. I had lost the taste for half-knowledge" (p. 191). In "Margaret Drabble and the journey to the self," Joan Manheimer nicely describes the problem in *The Millstone*:

> Against the background of a dreary catalogue of female characters whose happiness depends upon their fortuitous union with the proper man, Rosamund offers a refreshing image of a woman successful and satisfied without one. . . . Still this achievement signifies not a solution to the problem Drabble addresses, but an evasion of it. The cost of Rosamund's integrity is such that we must finally balk at the expense. Rosamund is a disappointingly asexual creation. (1978: 32)

Maternity takes a different turn in Drabble's novels of the 1970s. The tableau of the Madonna and infants give way to the mother and children with demands living in a larger social world. The engaging claustrophobia of Drabble's 1960s first-person narrators shifts to a chatty omniscience that allows for more complex sets of characters and issues. Take, for example, *The Needle's Eye*. As Ellen Cronan Rose notes:

> When *The Needle's Eye* was published in 1972, it must have surprised readers who thought they knew to expect from Margaret Drabble another novel about the situation of being a woman. For the first paragraph situates the reader in the consciousness of a man, Simon Camish, from whose point of view a large bulk of the novel is narrated. (*1980:* 71).

In addition to the uniqueness of the male consciousness in *The Needle's Eye*, the novel signals Drabble's turn to a wider reach of social interactions. That reach prompted Joyce Carol Oates to declare: "Here is a real novel," a declaration that the Popular Library edition proudly displayed on its back cover. Yet "the situation of being a woman" is still very much a thread in this "real novel," in the characterization of Rose Vassiliou, the mother of three children who is separated from an abusive husband and enmeshed in legal problems of Dickensian proportions. She is also less rhapsodic about motherhood. Rose decides to return to her husband and concludes bitterly that "She had ruined her own nature against her own judgement, for

Christopher's sake, for the children's sake" (1972: 378). In her reading of *The Needle's Eye*, Joanne Creighton argues that "children are the stabilizing force" (1985: 78). I differ, and believe that judgment is conditioned by the expectations readers bring from reading 1960s Drabble novels. Rose is trammeled by maternity.

Maternity is no obstacle for Frances Wingate, a celebrated archaeologist and central character in Drabble's widely acclaimed novel *The Realms of Gold* (1975). The mother of four children, Frances finds herself far removed from maternal care:

> It had been interesting, the experience of being programmed for maternity. She had been a fairly responsive case; yet not utterly responsive now that her younger child was seven, and some of her finer responses were no longer needed. She had felt, had noticed her heart hardening. She no longer softened at the sight of other people's babies: in fact she would avoid them and leave railway compartments when they entered. (1977b: 9)

Frances is more intent on coping with her own depression (a recurring illness in Drabble's fiction) and probing her family history, in particular the history of her father's family the Ollerenshaws of the East Midlands: "She had allied herself with the ill-connected Ollerenshaws, and the dull ditches of her father and his newts" (p. 267). She chooses a patrilineal rather than a matrilineal connection, a point I want to stress. Frances Wingate, the grown child, like so many of the central women characters in Drabble's fiction, sees her mother as the matriarch exercising power as the gatekeeper. Lady Ollerenshaw, "an intelligent, highly educated woman, from a family of famous names," devours others and is seen by her daughter as "a snake" (p. 80). While Lady Ollerenshaw's social appetites are insatiable, Rita Ablewhite, a matriarchal figure in *The Radiant Way* (1987), "'doesn't get out much'," according to Shirley Harper, one of her two daughters (agoraphobia also affects Kate Armstrong's mother in *The Middle Ground* (1980)). But for Liz Headleand, a successful London psychiatrist and the mother of two daughters and three stepsons, Rita Ablewhite, locked away at 8 Abercorn Avenue in Northam, is the enemy:

> She had succeeded in avoiding going to Northam for two years, on one pretext or another, and had managed to justify herself to herself, after a manner. She was, after all, very busy. She spoke to her mother on the telephone, but not often. The truth was, as she quite well knew, that she could not bear to see her mother. She hoped her mother would die, soon. (1989b: 124-5)

Why?

One reason is that Rita Ablewhite has helped her daughter become a success. Directed by her mother, "Liz Ablewhite was offered, and graciously accepted, the Alethea Ward Scholarship in Natural Sciences (an annual college award specifically designated by Dr. Ward, 1853–1935, for female students of medicine from the County of Yorkshire, her own home county), the goal towards which her mother had been directing her over the past ten years" (p. 82). In "Bleak houses: Doris Lessing, Margaret Drabble and the condition of England," Gayle Greene captures Liz's situation when she states: "Like many protagonists of contemporary women's fiction, her ambition is fuelled by matrophobia" (1992: 314). Her sister, Shirley Harper, who remains in Yorkshire, offers a similar, if simpler, judgment of Liz when she declares: "I do think you behaved appallingly to Mother" (1989b: 371).

Another element in the mother–daughter rupture in *The Radiant Way* is related to the secret of the father. After her mother dies, Liz and her sister ready their mother's house for sale, and Liz comes upon information about her long missing father, a pedophile and suicide – and her own molester. But the gravity of this discovery is never convincingly connected to Liz's total rejection of Rita Abelwhite. Much about the mother–daughter conflict is left unresolved in *The Radiant Way*, a novel Dominic Head calls Drabble's "most important political novel" (2002: 31).

Resolution of a sort – or at least tying up some loose ends – waits until *A Natural Curiosity* (1989), the second of the three novels (*The Gates of Ivory*, 1991, is the third) that ambitiously and compellingly map the state of the nation through the lives of Liz Headland, Alix Bowen, and Esther Breuer, three Cambridge friends. Liz attends a party near Northam and is introduced to Marcia Campbell, who turns out to be Rita Abelwhite's illegitimate daughter: "Marcia was, and indeed always had been, the oldest daughter of Rita Abelwhite, born out of wedlock a year before Liz herself" (1989a: 268). Seduced by an aristocratic employer, Rita Ablewhite was forced to give up her child and rushed into a marriage of convenience.

Here I want to inject some conjecture about Drabble's biography and attitudes toward matriarchy, particularly when Yorkshire is part of the landscape. Yorkshire is Margaret Drabble's home county; she was born in Sheffield at the beginning of World War II. Both of her parents were university graduates, and Drabble achieved great success at Cambridge University, where she won a "starred first." Marriage quickly followed graduation, in 1960. After a short stint in the theater at Stratford, Drabble and her family settled in London, where her success as a novelist quickly followed. But as Drabble indicated in a 1975 interview with Nancy Poland, success had its price:

> "It (achievement) has cost quite a lot, I think." Later she [Drabble] sounded wistful when she said, "It's sometimes such a misery to spend your life worrying about achievements, you know. My mother was always convinced that I was going to be something wonderful . . . perhaps I believed her, perhaps I simply took it all in with my mother's milk." (1975: 260–1)

But mother's milk can turn sour, and in that same interview, Poland goes on to reveal that Drabble's mother "still doesn't think 'Maggie' – despite her success – 'has ever been fully stretched'" (p. 261). As intimated in the Poland interview, Drabble had a very complicated relationship with her mother, Kathleen Marie Drabble (née Bloor). In her "Afterword" to *The Peppered Moth* (2001), her most complex dissection of matriarchy, Drabble speaks directly of that difficulty: "I think about my mother a great deal, uncomfortably. Night and day on me she cries" (2002: 367).

The almost pathological antipathy Liz Headland feels toward her mother has roots in Drabble's own biography. And Drabble often comments on the weight of biography in a writer's work, as, for example, in an interview with Gillian Parker and Janet Todd published in 1983. Asked "Do you see literature as text and context, or as text alone?" Drabble responded:

> No. I see it as social context. Also I see it a lot in terms of a writer's personal biography. I was taught not to pay any attention to it, but I find it increasingly interesting. It's so obvious that writers are influenced by the way their parents behaved. It seems to me ridiculous to isolate a text, in fact almost meaningless. (Parker and Todd 1983: 171)

Liz Headland is not the first of Drabble's protagonists to escape the North – and its association with matriarchal power – for the South and the possibility of self-creation. Amidst the 1960s novels so drenched in maternity and narrated in the first person is an anomaly, *Jerusalem the Golden* (1967), winner of the James Tait Black Memorial Award. The third-person narration follows the social progress of Clara Maugham, whose very name speaks to her relationship with her mother: "For Mrs. Maugham did not like the name any more than Clara and her school friends did, and she chose it through a characteristic mixture of duty and malice" (1987: 9–10). But Clara turns her name into an asset just as she turns the intelligence resented by her mother into the way out:

> So she cultivated, stubbornly, discreetly, her inclinations, and in the end it was this same intelligence which in her home town was so sourly disowned, so grudgingly deprecated, that got her out of it and transported her incredibly, mercifully, to London. When she received her first term's check for her state scholarship allowance, she stared at it for some time as she contemplated the fact, the printed fact before her, the final vindication of her lonely belief that there was more than one way of life in England. (1987: 10–11)

Meeting and being enfolded by the golden Denham family is another confirmation "that there was more than one way of life in England." Clara can't wait to leave home but the adult Denham children are ever returning home: "the Denhams seemed to be perpetually, intricately, shiftingly involved, each with the other, and each with a whole circle of cross-threaded connections" (pp. 126–7). It is a far cry from Northam, and Clara responds to the dramatic difference: "She had not been reared upon embraces. She took her place in the diversely-lit evening of the drawing room with a sense that if she belonged anywhere it was as much here as to those long and silent evenings in front of the derided, loquacious television" (p. 137). Clara has an affair with Gabriel Denham but is literally in love with the Denham family, another interesting link to Margaret Drabble's own experience. In a 1980 conversation with Sharon Whitehill, Drabble spoke of her first marriage to Clive Swift, the actor, and declared: "I loved my husband's family. Sometimes I think I really married *them*" (1984: 72). Drabble married Michael Holroyd, the biographer, in 1982.

Since I have quoted Drabble on the subject of her family, I will now take the liberty of introducing an observation made by A. S. Byatt, another distinguished novelist and Margaret Drabble's sister. (The sisters have long been rivals.) In an online LitChat, Byatt talks of her love-hate relationship with the work of D. H. Lawrence, a relationship she shares with Drabble. After scorning Lawrence's view of the novel's centrality, Byatt concludes: "But nevertheless, he did sort of put a kind of Blakeian vision into a world I knew, into a world of chapels and of very, very cautious lower-middle class values, and people who wanted to get out of something that they didn't want to hate" (1996: 2). Clara Maugham is certainly one of the people "who wanted to get out of something": "Her years in London had merely strengthened her desire to live there for the rest of her life, and while she was there her mother seemed, most of the time, to be no more than a dreadful past sorrow, endured and survived" (1987: 97). But what about hate? The novel is fairly steeped in it.

In what the narrative suggests will be Clara Maugham's final release from Northam and its limitations, a telegram brings Clara to her mother's hospital bedside. And Drabble attempts an explanation of the past with Clara rummaging through her mother's belongings and discovering photographs and exercise books that reveal something of Mrs Maugham's life before marriage and "before the end of her hopes" (p. 228). But the discovery seems forced; hate, or, to use Gayle Greene's word, "matrophobia," dominates *Jerusalem the Golden*. Ultimately, Clara concludes: "Her mother was dying, but she herself would survive it, she would survive because she had willed herself to survive" (p. 239). In *Writing of Women*, Phyllis Rose calls *Jerusalem the Golden* "perhaps the best of the five intense and closely focused novels Drabble wrote in the sixties" (1985: 109). I agree with that estimate. From my vantage point, *Jerusalem the Golden* is even more significant as a proleptic work that points to the more complicated and painful mother–daughter issues Drabble would explore in her later novels.

The Witch of Exmoor (1996), with its own formidable matriarch Frieda Haxby (married name Palmer), is one such novel. Mother of a son and two daughters whom she rears without a husband, Frieda has established herself as an independent woman through her will to succeed and her work as a writer. Her masterpiece is "that perennial and influential classic *The Matriarchy of War*" (p. 30); Frieda's book title refers to a work that addresses female employment during the World Wars but might also be appropriated to capture the combative state existing between many of the aging mothers and grown daughters in Drabble's fictional world. Matriarchy, more than patriarchy, is a persistent obstacle to female empowerment in Drabble's novels.

Frieda's son-in-law, Nathan Herz, is fascinated by Frieda and her brood:

Seen from afar, the Palmers – Daniel, Gogo, and Rosemary – might seem to carry the assumptions of the British middle classes, carried on from generation to generation. But they come from nowhere. They have turned themselves into members of the English middle class by sleight of hand. Their manner, their voice, their pretensions – they appear to date back from centuries, but, as Nathan knows quite well, they date back no further than Frieda Haxby Palmer and her missing husband, whoever he may have been. (1996: 20)

Interestingly enough, the omniscient narrator is also favorably disposed to the manipulative Frieda, who is presented as a woman of imagination and energy. She is unwilling to go gently into old age. Her grown children, however, have other views and expectations of Frieda. An absent father allows Frieda Haxby full control over her children – a power they, especially her grown daughters, have internalized. Gogo and Rosemary cannot resist "the game of Unhappy Families": "They could bring any topic home. They could lasso conversations about gardening, or the cinema, or the Hubble telescope, or the sugar industry, or Guyanese politics, or the slave-trade, and bring them home to graze about their mother" (p. 9).

But the lady's not for grazing. As *The Witch of Exmoor* opens Frieda Haxby has made herself the missing parent by taking herself into self-imposed exile to Exmoor and a derelict hotel by the sea that she has purchased. From her daughters' perspective, Frieda is using exile to best them by constructing a new narrative: "She has forced them into the role of Bad Children, and willfully, playfully, cast herself as a Neglected Mother" (p. 86). There is also a concern about money. Frieda's "vast, incoherent, over-researched baroque monstrosity" (p. 29) *Queen Christina* has a new reading audience, film producers. They have a different view: "At the very least, there was a fine vehicle here for a leading lady, and plenty of opportunities for feminist deconstruction of the past. Lesbianism and espionage, rape and assassinations, art and abdications – what more could you want?" (p. 151).

Frieda Haxby from the Fens goes to Exmoor to play her last game, to exercise a final control over her family: she has come to write her memoirs. She determines to expose the sleight of hand that Nathan Herz so admired, the Palmers' ease in passing into the English middle class:

> She sits here, and addresses herself to her final questioning, her last revenge. This must be clear, she believes, even to her own dim-witted family. She is here to summon her mother, her father, her sister, her husband from their graves and from their hiding places. As the Witch of Endor raised Samuel to terrify Saul, so she, the Witch of Exmoor, will raise Gladys Haxby, Ernest Haxby, Hilda Haxby, Andrew Palmer. Her nice clean ambitious well-educated offspring will be appalled by their hideous ancestry. (1996: 66)

With Frieda's fall and drowning, the memoir goes unwritten, but the dead are "summoned" and confronted by Frieda's granddaughter Emily Palmer, who hacks into Frieda's computer.

The story revolves around the sibling rivalry between Frieda and Hilda that peaks with Hilda's affair with Andrew Palmer and her subsequent killing of their child and her suicide. Hardly a "hideous ancestry" for Frieda's daughters: "They speak of poor Aunt Everhilda, whom they had never known, and their poor little nameless half-sister, who had died in a gas oven. They speak, obsessively, at length, of their vanished father, so little mentioned for so long"(p. 267). Ironically, Frieda's memoir-writing has made a common ground for sisters long separated by marriage choices and life-styles. Even more ironically, they are turned into historical researchers like Frieda: "They piece together their fears of the past and for the future, and each time a new pattern emerges, a new seam is stitched. One day they will make sense of their ancestry" (p. 267). Or so they think.

Frieda, too, has tried to make sense of her ancestry. She is the woman of action: writer, researcher, game player, and possesser of "many paged, richly stamped passports" (p. 73) who thinks she has escaped Dry Bendish and a domineering mother, described as a "tedious and armchair-bound old bloodsucker" (p. 29). Yet she spends her last days trying to understand that past: "Is this desire to write her memoirs a desire for revenge, or a desire to salvage her own self? She is not sure" (p. 69).

Frieda Haxby's uncertainty about her motives for trying to revisit the past is an apt introduction to Margaret Drabble's "Afterword" to *The Peppered Moth*. Therein, she writes of being encouraged by friends, one of whom urged, "Use your mother's blood for ink" (2002: 367), to face her difficult relationship with her own mother. Responding to that encouragement, Drabble wrote *The Peppered Moth*, a novel rather than "a factual memoir" (p. 367). The richly textured novel opens in South Yorkshire with a scientific lecture "upon the subject of mitochondrial DNA and matrilineal descent" (p. 2). Dr Hawthorn, the lecturer, tells his audience: "Where we come *from* is the most interesting thing that we can know about ourselves" (p. 63). And Drabble underscores the complexity of *from* as she combines material from archaeology, molecular biology, environmental science, and genealogy to explore the tension between nature and nurture. For my purposes, however, it is the novel's matrilineal history that is most absorbing.

The Peppered Moth amply supports the late Lorna Sage's positioning of Drabble in *Women in the House of Fiction*. Sage links Drabble, Iris Murdoch, Edna O'Brien, and Mary McCarthy, and notes: "In the end, perhaps, it's the relation between generations that counts most for the novelists of the middle ground – the past as construction, as context" (1992: 111). Drabble crafts a tale of four generations of mothers and daughters: Ellen Cudworth, Bessie Bawtry, Chrissie Barron, and Faro Gaulden (the names themselves point to the family movement from provincial North to cosmopolitan South). The omniscient narrator has clear loyalty to and affection for the younger (Chrissie and Faro) rather than to the older (Ellen and Bessie) generations. The narrator labels Ellen Cudworth and Bessie Bawtry "these dreadful people" (2002: 198), and not without reason.

The repressed and repressive Ellen Cudworth "did not like children, as a class" (p. 11), nor for that matter does she like them as individuals. She is interested in her elder daughter, Bessie, only because of the child's willfulness. The more docile and loving Dora is victim of both mother and sister:

> Months passed, years passed. Bessie came out from under the table, and forgot her cotton bobbin, and Dora woke up and began to try to make a noise. Ellen and Bessie

between them soon put a stop to that. Bessie had decided that she was the most important member of the family, and had already managed to impose her conception and her will on others. Dora must learn to stay in second place. (2002: 18)

Bessie is another matter: "Bessie Bawtry, from her earliest memories, thought of herself as special. And so she was" (p. 7).

Like Clara Maugham in *Jerusalem the Golden*, Bessie Bawtry's specialness is connected to will and intellect: "For her, it is college or death" (p. 69). But Bessie's ambition, which leads her to a Cambridge degree in the 1920s, is tainted by some vague limitation: "Bessie did not mutate. She seemed to thrive and prosper, according to her own lights and her own plans. But, gradually, almost inevitably, something seemed to begin to go wrong" (p. 109). That something is later connected to a depression that seriously affects her relationship with her husband Joe Barron, and her children. The "special" Bessie Bawtry, ahead of her time in laying intellectual claims to a university degree, becomes the Bessie Barron who "sank into depression with an almost voluptuous abandon" (p. 181).

Chrissie Barron, daughter of Bessie Bawtry and Joe Barron of Yorkshire, and Faro Gaulden, daughter of Chrissie Barron and Nick Gaulden of London, suffer little at the hands of the omniscient narrator. Indeed, Faro, described as "a bobby-dazzler" (p. 3), is the novel's golden girl, reminding the reader of Frances Wingate in *The Realms of Gold*. An historian of science, Faro Gaulden writes for "a scientific magazine called *Prometheus*" (p. 136) and finds herself in Dr Hawthorn's audience, beginning a journey that takes her into the past of the Cudworths and into an even more distant past as evidenced in the discovery of Cotterhall man in Yorkshire.

In the novel's fairly bleak depiction of mother-daughter relationships, only Faro's characterization offers the possibility of reconciliation among generations. Cleaning out her great-aunt Dora's house after Dora's stroke confines her to a home, Faro is at first impatient, even dismissive:

She has several plastic bags full of rubbish, and she is sure she is about to discard something important. Though how could any of this be of any importance? These are such little lives. Unimportant people, in an unimportant place. They had been young, they had endured, they had taken their wages and their punishment, and then they had grown old, and all for no obvious purpose. And now she is throwing them all into a plastic bag. (2002: 361)

Not quite all. Things as objective correlatives figure in this final scene in the narrative. First, there is a discolored sixpence; second, a watch come to life; and, finally, a photograph: "It is of the two sisters, taken on Grandma Barron's wedding day, for Bessie is wearing her wedding dress, and Dora is playing bridesmaid" (p. 364). Ultimately, the discolored sixpence opens the door to a happy memory of a Christmas long past:

Bessie, who had sliced the pudding, made sure that little Faro, who had noticed the manoeuvre, had nevertheless been pleased and excited to find the coin, hygienically wrapped in foil, half hidden in her rich brown fruity portion. Faro stands stock-still on the seventh step, for she can see Grandma's happy face, smiling as Faro cries out and unwraps the silver treasure. (2002: 364)

The potential for reconciliation pivots on the grandmother–granddaughter relationship, not the mother–daughter relationship, a potential underscored by Drabble's epigraph for *The Peppered Moth*. She uses a poem written by Rebecca Swift, her daughter. The poem, "On remembering getting into bed with grandparents," captures the different perspective of the granddaughter in its first lines: "It's amazing we got that far, loveless / As you were supposed to be." The placement of that different set of memories at the very beginning of the text offers another version of Kathleen Marie Bloor, but it is a version that is quickly overpowered by the Bessie Bawtry figure created by Kathleen Marie Bloor's daughter.

In the *New York Times Book Review*, quoted in the Harcourt paperback edition of *The Peppered Moth*, Daphne Merkin offers one way to view Bessie Bawtry when she writes: "Bad mothers, just as surely as absentee fathers or feuding siblings can make for good fiction." And by anyone's measure Bessie Bawtry is a bad mother. Her daughter, Chrissie Barron, sees her as "a real bloodsucker as well as a shrew" (2002: 221), while the omniscient narrator holds her at arm's length so that the reader knows little about her internal life and motives. In the "Afterword," Drabble offers an interesting description of her narrative predicament: "I encountered great difficulties. The worst was the question of tone. I find myself being harsh, dismissive, censorious. As she was. She taught me language" (p. 367).

Early in *The Peppered Moth*, the narrator describes the relationship between Ellen Cudworth and her daughter Bessie:

Ellen, like her daughter Bessie, disliked dirt. They were at one on this. Ellen had always been at war with dirt. She lost, but she fought on. Bessie would not respect her for these battles, because she was to observe only the defeat, not the struggle. Therefore she was to despise her mother. That is the way it is with mothers and daughters. (2002: 11)

I quote this passage because I think it captures some of Drabble's predicament. She "was to observe only the defeat, not the struggle" in her mother's life, and, ultimately cannot extend an imaginative sympathy to what "the battles" might have cost. Earlier I mentioned that Frieda Haxby in *The Witch of Exmoor* is brought to life by an omniscient narrator; not so Bessie Bawtry, who is more of a sociological and clinical study than a character in a novel. Drabble's depiction of the society that fosters Bessie's ambition is masterful; not for nothing did she publish a fine biography of Arnold Bennett. The scenes in pre- and post-World War I Yorkshire are filled with absorbing detail. But Bessie Bawtry eludes the reader and the author. Drabble herself describes that failure: "I wrote this book to understand my mother better. I went down into the underworld to look for my mother, but I couldn't find her. She wasn't there" (p. 369). In *The Picture of Dorian Gray*, Oscar Wilde observes that "Children begin by loving their parents; as they grow older they judge them; sometimes they forgive them" (1993: 48). In the later novels of Margaret Drabble, forgiveness between mothers and daughters is rare indeed.

REFERENCES AND FURTHER READING

Byatt, A. S. (1996) "LitChat: A. S. Byatt." *Salon*, February 15: 1–2. <http://www.salon.com/08/departments/litchat2.html>

Creighton, Joanne V. (1985) *Margaret Drabble*. New York: Methuen.

Drabble, Margaret (1972) *The Needle's Eye*. New York: Popular Library.

——(1977a) [1964] *The Garrick Year*. New York: Popular Library.

——(1977b) [1975] *The Realms of Gold*. New York: Popular Library.

——(1987) [1967] *Jerusalem the Golden*. New York: Plume Books.

——(1989a) *A Natural Curiosity*. New York: Viking.

——(1989b) [1987] *The Radiant Way*. New York: Ballantine Books.

——(1996) *The Witch of Exmoor*. New York: Harcourt Brace.

——(1998) [1965] *The Millstone*. New York: Harvest Books.

——(2002) [2001] *The Peppered Moth*. New York: Harvest Books.

Greene, Gayle (1992) "Bleak houses: Doris Lessing, Margaret Drabble and the condition of England," *Forum for Modern Language Studies*, 28 (October): 304–19.

Hannay, John (1986) *The Intertextuality of Fate: A Study of Margaret Drabble*. Columbia: University of Missouri Press.

Head, Dominic (2002) *The Cambridge Introduction to Modern British Fiction, 1950–2000*. Cambridge: Cambridge University Press.

Manheimer, Joan (1978) "Margaret Drabble and the journey to self," *Studies in the Literary Imagination*, 11 (Fall): 127–43.

Myer, Valerie Grosvenor (1974) *Margaret Drabble: Puritanism and Permissiveness*. New York: Barnes and Noble.

Parker, Gillian and Todd, Janet (1983) "Margaret Drabble," in Janet Todd (ed.) *Women Writers Talking*. New York: Holmes and Meier.

Poland, Nancy (1975) "Margaret Drabble: 'There must be a lot of people like me'," *Midwest Quarterly*, 16 (Spring): 255–67.

Rayson, Ann. (1978) "Motherhood in the novels of Margaret Drabble," *Frontiers*, 3: 43–6.

Rose, Ellen Cronan (1980) *The Novels of Margaret Drabble: Equivocal Figures*. Totowa, NJ: Barnes and Noble.

——(ed.) (1985) *Critical Essays on Margaret Drabble*. Boston: G. K. Hall.

Rose, Phyllis (1985) *Writing of Women: Essays in a Renaissance*. Middletown, CT: Wesleyan University Press.

Sage, Lorna (1992) *Women in the House of Fiction: Post-War Women Novelists*. London: Macmillan.

Schmidt, Dorey (ed.) (1982) *Margaret Drabble: Golden Realms*. Edinburg, TX: Pan American University.

Wilde, Oscar (1993) [1891] *The Picture of Dorian Gray*. New York: Dover Publications.

Whitehill, Sharon (1984) "Two for tea: an afternoon with Margaret Drabble," *Essays in Literature*, 11 (Spring): 67–75.

32
V. S. Naipaul

Timothy Weiss

When V. S. Naipaul was named the Nobel laureate in literature for the year 2001, it was an honor well merited and long overdue – as well as somewhat unexpected. After all, over a fifty-year period Naipaul has published important books, and these varied works address key social and cultural issues of the second half of the twentieth century: colonialism, decolonization, emigration, ideologies, and religious fundamentalisms, the need for a new universalism in a world submerged in murderous identities. For this reason, and perhaps others, he has been, at times, a controversial figure. He is a masterly writer of fiction, but he is more than a writer of fiction: he is also an historian, an analyst of culture and societies, and an intellectual spokesman beyond national frontiers. In short, he has a world presence, and he has, to a certain degree, established the paradigm of what it means today to be a world writer in English.

In "Two worlds," the author's Nobel Lecture 2001, and in a short piece entitled *Reading and Writing: A Personal Account* (2000), Naipaul explains that although fiction has allowed him to illuminate certain "areas of darkness" of his world, it has its limitations and has had to be complemented by other kinds of research and representation:

> As a child trying to read, I had felt that two worlds separated me from the books that were offered to me at school and in the libraries: the childhood world of our remembered India, and the more colonial world of our city. I had thought that the difficulties [of reading and becoming a writer] had to do with the social and emotional disturbances of my childhood ... and that the difficulties would blow away as I got older. What I didn't know, even after I had written my early books of fiction, concerned only with story and people and getting to the end and mounting the jokes well, was that those two spheres of darkness had become my subject. Fiction, working its mysteries, by

indirections finding directions out, had led me to my subject. But it couldn't take me all the way. (2000: 37–8)

A great appeal and strength of Naipaul's works is that they combine the imaginative reach of fiction with the sense of living testimony that one expects from history and social and cultural studies. If Naipaul's project as a writer had been wholly a rhetorical one – making stories, "getting to the end and mounting the jokes well," as he puts it – his works would not have the force of truth with which they strike us. His oeuvre has had to be about something more than the pleasure of the text: it is an investigation into the nature of a complex world that encompasses a distant past ("remembered India"), the West Indian colony (Trinidad), life in the metropolis (London), decades of decolonization and the beginnings of postcolonial readjustments, various travels and sojourns (in Asia, Africa, South America, and North America), globalization and wars of ideologies.

The Nobel Lecture 2001 reiterates and elaborates on this. "[A]s a child," Naipaul recounts, "I had a sense of two worlds, the world outside that tall corrugated-iron gate, and the world at home – or, at any rate, the world of my grandmother's house." Like others in the East Indian community of Trinidad, he continues, "the world outside existed in a kind of darkness" (2002: 482). "When I became a writer those areas of darkness around me as a child became my subjects. The land; the aborigines; the New World; the colony; the history; India; the Muslim world, to which I also felt myself related; Africa; and then England, where I was doing my writing" (p. 484). Today, in retrospect, this all appears clear-cut and unmistakable, but in looking back on a writer's career one traces a logic and connections that were not apparent at the moment of struggle and composition; so it is not contradictory to talk of the project of Naipaul's works on the one hand and the indeterminate nature of their inquiry and discovery, on the other. "I was an intuitive writer," he asserts:

> That was so, and that remains so now, when I am nearly at the end. I never had a plan. I followed no system. I worked intuitively. My aim every time was to do a book, to create something that would be easy and interesting to read. At every stage I could only work within my knowledge and sensibility and talent and world-view. Those things developed book by book. And I had to do the books I did because there were no books about those subjects to give me what I wanted. I had to clear up my world, elucidate it, for myself. (2002: 483)

In the following pages I will retrace steps in Naipaul's journey as writer. Along the way we might keep in mind two things: first, Naipaul's works have an intertextuality, that is, they tend to build, comment upon, and extend the subject matter and themes of previous books; second, his works combine fiction with autobiography, history, travel, and social and cultural commentary to the point that, although we can and should make a distinction between fiction and nonfiction, differences among these works have more to do with emphasis and highlighting than with hard-set generic boundaries.

Novels of the 1950s and 1960s: *Miguel Street, The Suffrage of Elvira, The Mystic Masseur, A House for Mr Biswas, Mr Stone and the Knights Companion, The Mimic Men*

Naipaul has called his 1950s novels – *Miguel Street* (1959), *The Mystic Masseur* (1957), and *The Suffrage of Elvira* (1958) – social comedies, and over the years these books have not lost their appeal, for they are infused with a delight and an inquisitiveness. Their humor has a double side, however, expressing both a joy of life and a malaise; they celebrate the richness of a multicultural society, yet they also show the traps and dead ends of this colonial world. The Trinidad of these 1950s novels combines an emigrant's distanced evaluation with a colonial's old uncertainties and fears. By way of the novels' split perspectives and polyphony, the author can write affectionately about the colony as well as satirize it. "To condemn the picaroon [colonial] society out of hand is to ignore its important quality," he writes in *The Middle Passage*; "And this is not only its ability to beguile and enchant. For if such a society breeds cynicism, it also breeds tolerance ... tolerance for every human activity and affection for every demonstration of wit and style" (1969c: 77). Of his fiction, the 1950s novels are perhaps most touched by the "wit and style" of a unique, multicultural society.

In *Miguel Street*, the author's first written but third published novel, the narrator recounts the story of his youth in an inner-city neighborhood of Port of Spain as if he were again a boy growing up there; in its split perspectives and interlinked stories of urban frustration and entrapment in the web of city life, the collection resembles James Joyce's *Dubliners*. What most strikes the reader about the stories of *Miguel Street* is perhaps less their variety – there is a richness of personalities and idiosyncrasies – than ultimately their sameness. Most of the stories end unhappily, and most treat frustrations and obsessions that the respective characters never quite overcome. In one way or another, these stories explore the limitations of the colony and the psychological mark that colonialism continues to imprint on the inhabitants of this neighborhood of Port of Spain. One of these psychological marks is the feeling that the metropolis is reality and that the colony only an imitation of that reality.

In *The Mystic Masseur* the conflict between colonial self and metropolitan other is played out in the main character, Ganesh, who combines aspects of both the past and the future of the colony. On the one hand, he is a masseur, or a folk healer, in the tradition of his father; on the other hand, he becomes a specialist in self-promotion and image-making. At the end of the novel, he is no longer the folksy Ganesh Ramsumair, for whom the narrator feels a certain sentimental attachment, but the formal G. Ramsay Muir, Esquire. Ganesh is a product of the tension between the colony and the metropolis; he is divided between his colonial self (i.e., the son who follows in the tradition of his father) and the metropolitan other that he at once mimics and makes fun of.

Considered by many as Naipaul's masterpiece, *A House for Mr Biswas* (1961) looks back to the East-Indian West-Indian colonial world of the author's grandparents and parents. Like the 1950s novels, it depicts communities being reshaped by larger cultural, social forces; moving from East Indian villages to Port-of-Spain city life, it records a colony's transition from a rural to an urban, industrialized society. Through the story of Biswas, the novel tells both an individual's story and a community's history, defining the colony-metropolis equation in terms of an internal exile engendered by the gap between the protagonist's desire and his life's responsibilities and limitations. Biswas feels a sense of not-belonging; he fits neither in the Tulsi family circle nor in the Trinidad community. For him, an imagined England is where life is to be found, not on a West Indian island-colony far from the currents of progress and modernity; Biswas dreams of living the life of the metropolitan other, with a success and dignity that the colony is denied and with which the world beyond is imbued. Highly biographical, the novel can be read as a collaborative creation between a son and his father's life and writings. In "Prologue to an autobiography" (1984), Naipaul calls *Mr Biswas* his "father's book": "written out of his journalism and stories, out of . . . knowledge he had got from the way of looking MacGowan [former managing editor at the *Trinidad Guardian*] had trained him in. It was written out of his writing" (1986: 60). This is not to say that the novel is strictly biographical, that Mohun Biswas and Seepersad Naipaul are the same, but that the fictional creation emerges from the son's "translation" of the father's life and writings and his transformation of their voices by filtering them through his own. The son inherits the father's dream of becoming a writer, and through becoming a writer he in turn creates a fiction of his father and his father's dreams. Biswas emerges, as well, from Naipaul's own experience of alienation: in Biswas's not-belonging is Naipaul's; his sense of being an outsider is also Naipaul's. *A House for Mr Biswas* is certainly biographical, but it is also certainly fictional. What is fiction? In *Reading and Writing* Naipaul replies with a quote from Evelyn Waugh: "experience totally transformed" (2000: 23).

So we can read Biswas's story with two different highlightings: as history informed by fiction, or as fiction informed by history. With the first, Biswas's story tells a specifically Trinidad Indian story. His struggles to educate himself and to secure a profession and a house of his own are largely the struggles of his fellow East Indians along the hard road from indentureship to middle-class independence. In *West Indian Literature* Bruce King observes that *A House for Mr Biswas* "has a reputation as a New World epic celebrating the struggles of an immigrant towards acculturisation and success"(1979: 165). Indeed, the narrative shows Biswas's successes and defends his ambitions, which sustain him, motivate him to become somebody other than a laborer, and give him the courage to strike out into the unknown beyond his rural East Indian community. A less dreamy, more malleable Biswas would not have resisted the pressures to be incorporated in the Tulsi family enterprise as a lifelong worker in the shops and fields; a less adventurous and resourceful Biswas would not have boarded the bus for Port of Spain and talked and written his way into a job as a reporter at the city newspaper. Yet the narrative also shows the fragility of Biswas's successes and his illusions. A careful, less impulsive Biswas would not have wasted his money building the Green Vale and Shorthills houses, and would not have looked so cursorily at the house on Sikkim Street before purchasing it. His dreams also betray him and isolate him from others. In *V. S. Naipaul: A Materialist Reading,* Selwyn Cudjoe calls the novel a "prose-tragedy." Biswas never really belongs within his family, community, or society; he remains the iconoclast, the outsider, the man on the margins. He is a fictional representation informed not only by the life of the author's iconoclastic, alienated father, but also by the son's experience of emigration/ exile. That experience overwrites the fictionalized biography of the father, superimposing one story of wandering on another. In this sense, it is Naipaul the emigrant/ exile who is Mr Biswas, the author creating a character in the spirit of his father yet also infusing that character with his own estrangement and wandering. A commemoration to the frustrations, qualified achievements, and, above all, survivalist spirit of his father, *A House for Mr Biswas* completes Naipaul's initial retrospectives on the colony.

An elaboration of this sense of belonging nowhere and a critique of England and Englishness become the project of *The Mimic Men* (1967) and *Mr Stone and the Knights Companion* (1963). Informed by the author's experience of the deleterious aspects of life in the metropolis, the two novels tell complementary stories of alienation. Ralph Kripal Singh of *The Mimic Men* is a political exile from the Caribbean island of Isabella and a disillusioned exile from his youthful, colonial vision of the metropolis as center of the world. Mr Stone, the protagonist of the eponymous novel, is a London office worker – "a gentle, endearing man...of no particular consequence" – who feels cut off from people and nature. In the absence of community and meaningful action, Stone and Singh become fragmented individuals and withdraw into various versions of aestheticism and fantasy. If the West Indian colony was flawed by a lack of order, as Singh claims, so too is the metropolis flawed by its numbing order and depersonalization, as the fate of Mr Stone illustrates. For the protagonists of these two satirical novels, the only relief lies within the realm of the imagination, where history, with its disappointments and horrors, can be momentarily absent. Singh dreams of retiring to a cocoa plantation on an idealized Caribbean island; for his part, Mr Stone loses himself in the Knights Companion project, a kind of imaginary return to the medieval camaraderie of King Arthur and the Round Table.

It is worth looking at *The Mimic Men*, one of Naipaul's most important novels, in a bit more detail. A middle-aged West Indian businessman and politician, Ralph Singh, recounts memoirs of his life on Isabella (a British colony), his business and political career there, and his exile in England. The memoirs commence with a recollection of post-World War II London, where Singh did university studies and later worked at the British Broadcasting Corporation, and reach back to his childhood, Isabellan friendships, his successful entrepreneurship, and his participation in the island's independence movement and his brief political career. When Singh and others in his party fail to satisfy the expectations of the newly independent island, he is removed from power and put on a plane for London (1985b: 242). Throughout his recollections, but especially in the novel's final pages, Singh contemplates his exile from the colony and bitter withdrawal from metropolitan English society, to which he once looked eagerly as the center of the "real world" beyond the "shipwreck" of his life in the West Indies. Ironically, exile in England becomes for Singh the "greater shipwreck"; there, without hope of going home, he lives cut off from any community, his thoughts turning idly between the poles of fantasy and nihilism. His critique of colonial societies is essentially the critique that Naipaul puts forward in *The Middle Passage*: the colony is inherently flawed – but neither is the metropolis a solution. Singh looks with disgust at London and longs for a blank, cold, people-less world; London and England are "the greater disorder, the final emptiness" in a fragmented life (1985b: 8). The dark, satirical mood of these two novels foreshadows the mood of much of Naipaul's writings from the late 1960s to the mid-1980s.

Expansion of Range and Subject Matter: Travel Writing, Social Commentary, History and Fiction from 1962 to 1985

During this period Naipaul expanded his range of writing and began to mix travel writing and social commentary with history and fiction. The works of these decades tend to fall into three groupings: works with the metropolis as their setting or subject matter; works about India and religious fundamentalisms in Asia; and works, whether fiction or nonfiction, that ponder the state of affairs in former colonies in Africa, Asia, the Caribbean, and South America. *The Middle Passage* (1962), *An Area of Darkness* (1964), *The Loss of Eldorado* (1969), *The Overcrowded Barracoon* (1972), and *A Wounded Civilization* (1977) are some of the important sociocultural, historical studies of this period, with which Naipaul intersperses novels and collections of stories. From dictatorships, to civil wars, to ethnic and ideological purifications, the subject matter of this fiction ponders a social breakdown and chaos that has come with decolonization, Cold War rivalries, and the impotence of Europe to respond to crises in its former colonies. In one sense, these works document a socioeconomic slide that began in the 1970s and accelerated during the 1980s, the beginning of the dead-end decades of the Third World. Naipaul traveled to and lived in newly independent nations in Africa and the Caribbean and former Spanish colonies in South America; the fruits of those experiences are the novels *In a Free State* (1971), *Guerrillas* (1975), and *A Bend in the River* (1979), and the essays collected in *The Return of Eva Perón* (1980). These fictional works often portray violence, with touches of the grotesque and the monstrous. Bobby of *In a Free State* (1971) is beaten up and humiliated; Jane of *Guerrillas* (1975) is sodomized then hacked to death; Father Huismans of *A Bend in the River* (1979) is beheaded. But this violence represents and testifies to the times: between 1945 and 1983, about 20 million people died in over a hundred major wars, military actions, or conflicts, the majority of which occurred in the Third World. During the 1970s, then, Naipaul wrote works about this troubling period of struggles for spheres of influence and cultural, socioeconomic change and breakdown. Events in countries such as Zaïre, Rwanda, Burundi, Liberia, and Sierra Leone have shown that, although

Naipaul has often been criticized for his gloomy portrayal of the developing world, he did not exaggerate the potential for catastrophe and horror.

The novel *A Bend in the River* makes reference to the sociopolitical turmoil of 1960s and 1970s postcolonial Zaïre: ethnic conflicts, secessionist movements and governmental retaliation, periods of boom-and-bust tied to the price of copper, a dictator's ideological program, the nationalization of businesses, corruption, and bribery. Salim, the novel's narrator and main character, a shop owner of Indian Muslim origin, tries to remain outside of this turmoil but is inevitably drawn into it. He recounts, in retrospect, his journey from an East African coastal community ("an Arab-Indian-Persian-Portuguese place") to a town at the "bend in the river" of a central African country where he reopens the shop of a friend and adviser, Nazruddin.

Like the characters in *In a Free State* and *Guerrillas*, those of *A Bend in the River* present various ideological attitudes and positions in a postcolonial world. Salim looks at the town at the bend in the river through the eyes of an emigrant; he seeks to prosper in that community, but he remains an observer and outsider. He belongs nowhere, neither in central Africa nor in the effete Indian Muslim community of the East African coast: "We couldn't protect ourselves; we could only in various forms hide from the truth. To stay with my community... was to be taken with them to destruction. I could be master of my fate only if I stood alone" (1980: 20). Salim conceives of history as a tide that is sweeping him, and other Indians like him in East and Central Africa, away. He rebels against the traditional ways of his ethnic group, with its authoritarianism, fatal acceptances, and self-contained vision; this restlessness and rebellion seem to serve him well, enabling him to break away from a dying, enclaved community, and to prosper in the midst of social instability and breakdown, but they carry with them a price, a sense of homelessness and a lack of a social sensibility.

Salim is a hybrid of voices and attitudes, a mixture of insight yet self-deception, practicality yet adventure, skepticism yet naivety. He is a shrewd shopkeeper who knows how to make a profit, yet he has a hunger for experience and can be reckless, as in his relationship with Yvette (the wife of a presidential adviser) and in his black marketing in ivory and gold. At times he seems not quite an adult, only partially developed intellectually and socially: he looks up the meaning of "uranium" in a children's encyclopedia, and is oddly attracted by the photos of Yvette as a girl. Yet he sees clearly the cracks in the facade of the expatriate Europeans at the Domain (a kind of central African research institute and think-tank) and the fallacies of the postcolonial African society. In the end, Salim manages to escape not through his own power of will but through a fortuitous coincidence and a powerful African acquaintance. The novel's final sentences, with their echo of *Heart of Darkness*, focus on the bush and jungle enveloping the steamer and Salim its passenger, making men seem small amid nature's profusion and gigantism: "The steamer started up again and moved without lights down the river, away from the area of battle. The air would have been full of moths and flying insects. The searchlight, while it was on, had shown thousands, white in the white light."

The novel's vision of postcolonial, ideologically tormented Africa can be viewed from three interpenetrating planes: myth, history, and autobiography. Naipaul's 1970s novels at once look back to western discourse about the "dark continent" and forward to a contemporary western evaluation of the illusion of development in the Third World. They put forward a scenario of the Africa of tomorrow in which development is, ironically, a movement backwards, dissolution. In the 1970s Naipaul observed what Africa would become in the 1980s and 1990s: a region of accelerating breakdown. Salim's image of Africa as a perpetual dawn fading into darkness is certainly a myth, but African countries' breakdown during this period was very much an historical reality. On this reality, Naipaul's 1970s novels superimpose myth and, perhaps, autobiography. The author brings his own sense of homelessness and a colonial's "fear of extinction" to this construction of a Third World regressing into a "Fourth World" of hopelessly fractured societies where, for most people, there is no longer even a home or a place to escape to. In *A Bend in the River*, then, travel writing, social commentary, history, and fiction mix; the final product is fiction, yet this fiction bespeaks the power of testimony, upon which autobiography and history depend.

Remembrance within Disorder: *The Enigma of Arrival* and Other Works from 1985 to 2000

"I am the sum of my books," Naipaul has said. "Each book, intuitively sensed and, in the case of fiction, intuitively worked out, stands on what has gone before, and grows out of it" (2001: 480). Certainly those readers who know Naipaul's oeuvre will perceive the intertextuality of works of the final period of his career. Although recalling previous books, *The Enigma of Arrival* (1987) and *A Way in the World* (1994) depart from them in important ways and occupy a twilight space with their particular sense of endings, softened moods, and commemoration. These novels emphasize memory's power to reach beyond the shortsightedness of the times and to enable human beings to reinterpret and understand their lives anew in the face of personal and social breakdown and disorder; they are end-of-the-century works not in the negative connotation of decadence, but rather in a neutral sense of a transition period in which endings and beginnings are mixed together. Beneath the mood of calm, there rustles a certain question or anxiety. These novels are about the dead – about those who have died (a brother and sister, Jack the Waldenshaw farm worker, Blair the Trinidad diplomat and international consultant), as well as things that have ceased to be (the narrator's colony-engendered myth of England, a Trinidad of rural ethnic communities, European colonies and empires). Yet they are also about beliefs to live by at a time of endings where old ideologies have collapsed and a sense of insecurity and uncertainty are the dominant moods in societies around the world. Throughout his long career Naipaul has explored the themes of the times; *The Enigma of Arrival* and *A Way in the World* explore personal change and the vacuum that the passing of empires has left behind. These novels lament losses, but they also project a moral, intellectual vision in a landscape where old orders have crumbled and where societies have become increasingly divided and directionless.

Written as a first-person narrative, *The Enigma of Arrival* is autobiographical fiction and fictional autobiography. The novel's long second chapter, "The journey," consists of a fictionally transformed account of Naipaul's career between his departure from Trinidad as a scholarship student bound for England in the early 1950s and the publication of *Among the Believers* in the early 1980s. The chapter continues, in fictional form, the narrative entitled "Prologue to an autobiography" in *Finding the Center* (1984) and, read today, recalls *Reading and Writing*. The titular motif of the journey forms the theme of this chapter and of the novel: the narrator's journey from Trinidad to England, return journeys to the West Indies and the Caribbean, journeys as part of his work as journalist and novelist to Central and South America, Asia, and Africa, the writer's journey of words about those worlds, and life itself as a journey. The narrator recalls his disillusionment upon arrival in England where, drawn by a colonial romance of faraway places, expecting to encounter a city like the literary London in the novels and short stories he has read, he finds instead a "strange and unknown" place. In his boardinghouse he meets not colorful, English personages waiting to be characters in a story, but immigrants from other countries, the "flotsam of Europe" after World War II. He describes his initial attempts to write "metropol-itan" stories according to his preconception of England and English writers, and his chagrin at not finding suitable material in this fractured, immigrant world. He explains his realization that his writer's subject matter was not "sensibility" – "the ideas of the aesthetic movement of the end of the nineteenth century and the ideas of Bloomsbury, ideas bred essentially out of empire, wealth and imperial security" – but the collision of incongruous "worlds" and his own life as a "version" of the "great movement of peoples" taking place "in the second half of the twentieth century" (1987: 141, 146–7).

The novel's narrator is truly a mélange of cultures and civilizations: Hindu, West Indian, English, American. His allegiances have been formed not only by his ethnic heritage but also by his experiences as an intellectual and writer – by his travel and life around the world – in the Caribbean, South America, Africa, Asia, England, and the United States. He retains ties with Trinidad, where he was born and grew up, and with England, where he has studied and resided, off and on, during his adult years, but these ties do not fix his identity. Rather, the community to which he pledges his allegiance is a composite construction, at once rooted in Caribbean culture – in its cosmopolitan spirit – and in humanistic traditions of India and Europe. One com-ponent of these broad allegiances is the narrator's attitude toward England and Englishness, as exemplified by his understanding of two personages, the Waldenshaw landlord and Jack the gardener. Although the narrator recognizes the landlord's attachment to the old England of empire, he views him not with the disdain of a former colonial but with the understanding of a person who is himself troubled by change and loss. The narrator comprehends the ironic imprint of the landlord (and empire) on his own self and destiny – and conversely, in the late twentieth century, the equally ironic imprint of former colonials and other emigrants on England's identity and destiny. With these people – emigrants of dismantled twentieth-century empires – and with Jack, the narrator shares a sense of life's unpredictability and sweeping changes; in Jack, who owns neither the cottage in which he lives nor the garden in which he toils, the author creates a basic symbol of the human condition and the individual's responsibility to live in his world.

Another hybrid work, *A Way in the World,* mixes autobiography, fiction, historical dramatizations, and stories that grow out of Naipaul's travels in and reflections on the West Indies and Africa during the 1960s. "History: a smell of fish glue" and the final chapter, "Home again," recount the book's most compelling story, that of Blair, a Trinidadian who rises in governmental ranks and becomes a diplomat and international consultant in sub-Saharan Africa. As in *The Enigma of Arrival,* it is death, Blair's murder in an African banana plantation, that inspires the narrator to express simply and movingly the memory of another's life and one's difficult, often awkward efforts to touch an honesty about one's self and relationship to others. In sum, both *A Way in the World* and *The Enigma of Arrival* seek – at the dead end of a century of clashes of ideologies – to plumb something precious that cannot be turned into a category or a classification. Neither novel proposes a new plan of living or a new vision of the world; rather, each exercises a long memory that has the capacity to measure and comprehend from new perspectives. Both could be called moral works in the sense that their stories incarnate certain values such as integrity, critical thinking, and independent-mindedness, and a willingness to encounter the individual as individual, not as a category or a representative of ethnic or national identity. A "way in the world" where individuals would discover individuals in their complexity, commonality, and uniqueness would reopen an imaginative space in which mystery could be brought back to life, saved from the ideologies that have fixed the world into camps and categorizations.

Into the Future

Is Naipaul a West Indian/Caribbean writer, a writer of the Indian diaspora, an English writer, or a postcolonial writer? The answer is perhaps all of these and no one of them solely. That Naipaul is a major writer of the second half of the twentieth century is widely recognized; what is less recognized is that he presents a certain paradigm of achievement that puts him in an even more select category. His works, spanning the second half of the twentieth century, have addressed important themes of the age; his literary achievement both predates and coincides with the broadening of English literature and English studies into other geographic and thematic domains such as West Indian and Caribbean literature, diasporic Indian literature, and postcolonial literatures. Naipaul has a status within these separate domains as well as an international status that exceeds them. So in response to the question, who is Naipaul, we must say he is a world writer in English. He has established the paradigm of the writer of English as a world literature, and for this reason and others, his place in its emerging canon is secure. His record of literary achievement stands as a model for millions of young learners of the English language in Asia and other parts of the world; moreover, his style is a style that they can read, and he writes about subject matter and themes with which they can identify. Naipaul continues to publish challenging books: the sociocultural study *Beyond Belief: Islamic Excursions Among the Converted Peoples* (1998), for example, develops further the spectrum of ideas of *Among the Believers: An Islamic Journey* (1981); both books address a central topic of the world today: identity and religious fundamentalisms. More recently, the novel *Half a Life* (2001) recalls parts of R. K. Narayan's *The Guide* as well as several of Naipaul's previous works, including *The Mystic Masseur*, *The Mimic Men*, and *A Bend in the River*. One cannot say how Naipaul's literary contributions will be assessed in years to come, but, as it now stands, his style and the paradigm of international writer that he has established make him an unavoidable figure for anyone who wants to examine the changes that have taken place in the world – and in "English literature" – during the second half of the twentieth century.

REFERENCES AND FURTHER READING

Cudjoe, Selwyn R. (1988) *V. S. Naipaul: A Materialist Reading*. Amherst: University of Massachusetts.

Hayward, Helen (2002) *The Enigma of V. S. Naipaul: Sources and Contexts*. New York: Palgrave Macmillan.

Hughes, Peter (1988) *V. S. Naipaul*. London: Routledge.

King, Bruce (1979) "V. S. Naipaul," in Bruce King (ed.) *West Indian Literature*. Hamden, CT: Archon Books.

——(1993) *V. S. Naipaul*. New York: St Martin's Press.

Mason, Nondita (1986) *The Fiction of V. S. Naipaul*. Calcutta: The World Press Private.

Morris, Robert K. (1975) *Paradoxes of Order: Some Perspectives on the Fiction of V. S. Naipaul*. Colombia: University of Missouri Press.

Mustafa, Fawcia (1995) *V. S. Naipaul*. Cambridge and New York: Cambridge University Press.

Naipaul, V. S. (1969a) *A House for Mr Biswas*. New York: Penguin. (First published 1961, London: André Deutsch).

——(1969b) *Miguel Street*. New York: Penguin. (First published 1959, London: André Deutsch).

——(1969c) *The Middle Passage*. New York: Penguin. (First published 1962, London: André Deutsch).

——(1980) *A Bend in the River*. New York: Vintage Books. (First published 1979, New York: Alfred A. Knopf).

.——(1984) *The Mystic Masseur*. New York: Vintage Books. (First published 1957, London: André Deutsch).

——(1985a) *Mr Stone and the Knights Companion*. New York: Vintage Books. (First published 1963, London: André Deutsch).

——(1985b) *The Mimic Men*. New York: Vintage Books. (First published 1967, London: André Deutsch).

——(1986) "Prologue to an autobiography," in *Finding the Center: Two Narratives*. New York: Vintage. (First published 1984, New York: Alfred A. Knopf).

——(1987) *The Enigma of Arrival*. New York: Alfred A. Knopf.

——(1994) *A Way in the World*. New York: Alfred A. Knopf.

——(2000) *Reading and Writing: A Personal Account*. New York: New York Review.

——(2001) *Half a Life*. New York: Alfred A. Knopf.

——(2002) "Two worlds," Nobel Lecture 2001, *PMLA*, 117: 479—86.

Nixon, Rob (1992) *London Calling: V. S. Naipaul, Postcolonial Mandarin*. New York: Oxford University Press.

Ramchand, Kenneth (1970) *The West Indian Novel and its Background*. New York: Barnes and Noble.

Rohlehr, Gordon (1977) "The ironic approach: the novels of V. S. Naipaul," in R. D. Hamner (ed.) *Critical Perspectives on V. S. Naipaul*. Washington, DC: Three Continents Press.

Weiss, Timothy (1992) *On the Margins: The Art of Exile in V. S. Naipaul*. Amherst: University of Massachusetts Press.

White, Landeg (1975) *V. S. Naipaul: A Critical Introduction*. New York: Barnes and Noble.

33
Salman Rushdie

Nico Israel

Before February 14, 1989, Salman Rushdie was merely a well-known British writer of Indian origin. He had, over the previous decade, won a Booker Prize for his novel *Midnight's Children*, attracted strong notice for his next novel, *Shame*, and written a handful of well-received essays published in British literary journals and magazines. His texts were taught in the United States in "Anglophone" and "Postcolonial" literature courses with increasing frequency, and he had written a book about his travels in Sandinista-led Nicaragua, establishing his credibility as a political journalist. His most recent novel, 1988's *The Satanic Verses*, had been published to wide acclaim in Britain, and sales, fueled in part by controversy over the satirical depiction of Islam in the novel, were quite brisk.

On that Valentine's Day, however, Rushdie was catapulted from the realm of "mere" writer to international political figure and celebrity. Iran's fundamentalist leader, the Ayatollah Ruhollah Khomeini, issued a *fatwa* or Islamic decree, sentencing the "apostate" Rushdie, who had been born to Muslim parents but was not himself religious, to death for *The Satanic Verses*'s alleged insult to the prophet Mohammed. In the following weeks, the death sentence was bolstered by a 2-million-dollar bounty. Suddenly, Rushdie, who had gone into hiding and was accompanied constantly by bodyguards, became, by name recognition, possibly the most famous writer in the world.

Fifteen years later, the urgency of the *fatwa* period has receded into near-oblivion, and Rushdie is no longer in hiding. His name is now less recognizable to the general public than it was, and he seems to be achieving the peculiar distinction of being a "mere" writer once again. Given the fact that he lives in New York and writes about America, the extent to which he is still a "British" writer is debatable. ("You're British, right?" an American asks Malik Solanka, the 55-year-old protagonist of Rushdie's latest novel, *Fury*; Solanka, the text informs us, "didn't get into the postcolonial, migrational niceties" (2002: 35).) In the intervening years, Rushdie published several novels, a book of stories, and numerous political and literary essays;

he also co-edited a volume of Indian fiction, publishing some of the writers whose work most influenced his own. Yet any attempt to discuss Rushdie's writing *qua* "literature" is confronted by the blunt power of the *fatwa* and the constellation of culture, politics, and history that it illuminated, a constellation Rushdie has forcefully explored throughout his literary career, particularly in his novels.

That novelistic career can perhaps best be divided into two periods: pre- and post-1989. The early, pre-*fatwa* novels focused on the triumphant and traumatic histories of two postcolonial nation-states (India and Pakistan) and the potent effects of migration on citizens of these formerly colonized countries and of the formerly colonizing power (Britain). The later, post-*fatwa* novels are less rooted in particular nation-states, addressing instead a kind of generalized migrancy; they typically emphasize the intersection between aesthetics (visual art, music, literature) and possibilities for personal and political expression. Such concerns are certainly germane to someone in Rushdie's unique position of having been at once jet-setting, in hiding, and censored. But more broadly, they also reveal much about contemporary international culture and politics. After all, 1989 was not only the year of the *fatwa*; it also marked the fall of the Berlin Wall and the beginning of the Soviet Union's decline, and with it the arrival of a new type of extra-national geopolitical structuring that social scientists and economists have examined under the rubric "globalization." If Rushdie's earlier texts expressed, in both their subject matter and their form, a kind of meeting place, appropriate to the 1970s and 1980s, between the postcolonial and the postmodern, his more recent texts give voice to a nascent global mode of sovereignty and resistance.

Novels of the 1970s and 1980s: *Grimus, Midnight's Children, Shame, The Satanic Verses*

Grimus (1975), Rushdie's first published novel, was written in the hope of securing a science-fiction prize that would have provided its author the financial means to devote himself to writing full time. Having recently graduated from Kings College, Cambridge University, with a degree in history, the Bombay-born Rushdie was working as a freelance advertising copywriter, scripting commercials for "cream cakes, hair colourants and the *Daily Mirror*." As if consequently, *Grimus* presents an unwieldy blend of technological fantasy, thickly veiled historico-political allegory, and unbridled self-advertisement. The text traces the epic journey of Flapping Eagle, a Native American boy who is orphaned by his parents, seduced and then abandoned by his older sister, and banished from his tribe. As he wanders into a southwestern American town, sometime in the 1970s, Flapping Eagle (who is also known as Born-from-Dead, and, because he was born a hermaphrodite, Joe-Sue) meets a stranger who gives him an elixir granting him immortality. Seven hundred and forty-three years later, having "fallen through a hole in the sea" in a suicide attempt, Flapping Eagle arrives, still in the body of a 34-year-old man, at the town of K on the slopes of the mythical Calf or Kâf Island. Here, he encounters Grimus, a twisted Prospero-like figure, infertile and exasperated with the tribulations of immortality, who rules the island's expatriate community with an iron fist and guards his secret weapon, the magical, all-powerful Stone Rose. Grimus has, it seems, chosen Flapping Eagle as his son and political successor, and drawn the latter toward him across time and space, yet Flapping Eagle, undesirous of power and exhausted with immortality, resists. After a lengthy battle of wills and might, Grimus's and Flapping Eagle's identities become merged into an "I-Grimus," but the Flapping Eagle determination within that merged being is able to destroy the Stone Rose, and Kâf fizzles into nothingness.

Grimus is notable primarily for its introduction of thematic preoccupations that would appear throughout Rushdie's later, better-known work. The novel features a confused and uprooted familial genealogy, a rival structure involving two male antagonists, a virtually omnipotent political leader, an incestuous relationship, and expressions of fear over biological impotence and paternity; it begins with a fall, ends with a quasi-apocalypse, centers on the activity of an expatriate society, portrays a raucous bordello as a kind of asylum, and, eventually, focuses on a high mountain as the site of a spiritual, as well as epic, quest. In addition to anticipating these eventually characteristic Rushdiean *topoi*, *Grimus* amply demonstrates Rushdie's propensity to draw on established "classical" texts (from both West and East) to propel his own narrative: Flapping Eagle's meanderings are filtered through those of the heroes of the *Odyssey*, the *Aeneid*, *The Inferno*, *Oedipus Rex*, the Koran, *The Thousand and One Nights*, *The Tempest*, and Kafka's *The Trial*; but the novel clearly also draws inspiration from such popular cultural sources as comic books, adventure tales, and Western movies.

Despite revealing tendencies that would prove more successful in later efforts, *Grimus* "bombed," as Rushdie himself put it, in terms of both book sales and critical response; the novel neither won the science-fiction prize nor granted Rushdie the status of full-time author. It seemed that the text's nomadic, spatio-temporally wayward narrative was simply too disjointed or unmoored for readers' (or critics') tastes. With *Midnight's Children* (1981), Rushdie jettisoned the science-fiction mode and turned toward a blend of national allegory and magical realism, anchoring his narrative in the territorial contiguity of an emerging nation-state (India) while maintaining a frequently fantastic, even hyperbolic tone. The predicaments of young Saleem Sinai, born at the moment India achieves independence, mirror those of his homeland: the text charts his various youthful adventures against the backdrop of the wars, crises, and political transformations of the nascent independent nation, from glorious liberation from colonialism through the mass imprisonments and sterilizations of the 1970s State of Emergency period.

The grim and violent history that it records notwithstanding, *Midnight's Children* is primarily a comic novel – often ebulliently so. The text's celebrated opening establishes its effusive narrator's tenuous relation to national historiography:

I was born in the city of Bombay... once upon a time. No that won't do, there's no getting away from the date: I was born in Doctor Narlikar's Nursing Home on August 15th, 1947. And the time? The time matters, too. Well then: at night. No, it's important to be more... On the stroke of midnight, as a matter of fact. Clock-hands joined palms in respectful greeting as I came. Oh, spell it out, spell it out: at the precise instant of India's arrival at independence, I tumbled forth into the world. There were gasps. And, outside the window, fireworks and crowds. A few seconds later, my father broke his big toe; but the accident was a mere trifle when set beside what had befallen me in the benighted moment, because thanks to the occult tyrannies of those blandly saluting clocks I had been mysteriously handcuffed to history, my destinies indissolubly chained to those of my country. For the next three decades, there was to be no escape. (1991b: 3, ellipses in text)

The passage is reminiscent of Laurence Sterne's *Tristram Shandy*, not only in its evasive, somewhat impatient narrative tone and in the direct address to its readers, but also in the slapstick "broken toe" and the mention of clocks, two motifs from *Shandy*'s early pages. Saleem's body, like poor Tristram's, is beset by various injuries, causing him to disintegrate, but Rushdie invests these corporeal wounds with a politico-geographical significance that goes beyond comedy; over the course of the narrative, which, like many of Rushdie's later texts, traces salient moments of twentieth-century Indian history, India becomes two countries (India and Pakistan) and then, with the secession of Bangladesh from Pakistan, three. Meanwhile Saleem loses various limbs and organs. Subject to partition at the very instant of his emergence into the world, he continues chronically to come undone straight through to the text's quasi-apocalyptic ending, in which, during a political demonstration, he is trampled by a rioting mob. "Handcuffed to history," his destinies "chained" to India's, Saleem embodies the often violent entwinement of the personal and the political.

Much of Rushdie's portrayal of this entwinement necessarily involves an element of "magic." The title characters, born in the hour after independence – chief among them Saleem (whose name comes from the Urdu word for "peace") and his antagonist Shiva (named after the all-powerful Hindu god of destruction) – have the capacity to communicate with one another across India through a radio network transmitted via their sinuses; it is as though the power of *Grimus*'s Stone Rose has been apportioned to these "midnight's children," who can intervene collectively to influence major historical events. However, unlike many Latin American "fantastic realists," whose surrealistically inflected narratives draw on supposedly indigenous South American traditions, Rushdie tends to turn to magic (which is undeniably also a part of Indian folkloric traditions) to describe moments of extreme historical violence: sectarian atrocities, mass slaughter, the creation of hundreds of thousands of refugees, forced or coerced sterilizations. Rushdie's deployment of "magic" is thus a question less of exoticization or narrative evasion than of literary ethics: magic is the only just way, the author suggests, to confront the representability of suffering.

In an elaboration of this issue of historical ethics, *Midnight's Children* demonstrates, through its tracing of Saleem's complex familial genealogy, the virtual unthinkability of a pure, unbesmirched "Indian" India. Saleem is the illegitimate child of William Methwold (a colonial English gentleman with a French grandmother) and Vanita, a ghetto-dwelling Hindu; he is switched at birth by a Catholic nurse named Mary Pereira, who acts out of love for a leftist political revolutionary, Joseph D'Costa; and he is raised by affluent Muslims Ahmed and Amina Sinai. It is as though not only, as with *Heart of Darkness*'s Kurtz, "all Europe went into the making" of Saleem, but also all of South Asia, as well as most of the world's major religions. Even in his earliest texts, Rushdie takes a stand against notions of ethnic or religious "purity": national identity (especially postcolonial national identity) is anything but fixed; it is precisely, and powerfully, open to interpretation.

Shame (1983), Rushdie's third novel, takes dead aim at supposed purity, with a scandal-drenched send-up of the secret and official history of Pakistan, the nation whose very name invokes a "land of the pure." The theocratic Muslim state, to which Rushdie's family moved when he was a teenager but by whose exclusionary hypocrisy he claims to have always been repulsed, had already been caricatured in *Midnight's Children*, when Saleem, AWOL from the Indian army, finds himself lost in an air-conditioned suburban-style wasteland in the Karachi of the 1960s. In his narrative return to Pakistan, Rushdie foregrounds the adventures of the "duelists," Iskander Harappa and Raza Hyder, transparent, almost comic-book renditions of dapper demagogue Zulfikar Ali Bhutto and sycophantic strongman Muhammad Zia ul-Haq, Pakistan's leaders for most of the 1970s and 1980s, respectively. The text follows Harappa and Hyder as their fortunes intertwine with the turbulent history of the nation: the rise of Iskander Mirza and his ousting by Ayub Khan; the discovery of natural gas in the region of Baluchistan, and the early secessionist movements; the 1965 war with India; the growing power of the Islamic clergy; the unbalanced economic development between East and West Pakistan and the subversion of the 1969 election victory of Sheikh Mujib; the war over what was to become Bangladesh; and, eventually, Zia's coup displacing Bhutto and the latter's execution by hanging. These episodes are filtered through and overshadowed by accounts of the fictionalized families of the two men, with characters' marriages and infidelities, family feuds and the birth of children expressing that history in a different, more intimate way. For example, Hyder's brutal killing of his wife's lover in Baluchistan coincides in the text with the actual war against Baluchi separatists; later, Harappa's abandonment of his decadent "playboy" life-style and return to his family heralds Bhutto's return to the fold of government in the 1970s.

In a manner recalling the conceptual pairing of *Midnight's Children*'s Saleem and Shiva, Rushdie portrays postcolonial history as circulating around an agonistic struggle between two powerful men, and here, as in *Midnight's Children*, the text relies on an alliance between the personal and the political to convey national history. But while Saleem's allegorical autobiography in the 1981 narrative was addressed (within the text) to his illiterate, salt-of-the-earth lover, Padma, who insisted on the "tick-tock" of linear, teleological time (which Rushdie calls her "what-happens-next-ism"), the national history of *Shame* proceeds by fits and starts, punctuated by extemporal leaps and narrative digressions delivered in the voice of the first-person storyteller-historian, Omar Khayyam Shakil, whose first two names, not incidentally, are those of the Sufi author of the *Rubaiyat*.

In one such digression early in the novel, Shakil speaks of his namesake, whose work was translated by the nineteenth-century British Orientalist scholar Edward Fitzgerald:

> Omar Khayyam's position as a poet is curious. He was never very popular in his native Persia; and he exists in the west in a translation that is really a complete reworking of his verses, in many cases very different from the spirit (to say nothing of the content) of the original. I, too, am a translated man. I have been borne across. It is generally believed that something is always lost in translation; I cling to the notion – and use, in evidence, the success of Fitzgerald-Khayyam – that something can also be gained. (1984: 24)

Reading this excerpt, it is hard not to think of Shakil as a stand-in for Rushdie, whose work had been banned in India (for its depiction of Indira Gandhi as akin to the wicked witch in *The Wizard of Oz*), and who had himself been "borne across" the ocean, his immensely successful *Midnight's Children* by then translated into dozens of languages. The metaphor of linguistic surplus and debt allows Shakil/Rushdie to "cling to" the potential positivity of translation, despite claims by anonymous critics that his voice is inauthentic (in Rushdie's case, for writing about Pakistan from abroad, in the colonizer's language, English). The text suggests that such translated status enables one better to bear witness, yet it also emphasizes the difficulty of bringing about political change from "outside." Born in a "border town," Shakil, fat, ugly, and repulsive to all, is plagued by the near-constant "feeling of being a person apart . . . a creature of the edge" (1984: 19). He is carried along by the momentum of history, without the power to change that history. At the end of the novel, Shakil, nearing death, admits that "other persons have been the principal actors in my life-story. I watched from the wings, not knowing how to act" (p. 313). These principal actors, partaking in political scheming and orgies of violence while clinging to a spurious notion of purity, eventually consume Shakil in a horrific act of rape and murder, amid a nuclear conflagration.

Shame addresses the question of the difficulties of resistance in the face of oligarchic political power; as with *Grimus* and *Midnight's Children*, it ends with violence and destruction. *The Satanic Verses* (1988) is Rushdie's first novel not to end with such a scene, yet it is one pointed irony among many others that the text provoked actual political violence. Between 1991 and 1993, *The Satanic Verses*'s Japanese translator was stabbed to death, its Italian translator was beaten and stabbed, and the publisher of the Norwegian translation was shot and seriously wounded. Meanwhile, in Ankara, several dozen people were killed in a fire set during a conference attended by the Turkish translator of the text. One salient aspect of the *Satanic Verses* "affair," then, is the *global* reach of its disastrous effects: effects that were, of course, distorted, on all sides, precisely for political purposes. It is further noteworthy that the violence occurred neither in Britain nor Iran, nor was it contained within any obviously demarcated zone of West or East (or "modern" or "traditional"); rather, it happened in borderline sectors of what used, optimistically, to be called the global village.

This is not the place for an extended reiteration of the controversy over *The Satanic Verses*. Neither is there room for a rectification of the "misreading" of the text by Islamic fundamentalists, many of whom admitted that they had not read, indeed would not read, the novel. One of the precious few benefits of the hubbub surrounding the novel is that Rushdie was prompted to articulate his rationale for writing it. In an open letter to Rajiv Gandhi, then prime minister of India, where the book had recently been banned, Rushdie insisted that *The Satanic Verses* "isn't about Islam, but about migration, metamorphosis, divided selves, love, death, London and Bombay." Some time afterward, he wrote, even more emphatically, "If [the book] is anything, it is a migrant's eye view of the world." These claims, however disingenuous or politically expedient they may appear to be in retrospect, gesture away from the text's familiar criteria of reception (blasphemy versus free speech, the sacred versus the profane, democracy versus tyranny, political satire versus cultural taboo) and toward the slippery arenas of cultural geography (imaginary national and extranational spaces, diasporic subjectivities) that were the chief topics of Rushdie's early works, and that were largely overlooked in debates about this novel.

The Satanic Verses features two central characters, Gibreel Farishta, an Indian Muslim movie star famous for his roles in filmic stories of Hindu Gods, and Saladin Chamcha, a naturalized British citizen and gratuitously Anglophilic radio and television voice-over specialist. Farishta, whose name in Urdu signifies "Angel," dreams he is present during the apocryphal satanic verses incident (disputed lines from the Koran that were later expunged in official versions), while Chamcha (Hindi for "spoon" or "toady"), absorbing the hatred of his British immigration-officer captors, becomes a horned, tailed, halitosis-suffering demon. The two characters seem initially to represent diametrically opposite principles, but as soon as they land on English soil after their plane is blown out of the sky by terrorists, all such rigid divisions between resister and toady begin to unravel, and physical and psychical transformations commence. Indeed, as the narrator of *The Satanic Verses* puts it, in a characteristic Rushdiean formulation, "Such distinctions, resting as they must on the idea of the self as being (ideally) homogenous, non-hybrid, 'pure' – an utterly fantastic notion! – cannot, must not suffice" (1992a: 427).

The text's land- and time-scapes include not only India and Britain in the twentieth century, but Arabia in the early Middle Ages, Argentina in the 1930s, and the Nepalese Himalayas around Mount Everest in the present. Given the plethora of miracles that occur – Gibreel and Saladin surviving a plane explosion, the Arabian sea apparently parting – it is Rushdie's most multinational and most "fantastic" text and, generally speaking, his most philosophically dense and best written. It asks, repeatedly and rhapsodically, "how does newness come into the world?" and suggests, powerfully, that newness comes into the world via the exuberant, hybrid commingling of cultures: a hybridity akin to the polyphony of the novel as form. Yet, "on the ground," such hybridity is often perceived as intolerable and is frequently and forcefully resisted – as the *Satanic Verses* affair amply, disastrously, demonstrates.

Novels after 1990: *The Moor's Last Sigh, The Ground Beneath Her Feet, Fury*

Rushdie's writing during the nearly decade-long *fatwa* period (1989–98) included a children's story, *Haroun and the Sea of Stories*, an extended analysis of *The Wizard of Oz* for the British Film Institute, and a short-story collection, *East West*. *Haroun* tells a tale of marital infidelity and familial reconciliation filtered through *The Thousand and One Nights*; *The Wizard of Oz* offers a reading of the film whose most famous line is "There's no place like home"; *East West* focuses on imagined cultural zones where the hemispheres meet and interpenetrate. Each of these texts allegorized Rushdie's own personal situation in the early 1990s as well as hoped-for solutions to his predicament; they also reflected on the mystery of his having become, after repeatedly proclaiming his marginality and inconsequentiality, an historical "actor," albeit an embattled one. But it is in the novels written after 1990 that Rushdie more fully examines the peculiarities of his banishment into the public sphere (which involved being simultaneously sent into hiding and thrust into the spotlight) and some of the lessons to be learned from that experience about the culture of globalized politics and the politics of globalized culture.

The Moor's Last Sigh (1995) relates the story of four generations of the Zogoiby and da Gama families set against the backdrop of twentieth-century Indian and global political and social history. The narrator, Moraes ("Moor") Zogoiby, half Sephardic Jewish and half Portuguese Catholic, with a Muslim name in a predominantly Hindu nation, is the youngest child of the modern artist Aurora da Gama and Abraham Zogoiby, a power-hungry spice merchant. (Some critics found Rushdie's representation of Abraham anti-Semitic, a charge Rushdie hotly disputed; in any case Rushdie's analogy between Jews and postcolonial migrants is salient and appears in several of his texts.) Moor writes the story while on the run in late twentieth-century southern Spain, his patrimonial homeland, having been forced to flee India by gangsters and their political cronies. Aging twice as fast as normal, and breathless because of an inherited asthmatic condition, Moor struggles to tell his family's and his nation's secrets before he is caught by his pursuers.

Rushdie told interviewers in the early 1990s that *The Moor's Last Sigh* was going to be set in fifteenth-century Spain, the era of the grand inquisitors and the expulsions by order of Ferdinand and Isabella of Muslims and Jews from what had once been a prosperous multicultural society. That the novel eventually focused on twenti-eth-century India, more familiar terrain for Rushdie, indicates the difficulty of representing late-medieval politics and maintaining allegorical linkages to his own decidedly contemporary predicament. In the text's final version, connections between obscure fugitive Moor and hunted author Rushdie are signaled throughout. On the first page of the text, for example, Moor (whose name alludes to both the tragedy of Othello and the idea of mooring and unmooring) writes, "On the run, I have turned the world into my pirate map, complete with clues, leading x-marks-the-spottily to the treasure of myself. When my pursuers have followed the trail they'll find me waiting, uncomplaining, out of breath, ready. – Here I stand. Couldn't have done it differently" (1997: 3). Such bounty-hunting scenes are plentiful in *The Moor's Last Sigh*; indeed, they are its predominant motif. Ugly and infirm (like many of Rushdie's textual stand-ins), Moor is hardly a "treasure," save as a dead man or captive. The text acknowledges its own condition of writing and posits a tone of resignation and inevitability: "Couldn't have done it differently."

Yet the novel is much more than a reflection on the personal effects of the *Satanic Verses* affair; it makes a strong case for Rushdie's deeply held belief that diasporic movement and the cultural hybridity that such movement provokes can and do produce positive social results. A description of Aurora Zogoiby's paintings makes this point clear:

> [T]hey were an attempt to create a romantic myth of the plural, hybrid nation; she was using Arab Spain to re-imagine India, and this land-sea-scape in which the land could be fluid and the sea stone-dry was her metaphor – idealised? sentimental? probably – of the present, and the future, that she hoped would evolve. (1997: 227)

This is not merely a description of the paintings, but of *The Moor's Last Sigh* itself. Such a "scape" is hardly without obstacles; like many of Rushdie's novels, the text blends an almost utopian hopefulness with extreme pessimism. Seeing his mother Aurora's paintings later, Moraes Zogoiby thinks of them as tragic, "the tragedy of multiplicity destroyed by singularity, the defeat of Many by One" (p. 408). In *The Moor's Last Sigh*, hybridity and multiplicity are synonyms for "love," singularity and Oneness for its antithesis. As its narrator puts it, "If love is not all, then it is nothing: this principle, and its opposite . . . collide down all the years of my breathless tale" (p. 28). Ultimately, the text valorizes the realm of imaginative art as the sole haven from the world: "I discover[ed] the one and only shore upon which I might be safe for ever, *the shore of Fancy itself*" (p. 290, emphasis in text). This valorization of imagin-ation may seem Romantic – indeed, perhaps idealized or sentimental – but for Rushdie it was all the more worth defending, passionately.

The Ground Beneath Her Feet (1999) was published shortly after Rushdie's self-declared "release" had been worked out covertly by British, American, and Iranian diplomats as part of a broader rapprochement among the states; it was hailed as a breakthrough text in which Rushdie returned to his pre-*fatwa* form and novelistic flair. But the novel, written during the *fatwa* period, still seems haunted by a sense of displacement. Its first sentence posits its hero's demise as occurring on "St. Valentine's Day, 1989," the date, as mentioned earlier, on which the *fatwa* was declared. *The Ground Beneath Her Feet*'s narrator, Umeed Merchant, is a photojournalist who silently records wars and political figures' dirty dealings, but also news made by celebrities and fashion mavens. Merchant, from an upper-middle-class Bombay Muslim family, tells of the lifelong love between two central characters, Vina Apsara and Ormus Cama. Vina is the American-born daughter of a poor white Southern woman and soon-to-be-gay Indian salesman; she is raised in the United States by her now-single mother before being shuttled off to Bombay as a teenager. Ormus is a rock-and-roll-obsessed son of a wealthy Bombay Parsi Anglophilic lawyer spending his retirement concocting theories about the fundamental similarity between western and eastern myths; unlike his father, Ormus wants to forget history and embrace the contemporary. The first half of the text takes place in Bombay, in some of the same upper-middle-class neighborhoods described in *Midnight's Children* and *The Satanic Verses*; in fact Rushdie reintroduces many of the characters from his earlier works (William Methwold and Aurora Zogoiby among them) in order to retell Indian history from the 1940s to the 1970s. The second half of the novel is set in England, Mexico, and, most notably, the United States: it is the first extended treatment of America in Rushdie's fiction. In this half of the text, Vina and Ormus become world-famous rock stars and lovers, until their excessive fame drives them apart.

The novel is a revised and updated Orpheus and Eurydice story, with Ormus's extraordinary musical talent paralleling that of the mythical lyre-player who went to the underworld to rescue his true love, only to lose her after glancing backward, breaking his agreement with the gods. In *The Ground Beneath Her Feet*, after the feisty, free-loving Vina dies in an earthquake – earthshaking events and the resultant geological and psychical unmoorings are the text's central motifs – Ormus tries to bring her back from the dead. The Orpheus-Eurydice theme allows Rushdie to delve into the commingling of various eastern and western classical narratives, a chief feature of much of his fiction, while the worldwide pervasiveness of rock music gives him a forum to reflect on the internationalization of culture and the lure and danger of celebrity, all the while indulging his love of corny ditties, which he writes with aplomb. (One example: *It's not up to you no more, you can't choose if it's peace or war, just can't make choices any more, your nightmare has come true; and when the day becomes the night, and when you don't know wrong from right, or blind from sight or who to fight, don't tell me you feel blue* (1999: 389).)

A journalistic sensibility has always informed Rushdie's writing, and it is no accident that the narrator of this tale is a photojournalist, who records irrevocable split-second transformations with a click of his shutter. But of all of Rushdie's fiction to date, *The Ground Beneath Her Feet* seems the least concerned with historical "events"; in comparison to, say, *Midnight's Children*, there are far fewer allegorical parallels between politically charged episodes and characters' lives. Instead, in a magnification of issues explored in *The Satanic Verses* and *The Moor's Last Sigh*, the text seems preoccupied by a sense of geographical movement from place to place, milieu to milieu, nation to nation, and it focuses on the effects of transnational migration on one's perceived picture of the world. As Umeed notes, "It is no longer possible to speak of places like Bombay, as people spoke of them in those days, as being situated on the *periphery*; or to describe Ormus's yearnings [to go to London], which were also Vina's and mine, as some sort of *centripetal force*" (p. 100, emphasis in text); indeed *The Ground Beneath Her Feet*, in its exposure of the effects of globalization on human lives, demonstrates the obsolescence of vocabularies of political and cultural centers and peripheries.

The Ground Beneath Her Feet also marks Rushdie's declared leave-taking from India as the central location of his fiction. In a moving if typically operatic conclusion to the first half of the text, its narrator addresses his home nation, "My mother, my father and my first great truth":

> It may be that I am not worthy of you, for I have been imperfect, I confess. I may not comprehend what you are becoming, what perhaps you already are, but I am old enough to say that this new self of yours is an entity I no longer want, or need, to understand. India, fount of my imagination, source of my savagery, breaker of my heart. Goodbye. (1999: 249)

This gesture of farewell to homeland allows for a focused reflection on America and particularly New York City, Rushdie's new home. At times America stands in the text for the geographic destiny for the world's outsiders and wanderers. Striking a familiar note, Rushdie's narrator declares that "I must believe – and in this I have truly become an American, inventing myself anew to make a new world in the company of other altered lives – that there is thrilling gain in this metamorphic destiny, as well as aching loss" (p. 441). But this ambivalent embrace of America's amenability to "makeovers" doesn't efface the political violence that the nation perpetrates, in the name of its capacity for newness, on the rest of the globe.

America is also the primary setting for *Fury*, Rushdie's latest novel at the time of this essay's writing. The novel concerns Malik Solanka, a former Cambridge University professor of philosophy who has quit his academic post because the wooden dolls he made as a hobby in his spare time eventually ended up as television personalities, and, once licensed and distributed worldwide, made him wealthy. Fifty-five years old, he has come to New York in a futile attempt to forget his past – both in Bombay, where he was born, and London, where he was educated and married, with a young child – and to clear his mind of the philosophical dilemmas that refuse to go away:

> To the devil with this classical mishmash, Professor Solanka silently exclaimed. For a greater deity was all around him: America, in the highest hour of its hybrid, omnivorous power. America, to which he had come to erase himself. To be free of attachment and so also of anger, fear, and pain. Eat me, Professor Solanka silently prayed. Eat me, America, and give me peace. (2002: 44)

This "eating" provokes indigestion, and Solanka cannot escape the furies hounding him: his ex-wife, his own fame, and his recollections conspire to render him a cantankerous late-middle-aged man alone in his overpriced sublet on Manhattan's Upper West Side. Two young women, sexual muses of a sort, eventually help to rescue him, and he begins to write again. His mode is science fiction, and the latter part of the text offers an inset narrative of evil puppet masters and the battle between political oppression and liberation. This, too, becomes immensely popular, the sci-fi narrative eventually influencing political events in far-flung nations. Ultimately, however, his muses abandon him, and Malik ends up alone in a London park, spying on his own child from a distance.

The novel is perhaps the least dynamic of all of Rushdie's efforts. It seems an almost willful attempt to focus on a single character in a single place during a time in which New York, Rushdie's then-new home, was "boiling with money" and confidence – a situation that would begin to change shortly after the text's publication in 2001, with the violent destruction of the twin towers of the World Trade Center. At times the text reads like a deliberately "American" novel; Rushdie demonstrates his debt not only to Thomas Pynchon (who has influenced almost all of his work) but to an older generation of writers such as Philip Roth and Saul Bellow, who, through their smart, kvetching, self-pitying old men, explore philosophical conundrums with cool precision and dark humor. Curiously, though, *Fury* features the first bit of sci-fi in Rushdie's writing since *Grimus*, and in a sense Rushdie has come full circle, back to the future via a propulsion into the past.

Describing the process of writing his sci-fi comic, which is to be published on the internet, Malik ponders the fact that

> the . . . story was a skeleton that . . . grew new bones, the framework for a fictional beast capable of constant metamorphosis, which fed on every scrap it could find: its creator's personal history, scraps of gossip, deep learning, current affairs, high and low culture, and the most nourishing diet of all – namely the past. (2002: 190)

This declaration, an anti-death-sentence, is a fitting summation of Rushdie's fiction. Rushdie, the former student of history, produces novels that hungrily feed on the past, drawing it toward the ever-metamorphosing shape of the present, opening a space for newness to enter the world.

REFERENCES AND FURTHER READING

Aravamudan, Srinivas (1989) "'Being God's post-man is no fun, yaar': Salman Rushdie's *The Satanic Verses*," *Diacritics*, 19/2: 3–20.

Baucom, Ian (1999) *Out of Place*. Princeton: Princeton University Press.

Bhabha, Homi K. (1994) *The Location of Culture*. London: Routledge.

Brennan, Timothy (1989) *Salman Rushdie and the Third World: Myths of the Nation*. Basingstoke: Macmillan; New York: St Martin's Press.

English, James F. (1994) *Comic Transactions: Literature, Humor, and the Politics of Community in Twentieth Century Britain*. Ithaca: Cornell University Press.

Gorra, Michael (1997) *After Empire: Naipaul, Scott, Rushdie*. Chicago: University of Chicago Press.

Israel, Nico (2000) *Outlandish: Writing between Exile and Diaspora*. Stanford, CA: Stanford University Press.

Rushdie, Salman (1975) *Grimus*. London: Gollancz.

——(1984) [1983] *Shame*. New York: Vintage.

——(1991a) *Haroun and the Sea of Stories*. London: Granta Books in conjunction with Penguin.

——(1991b) [1981] *Midnight's Children*. New York: Penguin.

——(1992a) [1988] *The Satanic Verses*. Dover, DE: Consortium Publishers.

——(1992b) *The Wizard of Oz*. London: British Film Institute.

——(1996) *East West: Stories*. New York: Vintage.

——(1997) [1995] *The Moor's Last Sigh*. New York: Vintage.

——(1999) *The Ground Beneath Her Feet*. New York: Henry Holt.

——(2002) [2001] *Fury*. New York: Modern Library.

Steiner, Wendy (1995) *The Scandal of Pleasure: Art in an Age of Fundamentalism*. Chicago: University of Chicago Press.

Suleri, Sara (1993) *The Rhetoric of English India*. Chicago: University of Chicago Press.

34

The Irish Novel after Joyce

Donna Potts

Joyce stands behind us like the ghost of the father
(John Banville)

Contemporary Irish fiction writers are often described as writing in the shadow of James Joyce. Although this claim has the potential to diminish their unique contributions to the Irish literary tradition, it nonetheless provides a useful starting point in any discussion of that tradition. The confluence of cultural influences on Joyce was powerful and pervasive enough to be felt by his successors, whose own expression of these influences was bound to be shaped by the author who is arguably the greatest and most stylistically versatile writer of the twentieth century. As the oldest colony of the British empire, Ireland has a broken tradition in terms of language, culture, and religion: in the sixteenth century, the Normans outlawed the native language, Irish-Gaelic, as well as native Irish dress, religion, and various cultural practices. The establishment of the English Protestant Church led to persecution of Irish Catholics, and ultimately to Ireland's self-identification as a Catholic nation in contrast to Protestant England. Joyce describes Irish art as "the cracked looking glass of a servant" (1934: 383); and his fiction, written during the period in which Ireland was still under English domination, but struggling for independence, reflects the broken tradition that results from colonization. In particular, Joyce's linguistic escapades, his preoccupation with representations of colonial Ireland, his depiction of the role of Catholicism in Irish life, his uncompromising realism that underscores class distinctions exacerbated by colonization, and his allusions to Irish mythology and folklore are all responses to a colonial legacy shared by his successors.

The stylistic and linguistic playfulness of Flann O'Brien's fiction owes an obvious debt to Joyce. Born Brian O'Nolan in 1911 in County Tyrone, O'Brien grew up in Dublin, and in the 1930s began writing a bilingual column for *The Irish Times* under the pseudonym Myles na Gopaleen (Myles of the Small Horses), the name of the

comic hero of Dion Boucicault's play *The Colleen Bawn* (1860). He is best known for
the novels *At Swim-Two-Birds* (1939) and *An Béal Bocht* ("The Poor Mouth," 1941),
the latter written in Irish, which O'Brien had spoken exclusively until the age of 6.
At-Swim-Two-Birds, the story of an Irish college student who writes an irreverent
novel in which the figures of Irish myth and legend come to life and riot against their
author, is reminiscent of Joyce's experimentation with language and genre (especially
the incorporation of Irish myth and legend into a realistic story line), particularly in
his later novels, *Ulysses* and *Finnegans Wake*. Declan Kiberd suggests that O'Brien's
decision to write *An Béal Bocht* in Irish was the means by which he provided the
Victorian stereotype of the stage Irishman, Myles na Gopaleen, the opportunity to
speak in his native language, the eclipsed "g" of his stage name now restored:
"Through the use of his once-despised but now-functional language, Myles succeeds
in depicting a world where all men, and not solely the Irish-speaking peasant, are seen
for the buffoons that they are" (Kiberd 1996: 498).

Although born into a Protestant family and emphatic about the role of the Anglo-
Irish ascendancy in the Irish literary tradition, most notably in his survey, *A Writer's
Ireland: Landscape in Literature*, William Trevor has relied on his position as an
outsider to predominantly Catholic Ireland to gain insights into the sources of its
religious and political tensions. Born William Trevor Cox in Mitchelstown, County
Cork in 1928, Trevor attended a convent school in Youghal, bringing him into direct
contact with rural Irish Catholic life. He continually exploits his position as "outsider," almost invariably preferring to write outside his own experience rather than
autobiographically. Although claiming to be "a short-story writer really who happens
to write novels, not the other way round" (Stout 1989: 143), Trevor has written
nineteen novels in addition to his fifteen collections of short stories. His early novels,
The Old Boys (1964), *The Boarding House* (1965), and *The Love Department* (1966), are
set in England, where he has lived since 1952; and although they include Irish
characters, these tend to be caricatures, featuring respectively an Irish maid, a blarney
spouting con-man named Studdy, and Septimus Tuam, whose "smooth Celtic voice"
enables him to seduce ostensibly happily married women. Tributes to Joyce appear
consistently in his early work, most explicitly in the form of echoes of the final lines of
"The dead."

During the 1970s, as Irish "troubles" increased in intensity, Trevor became increasingly interested in writing about Ireland and Irish problems, and he had also perhaps
gained sufficient distance from his country to write about it from the peripheral
position that he preferred, with the objectivity of an outsider. On a radio program in
1981 Trevor stated:

> As an Irishman I feel that what is happening in Ireland now is one of the great horrors of
> my lifetime, and I find it difficult to comprehend the mentality, whether Irish or
> British, that pretends that it will somehow all blow over. It will not. There will be more
> death, more cruelty, more fear, more waste. The nightmare will go on . . . Compassion is
> thrown to the winds, distortion rules. (MacKenna 1999: 110)

In fact, Trevor has since acknowledged that he regards himself as following in the tradition of writers such as Frank O'Connor and Sean O'Faolain, thereby associating himself with the Irish nationalist tradition rather than the Anglo-Irish one (p. 134).

The novel *Fools of Fortune* (1983), which grew out of his 1981 short story "Saints," addresses the troubled and complex relationship between England and Ireland through two families – the Irish Quintons and the English Woodcombes – from the famine of the 1840s to the Irish Civil War. The Irish Willie falls in love with his English cousin Marianne; and when his family home is destroyed by British soldiers in 1918, his subsequent revenge on a British officer results in his exile from Ireland, and separation from Marianne and their daughter Imelda. The Quintons' plight is emblematic of that of the Protestant minority during the Civil War: however well-intentioned they are toward one another, their country, and the cause of Irish nationalism, they inevitably become victims of a capricious fate.

In the novel *Felicia's Journey* (1994), Trevor's growing preoccupation with the fate of the Catholic majority, already evident in his short fiction, finds expression in his longer fiction. The novel concerns an unmarried, pregnant 17-year-old Irish Catholic girl who, searching in England for the father of her child, falls into the hands of an English serial killer, Mr Hillditch, survives the ordeal, and eventually has an abortion. The novel may be read as a postcolonial narrative: with each successive meeting between the English Hillditch and the Irish Felicia, Hillditch becomes more contemptuous of the cultural background of this "runaway from the Irish boglands" (Trevor 1994: 127) and whose impending return to her family begins to seem to him "a fate which is, literally, worse than death and one from which he, the enlightened colonial redeemer, must deliver her, the misguided postcolonial victim" (St. Peter 2002: 336).

Felicia's great-grandmother, with whom the girl is forced to live while in Ireland, represents traditional Ireland, and indeed bears a resemblance to various representations of Ireland, especially Yeats's Cathleen ni Houlihan, who, in the form of an old woman, seeks young men willing to die for her "four green fields." In her youth the grandmother had lost her husband in the struggle for Irish freedom and had subsequently endured a life of hardship, believing it to have been ennobled by her young husband's bloodshed – much as Cathleen ni Houlihan, upon persuading a young man to abandon marriage plans and risk death for her sake, departs with the "walk of a queen." The grandmother has outlived two generations and has also "outlived her own rational thought" (1994: 25). Her memorabilia of Ireland's history – newspaper clippings, photographs, and copies of documents – are the modern-day analogy of the compendium of Irish oral history traditionally possessed and recited by feminine representations of Ireland that appear in the traditional eighteenth century Irish *aisling*, or vision poem; in this the poet encounters a woman who is an allegorical representation of the country, and whose tale of subjection to a foreign entity, invariably male, is emblematic of the Irish colonial condition.

While Trevor writes as an outsider to the Irish Catholic tradition, Edna O'Brien's fiction is continually informed by her position as an insider. Born in Tuamgraney,

County Clare in 1930, O'Brien attended convent school before leaving for Dublin at 16 to attend Pharmaceutical College. Her *Country Girls* trilogy (*The Country Girls*, 1960; *The Lonely Girl*, 1962; and *Girls in their Married Bliss*, 1964), whose protagonist, Caithleen Brady, leaves convent school for Dublin, and later moves to London, closely parallels her own life story. James Joyce was an extremely important influence on O'Brien: her book about him was published in 1999, she wrote the introduction for Penguin's *Dubliners*, and, in an interview with Philip Roth, she stated that in the "constellation of geniuses, he [Joyce] is a blinding light and father of us all" (Roth 1984: 39). In many ways, her writing may be viewed as an attempt to accomplish the same goals for Irish literature, but to do so from a woman's perspective, with female protagonists. Frank Tuohy has suggested that while Joyce was the first Irish Catholic to make his experience and surroundings recognizable, "the world of Nora Barnacle" had to wait for the fiction of Edna O'Brien (quoted in O'Brien 1976b: 50).

O'Brien's trilogy is influenced by the tradition of autobiography in Ireland: Joyce's *Dubliners* features stories told from the first-person point of view of a child, full of autobiographical details and frequent references to actual places and people in Dublin; likewise, O'Brien's trilogy, which even includes a reference to Caitlin's reading *Dubliners*, is closely observed and steeped in realism. The journey to Dublin seems an essential rite of passage for Irish writers: William Carleton, author of the famous *Lough Derg Pilgrim*, writes in his *Autobiography* about making the journey from Country Tyrone to Dublin on foot. Patrick Kavanagh retraced most of Carleton's trek in the 1930s, coming to Dublin to pay homage to its writers, whom unfortunately he found only too content to idealize the Irish countryside and peasantry while condescending to authentic peasants like Kavanagh. Edna O'Brien is, however, the first Irish woman to write of leaving the countryside and going to Dublin, and she imbues the journey with the spiritual significance accorded to pilgrimages.

Although World War II extended through O'Brien's late childhood and early adolescence, the Republic of Ireland was neutral during the war, and thus isolated from the strife that prevailed in Europe and Britain. In 1941 O'Brien was enrolled in the Convent of Mercy, Loughrea, County Galway, "a place so remote from the world's strife that the drama of the year is the blooming of the rhododendrons, there to wait out the war in peace" (D. O'Brien 1982: 181). This idyllic setting, coupled with her reading there of romantic works, including *Gone with the Wind*, *Rebecca*, and *How Green was My Valley*, doubtless influenced her rendering of nature in *Country Girls*. Caitlin's subsequent move to Dublin, and then to London, are marked by her increasing estrangement from nature, which corresponds to her increasing self-destructiveness and sense of alienation. Although scenes in the first book are idyllic, O'Brien, like Kavanagh, depicts the Irish countryside as the site of labor and hardship: Caitlin's mother's shoulder is permanently lowered by constantly carrying a heavy bucket, and rural characters like the hired man Hickey, though kind to Caitlin, are too rough-hewn to appreciate the complexities of her character.

"Irish revel," one of the stories in O'Brien's first collection *The Love Object* (1969), is a tribute to Joyce's "The dead," and its protagonist, Mary, prefigures a number of

O'Brien protagonists. O'Brien's sense of Ireland as a land frozen in fear – "fear of church, fear of gombeenism, fear of phantoms, fear of ridicule, fear of hunger, fear of annihilation" (1976b: 127) – is echoed in lines such as "if only I had a sweetheart, something to hold on to, she thought, as she cracked some ice with her high heel and watched the crazy splintered pattern it made (1975: 114), which in turn echo Joyce's description of Ireland as "a cracked looking glass" and a land of stasis and "paralysis" (Gilbert 1957: 134). Mary's clutching to a sweetheart as an escape from a desperate situation forms one strand of a "crazy splintered pattern" of obsessive dramas in which O'Brien protagonists find themselves trapped. At the story's close Mary stops briefly for a view of the countryside from a hill above her home and surveys it in terms that clearly echo Joyce's language in "The dead." However, instead of the softly falling snow that Gabriel Conroy views from his hotel window, Mary witnesses an unforgiving frost in a setting that seems to deny any opportunity for spiritual enlightenment or redemption:

> The poor birds could get no food, as the ground was frozen hard. Frost was general all over Ireland; frost like a weird blossom on the branches, on the riverbank from which Long John Salmon leaped in his great, hairy nakedness, on the plough left out all winter; frost on the stony fields, and on all the slime and ugliness of the world. (1975: 113)

O'Brien's relationship to feminism is debated: some critics, Julia O'Faolain among them, praise her work as feminist – "[her] stories are bulletins from a front on which they will not care to engage, field reports on the feminine condition at its most acute" (O'Faolain 1974: 4) – while others, Anatole Broyard and Lotus Snow are examples, criticize her depiction of women either because her heroines are portrayed as "chasing after men" (Broyard 1986: 12) or because they select "one route only: sex. They never consider the professions, social service, art and music, politics, travel . . . A monomaniacal lot, these women reject all of life but sex" (Snow 1979: 83). Most critics, including Eckley and O'Brien herself, agree that her characters are more concerned with love and romance than they are with careers. O'Brien says, "I'm obsessed quite irrationally by the notion of love" (O'Hara 1993: 317).

Yet O'Brien's exploration of private obsessions is the means by which she addresses precisely the same public issues that her predecessors have. She regards her fiction as simultaneously addressing personal and public issues: "War, whether it's between a man or a woman, or different parts of a country, or different nations, is always, always more complicated than just the two sides. It is that I want to write about. It's the dilemma and conflict within the obvious dilemma that matters" (quoted in Hatheway 1999: 124). Even as early as her seemingly apolitical *Country Girls* trilogy, she confronts issues that are integral to public discourse in Ireland: religion, politics, and national identity. She presents Irish Catholicism as a source of guilt and fear, and she confronts Ireland's troubled political history through references to the Black and Tans as well as to Ireland's colonial legacy. "Mr. Gentleman," as the town has affectionately dubbed the wealthy and mysterious man over whom Caitleen obsesses throughout the trilogy, is the means by which O'Brien provides a chronicle and critique of the occupation of Ireland, first by the Normans and, later, by Anglo-Irish Protestants, spawning class and religious conflicts that have never been resolved.

O'Brien's female characters, who are reminiscent of traditional representations of Ireland, are the means by which she challenges the gendered nature of Irish national-ism and considers its effect on real women's lives. Fixed constructs of gender have been central to Irish nationalism: from the *aisling*, invariably featuring Ireland as female and its oppressor as male, to Ireland's various representations as Hibernia, Mother Ireland, the Poor Old Woman, the Shan Van Vocht, Cathleen ni Houlihan, the Dark Rosaleen, and even the Virgin Mary. Through Caitleen – also known as Kate and Cathleen – the *Country Girls* trilogy relies on and provides insight into traditional representations of Ireland. O'Brien invokes a number of traditional female representa-tions of Ireland in order to combat the destructive tendencies of such myths. Throughout her literary career, while her victimized or betrayed females may serve as representations of Ireland, they are nonetheless flesh and blood women whose tribulations reflect those visited on real women in Ireland. Her 1990s trilogy (*House of Splendid Isolation*, 1994; *Down by the River*, 1996; and *Wild Decembers*, 1999) explicitly addresses contemporary political issues, from Irish nationalism to the Catholic Church's role in abortion rights to the battles over the representation of women and of Ireland.

Like O'Brien, John McGahern explores traditional Irish themes: religion, Irish national identity, migration from the farm to the city, and exile. Born in Dublin in 1934 to John (a police officer) and Susan McManus McGahern, McGahern was raised in County Roscommon in western Ireland. His first novel, *The Barracks* (1963), received Ireland's highest literary prize, the AE Memorial Award. Written while he was a teacher at St John the Baptist Boys National School in Clontarf, *The Barracks* concerns an Irish boy whose father is a local police sergeant, and whose mother dies during the course of the novel. Though its plot closely parallels McGahern's own early life, the novel may also be read as a critique of de Valera's vision of a predominantly rural Catholic Ireland. The book is also notable for its confrontation of heretofore unspeakable issues such as parental and clerical sexual abuse of children.

After the publication of *The Barracks*, McGahern took a year's leave of absence from teaching and went to London to write. His next novel, *The Dark* (1965), a coming-of-age novel about an Irish adolescent boy, was banned by the Irish Censorship Board, resulting in the loss of McGahern's teaching position. *The Dark*, in terms of its subject and approach, is reminiscent of Joyce's *A Portrait of the Artist as a Young Man*. The novel revolves around two conflicts: that of the boy and his father, which in turn may be seen as analogous to the conflict between the individual and the paternalistic authority of Church and state; and that of the boy's desire to be a priest in order to fulfill a deathbed promise he made to his mother, and the natural sexual desires that are awakened in him during adolescence. Although he rejects the priesthood, both conflicts are to some extent resolved through the power of nature: near the end of the novel, when the young Mahoney helps his father with haymaking, he achieves a mystical harmony with the natural setting, which is the means by which he achieves reconciliation with his father (Sampson 1993: 79).

In addition to the censorship of his book, McGahern's marriage to the non-Catholic Finnish theatrical director Annikki Laaski during his leave contributed to the school administrators' decision to fire him. The issues raised by the censorship of *The Dark* provided material for two novels, *The Leavetaking* (1974) and *The Pornographer* (1979). In *The Leavetaking*, Patrick Moran is Dublin schoolteacher, who, like McGahern, is dismissed for choosing to marry a woman outside his faith. Denis Sampson observes that Patrick Moran's leavetakings entail a series of deaths to the self, which gradually allow his artistic consciousness to be born (1993: 125). Moran accepts the modern penchant for substituting art and love for religion, rejecting his religion and its promise of eternal salvation in favor of the daily renewal of life through love, the "only communion left to us now" (McGahern 1984: 168). Yet McGahern is aware of the limitations of Moran's choice: "Religion, in return for the imitation of the formal pattern, promises us the eternal kingdom. The Muse, under whose whim we reign, in return for a lifetime of availability, may grant us the absurd crown of style" (McGahern 1991: 12).

The Pornographer (1979), which concerns a failed poet who has turned to writing pornography, involves an intersection between events in the author's own life and those in his fictional account of his characters, two "sexual athletes," Colonel Grimshaw and Mavis Carmichael. His gradual recognition of the limitations in the pornography he writes coincides with his recognition of the shortcomings in his own approach to sexuality, both of which occur after he impregnates a woman whom he realizes he does not love: "By not attending, by thinking any one thing was as worth doing as any other, by sleeping with anybody who'd agree, I had been the cause of as much pain and confusion and evil as if I had actively set out to do it. I had not attended properly. I had found the energy to choose too painful . . . I had turned back, let the light of imagination almost out" (1979: 251).

Amongst Women (1990), McGahern's most acclaimed novel to date, concerns Michael Moran, a veteran of the Irish War of Independence, and the father of three daughters and two sons. The title is a reference to Moran's daily reciting of the rosary, "Blessed art thou amongst women," yet it is also an ironic reference to the fact that this patriarchal, nationalistic, devoutly Catholic figure's fate must ultimately be decided "amongst women" (Di Battista 1998: 25). Moran serves as a symbol of the paternalistic authority of the Church and state, yet, as the title suggests, the women in the novel ultimately usurp this power. Eamonn Wall observes that *Amongst Women* "is a mirror to the century – from the War of Independence to close to the present . . . an Irish world in its long moment of change from its frail postcolonial identity to its more confident one as part of Europe" (1999: 305).

While Patrick McCabe's novels are set in contemporary Ireland, they are preoccupied with Ireland's past role as a colony of England and its more recent role as a cultural colony of the United States. Born in County Monaghan in 1955, McCabe received the *Irish Times* Award for Fiction and was shortlisted for the Booker Prize in

1992 for his novel *The Butcher Boy*. In addition to *The Butcher Boy*, he has written *The Dead School* (1995), *Breakfast on Pluto* (1999), *Mondo Desperado* (2000), *Emerald Germs of Ireland* (2001), and *Call Me the Breeze* (2003). Titles such as *Emerald Germs of Ireland* – a pun on a popular book of Irish melodies, *Emerald Gems of Ireland* – reveal McCabe's penchant for parodying and debunking popular representations of Ireland.

Still widely regarded as his best novel, *The Butcher Boy* systematically explores the most popular representations of Ireland – as a pristine green landscape and as a woman – and of the Irish, as drunken ne'er do-wells and pigs. *The Butcher Boy* (the basis for a film by Neil Jordan in 1998) is the story of a 12-year-old Irish boy, Francie Brady, the only child of a terminally alcoholic father and a suicidally depressed mother, both of whom die during the course of the novel, leaving Francie alone in an ultimately destructive fantasy world populated by cowboys and Indians, bog men, space aliens, comic book heroes, and even the Virgin Mary herself. The book may be read as a chronicle of Ireland's cultural resistance to British imperialism as well as a commentary on Ireland's more recent role as cultural colony of the United States. Thus, while *The Butcher Boy* is about a boy caught between childhood and adolescence, it is also about a culture torn between Irish and English values, between the traditional and the modern, between ancient blood feuds and Cold War nuclear power struggles.

The novel begins in the hideaway near the river belonging to Francie and his best friend Joe, with pristine images of spring water, snowdrops, and bright green shoots, yet this apparent pastoral retreat is gradually corrupted by the adult world of conflict, destruction, and hypocrisy. With *post hoc, ergo propter hoc* logic, Francie places blame for the bewildering course his life takes on the Nugent family, who have just returned to the community after living in London, and whose son Philip, of Francie's age, is immediately regarded as a rival for the affections of Joe. Mrs Nugent's assessment of the Bradys as "pigs" invokes an English stereotype of the Irish popularized in *Punch* cartoons. The Nugents have heretofore been envied for their refinement, reserve, restraint, taste and order – the stereotypical English traits on which the old Celt/Saxon dichotomy depended – qualities that for centuries had presumably made the English eminently suited to govern the Irish. Francie's weeping mother, humiliated by the Anglicized Mrs Nugent, resembles the weeping woman in the Irish *aisling*, emblematic of an Ireland still trying to shake off English influence.

Images of stasis and paralysis that were employed by Joyce and Edna O'Brien appear in McCabe's novel as well: Francie is a static character, unable to leave the world of childhood, transfixed by static images such as a water drop on a leaf, the ashes of a fire (also the motif in Frank McCourt's *Angela's Ashes*), and the crazy, splintered patterns of a patch of ice at which he hacks. Francie refuses to acknowledge his father's death, and so continues to talk to him and behave as though he were still alive. McCabe's townspeople likewise seem paralyzed: the threat of the Cuban missile crisis leads them to deny the real world, to retreat into religious visions, and to channel their hopes into the possibility of seeing "our lady" Mary (1992: 31).

Whereas McCabe's fiction explores the Irish preoccupation with Catholicism, Roddy Doyle's fiction is equally notable for its conspicuous absence. Winner of the

Booker Prize for *Paddy Clarke Ha-Ha-Ha* (1993), Doyle was born in Killbarrack, North Dublin in 1958, and is also the author of *The Commitments* (1987),*The Snapper* (1990), *The Van* (1991), *The Woman Who Walked into Doors* (1996), and *A Star Called Henry* (1999). His first four novels are set in Barrytown, a fictionalized Dublin town whose name was inspired by a Steely Dan song, and which emblematizes an Irish working-class world increasingly disenchanted with the promises and claims of politics and religion. His first five novels all feature characters who are working-class or middle-class Dubliners whose immediate environment and familial relation-ships, good or bad, are central to their lives, whereas religion and Irish politics are peripheral. While Doyle claims that Joyce has had no conscious influence on him whatsoever (White 2001: 7), he readily acknowledges the importance of Flan O'Brien: "The work of Flann O'Brien was an enormous hit with me and the people I hung around with" (Sbrockey 1999: 541). Doyle's efforts to capture the nuances of Irish speech hearken back to the competing claims of Irish-Gaelic and English, as well as to the relatively long and influential Irish oral tradition.

Some critics have regarded the apparent absence of religion and politics in Doyle's novels as willful ignorance on Doyle's part, but Doyle himself avers that this absence is a reflection of reality: scandals in the world of politics as well as in the Church have led to a growing disillusionment, especially among the working class, with the traditional dominance of Church and state. In Doyle's novels, priests do not appear, few parishioners attend Mass, and the founder of Christianity is invoked only as a residual expletive, "Jaysis." Likewise, politics seems to be absent, although his characters' failure to discuss politics does not necessarily mean that Doyle's books are apolitical. Doyle himself contends that "It's the difference between politics with a little "p," or a big "P." But a book about a woman in a violent marriage [*The Woman who Walked into Doors*] is a political book. A book about two unemployed men [*The Van*] is a political book" (White 2001: 13). Doyle's construction of a common ancestry for the Irish and the African Americans in his novel *The Commitments*, in which a group of Irish young people form a soul band, is reminiscent of colonial discourse that identified the Irish as essentially black, "[as] epitomized in Edmund Spenser's *View of the Present State of Ireland* in which he uncovers an African ancestry for the Irish through methods of comparative anthropology" (Piroux 1998: 49). Furthermore,

> Doyle, while not 'political', is certainly aware of world politics: *The Van,* in which Jimmy Rabbit and his best friend Bimbo respond to their unemployment by opening a fish and chip van, offers a critique of capitalism and of Thatcher's warring UK, and Jimmy and Bimbo's disintegrating relationship, although not exactly allegorical, does lend itself to comparison with British politics in the 1980s. (White 2001: 95)

Despite Doyle's contention that James Joyce was not an influence on his writing, *Paddy Clark Ha Ha Ha* suggests otherwise: Doyle's account of Paddy's childhood parallels that of Joyce's Stephen Dedalus in *A Portrait of the Artist as a Young Man*, and its opening sentence even echoes Joyce's opening sentence. Paddy Clark is a young Irish boy who must come to terms with his parents' divorce in a society in which divorce was (until 1997) an impossibility. Hence, Doyle here confronts yet another political issue.

While Doyle's most recent novel, *A Star Called Henry,* is on one level a historical novel about the Irish struggles to achieve nationhood in the early part of the twentieth century, on another it offers a critique of Romantic Nationalism, drawing on Celtic myth and/folklore, particularly the Cuchulain legend, to which a number of the leaders of the Easter Rising were devoted (Dawson 2001: 169).

Born in 1969, Emma Donoghue deserves mention as a promising young writer who has already published three novels. The author of *Passions between Women: British Lesbian Culture 1668–1801* (1993), her first novel, *Stir Fry* (1995), concerns a lesbian rite of passage set at University College Dublin. Her more recent novel, *Slammerkin* (2000), is based on the true story of Mary Saunders, a girl who was executed in the eighteenth century in the Welsh Marches for killing her dressmaker mistress. Donoghue's setting, though not Irish, enables her to explore the class division produced by the colonial enterprise and emblematized by the Celt/Saxon dichotomy. The Welsh Marches – the borderland between England and Wales – has a distinctive geography and history. People living in the Marches were subject to "the customs of the March," while those in Wales proper still adhered to indigenous Welsh law. The Marches, we later learn in the novel, is also an area that has ignored calendar reform, preferring to follow the old calendar; and it occurs to Mary that if her father Cobb had never left the Marches, he could have saved time, as well as his own life (he died during the Calendar Riots in London). The book is thus divided into Part I, London, and Part II, Monmouth, emphasizing sharp distinctions between its two settings – London and the Welsh Marches – as well as the high cost of leaving one area for the other: Cobb's migration and subsequent death foreshadows Mary's own.

When Mary prepares to leave London for Monmouth she asks the driver where it is. He informs her that "Wales is where England runs out" (2000: 110). His bleak description resonates with what Margaret Atwood has called the "colonial mentality," the belief among the colonized that "the great good place is always somewhere else." The atmosphere of the book is pervaded by England's role as an imperial power, as when, earlier in the novel, Mary reads in the newspaper about the ascension of George III, "King of Great Britain, Ireland, Gibraltar, Canada, the Americas, Bengal, the West Indies, and Elector of Hanover" (p. 12). Donoghue's juxtaposition of the two settings enables her to render the English domination of the Celts as well as the way in which the Celts resisted domination: in the "Monmouth" setting, she introduces a body of Celtic folklore, custom, and mythology that imbues it, if not with political authority, then at least with imaginative authority, as a means of encoding resistance toward the imperial center and its totalizing systems of generic classification.

Donoghue's fascinating interplay between the language of the indigenous Celts and that of their English conquerors, her brutally realistic descriptions of life for the working Irish poor, her rendering of the colonial mentality, and her incorporation of

Celtic folklore and myth all hearken back to the preoccupations of Joyce, and reveal just how powerful and lasting these cultural influences have been on the Irish literary tradition of the past fifty years.

REFERENCES AND FURTHER READING

Broyard, Anatole (1986) "The rotten luck of Kate and Baba." Review of *The Country Girls: Trilogy and Epilogue*, *New York Times Review of Books*, May 11: 12.

Dawson, Janice (2001) "Aspects of the fantastic in *A Star Called Henry*: deconstructing Romantic Nationalism," *Journal of the Fantastic in the Arts*, 12/2: 168–85.

Di Battista, Maria (1998) "Joyce's ghost: the bogey of realism in John McGahern's *Amongst Women*," in Karen R. Lawrence (ed.) *Transcultural Joyce*. Cambridge: Cambridge University Press.

Donaghue, Emma (2000) *Slammerkin*. New York: Harcourt.

Eckley, Grace (1980) "Edna O'Brien," in Robert Hogan (ed.) *Dictionary of Irish Literature*. Westport, CT: Greenwood Press.

Fitzgerald-Hoyt, Mary (2002) "Making history: 'The News from Ireland'," *Colby Quarterly*, 38/3 (September): 315–28.

Gilbert, Stuart (ed.) (1957) *Letters of James Joyce*, vol. II. London: Faber and Faber.

Haberstroh, Patricia Boyle (1983) "John McGahern," in Jay L. Halio (ed.) *Dictionary of Literary Biography*, vol. 14: *British Novelists Since 1960*. Newark, DE: University of Delaware.

Hatheway, William K. (1999) "Breaking the tie that binds: feminine and national representation in Edna O'Brien's *House of Splendid Isolation*," *North Dakota Quarterly*, 66/1: 122–34.

Ingman, Heather (2002) "Edna O'Brien: stretching the nation's boundaries," *Irish Studies Review*, 10/3: 253–65.

Joyce, James (1934) *Ulysses*. New York : Modern Library.

Kearney, Richard (1984) *Myth and Motherland*. Belfast: Dorman.

Kiberd, Declan (1996) *Inventing Ireland: The Literature of the Modern Nation*. London: Vintage.

McCabe, Patrick (1992) *The Butcher Boy*. London: Picador.

McGahern, John (1979) *The Pornographer*. New York: Harper and Row.

——(1984) [1974] *The Leavetaking*. London: Faber and Faber.

——(1991) "The image," *Canadian Journal of Irish Studies*, 17/1 (July): 12.

MacKenna, Dolores (1999) *William Trevor: The Writer and His Work*. Dublin: New Island Books.

Martin, Augustine (1965) "Inherited dissent: the dilemma of the Irish writer," *Studies: An Irish Quarterly Review*, 54 (Spring): 1–20.

O'Brien, Darcy (1982) "Edna O'Brien: a kind of Irish childhood," in Thomas F. Staley (ed.) *Twentieth Century Women Novelists*. Totowa, NJ: Barnes and Noble.

O'Brien, Edna (1975) [1969] *The Love Object*. Harmondsworth: Penguin.

——(1976a) *A Fanatic Heart*. Harmondsworth: Penguin.

—— (1976b) *Mother Ireland*. New York: Plume.

O'Faolain, Julia (1974) Review of *A Scandalous Woman and Other Stories*, *New York Times Book Review*, September 22: 3–4.

O'Hara, Kiera (1993) "Love objects: love and obsession in the stories of Edna O'Brien," *Studies-in-Short-Fiction*, 30/3 (Summer): 311–25.

Piroux, Lorraine (1998) "I'm black an' I'm proud: re-inventing Irishness in Roddy Doyle's *The Commitments*, *College Literature*, 25 (Spring): 45–57.

Putzel, Steven D. (1982) "The black pig: Yeats's early apocalyptic beast," *Eire Ireland*, 17/3: 86–102.

Roby, Kinley (1993) *William Trevor*. New York: Twayne Publishers.

Roth, Philip (1984) "A conversation with Edna O'Brien: 'The body contains the life story'," *New York Times Book Review*, November 18: 39–40.

Sampson, Denis (1993) *Outstaring Nature's Eye: The Fiction of John McGahern*. Washington, DC: Catholic University of America Press.

St Peter, Christine (2002) "Consuming pleasures: Felicia's journey in fiction and film," *Colby Quarterly*, 38/3 (September): 329–39.

Sbrockey, Karen (1999) "Something of a hero: an interview with Roddy Doyle," *The Literary Review*, 42 (Summer): 537–52.

Sekine, Masaru (ed.) (1985) *Irish Writers and Society at Large*. Gerrards Cross, Bucks: Smythe; Totowa, NJ: Barnes and Noble.

Snow, Lotus (1979) "That trenchant childhood route?," *Eire-Ireland*, 14: 74–83.

Stout, Mira (1989) "The art of fiction CVIII: William Trevor," *Paris Review*, 110: 118–51.

Tracy, Robert (2002) "Telling tales: the fictions of William Trevor," *Colby Quarterly*, 38/3 (September): 295–307.

Trevor, William (1994) *Felicia's Journey*. New York: Penguin.

——(1996) *Three Early Novels*. New York: Penguin.

Wall, Eamonn (1999) "The living stream: John McGahern's *Amongst Women* and Irish writing of the 1990s," *Studies: An Irish Quarterly Review*, 88: 305–14.

White, Caramine (2001) *Reading Roddy Doyle*. Syracuse, NY: Syracuse University Press

35

Anita Brookner

Cheryl Alexander Malcolm

When Anita Brookner won the 1984 Booker McConnell Prize for *Hotel du Lac*, the battle lines between her admirers and detractors were drawn. Had Brookner won the prize for *Latecomers* (1988) – about two *Kindertransport* children who escape the Holocaust and become successful London businessmen – these divisions might well have been different. In spite of writing eighteen novels since *Hotel du Lac*, Brookner is identified most with her Booker Prize novel. This essay will explore the notion that *Hotel du Lac is* representative of Brookner's writing and will trace its impact on the author's career. But it will do so by examining the misconceptions that make Brookner, as her editor at Viking says, "the most misunderstood writer: people assume that all her books are the same and that they are peopled by lonely ladies in cardigans and are the most genteel fare" (J. Annan 2001: 1).

Spinster Fare

Brookner's admirers (who include authors ranging from David Lodge to Edna O'Brien) praise the elegance of her writing. Brookner's detractors dismiss her novels as tales of "spinsters doing not very much rather slowly" (Derbyshire 2001: 4). The extent to which Brookner is perceived to write about lonely women cannot be overstated. It is perpetuated even in a Penguin catalogue, which in 2000 referred to her work as "spinster novels." Yet, since *Hotel du Lac*, Brookner has written one family saga (*Family and Friends*, 1985), five novels with male protagonists (*Latecomers*, 1988; *Lewis Percy*, 1989; *A Private View*, 1994; *Altered States*, 1996; and *The Next Big Thing*, 2002); and five novels about marriage (*Brief Lives*, 1990; *A Closed Eye*, 1991; *A Family Romance*, 1993; *Incidents in the Rue Laugier*, 1995; and *The Bay of Angels*, 2001). That Brookner does not write only about single women is all too apparent. What is less obvious is that "spinster" is a misnomer even for the unmarried women in her novels. If the legacy of winning the Booker Prize for *Hotel du Lac* is that Brookner is perceived only to write about genteel English spinsters, this is indeed an ironic one. Edith Hope fits the stereotype of a spinster least of any of Brookner's single female protagonists.

The word "spinster," unlike its male counterpart "bachelor," designates not only an unmarried status but a sexless one. Whereas bachelors can be "eligible," spinsters are generally regarded to be too old or undesirable for marriage. Yet Edith Hope receives two offers of marriage from two separate men *and* she has a married lover. By naming the protagonist of *Hotel du Lac* "Edith," Brookner might seem to have been designating a spinster type. "Edith" is a fairly old-fashioned name, more usually given to women of an earlier generation than that of the protagonist. The implication is that she is somehow out of date. Edith's unwillingness to update her romance novels, in other words to reflect the social realities of sexually liberated career women, may make her appear prudish. Yet her refusal to cater to the tastes of "those multi-orgasmic girls with the executive briefcases" is rooted in her sense of justice (1985b: 28). By perpetuating the maxim that "the meek will inherit the earth" (in her books "it is the mouse-like unassuming girl who gets the hero"), she is effectively putting the world to rights (ibid.). Extracts from her letters to her married lover serve most of all to remind us that this is *not* a sexually inexperienced or repressed woman. Would the latter, after canceling her wedding, have her married lover back to the house to help her finish the party champagne before making love, as Edith Hope does? If belief in the supremacy of romantic love over casual sex or marriages of convenience makes Edith Hope seem old-fashioned, that does not make her pitiful. Rather, it is society that is to be pitied for continuing to regard married women with children as the norm and anything else as abnormal. This message is reinforced through the examples of the other residents at the Hotel du Lac, in particular by a young woman whose aristocratic husband wants her to get over her eating disorder in order to give him heirs, and by an aged Frenchwoman whose position in the family is taken over by a young daughter-in-law. Just as Edith Hope is marginalized by her single status, so these other women are similarly cast out from their homes because they are infertile or old.

Inherent in the disdain felt by some critics for Brookner's single female protagonists is, then, an ageism as well as a preconceived notion of what constitutes an acceptable woman. Given that Brookner did not write about the aged until long after *Hotel du Lac*, and that the first of these older protagonists (in *Latecomers* and *A Private View*) are male, it is surprising that the term "spinster" appears as often as it does in reviews of her novels. Brookner offers this explanation: "I think they [British reviewers] had made the initial mistake of identifying me with my female protagonists, so that the criticism that comes my way . . . is a semipersonal kind which does not rank as real criticism" (Guppy 1987: 165–6). Brookner has never been married nor does she have any children. She did, however, care for her ill parents for many years. In this regard, many of her heroines resemble her.

Reversal of parent/child roles is a common feature in Brookner's writing. This takes two forms, often in combination within one novel. Either the parents of the main characters do not care for them as children, or the characters have to care for their parents although they themselves are barely more than children, or both situations occur. As a consequence, Brookner's protagonists appear, in manner if not physically, aged beyond their actual years. The burden of such a predicament is both practical and psychological. Hindered from acting independently, such caregiver protagonists stop thinking of a future for themselves. This may well explain why "spinster" has been applied to Brookner women who are only in their twenties or thirties.

Whereas a strong sense of filial duty might, in some readers' minds, make the Brookner protagonist appear old-fashioned, a proclivity for finding lovers and having affairs should surely make them modern. Yet it would seem that many critics, like most characters in Brookner's novels, do not see past the respectable public image presented by her protagonists. The dichotomy between appearances and realities is most extensively dealt with in *Fraud* (1992), which begins like a detective novel. A missing person investigation is underway for "Miss Durrant, a woman in middle years, living alone in apparently comfortable circumstances," or what the police call "a funny type. Old fashioned. Looking after the mother, and so on. Unmarried. Typical spinster" (1993b: 5). The first indication that there may be a discrepancy between appearances and realities is in the first paragraph of the novel when, during a search of Anna Durrant's home, a policeman opens a cupboard.

> This was the first sight of anything unusual, the lavishness of the materials – the fine tweed, the cashmere, the silk – and the brilliance of the colours, surely a little exorbitant for a woman of Miss Durrant's presumed age. The bedroom of the little flat contained a long looking-glass on a stand, and a faint odour of gardenias issued from the opened door of the built-in wardrobe. In the bathroom they found several bottles of expensive scent, some of them still sealed and in their original packages. (1993b: 5)

The discovery, not of Anna Durrant's corpse but of her rich finery, foreshadows the discovery that Anna Durrant is alive and well in Paris where she has decided to move and become a fashion designer. The police officers' surprise suggests that such possessions are out of place in the home of a "typical spinster." Splendid and rich possessions are at odds with a life which convention says must be dull and poor. The implication is that a middle-aged woman who is single and has no children cannot be beautiful or sensual. She is barren and to be pitied. While it turns out that Anna Durrant is neither the victim nor the perpetrator of a crime that the detective style opening leads us to expect, both roles are conventionally assigned to the older single woman. By deviating from a norm of marriage and motherhood, she is seen either to have been wronged or to be committing some wrong against society.

While Brookner explores these attitudes in many of her novels, she is best at showing how flawed they are in *Fraud*. For crimes have been committed. Anna's mother is swindled by a bigamist, George Ainsworth. Anna's best friend, Marie-France, is exploited by an opportunist with a roving eye, Philip Dunoyer. Anna's doctor, Lawrence Halliday, is seduced into marriage by Vickie Gibson, who exudes sexuality but otherwise has no feelings for him. An acquaintance of Anna's called Philippa is caught in an affair with a married man who merely sees her as a recreation.

Throughout the novel, people who conform to the norm (for example, in terms of marriage or its pursuit) are duped and subjected to disappointment. Only the protagonist is happy and – as the final image of her "plunging" into the Paris traffic and "holding back" the cars with her hand "to ward them off" symbolizes – in control of her life (1993b: 262). The "typical spinster" who, we are at first led to believe, is a corpse proves to be more alive than anyone else in the novel.

The resemblance between the opening of *Fraud* and the short story "Illusion" by Jean Rhys is too striking not to mention and, given Brookner's professed admiration of Rhys's writing, is not accidental. In "Illusion," as in *Fraud*, the dresses are effectively skeletons in the closet, raising questions about the protagonist's "cool sensible, tidy English outside" (Rhys 1987: 2). They are flamboyant and fun; they are un-English. Like Rhys, Brookner repeatedly aligns England with conformity, drabness, and hypocrisy; France with emancipation, vitality, and truth. Brookner's is a harsh portrait of a nation, which may well account for the strong dislike that some British reviewers evince for her work. There is certainly a marked difference in reception between one side of the Atlantic and the other. Whereas to Americans, Brookner seems so English,

> to the English, Brookner essentially seems Continental, foreign; all her novels . . . are about exile. The families in them have attenuated roots in Vienna, Paris, somewhere unspecified further east; childhood holidays are recalled, not in Cromer or St. Ives, but Baden-Baden, Scheveningen, Veyey; they may or may not be Jewish, but Jewishness offers no background or support. (Dinnage 1989: 34)

Given how many of her protagonists have active sexual lives if not adulterous affairs, it is remarkable that Brookner ever gained a reputation for writing about genteel or stereotypical spinsters. Yet this is no less remarkable than that this Anglo-Jewish writer is considered so English when the focus of over twenty years of her writing has been on characters on the peripheries of English society. One wonders whether reviewers read her novels *from* beginning to end, not merely the beginning and end. If they read only the beginnings and ends they may well be duped. For example, *A Start in Life* (1981), *Brief Lives* (1990), and *A Closed Eye* (1991) feature an older single female protagonist although the main bodies of these novels are about her youth. Like the characters who think they know these protagonists, some reviewers may be falling for an appearance of respectability and Englishness, which Brookner's elegant prose and traditional narratives would seem to support. In fact, Brookner's novels are about individuals who are continually "performing" identities. Adulterers are performing their respectability. Sexually active daughters are performing their innocence. The immigrants and children of immigrants are performing their Englishness. Brookner is likened to Henry James in that her "fiction lies on the edge of the English social order, repeatedly speaking for those who can never feel quite at home in its settled landscapes" (Birch 2002: 31). Comparisons to Jane Austen, however, are misleading. Whereas Austen wrote about those who are "in society," those who "accept themselves as part of society, however uncomfortably placed in it they may be," Brookner writes about those who are "outside society, unable to believe they belong – even when they are married and rich" (G. Annan 1992: 25).

The Foreigner in the Attic

When the Caribbean-born Jean Rhys took the figure of Mrs Rochester and let us hear her side in *Wide Sargasso Sea*, she not only turned our attention (and sympathies) from *Jane Eyre*, she effectively exposed the madwoman in the attic for what she *really* was: the foreigner in the attic. Although less dramatically executed in Brookner's novels, foreign characters are also kept hidden (as, for example, happens to the Russian and French grandparents in *Providence (1982)*) or hide themselves under a show of English assimilation (as their granddaughter, Kitty Maule, does). *Hotel du Lac* is unique in that its protagonist practices self-concealment and is concealed by others when she is sent from England to a Swiss hotel in the off-season. The significance of the latter cannot be overstated. Edith Hope is half Austrian. Switzerland is not her home, but neither wholly is England.

Sent away on condition that she return contrite and well behaved, her lapse was to spurn a perfectly suitable (to her English friends) but (in her view) utterly dull English bridegroom at the altar. The link between foreignness and decadent behavior is made by the hotel owner, who upon seeing her name in the register muses, "Hope, Edith Johanna. An unusual name for an English lady. Perhaps not entirely English. Perhaps not entirely a lady. Recommended, of course. But in this business one never knew" (1985b: 23). In both instances he is correct. Edith Hope, as is characteristic of Brookner's protagonists, perfects an appearance of cool Englishness and propriety, both of which are false. As is seen from the letters she writes but does not send to her married lover, she can and does love passionately. She also knows the risks of confessing as much. In *The Rules of Engagement* (2003), Elizabeth Wetherall, who is married and having an affair, expresses the lot of the mistress thus:

> The agreement, or rather the agreement that had been imposed on me, was that we were two strangers who met from time to time for a specific purpose, but who did not otherwise intrude into each other's lives. In order to sustain my part in this bargain I had needed all my hard-won pragmatism, and this, so far, had not deserted me. What intimacy we shared was rigorously controlled, confined to the flat in Britten Street, and never referred to in a wider context. (2003: 79)

As passages such as this one suggest, control should not be confused with an absence of emotion, but may signify more powerful emotions than it is wise to show. Control, which is the hallmark of Brookner's writing, may be likened to a form of self-censorship. The amount of detail in Brookner's texts, from the precise cut and color of clothing to menus for whole dinners, for example, can lead us to think that all is revealed. Yet, frequently, the external details of her characters' lives function as a smokescreen, covering omissions and at the same time building the reader's trust in the narrator. The one certainty in Brookner's novels is that secrets abound. So do double lives.

Like so many of her characters, Brookner has herself had a double life. Although a native Londoner, she claims to have never felt completely at home there. Had Lilian Furst not used it already, *Home Is Somewhere Else* would be a fitting title for Brookner's life story. Yet Brookner is no Furst. Nor indeed is she an Anne Karpf or Eva Hoffman. Born to Polish Jewish parents in London in 1928, Brookner was spared the tremendous upheavals and dislocations of Jews who escaped the Holocaust, or whose parents were camp survivors, or who emigrated when anti-Semitism rose again in Central Europe after the war. Yet the major themes of these memorialists – displacement, loss, and witness – pervade Brookner's novels. Growing up in an extended household of family and friends, many of whom had fled the Holocaust, Brookner gained a sense of history, albeit second hand, but still too close for comfort. Brookner was "inculcated from an impressionable age with a sense of permanent dislocation" on account of being the daughter of Polish Jews (Oates 1999: 19). Feelings of being a part of two cultures – but also *apart* – is the single thread running through all of her novels since *A Start in Life* (1981) (or *The Debut* as it is known in the USA) was published.

It was Brookner's first novel, but not her first book. An outsider to literary circles but not the art establishment, Brookner had already published eight studies on French art and had been the first woman ever to be appointed Slade Professor of Art at the University of Cambridge. An eminent scholar with an international reputation and honors (she was made a fellow of New Hall, Cambridge and King's College, and, in 1990, a Commander of the British Empire) Brookner seems a far cry from the stereotypical English spinster with whom many critics identify her.

Brookner says that she has been most influenced by French writers, especially Proust, and that she is an admirer of Jean Rhys. Both were outsiders – Proust on account of his invalidism and his Jewishness, Rhys because she was a white in the Caribbean and a Caribbean in England – and both wrote about outsiders. Notwithstanding fame in two careers, as an art historian and a writer, Brookner continues to take up the cause of outsiders. Whether they are of foreign birth or background, or are single, or old, or seemingly damaged in some way, such outsiders tend to be the focus of her novels. That they are all assembled in *Hotel du Lac* may account for its unrelieved malaise, which leads to comparisons between reading it and "taking an ice-cold bubblebath" (Mars-Jones 2002). In terms of Brookner's literary career, however, it offers a window on to the major characters and themes of the twenty-two novels that she has written in as many years.

Hotel du Lac was Brookner's fourth novel about a single young woman of foreign background in England. The first, of what is loosely a cycle, *A Start in Life* is about Ruth Weiss, the only daughter of a German Jewish father and an English Catholic mother, who, raised neither Jewish nor Catholic, neither wholly German nor English, is virtually made a foundling in her own home. Her only happiness is in Paris where, as a foreigner, her outsider status carries none of the shame it does in her own country. With new-found confidence, she embarks on an affair and cuts her hair as if to symbolize the severing of even the tenuous ties she has to her family. In *Providence*, Kitty Maule, the only daughter of a French mother and an English father who died before she was born, has

> two homes; one, a small flat in Chelsea, where she kept her father's photograph ... the other, her grandparents' house in the suburbs, where, once inside the front door, one encountered the smells, the furnishings, the continual discussion that might take place in an apartment house in Paris or perhaps further east. (1990: 6)

The words "further east" are not explained until the next page, where we are told that Kitty Maule's grandfather is Russian. The importance of the vague and almost euphemistic language used to describe the grandfather is central to the underlying tension throughout the novel. Kitty Maule sees herself as English, but the English do not. Her frankness about her French background suggests that her Russian grandfather is the impediment to her being accepted in England. *Providence* begins, for example, with a reference to her grandparents' legacy of "racial memories" and a watchfulness and mistrust of anyone who is not family (1990: 5). Like Ruth Weiss, Kitty Maule is "troped as Jewish" by her difference, which she cannot renounce although it impedes her acceptance into a dominant culture for which Christianity is important (Sylvester 2001: 50).

Brookner most fully develops the theme of conversion in *Look at Me* (1983), in which a hedonistic and beautiful upper-class English couple briefly amuse themselves by befriending a young woman, until she fails to conform to all their principles. Just as Nick and Alix are aligned with England and its colonial past, Frances Hinton is associated with outsiders such as the peripheral British (the Irish Mrs Halloran), Eastern Europeans (Dr Simik), and Jews (Dr Leventhal and Olivia) with whom she works at a library. Her identification with Olivia (Alix, for example, speaks to Frances and Olivia as if they were twins when she first meets them) is especially significant because Olivia is severely disabled as a result of a car accident. Olivia's back brace, like the birthmark on Harriet Lytton's face in *A Closed Eye* (1991), is a visible reminder that she is outside a dominant culture in which wholeness, like beauty, is so important. After Frances takes a Christmas present to her retired predecessor, Mrs Morpeth, she is shunned by Nick and Alix. Whereas Frances might have seemed a candidate for conversion, she proves not to be by her continued association with those on the margins, such as Mrs Morpeth who is disqualified by her age. Brookner further explores how the aged are displaced from the center of society in *A Private View* (1994), *Visitors* (1997), *Falling Slowly* (1998), and *The Next Big Thing*. *Look at Me* above all foreshadows *Hotel du Lac*, however, because its protagonist is one in an ensemble of characters who are displaced and marginalized.

Brookner says that the contrast between the foreign protagonists and English men in her early novels is really "the contrast between damaged people and those who are undamaged" (Haffenden 1985: 150). The women with whom Edith Hope has the most affinity at the Swiss hotel can all be considered damaged to some extent. One is old and deaf, another, as a consequence of anorexia, is infertile. A common feature of all of them is childlessness.

Assimilation, however, is not especially difficult for the characters in Brookner's novels. Languages and customs can be learned, as is proved by, among others, Hartmann and Fibich in *Latecomers*, Dolly in *A Family Romance*, and Julius Herz in *The Next Big Thing*. Nonetheless, these characters, after they escape the Holocaust, are left effectively homeless for the rest of their lives. As Brookner writes at the start of *The Next Big Thing*, they "never went home, for home no longer existed, flattened by Allied bombs" (2000: 5). The words "How could such loyalty not be recognized, and if necessary protected?" earlier allude to the metaphorical bomb – the Holocaust – that destroyed all concept of home for these characters (p. 3). Brookner employs ambiguity (these words could be those of Herz's father or the omniscient narrator) and a rhetorical question (uncommon in her narratives) to draw attention to and signify not only the naivety of Herz's father, who will soon learn that the Final Solution treated assimilated and unassimilated Jews alike, but also one of the major questions of the twentieth century: how could the Holocaust have happened?

While Brookner does not write specifically about anti-Semitism, she does treat themes of conversion (most extensively in *Look at Me*) and the marginalization by the English of anyone deemed "a foreigner." In the following passage from *Altered States* (1996), a family's reaction to a man's choice of bride says more about their xenophobic Englishness than the character of the woman under scrutiny.

> "A foreigner," said Marjorie bitterly...
> "It was the holiday that brought it on," said Sybil. "That was your idea, Alice."
> (1996: 14)

The words "brought it on" liken the foreign spouse to an illness one might catch when abroad. It is a hazard to be avoided which, unlike their brother Humphrey, Marjorie and Sybil succeed in doing by planning but never actually going on any trips. While the use of "foreigner" in all its generality points to the undifferentiated xenophobia of Humphrey's sisters, it also functions like a euphemism to conceal as much as to reveal things about his wife. The suggestion that this female figure is best kept hidden because she is a threat and an embarrassment is conveyed in the following exchange:

> "...Are you planning any sort of reception for Humphrey and his, well, his bride?"
> "Certainly not."
> "Then perhaps I will invite them to a little party. You too, of course. Do we know anything about her?"
> "Not a thing," said Marjorie triumphantly.
> "I see," said my mother. "A foreigner, you said. And he met her in Paris. Is she French?"

"She may be," said Sybil. She was prepared to go no further.

"And has she got a name?" asked my mother, her patience beginning to wear thin.

"Edwige." This was offered reluctantly.

"But that is French. She must be French."

"Not quite, Alice," put in Marjorie. "Edwige is not her real name. Her real name is Jadwiga. Polish, you see." She pronounced this as if it were the ultimate proof of the bride's unworthiness. "Not quite what we're used to. Humphrey least of all. Still, we shan't wait around to see them make a mess of things. (1996: 17–18)

When speaking about the foreign wife, verbal concealment mirrors the sisters' wished-for physical concealment of her. Yet whereas the narrator's mother is described as having "her patience beginning to wear thin" because of Sybil's and Marjorie's uncommunicativeness, their reticence lends an air of mystery and suspense to the narrative. Brookner's writing has been called "suspenseful in spite of its lack of action" (Lopate 1990: 10). Her use of concealment, even in lengthy passages of dialogue, and omissions, in the most detailed narrative passages, make it so.

If a foreign wife, not to mention a Polish one, is an unsettling entity for Humphrey's sisters, she is also one for the reader – but for other reasons. Besides informing us about this character, the first-person narration rings with the narrator's own confusion as to who or what to make of this foreign wife. Even seemingly precise designations hint at uncertainty. Chapter three, for example, begins with the words "I first encountered Jadwiga/Edwige..." (1996: 19). While it may be more accurate to call her both names rather than one, the juxtaposition of the two suggests a choice which the narrator himself does not or cannot make. The choice is, in fact, nullified for him when his mother says

"...Now I want you to meet Jenny."

"Jenny?"

"Humphrey's wife, dear."

"I thought she was called something else?"

"We call her Jenny. That's what Humphrey calls her..." (p. 20)

Humphrey's rechristianing of his wife with the Anglo-Saxon name "Jenny" is comparable in *Wide Sargasso Sea* to the Rochester character's refusal to call his wife by her birth name, choosing instead to call her Bertha. Although "Jenny" may appear closer to "Jadwiga" than "Bertha" is to "Antoinette," it is just as remote. For the Polish pronunciation of "j" is equivalent not to "j" but "y" in English. As a choice, "Jenny" reveals Humphrey's mispronunciation of his wife's name or complete lack of regard for it. Where Rochester's renaming of Antoinette is comparable to the colonizer's raising the union jack over a new claim, Humphrey uses "Jenny" like a cloak on a naked figure to conceal the embarrassment of his wife's background.

What Humphrey does not know is that identities are not so easily adopted or discarded. Soon after hearing that Jadwiga/Edwige is now Jenny, the narrator, Alan Sherwood, is addressed by her for the first time.

"I have so wanted to meet you, Alan. My dear Alice talks of you all the time. Has she told you about me?"

"Yes indeed. Forgive me for mentioning this, but your accent is quite French. Mother told me you were Polish."

She laughed delightedly. "But my dear, I lived in Paris over thirty years. I went there as a young girl. I think of myself as a Parisienne." This last remark stirred Humphrey into some kind of protest. "But now of course I am English, an English wife with an English husband and an English family." She laughed again. (1996: 23)

Beyond the congeniality, even mundanity, of this exchange, a complexity of identity problems are introduced into the text. The first concerns speech. Humphrey's wife might speak fluent and grammatically correct English. She might even (as her first words to Alan prove) be able to speak in a distinctly English as opposed to, for example, an American manner, as shown in her use of "*so* wanted", "My *dear* Alice," and "*Has she told you*" instead of the more commonly used American form "Did she tell you." Nonetheless, her accent gives her away as a foreigner. Yet, although her accent is French it is not enough to *make* her French; neither does her having lived in Paris for "over thirty years," nor the fact that she thinks of herself as a Parisienne. By whatever means this English family has learned of her Polish background, it resurfaces like an "indelible ink" of Jewishness.

As several critics have noted, Brookner can write an entire novel about Jews without once using the word (Friedman 1988: 21). Such an omission in *Family and Friends*, for example, makes the death of the matriarch far more momentous than it might have been otherwise. After all, one expects someone to die in a deathbed scene. But when the traditional Jewish mourning rituals are enacted (the covering of mirrors, rending of clothing, etc.), the fact that this is a Jewish family is finally disclosed. Furthermore, when Lili and Ursie, two orphaned refugee girls, are described as "crying out of control . . . all night" as they "relive their history, their earlier losses," the Holocaust is firmly if elliptically evoked (1985a: 177). This has the effect of placing Sokfa Dorn in a context beyond merely the negative stereotype of an overbearing Jewish mother. In retrospect, keeping her two frailer children at her side was as much in their best interests as encouraging her two heartier ones to marry and leave. With returning to Germany out of the question and life in England uncertain, "marrying out," both figuratively and literally, offers a prospect of survival for her son Frederick and daughter Betty.

Brookner's refusal to dramatize the Holocaust directly in her novels has drawn criticism, however, from even her admirers. A reviewer for *The Jewish Chronicle*, for example, finds it unbelievable that, in *Family and Friends*, "Frederick runs a hotel in Italy during the war, without a single tremor of fear or foreboding," and that, in *A Family Romance*, Dolly and her seamstress mother were "unscathed" living in Paris throughout the war (Charles 1993: 9, 63). Yet, as Louise Sylvester writes in "Troping the other: Anita Brookner's Jews," "the privations associated with the Second World War for Jews living in Europe are alluded to in the urgency with which Betty and Max (who is Hungarian) leave Paris for America, and in the anxious question Sofka asks her friend Irma Beck when the latter knocks at her door selling lace: "At last, and fearfully, Sofka enquires, 'Your children?' For the first time the woman relaxes, and smiles. 'Safe,' she says. 'Here'" (Sylvester 2001: 51). In *A Family Romance*, Brookner tropes Jewishness with Dolly's urgent will to live. Without dramatizing how Dolly and her mother flee Belgium for France, gain the protection of local prostitutes servicing German officers, and conceal their German origins before the Occupation and their Jewishness afterward, Brookner depicts Dolly's resilience with images of movement. In stark contrast to her seemingly static English in-laws, Dolly is presented, like the figure of the wandering Jew, as continually on the move.

Not dramatizing the Holocaust or referring to it by name has a similar effect to Brookner's reluctance to use the word "Jew." Noting that Brookner only uses the word "Jew" once in *Latecomers*, Bryan Cheyette explains that "what is left unsaid in *Latecomers* becomes the subject of the novel. To this extent Brookner makes overt the silence that surrounds Jewishness within English national culture" (Cheyette 1998: xli). In the same way, Brookner makes overt the silence in England surrounding the Holocaust and its place in the nation's history.

In words that now sound prophetic, Lorna Sage observed in 1980 that "much of what's significant in English fiction is written with 'elsewhere' very much in mind; is, in a sense, written *from* elsewhere" (Sage 1980: 136). "[E]normous changes have taken place in what it means to be English ... you'd expect the novel to reflect on them, even if not comfortably or quickly or very directly" (p. 136). Brookner does not say that many of her characters are Jews, but designates them as such indirectly, which reveals how they are both inside and outside English culture. In *Falling Slowly*, for example, Beatrice is buried in a cemetery in Golders Green, a part of London largely inhabited by Jews; Max uses the expression "Nu?" meaning "So?" with the English, who "thought it quaint," but not with his brother who, like himself, comes from a German Jewish background that would have shunned Yiddish (1998: 90). Like Harold Pinter, Brookner writes from the "outside in," interrogating "the received cultural boundaries of Englishness" (Cheyette 1996: 308). She does so with an acuity that is not usually associated with English spinsterdom. One really does wonder whether some reviewers have actually read Brookner's novels.

One rereads Proust "almost with fear" according to Brookner (Guppy 1987: 157). The same can be said about rereading Brookner. Like Proust, who likens the dominant society to a kaleidoscope that keeps reversing "its coloured lozenges" – one moment including, the next moment excluding those, such as Jews, on the peripheries – Brookner depicts the English as a capricious lot (Proust 1987: 557). Each of her twenty-two novels presents a new turn of the kaleidoscope. In the perception that "strength and self-awareness are found not so much in finding an access to the inner circle, as in recognizing why you are on the periphery" lies their pain and their beauty (Baxter 1993: 137).

REFERENCES AND FURTHER READING

Annan, G. (1992) "Still life," *The New York Review*, May 14: 25–6.

Annan, J. (2001) *Anita Brookner*. <http://www.penguin.co.uk/static/packages/uk/readers/aug01/brookner.html>.

Baxter, G. M. (1993) "Clothes, men and books: cultural experiences and identity in the early novels of Anita Brookner," *English: The Journal of the English Association*, 42/173: 125–39.

Birch, D. (2002) "Wintry lessons," *London Review of Books*, June 27: 30–1.

Brookner, A. (1983) *Look At Me*. London: Jonathan Cape.

——(1985a) *Family and Friends*. New York: Pocket Books.

——(1985b) [1984] *Hotel du Lac*. London: Triad/Panther Books.

——(1990) [1982] *Providence*. New York: Vintage Contemporaries.

——(1993a) *A Family Romance*. London: Jonathan Cape. (Published as *Dolly* (1996) New York: Random House).

——(1993b) [1992] *Fraud*. Harmondsworth: Penguin.

——(1996) *Altered States*. London: Jonathan Cape.

——(1998) *Falling Slowly*. London: Viking.

——(2002) *The Next Big Thing*. London: Viking.

——(2003) *The Rules of Engagement*. London: Viking.

Charles, G. (1993) "Darkness and light," *The Jewish Chronicle*, September 10: 63.

Cheyette, B. (1996) "'Ineffable and usable': towards a diasporic British-Jewish writing," *Textual Practice*, 10/2: 295–313.

——(1998) Introduction, in B. Cheyette (ed.) *Contemporary Jewish Writing in Britain and Ireland: An Anthology*. Lincoln: University of Nebraska Press.

Derbyshire, J. (2001) "Hugging the shore," *Washington Post 'Book World,'* May 20: 4.

Dinnage, R. (1989) "Exiles," *New York Review of Books*, June 1: 34–6.

Friedman, R. (1988) "A portrait gallery of clearly drawn subjects," *The Jewish Chronicle*, September 23: 21.

Guppy, S. (1987) "Interview: the art of fiction XCVIII: Anita Brookner," *Paris Review*, 109: 146–69.

Haffenden, J. (1985) "Anita Brookner," in J. Haffenden (ed.) *Novelists in Interview*. London and New York: Methuen.

Hosmer, R. E., Jr. (1993) "Paradigm and passage: the fiction of Anita Brookner," in R. E. Hosmer (ed.) *Contemporary British Women Writers: Texts and Strategies*. Basingstoke and London: Macmillan.

Lopate, P. (1990) "Can innocence go unpunished?," *New York Times Book Review*, March 11: 10.

Malcolm, C. A. (2002) *Understanding Anita Brookner*. Columbia: University of South Carolina Press.

Mars-Jones, A. (2002) "Death of strong feelings," *The Observer*. June 30. <http://books.guardian.co.uk/critics/reviews/0,5917,746450,00.html>.

Oates. J. C. (1999) "Writing for the tortoise market," *The Times Literary Supplement*, July 30: 19.

Proust, M. (1982) "Within a budding grove," in *Remembrance of Things Past*, vol. I, trans. C. K. S. Moncrieff and T. Kilmartin. New York: Vintage. (Originally published 1919).

Rhys, J. (1987) "Illusion," in *Jean Rhys: The Collected Short Stories*. New York and London: W. W. Norton.

Sage, L. (1980) "Invasion from outsiders," *Granta* 3. Harmondsworth: Penguin.

Skinner, J. (1992) *The Fictions of Anita Brookner: Illusions of Romance*. New York: St Martin's Press.

Sylvester, L. (2001) "Troping the other: Anita Brookner's Jews," *English*, 50/196: 47–58.

36

Julian Barnes's *Flaubert's Parrot*

Merritt Moseley

Julian Barnes's *Flaubert's Parrot* was an unexpected masterpiece when it appeared in 1984: a surprise because its author, though a well-established figure in London's literary world – he had been deputy literary editor of *The New Statesman*, a restaurant and television critic and a book reviewer – lacked the visibility and esteem of such contemporaries as Martin Amis, Ian McEwan, and Peter Ackroyd. Barnes had in fact published four previous novels. *Metroland* (1981) is a beautifully written coming-of-age, and to some extent coming-to-terms, novel about a young man who stops trying to shock the bourgeoisie when he realizes he has joined them. *Before She Met Me* (1982) recounts the macabre story of a college lecturer obsessed with his wife's sex life; his determination to track her previous relationships both in and out of films becomes a form of ultimately violent insanity. Both novels, it might be worth noting, featured wifely adultery, real or imagined, and its effect on the husband (the imagined adultery causes much more trouble than the real).

Julian Barnes had written two other novels – *Duffy* (1980) and *Fiddle City* (1981), detective novels featuring a bisexual private eye called Duffy – but as they had appeared under the pseudonym Dan Kavanaugh, they would have done nothing to prepare readers for a witty, literate, generically ambiguous book like *Flaubert's Parrot*. *The Guardian* did not review the book until after the judges for the Booker Prize for Fiction had announced the shortlist, the six titles from which the 1984 winner would be chosen. (The Booker Prize for 1984 was chosen from the following list: Julian Barnes, *Flaubert's Parrot*; David Lodge, *Small World*; J. G. Ballard, *Empire of the Sun*; Anita Desai, *In Custody*; Penelope Lively, *According to Mark*; and Anita Brookner, *Hotel du Lac*, which was the surprising winner (Ballard's book had been the bookies' favorite).) Even after making this distinguished list, it shared a short group review with four other titles including such unliterary stuff as Tom Sharpe's most recent farce. The early British reviews struck several notes that would become familiar in discussions of *Flaubert's Parrot*. *The Guardian* reviewer referred to it as a "hybrid novel in which actuality and invention are merged" and a "fascinating, highly original, deliberately maddening book" ("Books" 1984). In *The Financial Times*, Ian Davidson commented:

> The first problem for the editors and salesmen would have been to assign it to a recognised category. Literary biography? Literary criticism? Epistemological philosophy? Belles lettres? Evidently, the publishers and the Booker Judges have accepted that it is in fact a novel, perhaps because the author is a 'novelist.' Most ordinary novel readers will find this a baffling judgment . . . one might say that this is the antithesis of a novel. (1984: 14)

This objection, that in some way *Flaubert's Parrot* is not a novel despite its claims to be one, has been a perennial and nagging accompaniment to the book's continued popularity. There are fifteen chapters. Two of them appeared as separate works, in the *London Review of Books* and *Granta*, before becoming chapters in this novel. The usual accusation levied against a novel in which the chapters are only loosely connected, and are so apparently detachable that some of them have been detached and published independently, is that it is not a novel but a collection of short stories. The accusation against Barnes's book is more likely to be that it is a collection of essays. That it won the Prix Médicis, a French award customarily given to a book of essays, assisted this accusation. Writing in 2002, reviewer Jason Cowley flatly declares:

> Julian Barnes's most celebrated novels – *Flaubert's Parrot* and *The History of the World in 10½ Chapters* – are not really novels, they are stylised essays in which Barnes excels at smoothing the world into knowing aphorism and smart generalisation. (2002: 15)

Barnes's exasperation aside – in 1991 he insisted to one interviewer that "my line now is I'm a novelist and if I say it's a novel, it is" (Lawson 1991: 36) – there are many other responses to such a cavil. One is that in a universe of celebrated novels that includes *Jalousie* and *Hopscotch* and *Pale Fire* and *Life: A User's Manual* and *The Dictionary of the Khazars*, there is nothing even particularly eccentric about Barnes's books. Answering the same kind of critique in 1989, on the publication of *A History of the World in 10½ Chapters*, Barnes defined it as "an extended piece of prose, largely fictional, which is planned and executed as a whole piece" (Sexton 1989: 42). Although that definition easily embraces all of the titles just mentioned, none of them are by British authors, and there is something provincial about what Barnes calls the " 'but-does-he-write-proper-novels?' school of criticism, which I get a bit, especially in England" (Smith 1989: 73). In 2002 he explained that

> I thought of *Flaubert's Parrot* when I started writing as obviously an unofficial and informal, non-conventional sort of novel – an upside-down novel, a novel in which there was an infrastructure of fiction and very strong elements of non-fiction, sometimes whole chapters which were nothing but arranged facts. (2002: 259)

Flaubert's Parrot as Miscellany

Flaubert's Parrot is a novel. It is, certainly, one that mixes disparate elements. It mixes fact and fiction: its fictional narrator Geoffrey Braithwaite is a student of the Gustave Flaubert who, in fact, lived in France and wrote novels. But then most novels mix fact and fiction: the fictional characters of *Midnight's Children* live in India, a real place, and the central event is the moment of separation between India and Pakistan, a real historical event. Michael Frayn's *Spies* sets fictional children loose during the (factual) Second World War. The real Emperor Napoleon is a character in *War and Peace*. Combination of the fictional and the empirical is one of the defining characteristics of western novels, and they differ primarily in the percentages in the mixture.

Barnes adds to his novel's miscellaneity by discontinuity of form. One chapter is an examination paper; another is a dictionary of received ideas about Flaubert; another is about animals in Flaubert's life and works, and yet another offers three alternative chronologies of his life. Malcolm Bradbury praises the book for this feature, calling it

> To date [1993] his best book. It is half critical text, half a human narrative, all based around the life and artistic impulse of the great nineteenth-century French realist, who also opened the door to fictional Modernism . . . the text itself takes multiple forms: it is a research, a meditation, an examination paper, a playful latter-day commentary, on Flaubert's own ambiguous realism, and on the strange stimuli of art. It busily plays with notions of the real and fictional, makes its own rules, breaks up its own discourse, leaves behind its own ambiguities: a postmodern "text" indeed. (1993: 437)

In a different tone – another "playful latter-day commentary," perhaps – Eric Metaxas satirized *"Flaubert's Panda* by Boolean Jarnes," declaring that "This one is part biography, part literary criticism, part prose poem, part fire hydrant, and part decayed wolf's pelt – in short, the post-modernist novel at its best" (1987: 36).

Flaubert's Parrot is a discontinuous novel, in which it is not just the disparate materials that create this effect but the arrangement of them. Chapter 2 has the three competing Flaubert chronologies; Chapter 3 contains the story of Julie Herbert, an English governess with whom Flaubert may have had an affair, the discovery of a cache of her letters and its later destruction; Chapter 4, "The Flaubert Bestiary," is about animals in Flaubert's novels and letters. Even as a fiction it undeniably lacks unity. The question is: why?

One reason has to do with its most fundamental mixture, that between the biographical and critical commentary on and speculation about Flaubert and the reticently autobiographical story of Geoffrey Braithwaite. These are also, roughly, the nonfiction and the fiction. Reading unsympathetic or bewildered notices of the novel one would hardly detect that all the biographical material about Flaubert, even the bestiary and the examination paper, are not presented by Julian Barnes, but by his narrator and protagonist Braithwaite, which means that the miscellaneousness of the organization, the fussiness of the curiosity about minor details – what color was redcurrant jelly in nineteenth-century France? – and the arguably essayistic quality of the book are phenomena attributable to the mind and concerns of Braithwaite rather than Barnes. Braithwaite is a fictional character who is naturally much less interesting than Gustave Flaubert. A retired physician, a widower, a bit of a train-spotter (Chapter 8 is "The Train-spotter's Guide to Flaubert") who has substituted Flaubert for locomotives, he also likes to draw attention away from himself.

His self-abnegation is hardly complete, and he unleashes vigorous opinions, ranging from the bluntly emotional – "Let me tell you why I hate critics" (Barnes 1984: 74) – to the politico-philosophical – "The greatest patriotism is to tell your country when it is behaving dishonourably, foolishly, viciously" (p. 131) – to the amusingly literary-critical. In Chapter 7, "Cross Channel," he announces the orders he would issue as literary dictator, ten of them, including a quota system on fiction set in South America, a twenty-year ban on novels set at Oxford or Cambridge (a less severe ban of only ten years on novels set at other universities), an absolute prohibition of novels about incest, bestiality scenes, and novels that identify the narrator only by an initial (pp. 98–9). Braithwaite needs opinions; he also needs great curiosity, patience, and freedom, to promote and permit his investigations. In interview, Barnes explained the reason for Braithwaite. The novel actually grew out of his own pilgrimage to Flaubert's home and his discovery of multiple modern parrots asserted to be the original of the bird in *Un coeur simple*;

> and then it came to me that there could be a story made from this, and as soon as I had the kind of person who, in my stead, would be able to write passionately about these two parrots – so, someone rather pedantic, rather obsessed, ready to draw the fullest meanings out of the smallest coincidence or ambiguity – I began to have Geoffrey Braithwaite . . . (Barnes 2002: 258)

But Geoffrey Braithwaite is far more than a man who, while sharing some of Julian Barnes's interests, is more pedantic and obsessed and therefore can make much out of the competing claims of two moldy parrots. He has his own story as well, and the relationship between that story and the story of Flaubert is crucial to the novel. The central fact about Braithwaite is that his wife Ellen was repeatedly unfaithful to him and killed herself. It takes quite a while to discover this, though. The first hint of their complex relations comes in Chapter 6, "Emma Bovary's Eyes": "I never thought my wife was perfect. I loved her, but I never deceived myself. I remember . . . But I'll keep that for another time. I'll remember instead another lecture I once attended . . ." (p. 76). That "instead" is a tantalizing hint. Later he explains a bit more:

> Three stories contend within me. One about Flaubert, one about Ellen, one about myself. Mine is the simplest of the three – it hardly amounts to more than a convincing proof of my existence – and yet I find it the hardest to begin. My wife's is more

complicated, and more urgent; yet I resist that too. Keeping the best for last, as I was saying earlier? I don't think so; rather the opposite, if anything. But by the time I tell you her story I want you to be prepared: that's to say, I want you to have had enough of books, and parrots, and lost letters, and bears, and the opinions of Dr Enid Starkie, and even the opinions of Dr Geoffrey Braithwaite. Books are not life, however much we might prefer it if they were. Ellen's is a true story; perhaps it is even the reason why I am telling you Flaubert's story instead. (pp. 85–6)

It finally comes out, as much of it as readers need, in "Pure Story." Geoffrey loved Ellen, she had lovers, he was unhappy but loved her still; eventually she killed herself. Apparently she was bored; and, as he wryly notes, "unlike me she didn't have some rash devotion to a dead foreigner to sustain her" (p. 166).

Thus Braithwaite's story is related to Flaubert's in two ways. One is the parallel between Ellen Braithwaite and Emma Bovary. She was an adulterous wife; her husband, a doctor (Charles Bovary was an *officier de santé*), was complaisant. Charles Bovary, in the only rhetorical flourish of his life, assigns the blame for Emma's infidelity and suicide to fate. Braithwaite stops short of that, offering the statement – hardly an explanation – that "I loved her; we were happy; I miss her. She didn't love me; we were unhappy; I miss her" (p. 161). He is clear on how she differed from Emma: "She wasn't corrupted; her spirit didn't coarsen; she never ran up bills" (p. 164). Did she, like Emma, rediscover in adultery all the platitudes of marriage? He doesn't know.

Another link between Braithwaite and Flaubert, and perhaps more important, particularly since Braithwaite resists all temptation to discover further homologies between his story and the one Flaubert told in *Madame Bovary*, is that thinking about Flaubert has helped him to avoid thinking about Ellen, and telling the reader about Flaubert is a way of delaying telling about Ellen. Braithwaite's unhappy marital history provides the etiology of the investigation, and then the transmission, of his findings and thoughts about Flaubert.

Flaubert's Parrot in the Barnes Canon

When he published *Flaubert's Parrot* in 1984, Julian Barnes was not utterly unknown. Both *Metroland* and *Before She Met Me* had achieved paperback publication and justified the publication of a further novel. When *Granta* magazine published its list of the Twenty Best Young British Novelists in 1983, Barnes was included in this arbitrary but nonetheless very influential compilation. Still, Barnes's publisher, Liz Calder, was uneasy about his third book, and he has said that he likewise had no great expectation of success. He may well have been liberated to write a different kind of work because of the modest success of the first two and his own still-moderate visibility.

In a 2000 profile he acknowledged his own awareness of *Flaubert's Parrot* as a departure, but explained,

It wasn't as if I was trying to follow up two international successes. I was following up two novels which had just stumbled into paperback and no one abroad wanted to buy. (Wroe 2000)

The results must have surpassed his fondest hopes. The acclaim of distinguished elder statespersons of the literary world was quick to arrive. Graham Greene called the book "intricate and delightful," while from Mexico Carlos Fuentes "saluted" him for work which was "at the forefront of a new internationalisation of British fiction" (Wroe 2000). Barnes has always acknowledged that *Flaubert's Parrot* was "the book that launched me" (Smith 1989: 74) while expressing some rue that its fame eclipses some of his other books, especially if they are less flashy. The novel became an international bestseller "and marked the point when Barnes changed from being a journalist who wrote novels to a novelist who did a bit of journalism" (Wroe 2000).

Now ranked with the best novelists of his generation, Barnes found not only worldwide acclaim and sales of millions of books. Expectations for his succeeding books were much higher; and the disappointment some reviewers expressed over *Staring at the Sun*, his next book, he attributed to its not being "*Victor Hugo's Dachshund*" (Smith 1989: 74). On the other hand, the ground had been prepared for his *A History of the World in 10½ Chapters*, another innovative book that appeared in 1989. David Sexton, among others, again raised the "is-it-a-proper-novel?" question:

Barnes writes books which look like novels and get shelved as novels but which, when you open them up, are something else altogether. *Flaubert's Parrot* was for the most part a set of studies of Flaubert and his parrot. His new book, *A History of the World in 10½ Chapters*, is even odder. The 10 chapters contain 10 quite different stories, some factual, some not. They are related only by image and theme. (Sexton 1989: 42)

By that time Barnes was unlikely to be ruffled by such quibbling and *A History* sold more copies than *Flaubert's Parrot*. He subsequently published four more novels, a book of short stories about French/English relations, a book of essays on the same theme, another book of essays written as the *New Yorker*'s London correspondent, and a collection of essays about food.

British literary culture is preoccupied with the Booker Prize for fiction, and Barnes is one of those regularly singled out for never having won it, despite making two shortlists, the other being for *England, England* in 1998. (Martin Amis is another novelist famous for this "failure"). Still, Barnes has been generously recognized with literary prizes, including the Somerset Maugham Award for *Metroland*, and *Flaubert's Parrot* won the Geoffrey Faber Memorial Award and the Grinzane Cavour (Italy) in addition to the Prix Médicis. Further evidence of his high esteem in France comes from his having won the 1987 Gutenberg Prize and been named a Chevalier de l'Ordre des Arts et des Letters in 1988 and an Officier de l'Order des Arts et des Lettres in 1995.

Flaubert's Parrot as Postmodernist Text

There are many reasons to admire *Flaubert's Parrot*. It is immensely intelligent. It is funny as well as sad. It contains more information about Gustave Flaubert than most readers will know already, along with some deeply thoughtful speculations on the meaning and value of that information, the importance of authors' lives, the possibility that loving an author is the purest love of all, and much more. And Geoffrey Braithwaite is an easily overlooked epigrammatist. Among his memorable observations: about writing: "Mystification is simple; clarity is the hardest thing of all" (p. 102); about the past: "The past is a distant, receding coastline, and we are all in the same boat" (p. 101), or "Sometimes the past may be a greased pig; sometimes a bear in its den; and sometimes merely the flash of a parrot, two mocking eyes that spark at you from the forest" (p. 112); and (about books? Life?): "Books say: She did this because. Life says: She did this. Books are where things are explained to you; life is where things aren't" (p. 168).

But despite its many virtues, there is no question that much of the continuing interest in the novel, at least among academic readers and critics, comes from the association of *Flaubert's Parrot* with the literature of postmodernism. This association demands some scrutiny, since some of the claims for the postmodernity of the novel are, it seems to me, overstated.

What does it mean to call a novel postmodern? Malcolm Bradbury and Eric Metaxas seem to agree: fragmentation of form and self-consciousness that calls attention to the work's fictive status. Bradbury points out that Barnes's postmodernist text mixes fiction and nonfiction; it takes multiple forms; and it "busily plays with notions of the real and fictional, makes its own rules, breaks up its own discourse, leaves behind its own ambiguities..." (1993: 437). If this is the agreed-upon definition of the postmodern then obviously *Flaubert's Parrot* qualifies, though it is much less insistent on breaking the frame or revealing its artificiality than many other comparable works.

But this is a soft notion of postmodernist fiction, and the harder-edged idea is much more concerned with epistemology, questions of what can be known and whether such concepts as truth and reality are anything other than linguistic constructs. James B. Scott begins his discussion of *Flaubert's Parrot* with the observation that

> much of postmodern literary theory would be predicated on that very principle [that] reality and truth are the illusions produced when systems of discourse (especially artistic discourse) impinge on human consciousness. In practice, this has led postmodern novelists to strive to undermine hermeneutic responses to art by foregrounding the discourse that informs their artifact, thereby implying that not only is the final "meaning" of a work of art forever unknowable, but also any orthodox truth is actually a discourse-generated fluke. (1990: 57)

Descending to cases, Scott insists that *Flaubert's Parrot* "evinces [the] conviction that words are empty signifiers never touching a final signified and that the self is a creature of discursive forces" (p. 59). Other commentators share Scott's interpretation. Andrzej Gasiorek refers to "Barnes's preoccupation with the inaccessibility of the past" (1995: 158); and asks rhetorically, "If interpretation is so problematic, if the seeker of knowledge (as figured in this novel) is confronted either by fifty parrots among which he cannot choose or by an abandoned perch, can he or she make any claim to knowledge at all?" (p. 161) Aleid Fokkema identifies the book as being about "the postmodern crisis of representation" (1999: 41); Alison Lee asserts that *Flaubert's Parrot* shows the reader that "Language creates 'reality,' and language is inescapably plural" (1990: 39), and places the novel in Linda Hutcheon's category of "historio-graphic metafictions," which "are irrevocably self-conscious, asserting through structure and conflicting information that the 'parrot' is a discursive construct" (p. 40).

Linda Hutcheon, in her turn, makes it clear in what sense the book is a historio-graphic metafiction. Turning from Hayden White's views of the unreliability of history, she concludes:

> The same questioning of the status of the document and its interpretation that is being conducted in historiography can be found in postmodern novels like Berger's *G* or Barnes's *Flaubert's Parrot*, or D. M. Thomas's *The White Hotel*. This sort of fiction has contributed to the now quite general reconsideration of the nature of documentary evidence. (2002: 77)

John Bayley seems more uneasy about the epistemological *mise en abysme*, but then he seems to conclude that Barnes has failed to mount a postmodern epistemological challenge despite his own best efforts.

> Flaubert's writings, and what the narrator makes of them, mingle with a sense of unreality presided over by the ambiguous legend of Flaubert, the disappearance of things under close scrutiny, the impossibility of the past itself.
>
>   These are the modish notions canvassed by the novel, but the impression it makes on the reader is rather different. The past, the parrot, and Flaubert himself all come most vividly to life, as if to confirm that there was a parrot, however now unverifiable, just as there was a real moment (among many others) when Flaubert sat down one afternoon to write *Madame Bovary*, the novel which neither he then, nor its readers now, have ever been quite sure about. The conscious implication of *Flaubert's Parrot* is that since we cannot know everything about the past we cannot know anything; but its actual effect – and its success – is to suggest something different: that the relative confirms the idea of truth instead of dissipating it, that the difficulty of finding out how things were does not disprove those things but authenticates them. (Bayley 1987: 12)

Whatever the modishness of the notions that the past is inaccessible, that reality and truth – or "reality" and "truth" – are no more than linguistic constructs, and that a seeker of knowledge can really make no claim to any knowledge at all, many critics find these embodied in *Flaubert's Parrot*. Yet the evidence for them is inadequate.

There are three major data from *Flaubert's Parrot* that seem to support indecidability and the epistemological dead end. One of these is the statements made by Geoffrey Braithwaite himself about the past. He says that the "past is a distant, receding coastline, and we are all in the same boat" (p. 101); he says, "I'm not sure what I believe about the past" (p. 91); strongest of all, he writes, in the context of a discussion of whether fat men were fatter in Flaubert's time than the present day,

> How can we know such trivial, crucial details? We can study files for decades, but every so often we are tempted to throw up our hands and declare that history is merely another literary genre: the past is autobiographical fiction pretending to be a parliamentary report. (p. 90)

More important than Braithwaite's statements – and we note that even this last questioning of history is only what he is *tempted* to declare *every so often* – is the evidence provided by the structure of the novel. The chief exhibit is Chapter 2, "Chronology," which contains three chronologies. The first one includes such entries as, under 1825, "Few servant problems will trouble his life" (p. 23), and, in 1874, "Publication of *La Tentation de saint Antoine*. Despite its strangeness, a gratifying commercial success" (p. 26). Chronology II is an alternative compilation of negative, unfortunate, or unhappy events, including "1839: Expelled from the College de Rouen for rowdyism and disobedience" (p. 28) and "1876: . . . Gustave's last years are arid and solitary" (p. 31). Chronology III consists of statements in the author's own words.

What are we to make of these three chronologies? Does one undermine the other, and does the inclusion of conflicting and contradictory chronologies alongside each other in turn undermine the idea of reliable chronology at all? Reviewing the novel on its American appearance, Peter Brooks identified it as "a kind of collage, pasted up from a multitude of quotations from Flaubert, "facts" from his life (often at odds with one another)" (Brooks 1985: sect. 7, 7). But are the "facts" at odds with one another, in a way that would deny them their claim to *be* facts? The answer is no.

As seductive as it may be to think of the chronologies as conflicting, they really are not. There is no conflict, to an informed mind, in the idea that a novel may be a commercial success and a critical failure, or that a person who is in the act of writing a book will, if he dies, leave it unfinished. A genuine challenge to the historicity of the past could have provided variant dates for the author's birth and death or caused the chronologies to disagree on whether Flaubert ever met Turgenev, lived in Rouen, or had an affair with Louise Colet. The facts are secure. What creates the great differences between the two chronologies is the attitude implied by their contents toward their subject. Each chronology proceeds from a *parti pris*.

A similar exercise produces the later chapter called "Louise Colet's Version." Braithwaite knows that he loves Flaubert and that his partisanship shapes his version.

He is in the act of refuting the accusation that Flaubert was beastly to women, particularly Louise Colet: "though admittedly we hear only Gustave's side of the story. Perhaps someone should write her account: yes, why not reconstruct Louise Colet's Version? I might do that. Yes, I will" (p. 135). Naturally Louise Colet's Version places the emphasis differently; it is partial, but though it casts a different light on Flaubert it does not cancel out any facts. For his part, Barnes has declared that "all the information that Geoffrey Braithwaite gives you about Flaubert is true, or as true as he and I together could make it " (2002: 261). That he acknowledges the possibility of some inadvertent factual mistakes that scholars might correct is a testament to the knowability of the past, not the opposite. It is true that those who read Barnes as deconstructing the past, or history, can find support in *A History of the World in 10½ Chapters*, in such passages as

> History isn't what happened. History is just what historians tell us. . . . The history of the world? Just voices echoing in the dark; images that burn for a few centuries and then fade; stories, old stories that sometimes seem to overlap; strange links, impertinent connections. (1989: 240)

But those universal assertions do not hold constant even in that book, much less provide retrospective support for a theory of reading the earlier novel.

There is another long interview bearing on this question, published in a 1999 book called *"Do You Consider Yourself a Postmodern Author?": Interviews with Contemporary English Writers*. Though Barnes never quite answers that question, he does insist on the knowability of some of the truth and he steadily resists the interviewer's efforts to relate his fiction to literary theory; he claims to be deliberately unaware of literary theory, because he believe it threatens to make his fiction arid; and he says (very un-postmodernly) that "novels come out of life, not out of theories about either life or literature" (Freiburg 1999: 52). (For the record, he told me in a May, 1992, telephone conversation that he did not consider his novels postmodernist.)

The third chief exhibit in the claim that *Flaubert's Parrot* demonstrates the unavailability of the truth is the parrot itself. Chapter 1 launches the story; Braithwaite, despite enough self-knowledge to ask himself "Why does the writing make us chase the writer?" (p. 12) is nevertheless on a relic-hunting pilgrimage. At the Hôtel-Dieu he sees a stuffed parrot; the label identifies it as the stuffed parrot borrowed by the author while he was writing *Un coeur simple*, in which a simple woman confuses her parrot with the Holy Spirit. Later, in another museum, he finds another parrot whose identifying label makes exactly the same claim. Only one of them can be the authentic parrot. At the end of the novel Braithwaite visits the Museum of Natural History, from which Flaubert borrowed the parrot in the first place, and finds three more claimants, remaining from an original fifty, each of which might have been the model for Loulou.

Here is a genuinely irreconcilable factual conflict. If the bird at the Hôtel-Dieu is Flaubert's parrot, the bird at the Flaubert museum is not, and neither is any of the birds at the Museum of Natural History. And there is no way to decide which is real, which an impostor. The question is whether this frustration means that all inquiry about the past – and, by extension, about the present, the real, the "true" – is inevitably as frustrating or, as Andrzej Gasiorek asks, "if the seeker of knowledge (as figured in this novel) is confronted either by fifty parrots among which he cannot choose or by an abandoned perch, can he or she make any claim to knowledge at all?" (1995: 161). The answer is yes. Geoffrey Braithwaite, the seeker after knowledge figured in this novel, knows many things about Flaubert as well as about his own wife and much else that inhabits the supposedly unknowable past.

In 1999 Barnes was asked if he thought history was a matter of taste. He replied:

> Well, the way history is remembered and therefore to a certain extent the way history is written about is a matter of taste, but I certainly don't believe that all tastes are equal, or that taste is any substitute for truth. I'm Orwellian in this respect, in that I think that one hundred percent truth is unreclaimable and unknowable, but we must maintain the superiority of a sixty-seven percent over a sixty-four percent of truth. (Freiburg 1999: 58)

This is a messy and, perhaps, unsatisfactory position by contrast with an absolutist denial that anyone can know anything at all. But Barnes is not an absolutist, nor is Geoffrey Braithwaite; and *Flaubert's Parrot* is more a demonstration of the difficulty of establishing meaning and the fragility of understanding than of their impossibility.

References and Further Reading

Barnes, Julian (1984) *Flaubert's Parrot*. New York: Alfred A. Knopf.

——(1989) *A History of the World in 10½ Chapters*. New York: Alfred A. Knopf.

——(2001) "Flaubert's Parrot." Broadcast on BBC Radio 4, December 5. Transcript at <http://www.bbc.co.uk/arts/books/club/flaubertparrot/transcript.shtml>

——(2002) "Julian Barnes in conversation," *Cercles*, 4: 255–69.

Bayley, John (1987). *The Order of Battle at Trafalgar*. New York: Weidenfeld and Nicolson.

"Books: a haunting and a hybrid" (1984) *The Guardian*, October 4: n.p.

Bradbury, Malcolm (1993) *The Modern British Novel*. London: Secker and Warburg.

Brooks, Peter (1985) "Obsessed with the Hermit of Croisset," *New York Times*, March 10: sect. 7, p. 7.

Cowley, Jason (2002) "New Gauls, please," *The Observer*, January 6: Review, p. 15.

Davidson, Ian (1984) "Passing the dummy," *Financial Times*, September 29: Books, p. 14.

Fokkema, Aleid (1999) "The author: postmodernism's stock character," in E. Paul Franssen and Ton Hoenselaars (eds.) *The Author as Character: Representing Historical Writers in Western Literature*. Madison, NJ: Fairleigh Dickinson University Press.

Freiburg, Rudolf (1999) "Julian Barnes," in Rudolf Freiburg and Jan Schnitker (eds.) *"Do You Consider Yourself a Postmodern Author?" Interviews with Contemporary English Writers*. Münster: Lit Verlag.

Gasiorek, Andrzej (1995) *Post-War British Fiction: Realism and After*. London: Edward Arnold.

Hutcheon, Linda (2002) *The Politics of Postmodernism*, 2nd edn. London: Routledge.

Lawson, Mark (1991) "A short history of Julian Barnes," *The Independent Magazine*, July 13: 34–6.

Lee, Alison (1990) *Realism and Power: Postmodern British Fiction*. London: Routledge.

Metaxas, Eric (1987) "That post-modernism!," *Atlantic Monthly*, January: 36–7.

Scott, James B (1990) "Parrot as paradigm: infinite deferral of meaning in 'Flaubert's Parrot'," *ARIEL: A Review of International English Literature*, 21 (July): 57–68.

Sexton, David (1989) "Still parroting on about God," *Sunday Telegraph*, June 11: 42.

Smith, Amanda (1989) "Julian Barnes," *Publishers Weekly*, November 3: 73–4.

Wroe, Nicholas (2000) "Literature's Mister Cool," *The Guardian* online, July 29: <http://books.guardian.co.uk/departments/generalfiction/story/0,6000,348186,00.html>

37

Kazuo Ishiguro's
The Remains of the Day

Cynthia F. Wong

After winning the 1989 Booker Prize for his third novel, *The Remains of the Day*, Kazuo Ishiguro remarked that his literary ascendancy depended on Salman Rushdie having won the Booker Prize in 1981 for *Midnight's Children*. In a 1991 interview Ishiguro observed that "everyone was suddenly looking for other Rushdies . . . [and] because I had this Japanese face and this Japanese name," and because late-twentieth century critics seemed to favor a writer's diverse ethnic origins, "I received a lot of attention, got lots of coverage, and did a lot of interviews" (Vorda and Herzinger 1991: 135). Malcolm Bradbury notes that Rushdie's novels had come to signify "a new spirit of ethnic and stylistic multiculturalism that has been widening the vision and range of [the British novel in] the Eighties" (Bradbury 1993: 422), and he includes Ishiguro's work as both contributing to and benefiting from that spirit. Bradbury also observes that the combination of Ishiguro's Japanese ancestry and British upbringing produces an artist with a unique vision and talent.

Born in Nagasaki in 1954, Ishiguro moved with his family to Great Britain in 1960 for what was to be a temporary stay. Ishiguro's early years were characterized by immersion in both Japanese and British cultures, but the former lapsed as the years passed and a return to Japan was nowhere in sight. At the University of Kent at Canterbury, Ishiguro earned his BA (Honours) in philosophy and English. At the University of East Anglia he received his MA in creative writing, and he names his tutors there, Angela Carter and Malcolm Bradbury, as important literary mentors. Barry Lewis deems Ishiguro's cultural identity as "neither Japanese nor English, somewhere in-between departure and arrival, nostalgia and anticipation," and calls the author "a displaced person, one of the many in the twentieth century of exile and estrangement" (2000: 1). Such displacement may account for Ishiguro's own declaration that he is an international writer, for such a detail is relevant when examining the contexts of his five novels up to 2000: the first two, *A Pale View of Hills* (1982) and *An Artist of the Floating World* (1987), are situated in Japan shortly after the Second World War; the third, *The Remains of the Day* (1989), in interwar England;

the fourth, *The Unconsoled* (1995), in an unidentified country in contemporary Middle Europe; and the fifth, *When We Were Orphans* (2000), in both post-imperial England and in occupied Shanghai. The protagonist of each novel struggles with understanding the conflation of past and future in the present moment of their narratives; each seeks to resolve relationships of people and of time, as well as his or her sense of self and belonging in their historical situations.

In addition to his critically acclaimed novels, Ishiguro has written numerous short stories and television scripts, and he was a consultant for the 1993 James Ivory and Ismail Merchant cinematic adaptation of *The Remains of the Day*, which was nominated for eight Academy Awards. His first four novels have won important literary prizes: the Winifred Holtby Award of the Royal Society of Literature for the first; the Whitbread Book of the Year for the second; the Booker Prize for the third; and the Cheltenham Prize for the fourth. Both his second and his fifth novels were shortlisted for the Booker prize as well. And all of his works have been translated into numerous other languages, insuring the author a genuinely international readership.

That Ishiguro's first-person narrators frequently practice elaborate forms of self-deception does not undermine the compassion that the author is able to evoke for his otherwise flawed characters. The first three novels all employ a complex narrative strategy in which the narrators both reveal their painful pasts yet manage to shroud the implications of these pasts. The next two novels employ even more striking narrative forms by which the narrators manipulate self-knowledge in such a way that they are able to rework an understanding that suits both their personal and public portrayals of "truth." In *When We Were Orphans*, for instance, Ishiguro uses a paradigm of detection as one mode by which humans construct an acceptable story of their lives. Christopher Banks, the world-class detective protagonist of that novel, is like Ishiguro's other characters in that he returns to a shadowy past in order to answer questions about his origins and a key event of his life, in his case the earlier disappearance of his parents. Prompted by a compelling desire to fill in the gaps of his life, Banks must determine what value he attributes to his discoveries, and he raises a question that confronts all of Ishiguro's characters: what constitutes a life worth living and how can one know and ascertain this value through experience?

Although Ishiguro has explicitly disavowed any efforts at social critique, he manages precisely that through the epistemological focus of each novel: the author accounts for the manner in which his characters muster a presentable story after having immersed themselves in painful knowledge about their lives. Perhaps the character who best represents the deep conflict between self understanding and public accounting is Mr Stevens of *The Remains of the Day*, a seemingly stoical butler who serves Darlington Hall between the two world wars and who, in 1956, embarks on a literal and figurative journey. Under the guise of a travelogue, Stevens's narrative unveils slowly the profound anguish to which his years of unquestioned servitude have reduced him. As a first-person narrator, Stevens partakes in a physical journey to the west of England as he simultaneously traverses and records an interior sojourn that is both an attempted redemption of a painful past and a confession as to his own complicity in world and private events. Not content to describe merely the spacious landscape laid out before him, Stevens finds himself thrust into a difficult temporal reexamination of his entire life. Ishiguro's portrayal of Stevens is simultaneously sympathetic to and critical of the blind errors to which humans succumb – willingly or unknowingly – in their ethical devotion to their country at the expense of private self-fulfillment.

Readers of *The Remains of the Day* follow Stevens's journey at spatial and temporal levels: first, as he heads west to persuade Mrs Benn (formerly Miss Kenton) to return to Darlington Hall; and second, as he formulates his tale of duty to his Nazi-sympathizer employer in the 1930s and 1940s. Both journeys, deeply emotional and psychological in essence, untangle the deep regret and shame that Stevens presently feels – yet manages to shroud – in the moment of his recounting. As he moves through the West Country, and as his remembrances of Lord Darlington and Miss Kenton are brought into focus in his own mind, the reader comes to understand the sadness and uncertainty now encircling his old age. Even as he hopes perhaps for a second chance at love with Miss Kenton, Stevens also seeks to explain his blind devotion to Darlington. In Stevens's tale are intertwined stories about paternal duty, professional devotion, national service, and amorous displacement. Stevens the man and Stevens the professional turn out to be the same person with a divided conscious-ness. In the end, Stevens is left empty-handed and must gather what vestige of courage he can in order to live out his remaining days at Darlington Hall under his new employer, the American Mr Farraday.

Not surprisingly, *The Remains of the Day* has generated a rich array of readings about Stevens's character and about Ishiguro's interpretation of Britain's role in the socio-political upheavals of the novel's period, between the 1920s and the 1950s. Many critics have noted that 1956, the year in which Stevens takes his holiday, is a crucial one for British history and, therefore, for the individual reconstruction of British national identity. As John McCombe explains, "The crisis that seemed to confirm Britain's decline erupted when Egyptian Prime Minister Gamel Abdel Nasser nation-alized the Suez Canal Company on July 26, 1956, the very month and year in which Ishiguro sets the novel's narrative frame" (2002: 79). Readings about the postcolonial attributes of Ishiguro's authorship and works are valuable for understanding the perplexity facing humans living in turbulent ages, even as critical paradigms them-selves are questioned in Ishiguro's novels. However, Ishiguro continually denies attempts to offer historical interpretations in his work, and he has noted frequently that he mainly intends to portray the complex emotions of his characters, each of whom is caught in turbulent times.

Despite the author's disclaimers, however, Ishiguro's novels are undeniably histor-ical in their contexts (and are often factually accurate); the types of situations in which his characters find themselves reveal how each is a historically constituted person grappling with fate and human will. In the first two novels – where the context of world events is significant to the protagonists' personal stories – Ishiguro situates the characters and main events in 1950s postwar Japan. The narrator of *A Pale View of*

Hills, Etsuko, is living in England in the decades following the war, and she reminisces about an extremely difficult period in her personal life that had its roots in Nagasaki shortly after its bombing in 1945. She attempts to reconcile her understanding of her life in war-torn Japan with the private devastation that she brought with her to England, where her eldest daughter committed suicide. In both Etsuko's narrative and in Ono's narrative in *An Artist of the Floating World*, the reader detects an immense bereavement experienced by the characters, even as they inadvertently reveal their guilt or complicity in shaping tragic events. At the end of their stories, the narrators express their general helplessness at changing the past, even as the memory of their stories serves briefly to displace the emptiness of their present lives. However, Ishiguro ends these novels not on a note of dark despair but with a hope that the emptiness might be countered by a cheerful, even if somewhat futile, attempt to live out what remains of their days.

A similar note of futile hopefulness is encountered at the end of *The Remains of the Day*, as Stevens practices new modes of bantering to try out with his new employer, convinced in a pathetic yet poignant fashion that "in bantering lies the key to human warmth" (1993b: 245). In response to Brian Shaffer's query about the equivocation produced in readers over his characters, Ishiguro responds, "Is it possible to contribute to the good of the world? How difficult or easy is it to make a contribution to a more civilized world? [My characters] do pose these questions, so it is justified for people to argue over whether these novels close on a hopeful note or not" (Shaffer 2001: 11). Even Stevens surreptitiously understands that time itself is a false healer, that "the wounds of bereavement [are] only superficially healed" (1993b: 41) in a given lifetime, and that whatever one chooses to do can only blunt momentarily the worst pain. Ishiguro's portrayal of Stevens as both a pawn and subject of imperial politics may be helpful for understanding the various crossroads in which Stevens finds himself. If Etsuko and Ono fail to provide a means by which troubled souls might seek consolation from engaging with labyrinthine memory, neither does Stevens serve the acolyte role we hope his eventual knowledge of self might prefigure.

In Ishiguro's next novel, *The Unconsoled*, he shows another protagonist, Ryder, who – like Stevens – struggles with his self-prescribed role as a healer of one society's ills. In Stevens's case, because he implies that his service to Lord Darlington is in large measure service to his country, he also infers his own greatness as a professional. Bruce Robbins denounces both Stevens's understanding of professionalism and Ryder's understanding of "cosmopolitanism" in *The Unconsoled*. He suggests that Stevens's self-representation is inherently dangerous, for his claim to serve larger humanitarian ends has taken a terrible toll not only on him but also on those whose lives were touched by the advent of fascist politics. A critical scene in the novel involves Stevens's adamant refusal to attend to his dying father upstairs as he is serving important political figures downstairs at the 1923 international conference at Darlington Hall. When Miss Kenton expresses her sympathy to Stevens upon his father's death, Stevens haplessly explains to her that his present service to Darlington is exactly what his father would have demanded of him. In effect, Stevens bases his inability to attend to his dying father on his own father's unrelenting adherence to professional duty, a vicious cycle of sorts that proves emotionally debilitating to both men. Stevens's ability to conceal his private grief at his father's passing is noticed both by the young Reginald Cardinal and by his employer, Lord Darlington, who just as easily ignores both the cause and implication of Stevens's grief. Remarkably, Ishiguro presents this scene as if Stevens himself is unaware of his own bereavement; even though the narrative is constructed through Stevens's eyes, the reader sees the protagonist's grief only indirectly, in the words and actions of others.

As the lord of the manor, Darlington is not obliged to be attuned to the emotional oscillations of the hired help. Even later in the narrative, when Stevens reveals how, in 1935, his lordship apologized for an event that transpired one evening when Stevens was queried about his political opinions, Darlington is less sensitive about Stevens's feelings than he is about affirming his own fascist politics (pp. 194–9). Stevens's acceptance of and public deference to the employer–employee relationship is a source of his deepening grief over the years, for he has had to shield from his professional self any and all personal feelings and views. Another telling incident concerning Stevens's disparate senses of self occurs when Stevens's suppression of his feelings not only validates Darlington's totalitarian views but also has damaging consequences to his relationship with Miss Kenton.

Prior to revealing this episode in his travelogue, Stevens propounds in Lord Darlington's defense as if to a "querulous interlocutor" (Wall 1994: 36): "It needs to be said too what salacious nonsense it is to claim that Lord Darlington was anti-Semitic, or that he had close association with organizations like the British Union of Fascists. Such claims can only arise from complete ignorance of the sort of gentleman his lordship was" (1993b: 137). Stevens continues for another several sentences in heated defense of Darlington's innocence, but then halts momentarily to qualify that, "except, perhaps, in respect to one very minor episode in the thirties," his lordship was correct in his judgments and was not under any undue influence by men like Sir Oswald Mosley and his Blackshirts. He pauses to point out that even that episode "was blown up out of all proportion" (p. 137). The episode in question is presented a few pages later: Darlington calls upon Stevens to tell Miss Kenton that two of the Jewish maids on the staff must be let go, for, as his lordship explains, "It's regrettable, Stevens, but we have no choice. There's the safety and well-being of my guests to consider" (p. 147). Darlington's couched explanation that the maids' (otherwise absent) presence might offend his pro-Nazi guests, when given by Stevens to Miss Kenton, raises her ire. In shock she replies to Stevens that firing them "would be simply – *wrong*" (p. 149). Although she eventually carries out the order, Miss Kenton threatens to leave her employ if the dismissal takes effect. When she still remains in her post as head housekeeper a year later, Stevens at first lightly chides her for remaining. When he tells her that he was "as distressed by the episode" (p. 153) as she was, she is astonished by his sentiment. When asked why he did not say so at the time, Stevens describes his effort to reply: "I gave a laugh, but for a moment was rather at a loss for an answer," and shortly later "excused myself and proceeded to make my exit" (pp. 153–4). Quelled by Miss Kenton's logic, Stevens retreats – as he does often through the years – when his own cool reasoning is questioned, or when the incongruity of his public and private selves is noticed.

Stevens's suppression of his emotions when fulfilling his lordship's request is revealed in this particular scene to impede his forming a deeper alliance – whether empathetic, romantic, or otherwise – with Miss Kenton. For Stevens to align with her in the above incident would have amounted to a betrayal of his loyalty to Darlington, which, in Stevens's mind, turns out to be a betrayal to the nation. However, in addition to experiencing the hardship of a suppressed emotional life at the time of his service to Darlington, Stevens finds that his employer's honor grows more questionable as time passes. Variously, during his 1956 journey, he finds himself disavowing any past association to Lord Darlington, particularly since public sentiment about his former employer's prewar activities has become hostile of late. In the privacy of his thoughts, however, Stevens grapples with the implications of his choice to conceal his formerly proud relationship with Darlington. During his travels in the present, when he is physically and historically outside the confines of Darlington Hall, Stevens questions his professional choices and personal sacrifices. Without a doubt, Stevens's awareness of the futility of undoing the past provides one of the deeply affecting turning points of the novel. While his claims for his professional behavior and actions are excessively pedantic, his eventual comprehension of loss and of his previously unexamined life are wrenching.

Interestingly, Stevens's expression of his emotional duress may be in line with a liberal humanist reading of the text, but his responsibility for the full extent of his life remains open for closer examination. His submission to the underlying principles of professionalism and honor is parallel to the deference that Darlington himself presents to the conference participants in 1923. Unable to foretell the probable harm that their allegiances might cause to a yet unknowable future, both Darlington and Stevens behave in accordance with what they deem to be the proper social ideals of the time. They espouse their ideals with limited knowledge of a much larger picture. For Darlington, appeasement of German powers might stifle an impending war; for Stevens, good service to Darlington is of utmost importance to ensuring world peace. For both, service to a national cause is the order of the day, although in 1923 such views could not be foreseen to turn out well by 1956.

Hindsight itself is a benefit viewed skeptically by Stevens late in the narrative. He notes that when "one begins to search one's past for such 'turning points,' one is apt to start seeing them everywhere" (p. 175). By massing the evidence of illumination as ubiquitous and therefore indiscriminate, Stevens forgives himself for either missing it when it occurred or for interpreting it too late to gain any value from it. Cleverly, he is able to sweep away his misfortunes, even as he tries to salvage what good remains of these insights. Significantly, Ishiguro seems sympathetic to the limitations of what humans can know; that his characters suffer for their narrow choices is evident in the dismal loneliness which eventually characterizes both Darlington's and Stevens's lives.

A reader's denunciation of Stevens's moral choices should be considered in light of Stevens's own calculated representation of his story. On the one hand, Stevens seems to strive for a clear and objective narrative; on the other he seems increasingly embarrassed by his own enlightenment of the past. In fact, he seems especially anxious to pardon his own naivety while also protecting his past allegiance to Darlington. James Lang explores the relationship of one's private history to the always evolving sentiments of public memory when he writes: "The competing strategies of historicization in *The Remains of the Day* – official, public, diplomatic history in contrast with the private memories of the diplomat's butler – find a parallel in the slow movement, on the part of twentieth-century historians, away from the grand narratives and grand characters of earlier historiography toward the lives and experiences of the ordinary, the mundane, the marginalized, and the dispossessed" (2000: 147). If Stevens had determined himself glorified by his lordship's political prominence in world events in the 1920s and 1930s, the same inflated pride diminishes considerably when, in 1950 (the time of Stevens's present narrative), the world understands the devastating results of fascist politics. The heightened political climate of the earlier period has produced in Stevens an exaggerated sense of self-importance; but with the vilification of Darlington's politics by the end of the World War II, when Darlington Hall is also empty and in disarray, Stevens is left with his own solitary self. Lacking a gilded employer to please and now managing a large and desolate estate with a greatly decreased work force, Stevens loses key gauges by which to measure his self-worth. If Stevens had built his life upholding the duties of his profession at the expense of all else, that commitment in the past now threatens to destroy entirely his very reason for being. Unable to eradicate the past completely in order to start afresh, Stevens must reinvent a new mode for the final years of his life. Momentarily, the holiday encounter with Miss Kenton/Mrs Benn serves as an impetus for just such a revision.

Ishiguro expresses Stevens's inevitable dispossession of a meaningful life with remarkable grace, and the portrayal of Stevens aligns with the author's critique of the British empire. As a *character*, Stevens is as odious and cold as the father he admires so much; as a *national character*, Stevens turns out to have played either an unimpressively small role in world events or a deeply wrong one in his service to the shortsighted, even if well-meaning, Lord Darlington. None of the roles he plays is especially admirable and all are overcharged by Stevens's own declaration of importance. By 1956, Stevens is stripped of the vestments that had granted a shred of meaningfulness to his life as a butler; it is a nakedness he tries hard to bear well. Even as this devastating news slowly but vividly manifests itself in Stevens's consciousness and makes its way into his narrative, he finds a way of diverting attention from it. In Moscombe, after Stevens's car runs out of petrol and he is invited to stay with the local Taylor family (who invite many of the townspeople to meet a gentleman who has landed in their midst), Stevens's exchange with Harry Smith reveals the great stress of his divided sense about what constitutes living a life of dignity. Only the following morning, when Dr Carlisle pointedly asks Stevens whether or not he is a "manservant of some sort" (p. 207) – in order to account for Stevens' references to many of the great men of history who had come to Darlington Hall – does Stevens feel unburdened after hiding from his past relationship with Darlington. The public's memory of men like Darlington is too strongly etched in the minds of local men who lost loved ones in the war; their overt condemnations of Nazi-sympathizers, past and present, overpower Stevens's feeble attempts to rework his own delusion about Darlington's naive and amateur politics.

Increasingly, as the voyaging Stevens moves physically closer to Mrs Benn, his memories of life with Darlington and his present encounters with the locals of each town undermine his determination to reconcile the present to an acceptable version of the past. Hidden in Darlington Hall all these years, Stevens, in his confrontation with the outside world, opens all the dark corners he had managed to avoid. Indeed, his growing repudiation of Lord Darlington and his growing excitement at meeting Miss Kenton confuse his purpose for undertaking both his physical and mental journeys. Yet, interestingly, by the end of the novel, Stevens manages to put even the shame of Darlington's memory behind him; he seems able to adopt a frame of mind in which he can be undaunted by his interpretation of *his* past, one that he has reconfigured through the space and time of his own travels.

Stevens's ability to sugar over a bitter past leads us to question whether Stevens is completely delusional. Kathleen Wall's illuminating essay about the novel's "challenges to theories of unreliable narration" dissects Stevens's speech patterns in order to show how "he has kept values, events, memories, and interpretation in separate mental 'boxes' in order to avoid the psychological conflict that inheres in being aware of one's fractured subjectivity" (1994: 23). In other words, Stevens would rather not show and tell all that he knows, even while he is painfully aware that he must cover up what he hopes never to know. Stevens's ability to adapt to whatever new situation he finds himself in seems to be his saving grace, a point thoughtfully developed by Adam Zachary Newton in his study of narrative ethics. Newton writes that the novel is filled with moments when "Stevens's voice conspicuously changes register, as a world of secrets newly discovered wells up from beneath its occluded surface" (1997: 273). Stevens is able to suppress, and even to *transform,* past disgrace into present acceptance. He is imbued with an authoritative sense of precisely how he might rewrite his past and present to better effect. He also is able to sift through knowledge, past and evolving, in order to survive the brutal confrontation with a difficult history.

The event that serves as the prime motivation for Stevens's journey to the west of England is the one that past memories of Darlington Hall in all of its glory had precipitated: Stevens's meeting with Mrs Benn/Miss Kenton after twenty years. This critical meeting is much anticipated from the novel's start but, unfortunately, as Stevens's memories of Lord Darlington surface, and as his encounters with the locals challenge those memories, Stevens loses courage. Not surprisingly, but with some disappointment, the reader encounters this meeting not in all of its immediacy and unrehearsed awkwardness, but as a reflected and neatly delivered account in Stevens's most *recent* memory of that event. The scene appears in the last section of the novel,

"Day Six. Evening. Weymouth." After a description of his present surroundings, Stevens tells us, "It is now fully two days since my meeting with Miss Kenton in the tea lounge of the Rose Garden Hotel in Little Compton" (pp. 231–2). While such a record of the event is true to the narrative device that Stevens is keeping a travelogue (and hence that he records in his diary experiences after they occur), the gap in the narrative between the event and its telling here is most striking. Stevens carefully orders the presentation of events in the hope of putting himself in the best possible light. First, Stevens's pleasure at this meeting is noted: "But it was not so much the content of our conversation as the little smiles she gave at the end of utterances, her small ironic inflexions here and there, certain gestures with her shoulders or her hands, which began to recall unmistakably the rhythms and habits of our conversations from all those years ago" (p. 233). After learning the details of her present existence, however, Stevens knows that it is impossible to ask her to leave the life she has spent two decades forging; the meeting confirms how hopeless is Stevens's original plan of rehiring her as head housekeeper to Mr Farraday's estate.

The narrative of this scene changes its tone momentarily, however, when Mrs. Benn herself reveals to Stevens that she regrets not having had an opportunity to share her life with him. Shocked, perhaps, because Mrs Benn has returned their discourse to that of lost love, while Stevens had been emphasizing the professional contribution she might make upon a return to Darlington Hall, Stevens's silence is filled only with the thoughts he records in his own mind : "[The] implications [of her words] were such as to provoke a certain degree of sorrow within me. Indeed – why should I not admit it? – at that moment, my heart was breaking" (p. 239). Despite the private tumult he feels, Stevens is able to put on a brave face, a *dignified* face, for, as he told Dr Carlisle earlier that day, dignity "comes down to not removing one's clothing in public" (p. 210). His refusal to let down his guard now takes the form of a benevolent yet rather patronizing aspect. He tells her what he might tell himself as a gesture of consolation: "We must each of us, as you point out, be grateful for what we *do* have. . . . You really mustn't let any more foolish ideas come between yourself and the happiness you deserve" (p. 239). Momentarily stunned by Mrs Benn's confession, Stevens formulates an appropriate reply to the loss he feels but cannot or will not express and, in this manner, he fortifies his ability to sidestep a painful reality. Rebecca Walkowitz identifies the inability to acknowledge loss as a complex psychological process which Ishiguro embeds in his narrators' consciousness: "[Ishiguro's protagonists all have an] inability to acknowledge that the past, always figured, cannot be faced. . . . [They cannot see] that one takes responsibility for the past only by acknowledging its loss: the attempt to deny this loss, and thereby to deny that there is any betrayal of self or community, turns out in Ishiguro's novels to be the worst evasion of all" (2001: 1050). This "evasion" that characterizes Stevens's entire life culminates in his eventual meeting with Mrs Benn, a meeting that presages a future of solitude for Stevens.

Finally, Stevens adjusts his present physical surroundings so that these correspond to his role as diarist, rather than as confessor. Metaphorically, he finds in the very physical landscape a way to produce a stable narrative to which he might make present correspondence and reference. Indeed, Stevens's own past is realigned by the journey he undertakes. He knows (now) that his life with Darlington had unequivocally shaped his life in negative ways. At the end of the novel, Ishiguro allows Stevens to make a final expiation of his complicity with Darlington in a single scene at the pier in Weymouth, when Stevens admits to a retired footman whom he has befriended: "You see, I *trusted*. I trusted in his lordship's wisdom. All those years I served him, I trusted I was doing something worthwhile. I can't even say I made my own mistakes. Really – one has to ask oneself – what dignity is there in that?" (p. 243). After accepting some consoling words from his newfound companion, Stevens determines to "adopt a more positive outlook and try to make the best of what remains of my day," and then adds this sardonic comment: "After all, what can we ever gain in forever looking back and blaming ourselves if our lives have not turned out quite as we might have wished?" (p. 244). What would have been an alternative existence for Stevens? He never says exactly. How can one change a life that is already lived? One cannot. Yet, throughout *The Remains of the Day*, Stevens nevertheless attempts just such a thing, a version of perpetual revision until the best text emerges, akin to attempts, Ishiguro seems to hint, to revise and place in a better light the decisions Britain itself made between the wars.

References and Further Reading

Bradbury, Malcolm (1993) *The Modern British Novel*. New York and London: Penguin.

Davis, Rocio (1994) "Imaginary homelands revisited in the novels of Kazuo Ishiguro," *Miscelanea*, 15: 139–54.

Gorra, Michael (1997) *After Empire: Scott, Naipaul, Rushdie*. Chicago and London: University of Chicago Press.

Griffiths, M. (1993) "Great English houses/new homes in England? Memory and identity in Kazuo Ishiguro's *The Remains of the Day* and V. S. Naipaul's *The Enigma of Arrival*," *SPAN*, 36: 488–503.

Guth, D. (1999) "Submerged narratives in Kazuo Ishiguro's *The Remains of the Day*," *Forum for Modern Language Studies*, 35: 126–37.

Habib, C. (1991) "Nagasaki and more: on the English novels of Kazuo Ishiguro," *Esprit*, 2: 114–20.

Head, Dominic (2002) *The Cambridge Introduction to Modern British Fiction, 1950–2000*. Cambridge: Cambridge University Press.

Holdheim, W. Wolfgang (1984) *The Hermeneutic Mode: Essays on Time in Literature and Literary Theory*. Ithaca and London: Cornell University Press.

Ishiguro, Kazuo (1981a) "A strange and sometimes sadness," *Introduction 7: Stories by New Writers*. London: Faber and Faber.

——(1981b) "Getting poisoned," *Introduction 7: Stories by New Writers*. London: Faber and Faber.

——(1981c) "Waiting for J.," *Introduction 7: Stories by New Writers*. London: Faber and Faber.

——(1983) "Summer after the war," *Granta*, 7: 120–37.

——(1989) *An Artist of the Floating World*. New York: Vintage. (First published 1986, London: Faber and Faber; New York: Putnam).

——(1990a) "A family supper," *Esquire*, March: 207–11.

——(1990b) *A Pale View of Hills*. New York: Vintage. (First published 1982, London: Faber and Faber; New York: Putnam).

——(1993a) "The gourmet," *Granta*, 43: 89–127.

——(1993b) *The Remains of the Day*. New York: Vintage (First published 1989, London: Faber and Faber; New York: Alfred A. Knopf).

—— (1996) *The Unconsoled.* New York: Vintage. (First published 1995, London: Faber and Faber).

—— (2000) *When We Were Orphans.* New York: Alfred A. Knopf; London: Faber and Faber.

Janik, Del Ivan (1995) "No end of history: evidence from the contemporary English novel," *Twentieth Century Literature,* 22: 1–27.

King, Bruce (1991) "The new internationalism: Shiva Naipaul, Salman Rushdie, Buchi Emecheta, Timothy Mo and Kazuo Ishiguro," in James Acheson (ed.) *The British and Irish Novel since 1960.* New York: St Martin's Press.

Krider, Dylan Otto (1998) "Rooted in a small space: an interview with Kazuo Ishiguro," *Kenyon Review,* 20: 146–54.

Lang, James M. (2000) "Public memory, private history: Kazuo Ishiguro's *The Remains of the Day,*" *Clio,* 29: 143–65.

Lewis, Barry (2000) *Kazuo Ishiguro.* Manchester: Manchester University Press.

Mallett, Peter J. (1996) "The revelation of character in Kazuo Ishiguro's *The Remains of the Day* and *An Artist of the Floating World,*" *Shoin Literary Review,* 29: 1–20.

Mason, Gregory (1989a) "An interview with Kazuo Ishiguro," *Contemporary Literature,* 30: 335–47.

—— (1989) "Inspiring images: the influence of Japanese cinema on the writings of Kazuo Ishiguro," *East-West Film Journal,* 3/2: 39–52.

McCombe, John P. (2002) "The end of (Anthony) Eden: Ishiguro's *The Remains of the Day* and mid-century Anglo-American tensions," *Twentieth Century Literature,* 48: 77–99.

Newton, Adam Zachary (1997) *Narrative Ethics.* Cambridge, MA: Harvard University Press.

O'Brien, Susie (1996) "Serving a new world order: postcolonial politics in Kazuo Ishiguro's *The Remains of the Day,*" *Modern Fiction Studies,* 42: 787–806.

Oe, Kenzaburo and Ishiguro, Kazuo (1991) "The novelist in today's world: a conversation," *Boundary Two,* 18: 109–22.

Patey, Caroline (1991) "When Ishiguro visits the west country: an essay on *The Remains of the Day,*" *Acme,* 44: 135–55.

Robbins, Bruce (2001) "Very busy just now: globalization and harriedness in Ishiguro's *The Unconsoled,*" *Comparative Literature,* 53: 426–40.

Rothfork, John (1996) "Zen comedy in postcolonial literature: Kazuo Ishiguro's *The Remains of the Day,*" *Mosaic,* 29: 79–102.

Rushdie, Salman (1991) " 'Commonwealth literature' does not exist" and "Kazuo Ishiguro," in *Imaginary Homelands: Essays and Criticism, 1981–1991.* London: Viking.

Shaffer, Brian W. (1998) *Understanding Kazuo Ishiguro.* Columbia: University of South Carolina Press.

—— (2001) "An interview with Kazuo Ishiguro," *Contemporary Literature,* 42: 1–14.

Smitten, Jeffrey R. and Daghistany, Ann (eds.) (1981) *Spatial Form in Narrative.* Ithaca and London: Cornell University Press.

Su, John J. (2002) "Refiguring national character: the remains of the British estate novel," *Modern Fiction Studies,* 48: 552–80.

Tamaya, Meera (1992) "Ishiguro's *Remains of the Day*: the empire strikes back," *Modern Language Studies,* 22: 45–56.

Vorda, Allan and Herzinger, Kim (1991) "An interview with Kazuo Ishiguro," *Mississippi Review,* 20: 131–54. Also in Vorda, Allan (ed.) (1993) *Face to Face: Interviews with Contemporary Novelists.* Houston: Rice University Press.

Wain, Peter (1992) "The historical-political aspect of the novels of Kazuo Ishiguro," *Language and Culture,* 23: 177–205.

Walkowitz, Rebecca (2001) "Ishiguro's floating worlds," *English Literary History,* 68: 1049–72.

Wall, Kathleen (1994) "*The Remains of the Day* and its challenges to theories of unreliable narration," *Journal of Narrative Technique,* 24: 18–42.

Wong, Cynthia F. (1995) "The shame of memory: Blanchot's self-dispossession in Ishiguro's *A Pale View of Hills,*" *Clio,* 24: 127–45.

—— (2000) *Kazuo Ishiguro.* Tavistock, Devon: Northcote House.

—— (2001) "Like idealism is to the intellect: an interview with Kazuo Ishiguro," *Clio,* 30: 309–25.

38

Ian McEwan

Rebecca L. Walkowitz

Given his exceptional success, it is all the more notable that Ian McEwan writes stirringly, even frequently, of unexceptional failure (Lee 1978). From his first collection of short stories, which he published in 1975 at age 27, to the novels he published two or more decades later, McEwan focuses on creative acts and social gestures that are, as he puts it, "inept, but hauntingly so" (McEwan 2001: 6). There is a remarkable contrast between the perennial impudence of his subject matter and the consistent polish of his style. McEwan is generally praised as "the most technically accomplished of all modern British writers" (Winder 2001). One critic has called him "the cool, clinical technician of contemporary English prose" (Cowley 1998). Early reviews of McEwan's work tend to speak of "fine effects" and of his "power to shock," while more recent assessments celebrate above all his mastery of narrative form: his ability to capture, for example, a child's point of view, the mannered politeness of a rejection letter, or the tone of "sexual unease" (Barnes 1975; Lee 1978; Kermode 2001; Lancaster 2002; McGrath 2002). There is little doubt that McEwan is flourishing; he has won most of the literary awards available to him in Britain and the United States, including the Booker Prize for *Amsterdam* (1998), the Somerset Maugham Award for *First Love, Last Rites* (1975), the Whitbread Novel of the Year Award for *The Child in Time* (1987), and the National Book Critics Circle Award for *Atonement* (2001). Yet he directs his attention in each of these texts to episodes of carelessness and deflated triumph.

McEwan announced in 1978, two books into his career, "I would like to see the novel less urbanely celebratory of our times and more critical" (McEwan 1978a). This is a telling comment for two reasons. First, it suggests that there is more to McEwan's literary project than the technical accomplishment for which he has been applauded and sometimes disparaged. Second, it suggests that, for McEwan, urbanity and celebration can stand in the way of social critique, while stories of crudeness and clumsiness, which pervade McEwan's novels, may offer new opportunities both for critique and for innovation. Over three decades, McEwan's stories and novels have developed a strategic vocabulary for the pathos of unimpressive or unspectacular achievements, like the orgasm that is "miserable, played-out, barely pleasurable" or the "reverie, once rich in plausible details," which becomes "a passing silliness before the hard mass of the actual" (McEwan 1975: 29; 2001: 76). One of the most important words in McEwan's lexicon is "homemade": it is the title of his first published story, which he later reprinted as the opening tale of _First Love, Last Rites_. As any dictionary will confirm, homemade objects are plain, simple, crude, or, literally, made for domestic use or in a domestic setting. They tend to be imperfect because they are prepared not from the best ingredients but from the ingredients at hand, not with the practiced skill of the expert but with the ingenuity and enthusiasm of the amateur.

In McEwan's work, homemade objects generate situations that are unexpected and often inappropriate. McEwan's inaugural story features a 14-year-old narrator who, in a pathetic imitation of sexual conquest, loses his virginity to his 10-year-old sister. The narrator's imitation is based on tales of sexual adventure that he has overheard while sitting among a crowd of workmen in a local café. McEwan's wry presentation of these tales deflates the bravado of the workmen, of the boy, as well as of the story: there is no real conquest, but there is also no moral; there is no sense that maturity or expertise leads to sexual attitudes that are preferable to the boy's absurd triumph. The narrator reports that he and his friend

> listened to who and how the dustmen fucked, how the Co-op milkmen fitted it in, what the coalmen could hump, what the carpet-fitter could lay, what the builders could erect, what the meter man could inspect, what the bread man could deliver, the gas man sniff out, the plumber plumb, the electrician connect, the doctor inject, the lawyer solicit, the furniture man install – and so on, in an unreal complex of timeworn puns and innuendo, formulas, slogans, folklore, and bravado. I listened without understanding, remembering and filing away anecdotes which I would one day use myself... (1975: 15–16)

That the narrator "listened without understanding" tells us that these "timeworn puns" constitute an adult sexuality that is no less absurd and no less superficial than the experimentation of a naive 14-year-old.

The sentence as list, the sexual irreverence, the perversity of manners – all of these elements betray the strong influence of Vladimir Nabokov on McEwan's early work. No story suggests this more than the wonderfully horrible anecdote "Butterflies," which is also part of the _First Love, Last Rites_ collection. "Butterflies" takes the plotline of Nabokov's _Lolita_ and replaces the winning sophistication of Humbert Humbert with the unintelligent meanness of an unnamed narrator, who lives not in the enchanted world of a rich imagination but in the desolate, ugly world of post-industrial London. McEwan's narrator lures a young girl to an abandoned canal, where he molests her and indirectly causes her death; the title of the story is a nod to Nabokov, novelist and famous lepidopterist, and it is also a reference to the narrator's ruse: he tells the girl that there will be butterflies at the canal, but of

course there is only stagnant water and menace. The story is interesting as an example
of what McEwan will call "impartial psychological realism" (2001: 41). It is interesting, also, because it prepares us for McEwan's later, more extensive efforts to display
the literary and social expectations – about family, sexuality, and heroism – that
readers take for granted.

"Butterflies" lures the reader, who initially trusts the narrator much as the girl does
and who initially imagines that our concern – the molestation and death of the girl –
is also his. The story begins with a whiff of Proust, "I saw my first corpse on
Thursday" (1975: 79). One assumes that the narrator is remembering, simply, that
on Thursday he saw a corpse for the first time. One realizes later that he is
remembering, instead, that on Thursday he saw the first corpse for which he is
responsible: the corpse belongs to him not because he has seen it but because he has
made it; it could be no one else's "first corpse" in quite the same way. "Butterflies" is
full of duplicitous language, phrases that seem harmless or beautiful in one moment
and then menacing or ugly in another. Like butterflies, whose imitative patterns make
them difficult to see, these phrases are at first unremarkable: their duplicity can be
perceived only by those attentive readers who notice the difference, as Nabokov
writes, between "a twiglike insect" and "a dead twig" (Nabokov 1980: 377). In
McEwan's story, butterfly-phrases include the first sentence ("I saw my first corpse
on Thursday") and also other sentences, such as "I had time to kill" or "I ran through
what had happened, and what I should have done" (1975: 81, 96). The last comment
refers not to the narrator's remorse about the girl but to his far less sympathetic
remorse about his failure to befriend a group of West Indian boys on the street. For
the reader, though not for the girl, the story is full of butterflies, but they are
metaphorical and in no way benign.

It is important to see that McEwan's story aims to transform both characters and
readers: one comes to notice that menace extends, beyond the unconventional narrator,
into the conventional world that passes for normal. The landscape of London, whose
physical beauty might provide some contrast to the narrator's moral blight, in fact
seems to resemble it. The narrator reports,

> There are no parks in this part of London, only car parks. And there is the canal, the
> brown canal which goes between factories and past a scrap heap, the canal little Jane
> drowned in. (1975: 80)

Later, he adds: "I drank water from the kitchen tap. I read somewhere that a glass of
water from a London tap has been drunk five times before. It tasted metallic" (p. 81).
Interspersed among the details of the narrator's encounter with the girl are remarks
about the Pakastani family that owns a shop they call "Watson's" and whose "two sons
were beaten up by local skinheads" (p. 86). The narrator's actions are horrible,
McEwan suggests finally, but they are also ordinary, part of a damaged environment
made up of asphalt, recycled water, and brutal incivility.

In his later work, McEwan has continued to focus on social or sexual relationships whose state of damage a new calamity does not *introduce* but rather *displays* and *exaggerates*. His first two novels, *The Cement Garden* (1978) and *The Comfort of Strangers* (1981), present in one case a family and in the other a romantic couple, both of which are living uneasily even before they encounter the agents of more explicit or more extravagant disorder. The plot of *The Cement Garden* involves four children who live alone in a house after their parents have died; in *The Comfort of Strangers*, an unmarried couple on holiday in Venice meets two strangers who lead them into cruelty, mutilation, and death. The titles of the novels alert us to intimacies that are unconventional or unsuccessful, like a garden made of cement or like the comfort of a stranger. The first half of *The Cement Garden* concerns the death of the parents: the father dies of a heart attack while mixing cement that he is using to cover over his weed-infested garden; the mother dies of some unspecified disease, and then she is buried in the cement by her children, who wish to avoid the so-called "care" of state intervention (1978a: 66). The second half of the novel follows the children as they bury themselves in wild intimacy and social isolation.

McEwan's novels often begin with an efficient, prophetic set piece: a careful scene that gestures to a future it is just about to determine through some episode of failure or pathetic achievement. The narrator of *The Cement Garden* explains in the first paragraph of the novel that his father's death, which he has not yet recounted, "seemed insignificant compared to what followed" (p. 13); likewise, the narrator of *Enduring Love* (1997) announces on the second page, "I'm lingering in the prior moment because it was a time when other outcomes were still possible" (1997: 2); and the narrator of *Atonement* says of the heroine's elaborate plans, "Briony was hardly to know it then, but this was the project's highest point of fulfilment" (2001: 4). In each case, the narrator is looking back on an event that comes to shape the perspective from which the novel has emerged. The first chapter of *The Cement Garden* includes a minor achievement and a major failure whose contiguity is, like the cement garden itself, a "fascinating violation" (1978a: 21). While the adolescent narrator is ejaculating in the bathroom, having taken a break from mixing cement for the garden, his father collapses; the narrator returns from his triumph to find his father, whom he should have been helping, face-down in the soft concrete.

In *The Cement Garden*, McEwan's narrator is more absorbed by his own sexual acts and fantasies, which are vulgar rather than ominous, than he is by the conditions of economic, emotional, or social damage in which he and his family live. Readers have been shocked by McEwan's explicitness, by which they usually mean his description of the sexual games the narrator "knowingly, knowing nothing" plays with his two sisters, one older and one younger (1978a: 16; Byrnes 1995). Yet the focus of our dismay, McEwan suggests, should be elsewhere: with the father, who loses his temper frequently, cruelly taunts the narrator and his siblings and their mother, and has spent the family's little money on the cement scheme for his garden rather than on school clothes for his youngest son (1978a: 15, 19, 41); with the neighborhood, "where stinging nettles grew round torn corrugated tin" and where "other houses were knocked down for a motorway they never built" (pp. 27–8); or with Derek, the older sister's boyfriend who alerts the authorities at the end of the novel not out of sympathy or moral concern but out of jealousy, greed, and conventional disgust. The novel even suggests that the family of children provides more intimacy and nurture than the parents provided in the past or that the community will provide in the future: for example, the sisters show sympathy to their youngest brother, 6-year-old Tom, who is bullied at school and wants to dress like a girl, whereas the parents and the teacher offer in matters of sexuality only diagnosis or condemnation.

Characters who adopt a pious or too-earnest relation to sexuality and social behavior are generally marked as hypocrites or as naive strivers in McEwan's texts. Thus Derek only "saves" the children from their isolation and incest because he has been rebuffed by the sister and because he sees the children's house as a financial opportunity for himself (1978a: 116, 150). In the later novels, such as *Black Dogs* (1992) and *Enduring Love*, would-be heroes are thwarted by minor accidents and persistent uncertainties. These novels offer a critique of chivalry, on the one hand, and of rationalism, on the other. McEwan may acknowledge the attraction of rationalism, as Michael Wood has argued, but he cannot share its confidence in the social efficacy of analysis and quantification (Wood 1997: 9). Visiting a former extermination camp while on a visit to Poland in 1981, the narrator of *Black Dogs* feels that he and his companion are "like tourists" because his emotions are dulled by the enormous weight of numbers, as he looks at the "shoes, tens of thousands of them, flattened and curled like dried fruit" (1992: 93). The narrator explains:

> The extravagant numerical scale, the easy-to-say numbers – tens and hundreds of thousands, millions – denied the imagination its proper sympathies, its rightful grasp of the suffering, and one was drawn insidiously to the persecutors' premise, that life was cheap, junk to be inspected in heaps. (1992: 93)

McEwan's novel does not discard the need for numbers but it finds them insufficient to communicate the experience of extermination camps or of the people who perished there. One alternative that the novel offers to numbers that are "easy-to-say" are those words whose many meanings prod the imagination, as in the novel's title, which refers to a bout of depression, a dishonorable person, a symbol of evil in a nightmare, and attack animals trained by Nazi soldiers. McEwan offers all of these meanings for "black dogs" and then also attaches them to other, less dramatic objects, such as the proverbial "patience of a dog" and a "hot dog" bought in a city street (1992: 69, 72). Allowing his metaphor to register as both transcendent evil and fast-food dinner, McEwan emphasizes the blasphemy of narrative: a rational story of visceral events, a personal account of universal or collective incident, the mix-up of colloquial idiom and moral symbolism (Walkowitz 1998: 108). "Blasphemy," too, is a term that proliferates in the novel: it refers to profanity against God or religion but also to the refusal of other, more secular orthodoxies, including the "sonorous platitudes" of atheism and rational explanation (McEwan 1992: 124).

Black Dogs resists triumphant religion as well as triumphant rationalism, much as *Enduring Love* refuses to allow the practiced reasonableness of its science-writer protagonist to trump either the humanism of his wife, a literary critic, or the insanity of an evangelical stalker. The novel opens with the meticulous description of a ballooning accident in which Joe Rose, the science writer, and his wife Clarissa witness the gruesome death of a rescuer. The initial scene introduces Jed Parry, the stalker, who sees in the disaster a divine manifestation of the love he must share with Joe. McEwan alerts us to the continuity between scientific rationalism and religious triumphalism by suggesting that Jed's obsession with details – the so-called signs of Joe's love, which he finds in a glance or in a smile – is much like Joe's obsession with proof and enumeration. While adding up the "twenty-nine" messages that Jed has left on his answering machine, Joe receives yet another call. It is Jed, who has, he says, received Joe's message: "Joe. Brilliant idea with the curtains. I got it straight away? All I wanted to say is this again. I feel it too. I really do" (1997: 78). Jed imagines that the slightest twitch in the curtains of Joe's apartment is an intentional communication, Joe's sign that he wants to be rescued from his marriage and from his atheist convictions. This seems, of course, crazy, but McEwan would have us notice that Jed's stalking of Joe is only a little more hyperbolic than Joe's manic "investigation" of Jed, his acquisition of a gun (not so easy in England), and his decision to shoot Jed while Jed is holding a knife to his own throat. The novel is full of rescues that go awry, and McEwan attributes these failures to the psychology of heroic achievement: the assumption of certainty and selflessness that excludes ambivalence but also cooperation.

In *Atonement*, McEwan's first novel of the twenty-first century, the critique of rational calculation is indirect but devastating: most of the story takes place in 1935 and in 1940, just before and during World War II, and in this context detached enumeration is a characteristic either of unfeeling bureaucracy (the too-calm estimation of casualties) or of self-interested capitalism (the too-pleased estimation of wartime profit). The novel may focus our attention on the crime of its narrator, Briony, who as a child falsely accuses her sister's lover of being her cousin's rapist, but McEwan suggests that rigid social attitudes, including sexual hypocrisy and class prejudice, have made Briony's accusation almost inevitable. *Atonement* brings together many of the concerns that McEwan has explored in later and in earlier work: the critique of urbane celebration; the resistance to correction or "atonement" and to the idealization of the past; and the assertion that sexual moralism and social complacence are embedded in and generative of the economic and political conditions of twentieth-century Britain.

Atonement opens in an English country house. In the foreground is a play, "The trials of Arabella," which 13-year-old Briony Tallis has composed for the occasion of her older brother's visit. In the background are preparations for war, which McEwan presents indirectly: we hear of government documents prepared by Briony's father, a minister who remains in London, and of business plans prepared by Paul Marshall, the chocolate manufacturer whom Briony's brother Leon has brought to the Tallis estate. Briony's mother, who suffers from nervous headaches and whose husband is having the kind of discreet affair everyone recognizes and no one discusses, finds the government documents by accident. Their practiced indifference matches her own:

> It was only the mildest of wifely curiosity that prompted her to peep, for she had little interest in civic administration. On one page she saw a list of headings: exchange controls, rationing, the mass evacuation of large towns, the conscription of labour. The facing page was handwritten. A series of arithmetical calculations was interspersed by blocks of text. Jack's straight-backed, brown-ink copperplate told her to assume a multiplier of fifty. For every one ton of explosive dropped, assume fifty casualties. Assume 100,000 tons of bombs dropped in two weeks. Result: five million casualties. (2001: 149)

The casual, "straight-backed" prose of this passage should recall the numbing calculations from *Black Dogs* and *Enduring Love*: McEwan suggests that human suffering and political causality have been muted by the detached contemplation of "multipliers."

One hears in Jack's estimations and in his transformation of death into "casualties" an echo of Paul Marshall's estimations, which manage in the course of a single, very long sentence to transform the calamity of possible war into the fantasy of possible wealth. In a "ten-minute monologue" presented by McEwan as free indirect discourse, Marshall describes his plan for "Army Amo," a chocolate bar coated in green candy from which he hopes to profit extravagantly, if, as he hopes, there is a war:

> The launch of Rainbow Amo had been a triumph, but only after various distribution catastrophes which had now been set right; the advertising campaign had offended some elderly bishops so another was devised; then came the problems of success itself, unbelievable sales, new production quotas, and disputes about overtime rates, and the search for a site for a second factory about which the four unions involved had been generally sullen and had needed to be charmed and coaxed like children; and now, when all had been brought to fruition, there loomed the greater challenge yet of Army Amo, the khaki bar with the Pass the Amo! slogan; the concept rested on the assumption that spending on Armed Forces must go on increasing if Mr Hitler did not pipe down; there was even a chance that the bar could become part of the standard-issue ration pack; in that case, if there were to be a general conscription, a further five factories would be needed; there were some on the board who were convinced there should and would be an accommodation with Germany and that Army Amo was a dead duck; one member was even accusing Marshall of being a warmonger; but, exhausted as he was, and maligned, he would not be turned away from his purpose, his vision. (2001: 49–50)

Whereas Jack Tallis seems more concerned about the exact number of victims than he is about the death of the victims themselves, Paul Marshall thinks more about the chocolate bars he will sell than about the soldiers who will die eating them.

McEwan adds to these euphemistic and triumphant visions of war several visions of art, whose abstract triumphalism the novel will likewise reject. It will turn out that Briony is not only the author of a play but also of a novella and of the novel we are reading. The play is a rehearsal, as it were, for Briony's later work, and its story displays values that she, and *Atonement*, will later discard in favor of other, less insular sentiments. "The trials of Arabella" celebrates above all the value of endogamy: a young maiden develops a "reckless passion" for a foreign count; she elopes with the count against the wishes of her family; when Arabella falls ill, the count deserts her, but she is rescued by a prince, disguised as an impoverished doctor, whom she learns to love and eventually marries; the marriage to the prince reconciles Arabella to her family (2001: 3). The heroic resolution of the play will resonate throughout McEwan's novel against the unheroic, uncorrected mistakes that suffuse every other episode, both of war and of romance, in the text.

With her play, Briony hopes to rescue her brother by teaching him to embrace the tradition of marriage and family; her later novella, though more sophisticated in its style and approach, also conforms to a rescue plot, at least in its intentions. In the third section of *Atonement*, set in late April and early May of 1940, Briony is training as a nurse in a London hospital. She has just completed a novella based on events at the Tallis house. Her vision of this novella comes to her in a moment of quiet, which exists because Briony is running an errand rather than cleaning bed pans and also because the news from Dunkirk – known to the reader from the previous section of the novel – has not yet arrived, while the bombing of London, in which her sister will die, has not yet begun. In the context of this pause, on the edge of hospital routine and wartime disaster, Briony begins to gush about her literary "achievement":

> What excited her about her achievement was its design, the pure geometry and the defining uncertainty which reflected, she thought, a modern sensibility... The novel of the future would be unlike anything in the past. She had read Virginia Woolf's *The Waves* three times and thought a great transformation was being worked in human nature itself, and that only fiction, a new kind of fiction, could capture the essence of the change. To enter a mind and show it at work, or being worked on, and to do this within a symmetrical design – this would be an artistic triumph. (2001: 281, 282)

Briony's fantasy of geometric achievement clashes with the corporeal rawness of the events she is representing and of those that, we know, will soon take place. It might seem that Briony's aspiration is shallow because it focuses on the wrong object: winning a writing prize, say, rather than winning the war. But, for McEwan, the problem is not the endeavor but the affect: the problem is "triumph."

Alongside these visions of triumphant design, McEwan will display the mindless routine of the war hospital and the British army's unglorious "rescue" at Dunkirk. McEwan repeats the word "rescue" here and elsewhere to draw the reader's attention to the continuity between the politics of chivalry and the politics of war (pp. 227, 349). McEwan will inform us at the end of the novel that Cecelia, Briony's sister, dies a "casualty" (her father's word) of the blitz and that Cecelia's lover Robbie dies in the Dunkirk retreat. The scenes of wartime serve to replace the earlier visions with explicit, embodied sights: a leg hanging in a tree; a soldier with a gaping head wound (pp. 192, 308). They serve, also, to deflate heroic images of family, romance, and art. It is noticeable, for example, that the make-shift, transient families that Robbie and Briony develop during the war are far superior to the conventional family they have left behind, and one should think here of McEwan's work in *The Cement Garden*: Robbie makes friends with two corporals who protect him and whom he, though a private, leads to the beach at Dunkirk; Briony allows a dying French soldier to imagine that she is his fiancée. These arrangements, McEwan suggests, are not compensatory: they do not simulate or reconstitute the prewar family; rather, they demonstrate more flexible, more inclusive, and more imaginative relationships than those that the war disrupts.

Robbie's experience of the war leads him to adjust his memory of intimacies in his past, purposefully shattering pathos and delicacy where he had only accidentally shattered them before. Retreating to Dunkirk, Robbie decides that he will no longer remember having "made love to Cecelia," but will embrace the language of the corporals and remember instead that "they had fucked while others sipped their cocktails on the terrace" (p. 227). It is worth noting here that the deflation of heroic diction is focused not on the language of war but on the language of sex and social intimacy. McEwan uses the war to criticize the peace and to refocus our attention on relations between men and women; on rules of sexuality and marriage; and on the concept of the family, writ small and writ large. Briony has composed her novel, she tells us in a coda, to atone for her crime and to reanimate the marriage plot – the love story of Robbie and Cecelia – that her accusation had forestalled. In the novel, as we read it, Robbie survives Dunkirk, and he and Cecelia are reunited in London; in the coda, a diary entry from 1999, Briony acknowledges that she has invented this ending to give the couple in fiction what she took from them in life.

At the beginning of *Atonement*, Briony's play is most significant as an event that does not take place. It is delayed by an avalanche of social disasters, including the love affair between Cecelia and Robbie, the charlady's son; the elopement of Briony's aunt, who has run off to Paris with a man said to work in the wireless; the disappearance of Briony's young cousins, distressed by their parents' divorce; the rape of cousin Lola by Paul Marshall; and the arrest of Robbie, who is accused of Marshall's crime. In the final scene of McEwan's novel, the play is performed but sixty-four years late. Of the original cast, at least one member has died; some but not all of the remaining cast are now in the audience; their great-grandchildren are the new players; and the family – as a group and as a paradigm – has changed altogether. The belated performance of the play registers the difference between its endogamous fantasy and the exogamous family that watches it.

The prologue of the play, in rhyming pentameter, is given at the beginning of *Atonement* and then again at the end. It tells of "Arabella" and her "extrinsic fellow," from whom she has to be rescued by the doctor-prince (2001: 16, 367). In the first casting of the play, the prologue is to be read by Briony; in the final casting, the prologue is read by a cousin's great-grandson, who has a Cockney accent and who also plays the extrinsic count. As the performance suggests, the family has become extrinsic: the scene remains at the Tallis house, but the house has become a hotel, while the park has become a golf course; Briony is brought to the hotel by a West Indian taxi driver with a law degree from the University of Leicester, whose conversation makes her realize that talk and dress and taste in music no longer convey educational level or even citizenship (p. 362); while a boy with a Cockney accent plays the foreign count, a half-Spanish girl plays the English maiden. Trumping Briony's novel, which strives for apology, reconciliation, and heroism, the belated play values mix-ups rather than correction.

Like the young Briony, who uses a thesaurus to replace simple words with jarring but equivalent terms, McEwan updates worn images by introducing indecorous phrases in the middle of romantic fantasies or delicate social gestures. The intrusion of "fucking" in the middle of Robbie's daydream is good example of this strategy. McEwan punctuates his novel with semantic constructions, social acts, and works of art that are, as he says throughout the novel, "homemade," much like Briony's play or like Cecelia's "endearing attempt to seem eccentric, her stab at being bold," which is "exaggerated" but effective in unexpected ways (p. 80). The homemade play is effective because it depicts, in exaggerated fashion, the fantasy of heroic rescue that Briony's novel had led us to embrace. Refusing to endorse this fantasy, except in fiction, McEwan won't give celebration the final word. For all the impartiality of McEwan's "psychological realism," *Atonement* displays a critical target that is hard to miss. Call it chivalry or call it triumphalism, McEwan prefers to the disciplines of unwavering success the innovations of unexpected failure.

References and Further Reading

Barnes, Julian (1975) "Tall truths," *New Statesman*, May 2: 600.

Bewes, Timothy (2000) "What is 'philosophical honesty' in postmodern literature?," *New Literary History*, 31: 421–34.

Byrnes, Christina (1995) "Ian McEwan – pornographer or prophet?," *Contemporary Review*, 266: 320–3.

Cowley, Jason (1998) "Portrait: Ian McEwan," *Prospect*, December: 42–5.

Kermode, Frank (2001) "Point of view," *London Review of Books*, 23 (October 4): 8–9.

Lancaster, John (2002) "The dangers of innocence," *New York Review of Books*, 49 (April 1): 24–6.

Lee, Hermione (1978) "Shock horror," *New Statesman*, January 20: 86–7.

——(2001) "If your memories serve you well . . . ," *The Observer*, September 23: 16.

McEwan, Ian (1975) *First Love, Last Rites*. New York: Random House.

——(1978a) *The Cement Garden*. New York: Random House.

——(1978b) "The state of fiction: a symposium," *The New Review*, 5: 50–1.

——(1981) *The Comfort of Strangers*. New York: Random House.

——(1987) *The Child in Time*. New York: Penguin.

——(1992) *Black Dogs*. New York: Bantam.

——(1997) *Enduring Love*. London: Jonathan Cape.

——(1998) *Amsterdam*. London: Jonathan Cape.

——(2001) *Atonement*. London: Jonathan Cape.

514   *Rebecca L. Walkowitz*

McGrath, Charles (2002) "Not quite right for our pages," *New York Times Book Review*, October 27: 31.

Nabokov, Vladimir (1955) *Lolita*. New York: Vintage.

——(1980) "The art of literature and commonsense," in Vladimir Nabokov, *Vladimir Nabokov: Lectures on Literature*, ed. Fredson Bowers. New York: Harcourt Brace.

Proust, Marcel (1993) *Time Regained*, trans. Andreas Mayor and Terence Kilmartin. New York: The Modern Library. (Original work published 1927).

Ricks, Christopher (1979) "Adolescence and after – an interview with Ian McEwan," *The Listener*, 101 (April 12): 526–7.

Seaboyer, Judith (1999) "Sadism demands a story: Ian McEwan's *The Comfort of Strangers*," *Modern Fiction Studies*, 45: 957–86.

Updike, John (2002) "Flesh on flesh: a semi-Austenesque novel from Ian McEwan," *The New Yorker*, 78 (March 4): 80–2.

Walkowitz, Rebecca L. (1998) "A fine romance," *Soundings*, 8: 107–10.

Winder, Robert (2001) "Between the acts," *New Statesman*, 14: 49–50.

Wood, Michael (1997) "When the balloon goes up," *London Review of Books*, 19 (September 4): 8–9.

39

Graham Swift

Donald P. Kaczvinsky

In "Margins and the millennium: towards 2000," the concluding chapter of Randall Stevenson's overview of twentieth-century British literature, the author states that British literature in the twentieth century "not only reflects but seeks to compensate for the problems and anguish of history, reshaping in imagination what is lost or intractable in fact" (1993: 127). The primary source of anguish is found in "the final flourishing, later decline and eventual loss of Empire" (p. 126). One clear effect of this loss, Stevenson suggests, is simply that British fiction became impoverished, having been robbed of the opportunity to encounter unfamiliar subjects, settings, and characters as well as losing a distanced objectivity in the scrutiny of Britain's own culture. For Stevenson, the anguish is compensated for nostalgically in British pop culture, in spy thrillers such as Ian Fleming's James Bond, and in 1980s films such as *Gandhi* and *A Passage to India.* He also finds a consequence likely to be more lasting and much more significant in the cross-cultural awareness of transplanted writers or in writers "from national and post-colonial minorities" (p. 140). In this chapter, Stevenson never mentions the novels of Graham Swift. Yet few contemporary writers consider the "problems and anguish of history" more acutely, or articulate the sense of loss more fully, than Swift.

Stevenson's omission is perhaps understandable. Swift writes from the middle, not the margins. His novels focus on the lives of middle-aged and middle-class men living in South London, where Swift himself was born in 1949 and where he resides. Rarely does Swift depict scenes in the former colonies or include non-white characters. Although it is difficult to say exactly where the plots of Swift's novels begin, the critical moment in the major characters' lives comes during or just before World War II. While Swift does not write war novels or depict battle scenes, and while his characters remain physically unscathed by combat, they often suffer from personal and psychological problems stemming from events in the middle of the century. Swift's fiction, however, does not offer compensation for the anguish of history, as Stevenson suggests is the case in pop culture. Rather, his seven novels confront the tremendous devastation throughout the century and ask, as we head into the twenty-first century, whether there is any future for "middle class" England and for the English novel.

Origins and Ends: The Minor Novels

In *The Sense of an Ending* Frank Kermode argues that "Men . . . rush 'into the middest', *in medias res*, when they are born; they also die *in mediis rebus,* and to make sense of their span they need fictive concords with origins and ends, such as give meaning to their lives" (1966: 7). This is never truer than in Swift's fiction.

The combination of a man from the middle who is nonetheless conscious of his end is found in Swift's first novel, *The Sweet-Shop Owner* (1980). The narrative begins with Willy Chapman reading a letter from his daughter Dorry. He reflects on her words, with an ironic parody of *Genesis*: "'In the end.' 'In the end?' What did she mean – in the *end* he would see?" (1985a: 9).

The novel recounts the last day of Willy's life. Superficially, he possesses all of the trappings of middle-class success; at a deeper level, however, his personal life has been a failure. Willy serves in the army during World War II, which has little effect on him; yet the general violence that characterizes much of the twentieth century has destroyed his marriage. While a young woman, Irene, his wife, was raped by a family friend; the sexual battle has left her psychologically and sexually scarred for life, and that is manifest in her bouts of asthma. She marries Willy because she knows he will demand nothing of her. Irene sets up Willy with his sweet-shop and bears him a daughter on whom he can bestow his love. But Dorry turns out to be as cold and as unfeeling as her mother. In his youth, Willy won long-distance running races by his ability to time perfectly his kick to the finish line, and he remembers fondly a race he ran against his future brother-in-law, though we do not know the outcome. On this last day of his life, he times his death by walking around the city in the summer heat, getting his affairs in order, and trying to induce a heart attack. Willy's hope is, after sending Dorry £15,000, an inheritance from her mother, that she will return home on her birthday, only to find him dead. "He would be history" (1985a: 10), but his life would have a sense of an ending.

David Leon Higdon, in an essay on the "double closures" of Swift's novels, suggests that the conclusion of *The Sweet-Shop Owner* typifies Swift's technique, in which "the open ending appears to be closed and the closed ending open" (1991: 93). Yet Swift subtly hints that Willy's attempt to construct his life as a narrative will fail. More than likely, Dorry will not return home to find Willy dead: he will be lucky if she even shows up for his funeral. The novel is told almost exclusively from an omniscient point of view, so we know, especially in the light of Swift's later fiction, that there will be no one left to recall Willy Chapman's life. Ironically, Willy will not be "history" but a fading memory, remembered only by Mrs Cooper, his shop assistant who is secretly in love with him, who will keep her feelings to herself. The narrative of Willy Chapman is a dead-end for England and English literature, but *The Sweet-Shop Owner* anticipates many of the themes and situations Swift will explore in his later works. Particularly significant is the father's desire to contact an estranged daughter, a subject reworked to better effect in Swift's masterpiece, *Last Orders* (1996).

As Stevenson suggests, the prolific output of postcolonial and transplanted writers is one of the major literary consequences of the end of empire, as such writers often create a personal as well as national identity, separate and in opposition to the dominant British tradition. Perhaps the best example of this in contemporary British literature is Salman Rushdie's *Midnight's Children* (1981). The constructing of national identity is, in many ways, a greater challenge for English than for post-colonial writers, or even for writers from formerly subordinate nations of the United Kingdom. Jim McGuigan explains:

> Quite apart from the dynamics of cultural mixing and crossover, the Scots, the Welsh and the Irish seem to know who they are wherever they are – but do the English? The apparent vacuity of contemporary Britishness derives, in part, from the hollowing-out of Englishness. While it is no longer credible to simply represent Britain as England, the fact of the matter is that 'the English' themselves do not have a strong sense of identity as the Scots, the Welsh and the Irish. (McGuigan 2003: 285)

This challenge is taken up in Swift's minor novels – *Shuttlecock* (1981), *Out of This World* (1988), *Ever After* (1992), and *The Light of Day* (2003) – which are supremely concerned with questions of English identity. The plots or subplots of these works revolve around a son's investigation of his father's glorious past, often his celebrated career as a spy or war hero. Acting as a detective, the narrator-son discovers that his father is not the person he took him to be. The son deconstructs his father's identity until he recognizes the textual nature of identity and the mystery of origins. While the scope of this essay does not allow for a thorough consideration of all of Swift's minor works, his fifth novel, *Ever After,* provides one of the best examples of his technique.

Ever After weaves together fairy tale and romance, murder mystery and academic spoof, spy thriller and high tragedy. Bill Unwin narrates his story from a college garden as he convalesces after a failed suicide attempt. His words are, he warns us, "the words of a dead man" (1993: 3). At the age of 9, Bill lost his father in a gun accident and from then on was cared for by his mother and Sam Ellison, his mother's lover and later Bill's stepfather. Uncle Sam is a successful American businessman who sells plastic "substitoots" for a world that has squandered its natural resources. Colonel Unwin, Bill's father, was a distinguished leader of the empire, "formerly of the regular army, latterly of some ill-defined, semi-civilian sphere of duty between the military and the diplomatic services" (p. 38); but upon his death, Bill creates a family romance. "He was a spy, an undercover agent, he was on some hush-hush mission" (p. 23). Bill discovers days later, however, that his father's death was no accident: Colonel Unwin committed suicide after learning of his wife's infidelity with Sam. Bill begins to fancy himself a latter-day Hamlet, taking revenge on the devious Claudius.

Yet the novel juxtaposes a Cinderella story with this Shakespearean tragedy (Swift's postmodern novels frequently combine high and low literary genres, which often work at cross-purposes to resist pat endings). Born in December 1936 during the Abdication Crisis, Bill maintains that his life was imbued, "for better or worse, with a sort of fairy-tale propensity" (p. 63). While working at The Blue Moon Club in Soho, he meets Ruth Vaughan, a first-year drama student. The two fall in love and, while Bill pursues an academic career, Ruth becomes a celebrated actress. They marry and settle into a happy life together; but then Ruth, who is diagnosed with lung cancer and given only a few months to live, commits suicide. The traditional conclusion to Bill and Ruth's fairy-tale life is short circuited by the last and greatest role Ruth plays, Shakespeare's tragic queen, Cleopatra.

The Cinderella motif, however, continues in Bill's life even after Ruth's premature death. Uncle Sam, Bill's fairy godfather, names Bill as his heir and offers to endow his college, with the stipulation that Bill is named the first Ellison Fellow. As Fellow, Bill edits the diary of Matthew Pearce, his maternal ancestor. Pearce's diary records how his Victorian world is destroyed by the premature death of his son and by questions of human origins: he sees the skeleton of an ichthyosaurus and reads Darwin's *On the Origin of Species*. In the major plot, Sam, just before his death, completely shatters Bill's sense of identity by revealing the secret of Bill's origins. He reveals that Bill's real father was not Colonel Unwin but an engine-driver, and that Bill's mother told her husband this news just before the "accident" that killed him. Hamlet, Cinderella, prematurely aging professor, third rate academic, heir to a plastics business, Ellison Fellow, husband to Ruth Vaughan, a "dead man" (p. 3): Bill Unwin is all of these, and none of them, for he does not even know his father's name.

Stevenson suggests that, for a postwar audience, popular forms of literature, like the spy thriller, offer "a kind of myth or collective wish-fulfillment in which British dominion secretly continues in the shadow world of agents and espionage" (1993: 127). For Swift's narrators, however, the romance of British military glory no longer operates in a shadow world, or in any other world. As Bill Unwin puts it of Colonel Unwin's vaunted career:

> And what world was he sorting out? Some new, rebuilt world which would one day be unveiled to the dazzlement and shame of such backsliders as Mother and me? Or some old, dream-world restored, in which implacable British sergeant-majors bawled for ever over far-flung parade grounds and men followed well-trodden paths to glory and knighthoods?
>
> He was fifty-five. And I had the insight of an infant. But it seems, now, that I could have told him then: that world was gone. An axe had dropped on it. (1993: 20–1)

Or perhaps a bomb. For Bill learns, through his own inquiries of the government, acting not the part of Prince Hamlet but of a "prating Polonius" (pp. 188–9), that his "father" was involved in intelligence – was "[a] reluctant, a regretful, a squeamish spy" (p. 205) – whose duties helped create atomic weapons. Bill is informed that Colonel

Unwin "may have harboured ... a growing aversion, on conscientious grounds, to the nature of his special duties, which, conflicting intolerably with his considerable dedication and ambition, may ultimately have contributed to his suicide" (p. 204). Colonel Unwin's Victorian world, professionally and personally, is blown to pieces by the realities of late twentieth-century existence – unhappily "ever after."

The Loss of Grand Narratives: *Waterland* and *Last Orders*

Swift's two major novels explore origins and ends, questions of identity, and the textual nature of the self. However, what constitutes the most acute source of anguish for the characters is the realization that we may be at the end of history. Jean-François Lyotard has famously proposed that what characterizes the postmodern condition is "an incredulity toward metanarratives" (1984: xxiv) or Grand Narratives – universal and totalizing stories that give direction to the historical process and legitimize statements of truth. Such narratives provided the comfort, even with the violence and apparent chaos of the world around us, that we were moving toward some definable and beneficial goal, that history was teleological and that the future, ultimately, was predictable.

Critics have addressed the theme of the end of history more often than any other in Swift's novels, generally with the intention of showing how Swift's fiction reshapes our understanding of historical consciousness (Schad 1992; Janik 1995; Osuna 1999; DeCoste 2002). Swift's novels are frequently used as an illustration of what Linda Hutcheon has called "historiographic metafiction." In Hutcheon's view, postmodern fiction does not reject or ignore history but actively engages with history, setting its characters within specific historical settings while at the same time, and paradoxically, subverting the objectivity of historical narratives. Such self-reflexive texts expose the conventions by which stories – whether supposedly nonfictional or fictional – organize, structure, and shape reality. Swift's two major novels, *Waterland* (1983) and *Last Orders*, respectively, illustrate the two modes of narration favored by "historiographic metafiction": an "overtly controlling narrator," on the one hand, and "multiple points of view," on the other. In neither mode, suggests Hutcheon, "do we find a subject confident of his/her ability to know the past with any certainty" (1988: 117).

Waterland, which was shortlisted for the Booker Prize, is a valediction to the British empire and the Grand Narratives that supported it: both Christianity and Enlightenment Progress. Tom Crick, the novel's narrator, is a history teacher at a London comprehensive, where, ostensibly owing to budget cuts, he has been offered early retirement. In fact, the more pressing reason for his dismissal is that Tom's wife, Mary, has been caught kidnapping a child from a pram at a Safeways in Lewisham. She believes that God has told her that she will miraculously have a child, a parody of the annunciation that trumpets not the incarnation but her admission into an insane asylum. Lewis Scott, the school's headmaster, fears the repercussions that such a scandal will have upon the school. But Scott hopes not only to retire Crick but to merge History with General Studies – literally putting an end to "history" – and to replace their curricula with a curriculum based on technical, pragmatic, utilitarian knowledge, rather than "a rag-bag of pointless information" (1985b: 17).

The critical moment comes when Price, Crick's rebellious student and the president of the Holocaust Club at Crick's school, interrupts his lesson on the French Revolution, saying: "The only important thing about history, I think, sir, is that it's got to the point where it's probably about to end" (p. 5). Crick answers Price's criticism later over a drink, pointing out that Price's feelings and fears are not new. More immediately, Crick confesses his own loss of faith in the Grand Narrative of History:

> So I shouldered my Subject. So I began to look into history – not only the well thumbed history of the wide world but also, indeed with particular zeal, the history of my Fenland forebears. So I began to demand of history an Explanation. Only to uncover in this dedicated search . . . that history is a yarn. And can I deny that what I wanted all along was not some golden nugget that history would at last yield up, but History itself, the Grand Narrative, the filler of vacuums, the dispeller of fears of the dark? (1985b: 46–7)

Finding himself at the end of both a career and a marriage, and on the defensive with his students about the very relevance of his discipline, Crick deviates far from his syllabus to give them a history of his past in an attempt to explain how things turned out so badly.

The two epigraphs to the novel provide the key to understanding Crick's narration. The first offers several definitions of "Historia" that, taken together, underscore the fact that History is neither objective nor teleological, but, more in line with the claims of postmodernism, multiple, open-ended, tentative: History is "an inquiry," a "narrative of past events," or any kind of "account, tale, story." The second epigraph is from Dickens's *Great Expectations*, linking Crick's narration to Pip's. Both narrators must confess their own culpability in and connection to past crimes and murders. Tom's story concerns a love triangle between two brothers and the girl next door. As adolescents, Tom Crick and Mary Metcalf satisfy their sexual curiosity, after school in an abandoned windmill. Tom's brother, Dick, who is a "potato head," is also in love with Mary; and Mary is decidedly curious about Dick. But Dick is "too big" to fit in Mary's "hole" (or so Mary says), while Tom's "thing" is smaller but more penetrating, exploring places Dick cannot go. When Mary becomes pregnant, she tells Dick, in an effort to protect Tom, that Freddie Parr, a mutual friend, is the father. In jealous anger, Dick kills Freddie, striking him over the head with a bottle of ale and leaving him to drown in the river Leem. Tom, realizing what his brother has done, will use his intelligence as a weapon to destroy Dick, telling Dick that his father is not really his Dad and thus driving Dick to suicide. Mary has the fetus aborted by a Fenland witch, who spits the string of blood into a pail and disposes of it in the river Leem.

The watery fens of East Anglia, which provide the setting for the novel, are the dominant metaphor for Crick's own complex understanding of history. Indeed, the marshy fens are in a constant state of recovery and loss; and their "silt" needs to be endlessly dredged. Tom Crick's word for the historical process is "reclamation," an ongoing battle, a fight against silt, which clogs the waterways and swamps out usable land. The fens are at once "nothing" and everything, water and land, silt and sea, a combination of elements as contradictory and paradoxical as history itself. Tom Crick's stories dredge up the past, winding through the novel, like the rivers of the Ouse and Leem wind through the fens, flooding the work with meaning. Even relatively brief chapters of only a few paragraphs long – "About phlegm," "Quatorze juillet," and "About natural history" are examples – form rivulets and tributaries that swell the novel's tide of information and historical import. Tom Crick's narration, in fact, follows his conception of history: "It goes in two directions at once. It goes backwards as it goes forwards. It loops. It takes detours. Do not fall into the illusion that history is a well disciplined and unflagging column marching unswervingly into the future" (p. 102). In Chapter 48, Lewis Scott's hypocritical introduction of Crick at the school's Easter assembly is interrupted by Price and his Holocaust Club, who chant, "Fear is here!" and "No cuts! Keep Crick!" Crick clears his throat, stands, and begins his valediction: "Children" (pp. 251–2). We expect the full valedictory address in the next chapter. But the text suddenly turns "in two directions at once." Chapter 49 begins "–Who will inherit the world" (p. 253). But we must also look back to Chapter 2, which opens, "Children. Children, who will inherit the world" (p. 4), thus providing a second, alternative, farewell address. Which is the "real" valediction and which one flows into the other are ultimately impossible to ascertain. Crick's powerful intellect keeps the narrative stream flowing, but the origin and ontological status of the narration is as mysterious as the birth and sex of the European eel, yet another obsession of Swift's narrative.

Crick's tale of adolescent love is juxtaposed to the tragic rise and fall of the Atkinsons, his maternal ancestors. Unlike the Cricks, who reclaim the land through stories, the Atkinsons reclaim the land through action. Through his shrewd business maneuvering and the superior quality of his barley, Thomas Atkinson built a financial empire based on that most English of all industries, the brewing of ale. He tries to control the flow of the Leem, making it navigable, by financial means and by developing technology. His sons, George and Alfred, continue to build their father's business empire. Behind the business success of the Atkinsons is their Victorian faith in "that noble and impersonal Idea of Progress" (p. 69). Where Crick's private story of failure winds and twists, the rise and fall of the Atkinson's is told in a straightforward way, suggestive of their own intention to straighten the tortuous flow of the river. Tom Crick warns us, however, against "mistaking the reclamation of land for the building of empires" (p. 254).

The Atkinsons' attempt to control Nature ends in disaster. In January of 1820, irritable with gout, Thomas Atkinson strikes his wife Sarah, who falls and knocks her head against the corner of a writing table. She remains silent forever afterward, except for periodic outbursts of the words "Smoke," "Fire," or "Burning!" Sarah's premonitions come true when Ernest Atkinson, the grandchild of Sarah and Thomas and the grandfather of Tom Crick, serves a potent ale to the public to commemorate the coronation of George V. The citizens get wildly drunk and set fire to the brewery, marking the end of Atkinson power and dominion. A conscientious objector to World War I, Ernest Atkinson retreats into his estate and places all of his love on his daughter, who, in order to get her father to approve her marriage to Henry Crick, agrees to commit incest with him. Ernest believes the incestuous union will give birth to a "savior of the world" – a man who will bring an end to the violence and carnage of the Christian era and usher in a reign of peace. Instead, it eventuates in the birth of Dick and the tragedies that will haunt Tom's own life.

David Leon Higdon suggests that in Tom's speech and in his adoption of Price that "Crick has won a major victory for himself" (1991: 92). But whether Price or any of Tom's students will take the lesson past the Easter assembly, whether there will be a resurrection of history or whether this is just another parody of the Christian metanarrative of salvation, remains uncertain. With Dick dead, Mary left sterile from the abortion, and Tom near a nervous breakdown, the possibility of future Cricks is slim indeed.

Last Orders is at once more poignant and more optimistic than *Waterland*. When the novel won the Booker Prize, in 1996, a debate erupted in the British press over the question of whether Swift plagiarized William Faulkner's *As I Lay Dying* (1930). Early in his career, Swift acknowledged his admiration for Faulkner's novel (Crane 1988: 9), and, in *Last Orders*, he adopts Faulkner's technique of allowing the readers to overhear the inner thoughts of the various characters as they travel to dispose of the remains of a dead relative or friend. Also like Faulkner's work, each chapter of Swift's is narrated from one character's point of view, providing multiple perspectives over the course of the novel.

Jack Dodds's "last order" before his death has brought his son and his Bermondsey friends together on a journey to Margate Pier, where they are to scatter his ashes. On the trip, they come to terms with their lives, their deaths, and, most of all, their relationship to Jack. His very name, Jack Arthur Dodds, suggests that he represents all of the "jacks" and royalty of British history. As Wendy Wheeler has noted, Dodds is an "amalgamation for Dads and Gods" (1999: 76), and so Jack's death announces not only the end of the British empire, but the death of God and the end of the British paternal line. In the one chapter that Jack himself "narrates" (Faulkner's deceased Addie Bundren also narrates one chapter), he offers from beyond the grave a final assessment of the imperial enterprise and the entire twentieth century, through the remembered advice of his own father on the art of butchery: "'Jack boy,' he says, 'it's all down to wastage.... What you've got to understand is the nature of the goods. Which is perishable'" (1997: 285).

Of far more interest than Swift's Faulknerian techniques are his allusions to Chaucer, and to the origins of English literature. Like Chaucer's *Canterbury Tales*, *Last Orders* is a frame story. The pilgrimage begins in a Southwark pub on an April day and travels through Kent. But if Chaucer's fourteenth-century work is supported by the sacred metanarrative of Christian salvation, Swift's late-twentieth-century one offers a secular journey of postmodern pilgrims who have lost faith. The morning is sunny, but by the time the men arrive at Margate Pier, the heavens open up and unleash an apocalyptic storm – all in view of *Dreamland*, a kitschy version of heaven on earth that they see across the water. The travelers visit Canterbury Cathedral, but the holy site has now become a mausoleum; and the men need a tourist guidebook to recall the history entombed there.

As in Chaucer, the sexual life of the characters is an index of their spiritual life. The marriage of Jack Dodds and Amy Mitchell is cursed from the start. The two meet while picking hops at Wick's Farm. On a warm August night, while flirting with Jack, Amy sees a gypsy whom she fancies but who does not return her favors. Excited by the sight of Romany Jim, she makes love to Jack in a hop bin near an old windmill. She will keep the secret of her real desire, and the relationship between Jack and Amy is all downhill from there: the product of their first love-making is daughter June, an idiot. The crisis comes when Jack and Amy take a belated honeymoon in 1939 to Margate. Jack tells Amy, the "Best thing we can do . . . is forget all about her [June]" (1997: 253). Amy, in effect, must choose between her husband and her daughter. June is institutionalized and Jack's and Amy's fifty-year marriage is defined by mutual silence: Jack will not mention June; and Amy will visit a daughter twice weekly who cannot not even say "Mum."

In its postmodern way, the novel provides, through the several lives and fortunes of its characters, the multiple possibilities for England after the death of Jack Dodds. Vince Pritchett, who lost his parents in June of 1944 during the bombing of London and was subsequently adopted by Jack and Amy, has moved the culture from its reliance on meat to motors: rather than follow Jack's trade, he sells used cars for a living. He pays his respects to Jack, ironically driving a Mercedes, a German car, on this errand to deliver Jack's ashes to the sea. More importantly, Vince, after years of bitterness and resentment, can pay tribute to Jack by scattering some of his ashes at Wick's Farm. Without Jack, Vince, one of the orphans of the war, will keep fighting the world. Bitter over his lot in life, Vince constantly grouses about the "Ayrabs," whom he used to shoot in Aden but whom he now serves, selling them his used cars – and his daughter – for the right price.

At the end of the century, Vic Tucker, the undertaker, another of the novel's characters, is "looking the best of [them] all, by a long chalk" (p. 74). His family is intact, and his sons are going to follow him in the trade. He directs the show, acting the part of a secular "vicar" as he "tucks" up the casualties of the century, one by one, into their grave, giving them a decent funeral. Lenny "Gunner" Tate, yet another character, is probably going to be the next to die, and, like Willy Chapman, will soon be history. Indeed, early in the day of their group errand, Lenny climbs the hill to the naval memorial in Chatham – on Vic's recommendation – nearly bringing on a heart attack. Lenny's home-life is in ruins. His daughter, Sally, became pregnant by Vince and is now married to a criminal. She is a reincarnation of the estranged daughters to be found throughout Swift's fiction. On the journey, Lenny takes out his entire life's frustrations on Vince, tauntingly calling him "Big Boy," "toe-rag," and "pillock," and even challenging him to a fight. But Lenny is really beating up himself: he feels guilty for demanding that Sally have an abortion. The faithless "Gunner" Tate does not have a prayer, yet he suggests that they stop by Canterbury Cathedral anyway, for Jack's sake – but perhaps more for his own.

By far the most important character on the journey is "Lucky" Ray Johnson. The relationship between Ray and Jack most fully suggests the intimate link between England and Britain. Although they grew up only blocks apart, Jack, who is a "big bloke" (p. 4), and Ray, "a small feller" (p. 87), never met until they served together in North Africa; thereafter they become inseparable. During that first meeting, Jack shows Ray a picture of Amy, and Ray falls in love with her. Later, he even has a 14-week affair with her, driving her twice a week in his camper to see her institutionalized daughter June.

Lying in St Thomas's hospital, Jack confesses to Ray that he took out a loan five years ago to save the shop and that he has a debt of £20,000 that has now come due. In *The Canterbury Tales*, the sick seek aid through the intervention of a saint; in *Last Orders*, Jack turns to Ray for help. Ray is a gambler, who has every race-track in England memorized. With £1,000 borrowed from Vince, Jack asks "Lucky" to pick a winner, cover the loan, and save Amy a knock on the door. Ray puts all the money on a long shot, *Miracle Worker*, at thirty-three to one. By the time the horse wins, however, Jack has already died. In Africa, Ray once saved Jack's life; now, Jack's death may save Ray's. With Jack gone, Ray has some ready cash and the unique opportunity to marry Amy, the only woman he has ever loved. He plans a honeymoon to Australia where he can visit his daughter, Susie, and maybe even see his grandchildren, if he has any.

Randall Stevenson in 1993 worried that the loss of empire threatens British literature by robbing it of the opportunity to encounter unfamiliar subjects, settings, and characters. But Stevenson assumes, with the end of empire, that its citizens will, like Willy Chapman, simply sit back and die. Ray's story suggests another possibility. He is "a little ray of hope" (p. 284), as Amy calls him, for England. After properly mourning Jack, Ray is free to travel; he can visit the former colonies and dominions not as soldier, conqueror, or oppressor, but as father, grandfather, husband, and mate. He has stories to tell, and, at the end of his life, he has a chance to achieve genuine happiness and the prospect of future generations. If, then, as a rule, Swift's novels offer little promise for "middle class" English culture and English literature as it moves "towards 2000," we should always keep in mind the last of Ray's Rules for gamblers: "You can blow all the rules if you're Lucky" (p. 202).

References and Further Reading

Crane, John Kenny (1988) "Interview with Graham Swift," *Cimarron Review*, 84: 7–15.

DeCoste, Damon Marcel (2002) "Question and apocalypse: the endlessness of *Historia* in Graham Swift's *Waterland*," *Contemporary Literature*, 43/2: 377–99.

Higdon, David Leon (1991) "Double closures in postmodern British fiction: the example of Graham Swift," *Critical Survey*, 3: 88–95.

Hutcheon, Linda (1988) *A Poetics of Postmodernism: History, Theory, Fiction*. New York and London: Routledge.

Janik, Del Ivan (1995) "No end of history: evidence from the contemporary English novel," *Twentieth Century Literature*, 41/2: 160–89.

Kaczvinsky, Donald P. (1998) "'For one thing, there are the gaps': history in Graham Swift's *Shuttlecock*," *Critique*, 40/1: 3–14.

Kermode, Frank (1966) *The Sense of an Ending: Studies in the Theory of Fiction*. New York: Oxford University Press.

Lyotard, Jean-François (1984) *The Postmodern Condition: A Report on Knowledge*, trans. Geoff Bennington and Brian Massumi. Minneapolis: University of Minnesota Press.

McGuigan, Jim (2003) "Cultural change," in Jonathan Hollowell (ed.) *Britain Since 1945*. Malden, MA: Blackwell.

Osuna, Juan Jesús Aguilar (1999) "Graham Swift's *Waterland*: the pessimistic end of history, or the optimistic reclamation of (hi)story/-ies?," *Revista Canaria de Estudios Ingleses*, 38: 183–94.

Schad, John (1992) "The end of the end of history: Graham Swift's *Waterland*." *Modern Fiction Studies*, 38/4: 911–25.

Swift, Graham (1985a) [1980] *The Sweet-Shop Owner*. New York: Washington Square Press.

——(1985b) [1983] *Waterland*. New York: Washington Square Press.

——(1986) [1982] *Learning to Swim and Other Stories*. New York: Washington Square Press.

——(1988) *Out of this World*. New York: Poseidon.

——(1991) [1981] *Shuttlecock*. New York: Poseidon.

——(1993) [1992] *Ever After*. New York: Vintage.

——(1997) [1996] *Last Orders*. New York: Vintage.

——(2003) *The Light of Day*. New York: Alfred A. Knopf.

Stevenson, Randall (1993) *A Reader's Guide to the Twentieth Century Novel in Britain*. Lexington: University Press of Kentucky.

Wheeler, Wendy (1999) "Melancholic modernity and contemporary grief: the novels of Graham Swift," in Roger Luckhurst and Peter Marks (eds.) *Literature and the Contemporary: Fictions and Theories of the Present*. Harlow: Longman.

40

The Scottish New Wave

David Goldie

Scotland is a country with a long and sometime troubled history of Reformations and literary renaissances. As the inhabitants since 1707 of a nation without statehood, the Scots have, like the stateless Irish of a century or more ago, often looked to their writers for a strong, independent cultural ideal that will compensate for the absence of a clearly defined political identity. Until recent times, the most celebrated attempt to generate a reborn Scottish identity through literature was that made by the poets and novelists grouped around Hugh MacDiarmid; it flourished in the years before the Second World War but withered in the postwar settlement. The last quarter of the twentieth century, and the early years of the new millennium, however, have seen the emergence of a new, confident Scottish voice – or more accurately, a range of Scottish voices – in a revivified and re-orientated national literature (Carruthers 2004). This is a literature that has a strong poetry and a cutting theatrical and cinematic edge, but its most noted and sustained component is the short story and the novel. An unprecedented number of writers of literary and genre fiction, from Janice Galloway, Alasdair Gray, James Kelman, and Andrew O'Hagan to Iain Banks, Ian Rankin, Irvine Welsh, and Alan Warner, have in recent years risen to national and international acclaim. All have placed Scottish life firmly at the center of their work and have turned a literature that had, under the uneasy political and social conditions of the third quarter of the century, often been characterized by defeat and resignation into one that has become more notable for its imaginative boldness, the confidence of its voice, and its freedom with formal experiment. The continuing strength of this new wave can be found in range and diversity of contemporary work, such as Ali Smith's *Hotel World* (2001), which employs an experimental poetic prose to inter-weave the thoughts of five women – one of them dead – into a compassionate meditation of love and loss; or Alan Warner's *The Man Who Walks* (2002), in which the encounter of postmodernity with the highland landscape and history is rendered with an outrageous, Pynchonesque surrealism; or Andrew O'Hagan's sophisticated *Personality* (2003), which mingles intimate personal and family memory with the public discourses of showbiz and stardom in its monologues and lyrical narrative fragments.

It is always a little arbitrary to attempt to locate the point at which movements begin, but in the case of the Scottish novel's new wave most commentators agree on the seminal importance of two writers: Alasdair Gray and James Kelman. In particular, Alasdair Gray's novel *Lanark* (1981) is often cited by critics and other Scottish novelists (Galloway 2002) as the work that widened the doors of perception and encouraged new types of Scottish fiction to come into being; he detonated, as Gavin Wallace has put it, "a cultural time-bomb which had been ticking away patiently for years" (Wallace and Stevenson 1993: 4). *Lanark* is a large, ambitious work that combines elements of classical epic, *Bildungsroman* and *Künstlerroman*, with science fiction fantasy and political allegory. It comprises four books, printed out of chronological order, which tell two related life stories. The first, told in a largely realistic fashion, is that of Duncan Thaw, a young man growing up in a suburb of Glasgow's East End. Thaw bears a similar relation to Alasdair Gray as Stephen Dedalus does to James Joyce; that is to say, he offers a semi-autobiographical portrait of the artist as a young man, tormented by adolescent sexual anxiety and a yearning for aesthetic affirmation in a context of religious and national-political uncertainty. This narrative, which takes up half the novel, provides an often beautifully wrought account of adolescent yearning and despair alongside a meditation on thwarted artistic aspiration. It is poised within a second story, a science fiction fantasia in which a self-named character of obscure origin, Lanark, struggles to come to terms with a nightmare city, Unthank, and the sinister Institute that underlies it. The world of Unthank is one in which constants such as time and the stability of human form do not operate; it functions according to a kind of dream logic with an economy whose currency is energy and a politics which is governed in the interests of a cartel of multinational companies known collectively as the Creature. Unthank is clearly a phantasmagoric rendering of the other narrative's Glasgow, and Lanark a reincarnated, or transmigrated, version of the artist Thaw. Ironically, the mundane world that Thaw has tried to encompass in art has been transformed into something far more uncanny than his imaginings. The prevailing metaphors of Glasgow's sociopolitical life, metaphors of exploitation and consumption, are actualized in Unthank's ruinous political ecology, which uses human bodies as the staple sources of food and energy. The old world's psychological states are hypostatized into fantastic physiological conditions in the new; people in this world, for example, do not secrete anxiety in neurosis but as scaly exoskeletons of dragonhide.

Gray's novel is, in some ways, a typical example of the Scottish fiction of the 1960s and 1970s: a fiction haunted, as Liam McIlvanney has noted, "by the figure of the failed artist" (McIlvanney 2002: 182). Thaw and Lanark are both dreamers whose imaginative impracticality unsuits them for the social and political worlds in which they find themselves. What sets *Lanark* apart from other novels of this type, such as Archie Hind's *The Dear Green Place* (1966) and George Friel's *Mr Alfred M.A.* (1972), however, is the brio and the imagination with which it treats these familiar themes of artistic failure and political impotence. Where other novels of this kind offer physical escape as the only alternative to the defeat of creativity, Gray proposes a solution of imaginative re-engagement and transformation. Unlike Joyce, who had to fly the constraining nets of Ireland before he could be free to write, Gray showed Scottish readers and writers the imaginative possibilities of staying put. The implicit argument of this book, and the ones that followed it, is that, invested with sufficient imaginative power, the material of ordinary Scottish life, even of the failure of its artistic aspirations, can become the proper ground for a sophisticated and challenging literature.

It is important to realize just how important such a recognition was in Scotland in the late 1970s, an era in which it was widely felt that writers could "do no more than reflect a way of life that is lived more intensely and more urgently elsewhere" (Massie 1982: xxii). In locating such an intensity and urgency in Scotland Gray helped put the country, imaginatively speaking, back on the world's literary map. The significance of this act of cultural mapping is a governing theme of *Lanark*, and is instantiated in one of the novel's key – and most often quoted – exchanges:

> "Glasgow is a magnificent city," said McAlpin. "Why do we hardly ever notice that?" "Because nobody imagines living here," said Thaw. . . . "think of Florence, Paris, London, New York. Nobody visiting them for the first time is a stranger because he's already visited them in paintings, novels, history books and films. But if a city hasn't been used by an artist not even the inhabitants live there imaginatively. What is Glasgow to most of us? A house, a place we work, a football park or golf course, some pubs and connecting streets. That's all. No, I'm wrong, there's also the cinema and library. And when our imagination needs exercise we use these to visit London, Paris, Rome under the Caesars, the American West at the turn of the century, anywhere but here and now. Imaginatively Glasgow exists as a music-hall song and a few bad novels. That's all we've given to the world outside. It's all we've given to ourselves." (Gray 1982: 243)

There are perhaps intimations of authorial irony here, comparable to those that color our understanding of Stephen Dedalus's declarations of artistic intent towards the end of Joyce's *Portrait*. After all, Thaw dies in despair, having failed in the attempt to construct his perfect work of art. But for all its modernist hubris, the claim that Gray makes through Thaw is one that has been largely fulfilled by his novel. Thaw fails in his dream of creating "a modern Divine Comedy with illustrations in the style of William Blake" (1982: 204), but Gray doesn't – for this is, in fact, a fairly apt description of the novel that Gray, as a writer and illustrator, has shaped around Thaw's inadequacies. Gray, paradoxically, has made an imaginative triumph from an all-too familiar tale of artistic failure. In so doing, he points the way to a reimagined Scotland, a place in which culture is generated rather than merely reflected or consumed.

Having taken some twenty years to complete *Lanark*, Gray followed it up rapidly with a number of works that have built upon that first novel's imaginative foundations. The most noteworthy are *1982 Janine* (1984) and *Poor Things* (1992), the latter a historical novel that amalgamates elements of *Frankenstein, Pygmalion, Trilby*, and *The Strange Case of Dr Jekyll and Mr Hyde* into the mutually-contradictory accounts of two unreliable narrators and – in a typical Gray touch – a series of misleading notes, maps, and illustrations contributed by the author. *1982 Janine* follows *Lanark* in featuring a central character who is out of his depth in the modern world, and whose compensatory fantasies – in this case of a troubling pornographic nature – occupy much of the narrative. Taking the playful textual tricks and allusiveness of *Lanark* further, however, the novel redeems its central character, Jock McLeish, through a virtuoso formal experiment, presenting his redemptive long night of the soul in a thematic and typographical extravaganza. Whole pages of the novel's eleventh chapter look like the *parole in libertà* experiments of Futurism, but here they are put to a mimetic purpose in constructing a threatening, interior "ministry of voices" that McLeish must exorcise before he can narrate himself back into meaningful being in the book's twelfth chapter with the retelling of his life story: "the story of *how I went wrong*" (1985: 191).

James Kelman has played a similarly significant and complementary role in developing this sense of cultural self-confidence and encouragement to literary innovation through his attempts to focus the modern Scottish novel on the intricate particulars of contemporary Scottish life. Kelman's work is founded in a belief that for a working-class writer such as himself "there is a massive KEEP OUT sign hoisted above every area of literature" (Kelman 2002: 68). In his novels, which include *The Busconductor Hines* (1984), *A Chancer* (1985), *A Disaffection* (1989) and the Booker Prize-winning *How Late it Was, How Late* (1994), he has made it his business to knock down that sign of exclusion, to document the lives of characters living outside the traditional purviews of literary writing and reveal their complex, conflicted subjectivities. His achievement, and it is a considerable one, has been to invest those who have conventionally occupied a negligible margin with full seriousness and dignity, and allow them to speak to us in their own voices. The reader who might in normal life ignore or overlook characters like Kelman's bus worker Rab Hines, small-time gambler Tammas, disaffected teacher Patrick Doyle, and blind benefits claimant Sammy Samuels is brought into an intimacy, and indeed a society, with them, and comes, through a prolonged exposure to their world and thought, to comprehend the repetitious, frustrated, alienated condition in which they live.

An important part in the construction of this socialized intimacy is Kelman's use of demotic speech. Kelman, like many earlier Scottish writers, strives for verisimilitude by rendering direct speech in dialect. But where previously writers tended to enclose that vernacular speech within a narrative of standard English, Kelman uses dialect forms throughout. For Kelman this is a gesture against the conventional workings of power, the power that seeks to circumscribe experience and speech by authorizing only its more privileged forms. The result is a narrative style that does not seek to raise narrator over character, to allow one to dominate the speech of the other, but which instead attempts to merge the two voices: to construct a linguistic and perhaps political solidarity through the extensive use of the free indirect voice. This applies to dialect form and to lexical choice; Kelman's narrators not only speak the same language as his characters, they also share with them the use of the profanities that Kelman considers fundamental constituents of ordinary speech:

> So what Sammy was feeling was the opposite of the opposite, in other words he fucking was hemmed in man know what I'm saying, hemmed in; and it was gony get worse, afore it got better; that was a certainty, it was gony get worse. (Kelman 1994: 133)

Kelman has stated that he sees "the distinction between dialogue and narrative as a summation of the political system" (2002: 40), an argument that is given fictional form in *A Disaffection* when Patrick Doyle attempts to demystify his authority over a class of 13- and 14-year-old pupils:

> Okay. What time is it now? Patrick looked at his watch. He wanted to get out and away. He needed to think things out. He opened the pages of the book and closed them at once. He smiled at the class: they were that fucking wee! I'm so much bigger than you, he said, these are my terms. My terms are the ones that enclose yous. Yous are all enclosed. But yous all know that already! I can tell it just by looking at your faces, your faces, telling these things to me. It's quite straightforward when you come to think about it. Here you have me. Here you have you. Two sentences. One sentence is needed for you and one sentence is needed for me and you can wrap them all up together if you want to so that what you have in this one sentence is both you and me, us being in it the gether. (Kelman 1989: 26)

It is this desire to create a subversive commonality, an anti-authoritarian sense of "being in it the gether" quite different from the conventional organization of political socialism, that has driven Kelman's work and that has made him, like Gray, an important influence on a younger generation of Scottish novelists whose books began to appear in the 1990s, among them Irvine Welsh, Alan Warner, Duncan McLean, and Des Dillon. These writers have all taken on board the new freedoms with demotic speech and the commitment to keep faith with working-class experience expounded by Kelman. They have also taken on some of his prickliness and his forceful, sometimes incoherent, advocacy of a kind of vague leftism without commit-ment, writing out of a red-mist Nietzschean *ressentiment* that takes the place of a thoroughgoing politics or social vision. Kelman has stated a belief that "genuine creativity is by its nature subversive," that "good art can scarcely be other than dissident" (2002: 363–4). Rather like the controversial conceptual artists of the Britart movement, these writers have taken that subversive attitude as their own and have deliberately pushed at the overlapping boundaries of dissidence and art, creating work – if not art – that offers a calculated affront to the expectations of conventional readers.

One of the principal dissident voices in the Scottish novel of the 1990s was Duncan McLean, a writer from the rural Northeast who described his work as an attempt to "do for the country what Kelman had done for Glasgow" (March 2002: 41). The influential British style magazine *The Face* described McLean's collection of disturbing contemporary short stories, *Bucket of Tongues* (1992), as "the Scottish Tourist Board's worst nightmare" (McLean 1994: back cover). His subsequent novels, *Blackden* (1994) and *Bunker Man* (1995), offered further discomfort for the heritage industry in their depictions of a countryside devoid of natural and social consolation. *Bunker Man* in particular is a deeply troubling account of aggressive delusion and sexual violence in a small-town Scottish setting. Here the latent paranoia and frustration of Kelman's work is given explicit physical form, culminating in a willfully shocking ending, in which the central character Rob Catto arranges for the violent rape of his wife by a shadowy *Doppelgänger*, the Bunker Man, whom he then murders with a meat cleaver.

McLean's use of extreme violence as a metaphor for, and expression of, social alienation is shared with perhaps the most celibrated *enfant terrible* of the Scottish new wave, Irvine Welsh. Welsh's novels contain a great deal of explicit and shocking violence, and a determination to explore scenes of degradation and misery. If Kelman can be thought of as a Zola, then Welsh is a Céline or a Genet who tests his readers' hope by dragging it through the worst he has seen and can imagine – as instanced, for example, in his novella "A smart cunt" (1994):

> When we get to Veitchy's place Denise and Penman are there. They're all quite high, through snorting coke. Ronnie can go and get fucked. No way we would consider wasting coke on him. He'd have to sleep his way through this gig. Veitchy helps me to put him on the couch, and he just crashes out unconscious. Denise puckers his lips, – My my my, Brian's brought us a trophy. Is that what Ronnie is, Brian, our ain wee trophy?
>
> – Yeah, that's it, I say, catching Penman's eye. He chops out a line for me and I go down on it like it was a fanny that pished Becks. Suddenly, everything's better.
>
> – What have we here? Denise has unzipped Ronnie's flies and taken his floppy dick out. It looks pretty repulsive, bouncing around on his thighs like a broken jack-in-the-box.
>
> Veitchy laughs loudly, – Ha ha ha ha ha ha perr Ronnie ha ha ha ha, no real. Denise yir some cunt so ye are ha ha ha ha.
>
> – Now that's a whopper, Denise pouts with a saucy wink, – but it'll be even bigger erect. Let's see if ah kin breathe some life into poor old Ronnie.
>
> He starts sucking on Ronnie's cock. Veitchy and I check Ron's face for signs of recognition, signs of enjoyment, but it seems dead to me. Veitchy then produces a magic marker and draws glasses and a Hitler moustache on Ronnie's coupon. (Welsh 1995: 218–19)

Though it is redeemed, perhaps, by the vivid similes, Welsh's prose offers a relentlessly hopeless vision, suggesting not the absence of hope but its negation. This is apparent again in his *Marabout Stork Nightmares* (1995), a novel somewhat akin to Gray's *1982 Janine* in its presentation of a fantasy world constructed by an individual (in a typographically experimental form reminiscent of Gray) in the attempt to escape a troubled personal history. Welsh's protagonist, Roy Strang, uses his imagination as a jungle in whose thickets he can hide from and deny painful memories of childhood sexual abuse and his subsequent sexual violence toward others, particularly to Kirsty, a girl in whose gang-rape he has participated. But while Gray opens the door far enough for redemption to be glimpsed, Welsh slams it firmly shut. When the novel ends Roy is not redeemed but is instead mutilated and murdered in a lurid authorial revenge fantasy: dying, suffocated by his own severed penis, at the hands of the woman he has raped.

This uncompromising, confrontational hyperrealism is what underpins Welsh's most successful novel, *Trainspotting* (1993), an account of the lives, and sometimes deaths, of a group of Edinburgh drug and alcohol addicts. Where Kelman has, for the most part, relied on the relentless monotony of the free indirect monologue to persuade the reader of the awfulness of the situation he describes, Welsh in *Trainspotting* employs a welter of voices, a series of overlapping monologic fragments, that amount to the same thing, providing a witty and intelligent, but also often macabre and violent, aggregation of all the reasons for despairing of being brought up in a modern Scottish housing scheme. Welsh's Mark Renton, the pivotal character around whom most of the novel's fragments revolve, is more intelligent and articulate than Kelman's antiheros. He is a university dropout who can, when he wants, turn the politics of dialogue to his own ends, code-switching like a virtuoso between the cynical patter of the streets and an Anglicized English that gets him off the hook in his brushes with authority. He is a capable manipulator and is therefore more than merely a passive victim like the sympathetic Spud or the inarticulate Second Prize. It is Renton's intelligence and potential redeeming qualities that make his hopelessness, his dependency on hard drugs and bad company, the more striking. His refusal to better himself in the conventional way is one of the most intriguing aspects of this insightful and powerful novel. Is his refusal to get out when he can, his refusal to "sell out" on a subculture he knows is inimical and destructive of hope, simply the wilfulness of extended adolescence, a form of *nostalgie de la boue*? Or is he, after all, for all his independent qualities and rebellious intelligence, a victim of his upbringing just as much as Spud or the psychopathic Begbie or monstrous Sick Boy (an institutionalized life sentencer incapable of living in the normal world outside the prison walls)? Renton does eventually escape at the end of *Trainspotting*, ripping off his friends in a drug deal and absconding to Amsterdam. The reader's feeling that this is in fact only a temporary separation, however, is confirmed by Renton's reappearance in the scheme in *Porno* (2002).

Welsh's fiction is subtle and ambiguous because it hovers between extreme rage at the dependency culture he describes and a desire to celebrate the saving graces of wit, humor, and humanity it nevertheless occasionally inspires. He explores a world at once similar to, but fundamentally different from that of Gray and Kelman. The crisis of identity that much of their fiction explores is a recognizably modernist one, in which anxiety is expressed as the threat to the integral subject posed by the destabilizing forces of modernity. As writers Gray and Kelman can still derive consolation from the humanist tradition in which this contest has been rehearsed for centuries; both are highly self-conscious about their literary antecedents. Welsh, however, writes out of a more self-consciously postmodern sensibility, which is less inclined to take personal identity as the gift threatened by circumstance and more disposed to see it as a contingent position constructed *from* circumstance. His characters are merely desperate people whose formative circumstances are particularly bad, people divorced from literary and cultural history whose only reference points are the songs and football matches that popular culture puts in their way. The life that they make for themselves is enlivened by its moments of linguistic or humorous invention and its thrills, but is ultimately limited by the extreme poverty of the resources out of which it is made.

This is an attitude also explored in the novels of Alan Warner, particularly in his brilliant debut novel *Morvern Callar* (1995). As writers like Kelman and Welsh meet the inequities of modern life with something like rage, Warner responds in *Morvern Callar* with a more coolly measured rejection. His title character moves through the novel meeting the accidents of circumstance, including the recent suicide of her boyfriend, with an affectless self-assurance, contenting herself with the unreflexive sensual pleasures of grooming and dressing, sunbathing and dancing, and getting lost in the obsessively-listed music tracks that play through the headphones of her Walkman. It would be a mistake to think of her as alienated, for she offers little sense of an awareness of lack or consciousness of a distance from authentic being. Rather she is coolly adaptive, feeling little nostalgia for what she leaves behind and making a complete, if wholly solipsistic, life out of what little comes her way.

Welsh and Warner have shown the different ways in which a younger disaffected generation have opted out; theirs is a disintegrative vision that is vital and imaginative but that offers few prospects of social hope. For a reintegrative vision, the opting back in that comes after the wreck of hope, it is necessary to look elsewhere. One place in which it can be found is Janice Galloway's *The Trick is to Keep Breathing* (1989). This novel has some surface similarities with *Morvern Callar*. Both novels focus on a female character coming to terms with a sense of anomie precipitated by the recent death of a lover, but where Warner allows his character a fairly easy opt out, Galloway's character, Joy Stone, has the more difficult task of re-establishing connection. Broken down by the oppressive, often male, discourses of work, social expectation, and psychiatry she must recover a sense of herself and make a new social connection based on a rejection of these discourses. The novel does not shirk the difficulties this involves, and is an often painful read; but in achieving a situation in which Joy can forgive rather than condemn, Galloway points the Scottish novel toward a more Forsterian, connective ideal. This sophisticated feminism, a feminism in which Galloway has been followed by Ali Smith and, to some extent, A. L. Kennedy, has a connective rather than a disjunctive purpose, aiming not merely to expose patriarchy but to insist on the possibility of a humane, interconnected culture beyond its narrowing confines.

This subtle interrogation of patriarchy and power is carried on in Andrew O'Hagan's *Our Fathers* (1999). At first glance this seems a rather conventional story, in which a young man, Jamie Bawn, must come to terms with and grow past the patriarchal forces that have shaped him. The principal symbol of this patriarchy is his biological father, Robert, a hopeless alcoholic cast in a familiar tradition of west-of-Scotland male chauvinism and familial abuse. It is fairly simple for the young Jamie to recognize and reject such a blatantly oppressive patriarchy. He moves from his parental home to that of his grandparents, exchanging the brutality of his father for the benevolent patronage of his grandfather, Hugh Bawn, a lifetime socialist and pioneering builder of modernist municipal housing. As the novel progresses, however, and as Jamie Bawn returns as an adult to comfort his dying grandfather, this schematic polarity unravels. The flaws in the grandfather's idealism become apparent. In his single-minded pursuit of the political and social ideal of cheap municipal housing, Hugh Bawn has cut corners and created high-rise buildings and whole estates – "street after modern street, named for the receding glory of dead socialists" (O'Hagan 1999: 45) – which have rapidly become unfit for habitation. Rapt in a grand utopian dream, he has also trodden down the modest and tender imaginative life of his wife, Margaret, and has undermined the self-esteem of his son. His earnest desire to do good, and blind self-belief in the rightness of his actions, have resulted in a subtle steady oppression that has been felt down two generations. The suggestion that the novel makes is that the resolution of such oppression – an oppression all the more subtle for being unintended – does not lie in judgment but in forgiveness: a forgiveness akin to the resolution, "I will be gentle. I will be kind," that marks the end of Jock McLeish's struggle in *1982 Janine* or the human voice of Joy Stone whispering, "I forgive you," which closes Galloway's *The Trick is to Keep Breathing*. Jamie learns that he cannot break free by repudiating or rejecting his background, but rather by coming to a sympathetic understanding of its complexities. "I came home to Ayrshire," he writes, "thinking I would take a stand against Hugh's delusions. But that is not what happened. I stood beside him, and listened to his life, and I held his hand, and I finally grew up" (O'Hagan 1999: 221).

O'Hagan's unsentimental tenderness offers an alternative to Welsh's combativeness; his fiction provides subtle coloring and shadings of grey to set against Kelman's harsh blacks and whites. Kelman's fiction offers a forceful, almost visceral account of the tyranny of power as it is experienced by the powerless, but it does not have the tools to comprehend the workings of that power and end its abuses. In the world of his fiction social process is as opaque to those on whom it operates as it is in the work of Kafka or Beckett. This makes his works powerful aftershocks of the existential quakes of the mid-century, but it also robs them of crucial contextual detail and diminishes their impact as contemporary documents. Oppression is rarely documented in detail in Kelman; it is more often evoked abstractly, a tendency epitomized in the contextless testimonies of abuse in his *Translated Accounts* (2001). For Kelman's characters and narrators, political and social oppression is keenly felt but is rarely understood. O'Hagan, on the other hand, has a nuanced understanding of how what might seem to be the repressive monolith of power is actually constructed by the individual work of human hands. Some of these may mean ill, but some may mean well; power is as much about unintended consequences as it is a sinister racket perpetrated on its helpless victims by the hidden agencies of business or the state.

O'Hagan also offers a different take on the language problems raised by Kelman and his followers. O'Hagan's approach to the subject comes in the form of a scene often found in the traditional Scottish novel, the confrontation of teacher and pupil on the issue of the appropriate use of the Scottish language. In its common form this is a variation on a theme by Joyce, an adaptation of the scene in Joyce's *Portrait* in which Stephen Dedalus talks with the dean of studies and is mistakenly shamed into subordinating his own language to that of his English educator. In O'Hagan's version, however, the usual contrast between native Scots-speaker and English-speaking teacher is reversed. The children in Jamie Bawn's class are oppressed not by an English voice, but the insistent hectoring Scottish tones of Mr Buie. "Buie," we are told, "believed in a grand commonness: he spoke of real people; he spoke of oppression. We had never known anyone like that before. He wanted us to know that the way we spoke was a political matter" (p. 28). Like Hugh Bawn, Buie is a utopianist whose well-meaning commitment to a single idea results in unintended tyranny; his narrow interpretation of Scots linguistic freedom entails the banning of Hugh MacDiarmid's "English poems," the dismissal of all works of Robert Louis Stevenson that are not in "braid Scots," and the branding of Anglo-Scottish authors such as Walter Scott, John Buchan, and Muriel Spark as fascists, swine, and turn-coats. The class is saved from this unrelieved diet of dogma by a supply teacher.

> She spoke of American things. She spoke of Norwegian plays. And next day too she came in with her strangeness. She had gathered something of our class's infatuation with the native voice. "Speech is not all there is," she said. She went to the board and held up a book. "This nation was not always so obsessed with the way it *sounded* on paper. For many years it paid great attention to other things as well. To the way it *thought*. The Scottish Enlightenment shows us that there is more than one way to write Scottish English. *A strong Scots accent of the mind*," she wrote. "Discuss."
>
> Buie came in before the end of the lesson. He listened a moment. His face was grey. He dismissed the girl with the bangled wrists. He asked me to wipe the board of words.
>
> "That is my blackboard," he said. "It belongs to me."
>
> And he told me to leave not a trace of her chalk. "A very good example," he said, "of the English propaganda." (O'Hagan 1999: 29–30)

The notion of a "strong Scots accent of the mind" comes from Robert Louis Stevenson, but in the mouth of this female teacher it becomes the token of a new dispensation, a gentle rejection of the stridencies of a Scottish culture defined through conflict and opposition to its English other.

The Scottish new wave novel grew out of a widespread feeling of exclusion, a trepidation about Scotland's political and economic status and a pained awareness of a Scottish cultural cringe in the face of English and international culture. As might be expected, then, much of its initial impulse was reactive, consisting of a rejection of English models and a compensating valorization of the native culture and language. The result, set in motion by the crucial visionary and revisionary work of Gray and Kelman, was a liberating, uninhibited literature marked by a willingness to experiment and an urgent desire to root itself in a previously underexplored experience. But it was also a literature that took little account of female experience and of the middle class, that tended to reduce political and social complexity to a vague, gestural leftism or a despairing pessimism, and that rarely dwelt on the positive aspects of the British culture that has continued to shape so much of Scottish life.

But this has begun to change. At the beginning of their travels in France in *Foreign Parts* (1994) Janice Galloway's characters Cassie and Rona encounter an unfamiliar word on an advertising hoarding: "BRICOLAGE." This word, denoting a principle of constructing functional objects and social practices from the fragments that come to hand becomes, as Glenda Norquay has noted (Christianson and Lumsden 2000: 131–43), the sign under which their journey of mutual discovery proceeds and the novel itself operates. In one regard, the narrative and typographical fragmentation of the novel implies a deconstructive intent: a correlative of the characters' isolation and alienation; but in another sense it signals a commitment to imaginative reconstruction: a determination to make over the fragments of existing discourse into a newer, more integrative whole. In finding each other through the fragments of their shared experience, Rona and Cassie have by the novel's end constructed for themselves an identity and a relationship that goes against convention but that suits the particular needs of both. They have discovered that they need not be defined by the discourses of the old world but can rather, as bricoleurs, make the most of the possibilities available to them to construct a habitable world out of what they find.

One of the most welcome developments of the later work of the Scottish new wave has been in taking this spirit on board and making Scottish writing less fixated on a single idea of Scottish culture: not to linger on the failures, real or imagined, of a historical culture, or to limit expression to one authentic voice, but to look outward and explore the imaginative possibilities of making a culture out of a wider range of literary and linguistic materials. This takes it beyond the despair of Kelman and the nihilism of Welsh; and though it is not quite the literature of the socialist cooperative republic once hoped for by Alasdair Gray, it is nevertheless a worthwhile response to his injunction to "work as if you lived in the early days of a better nation."

References and Further Reading

Baker, Stephen (2000) *The Fiction of Postmodernity.* Edinburgh: Edinburgh University Press.

Bernstein, Stephen (1999) *Alasdair Gray.* Lewisburg, PA: Bucknell University Press.

Carruthers, Gerard (forthcoming) "Second renaissance: Scottish literature since 1968," in Laura Marcus and Peter Nicholls (eds.) *The Cambridge History of Twentieth-Century Literature.* Cambridge: Cambridge University Press.

Carruthers, Gerard, Goldie, David, and Renfrew, Alastair (eds.) (forthcoming) *Beyond Scotland: Scottish Literature in the Twentieth*

Century. New York and Amsterdam: Rodopi.

Christianson, Aileen and Lumsden, Alison (eds.) (2000) *Contemporary Scottish Women Writers.* Edinburgh: Edinburgh University Press.

Craig, Cairns (1999) *The Modern Scottish Novel: Narrative and the National Imagination.* Edinburgh: Edinburgh University Press.

Galloway, Janice (1991) [1989] *The Trick is to Keep Breathing.* London: Minerva.

——(1995) [1994] *Foreign Parts.* London: Vintage.

——(2002) "Rereadings: Glasgow belongs to us," *The Guardian,* Review section, October 12.

Gifford, Douglas and McMillan, Dorothy (eds.) (1997) *A History of Scottish Women's Writing.* Edinburgh: Edinburgh University Press.

Gray, Alasdair (1982) [1981] *Lanark: A Life in Four Books.* London: Granada.

——(1985) [1984] *1982 Janine.* Harmondsworth: Penguin.

——(1992) *Poor Things.* London: Bloomsbury.

Kelman, James (1989) *A Disaffection.* London: Secker and Warburg.

——(1994) *How Late It Was, How Late.* London: Secker and Warburg.

——(2002) *'And the Judges Said...': Essays.* London: Secker and Warburg.

MacDougall, Carl (2001) *Painting the Forth Bridge: A Search for Scottish Identity.* London: Aurum.

March, Cristie L. (2002) *Rewriting Scotland: Welsh, McLean, Warner, Banks, Galloway, and Kennedy.* Manchester and New York: Manchester University Press.

Massie, Allan (1982) Introduction, to Edwin Muir, *Scott and Scotland: The Predicament of the Scottish Writer.* Edinburgh: Polygon.

McIlvanney, Liam (2002) "The politics of narrative in the post-war Scottish novel," in Zachary Leader (ed.) *On Modern British Fiction.* Oxford: Oxford University Press.

McLean, Duncan (1994) [1992] *Bucket of Tongues.* London: Minerva.

O'Hagan, Andrew (1999) *Our Fathers.* London: Faber and Faber.

Wallace, Gavin and Stevenson, Randall (eds.) (1993) *The Scottish Novel since the Seventies: New Visions, Old Dreams.* Edinburgh: Edinburgh University Press.

Welsh, Irvine (1995) [1994] *The Acid House.* London: Vintage.

41

A. S. Byatt's
Possession: A Romance

Lynn Wells

A reviewer of A. S. Byatt's novel, *A Whistling Woman*, quipped that "Fans of [her] fiction can be divided into two groups: Those who cannot understand her novels and those who lie" (Charles 2002: 1). Even *Possession*, with its Booker Prize-winning success, huge international sales, and adaptation into a Hollywood film, has been singled out by the same reviewer as "demanding" (p. 1), and he is not alone in his assessment of Byatt's most widely known novel as densely literary and difficult to read. For example, an early review of the novel proclaimed that "*Possession* falls with a leaden thump as a romance; it succeeds as an exposition of the post-doctoral malaise – what happens when a naïve intellectual is swallowed into the bowels of the British Museum Reading Room and starts to live life backwards" (Smith 1990: 29). On the other hand, the *New York Times Book Review* called *Possession* a "gorgeously written novel," a "tour de force that opens every narrative device of English fiction to inspection without, for a moment, ceasing to delight" (Parini 1990: 3). This unusual collusion between the complexity of high art and the allure of popular fiction is only one of many paradoxes generated by the text.

In many respects, *Possession* is the quintessential contemporary novel. The primary setting will be recognizable to most readers: the London of the 1980s, in which traditional British culture is being gradually influenced by such global trends as consumerism and multiculturalism. The main characters, Roland Michell and Maud Bailey, are preoccupied with many of the problems commonly associated with life in the late twentieth century. They suffer, quite self-consciously, from a radically unstable sense of their own identities and lament their inability to regard concepts such as love or creativity without jaded skepticism; they pine for the past, when they believe people "valued themselves" (Byatt 1990: 277) and felt secure in the meaning of the world around them. Many of these anxieties are couched in the terms of what is broadly labeled "literary theory," a diverse field of contemporary intellectual inquiry that deals with identity, ideology, language, and representation in literature and other forms of discourse. Like much of the fiction written in the past few decades in

England and elsewhere, Byatt's novel clearly engages with the thought of contemporary historiographic theorists such as Hayden White, who have examined the relationship between literary and historical narratives, and have found that the presumed line between fiction and fact is a permeable one. By drawing attention to the processes involved in rediscovering the past and then shaping those discoveries into a story, writers of "historiographic metafiction" (Hutcheon 1988: xii) such as Byatt expose the essential constructedness of all historical narratives, even those that make claims to objectivity and verifiability.

Not only does *Possession* have as its central focus the pursuit and interpretation of the past, but it is also a self-consciously literary text. Roland and Maud are academics who study, respectively, the Victorian poets Randolph Henry Ash and Christabel LaMotte; and nearly all the other characters are involved in some way with literary study. All of the main characters are based on one or more author or literary character: Roland has his antecedents in Robert Browning's poem "Childe Roland to the dark tower came" and in the failed intellectual Leonard Bast from E. M. Forster's *Howards End*; Maud recalls Alfred Lord Tennyson's eponymous long poem; Ash bears a close resemblance to Tennyson but more particularly to Robert Browning (who makes an early appearance in the novel in the form of the epigraph from his poem "Mr Sludge, 'the Medium'," which castigates literature as a form of deliberate lying about the past); and Christabel, who has elements of Christina Rossetti, Elizabeth Barrett Browning, and Emily Dickinson, is named after Samuel Taylor Coleridge's mysterious poetic character. This high degree of overt intertextuality contributes to the novel's metafictional and parodic qualities, both of which are hallmarks of postmodern writing.

On the other hand, this very contemporary text is also noticeably traditional, both in its content and form. The novel evinces a deep nostalgia for the seemingly more vibrant world of Ash and LaMotte, who act as superior images of their modern counterparts. Unlike the twentieth-century couple, LaMotte and Ash apparently enjoy a stable sense of their own identities and of the values of their culture, and are curious, creative, and passionate, despite their Victorian ways. Their forbidden love affair, discovered by Roland and Maud a century later, provides much of the novel's seductive popular attraction. *Possession*'s fascination with Victoriana is reflected in Byatt's conscious formal emulation of the nineteenth-century novel within a contemporary framework, a style inaugurated by her fellow English writer John Fowles in *The French Lieutenant's Woman* (1969). In *Passions of the Mind,* Byatt asserts, "Respect for the tradition of the realist novel is apparently a very rooted fact" (1992: 149) in England, and the strong, continuing influence and popularity of nineteenth-century fiction and its imitations (such as Charles Palliser's 1989 novel, *The Quincunx*) contribute to *Possession*'s passéist allure. In addition to her skillful recreation of some of the nineteenth-century novel's characteristic techniques – rounded characters, a *bildungsroman* plot, and multiple coincidences – Byatt masterfully manipulates the conventions of a wide array of literary genres – detective fiction, the Gothic, and even the Western – to keep readers enthralled, despite the text's more challenging elements.

In general, Byatt's fiction holds a special appeal for female readers, since her work deals with the power that stories can have to suggest new possibilities, beyond historical constraints, for women's lives. LaMotte's various tales and poems, reproduced as part of the novel's narration of the past, create imaginative scenarios in which female figures overcome patriarchal restrictions and triumph over repressive males. Yet *Possession*, with its lampooning of contemporary feminist theory and its practitioners, has been criticized for its unfair depiction of current gender relations. The reaction against the novel's apparent conservatism in this regard is directed at the book's conventional romantic ending, in which the icy and independent Maud succumbs to Roland's sexual possession of her (Buxton 1996).

It would seem, then, that *Possession*, for all of its commercial and academic success, is a novel deeply at odds with itself, as evidenced by the often conflicting critical responses to it. One way of approaching this somewhat puzzling text is to study its own internal indicators of how the apparently contradictory elements can be resolved through attentive, interpretive reading. With her epigraph from Nathaniel Hawthorne's Preface to *The House of the Seven Gables*, Byatt goes out of her way to insist that her text is not meant to be a "novel" in the sense associated with the style known as realism, but rather a "romance," as signalled by *Possession*'s subtitle. This non-realistic fictional mode gives the author, Hawthorne says, "a certain latitude" to present "the truth of the human heart . . . under circumstances, to a great extent, of the writer's own choosing or creation" (Byatt 1990: n.p.).

Implicit in Byatt's choice of romance as the dominant mode for her work is a movement towards a more symbolic form of representation. *Possession* abounds with metaphors and symbols, many of which relate in some way to contact with the past and the recovery of lost voices and origins: mesmerism (introduced by the Browning epigraph), spiritual possession, resurrection, ventriloquism, myths and fairy tales, evolution, genetics and paleontology, to name a few. It would be tempting to read this nexus of symbols, all connected with the nineteenth-century scenes, as a sign of the novel's intense nostalgia; yet it is important to bear in mind another significant image pattern, that of the Garden of Eden. Near the end of novel, Maud and Roland assume their place in a long line of Adam and Eve figures in the novel, as the narrator suggests:

> In the morning, the whole world had a strange new smell. It was the smell of the aftermath, a green smell . . . which bore some relation to the smell of bitten apples. It was the smell of death and destruction and it smelled fresh and lively and hopeful. (Byatt 1990: 551)

This passage positions the central characters as the representatives of a contemporary world on the verge of a new beginning, seemingly in direct contrast to the negative images associated with postmodernity to that point.

This renewal of a moribund culture is made possible by a "dialogue," to use another of the book's key motifs, with the thoughts and traditions of earlier times, accessible in the form of written texts. As I have argued elsewhere (Wells 2003), this beneficial contact with the past is related to another important subtext, the notion of the *ricorso* developed in Giambattista Vico's eighteenth-century work on historical theory, *The New Science*, which is mentioned in *Possession's* opening pages. Vico viewed human history as occurring in cycles, or *corsi*, beginning in a state of mythical simplicity in which language and world are completely in tune, and ending in a state of near collapse when language has lost its power of correspondence and society has fallen into barbaric disarray. Disaster is averted only by the *ricorso*, a self-conscious reflection on lost values through the sympathetic reading of ancient texts. Byatt clearly draws on Vico's system to project a fantasy situation in which her rather dystopic postmodern world can reclaim from the past the linguistic, cultural, and personal stability that its citizens lack.

This essay will map out a way of reading *Possession* such that Byatt's projected, ultimately idealistic vision of contemporary reality is revealed. *Possession* is not so much a "description" of reading as an *"enactment"* (Kelly 1996: 95) of it; the main characters in both the Victorian and modern periods devote much of their time to the reading of texts, as well to the writing of them for others to read. *Possession* invites us to form part of this generational sequence of readers, to engage self-consciously with the novel's paradoxes in order to learn how appropriate "possession" of and by the past can, in fact, be the salvation of the present.

By setting the contemporary scenes of the novel in the fractious world of academic literary scholarship in the 1980s, Byatt crystallizes many of the anxieties characteristic of postmodern life. According to the multiple strains of literary theory that were flourishing around that time under the broad rubric of "poststructuralism" – including deconstruction and psychoanalytic and feminist theories – certain long-held assumptions, under pressure since at least the early twentieth century, finally gave way, seemingly for good. Chief among these vanishing ideals was the concept that language could relate in any direct way to the world it represented; in the terms of Ferdinand de Saussure's linguistics, which informed much deconstructive thought, the "signifier," or word, no longer could be said to correspond in any meaningful way with the "signified," the mental image one has of a real object in the world.

Earlier I mentioned how in Vico's eighteenth-century system such a breakdown in linguistic coherence heralded a culture's imminent dissolution. In this "age of irony" (Vico 1984: 131), community members turn to deceitful, unethical, and egotistical practices, using the slipperiness of language to further their own designs. Certainly, Byatt's predatory cast of academics fits with Vico's description. The rapacious Fergus Wolff exploits the trendiness of theoretical scholarship to advance himself professionally, and Mortimer Cropper, Ash's biographer, takes advantage of the self-serving intellectual climate to procure and fetishize objects once owned by the great poet, transforming some of them into "virtual," holographic exhibits. Neither has any sincere desire to come to know the historical texts or personages on their own terms; rather, they want to dominate the past, and to impose their own worldviews on it.

This narcissistic approach to history is most broadly caricatured in Leonora Stern, whose critical standpoint amalgamates the ideas of various influential feminist theorists, such as Luce Irigary and Hélène Cixous. In LaMotte's epic poem *The Fairy Melusine*, Stern finds, as she inevitably would in anything she read, the very suppressed images of female bodily experience that she expects are there, with little regard for the text's actual content. During his visit to Yorkshire with Maud, Roland reads Stern's analysis of the poem and reacts to it with discouraged acceptance of its contemporary relevance:

> He had a vision of the land they were to explore, covered with sucking human orifices and knotted human body-hair. He did not like this vision, and yet, a child of his time, found it compelling, somehow guaranteed to be significant... (Byatt 1990: 267)

In her essay collection *On Histories and Stories*, Byatt notes that "Modern criticism is powerful and imposes its own narratives and priorities on the writings it uses as raw material, source or jumping-off point" (Byatt 2001: 45). With her inability to see beyond her own feminist perspective, Stern embodies the narrow-mindedness that Byatt perceives in the universities and, by extension, the wider culture of her day.

Stern's domineering nature goes beyond her academic work. Like Cropper, she is an American, a nationality associated in the novel with rampant commercial greed; and like him she is portrayed as pushy and sexually possessive, foisting her lesbian orientation on an uninterested Maud. Read carefully, however, Byatt's critique of Stern's character, beyond poking fun at the sometimes-ludicrous excesses of certain theorists, need not be taken as a condemnation of feminism, with which Byatt clearly has sympathies. Rather, the depiction of Stern appears more to be an indictment of any system of thought that seeks to obliterate or repress the Other, whether historical, cultural, or personal, through the imposition of self-serving views.

Surrounded by egotistical yet successful characters such as Wolff and Stern, Roland seems like a man out of step with his times. As a white, male postgraduate at a time when affirmative action hirings were prevalent in universities, he is disadvantaged in his pursuit of an academic position. Instead, he is condemned to work as an ill-paid researcher under the Leavisite critic James Blackadder in the subterranean "Ash factory" in the British Museum. Both this location, described as the "Inferno" (Byatt 1990: 31), and the basement apartment that Roland shares with his embittered girlfriend Val, who nicknames him "old Mole" (p. 24), associate him with the underworld, a conventional part of a romance quester's journey. Yet the knight on whom Roland is modeled, Browning's "Childe," is an apparent failure, stymied at every turn by challenges that do not conform to his romantic vision of what will be expected of him. Byatt's Roland, too, seems destined to fail; he feels himself irresistibly drawn to the life of the past as he perceives it in Ash's poetry, but is constantly told that his approach to literature is hopelessly obsolete. Like his supervisor Blackadder, Roland finds that Ash has supplanted his own sense of identity; his apartment is dominated by images of the great poet, whose prose "sang in his head" (p. 99), blocking out any creative potential of his own. When Roland discovers the mysterious love letters tucked inside Ash's copy of *The New Science*, he finds himself irresistibly drawn to a somewhat outmoded pursuit of biographical literary scholarship that puts him in competition with the professional forces threatening to engulf him.

Roland's investigation into the identity of the mysterious female poet addressed in Ash's letters leads him into contact with Maud, a feminist scholar whose specialty is LaMotte, a supposedly distant relative. Like the other women in Roland's life – Val and his mother, who both bullied him throughout his academic career – Maud contributes to Roland's feelings of inadequacy. During his visit to her at Lincoln University, with its significantly named Tennyson Tower, Maud demonstrates her superiority, settling him "like a recalcitrant nursery-school child" (p. 49) before the boxes of LaMotte's papers. Despite her condescension and relative professional success, Maud has a sense of inferiority similar to Roland's; she allows herself to be intimidated not only by Stern but also by Wolff, with whom she had an affair in which he was the dominant partner, and she bows to pressure from feminist peers to conceal her naturally blonde hair, which they misconstrue as an artificial attempt at conventional femininity. Maud defines herself through her theoretically oriented work on LaMotte's poetry, especially its motifs of confinement and liminality, the transitional space between one state and another, as they relate to women's empowerment. Yet, as Roland does with Ash, Maud acts as a kind of shadow or weak repetition of LaMotte, dependent on the genius of the past but without originality or autonomy of her own (a charge frequently made against many facets of postmodern culture). This generational mirroring and decline is consistent with Vico's system, in which each successive age leading up to the crisis before the *ricorso* grows more sophisticated in terms of its linguistic conception of the world but at the same time deteriorates in individual and social terms. With Maud, this diminishing echo effect is even more pronounced, given her similarities not only to LaMotte but also to her primary poetic creation, the Fairy Melusina, whose blonde hair and serpentine qualities reflect those of her creator. Both Roland and Maud, then, exist in an "uneasy relation to the afterlife" (Byatt 1992: 149) of their Victorian counterparts, as Byatt says English contemporary fiction does to that of the nineteenth-century novel; their attitude to the past is one of longing for a lost ideal represented by the two poets.

The nineteenth-century scenes in the novel are characterized by an apparent sense that that period is securely grounded in the past, and that language, as well as all other systems of signification, is coherent and meaningful. Ash epitomizes the avidly curious Victorian scholar, with interests ranging from biology and paleontology, to the occult and mythology. All of these subjects figure prominently in his Browning-esque poems, masterfully ghost-written by Byatt, in which Ash creatively ventriloquizes voices from the past. He writes to LaMotte that he is "at ease with other imagined minds – bringing to life, *restoring* in some sense to vitality, the whole vanished men of other times" (Byatt 1990: 174). Central to Ash's approach to history is a respect for its distinctive nature, which he as a researcher must meet on its own terms. Blackadder says of Ash that "He wanted to understand how individual people at any particular time saw the shape of their lives – from their beliefs to their pots and pans" (p. 433); this attitude sharply contrasts with the narcissistic imposition of self upon the world practiced by some of the twentieth-century characters. Ash's fascination with reviving the past often leads him to investigate stories about the origins of various cultures. In his poems that are influenced by Icelandic mythology, the epic *Ragnarök* and the lyric series *Ask to Embla*, Ash draws on narratives familiar to the Judeo-Christian tradition: the resurrection and the apocalypse, but especially the creation. The poems' main characters are a pair of original humans, like Adam and Eve, who are loved by the gods who brought them into being and who share both innate sympathy and a recognition of each other's essential difference. The theme of creation is also the focus of the first of Ash's texts cited in the novel, *The Garden of Proserpina*, which describes an Edenic situation in which the world and words are in perfect harmony:

> The first men named this place and named the world.
> They made the words for it: garden and tree
> Dragon or snake and woman, grass and gold
> And apples. They made names and poetry.
> The things *were* what they named and made them. (Byatt 1990: 504)

This poem suggests Ash's affinity with the mythical unity of Vico's first time-form, a historical golden age that is still seemingly accessible to Victorians, and is articulated for them by Ash as their societal representative.

LaMotte, too, has an intimate relationship with the past as it is preserved in mythological terms. From her father, the mythographer Isidore LaMotte, she learned ancient stories from his native Brittany and from England, where her mother was born. Like Ash's encyclopedic knowledge, Isidore's exhaustive cataloguing of myths and legends, labeled the "Key to all mythologies" (p. 35) by Blackadder in an ironic reference to Casaubon's ultimately futile project in George Eliot's *Middlemarch*, exemplifies the urge towards coherent, meaningful systems that characterizes the nineteenth-century sections of the novel, in contrast to the disorderly, contingent world of the contemporary characters. While the Victorians reveled in taxonomies and other monuments of order, Cropper's father in the twentieth century, for example, "could never establish any guiding principle" (p. 112) for the artifacts in his private museum. From her father's research, LaMotte is aware of many of the archetypal figures, such as Melusina and the drowned women of the City of Is, through which women have conventionally been represented as seductive, evil, and monstrous. LaMotte revises these figures – "Metamorphoses interest me" (p. 305), she tells Ash – in keeping with the shifting roles and perceptions of women in her own time. Under the influence of fictional pioneers such as Priscilla Penn Cropper, the critic's proto-feminist great-grandmother, and of actual radicals such as Christina Rossetti and George Sand, whose presences are felt throughout the text, the world of nine-teenth-century women in the novel is slowly becoming more liberated, as evidenced by LaMotte's ability to live in celibate, artistic isolation with her friend and likely sexual partner, Blanche Glover. This utopian feminine community is disrupted only by Ash, whose introduction into LaMotte's life betokens an even more fulfilling union for her both personally and in terms of her connections with writing and the past.

In many respects, LaMotte and Ash's relationship epitomizes the ideal interplay between self and other, and by analogy between present and past, that seems to be possible in the novel's nineteenth-century scenes. Married to Ellen Ash, a repressive virgin with no serious artistic pretensions of her own, Ash finds in LaMotte a partner who shares his passion for writing. Their affair begins through a lengthy exchange of letters, through which they discover and cherish their differences over such issues as religious faith, as well as their joint fascinations. When Roland retrieves the corres-pondence a century later with Maud, he muses about how "true" letters are written "for *a* reader" (p. 145) who will implicitly grasp the writer's intention. Unlike Maud and Roland, who at first cannot establish any kind of dialogue, even with regard to the letters themselves, LaMotte and Ash exist in almost perfect reciprocity, like Ask and Embla, acting as each other's model reader. This collaborative, mutually sustain-ing sense of self – what theorist Mikhail Bakhtin calls "dialogism" – intensifies during the poets' journey to Yorkshire, necessitated by Blanche's growing jealousy and the need to shelter Ellen from knowledge of Ash's infidelity.

In Yorkshire, Ash reconciles himself to LaMotte's radical distinctness from him, resulting in a seemingly perfect act of "possession," both spiritual and sexual. Even more than her persona in the letters, Lamotte's physical presence is enigmatic yet enticing; Ash finds himself "voracious for information" (p. 301), greedily trying to learn all he can about her. Despite Lamotte's proximity, she is always on the verge of slipping away from him, of changing shape like the Greek god Proteus, or of metamorphosing like the "selkies" (p. 305), seal-women whose legends are prevalent in northern England. Post-coitus, Ash becomes vividly aware of LaMotte's probable experience as a lesbian, yet restrains his curiosity, knowing that she has secrets that he must not attempt to penetrate. Still, he feels that he "know[s]" (p. 308) her, and she concedes that he does; their union seems to them both to be the fulfillment of a sacred quest, a rediscovery of a lost origin, "where . . . desire has its end" (p. 312).

Yet the romance between LaMotte and Ash is doomed from the outset by the restrictive mores of Victorianism. The failure of their union demonstrates the impos-sibility of a truly dialogic relationship in actual social terms, since, as Lynne Pearce points out in *Reading Dialogics*, "in any exchange between two or more persons/ discursive positions a power dynamic is inevitably involved" (1994: 12). Further, as LaMotte has made clear from the time of their early correspondence, as a female writer in a patriarchal world she cannot stay long in the "hot light" (Byatt 1990: 310) of Ash's overwhelming influence. To survive as a poet, she must return to her autono-mous life, but finds even that marred by her relationship with Ash, since Glove has committed suicide in her absence, marking the demise of their early feminist utopia. In fact, all of the Victorian characters suffer distressing fates. LaMotte is unable to acknowledge as her own her child by Ash, Maia; she ends her days alone as the girl's putative aunt, "in a Turret like an old Witch" (p. 489). Her final message sent to Ash on his deathbed is intercepted by Ellen and never delivered, just as his final message to LaMotte, described in the novel's "Postscript" (another nineteenth-century convention), is forgotten by the young Maia after her unknowing encounter with her father. The nineteenth-century characters' unfortunate endings work counter to the text's superficial impression that the Victorian era, as presented by Byatt, is completely vital and free from difficulties.

In fact, if one reads the nineteenth-century sections of the novel closely, it becomes clear that Byatt has intentionally written them in such a way that the problems faced by her postmodern characters are already visible in the earlier period. Again, this gradual cultural deterioration is in keeping with Vico's system, in which the intermediary time-forms between the age of mythical simplicity and the age of irony undergo a progressive collapse of meaning and stability, despite their enhanced linguistic sophistication. This feeling of decline resonates in Ash and LaMotte's written exchange about religion, in which she, as a believing Christian, articulates her discomfort over the suggestions in his poetry that the story of the resurrection is just one of many such narratives constructed by people to reflect their desires and assuage their fears. Although Ash is careful to affirm his faith, his response to her that they live in "an *old* world – a tired world" (p. 181) reinforces the impression that religion is losing its potency in the Victorian era, at least in the eyes of one of its most eminent representatives. Ash himself, for all of his stature as an original man of letters, devotes much of his talent to the replication of other styles and voices, creating what postmodern theorists call "simulacra": copies that are reproduced to the extent that they displace all memory of the authentic artifact. Ash's choice of artistic approach is a sign that the holisitic relationship between language and the world that his period seems to enjoy is starting to come apart. Instead of displaying referential certainty, Ash's texts about the act of naming, such as *The Garden of Proserpina*, can be read as expressions of the fact that his world is on the verge of what Frederick Holmes calls the "schismatic fall into modernity" (Holmes 1997: 53), in which the bond between signifier and signified is irreparably breached.

While Roland and Maud are inclined to compare their world unfavorably to that of their precursors, through their pursuit to learn more about LaMotte and Ash they gradually lose their nostalgic longing for a lost, and in fact nonexistent, past in which none of the shortcomings of their own culture existed. Rather, they come to see the nineteenth century on its own terms, uncolored by their contemporary prejudices. During their parallel trip to Yorkshire, the scholars seem merely to be following in their predecessors' footsteps, as had Cropper some years before in his efforts to retrace every moment of Ash's life; yet unlike Cropper, Maud and Roland become willing to put aside their modern academic perspectives and try to understand the Victorians' point of view. Roland takes the lead in this shift, explaining to Maud, "Everything relates to *us* and so we're imprisoned in ourselves — we can't see *things*. . . . It makes an interesting effort of imagination to think how they saw the world" (p. 276). In adopting this stance, the twentieth-century couple unknowingly emulates the dialogic attitude towards the past common to both Ash and LaMotte; in the process, Maud and Roland also develop a new consideration for one another, their romantic reciprocity mirroring the respect for the past, as it did with the Victorians.

This relationship deepens throughout their subsequent journey to Brittany to pursue the secret of what happened to LaMotte after the affair in Yorkshire. While there, the two discover the journal of Sabine de Kercoz, LaMotte's cousin with whom she stayed during her pregnancy, which fills in missing information while giving readers more insight into LaMotte's Breton heritage, especially through the interpolated tales of the witch-like character, Gode. The contribution of the Brittany section to the novel, though, goes beyond providing useful plot details and Gothic atmosphere: as LaMotte's younger contemporary who is also a poet, de Kercoz stands as a clear reworking of the female artist figure, only with a modernist twist; she writes in her journal that she "would like to write the history of the feelings of a woman. A modern woman" (p. 377).

This deliberate repetition and updating of LaMotte's Victorian authorial persona forms part of a trend in the latter part of the novel towards overt self-consciousness, particularly with regard to the twentieth-century couple. Roland, especially, becomes aware of his and Maud's roles as characters in a pre-written narrative, the unfinished story of Ash and LaMotte: "[He] thought, partly with precise postmodernist pleasure, and partly with a real element of superstitious dread, that he and Maud were being driven by a plot or fate that seemed, at least possibly, to be not their fate but that of those others" (p. 456). In even more specifically literary terms, Roland suddenly understands that "He [is] in a Romance, a vulgar and a high Romance simultaneously; a Romance [is] one of the systems that control[s] him" (p. 460). With this recognition, Roland deepens his association with his namesake from Browning's poem, whose real success in his quest comes from in-depth reflection on his psychological state and the announcement of his identity, which is coterminous with his arrival at his goal. While on the physical level, Roland and Maud's activities towards the end of the novel play out a conventional romance narrative — the "Chase and race" (p. 460) that ends with the defeat of the villainous Cropper and the exhumation of Ash and LaMotte's buried secrets — on a more profound level, the twentieth-century pair's mutual quest, like that of Browning's knight, involves a process of self-discovery that in their case also leads to a new appreciation of the creative and romantic potential of their own time.

What Roland realizes by the end of the novel is that while Ash and his contemporaries may have enjoyed vibrancy and stability that the postmodern era lacks, he can reclaim some of those elements through a reassessment of the past and of his own identity in the present. This act of retrospection resulting in personal and cultural renewal corresponds, as I noted earlier, to Vico's concept of the *ricorso*, which stops the cycle of linguistic and social deterioration. For Roland, this engagement with the past culminates in his epiphanic rereading of Ash's *The Garden of Proserpina* during his last visit to the basement apartment. The intense self-consciousness of this scene is underscored by Byatt's lengthy narratorial interjection on the act of reading, calling attention to the parallel between Roland's actions and our own as readers. The kind of reading that the narrator promotes as the most revelatory, and that Roland finds himself experiencing, is one in which the reader sees the words as "hard and clear and infinite and exact, like stones of fire" (p. 512). By becoming aware of the words as things, almost like material objects, Roland gains a fresh cognizance of the connectedness of language and the world, despite the pronouncements of poststructuralist theory to the contrary:

> He had been taught that language was essentially inadequate, that it could never speak what was there, that it only spoke itself. . . . What had happened to him was that the ways in which it *could* be said had become more interesting than the idea that it could not. (Byatt 1990: 513)

With this unaccustomed sense of representational coherence, Roland is able not only to free himself finally from Ash's influence and become a poet in his own right, but also to face his culture's other deficiencies with a new optimism, emerging from the underground into a garden redolent of possibilities.

One of those possibilities, of course, is his relationship with Maud, which is only consummated once they are both able to imagine "a modern way" (p. 550) of being together, involving respect for each other's ambitions. Maud and Roland's lovemaking following the making of this pact heralds the end of the former character's divisive feminist attitude towards men and a return of romantic desire to the emotionally sterile postmodern world. This recovery of a historically valuable element comes about, as does Roland's re-engagement with language, because of a renewed awareness about the present's potential both to emulate the past and to grow beyond its own cultural limitations. While critics are correct to point out the gender imbalance in this scene, in which Roland takes the dominant sexual role, it is important to note that Byatt is careful not to project a truly dialogic relationship for her characters, since they are still inextricably tied to the social inequities of the foregoing generations. The narrator comments, quite self-consciously, on the "outdated" nature of the phrase "took possession" (p. 550) in this context, suggesting a future when such conceptions of gender relations would become obsolete.

After learning of her lineage as a descendant of both LaMotte and Ash, Maud feels that her ancestors have "taken [her] over, possessed her in almost a 'daemonic'" sense (p. 548). The challenge to Maud at the end of the story is to come to terms with her heritage, discover its benefits, and then forge an identity that combines the best of the past with autonomous self-awareness in the present. We can read Maud's situation as emblematic of the novel as a whole, on the level of both content and form. Despite its apparently nostalgic sensibility, *Possession* is very much a book about contemporary western culture, and about the power of the past to play a role in solving the problems of the present. Love, imagination, stable meaning, community – all of these things, Byatt implies, can be recovered in the postmodern world through respectful understanding of our predecessors and a willingness to see ourselves anew. By bringing together contemporary concerns and literary techniques with appealing Victorian characters and traditional narrative forms, Byatt has created an intriguingly paradoxical text, one that points us to a fantasized future of cultural rehabilitation.

REFERENCES AND FURTHER READING

Byatt, A. S. (1990) *Possession: A Romance*. New York: Random House.

——(1992) *Passions of the Mind: Selected Writings*. New York: Turtle Bay.

——(2001) *On Histories and Stories: Selected Essays*. London: Vintage.

Buxton, Jackie (1996) "'What's love got to do with it?': postmodernism and *Possession*," *English Studies in Canada*, 22/2: 199–219.

Charles, Ron (2002) "Frederica in wonderland," *Christian Science Monitor*, December 19. <http://www.csmonitor.com/2002/1219/p15s02-bogn.html> July 30, 2003.

Holmes, Frederick (1997) *The Historical Imagination: Postmodernism and the Treatment of the Past in Contemporary British Fiction*, English Literary Studies Monograph Series 73. Toronto: University of Victoria.

Hutcheon, Linda (1988) *A Poetics of Postmodernism: History, Theory, Fiction*. New York and London: Routledge.

Kelly, Kathleen Coyne (1996) *A. S. Byatt*. New York: Twayne.

Parini, Jay (1990) "Unearthing the secret lover," *New York Times on the Web*, October 21. <http://www.nytimes.com/books/99/06/13?specials/Byatt-possession.html> February 6, 2003.

Pearce, Lynn (1994) *Reading Dialogics*. London: Edward Arnold.

Smith, Anne (1990) Review of *Possession*, *The Listener*, March 1: 29.

Vico, Giambattista (1984) *The New Science of Giambattista Vico*, 3rd edn., trans. Thomas Goddard Bergin and Max Harold Fisch (unabridged). Ithaca and London: Cornell University Press. (Original work published in 1744).

Wells, Lynn (2003) *Allegories of Telling: Self-Referential Narrative in Contemporary British Fiction*. Amsterdam: Rodopi.

42

Pat Barker's *Regeneration* Trilogy

Anne Whitehead

Pat Barker's *Regeneration* trilogy – *Regeneration* (1991), *The Eye in the Door* (1993), and *The Ghost Road* (1995) – explores the history of the First World War by focusing on the condition and effects of trauma. The trilogy is an unusual blend of history and fiction and Barker draws extensively on the writings of the First World War poets and W. H. R. Rivers, an army doctor who worked with traumatized soldiers. The main characters are based on historical figures, with the notable exception of Billy Prior, whom Barker invented to parallel and contrast with the life of Wilfred Owen. Barker explores Rivers's medical treatment of shell-shocked officers at Craiglockhart military hospital in Scotland, and in particular his encounter with Siegfried Sassoon, which challenged Rivers's view of the war and of his own role as an army doctor. Barker powerfully dramatizes Rivers's growing doubt concerning the justifiability of the war. In the trilogy, the officers whom Rivers treats are normal men who are placed in situations of overwhelming pressure, and they suffer illness as a response to intolerable circum-stances. Rivers's understanding of the meaning of recovery is initially based on his early experiments with Henry Head on the regeneration of nerves. The early stages of recovery are defined by the restoration of the protopathic sensibility, a primitive level of sensation that has an all or nothing quality, so that extreme levels of pain are experienced. At a later stage, the epicritic sensibility returns, which is more finely discriminating and distinguishes between different levels of pain. In Barker's writing, the protopathic symbolizes the emotional, the sensual, the chaotic, and the primitive, while the epicritic comes to stand for the rational, the ordered, the cerebral, the objective, the civilized. For Rivers, the protopathic is a positive force, but it must nevertheless "know its place" (Barker 1991: 74). Rivers's own health, and that of his patients, depends on emotional containment, and his treatment both endorses and reinforces a traditional model of masculine behavior.

Rivers subsequently recognizes that internal division can represent a healthy and adaptive response to the war experience. The epigraph to *The Eye in the Door*, taken from Robert Louis Stevenson's *Dr Jekyll and Mr Hyde*, emphasizes the "duality" of man, and suggests that health lies in recognizing that "two natures" contend in the field of consciousness (Barker 1993: unnumbered). This refers most obviously to Prior, who develops a split personality in the novel. Although Prior invests his double with a demonic aspect, Rivers reveals that his dissociation originates in a traumatic situation, and enables Prior to cope with the conflicting demands placed upon him. Prior's alter ego emerges from a shell hole in the battlefields of France and allows him to survive combat, and to betray his childhood friends in his work for the Intelligence Services of the Ministry of Munitions. Prior's internal division is initially a healthy adaptation and only becomes pathological when he can no longer access the experiences of his double. Rivers recognizes that internal division is essential to performing a number of tasks. Observing Head's suspension of empathy in treating a patient, Rivers acknowledges that dissociation is vital to medical practice and research. His own treatment of war neurosis requires personal detachment and he describes the "split face" of medicine, suspended between involvement and objectivity (Barker 1993: 233). The soldier relies on the same detachment in order to perform his duty. This is exemplified in Siegfried Sassoon, who is two entirely different people at the front: a successful and bloodthirsty platoon commander and an anti-war poet. His ability to function within this duality renders him comparatively resilient to the war experience. More broadly, the process of writing itself relies on a mixture of empathy and detachment. In writing the trilogy, Barker deliberately deployed the figure of Rivers as a distancing device from the traumatic content of the war material, and the direct portrayal of combat is consciously delayed until the closing pages of *The Ghost Road*.

In the course of the trilogy, Rivers discovers that dissociation is a healthy and adaptive state, and only becomes pathological in extreme circumstances. The novels are centrally concerned with duality and each of the characters, including Rivers, leads a double life, a Jekyll-and-Hyde existence. In *Dr Jekyll and Mr Hyde*, Stevenson frames the "strange case" of Henry Jekyll within the interpretative paradigms of medicine, psychoanalysis, and law. Barker draws on Stevenson's story to explore the discursive and epistemological framing of those who do not conform to social norms. The trilogy critiques the legal and medical discourses that were deployed to frame, and contain, those who protested against the war. Barker reveals that these discursive structures, which pretended to objectivity and neutrality, were in reality both disciplinary and coercive. One of the central questions posed by the trilogy concerns the degree to which an effective protest against the war could be made and, if so, what form such a protest might take.

Forging a Language of Protest

At various points in the trilogy, Barker contends that language is no longer adequate in the face of the unprecedented horrors of modern, mechanized warfare. Watching Oscar Wilde's *Salome*, Charles Manning reflects that the former language of violence is no longer appropriate or possible, while Prior asserts that a new language must evolve, and the only words that currently hold any meaning are the names of battles: "Mons, Loos, the Somme, Arras, Verdun, Ypres" (Barker 1995: 257). Barker is not concerned with the evolution of the new literary language of modernism *after* the First World War; rather, she is concerned with the language of protest that emerged *during* the conflict. Her interest is clearly signalled in the opening words of *Regeneration*, which quote Sassoon's "Declaration of Protest." Sassoon protested not against war in general (he was not a pacifist) but against the continuation of the current war. He argued that the perpetuation of the conflict was in the interests of conquest, rather than in pursuit of the original, stated aims. In the trilogy, Sassoon's protest is contained, in the first instance, by Robert Graves, who seeks to protect his friend by ensuring that his case comes under the jurisdiction of the Army Medical Board, rather than a military tribunal. Sassoon is effectively silenced by his confinement at Craiglockhart, for it implies that the "Declaration" was the result of mental illness or insanity. Sassoon's anti-war sentiments also find powerful expression in his poetry. Barker demonstrates that his revisions to Wilfred Owen's "Anthem for doomed youth" subtly transform the clichés of war propaganda. The semantic shifts from all "our" dead to all "the" dead, and from the "solemn" to the "monstrous" guns, reveal that the enemy is no longer the German troops, but the generals who continue to sacrifice the young men of both sides (Barker 1991: 141). Those who die "so fast" in Owen's draft of the poem die "as cattle" in the final version; they are denied the dignity of a clean, quick death and are slaughtered like animals (p. 141). In working on the poem, Sassoon and Owen break away from traditional literary forms and models to forge a new language of anti-war protest.

An alternative, equally eloquent, language of protest is articulated in the symptoms of shell shock: stammering, mutism, seizures, and paralysis. Eric Leed has observed that for the soldiers, war neurosis was a "functional disorder" which removed them from the war, and this was the conscious or unconscious "aim" of the symptom (Leed 1979: 167). In his reflections on Lewis Carroll's *Alice in Wonderland*, Rivers clearly recognizes the functional nature of shell shock, observing that the soldiers, like Alice, solve their problems by transforming and changing their bodies (Barker 1995: 24). The most common symptoms of war neurosis were mutism and speech disorders, and Leed reveals that these conditions were the only form of protest available to the men:

> [T]he soldier was required to keep silent, to accept the often suicidal edicts of authority and to hold back or severely edit any expression of hostility toward those who kept him in a condition of mortal peril. Rather than cursing, striking or shooting his superior officer, he distorted his speech or completely denied himself that faculty. (Leed 1979: 167)

John Brannigan astutely observes that open mouths figure repeatedly throughout the trilogy and function, particularly in *Regeneration*, as powerful images of protest and control (Brannigan 2003: 18). Rivers interprets Prior's mutism as springing from the conflict between desire for protest and fear of the consequences. Prior is the only officer in Craiglockhart to be afflicted with mutism rather than stammering, and Rivers regards his condition to be symptomatic of the class conflict he experiences as a working-class officer. In his medical examination of Prior, Rivers inserts a spoon into his open mouth, causing him pain as he scrapes it across the back of his throat. Reflecting on the incident, Rivers recognizes that his momentary pleasure in Prior's discomfort is indicative of his own power over his patients and he feels "discontented with his own behaviour" (Barker 1991: 237).

At the close of *Regeneration*, Prior's open mouth becomes indissociable from that of Lewis Yealland's patient, Callan. Rivers sits in as the young soldier, who has endured all the major battles of the Western Front, is subjected to Yealland's electrical treatment. As he witnesses the session, Rivers is split between identification with the patient – remembering his own chronic, childhood stammering – and identification with the doctor, as he reflects on his own medical practice. He recognizes that Callan's mutism is itself a powerful form of protest, and that Yealland's treatment paradoxically acts as a form of silencing. During the session, Callan's protest is subtly voiced in his articulation of the sound "ba," which modulates from the contemptuous "Bah," to an imitation of a lamb led to slaughter, "Baaaa!" (Barker 1991: 232). In a dream that follows his visit to Yealland, Rivers connects Callan to Sassoon and is troubled by the underlying violence of his own methods of treatment, which may on the surface appear kinder than his colleague's explicit brutality and bullying, but which nevertheless aim to silence protest. Leed's distinction between "disciplinary" and "analytic" treatments (Leed 1979: 170) is helpful in distinguishing between Yealland's and Rivers's methods. If Yealland's "disciplinary" treatment assumes that the patient's protest is conscious and willed, Rivers's "analytic" approach is based on the principle that the patient's protest is unconscious, outside of his own control. In spite of this fundamental difference in viewpoint, however, Rivers is justified in his suspicion that both methods are forms of coercion and silencing. Rivers, like Yealland, is an agent of social discipline and occupies a position of authority and control over his patients.

Rivers succeeds in changing Sassoon's position so that he returns to combat, although he does not relinquish his anti-war protest. However, Rivers is also fundamentally changed by his contact with Sassoon. As Elaine Showalter observes, Rivers "caught Sassoon's anti-war complex in the process of treating it" (1987: 188). Barker is interested in Rivers's highly compromised position as an army doctor. In peacetime, the analyst heals or cures the patient. In wartime, however, he represents the official view of the conflict and his task is to induce the patient to resume a (frequently suicidal) military role. In the course of the trilogy, Rivers is increasingly confronted with his own doubts concerning the justifiability of a war that causes the breakdown of men in such great numbers. If he was previously able to suppress his misgivings, this is no longer possible when he is confronted with treating Sassoon. His first articulation of protest arises in response to David Burns's suffering, when Rivers voices his growing conviction, *"Nothing justifies this. Nothing nothing nothing"* (Barker

1991: 180). He feels increasingly trapped or locked into his official role. In *The Ghost Road*, Rivers uncovers the traumatic experience in which his stammering and loss of visual memory originated. His childhood protest at having his hair breeched was silenced by his father, who showed him the portrait of his ancestor and namesake William Rivers, who had his leg amputated without anaesthetic and did not complain. Focusing on the "resolutely clenched mouth" at the center of the picture (1995: 96), Rivers recognizes that his own work simultaneously legitimates and silences protest. At the close of the trilogy, Barker powerfully intercuts Prior's death at the front with Matthew Hallet's death on the ward of Rivers's hospital. Rescued from No Man's Land by Prior, Hallet becomes his substitute and screams his protest to Rivers: "It's not worth it" (p. 274). The protest is taken up by the other men on the ward, and it seems that Rivers himself can no longer uphold his official position. He feels an overwhelming "pressure building in his own throat" (p. 274), as his feelings against the war struggle to find expression.

Barker demonstrates that the protest of the soldiers – whether it was expressed through the symptoms of shell shock or in the form of Sassoon's "Declaration" – was medicalized. For those in authority, this served to delegitimize the protest, by classifying it as illness, and it also circumvented the problem of executing large numbers of men for cowardice or desertion. In *The Eye in the Door*, Barker explores the criminalization of the war protest of civilians, portraying the harsh treatment and imprisonment of Beatie Roper and her family. War propaganda viewed pacifism, socialism, and homosexuality as equally harmful to the war effort, and Barker powerfully depicts the ferocious climate of intolerance that prevailed. Rivers understands that the wartime anxiety whether love between men is "the right kind of love" (Barker 1993: 156) leads to harsh penalties against homosexuality, which is (like pacifism) subject to the legal/criminal discourse. Blackmailed and persecuted, Manning leads a "double life" of married respectability and illicit homosexual encounters (p. 155). His "case" is medicalized and he, like Sassoon, is referred to Rivers for treatment and "cure." In both cases the alternative is imprisonment.

As John Brannigan observes, the motif of visualization is foregrounded in *The Eye in the Door*. The novel centers on the image of the panopticon, which is explicitly depicted in Prior's visit to Beatie Roper at Aylesbury prison: "In the centre of the pit sat a wardress who, simply by looking up, could observe every door" (Barker 1993: 29). In *Discipline and Punish*, Michel Foucault interprets the panopticon as the model of modern authority and control. It substitutes an oppressive watchfulness in place of physical violence, and this authoritarian gaze is gradually internalized so that the individual becomes self-regulating. The painted eye on the door of the prison cell disturbs Prior not simply because it reminds him of finding his comrade's eyeball in the trench, but because it signals the surveillance and social control to which he himself is subject. From the opening of the novel, Prior is convinced that he is being followed, and he is also under observation by Rivers's disciplinary gaze. Prior's connection of the "misleading emptiness" of the prison with the landscape of No Man's Land (p. 30) recognizes that the soldiers and the conscientious objectors are

regulated by the same authoritarian systems of surveillance. Barker clearly demonstrates that all forms of anti-war protest were effectively silenced by disciplinary and
coercive medical or legal authorities. The hospital and the prison act as sites of
negotiation between the state and the individual. In Barker's fiction, nobody operates
outside this system: all of her characters, including Rivers, are locked into the
demands of repressive and authoritarian structures, and they necessarily operate or
respond within the constraints which they impose.

Dethroning the White, Male God

In the *Regeneration* trilogy, Barker rewrites the masculine narrative of the First World
War. As Catherine Lanone observes, she focuses on the symptoms of shell shock such
as paralysis, aphasia, and nightmares, which were traditionally associated with the
"feminine" disorder of hysteria, and thereby explores "the way masculine identity too
is distorted by patriarchal, phallocentric demands" (1999: 259). Analyzing the high
diction that was one of the casualties of the First World War, Paul Fussell has pointed
out that to be "manly" meant "not to complain" (1975: 22). In a situation in which all
signs of physical fear were interpreted as cowardice and all alternatives to combat,
such as pacifism, conscientious objection, desertion, or suicide were considered
unmanly, men were forced, like women, to express their conflicts through the body.
Showalter has pointed out that the nature of combat in the First World War rendered
the soldiers particularly susceptible to the development of "hysterical" symptoms,
because it "feminized the conscripts by taking away their sense of control" (Showalter
1987: 173). Men signed up expecting to take part in the Great Adventure. The
language of military attack has always significantly overlapped with the language of
male sexuality, with its references to assault, impact, thrust, and penetration. Prior
accordingly speaks of the experience of attack, or going over the top, as "sexy," because
of the exhilarating feelings of exposure and risk involved (Barker 1991: 72). In reality,
however, the men were mobilized into trenches and shell holes, and the predominant
experience of the war was one of passivity. For Rivers, shell shock originates in the
prolonged immobility, helplessness, and inactivity of the soldiers, and his diagnosis is
confirmed by the fact that its highest incidence occurs among the men manning the
observation balloons. The constriction of the trenches paralleled women's prewar
experiences, and Rivers recognizes this in connecting the symptoms of his patients
with his sister's hysteria, which results from her increasing confinement. If men are
restricted by the war, "shrunk into a smaller and smaller space," women's lives, on the
contrary, are opening up, "expand[ing] in all kinds of ways" (p. 90). Sarah Lumb
typifies the new generation of women, who have escaped from the confinement of
domestic service and entered the world of work. Employed in a munitions factory, she
is able to take home higher wages than she could possibly have earned before the war.
Barker's feminist intervention into history makes clear that if the men are suffering
from the pathological conditions of women in peacetime, it is because they are faced

with the same experiences of powerlessness and immobility, so that illness becomes the only available mode of protest.

Rivers's methods of treatment both challenge and reinforce received notions of masculinity. He demands that his patients admit their emotions into consciousness, which can only be achieved "at the cost of redefining what it meant to be a man" (Barker 1991: 48). However, the soldiers are still expected to perform their duty and return to France. As Greg Harris points out, Rivers's implicit affirmation of a traditional model of masculinity is most clearly brought out in his treatment of Ian Moffet. Seeking to cure Moffet's paralysis of the legs, Rivers deliberately shames him by drawing stocking tops on his legs, which draw attention to the "feminine" nature of his hysterical symptom. Moffet clearly recognizes that Rivers aims to humiliate him, observing: "You are consciously and deliberately destroying my self-respect" (Barker 1995: 52). According to Rivers's logic, Moffet's "self-respect" can only be restored by overcoming his paralysis and getting back on his feet. However, Rivers's "cure" effectively denies Moffet his means of protest, and the only recourse left to him is to attempt suicide. In the course of the trilogy, Rivers painfully learns the extent to which he himself has invested in the very notions of masculinity that he seeks to lead his patients to reject. Although he recognizes the shortcomings of traditional models of masculinity, they are nevertheless deeply rooted in his own consciousness, dating from his father's lesson in "appropriate" masculine behavior based on the picture of William Rivers.

Rivers's anti-war feeling derives less from a critique of traditional masculinity based on his work at Craiglockhart than from a postcolonial perspective originating in his anthropological work in Melanesia and the Solomon Islands. Conversing with the natives in Melanesia, Rivers recognizes that the West is not the "measure of all things" and his vision of the "Great White God" is "de-throned" (Barker 1991: 242). His anthropological travels and experiences surface in *The Ghost Road* to challenge the official view of the war. As Lanone points out, the story of Abraham and Isaac forms an important motif in the trilogy and registers the change in Rivers's viewpoint. Barker's treatment of the biblical account is strongly influenced by Wilfred Owen's poem, "A parable of the old man and the young," which emphasizes the betrayal and sacrifice of the young men of Europe by the older generation. Barker's emphasis shifts, however, from the pain of the betrayed to the conflict experienced by the betrayer. For Rivers, the story of Abraham and Isaac initially symbolizes civilization, for the hand of God intervenes and prevents the sacrifice. In primitive societies, by contrast, savagery prevails and the sacrifice of the young takes place. This contrast begins to collapse, however, in the context of the First World War, for the old men are "breaking the bargain" (p. 149) and slaughtering the young men across the battlefields of northern France. In *The Ghost Road*, Rivers recalls the death of the clan chief in the village of Narovo. By tradition, this demands a human sacrifice and the men of the community embark on a head-hunting raid. The small boy whom they capture is not killed by the natives, however, but adopted as the mortuary priest. His head is spared, but Rivers cannot say the same of his own patients. The memory of Navoro surfaces as Rivers watches the disembodied head of Prior disappearing down the road, and signals his awareness that he himself occupies the position of the "father" who has betrayed and sacrificed his "sons." Sassoon returns to France to narrowly escape death, while Prior dies in the same suicidal attack that kills Owen. If the war has been unnecessarily prolonged, as Sassoon claims, and the young men are being sacrificed to "the subclauses and the small print" (Barker 1995: 249), then Rivers is complicit in this attitude. Writing from a postcolonial perspective, Barker revises the story of Abraham and Isaac to demonstrate that western culture is characterized by barbarity and savagery, qualities that it routinely projects on to so-called "primitive" civilizations.

In *The Ghost Road*, Barker also counterpoints western and non-western paradigms in order to explore the theme of death. Through his Melanesian counterpart, the village healer Njiru, Rivers learns that *mate* designates a state of which death is the appropriate outcome, such as terminal illness or extreme old age. The moment of death itself is referred to as *mate ndapu*, "die finish" (Barker 1995: 135). Critically injured in France, Hallet has entered the state of *mate*, and Prior acts contrary to Njiru's beliefs in sending him back to England. Rivers's code of medical practice likewise emphasizes the duty of saving life. Barker calls Rivers's ethics into question by suggesting that, in terminal cases, it may be more merciful to hasten death than to prolong life. She also makes clear that Prior and Owen exist in a state of *mate*; they march along the ghost road and death is the inevitable outcome of their return to France. The gunfire that ends their lives merely marks the moment of death itself, *mate ndapu*. The trilogy closes with Rivers's powerful vision of Njiru on the ward of the hospital, which signals the return of his visual memory and suggests that he himself steps into *mate* and joins the ghost dance of the dead, as he gives up his last belief in the justifiability of the war. The scene also marks Rivers's articulation of his protest, and the vision of Njiru indicates the role of non-western paradigms and modes of understanding in the critique of the nation. Brannigan argues, further, that the final scene of the novel marks a shift in historical consciousness, so that time no longer unfolds progressively towards healing, but is structured around traumatic absence and otherness. When Owen and Sassoon share their experiences of the war, they project their visions either back or forward in time, envisioning "something ancient" or a time "[a] hundred years from now" (Barker 1991: 77). In order to situate themselves, it is necessary to conceive of the radical "hauntedness" of their own time (Brannigan 2003: 22). Through the motif of the ghost road, Barker suggests that history, after the First World War, is haunted by the memory of loss and is constantly striving to regenerate the past. Her own trilogy insists on the importance of the project of "regeneration," but simultaneously reveals that it is an ongoing venture, that "the process of regeneration is never complete" (Barker 1993: 147).

The Afterlife of the Trilogy

The *Regeneration* trilogy received a great deal of publicity, in part because of the prizes it was awarded. *The Eye in the Door* won the 1993 Guardian Fiction Prize, while *The*

Ghost Road received the 1995 Booker Prize. The Booker, in particular, attracted media attention to the trilogy but it also encouraged an erroneous reading of Barker's work. In his presentation speech, George Walden, the chairman of the Booker judges, attacked the "tyranny of ordinariness" and the "flight from the present" in contemporary fiction, and bemoaned the fact that so few of the Booker entries had "tackled modern England." Boyd Tonkin defends Barker's trilogy, arguing that the novels engage with the same issues – masculinity, violence, and the roots of conflict – as the rest of her fiction, which is set in the modern day. He contends that Barker had to enter the genre of historical fiction in order for her voice to be heard: "Only when Barker made her peace with the 'heavy industry' of period nostalgia...did the bookish powers that be salute her talent" (Tonkin 1995: 41). However, the trilogy also powerfully revises the genre of historical fiction. As Sharon Monteith observes, the issues in the trilogy were very much at the forefront of public consciousness, in the debates taking place in relation to Gulf War Syndrome. Emerging in early 1991, Gulf War Syndrome described a range of chronic illnesses that affected soldiers who had served in the Iraqi conflict. The cause of the symptoms could not be identified, but suspicion focused on four factors: the enriched uranium shells handled by servicemen; the vaccines used to protect the troops from chemical or bacteriological weapons; the organo-phosphate chemicals that were used during the campaign; and the Iraqi nerve agents in a bunker that was blown up by the Allied troops. Showalter controversially argued, however, that Gulf War Syndrome was a form of hysteria, and that its symptoms were remarkably similar to those of shell shock during the First World War. She believed that the condition was caused by the immobility and passivity of the troops stationed in the desert, and the "months of fearful anticipation" of being gassed or poisoned (1997: 141). Far from being engaged in a "flight from the present," Barker's trilogy comments indirectly on the contemporary conflict. Monteith points out that Barker's emphasis on the psychological consequences of war reflects the debates about Gulf War Syndrome, and that the trilogy powerfully indicates "the need to address society's expectations of combatants" (2002: 55).

In 1997, Gillies MacKinnon released his screen adaptation of *Regeneration*. The novel lends itself to film with its strong emphasis on dialogue and its powerful visualization of Craiglockhart. However, Karin Westman is justified in her observation that the film "streamlines Barker's complex novel considerably" (2001: 69). MacKinnon emphasizes the betrayal of the younger generation, drawing out the relationships between Rivers and Sassoon, and Rivers and Prior. As the most famous of the war poets, Owen's role is highlighted and his relationship with Sassoon is developed, although the film does not pursue the homoeroticism between them. Sarah Lumb's role is considerably reduced and, in the interests of the beautiful heroine, her skin is not yellowed by her work at the munitions factory. The film does not tackle Prior's bisexuality, but focuses instead on his class conflicts. In the interests of plot closure, the ending of the film shows Owen's death, and it implies that Prior survives the war, although Barker's character is killed alongside Owen in the attack on the Sambre-Oise canal. Barker's main concern with regard to the film was to ensure historical accuracy. In a 1998 interview, she observed that she made three key interventions with regard to the original script. She protested against the inclusion of a woman psychiatrist, because none existed. She criticized the device of Rivers telling patients information about other patients, on the grounds that it did not observe the rules of confidentiality and made Rivers appear unprofessional. She was also concerned that the Yealland scene should not come across to the viewer as torture: electricity was not used for torture or ECT until the 1930s and, in 1918, the only association with electricity was as a beneficial health treatment.

Barker has argued in interview that the film was most successful in visually distilling key aspects of the novel. In the opening scenes, the camera pans slowly across No Man's Land, and then cuts to Owen's encounter with Burns in a ring of dead animals. The juxtaposition powerfully suggests that the horror of the war is not confined to the trenches. The opening sequence of No Man's Land is filmed with an aerial tracking shot, which is only used elsewhere in the film to show Prior and Sarah making love. The repetition of the device signals the connection for Prior between "going over the top" and sex. The uniforms of the men have a strong visual impact, for they are impractical and constricting, and convey the extent to which the men are confined in their masculine and soldierly roles. However, the film goes further than the trilogy in depicting the potentially deadly consequences of protest against the war. Sassoon reads to Rivers from the newspaper the fate of a 17-year-old soldier who was executed for desertion. The camera cuts to a silhouetted sequence of the underage soldier being bound to a stake in No Man's Land, to await his death. This striking image provides a powerful symbol for Barker's vision of all the men involved in the war, including Rivers, who are silenced by authority, and who are inescapably bound to their official role and to their duty.

REFERENCES AND FURTHER READING

Barker, Pat (1991) *Regeneration*. London: Viking.

——(1993) *The Eye in the Door*. London: Viking.

——(1995) *The Ghost Road*. London: Viking.

——(1998) "Interview on the filming of *Regeneration*," *Regeneration* Gala. Tyneside Cinema, Newcastle upon Tyne.

Brannigan, John (2003) "Pat Barker's *Regeneration* trilogy," in Richard J. Lane, Rod Mengham, and Philip Tew (eds.) *Contemporary British Fiction*. Cambridge: Polity.

Foucault, Michel (1991) *Discipline and Punish: The Birth of the Prison*, trans. Alan Sheridan. Harmondsworth: Penguin.

Fussell, Paul (1975) *The Great War and Modern Memory*. Oxford: Oxford University Press.

Harris, Greg (1998) "Compulsory masculinity, Britain and the Great War: the literary historical work of Pat Barker," *Critique: Studies in Contemporary Fiction*, 39/2: 290–303.

Lanone, Catherine (1999) "Scattering the seed of Abraham: the motif of sacrificing in Pat Barker's *Regeneration* and *The Ghost Road*," *Literature and Theology*, 13/3: 259–68.

Leed, Eric (1979) *No Man's Land: Combat and Identity in World War One*. Cambridge: Cambridge University Press.

Monteith, Sharon (2002) *Pat Barker*. London: Northcote House.

Mukherjee, Ankhi (2001) "Stammering to story: neurosis and narration in Pat Barker's *Regeneration*," *Critique: Studies in Contemporary Fiction*, 43/1: 49–62.

Showalter, Elaine (1987) *The Female Malady: Women, Madness and English Culture 1830–1980*. London: Virago.

——(1997) *Hystories: Hysterical Epidemics and Modern Culture*. London: Picador.

Stevenson, Robert Louis (1987) *Dr Jekyll and Mr Hyde* and *The Weir of Hermiston*, ed. Emma Letley. Oxford: Oxford University Press.

Tonkin, Boyd (1995) "Fiction on the Ghost Road," *New Statesman and Society*, November 10: 41.

Westman, Karin (2001) *Pat Barker's* Regeneration: *A Reader's Guide*. New York: Continuum.

Whitehead, Anne (1998) "Open to suggestion: hypnosis and history in Pat Barker's *Regeneration*," *Modern Fiction Studies*, 44/3: 674–94.

Index